D1230679

"*Juvenile Justice: An Introduction* gives a comprehensive review of the juvenile justice system, covering the extent of juvenile delinquency, the history of juvenile justice, theories explaining juvenile delinquent behaviors, topical issues such as juvenile gang involvement, juvenile drug use, and juveniles and the police. The juvenile justice process and the system's response to juvenile delinquency are clearly outlined. I also appreciate how the authors interweave the juvenile justice landmark cases into the discussion. The book also discusses restorative justice as an alternative approach to dealing with juvenile delinquency.

Another positive for me is the in-depth coverage of the theories explaining delinquency. While students in this course (usually sophomore or junior) would have already taken their theory course (Criminology) in their second semester, many do not recall even hearing about these theories. This gives me a chance to present this to them a second time."

Sherill Morris-Francis, *Ph.D., Associate Professor and Graduate Coordinator, Mississippi Valley State University*

Juvenile Justice

Juvenile Justice: An Introduction, Tenth Edition, presents a comprehensive picture of juvenile offending, delinquency theories, and the ways juvenile justice actors and agencies react to delinquency. Whitehead and Lab offer evidence-based suggestions for successful interventions and treatment and examine the prospects for rebalancing the model of juvenile court.

This new edition includes insightful analysis and the latest available statistics on juvenile crime and victimization, drug use, court processing, and corrections. Special attention is given to female involvement, disproportionate minority contact, and diversity issues. The text also includes extensive discussion of police shootings, the issue of race, probation reform, life sentences for juveniles, recent Supreme Court decisions, and reform suggestions from Currie and Feld.

An essential text for undergraduate juvenile justice courses, this book offers rich pedagogical features and online resources. Each chapter enhances student understanding with Key Terms, a What You Need to Know section, and Discussion Questions. Links at key points in the text show students where to get the latest information.

John T. Whitehead is Professor Emeritus and former Chair in the Department of Criminal Justice and Criminology at East Tennessee State University. He completed his M.A. at the University of Notre Dame and earned his Ph.D. in Criminal Justice from the University at Albany. He has published articles about corrections, probation, and the death penalty. He is co-author of *Ethics in Criminal Justice: The Search for the Truth*, *Report Writing for Criminal Justice Professionals*, and *Teaching Criminal Justice*.

Steven P. Lab is Professor of Criminal Justice at Bowling Green State University. He holds a Ph.D. in Criminology from the Florida State University School of Criminology and Criminal Justice. Lab is the author or co-author of eight books, co-editor of one encyclopedia, and the author of more than 50 articles or book chapters. He is a past editor of the *Journal of Crime and Justice* and is the assistant editor of *Crime Prevention and Community Safety: An International Journal*. Lab has been a visiting professor at the Jill Dando Institute of Crime Science of University College London and at Keele University, as well as Visiting Fellow at Loughborough University and a research consultant with the Perpetuity Research Group at Leicester University. Lab is also a past president of the Academy of Criminal Justice Sciences.

Juvenile Justice

An Introduction

Tenth Edition

John T. Whitehead
Steven P. Lab

Routledge
Taylor & Francis Group

NEW YORK AND LONDON

Cover image: © Getty Images

Tenth edition published 2022
by Routledge
605 Third Avenue, New York, NY 10158

and by Routledge
4 Park Square, Milton Park, Abingdon, Oxon, OX14 4RN

Routledge is an imprint of the Taylor & Francis Group, an informa business

First edition published by Anderson Publishing 1990
Ninth edition published by Routledge 2018

Library of Congress Cataloging-in-Publication Data
Names: Whitehead, John T., author. | Lab, Steven P., author.
Title: Juvenile justice : an introduction / John T. Whitehead, Steven P. Lab.
Description: Tenth edition. | New York, NY : Routledge, 2022. |
Includes bibliographical references and index.
Identifiers: LCCN 2021036822 (print) | LCCN 2021036823 (ebook) |
ISBN 9780367764777 (hardback) | ISBN 9780367763756 (paperback) |
ISBN 9781003167112 (ebook)
Subjects: LCSH: Juvenile delinquency. | Juvenile justice, Administration of. |
Juvenile justice, Administration of–United States.
Classification: LCC HV9069 .W46 2022 (print) |
LCC HV9069 (ebook) | DDC 364.36–dc23
LC record available at https://lccn.loc.gov/2021036822
LC ebook record available at https://lccn.loc.gov/2021036823

ISBN: 9780367764777 (hbk)
ISBN: 9780367763756 (pbk)
ISBN: 9781003167112 (ebk)

DOI: 10.4324/9781003167112

Typeset in Giovanni
by Newgen Publishing UK

Access the companion website: www.routledge.com/cw/whitehead

To Pat, Dan, and Tim
and
To Bryce, Madison, and Rylee

Contents

Preface

When we wrote the first edition of this book over 30 years ago, we never imagined it would still be going at this point. This tenth edition of *Juvenile Justice: An Introduction* is a testament to the fact that we must have done something right. We are thankful that our peers have found value in our work. As in the past, this tenth edition reflects changes in the juvenile justice landscape and we have attempted to offer insight of value to the students who will use this book. We have updated materials and statistics throughout the text. Highlights of the changes include:

- Chapter 1 offers updated materials on the definition of delinquency and juvenile across jurisdictions; adds material on the emerging use of the NIBRS for measuring delinquency and crime; and provides updated statistics.
- Chapter 3 includes expanded sociobiological discussions of delinquency.
- Chapter 4 updates discussions on sociological explanations for delinquency and adds discussions on social support and social concern theory.
- Chapter 6 updates information on substance use and abuse by youths.
- Chapter 7 incorporates an extensive discussion of the race issue and how it affects policing; includes a discussion of possible reforms that are needed; and discusses police shootings.
- Chapter 8 adds an enhanced discussion of disproportionate minority contact and race.
- Chapter 9 includes an expanded discussion on juvenile life without parole, including life with parole and virtual life sentences; and adds the most recent Supreme Court decision on the issues.
- Chapters 10 and 11 update materials on issues in corrections, such as blended sentencing and Mendel's reform proposals.
- Chapter 12 has updated materials on restorative justice as it relates to delinquency with emphasis on family group conferencing.
- Chapter 13 has updated materials on victimization in school, especially as it relates to school shootings.
- The final chapter, Chapter 14, incorporates new reform proposals by Berry Feld and Elliot Currie; a discussion of police reform in light of police shootings and the killing of George Floyd; and the issues of life without parole and death sentences for juveniles.

Throughout the changes we recognize that we are often addressing some politically charged topics in today's world. We recognize there is a great deal of debate and strong differences of opinion on many of the issues. Our intent is not to take a side in the debate. Rather, we see the presentation as an academic treatise that sets forth the material and engenders debate. At the same time, we also recognize the long-standing debate about value-free research and the difficulty all academic writers have to totally subjugate their personal opinions when talking about charged issues. We have attempted to stay neutral and simply put forth the issues. Hopefully our readers can use this to prompt academic debate in the classroom.

In summary, we have tried to maintain a book that offers a comprehensive picture of juvenile offending, delinquency theories, and how juvenile justice actors and agencies react to delinquency. But we have also tried to introduce students to the controversial issues that arise as society attempts to prevent delinquency and to respond to delinquents in the most positive ways possible. We would like students to be both knowledgeable and critical; to understand how juvenile justice operates; and to be able to think about ways to improve what we have. Our hope is that professors can use this text as a starting point to help students think more deeply about the critical issues surrounding delinquency.

As with previous editions, there is instructional material that is available on the publisher's website for the book. There we have materials for both the instructor and the student. These materials supplement the book and can be incorporated into regular class activities or can be used by the individual for study and further exploration. Some of these materials are directed specifically to the student, while others are for the instructor.

We need to thank a lot of people who have provided insight on this edition, as well as all the past editions. No textbook is a success without support from others and the scholarship of countless academics and practitioners over the years. Attempting to name all the people who deserve to be mentioned is impossible without missing many individuals. We want to thank all of our colleagues with whom we have worked over the years and who have supported us. We especially need to acknowledge our editor Ellen Boyne and all of the people at Routledge (Anderson Publishing) for their support and hard work, as well as the reviewers of the book who offered important suggestions and insight. Finally, we want to thank our families for their support and understanding of the time we spend working on this book.

Preface

When we wrote the first edition of this book over 30 years ago, we never imagined it would still be going at this point. This tenth edition of *Juvenile Justice: An Introduction* is a testament to the fact that we must have done something right. We are thankful that our peers have found value in our work. As in the past, this tenth edition reflects changes in the juvenile justice landscape and we have attempted to offer insight of value to the students who will use this book. We have updated materials and statistics throughout the text. Highlights of the changes include:

- Chapter 1 offers updated materials on the definition of delinquency and juvenile across jurisdictions; adds material on the emerging use of the NIBRS for measuring delinquency and crime; and provides updated statistics.
- Chapter 3 includes expanded sociobiological discussions of delinquency.
- Chapter 4 updates discussions on sociological explanations for delinquency and adds discussions on social support and social concern theory.
- Chapter 6 updates information on substance use and abuse by youths.
- Chapter 7 incorporates an extensive discussion of the race issue and how it affects policing; includes a discussion of possible reforms that are needed; and discusses police shootings.
- Chapter 8 adds an enhanced discussion of disproportionate minority contact and race.
- Chapter 9 includes an expanded discussion on juvenile life without parole, including life with parole and virtual life sentences; and adds the most recent Supreme Court decision on the issues.
- Chapters 10 and 11 update materials on issues in corrections, such as blended sentencing and Mendel's reform proposals.
- Chapter 12 has updated materials on restorative justice as it relates to delinquency with emphasis on family group conferencing.
- Chapter 13 has updated materials on victimization in school, especially as it relates to school shootings.
- The final chapter, Chapter 14, incorporates new reform proposals by Berry Feld and Elliot Currie; a discussion of police reform in light of police shootings and the killing of George Floyd; and the issues of life without parole and death sentences for juveniles.

Throughout the changes we recognize that we are often addressing some politically charged topics in today's world. We recognize there is a great deal of debate and strong differences of opinion on many of the issues. Our intent is not to take a side in the debate. Rather, we see the presentation as an academic treatise that sets forth the material and engenders debate. At the same time, we also recognize the long-standing debate about value-free research and the difficulty all academic writers have to totally subjugate their personal opinions when talking about charged issues. We have attempted to stay neutral and simply put forth the issues. Hopefully our readers can use this to prompt academic debate in the classroom.

In summary, we have tried to maintain a book that offers a comprehensive picture of juvenile offending, delinquency theories, and how juvenile justice actors and agencies react to delinquency. But we have also tried to introduce students to the controversial issues that arise as society attempts to prevent delinquency and to respond to delinquents in the most positive ways possible. We would like students to be both knowledgeable and critical; to understand how juvenile justice operates; and to be able to think about ways to improve what we have. Our hope is that professors can use this text as a starting point to help students think more deeply about the critical issues surrounding delinquency.

As with previous editions, there is instructional material that is available on the publisher's website for the book. There we have materials for both the instructor and the student. These materials supplement the book and can be incorporated into regular class activities or can be used by the individual for study and further exploration. Some of these materials are directed specifically to the student, while others are for the instructor.

We need to thank a lot of people who have provided insight on this edition, as well as all the past editions. No textbook is a success without support from others and the scholarship of countless academics and practitioners over the years. Attempting to name all the people who deserve to be mentioned is impossible without missing many individuals. We want to thank all of our colleagues with whom we have worked over the years and who have supported us. We especially need to acknowledge our editor Ellen Boyne and all of the people at Routledge (Anderson Publishing) for their support and hard work, as well as the reviewers of the book who offered important suggestions and insight. Finally, we want to thank our families for their support and understanding of the time we spend working on this book.

CHAPTER 1

Introduction: The Definition and Extent of Delinquency

WHAT YOU NEED TO KNOW

- Delinquency can be defined in terms of: criminal laws, just like for adults; status offenses, which are applied only to youths; or sociological/criminological definitions, which take on a specific meaning depending on the interests of the individual or group studying delinquency.

- Defining delinquency requires one to define who is a juvenile. Most states outline minimum and maximum ages as well as exceptions in which the youth can be handled as an adult.

- Measures of delinquency include official records of the juvenile justice and criminal justice system and self-report surveys.

- According to the UCR NIBRS data, roughly 8.9 percent of all arrests are of youths under the age of 18, with 2 percent of all arrests for personal crimes and 8 percent for property crimes.

- Court and correctional statistics also provide insight to the extent of delinquency, although the magnitude of the problem appears much less due to the funneling effect of system involvement.

- Self-report measures reveal that virtually all youths offend, although this is true only when status offenses are included. Otherwise, the results are remarkably similar to official figures when serious crimes are considered.

- Regardless of the measure used, the trend in delinquency has been one of large increases since the 1960s with some leveling off and decreases since the late 1990s.

KEY TERMS

dark figure of crime

delinquency

disproportionate minority contact (DMC)

Index crimes

juvenile

Monitoring the Future (MTF)

National Incident-Based Reporting System (NIBRS)

National Youth Survey (NYS)

offense rate

panel design

Part I offenses

Part II offenses

self-report measures

sexting

Short–Nye instrument

status offense

Summary Reporting System (SRS)

transfer

Uniform Crime Reports (UCR)

victimless crimes

waiver

DOI: 10.4324/9781003167112-1

INTRODUCTION

Discussions of the juvenile justice system cannot proceed without a clear understanding of the behaviors that it is tasked to address. The juvenile court and the juvenile justice system are relatively recent inventions, tracing their history back to the late 1800s. Prior to that time, youths who broke the law were handled in the same system and in the same ways as adults. "Delinquency" was born in the late 1800s when crime and misbehavior by youths were redefined as separate and distinct from adult offenses, and new mechanisms of social control were developed to address problem children.

Youthful offenders, who used to be seen as simply young "criminals," have been transformed into "delinquents." The label of "delinquent," however, represents a variety of different behaviors and means different things at different places and points in time. It is important to understand the diversity in definitions of delinquency in order to examine the workings of the juvenile justice system adequately.

DEFINING DELINQUENCY

As already noted, **delinquency** has a number of different meanings. These various interpretations appear both in state statutes and criminological discussions of juvenile behavior. State statutes typically offer two sets of definitions for delinquency—a criminal law definition and a status offense definition. Beyond the codified legal definitions are social/criminological definitions that are used in research on juvenile misconduct.

Criminal Law Definitions

A criminal law definition of delinquency delineates activity that is illegal regardless of the age of the offender. "Delinquency" is simply a substitute label for criminal behavior by a juvenile. The only distinction between being a delinquent and being a criminal is the age of the individual.

WEB ACTIVITY

You can go to your state's statutes and look up the definitions of "delinquency," "status offense," and "juvenile."

Criminal law definitions of delinquency typically define a delinquent as someone who violates the criminal laws of the jurisdiction (see Box 1.1). The key to these statutes is the idea that a juvenile violated the criminal law. The fact that a juvenile committed the offense means that a different label will be imposed (delinquent versus criminal) and a different system will handle the individual (juvenile versus adult). A criminal law definition explicitly extends the criminal statutes to the juvenile population.

Status Offense Definitions

Besides criminal actions that can be committed by a juvenile, there are other behaviors for which only juveniles can be held accountable. This type of behavior is usually referred to as a **status offense** because it is only illegal if it

BOX 1.1 A CRIMINAL LAW DEFINITION OF DELINQUENCY

"Delinquent child" includes any of the following:

- Any child, except a juvenile traffic offender, who violates any law of this state or the United States, or any ordinance of a political subdivision of the state, that would be an offense if committed by an adult;

- Any child who violates any lawful order of the court, including a child who violates a court order regarding the child's adjudication as an unruly child for being an habitual truant;

- Any child who violates any lawful order of the court …;

- Any child who violates [prohibitions against purchasing or owning a firearm or handgun (Section 2923.211)].

Source: Ohio Revised Code (2017). Section 2152.02. Available at http://codes.ohio.gov/orc/2152.02Status.

BOX 1.2 A STATUS OFFENSE DEFINITION OF DELINQUENCY

Ohio Chapter 2151.022 defines an "unruly child" as:

- Any child who does not submit to the reasonable control of the child's parents, teachers, guardian, or custodian, by reason of being wayward or habitually disobedient;

- Any child who behaves in a manner as to injure or endanger the child's own health or morals or the health or morals of others;

- Any child who is an habitual truant from school;

- Any child who violates a law … that is applicable only to a child.

Source: Ohio Revised Code (2017). Section 2152.02. Available at http://codes.ohio.gov/orc/2152.02.

is committed by persons of a particular "status." Thus, juvenile status offenses represent acts that are illegal only for juveniles. Adults who take part in these acts are not subject to sanctioning by the formal justice system.

While "status offender" is the most common term for those who violate these acts, a variety of other names are applied to these individuals. Among the more common names are "unruly," "dependent," and "incorrigible," as well as acronyms such as PINS (person in need of supervision) or CHINS (child in need of supervision). One common criticism of status offense definitions is that they are ambiguous, and the language is so vague that they allow wide latitude in interpreting what is and is not a violation (see Box 1.2). Such statutes allow the juvenile justice system to intervene in the life of almost any youth. The behaviors outlined by status offense statutes make virtually any behavior of a juvenile sanctionable by the state. The definitions are all-encompassing and have been criticized for being overly broad (see, e.g., the President's Commission on Law Enforcement and the Administration of Justice, 1967). Arguments for eliminating such overly broad language have resulted in some courts ruling that the statutory language, such as that referring to "leading an idle, dissolute, lewd, or immoral life," is unconstitutionally vague (*Gonzalez v. Mailliard*, 1971).

School-age children are searched by a truancy task force in Richmond, Virginia, before being loaded into a van to be processed at the truant center. Truancy is a status offense, as it is a behavior for which only juveniles can be held accountable.

CREDIT: AP Photo/*Richmond Times-Dispatch*, Don Long

Actions that typically fall under the heading of status offenses include truancy; smoking; drinking; curfew violations; disobeying the orders of parents, teachers, or other adults; swearing; running away; and other acts that are allowable for adults. Most, if not all, juveniles violate these statutes at one time or another. Normal youthful behavior includes many of these activities. It is possible that all youths could be subjected to system intervention under these types of "status" definitions.

Social/Criminological Definitions

The study of delinquency and juvenile justice often relies on definitions of delinquency that do not conform precisely to the legal definitions of delinquent or status offenses. The definition of delinquency often takes on a specific meaning depending on the interests of the group or individual examining juvenile misconduct.

In one respect it is possible to define delinquency in terms of who is officially recognized as such. Cloward and Ohlin (1960), for example, define delinquent acts as those "that officials engaged in the administration of criminal justice select … from among many deviant acts, as forms of behavior proscribed by the approved norms of society" (Cloward & Ohlin, 1960:2–3). This means that the police, court officials, corrections officers, and others determine which actions are to be considered delinquent when they decide to take action. This limits delinquency to those actions that are handled by the justice system. Juvenile behavior that is ignored by the system is not to be considered delinquent.

Most definitions of delinquency present juvenile behavior as either delinquent or nondelinquent, with no middle ground. In reality, most individuals fall in between these extremes, having violated some laws and conformed to others. Most juveniles are involved, to varying degrees, in some form of delinquent behavior. Cavan and Ferdinand (1981) offer a continuum of behavior that ranges from extreme delinquency on one end to extreme "goodness" on the other (see Figure 1.1). The shape of the continuum, a bell curve, represents the proportional distribution of juveniles along the continuum. It is assumed that the largest group of youths would fall into the middle category of "normal conformity." The left-hand portion of the curve represent youths who run the risk of being apprehended and labeled delinquent. Minor underconformity may include such acts as status and victimless offenses while the delinquent contraculture category includes serious acts such as murder and rape and suggests organized involvement in deviance. The right side of the curve represents individuals who do not become involved in delinquency. Few

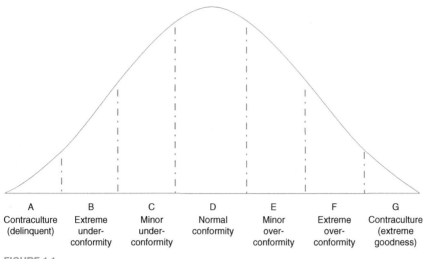

A	B	C	D	E	F	G
Contraculture (delinquent)	Extreme under-conformity	Minor under-conformity	Normal conformity	Minor over-conformity	Extreme over-conformity	Contraculture (extreme goodness)

FIGURE 1.1
Behavior Continuum

Source: Cavan and Ferdinand (1981).

juveniles appear in either of the "contraculture" categories of extreme delinquent or extreme goodness.

Today, most criminological research considers delinquency in terms of Cavan and Ferdinand's continuum. It does not limit the researcher to a simple legal definition or an either/or dichotomy. Instead, it allows the inspection of various types of delinquent activity as well as activity that is highly over-conforming. Seen as a continuum, juvenile activity can be subdivided into various parts and phases that change over time and can be compared to one another.

DEFINING A JUVENILE

In every definition of delinquency there is an implicit assumption of what constitutes a **juvenile**. Interestingly, the legal definition of a juvenile for juvenile court purposes varies from jurisdiction to jurisdiction. This means that persons subject to the juvenile statutes in one location may not be in another place. The majority of states (41) and the District of Columbia recognize the upper age for delinquent juveniles as individuals below the age of 18 (see Figure 1.2). Eight states list the age of majority below age 17 and one state considers anyone under 16 as a juvenile. Under these ages the individual is considered a juvenile and is handled in the juvenile justice system.

Besides setting an upper age for juvenile delinquency status, other factors influence whether an individual can be handled in the juvenile justice

WEB ACTIVITY

The Office of Juvenile Justice and Delinquency Prevention's *Statistical Briefing Book* provides access to a wealth of data on juveniles, including juvenile justice jurisdiction. Investigate the criteria for your state using that information (www.ojjdp.gov/ojstatbb) or go to your state's statutes for this information.

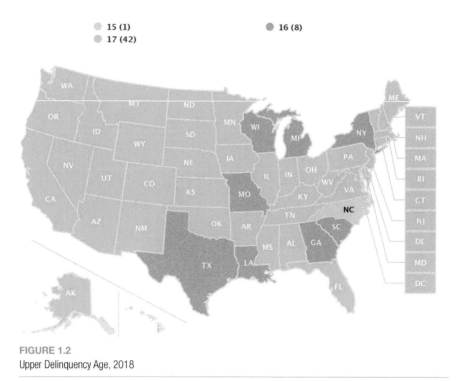

FIGURE 1.2
Upper Delinquency Age, 2018

Source: *OJJDP Statistical Briefing Book.* Online. Available at www.ojjdp.gov/ojstatbb/structure_process/ qa04102.asp?qaDate=2018. Released on December 13, 2019.

system. Thirty-two states and the District of Columbia set no lower age limit for being subject to juvenile justice intervention (see Figure 1.3). Eleven states set age 10 as the minimum for jurisdiction, four set age seven, one sets age 12, one sets age 11, one sets age eight, and one sets age six. In those states with a lower age level, any juvenile below the minimum age who exhibits deviant behavior is simply returned to his or her parents or guardian for handling.

Another age consideration is the termination of the juvenile system's intervention with an individual. Most state statutes allow the juvenile system to continue supervision and intervention with individuals who have passed the maximum age limit. Over two-thirds of the states (34) set the maximum age at which juvenile court jurisdiction is relinquished at age 20 (see Figure 1.4). Four states allow jurisdiction until age 24. Maintaining jurisdiction occurs mainly when that person committed his or her act as a juvenile and/or is being handled as an extension of intervention begun when he or she was a juvenile.

A final factor influencing juvenile court jurisdiction involves **waiver** or **transfer** provisions that may send a youth to adult court. Waiver is a process by which an individual who is legally a juvenile is sent to the adult criminal system for disposition and handling. The minimum age for transfer varies from state to state, with 24 states and the District of Columbia setting no minimum age. The most common minimum age set is 14.

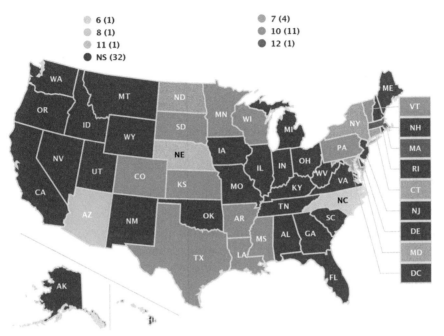

FIGURE 1.3
Lower Delinquency Age, 2018

Source: *OJJDP Statistical Briefing Book*. Online. Available at www.ojjdp.gov/ojstatbb/structure_process/qa04102.asp?qaDate= 2018. Released on December 13, 2019.

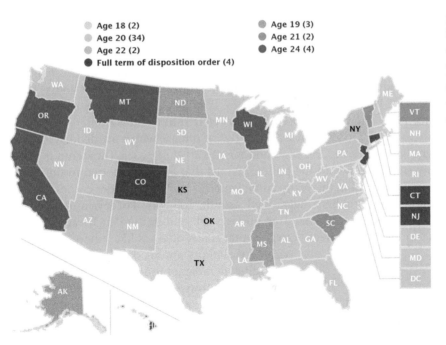

FIGURE 1.4
Extended Age of Juvenile Court Jurisdiction, 2019

Source: *OJJDP Statistical Briefing Book*. Online. Available at www.ojjdp.gov/ojstatbb/structure_process/qa04106.asp?qaDate= 2018. Released on December 13, 2019.

The varying definitions of delinquency and the consideration of what age constitutes being a "juvenile" have a major impact on any study of juvenile justice. The definitions alter the type of behavior with which we are concerned, the practices and interventions used in the treatment of delinquency, and the number of problems and youths subjected to intervention and study. It is the effect of the definition of delinquency on the measurement of delinquency to which we now turn.

THE EXTENT OF DELINQUENCY

There are various ways to measure delinquency, each of which produces a different picture of the delinquency problem. The different methods for measuring delinquency result in different absolute levels of delinquency as well as different information on the offense, the offender, and the victim. The two basic approaches to measuring delinquency are the use of official records and the administration of self-report surveys.

Official Measures of Delinquency

Official measures of delinquency are based on the records of various justice system agencies. Consequently, the level of delinquency reflects both the activity of juveniles and the activity of the agency that is dealing with the youths. The degree of detail in the records also varies by agency. The police, courts, and corrections each have different sets of priorities and mandates under which they operate. As a result, the data compiled by the agencies differ from one another. The following pages will consider data from each of these official sources.

Uniform Crime Reports

The **Uniform Crime Reports (UCR)** provide information on the number of offenses coming to the attention of the police, the number of arrests police make, and the number of referrals by the police to the juvenile court. These data have been collected yearly by the Federal Bureau of Investigation (FBI) since 1931. The traditional UCR (now referred to as the **Summary Reporting System [SRS]**) focuses on 29 categories of offense which are divided into the eight **Index**, or **Part I, offenses** and the 21 **Part II offenses**. These counts reflect only crimes known to the police. Actions that are not reported to the police are not included in the yearly crime figures. The Part I or Index crimes, include murder, rape, robbery, aggravated assault, burglary, larceny, motor vehicle theft, and arson. All remaining offenses fall within the Part II category. It is within the Part II offense category that status offenses like running away and curfew violations appear. Extensive information, including demographic data on the victim and offender (if known), circumstances of the offense, the use of a weapon, and the time and place of the offense, is gathered for the Part I offenses. For Part II offenses, only information on offenses for which a suspect has been arrested are tabulated.

Only 46 percent of all violent crime and 17 percent of all property crimes were cleared by an arrest in 2019, and this is limited to the Part I offenses. Little information, therefore, is known about the

WEB ACTIVITY

Extensive UCR data can be found at https://ucr.fbi.gov/crime-in-the-u.s/2019/crime-in-the-u.s.-2019/topic-pages/persons-arrested for information on age, sex, race/ethnicity, and other factors related to offending.

Information on the NIBRS system can be found at https://ucr.fbi.gov/nibrs/2018.

TABLE 1.1 Number and Percent of Arrests of Persons under 18 Years of Age, 2019

	Number	Percent
Violent Crime	35,253	9.8
Murder and Non-negligent Manslaughter	601	7.8
Forcible Rape	2,887	17.0
Robbery	12,266	21.6
Aggravated Assault	19,499	7.0
Property Crime	87,710	11.1
Burglary	14,504	12.1
Larceny-Theft	62,200	10.3
Motor Vehicle Theft	9,742	16.9
Arson	1,264	19.8
Total Part I Offenses	122,963	10.7

Source: Constructed by authors from FBI (2020b).

offender in most crimes. (Table 1.1 provides data on arrests involving persons under age 18 for the Part I crimes.) Juveniles constitute roughly 10.7 percent of the arrests for both Part I violent and property crimes in 2019.

The use of arrest data for measuring youthful offending is problematic mainly due to the focus on the Part I crimes listed in the UCR SRS. Beginning in 2021, the **National Incident-Based Reporting System (NIBRS)** replaces the SRS. The NIBRS data have several major advantages over the traditional UCR SRS data. First, the NIBRS collects detailed information on 23 categories with 52 total offenses (see Box 1.3) rather than just the eight Index Offenses. The offenses are grouped into three categories: Crimes against Persons, Crimes against Property, and Crimes against Society. Second, rather than abiding by the hierarchy rule and counting only the most serious Index Offenses, the NIBRS counts up to 10 offenses per criminal incident. Third, the NIBRS collects over 50 data elements, most of which are not found in the traditional SRS data, for each crime incident. Among the information included in this expanded data collection process is detailed information on the victim, the victim–offender relationship, injuries, and property loss (see Box 1.4). Other information collected includes the location of the offenses, the presence of weapons, property lost, number of victims and offenders, and arrestee information.

The great advantage of the NIBRS data is the ability of law enforcement and researchers to gain a more in-depth picture of the crime problem and to use that information to decide on appropriate courses of action. Unfortunately, participation in the NIBRS involves increased data entry requirements and data-processing abilities on the part of local law enforcement. The agencies must also meet stringent guidelines for participation. Because of these requirements,

BOX 1.3 NIBRS OFFENSE CATEGORIES

Crimes against Persons

Assault Offenses
Homicide Offenses
Human Trafficking Offenses
Kidnapping/Abduction
Sex Offenses

Crimes against Property

Arson
Bribery
Burglary/Breaking and Entering
Counterfeiting/Forgery
Destruction/Damage/Vandalism
Embezzlement
Extortion/Blackmail

Fraud Offenses
Larceny/Theft Offenses
Motor Vehicle Theft
Robbery
Stolen Property Offenses

Crimes against Society

Animal Cruelty
Drug/Narcotic Offenses
Gambling Offenses
Pornography/Obscene Material
Prostitution Offenses
Weapon Law Violations

Source: FBI (2019).

as of 2018 only 43 percent of the police agencies participate in the NIBRS (Federal Bureau of Investigation, 2019). Increased involvement in the NIBRS will enhance the value of official police crime data.

Table 1.2 presents juvenile offender data from the NIBRS for 2019. Roughly 585,000 arrests, or 8.9 percent of the total arrests, were of juveniles under the age of 18. Juveniles make up 12 percent of crimes against persons and 8 percent of crimes against property and crimes against society. A closer inspection of the arrest data reveals the extent to which youths were involved in crimes against persons. For the violent crime of murder, youths comprise 7 percent of the total arrests. They account for 12 percent of assault offenses, 21 percent of sexual offenses, and 4 percent of kidnapping/abductions. In total, this represents over 305,000 offenses. In addition, youths represent almost 8 percent of all arrests for property offenses and crimes against society.

Sex Distribution

The UCR routinely presents breakdowns of crime by sex of the offender. NIBRS data for 2019 show that juvenile females made up roughly 30 percent of all juvenile arrests. A much greater percentage of males are arrested for every offense category. The only offense for which females are more often arrested is prostitution offenses.

Race Distribution

The UCR also provides information on the race of juvenile arrestees. Table 1.2 presents data on arrests for white, black, and other youths. White youths make up almost two-thirds of all arrestees (62.1 percent), and account for roughly 60 percent of the crimes against persons and crimes against property. Black

BOX 1.4 INFORMATION COLLECTED BY NIBRS

Offense Information:

Bias motivation

Location type

Number of premises entered

Method of entry

Type of criminal activity/

   Gang Information

Type of weapon/Force involved

Property Segment:

Type of property loss/etc.

Property description

Value of property

Date recovered

Number of stolen motor vehicles

Number of recovered motor vehicles

Suspected drug type

Estimated drug quantity

Type of drug measurement

Offender Segment:

Age, sex, race, ethnicity

Arrestee Segment:

Arrest date

Type of arrest

Multiple arrestee segments indicator

Arrestee was armed with

Age, sex, race, ethnicity

Resident status

Disposition of arrestee under 18

Victim Segment:

Type of victim

Age, sex, race, ethnicity

Resident status

Aggravated assault/Homicide circumstances

Additional justifiable homicide circumstances

Type of injury

Relationship of victim to offender

Source: FBI (2015).

youths, however, are greatly overrepresented in most offenses when considering their numbers in the population—roughly 15 percent of the youths in the U.S. (U.S. Bureau of the Census, 2011). All other racial groups, which include native Americans, Asians, Pacific Islanders, and others, account for a relatively small percentage of arrests (typically less than 3 percent combined). Only for gambling offenses are numbers of the "other" category significant contributors (21 percent).

An examination of individual Part I offenses in the SRS provides a more detailed look at the data. While a greater percentage of white youths commit every type of offense than do blacks, except for murder and robbery, offending by black youths far surpasses their population representation for all Part I offenses. Arrests of black youths also exceed that of white youths in the Part II categories of stolen property offenses, prostitution and commercialized vice, and gambling.

TABLE 1.2 Distribution of Juvenile Arrests, 2019 NIBRS

Offense Category	Percent					
	Juvenile	Male	Female	White	Black or African American	Other
Total Offenses	**8.9**	**70.8**	**29.1**	**62.1**	**35.1**	**2.7**
Crimes against Persons	**12.0**	**72.0**	**28.0**	**58.4**	**38.8**	**2.8**
Assault Offenses	11.5	70.2	29.8	57.8	39.4	2.8
Homicide Offenses	7.0	86.6	13.4	44.2	53.8	2.0
Human Trafficking Offenses	4.4	80.0	20.0	49.5	45.5	5.0
Kidnapping/Abduction	3.7	82.9	17.8	59.7	37.3	3.0
Sex Offenses	20.9	93.8	6.2	69.3	27.8	2.9
Crimes against Property	**7.9**	**69.0**	**31.0**	**60.0**	**37.2**	**2.8**
Arson	19.3	78.1	21.9	68.4	28.9	2.7
Bribery	5.5	71.9	28.1	78.4	18.4	3.2
Burglary/Breaking & Entering	7.2	80.8	19.2	63.6	34.0	2.4
Counterfeiting/Forgery	2.0	62.9	37.1	65.4	32.1	2.5
Destruction/Damage/Vandalism	11.8	74.1	25.9	60.3	37.1	2.6
Embezzlement	3.2	50.5	49.5	60.4	37.4	2.2
Extortion/Blackmail	6.4	64.3	35.7	69.2	25.1	5.7
Fraud Offenses	2.9	62.0	38.0	63.4	33.3	3.3
Larceny/Theft Offenses	7.1	63.7	36.3	61.1	36.2	2.7
Motor Vehicle Theft	9.2	76.0	24.0	63.7	33.1	3.2
Robbery	13.5	87.6	12.4	30.5	67.3	2.2
Stolen Property Offenses	10.7	76.2	23.8	62.4	33.7	3.9
Crimes against Society	**7.6**	**72.4**	**27.6**	**69.4**	**28.1**	**2.5**
Animal Cruelty	2.9	59.8	40.2	71.9	25.9	2.2
Drug/Narcotic Offenses	6.8	71.1	28.9	71.7	25.8	2.5
Gambling Offenses	2.8	78.0	22.0	45.3	33.4	21.3
Pornography/Obscene Material	42.0	76.2	23.8	76.4	21.5	2.1
Prostitution Offenses	1.3	46.5	53.5	53.7	37.4	8.9
Weapon Law Violations	10.8	86.1	13.1	51.0	47.1	1.9

Source: Constructed by authors from FBI (2020a).

Trends in Delinquency

The trend in youthful crime has changed in recent years. The change in the number of violent offenses since 1988 appears in Figure 1.5. Arrests for both murder and rape have remained relatively stable, while robbery and aggravated

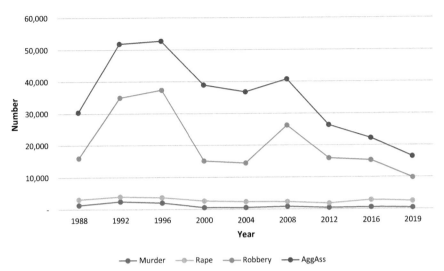

FIGURE 1.5
Trend in Juvenile Violent Crime, 1988–2019

Source: Constructed by authors from UCR SRS data.

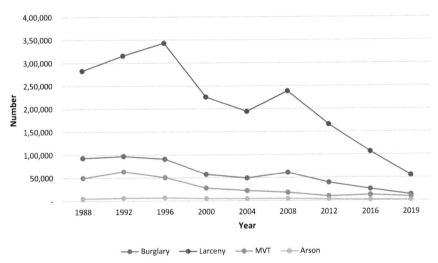

FIGURE 1.6
Trend in Juvenile Property Crime, 1988–2019

Source: Constructed by authors from UCR SRS data.

assault arrests increased from 1988 to 1996, dropped until 2004, rose until 2008, and dropped again over the following 11 years. Data on property crimes (see Figure 1.6) show general declines since 1986, except for a slight increase in 2008 for both larceny and burglary. Similar trends are evident when considering the **offense rate** (typically the number of offenses per 100,000), which eliminates the influence of any changes in the number of potential offenders on the delinquency data. One thing that is clear in both the raw number of arrests and the arrest rate figures is that official juvenile offending is higher today than 40 years ago, although the recent trend has been toward lower arrests.

A Critique of the UCR

The UCR is the longest running and most widely known and cited method of collecting information on crime in the United States. It began in 1931 and has continued on a yearly basis since that time and is undergoing major changes with the advent of the NIBRS. Despite this longevity, the UCR has a number of flaws that must be considered when using the data (see O'Brien, 1985). The most frequent criticism is the fact that it reflects only those offenses known to the police. Many individuals, for whatever reason, opt not to contact the police when they are a victim of or a witness to a crime. This failure to bring crimes to the attention of the police results in an undercount of crime in the United States. The unreported crimes are typically referred to as the **dark figure of crime**. In terms of juvenile behavior, the UCR focuses on more serious offending, since that is the focus of police activity, and it fails to consider the vast array of status offenses committed by youths (see Box 1.5).

A second concern with the UCR is that it is voluntary, and it relies on the individual agencies to report their data accurately. Each agency tabulates and forwards its own data to the FBI. Political and economic pressures have been known to influence the accuracy of counts submitted to the UCR system. For example, changes in police procedure due to political decisions can alter the amount of attention a police department pays to a certain form of crime. Similarly, the simple reclassification of offenses from one category to another (i.e., listing "rapes" as "other sex offenses," or "aggravated assaults" as "simple assaults") can alter the reported crime rates. Decisions like these can greatly alter the annual offense counts and have an impact on trend data over time.

BOX 1.5 CRITICISMS OF THE UCR

Dark Figure of Crime	Offenses that are not reported to the police and therefore are not reflected in UCR data
Voluntary	Agencies do not have to report their figures to the UCR and can manipulate the data that they do report
Limited Offender Data	Data available only on those offenders who are arrested; unable to know if those arrested are representative of all offenders
Focus on Offenses	Counts offenses and not offenders; fails to consider the fact that one offender can be responsible for multiple offenses
Changing Crime Definitions	Changes in the legal definitions of crimes over time and jurisdictions makes comparison of crime data difficult
Data Collection Techniques	There is a lack of knowledge on what impact changing methods for data collection (such as from hand to computers) can have on the data reports
System Bias	Impact of system policies on data collection is not clear

Another concern in using the UCR is the lack of information on offenders in much of the data. Arrest data reflect only those offenders who were caught in the course of the crime or ensuing investigation. The fact that less than 20 percent of all crimes are cleared by an arrest means that little is known about the offenders in most crimes. It is possible that UCR figures are distorted in terms of the age, race, and sex distribution of the total offending population. The UCR provides no information about the offender in more than 80 percent of the crimes committed each year.

Another serious problem entails the fact that the UCR counts offenses and not offenders. It would be easy to claim that the number of offenders is equal to the number of reported offenses, but unfortunately this would provide a highly inaccurate picture. Many offenders commit more than one offense over a period of time. As illustrated in the NIBRS, some individuals commit multiple crimes during a single criminal incident (such as bank robbery), with robbery, assault, and possibly kidnapping all occurring at the same time. These problems make it difficult to estimate the number of offenders over any period of time using the UCR. The number of offenders is clearly not equal to the number of offenses.

A variety of other concerns must be considered in using the UCR data. Among these is the fact that legal definitions of crime change over time and vary from place to place. In addition, the methods of data collection have changed over time (particularly from hand to computer tabulation). A further concern is the fact that any selective enforcement of the law or bias in making arrests can result in an overrepresentation of certain individuals (such as lower-class youths) in the UCR figures.

The most problematic aspect of official police data for the study of delinquency is the combined issues of the dark figure of crime and the failure to identify offenders in the vast majority of all cases. It is due to these problems that alternative methods of unofficial crime and delinquency data have been developed. Before turning to these types of data collection, we will look at two additional official measures of delinquency.

Juvenile Court Statistics

Juvenile court data present a picture of the cases and the juveniles who reach the adjudication stage of the system. The numbers of juveniles who appear in these records are smaller than those found in police data. This is due primarily to the fact that most juveniles reach the court through contact with the police who filter and screen cases. Relatively few youths are referred to court directly by their families, schools, or other associates. At the same time, court data offer more insight to status offending.

Table 1.3 presents data on delinquency cases in juvenile court. In 2018, almost 745,000 youths reached the juvenile court for delinquent offenses. This translates into a rate of 23.5 out of every 1,000 youths. An additional 100,400 youths reached the court for status offenses (a rate of roughly 3.2 per 1,000 youths). There is almost an equal number of personal and property crimes in

TABLE 1.3 Number and Percent of Youths in Juvenile Court, 2018

Most serious offense	Number	Percent of Cases Handled by Juvenile Courts					
		Female	White	Black	American Indian	Asian/ Pacific Islander	Hispanic
Total Delinquency	744,500	27	44	35	2	1	18
Person Offenses	232,400	30	41	38	2	1	18
Violent Crime Index*	54,400	16	29	47	1	1	21
Property Offenses	225,900	25	43	38	2	1	16
Property Crime Index**	156,200	27	41	39	2	1	17
Drug Law Violations	101,000	25	55	19	2	1	23
Public Order Offenses	185,100	28	43	36	1	1	19

* Includes criminal homicide, rape, robbery, and aggravated assault.
** Includes burglary, larceny-theft, motor vehicle theft, and arson.

Source: Adapted by authors from Sickmund, Sladky, and Kang (2020).

court, followed by public order offenses (e.g., disorderly conduct and liquor law violations) and drug law violations. Information on type of offense, sex, and race is also available in the court statistics. Like the UCR data, males dominate throughout the juvenile court statistics and typically account for at least three-quarters of offenses. While white youths dominate in all categories of delinquent offenses (40 percent or more), black youths are overrepresented relative to their proportion of the population.

The number of delinquency cases today far exceeds that of four decades ago (see Figure 1.7). The number of property cases peaked in 1994–1996 and has generally fallen since that time. The number of person, drug, and public order cases increased from 1960 to roughly 1996 and generally remained steady until 2008, when they started to decline. While the number of property cases in 2018 is almost 400,000 less than in 1985, the level of all other cases is still higher than in 1985. Taking a longer time period into consideration, the number of cases in 2014 remains significantly higher than in 1960. While the trend in delinquency caseloads has been declining since 2005 for both males and females, the decline is more pronounced in the male data. This is due mainly to the fact that the raw number of offenses for males is higher. There has been a similar decline in delinquency cases for all racial groups over the past 10 years (Hockenberry & Puzzanchera, 2017).

WEB ACTIVITY

Additional juvenile court statistics are available at: www.ojjdp.gov/ojstatbb/ezajcs/asp/selection.asp.

Juvenile Corrections Statistics

A third official source of information on juveniles coming into contact with the juvenile justice system is records kept on juvenile correctional facilities. The U.S. Justice Department routinely conducts a census of the population of

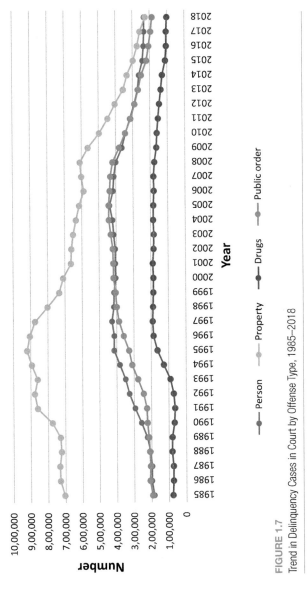

FIGURE 1.7

Trend in Delinquency Cases in Court by Offense Type, 1985–2018

Source: Constructed by authors from Sickmund et al. (2020).

juvenile facilities. As with juvenile court statistics, the numbers of youths who appear in these statistics are smaller than the UCR and court figures. Juvenile facilities rely heavily upon the juvenile court for their clients, and few of the youths coming into contact with the court are sentenced to confinement. Therefore, the figures found in data from juvenile facilities represent only a fraction of all the youths having contact with the juvenile system.

Table 1.4 presents data on youths in public and private juvenile facilities in 2017. The data in the table represent an average one-day count, and the daily totals would vary around these figures. Public facilities handled roughly 31,000 youths, and private institutions dealt with almost 13,000 youths on any one day (Sickmund, Sladky, Kang, & Puzzanchera, 2019). There are no significant differences between types of facilities in terms of sex of juveniles held, while private facilities handle a larger percentage of whites and a lower percentage of Hispanics youths. Few differences appear in the reason for admission when comparing public and private institutions. Each type of institution handles roughly the same proportion of youths committing different types of offenses. The only significant difference appears in status offenses (where private facilities handle a greater percentage) and personal offenses (where public facilities handle a greater percentage) (Sickmund et al., 2019).

TABLE 1.4 Characteristics of Juveniles in Correctional Facilities: Average One-Day Counts (and Percentages), 2017

Characteristic	Public Facility	Private Facility
Number of Juveniles	30,896 (70.9%)	12,684 (29.1%)
Sex		
Males	26,331 (85.2)	10,651 (84.0)
Females	4,565 (14.8)	2,033 (16.0)
Race		
White	9,162 (29.7)	5,053 (39.8)
Black	12,889 (41.7)	4,952 (39.0)
Hispanic	7,241 (23.4)	1,920 (15.1)
Other	1,604 (5.2)	759 (6.1)
Reason for Admission		
Person Offense	13,401 (43.4)	4,558 (35.9)
Property Offense	6,745 (21.8)	2,823 (22.3)
Drug Offense	1,371 (4.4)	769 (6.1)
Public Order Offense	3,742 (12.1)	1,830 (14.4)
Status Offense	465 (1.5)	1,225 (9.7)
Technical Violation	5,172 (16.7)	1,479 (11.7)

Source: Compiled by authors from Sickmund et al. (2019).

Not unlike UCR or court statistics, correctional figures show that most offenders are male. Females make up roughly 15 percent of institutionalized youths. In terms of types of offenses, males greatly outnumber females for every category except status offenses, where females make up 15 percent of those in custody (Sickmund et al., 2019). The racial breakdown for youths reveals that blacks are committed to a facility more often than any other group. Indeed, roughly 40 percent of all committed youths are black, followed by whites (30 percent), Hispanics (21 percent), and all other racial/ethnic groups (Sickmund et al., 2019).

The trend in correctional figures is somewhat interesting. Figures indicate that the number of incarcerated youths steadily increased from 1983 to 1999, with steady reductions since. The one-day count of youths in public and private facilities increased from 80,091 in 1983 to 99,008 in 1993

WEB ACTIVITY

Correctional data are available at www. ojjdp.gov/ojstatbb/ezacjrp.

(a 24 percent increase) to 120,563 in 1999 (a further 22 percent increase), although the number decreased by 64 percent to 43,580 in 2017. The earlier increases may be due to the increased violence and drug problems in the late 1980s and early 1990s. Recent moderation in incarceration mirrors the reduction in arrest statistics.

Summary of Official Statistics

Each of the various official measures of delinquency presents a slightly different view of juvenile offending. In terms of numbers of offenses, the UCR presents the most disturbing picture due to the large numbers of offenses it reflects. In addition to the number of offenses, the UCR provides detailed information on a variety of demographic and crime-related characteristics. Unfortunately, as noted earlier, this source of data has a number of inherent defects that limit its usefulness, in particular its reliance upon offenses known to the police.

Juvenile court statistics and correctional facility data also present a picture of juvenile misconduct that is somewhat narrow. A large part of the problem with these figures lies in the fact that they are greatly dependent on the productivity of the police. Most youths entering the courts and institutions initiate their journey by way of police contact. Any failure at the police level, therefore, carries over to these other counts. The increased levels of status offenses in court and correctional data is one point at which discrepancies with the arrest data appear. This is probably due to court referrals from sources other than the police. The problems and differences do not make the information useless, though. Rather, the data can be used to assess the workings of the institutions over time and provide insight into the juvenile system. They cannot be used to portray the extent of the juvenile crime problem accurately.

The fact that more minority youths, particularly African-American youths, are found in official data than their population representation is one that has long been recognized in the literature. This situation was first formally recognized in the 1980s and labeled as disproportionate minority confinement reflecting the number of youths in secure custody. This term as been expanded to **disproportionate minority contact (DMC)**, which recognizes the overrepresentation of minority youths at almost all stages of the juvenile justice system, including arrest, court referral, and detention.

The extent and level of DMC is evident throughout the juvenile justice system data and over time, although the level is not stable across jurisdictions or time. Leiber and Fix (2019), looking at data from 2005 to 2015, report that DMC is found across the states and that the African-American contact is often more than three times that for whites and/or twice the African-American proportion of the population. Comparing the data over time shows increasing levels of disproportionate contact for African Americans. Similar disparities are also found when considering other minority youths (such as Hispanic youths). Some points in the juvenile justice system have shown reductions in disproportionality while others show increases. The issue of DMC will appear at various points in this book and will be discussed in more detail in relation to other topics.

Self-Report Measures of Delinquency

Self-report measures attempt to gauge the level of delinquency by asking individuals to tell of their participation in deviant activity. This approach has a number of advantages. First, it is possible to measure both actions "known to the police" and those that are not known by official agents of social control. Second, it becomes possible to gather information on all offenders and not just those few who are arrested for an offense. Self-reports do not need an arrest in order to have information on the perpetrator. Third, self-report surveys can ask a variety of questions designed to elicit information useful in understanding why an individual violates the law. Information routinely collected includes data on family background (such as broken home, parental affection), economic status (occupation, income), education, attitudes (toward school, family, or work), friends' behavior, and others, as well as direct questions about the individual's behavior. This type of information is not available from most official delinquency measures. For these and other reasons, self-report methods have proliferated in recent years.

Self-report surveys have a fairly long history in juvenile justice. One of the earliest surveys was developed by James Short and Ivan Nye (1958; see Box 1.6). This survey asked youths to note the frequency with which they committed each of 24 items. The items in the scale were dominated by status and minor offenses. The few serious crimes included in the original list (such as stealing over $50) were deleted in subsequent forms of the scales, which included only seven items.

Self-report scales like the **Short–Nye instrument** invariably uncover a great deal of delinquent activity. Indeed, various studies using these types of scales show that virtually every person is a delinquent. This is due to the fact that it is hard to conceive of anyone saying they never committed any of the behaviors

BOX 1.6 SHORT AND NYE SELF-REPORTED DELINQUENCY ITEMS

- Defied parents' authority*
- "Run away" from home
- Driven a car without a driver's license or permit*
- Skipped school*
- Had a fist fight with one person
- Taken little things (worth less than $2) that did not belong to you*
- Taken things of medium value ($2–$50)
- Taken things of large value ($50)
- School probation or expulsion
- Used force (strong-arm methods) to get money from another person
- Driven too fast or recklessly
- Taken part in "gang fights"
- Taken a car for a ride without the owner's knowledge
- Bought or drank beer, wine, or liquor (including drinking at home)*

- Bought or drank beer, wine, or liquor (outside your home)
- Drank beer, wine, or liquor in your own home
- Deliberate property damage*
- Used or sold narcotic drugs
- Had sex relations with another person of the same sex (not masturbation)*
- Had sex relations with a person of the opposite sex
- Gone hunting or fishing without a license (or violated other game laws)
- Taken things you didn't want
- "Beat up" on kids who hadn't done anything to you
- Hurt someone to see them squirm

* Commonly used items in self-report surveys.

Source: Compiled by authors from Short and Nye (1958).

asked, particularly the status offenses. Defying parental authority or trying alcohol at some time are rather universal activities by juveniles. Asking if the individual has "ever" committed an act contributes to the high levels of positive responses. Compared to official counts of delinquency, such self-reports show a great deal more deviance.

Criticism of early self-report surveys, particularly due to their focus on minor activities and their exclusion of major delinquent/criminal offenses, prompted some researchers to develop surveys that more closely mirrored actions covered in the UCR. Two of these early surveys were the Monitoring the Future (MTF) survey (started in 1975) and the National Youth Survey (NYS) (started in 1976). Both of these include many more serious offenses and elicit significantly fewer positive responses. These surveys include questions on hitting teachers, group fighting, use of weapons, robbery, and aggravated assault.

The NYS used a panel design, beginning with a group of 11- to 17-year-olds from across the United States. A panel design means that the same set of individuals are interviewed repeatedly over a period of time. In the case of the NYS, this was over a number of years. This allowed researchers to compare the number of offenses and changes in offending over time. The NYS eventually became known as the NYS Family Study (NYSFS) and reflected the individuals as adults age 39–45. (A list of the kinds of behaviors probed by the NYS can be found in Box 1.7.)

BOX 1.7 NATIONAL YOUTH SURVEY ITEMS

Aggravated assault	Joyriding	Had sexual intercourse
Sexual assault	Damaged family property	Cheated on school test
Gang fights	Damaged school property	Stole at school
Hit teacher	Damaged other property	Thrown objects
Hit parent	Drug use	Carried hidden weapon
Hit student	Prostitution	Stole from family
Strong-armed robbery of student	Drug sales	Threatened physical violence for sex
Strong-armed robbery of teachers	Hitchhiked	
Strong-armed robbery of others	Disorderly conduct	Pressured someone for sex
Stole motor vehicle	Public drunkenness	Credit card fraud
Stole something over $50	Panhandled	Used checks illegally
Broke into building or vehicle	Made obscene phone calls	Fraud
Bought stolen goods	Runaway	**Arson**
Theft under $5	Skipped class	
Theft between $5 and $50	Lied about age	

Source: Jamieson and Flanagan (1987).

WEB ACTIVITY

Data from Monitoring the Future can be found at the MTF website at www.monitoringthefuture.org/datavolumes/2012/2012dv.pdf.

The MTF project surveys a national sample of youths and young adults each year. At its initiation, the project surveyed 12th graders each year. In 1991, the survey was expanded to include 8th and 10th graders and young adults. The MTF focuses primarily on drug use, although it also probes delinquent behavior. While different respondents participate each year, it is possible to examine general trends and changes over time.

Self-report surveys such as the NYS and MTF uncover much less offending than found in surveys that focus on minor offenses, such as status offenses. This is due to the inclusion of more serious offenses such as using a knife or gun in a robbery or hitting a teacher. Alternatively, items like arguing with your parents elicit much higher levels of behavior. Table 1.5 presents results for high school seniors in the 2012 MTF data. Less than 3 percent report ever using a weapon to steal something or hitting an instructor or supervisor, while 85 percent admit to arguing or fighting with parents. The data reveal similar levels of offending for males and females and for whites and blacks in most categories. Most racial breakdowns also reveal similar offense patterns.

Official and Self-Report Comparisons

Self-report data show that, although many persons commit various deviant acts, the majority of subjects confine their activity to minor offenses. Indeed, when major, serious offenses are included, there is a great decrease in the level of reported offending. The figures become much more similar to those in official statistics.

TABLE 1.5 Monitoring the Future, 2012

In the past 12 months:	Total	Sex		Race	
		Male	Female	White	Black
Argued or had a fight with either of your parents	85.0	83.3	88.0	88.5	69.1
Hit an instructor or supervisor	2.5	3.6	1.2	2.2	1.8
Gotten into a serious fight in school or at work	11.1	14.4	7.4	11.1	9.9
Taken part in a fight where a group of your friends were against another group	14.3	16.0	12.7	13.9	10.6
Hurt someone badly enough to need bandages or a doctor	10.3	14.9	5.4	9.4	12.5
Used a knife or gun or some other thing (like a club) to get something from a person	2.7	4.3	1.0	2.3	3.0
Taken something not belonging to you worth under $50	22.1	27.8	16.4	23.3	19.0
Taken something not belonging to you worth over $50	7.3	10.5	4.1	6.6	6.9
Taken something from a store without paying for it	22.9	23.3	20.8	20.0	26.3
Taken a car that didn't belong to someone in your family without permission of the owner	3.9	5.4	2.3	2.9	3.0
Taken part of a car without permission of the owner	2.3	3.3	1.3	1.8	2.7
Gone into some house or building when you weren't supposed to be there	21.1	26.1	16.6	20.7	17.3
Set fire to someone's property on purpose	2.0	3.3	0.9	1.6	1.7
Damaged school property on purpose	7.6	9.4	5.8	7.3	8.5
Damaged property at work on purpose	2.7	4.1	1.6	2.4	1.7
Been arrested and taken to a police station	5.6	8.8	2.7	5.7	5.5

Source: Compiled by authors from Bachman, Johnson, & O'Malley (2014).

The age distribution of offending in self-report data generally mirrors that of official data. Offending increases as individuals reach later teen and young adult years. Some variation emerges when the content of the self-report survey changes. Younger respondents tend to report less offending when serious offenses (such as aggravated assault and felony theft) are considered. Older youths report more serious offending and substance use. Unlike in official data, most differences in offending by race are modest in size. Data from the MTF project show only minor variation between black respondents and white respondents. The self-report data do not show the evidence of DMC seen in official data, thus suggesting the juvenile justice and criminal justice systems respond more to misbehaviors by minority youths. Self-report surveys display sex differences similar to those found in official data. Almost without exception, males report higher involvement in offending than females, although the differences are dependent on the type of behavior.

Self-report studies provide a means of examining youthful behavior in ways not available in official figures. Self-reports are useful in investigating so-called "victimless" crimes. **Victimless crimes** are behaviors in which the offender does not typically have a victim besides himself/herself. Drug offenses are one good example of a victimless crime where the offender/user is not one who calls the authorities to make a complaint about the behavior. The MTF survey is a prime example of a self-report survey providing information on drug use. That does not always draw the attention of the formal social control agencies, at least initially.

Another topic receiving increased attention through self-report surveys is **sexting**. Döring (2014) defines sexting as "the interpersonal exchange of self-produced sexualized texts and above all images (photos, videos) via cell phone or the internet." Besides by a cell phone, sexting can be by email, social networks, online postings, or faxing, among other electronic means. Data on sexting typically rely on surveys of youths and young adults. These surveys may combine a self-report survey on the extent to which respondents report being involved in sexting and a victimization survey in which respondents are asked if they have been the target of sexting. Asking youths about their lives and behaviors can open up new avenues for exploration.

Critique of Self-Report Data

Self-report data pose separate problems for researchers (see Box 1.8). The most common concern with self-report data involves the truthfulness of the respondents. Interestingly, most investigations into the validity of the self-report data show that the figures are fairly accurate. This assessment is based on studies that compare self-report results to lie-detector tests, repeated measures, and cross checks with other forms of data (Clarke & Tifft, 1966; Gold, 1970; Hardt & Peterson-Hardt, 1977; Hindelang, Hirschi, & Weis, 1981; Lab & Allen, 1984). The greatest discrepancies between self-report and official figures can be attributed to the different domains of behavior that are tapped by the two methods. Official records focus more on serious offenses, while self-reports often probe more minor offending.

BOX 1.8 CRITICISMS OF SELF-REPORT SURVEYS

Truthfulness	Respondents can falsify their answers, although research shows high levels of accuracy when checks can be made
Limited Respondents	Mostly youthful respondents; lack of adult respondents
Representativeness	Miss different groups in society, such as youths not in school, adults not in college; use of institutionalized populations not representative
Limited Domains	Focus on minor crimes; miss major offenses
Non-Systematic	With a few notable exceptions, self-reports are one-shot studies and there are no repeats against which to compare the results

An additional shortcoming of self-report data is the focus on juveniles. Due to the problems of locating accessible groups of adults, most self-report research has been carried out on youths. Although the data are rich with information on children, there is little opportunity to compare the findings to those found on adults. Typical adult samples found in self-report surveys deal with institutionalized adults or young adults in college settings. Neither of these two groups are representative of the general adult population. The method of selecting youths for self-report surveys may also bias the results. The typical use of school students in surveys may inadvertently miss high-rate offenders who are truants or dropouts and not present at the time of data collection.

COMPARING THE DELINQUENCY MEASURES

The different types of delinquency measures (official and self-report) show both similarities and differences. In general, they show that delinquency is a widespread problem. It is not restricted to any one group, area, or type of offense. The level of offending increased throughout the 1960s and early 1970s, leveled off and showed some decreases in the late 1970s and 1980s, increased in the late 1980s and early 1990s (particularly in serious personal offenses), decreased until about 2004, increased from 2004 to 2008, and has decreased since 2008. There is a clear diversity in offending. Youths are involved in all types of behavior—from status offenses to serious personal crimes. Property crimes dominate in all measures, and personal offenses are the least common.

The differences between the measures are a result of the measurement techniques. Official records provide an ongoing look at the level and change in delinquency from year to year according to the formal justice system. These records reflect offenses that are brought to the attention of the authorities. Actions that are not reported but are withheld from public officials are lost to these records. Self-reports typically portray a larger delinquency problem than official figures. The cause of this is the type of activities that are probed in the survey. Surveys that inquire about minor status offenses will always find high delinquency levels. When more serious offenses form the core of the self-report questionnaire, however, the number of delinquents falls to lower levels.

Most differences in the measures appear in the relative magnitude of offending and by offending subgroups in the population. Official measures differ in magnitude, with police figures leading court and correctional data. In terms of demographics, official figures show a much larger number of minority black offenders than self-report measures. Self-report statistics find little racial difference in offending. Similar discrepancies emerge when considering the sex of the offenders. While males dominate in magnitude of offending, official figures show the sexes committing different types of offenses. Self-report data, however, tend to portray the sexes as participating in the same types of behavior.

No single method of measuring delinquency should be considered better than the others. The usefulness of the measures depends entirely on the question that is being answered. Each method provides a different set of information about delinquency. Official records are useful for noting change in official processing and handling of youths over time. They also provide a long-term set of data that allows the inspection of changes over time. Official data are also rich in information about various demographic and offense factors not found in other measures. Self-reports provide a measure of delinquency based on the offender's viewpoint. They are capable of addressing behaviors that may not result in arrests and lead to official records. These measures are rich in data on minor crimes, the number of offenses an individual commits, demographics on offenders, and why an individual acts in a certain way.

SUMMARY

The study of delinquency depends heavily on the definition of delinquency and the measurement of the problem. Delinquency can be limited to those acts that are violations of the criminal code, focus on actions that are illegal only for juveniles, represent some combination of both criminal and status offenses, or can be molded to fit the criminological question of each researcher.

The outcome of this search for a definition of delinquency is a vast array of different measures of delinquency and resultant claims about the level of delinquent activity. The major methods of measuring delinquency—official and self-report—rely on somewhat different conceptions of what constitutes delinquency. The UCR, for example, is oriented more toward a criminal law point of view. The SRS considers only two very broad status offense categories (runaway; and curfew and loitering) among the 29 offense categories. The NIBRS expands the number of categories and crimes but is still oriented toward criminal law definitions of delinquency. Conversely, self-reports often rely heavily on status offenses in their surveys and include only a few (mostly property) criminal offenses.

Perhaps the reason behind the great discrepancies in definitions and measures can be found in the history of juvenile justice. The juvenile system has grown quickly since its inception and has seen many changes. Part of this is due to changes in the view society holds of youthful offenders. It may also be attributable to changes in the field of criminology and corrections. The changes in the juvenile system and the impact of various factors on the definition and extent of delinquency make up the substance for the next chapter on the history of juvenile justice.

DISCUSSION QUESTIONS

1. You have been appointed to write a definition of delinquency for the state legislature. You can either propose a new definition or rely on the existing definition. What is your definition? Why is it best, and why should it be accepted?

2. You have been asked to research each of the following questions or issues. What type of delinquency measure(s) will you use and why?

   • How much delinquency is there in the country?
   • What characterizes the typical juvenile offender?
   • Has the delinquency rate increased or decreased over the past 15 years?

3. A discussion has arisen over the best measure of delinquency. As an expert on such matters, you are asked to present an unbiased view of the strengths and weaknesses of official and self-report measures. Be as thorough as possible.

CHAPTER 2

The History of Juvenile Justice

WHAT YOU NEED TO KNOW

- Throughout most of history, youthful offenders were handled under the same laws and system as adults.

- The early institutions for handling juveniles (houses of refuge and reformatories) emerged in the 1800s as an outgrowth of concern over poverty and the need to train youths to be productive members of society.

- The first recognized juvenile court was in Cook County, Illinois, in 1899, with a focus on helping youths and not punishment.

- *Parens patriae* became the philosophical basis for the new juvenile court, with a focus on handling youths as parents would handle their children.

- The early court cases of *Ex parte Crouse* and *Commonwealth v. Fisher* affirmed the right of the state to intervene in a child's life even if the parents objected.

- Platt and others argue that the juvenile court was not developed solely out of the benevolent intentions of those involved; rather, it was developed as a tool of capitalism to ensure a complacent work force.

- Today, juvenile courts operate under a number of different rationales besides *parens patriae*, including punishment, deterrence, child welfare, restorative justice, and rehabilitation.

KEY TERMS

abandonment

apprenticeship

Bridewell Institution

Chancery Court

child savers

cottage system

dowry

Due Process Period

houses of refuge

infanticide

involuntary servitude

Lancaster State Industrial School for Girls

Lyman School for Boys

nullification

parens patriae

probation

Punitive Period

right to intervention

wet-nursing

DOI: 10.4324/9781003167112-2

INTRODUCTION

There is no question that juvenile misbehavior is a major concern in modern American society. No matter which definition of delinquency or which form of measurement is used, the level of delinquent activity is high. Any understanding of the juvenile justice system must begin with an analysis of delinquency in a historical framework. Interestingly, the history of juvenile delinquency and juvenile justice is a relatively short one. While deviance on the part of young persons has always been a fact of life, societal intervention and participation in the handling of juvenile transgressors has gained most of its momentum in the last 100–150 years. This chapter will discuss the state of affairs leading to the development of a juvenile justice system and briefly examine the early workings of that system.

PROPERTY AND PERSON

An understanding of the development of juvenile justice must begin with an understanding of the place of children in society. Throughout most of history, there was no such status as "child." Youthful members of society did not enjoy a separate status that brought with it a distinct set of expectations, behaviors, and/or privileges. Rather, the young were considered either property or people. The very young, from birth to age five or six, held much the same status as any other property in society. They were subject to the same dictates as other property—bought, sold, and disposed of according to the needs of the owner. Once the individual reached the age of five or six, he or she became a full-fledged member of society and was expected to act according to the same mandates placed on all "adult" members of society (Aries, 1962).

The state of indifference toward the young and the absence of any separate status are easy to understand within a historical setting. First, the life expectancy of the average person was short. More importantly, the infant mortality rate exceeded 50 percent. The failure to develop a personal, caring attitude for infants, therefore, can be viewed as a defense mechanism. Indifference reduced or eliminated the pain and sorrow that would accompany the loss of the infant. A second explanation for the lack of concern over the young entailed the inability of many families to provide for the young. Families lived from day to day on what they could produce. Each child represented an increased burden to the already overburdened family.

The inability to provide economically for a child led to a variety of practices. Infanticide, or the killing of young children, was a common response to the appearance of an unwanted and demanding child prior to the fourth century (and continued in some places into the fourteenth century) (Mause, 1974). Mothers would kill their young in order to alleviate the future needs of providing for the child. The great chances that the infant would die anyway from disease or illness made this practice easier for the parents.

The killing of female offspring was especially prominent. Females were considered more burdensome than males. This was because they would not be as productive as a male if they lived and because of the dowry practice. The marriage of a daughter often necessitated the provision of goods by the female's family to the groom. The basic rationale was that the groom and his family were assuming the burden of caring for a marginally productive female. The dowry practice was especially problematic for the poor, who could not provide a sufficient enticement for a prospective husband. The killing of a female infant, therefore, not only removed the immediate needs of caring for the infant but also eliminated the future need of a dowry.

A practice similar to infanticide was abandonment. Parents would abandon their children to die for the same reasons underlying infanticide. Abandonment grew to be the more acceptable practice in the fourth to thirteenth centuries and appeared as late as the seventeenth and eighteenth centuries. Infanticide and abandonment were not restricted to the poor members of society. Historical records show that even the affluent accepted the killing of infants. One prime example of this is the story of Oedipus the king. Oedipus, the son of the Greek king and queen, was destined to kill his father and marry his mother. In order to avoid this fate, the parents had the infant Oedipus bound at the ankles, taken to the mountains, and abandoned.

Another method that appeared for handling youths was wet-nursing. A wet-nurse was a surrogate mother paid to care for a child (Mause, 1974). Wealthy families would hire other women to raise their children until they had reached the stage of "adulthood," at which time the child would return and assume a productive role in the family. Poor women, who assumed the role of wet-nurses, would kill their natural offspring in order to save their mother's milk for the "paying" youths. The arrangement served a monetary purpose for the poor while relieving the wealthy of an unwanted responsibility.

Children who survived the first few years of life were subjected to a new set of activities. These new actions, however, retained the economic concerns that allowed for infanticide and other practices. The inability to provide for the needs of the family prompted the development of involuntary servitude and apprenticeship for the young. In essence, these actions were nothing more than the sale of youths by the family. The father, by selling the children, accomplished two things. First, he alleviated the burden of having to feed and clothe the person. Second, he gained something of "greater" value in return—money, a farm animal, food, or some other necessity of life. Such practices also were promoted as a means of providing labor for those in need. The rise of industrialization created a need for skilled labor, which could be learned by children through apprenticeships.

A second set of reasons behind the apprenticeship and servitude of youths was the general view that individuals who survived the years of infancy were simply "little adults." Indeed, children participated in the same activities as adults. Children worked at trades, drank alcohol, dueled, and participated in sex with adults and other young people. Part of this can be attributed to the lack of distinct expectations for youths. There was no period of schooling or education that separated the young from the actions of adults. Additionally, the living conditions of the family placed all ages within the same set of social conditions. The family home was typically a single room used for all activities. Eating, sleeping, and entertaining occurred in the same place and in view of everyone. The youthful members of society, therefore, learned and participated early in life.

The general view that children were the same as adults extended to the realm of legal sanctioning. Children were viewed as adults and were subject to the same rules and regulations as adults (Empey, 1982). There did not exist a separate system for dealing with youthful offenders. At best, the father was responsible for controlling the child and his choices for punishment had no bounds. Additionally, society could sanction youths in the same way as adults. The law made no distinction based on the age of the offender. In fact, youths could be (and were) sentenced to death for various deviant actions. While the law allowed for and prescribed harsh punishments, there is some question as to how frequently the more serious actions were actually used. Platt (1977) suggested that, while many youths could be sentenced to death, few received such a sentence, and most of those who did were never put to death. Similarly, Faust and Brantingham (1979) claimed that a process of **nullification**, or refusal to enforce the law against children, took place because of the lack of penalties geared specifically for juvenile offenders.

Throughout most of history, children held no special status in society. They did not receive any special, protected treatment. If anything, they were subjected to harsher treatment than adults. In terms of legal proscriptions, children could be held liable for the same actions and in the same fashion as adults. There was no legal term of "delinquency" under which the state could intervene with youths. Youths fell under the same statutes and guidelines that were used with adult offenders.

The concept of childhood began to emerge in the sixteenth and seventeenth centuries. It was during this time that medical advancements brought about a lengthening of the life expectancy of youths. Youths also began to be viewed as different from adults. They were in need of protection, assistance, and guidance in order to grow up uncorrupted by the world. This movement was led by clergy and scholars of the time. These leaders saw the young as a source of attack on the immoral and sinful aspects of society. Youths, who were not yet corrupted, had to be shielded from society and trained for their future role in the world. Children were seen as a catalyst for general social change. Childhood came to be seen as a period of time during which the young could receive an education and moral training without the pressures of adulthood.

Accompanying these changes were alterations in how youthful offenders should be disciplined. Responses to misbehavior began to be tailored to fit the age of the offender. In England, youths under the age of seven could not be held responsible for their actions, individuals between 8 and 14 could be held responsible only when it could be shown they understood the consequences of their actions, and youths age 14 and over were considered adults (Empey, 1982). While these types of changes began to recognize the difference between juveniles and adults, the actions taken against offenders remained the same, regardless of the age of the offender.

THE RISE OF JUVENILE INSTITUTIONS

Changes in the methods of dealing with problem youths corresponded to the changes occurring in American society of the early 1800s. During this time, there was a great movement toward the cities. Industrialization was drawing families out of the countryside and to the cities. The cities were growing in both size and density. In addition, the individuals moving to the cities brought with them a variety of outlooks and ideas. This growing diversity in the population was especially true of the cities in the United States, which were attracting immigrants from a wide range of European countries. The promise of a better life in the new world also brought with it a great deal of poverty (see Box 2.1).

Methods for dealing with problem youths grew out of the establishment of ways to handle poor people in the cities (see Rothman, 1971, 1980). The poor were seen both as a threat to society and in need of help. The primary response for dealing with the poor entailed training them and making them productive members of society. Unfortunately, there was little that could be done with the adult poor. They were beyond the training stage and were set in their ways. The children of the poor, however, were viewed as trainable. A key aspect of this training was the removal of the child from the bad influences and substandard training of the poor parents. While this view became prominent in the 1800s, Krisberg and Austin (1978) noted that as early as 1555 the English established the **Bridewell Institution** in London to handle youthful beggars. The primary emphasis of the institution was the handling of poor and destitute youths, although in practice the institution handled all problem youths, including

BOX 2.1	MAJOR MILESTONES/EVENTS/DATES IN JUVENILE JUSTICE, 1825–1899
1825	Houses of Refuge established New York: 1825 Boston: 1826 Philadelphia: 1828
1838	*Ex parte Crouse* rules in favor of *parens patriae*
1848	Lyman School for Boys established
1841	Probation initiated in Boston
mid-1800s	Institution of reformatories
1855	Chicago Reform School Act established reform schools in Chicago
1869	Massachusetts State Board of Charities takes control of juvenile probation
1870	*People v. Turner* rules against *parens patriae*
1892	New York separates trials of juveniles and adults
1899	First juvenile court established in Cook County (Chicago), Illinois

delinquents. The Bridewell Institution was envisioned as a place where the youths would be trained in a skill that they could use after they were released.

The establishment of institutions in the early 1800s in the United States closely followed the ideas of the Bridewell Institution. The institutions were viewed as places for training those individuals who were not productive and who seemed to pose a threat to society. There was a heavy emphasis on the problems of the poor. The establishment of institutions for the poor and delinquent also reflected a shift in the view of causes of deviance. Throughout most of history, deviance was viewed as a result of problems inherent in the individual. The 1800s, meanwhile, witnessed a growth in the belief that deviance was a result of poor environmental conditions. A change in the environment, therefore, should result in changed behavior. The earlier the individual was placed into a new environment, the better the chances of having a positive impact on the person's actions. The establishment of new institutions also provided the court with an alternative to doing nothing with juveniles or placing them in adult institutions.

Houses of Refuge

The establishment of institutions for children in the 1800s clearly conformed to these ideas. These early institutions were called **houses of refuge** and were envisioned as a place for separating the youth from the detrimental environment of the city. The first house of refuge was established in New York in 1825 and was followed by institutions in Boston (1826) and Philadelphia (1828). The rationale and setup of the houses of refuge closely followed the concern for the poor and the need for training discussed above.

Central aspects in the handling of youths were indeterminate sentences, education, skills training, hard work, religious training, parental discipline, and apprenticeships (Pisciotta, 1983). The use of education, skills training, hard work, and apprenticeships were clear indications that the goal was to produce a productive member of society. Indeterminate sentences allowed the institution to work with each person on an individual basis. Where one youth may benefit from a short period of intervention, another child may require extended work and assistance. The interest in religious training and parental discipline carried over the historical ideas that the best methods of training lay in the realm of the family and the church. The families of the youths in the institution were considered to be lacking in the ability to provide these basic needs. The houses of refuge were envisioned as shelters and sanctuaries that would protect and nurture their wards away from the corrupting influences of the city and the poor family (Rothman, 1971).

The establishment of the houses of refuge was also seen as a means of removing children from the criminogenic influences of the workhouses and adult jails (Krisberg & Austin, 1978). Reformers saw the prior methods of handling youths through the adult system as nothing more than placing poor and problem juveniles in contact with adult criminal offenders. The natural outcome would be "schools for crime" that produced more problems than they solved. The houses of refuge supposedly differed by offering education and training in useful skills within a setting that allowed for control and discipline of the children.

While the rationale and the goals of the houses of refuge were laudable, the daily operations and the impact of the institutions were questionable. Many of the activities were far removed from the real world. Inmates had little, if any, contact with members of the opposite sex. Military behavior was the norm. This included enforced silence, marching to and from different activities, the wearing of uniforms, and swift and habitual corporal punishment (Rothman, 1971). Apprenticeships often failed to be more than simple slave labor. Many of the apprenticeships were on farms in the country. Problem youths were apprenticed to ship captains and sent to sea. In general, there was no quality control or oversight for the apprenticeships. The institutional labor was often dictated by contractual obligations that led to exploitation of the youths by the institutional masters. Children were bribed, beaten, and even subjected to extended incarceration if the monetary interests of the administrators were at stake (Pisciotta, 1982).

Besides failing to provide the basic tools that they promised, the houses of refuge also failed in other respects. For the most part, these institutions were nothing but new prisons. They were tremendously overcrowded. This overcrowding was partly due to the admission of persons not suited for the goals of the institutions. The houses of refuge served the poor and destitute, and the delinquent youths. At the same time, they handled poverty-stricken adults and adult offenders. The overcrowding of the facilities by such diverse groups of inmates changed the focus of daily operations from the goals of education and training to that of simple custody and discipline. The establishment of institutions like the **Lyman School for Boys** in 1848 by the state of Massachusetts eliminated the housing of adult and juvenile offenders in the same facility but carried on the tradition of overcrowding and related problems. In general, the early houses of refuge failed to provide their stated goals and settled into a process very reminiscent of that of the adult prisons and jails that had previously been the norm for handling youths.

New Reformatories

The failure of the early houses of refuge did not lead to the end of juvenile institutions. The problems of the houses of refuge were well known by the mid-1800s. While the practice of the institutions had failed, proponents argued that the principles underlying intervention were correct. The issue, therefore, was in proper implementation of intervention. Emphasis on education, training, and parental discipline led to the establishment of "cottage" reformatories.

The **cottage system** was intended to closely parallel a family. Concerned surrogate parents would oversee the training and education of a small number of problem youths. Discipline would be intermixed with the care and concern typical of family life. Most of the cottages were located in the country and emphasized work on the farm. This was supposed to separate the youth from the criminogenic features of the urban environment and instill a sense of hard, honest work in the charges. The idea of indeterminate sentencing carried over to the cottage approach.

Other changes in the handling of youths accompanied the growth of these cottage reformatories. Foremost among these features was the development of **probation** in 1841 by John Augustus. While the early use of probation was centered on adult offenders, by 1869 the state of Massachusetts dictated that the State Board of Charities would participate in, and take charge of, court cases involving youthful offenders (Krisberg & Austin, 1978). Probation officers would assist in the gathering of information on the youths, suggest alternative means of intervention, and oversee the placement of juveniles in reformatories and apprenticeships. Another method of dealing with youths, in accordance with the cottage idea, entailed the "placing out" of juveniles into foster homes. For the most part, these placements were the same as apprenticeships. Such placements were seen as an alternative to institutionalization and allowed for the training of youths in a worthwhile occupation.

Unfortunately, like the earlier houses of refuge, these new alternatives for handling youths faced many of the same problems. The institutions and cottages became terribly overcrowded to the point that custody became the primary concern. Apprenticeships proved to be little more than slave labor, and youths often fled at the first opportunity. One analysis of 210 apprenticed individuals found that 72 percent of the youths either ran away or returned to the institution (Pisciotta, 1979). The harsh treatment of the youths in the institutions led to running away, the setting of fires, and various sexual problems (Pisciotta, 1982). The inability to handle some youths prompted the establishment of special facilities such as the Elmira Reformatory in 1876. Unfortunately, Elmira accepted both juveniles and young adults and negated the premise of separating youths from criminogenic older offenders. A final problem with the institutions was the continued mixing of both deviant and destitute youths in the same facilities. The institutions considered that being poor was closely tied to deviant activity and, as a result, intervened in the lives of lower-class individuals regardless of the existence (or lack) of a delinquent or criminal act.

Institutions for Females

Throughout the development of alternatives for handling boys, little attention was paid to females. Problem girls were dealt with in the same institutions as males and adults. Part of the reason for this was the relatively small number of females officially handled by agents of social control. Exceptions to this situation began to appear in the mid-1800s with the establishment of separate institutions for girls. One of the most well-known facilities for females was the **Lancaster State Industrial School for Girls** in Massachusetts. The girls committed to Lancaster had the same basic background as boys found in other institutions. They were mostly from poor, immigrant families who were faced with the vagaries and problems of the urban environment (Brenzel, 1983). The institutions were set up as family cottages in order to deal with these problems.

The hoped-for end product of the institutions for girls was the production of females capable of fulfilling their place in society. Where boys were to become productive laborers, females were to learn how to be good housewives and mothers (Brenzel, 1983). Success with the girls was gauged by successful marriage and parenthood. Much of the concern centered on the plight of future generations that were to be raised by the problem girls and not on the girls themselves. Unfortunately, these institutions fared no better than those handling boys. While some girls successfully graduated from the institutions, married, and became mothers, others did not realize the goals set by the institutions. In addition, Lancaster and similar institutions tended to be little more than prisons for youths. They were characterized by overcrowding, lack of treatment, and strict discipline. The differing focus from male institutions did not result in different outcomes.

THE ESTABLISHMENT OF THE JUVENILE COURT

The juvenile court arose in response to the failure of the earlier interventions with juveniles and to address the issues of the era. The late 1800s continued to experience great levels of immigration by lower-class Europeans to the industrial cities of the United States. Environmental factors remained at the head of the list of causes for deviant behavior. In addition, the emergence of psychological and sociological explanations for behavior suggested that the problems of society could be fixed. Finally, middle- and upper-class individuals (primarily women) were interested in doing something to help the poor and destitute. The new court system utilized many of the earlier intervention ideas. Consequently, the expansion of juvenile justice was subjected to many of the same problems of the earlier interventions, as well as new concerns. Box 2.2 provides a timeline of major dates in juvenile justice.

The Growth of the Juvenile Court

The first recognized individual juvenile court was established in Cook County, Illinois, in 1899. While this represented the first official juvenile court, a variety

BOX 2.2 MAJOR MILESTONES/EVENTS/DATES IN JUVENILE JUSTICE, 1900–PRESENT	
1901	Illinois State School for youths established
1903	Illinois expanded juvenile court jurisdiction to status offenses
1905	*Commonwealth v. Fisher* upheld *parens patriae*
1909	Establishment of child guidance clinics
1912	U.S. Children's Bureau established
1920	All but three states have separate juvenile courts
1966	*Kent v. United States* raises concerns about *parens patriae*

of jurisdictions implemented and experimented with similar institutions. Between 1870 and 1877, the state of Massachusetts established separate court dockets, separate hearings, and separate record keeping for cases involving juveniles under the age of 16 (Ryerson, 1978). New York passed legislation in 1892 that provided for separate trials for juvenile offenders, although juveniles continued to be held in the adult system (Platt, 1977). Similarly, Judge Ben Lindsey of Colorado, a leading advocate of juvenile court, operated a quasi-juvenile court for a number of years prior to the establishment of the court in Illinois (Parsloe, 1978). Regardless of the initial beginnings, by 1920 all but three states had juvenile courts, and there were more than 320 separate juvenile courts in the United States (Ryerson, 1978).

The legislation that established the Illinois court reflected the general belief in the ability to alter youthful behavior. First, the court was to operate in a highly informal manner without any of the trappings of the adult court. Lawyers and other adversarial features of the adult system (such as rules of evidence and testimony under oath) were discouraged. The judge was to take a paternal stance toward the juvenile and provide whatever help and assistance were needed. The emphasis was on assisting the youth rather than on punishing an offense. Second, all juveniles under the age of 16 could be handled by the new court. The court was not restricted to dealing with youths who committed criminal acts. Rather, the court could intervene in any situation in which a youth was in need of help. In practical terms, this allowed intervention into the lives of the poor and immigrants, whose child-raising practices did not conform to the ideas of the court. Third, the new court relied extensively on the use of probation. Probation continued to serve both administrative functions for the court as well as supervisory actions with adjudicated youths.

While no two juvenile courts could claim to have the same program, the courts all held the same general principles of providing assistance for the juveniles. Julian W. Mack of the Chicago juvenile court aptly portrayed the role and methods of the court when he stated:

> Most of the children who come before the court are, naturally, the children of the poor. In many cases the parents are foreigners, frequently unable to speak English, and without an understanding of American methods and views. What they need, more than anything else, is kindly assistance; and the aim of the court, in appointing a probation officer for the child, is to have the child and the parents feel, not so much the power, as the friendly interest of the state; to show them that the object of the court is to help them to train the child right. (Mack, 1909)

WEB ACTIVITY

Read the entire statement of Judge Mack at www.routledge.com/cw/whitehead.

Within this statement, Mack noted the minor concern over the deviant act in the court, the goal of providing assistance to both the youth and the family, the place of probation in the court, and the typical youth who was subjected to court intervention. The shift from the adult orientation is evident in the new terminology that developed in the juvenile court (see Table 2.1).

The progressive reforms that led to the establishment of the juvenile courts also had other influences. One of the impacts was a gradual widening of the juvenile court's mandate. The original Illinois statute allowed intervention for criminal activity, dependency, and neglect. In 1903, Illinois added such actions as curfew violation and incorrigibility (status offenses) to the situations allowing intervention. A second area of change involved the development of new institutions for handling youths who needed to be removed from their families. One of the first new institutions was the Illinois State School at St. Charles, Illinois, which was funded in 1901 and opened in 1905 (Platt, 1977). These institutions closely followed the family/cottage model used throughout the late 1800s. The greatest distinction was in the administrative unit (the juvenile court versus the adult court) and not in orientation. A move toward using full-time, paid probation officers also occurred shortly after the court's beginnings. By 1912, the federal government established the U.S. Children's Bureau to oversee the expanding realm of juvenile justice (Ryerson, 1978).

A final major movement coming from the progressive reforms was the institution of court-affiliated guidance clinics. The first of these was established in Chicago by William Healy, a leading proponent of the juvenile court, in 1909. These clinics relied on the new psychological and sociological explanations emerging during this time. Central to these explanations was the need for the expert analysis of each juvenile in order to identify the unique factors contributing to the individual's behavior. Following Healy's example, 232 clinics were established by 1931 (Krisberg & Austin, 1978).

The Legal Philosophy of the Court

Perhaps the greatest challenge to the growth of the juvenile system entailed debate over the philosophy of the court and the question of a juvenile's constitutional rights. Critics of the court and earlier interventions often claimed that the state was subjecting juveniles to intervention without regard to their rights and those of the family. In many instances the state was forcibly removing a youth from his or her parents' custody. These new interventions were viewed as an abrogation of the family's position in society. The problems of constitutional rights and the new juvenile justice system were deemed inconsequential compared to the possible benefits that could accrue from intervention. Indeed, the state relied on the doctrine of *parens patriae* for justification of its position. Table 2.2 presents key factors in the growth of *parens patriae* and its application to the juvenile court.

TABLE 2.1 Comparative Terms in the Juvenile and Adult Systems

Juvenile System	Adult System
Adjudication	Conviction
Hearing	Trial
Aftercare	Parole
Commitment	Sentence
Delinquent	Criminal
Petition	Indictment
Custody	Arrest

TABLE 2.2 Factors in the Growth of *Parens Patriae*

English Chancery Court (Middle Ages)	Basis of state intervention for welfare of children, particularly in cases of property rights and orphans
Ex parte Crouse ([1838] 1839)	Pennsylvania Supreme Court rules that *parens patriae* is sufficient basis for intervening in the lives of juveniles without parental consent
People v. Turner (1870)	Illinois Supreme Court rules against *parens patriae* in favor of parental rights to raise and care for offspring; largely ignored by the courts
Commonwealth v. Fisher (1905)	Pennsylvania Supreme Court rules that the court can intervene without impunity when the objective is to help the youth, i.e., if the intent is good the juvenile court can act
Kent v. United States (1966)	*Parens patriae* is seriously questioned in light of the lack of adequate help and treatment provided by the juvenile court coupled with the lack of due process applied in juvenile cases

Parens patriae, or the state as parent, was based on the actions of the English **Chancery Court**. The Chancery Court was primarily concerned with property matters in feudal England. One aspect of the court's function was to oversee the financial affairs of juveniles whose parents had died and who were not yet capable of handling their own matters. The court acted as a guardian until such time that the youth could assume responsibility. In practice, the court dealt only with matters involving more well-to-do families. The offspring of the poor did not have any property to protect. As an arm of the state, the Chancery Court often converted much of the property to the ownership of the state. There would be little to gain in overseeing the needs of the poor. Regardless of the intention of the Chancery Court, the precedent was set for intervention into the lives of children.

Movements to intervene in the lives of children in the United States were quick to rely on *parens patriae* for justification. The earliest example of this involved the case *Ex parte Crouse*. Mary Ann Crouse was incarcerated upon her mother's request but against her father's wishes. Her father argued that it was illegal to incarcerate a child without the benefit of a jury trial. In rejecting the father's argument, the court denied that the Bill of Rights applied to youths. The Pennsylvania Supreme Court ruled in 1838:

> May not the natural parents, when unequal to the task of education, or unworthy of it, be superseded by the *parens patriae*, or common guardian of the community? It is to be remembered that the public has a paramount interest in the virtue and knowledge of its members, and that of strict right the business of education belongs to it. That parents are ordinarily entrusted with it, is because it can seldom be put in better hands; but where they are incompetent or corrupt, what is there to prevent the public from withdrawing their faculties, held as they obviously are, at its sufferance? The right of parental control is a natural, but not an inalienable one. It is not excepted by the

declaration of rights out of the subject of ordinary legislation. (*Ex parte Crouse*, [1838] 1839)

The *Crouse* opinion set the tone for intervention with juveniles in the United States. In essence, the state could intervene, regardless of the reason, if it found that the child was in need of help or assistance that the parents and family could not provide. The decision relied solely on the good intentions of the state and the need to provide the proper training for the child.

Intervention based on *parens patriae* did not go completely unchallenged. Critics charged that the state was overextending its rights by intervening in many minor matters that should be simply ignored. More importantly, the argument was made that the state provided little more than incarceration and was not providing the education, training, and benevolent care that was required under the *parens patriae* doctrine. In *People v. Turner* (1870), the Illinois Supreme Court stated:

> In our solicitude to form youths for the duties of civil life, we should not forget the rights which inhere both in parents and children. The principle of the absorption of the child in, and its complete subjection to the despotism of, the State, is wholly inadmissible in the modern civilized world. The parent has the right to the care, custody, and assistance of his child. The duty to maintain and protect it, is a principle of a natural law.

In this instance the court affirmed the rights of the parent to care for the child. The intervention of the state was to be reserved for instances in which the youth had violated a criminal law and after the application of due process concerns. The good intentions of the state and the needs of the youth were not enough to warrant unfettered intervention into the family unit. Despite this apparent shift in legal concerns, most jurisdictions ignored the opinion and continued to follow the general guidelines set forth in the *Crouse* decision.

The issues of a child's and parent's rights were largely settled in the 1905 case, *Commonwealth v. Fisher*. In this case the Pennsylvania Supreme Court directly addressed the question of a juvenile's behavior, his or her constitutional rights, and the intent of the juvenile system in intervention. The court said:

> The design is not punishment, nor the restraint imprisonment, any more than is the wholesome restraint which a parent exercises over his child. The severity in either case must necessarily be tempered to meet the necessities of the particular situation. There is no probability, in the proper administration of the law, of the child's liberty being unduly invaded. Every statute which is designed to give protection, care, and training to children, as a needed substitute for parental authority, and performance of parental duty, is but a recognition of the duty of the state, as the legitimate guardian and protector of children where other guardianship fails. No constitutional right is violated. (*Commonwealth v. Fisher*, 1905)

The key concern was over the intent of the intervention and not the rights of the juvenile, his or her parents, or the effectiveness of the system. In essence, the child had a **right to intervention** and not a right to freedom. Moreover, the parents had little, if any, rights in the disposition of the child. The juvenile court was viewed as providing help in the most benevolent fashion possible. The Pennsylvania Supreme Court was granting the juvenile system a free hand in dealing with youths.

The basic constitutionality of the juvenile system went largely unchallenged after the *Fisher* decision. Those cases that did arise were met with the same rationale and outcome of the earlier case. It was not until the mid-1960s that the courts began to alter their views and grant some constitutional rights to juveniles. Indeed, not until 1966 was the benevolent premise of the juvenile system adequately challenged. In the U.S. Supreme Court case of *Kent v. United States*, Justice Abe Fortas said:

> There is evidence, in fact, that there may be grounds for concern that the child receives the worst of both worlds: that he gets neither the protections accorded to adults nor the solicitous care and regenerative treatment postulated for children. (*Kent v. United States*, 1966)

As will be seen in Chapter 9, the constitutional rights provided to juveniles in the last two decades are not equal to those provided to adults. The courts have continued to reserve various powers for the state and treat juveniles as a separate class of citizens with different rights and expectations.

Problems of the Court

Despite the swift adoption of the juvenile court and its related components, the new system was faced with a number of problems and failures. A major problem involved the extent to which the various operations were initiated. Many of the courts and agencies relied solely on untrained volunteers. The number of full-time, paid juvenile court judges, probation officers, and trained clinicians was small. Ryerson (1978) cited one survey (Beldon, 1920) that found that only 55 percent of the courts provided regular probation services and, of those with probation, less than 50 percent of the officers were full-time employees. The same survey reported that there were only 23 full-time juvenile court judges in the United States in 1918 (Beldon, 1920). The child guidance clinics experienced the same shortage of trained professionals. As a result, most youths did not receive any evaluation. Most evaluations that occurred took place after a child was incarcerated (Ryerson, 1978). This lack of adequate staff was accompanied by inadequate facilities and resources. While the juvenile court retained the use of institutionalization, the choice of placement usually rested on those institutions that had existed prior to the court's establishment. The problems of these institutions were the same as before. Harsh treatment, military regimentation, lack of training and education, high recidivism, and running away all continued. The new agencies, such as the child guidance clinics, similarly failed to provide the treatment and supervision they promised. Criticism of the court also focused on its expanded jurisdiction. As noted above, new statutes outlined juvenile behavior that had previously been left to the family for correction. The expanded jurisdiction of the court based on *parens patriae* also led to an increase in unofficial dispositions and handling of youths. There is evidence that many proceedings took place without the presence of a judge or the keeping of records. Such actions were justified on the basis of relieving the burden of the court and the desire to avoid the stigma of a more formal procedure. While these reasons may have been laudatory, they encouraged the handling of more juveniles with very minor transgressions. Many trivial actions, such as making noise, sledding in the street, playing in the street, riding bicycles on the sidewalk, and throwing paper into the sewers, became the subject of these unofficial cases (Rothman, 1980).

BENEVOLENCE OR SELF-INTEREST?

The institution of the juvenile court has generally been held as a progressive, humanitarian development. Most historians refer to the time period from about 1880 to the 1920s as the Progressive Era. It was during this time that many laws were passed mandating apparently humanitarian reforms. Actions such as mandatory schooling, regulations on working conditions for both adults and juveniles, concern over the plight of the poor and immigrants, the growth of agencies dealing with health concerns, and the establishment of the juvenile court were listed as examples of the benevolent actions of the reformers and society. Coercion within the juvenile justice system, and other forms of intervention, were considered a necessary evil for improving the lot of those who did not know any better (Rothman, 1980). Schlossman (1977) went so far as to label the benevolent movement in juvenile justice as an exercise in love. He plainly stated that institutions and the court needed to provide the type of love, affection, and concern found in the family setting.

According to other writers, however, benevolence was not the driving factor. Anthony Platt (1977) referred to the persons involved in the development of the juvenile court as **child savers**. The issue he addressed was the rationale for saving the youths. Platt viewed the growth of juvenile justice as a part of larger social movements that attempted to solidify the position of corporate capitalism in the United States. Rather than being a humanistic endeavor to help the less fortunate societal members, intervention through the courts allowed the powerful classes in society to mold a disciplined, complacent labor force. The juvenile court was a means of preserving the existing class system in the United States (Platt, 1977). Krisberg and Austin (1978) essentially made the same argument. They saw the system as a vehicle of the upper classes for controlling the "dangerous" (lower) classes in society.

Both Platt (1977) and Krisberg and Austin (1978) pointed to a variety of factors in support of their contentions. First, the driving force behind the growth of the juvenile system, especially the juvenile court, were middle- and upper-class individuals. Middle-class women formed one key group in the system's development (Platt, 1977). These women were the wives and daughters of the industrialists and landed gentry who controlled production and had the greatest say in government. A second form of support rested on the fact that the system grew during the time when the lower-class ranks were swelling with new, poor immigrants. In essence, the lower class was growing to a point at which it could pose a threat to the status quo. Third, and related to the second, was the establishment of new laws that addressed the activity of the lower classes. Statutes governing youthful behavior primarily addressed the actions of the poor and immigrants. The government extended control over entirely new classes of behaviors in the juvenile justice statutes. A fourth indication of the juvenile system's inherent bias was the exploitive use of children who were incarcerated or under the care of the system. Youths were placed in involuntary servitude, indentured, and apprenticed, all under the argument that they would benefit from learning a trade. Realistically, according to Platt (1977) and Krisberg and Austin (1978), these actions supplied immediate cheap labor and indoctrinated the youths in the capitalistic ideology of the upper classes. It was upon these, and similar, arguments that various writers question the benevolent intentions of those individuals involved in the juvenile justice system movement.

Additional support for the argument that the system lacked the benevolence purported in many studies comes from an evaluation of the treatment of females and blacks. Pisciotta (1983) offered evidence that the juvenile justice system had been both racist and sexist. The author noted that most residential institutions in the early 1800s refused to admit blacks. Instead, black youths were subjected to continued incarceration in adult facilities until special institutions for blacks could be built. One of the earliest separate black institutions was opened in Philadelphia in 1848. Exceptions to this rule of separating whites and blacks were restricted to instances in which the admittance of blacks was economically advantageous to those in charge. Once admitted to an institution, little education was supplied. Intervention with blacks revolved around training them in menial labor and to learn their "proper place" in society. Females were handled in a similar fashion (Pisciotta, 1983). Academic education was minimized while religious, moral, and domestic training was emphasized. This view of proper training for women rested on the expectation that females were to stay in the home and raise the next generation of children (Brenzel, 1983; Pisciotta, 1983).

One possible problem with the proposal that the juvenile court was a self-serving invention of the powerful involves the place of the new professionals in the growth of the system. As noted earlier, the emergence of the new psychological and sociological explanations for behavior played a major role in the direction of the juvenile institutions and court. Why did these professionals not criticize the growth of juvenile justice if, indeed, it was simply a means for the powerful to control the masses? Platt (1977) addressed this issue by pointing out that the professionals received a great deal of benefit from juvenile justice, regardless of the driving forces. These individuals gained the reputation as experts, secured employment as either full-time employees or paid consultants, gained access to data and information otherwise denied to them, and found a forum willing to let them advance their theories and ideas.

It was not that these professionals may not have objected to the biased premise of the system, they simply found more personal benefits in allowing the system to be instituted and advanced.

The debate over the intent of those forming the juvenile court has not been resolved. The usefulness of recognizing the difference in opinion is in opening the way for varied suggestions about dealing with problem youths. Individuals who assume the benevolence point of view turn to a variety of theoretical explanations and the accompanying forms of intervention. Advocates of the self-interest perspective focus on the actions of society and not the individual offender. Instead of looking for ways to help the youth, these writers suggest that changes in the social structure account for variation in the levels of deviance. This approach will be further explored in Chapter 4.

JUVENILE JUSTICE FROM 1920 TO THE 1960S

Most of the great movements and changes in juvenile justice were completed by the early 1920s. By this time, the juvenile court was solidly entrenched as the proper institution for dealing with problem youths. The problems and criticisms directed at the court and its institutions were passed off as the failure to implement the programs properly. The shortcomings were not inherent features of the system. Advocates called for increased resources, time, and patience. Society and the legal system were content to leave the juvenile justice system alone to search for effective interventions, provided the system continued to act in the best interests of its youthful clients. Changes in the handling of youths over the next few decades, therefore, were restricted to generating new theories of behavior, attempting new types of treatment, and evaluating their efforts.

Various new institutions were established for handling problem youths. These were necessitated both by increased numbers of youths entering the system and differing approaches to treating youths. Psychological explanations and perspectives led to the growth of various training and counseling (group and individual) programs. Psychotherapeutic interventions gained prominence in the 1940s and led to private and public institutions based on these ideas. The use of such interventions as guided group interaction and peer pressure formed the basis of programs such as the Highfields Project in 1950. Highfields was a short-term, residential facility that allowed the youths to visit their families and remain a part of the community. This type of program helped form the basis for halfway houses and other community interventions. Later chapters will address such actions in more detail.

CHANGES SINCE THE 1960S

Challenges to the *parens patriae* doctrine through a growing number of court cases in the late 1960s and early 1970s were early signals of major changes in society's approach to both juvenile misbehavior and adult criminality. The period from 1967 to the early 1980s has been referred to as the **Due Process Period**. The federal courts ruled in a number of key cases that juveniles had to be offered some procedural rights similar to those enjoyed by adults. The 1980s returned to an approach that was more punishment-oriented and ushered in what is referred to as the **Punitive Period**. Actions during this period included increased use of waiver, mandatory sentencing, and less emphasis on rehabilitation and treatment.

Clearly, the strong reliance on and belief in rehabilitation and treatment that dominated throughout the twentieth century has given way to more punitive responses (Garland, 2001). Retribution, just deserts, and deterrence have emerged as the watchwords for both the juvenile and criminal justice systems. Rather than look for the causes of deviant behavior in the inequities of society or the surroundings of the offender, there is a stronger belief that individuals of all ages choose to commit offenses and need to be held responsible for their actions.

Garland (2001) views these changes in social control as a result of numerous changes and forces over the past 30 years. Among those influences have been rising crime rates, changing economic conditions that marginalize greater numbers of individuals, challenges to the welfare state, growing concern for victims, the diversification of the population, the perceived inability of the state to control the citizenry, and the perception that families and other institutions have lost their ability to control the behavior of their members. Passing new laws, increasing the use of punishment, and similar responses have emerged as responses to these and other perceived problems. Changes in the juvenile justice system and society's response to youths are a clear reflection of these broad social changes.

WEB ACTIVITY

You can find out more about the general purpose clauses for juvenile courts and the purpose clauses for different states at www.ojjdp.gov/ojstatbb/structure_process/qa04205.asp?qaDate=2016.

Despite the movement to include greater emphasis on retribution and punishment in the juvenile justice system, *parens patriae* remains the key philosophy underlying juvenile courts in the United States. This is illustrated in an analysis of the "purpose clauses" for juvenile courts found in state statutes. Four general categories of juvenile court purpose clauses are identified by the Office of

The Cuyahoga County Juvenile Justice Center in Cleveland, Ohio, houses 36 courtrooms with associated chambers and magistrate offices as well as a treatment-focused 180-bed juvenile detention facility.

CREDIT: AP Photo/Tony Dejak

TABLE 2.3 Categories of Juvenile Court General Purpose Clauses

Balanced and Restorative Justice Clauses:
- Focus on balancing the needs of the youth, the victim, and public safety
- Typically includes an emphasis on treatment, care, and guidance of the youths
- Found in 28 states

Parens Patriae Clauses:
- Emphasis on "care, guidance, and control" to ensure the welfare of the youth
- Offer care similar to that which would normally be supplied by the parents
- Found in eight states

Due Process Era Clauses:
- Criminal court orientation
- Focus on community safety and offender accountability
- Found in seven states

Developmental Approach Clauses:
- Elements of most other approaches
- Focus on adolescent development and research for interventions
- Evidence-based practices
- Found in five states

No Clause:
- Found in two states

Source: Constructed by authors from *OJJDP Statistical Briefing Book* (2018).

Juvenile Justice and Delinquency Prevention (see Table 2.3). In only one of the four categories is *parens patriae* largely excluded and the emphasis shifted to an adult court/criminal law orientation for the juvenile court. The other three categories maintain *parens patriae* as at least a key component (if not directly named) in addressing problem youths.

SUMMARY

The growth of juvenile justice from the 1920s to the early 1960s followed a pattern of new programs, all within the original mandate and scope of the early reformers. The issues that fueled debate in the early years have returned to be debated in recent years. While there has been an increased emphasis on punishment and due process in the system, many of the rehabilitation and treatment ideas are still being tried and adapted in an attempt to live up to the *parens patriae* ideals that still underlie the juvenile justice system. The remainder of the text will look at the varied issues and the operation of the juvenile system, primarily since the early 1960s. Questions of theory, implementation, practice, and evaluation form the core of the discussion.

DISCUSSION QUESTIONS

1. Concern over child abuse has greatly increased over the past two decades. Many people argue that society's young are treated worse today than at any time in history. Based on your knowledge, place this view within a historical framework. That is, outline the historical view of children and some of the major practices for handling them.

2. You are an administrator of an early house of refuge and are asked to give a dispassionate view of your institution. What are the strengths and weaknesses of this type of institution? What problems do you face, and how can you correct them?

3. The legislature is proposing to abolish the juvenile court. Argue in favor of the legal philosophy that is the basis for the court. What is the philosophy? Why has it been legally upheld throughout the years? And why should it be maintained?

CHAPTER 3

Explaining Delinquency: Biological and Psychological Approaches

WHAT YOU NEED TO KNOW

- The Classical school of thought holds that humans are free-willed and choose their behavior, while the Positivist school sees behavior as dictated by outside causes beyond the control of the individual. Neoclassicism takes a middle ground where choices can be made from limited options.

- Early theories of behavior relied on biological explanations. Lombroso and others relied on physical features to identify criminals.

- Modern biological theories are best considered as biosociology, which refers to the fact that there are both biological and environmental influences on behavior, and it is necessary to consider the interaction of these factors.

- While psychological theories have a long history, they are limited by three common features—they focus largely on early life experiences to the exclusion of other variables, they are highly individualistic, and they are most useful in treatment settings.

- Freudian psychoanalysis seeks the cause of behavior in the unconscious/ instinctual parts of humankind, particularly in the battle between the id, ego, and superego.

- Developmental explanations argue that everyone develops through certain stages, with each stage contributing to the knowledge a person needs to be a successful conforming member of society. Deviance results when an individual fails to advance successfully through all the stages.

- Attempts to identify antisocial personalities have been common but have not succeeded in being able to assess adequately who will and will not be deviant.

- Low IQ has often been used as an argument for why some people break the law; however, a key unknown is the extent to which IQ is inherited or is a result of one's environment.

KEY TERMS

Antisocial Personality Disorder (APD)

atavistic

Attention Deficit Hyperactivity Disorder (ADHD)

biosociology (sociobiology)

Classicism

concordance

determinism

dopamine

ego

epigenetics

epinephrine

free will

hedonistic calculus

hormones

hypoglycemia

id

Interpersonal Maturity Levels (I-levels)

intelligence quotient (IQ)

medical model

meta-analysis

Minnesota Multiphasic Personality Inventory (MMPI)

DOI: 10.4324/9781003167112-3

INTRODUCTION

Throughout the history of juvenile justice, criminologists and others interested in deviant behavior have sought to explain why certain individuals act in certain ways at certain times. The number of theories for deviant behavior has grown considerably over the past 100 years as the field of criminology has progressed and the level of research has improved. A theory can be described as an attempt to answer the question "Why?" Why does an individual violate the norms of society? Why do certain conditions seem to accompany deviant behavior? Why does deviance occur when it does? These and other "why" questions form the basis for the theories that have been proposed for explaining delinquent behavior.

The types of factors that have been used to explain delinquency take a wide variety of forms. Early spiritualistic or demonological explanations reflected the belief that deviant acts were the result of the battle between good and evil—God and the devil. Individuals who committed crimes were possessed by the devil. Consequently, the solution to deviance involved exorcizing the devil and delivering the individual back to God. Often this could only be accomplished through the death of the devil's vessel—the individual. The soul would then be freed to join God.

These nonscientific explanations gave way in the 1700s with the advent of Classicism and the movement into Positivistic approaches in the later 1800s. Classicism and Positivism are "schools of thought" rather than specific theories of behavior. These schools lay out general beliefs about people and the world that shape the form that individual theories will take.

THEORETICAL SCHOOLS OF THOUGHT

Every explanation of behavior, whether it be conventional or deviant behavior, rests on a number of implicit assumptions about individuals and the world within which they operate. These beliefs form the core of many arguments about the causes of crime and how to deal with offenders. For example, differences in opinions about the death penalty often boil down to different beliefs about whether punishment can deter people. Every science has schools of thought that organize its ideas. In criminology the two schools are Classicism and Positivism (see Table 3.1).

The Classical School

Classicism finds its roots in the writings of Cesare Bonesana Marchese de Beccaria (1738–1794) and Jeremy Bentham (1748–1832). Beccaria was an Italian aristocrat who broke with the ruling classes to condemn the methods of dealing with crime and morals in society. In outlining a new set of criminal and penal practices, he set forth a number of beliefs about humankind and the function of society in dealing with deviance.

Under Classicism, humans are viewed as being hedonistic and having free will. Under the hedonistic calculus, individuals seek to maximize pleasure and

TABLE 3.1 Major Elements of Classicism and Positivism

Classicism	Positivism	Neoclassicism
Free will	Determinism	Soft determinism
Hedonism	Multiple causation	Free will with limited choices
Rational offender	Emphasize offender/situation differences	Punishment or treatment
Emphasis on offense	Medical model—Crime as "symptom"	
Legal responses—Clear laws and procedures	Individualized response	
Punishment for prevention and deterrence	Rehabilitation and treatment	

minimize pain (Bentham, 1948). Being free-willed, individuals choose activities and behaviors based on their calculation of the amount of pleasure and pain that will result. Pleasurable behaviors will be undertaken and repeated, while painful activities will cease. Under Classicism, individuals make a conscious, *rational* decision to commit crime based on the expectation of a pleasurable outcome.

These beliefs about free will and hedonism suggest that the solution to crime requires increasing pain and reducing pleasure, thereby eliminating deviant behavior. Beccaria and other Classicists, therefore, focused their efforts on making laws and setting punishments that would alter the choices of individuals. The emphasis must be on the offense and the legal system, not the offender. Beccaria felt that individuals could not make an informed decision to avoid crime unless they were presented with a clear set of laws and punishments. There must be a set punishment for each crime, and the level of punishment must be sufficient to offset any pleasurable consequence of an individual's behavior.

Classicism dominated discussions of crime, deviance, and the law in the 1800s. Indeed, changes in laws reflected the general belief in free will and attempts to deter individuals from becoming involved in crime. Punishment was not meant to be a form of retribution or retaliation by society. Instead, punishment was solely for the purpose of altering the outcome of the "hedonistic calculus."

Classical elements still drive deterrence arguments in modern society. Certainly, the moves toward incarceration, treating youths in adult court, and emphasis on punishment are based on Classicism. The fact that crime did not disappear under Classical approaches led to new ideas about behavior in the late 1800s. Much of this movement toward a new "school of thought" grew out of the developing medical sciences.

The Positivistic School

The basic tenets of Positivism are diametrically opposed to those of Classicism. Rather than hold the individual responsible for his or her actions, Positivists believe in **determinism**—that is, behavior is caused by factors beyond the control of the individual. Simply raising the amount of pain a person will receive if caught and punished will not alter behavior. Instead, changing behavior can be accomplished only by identifying and eliminating the factors that are causing the individual to act in a certain way.

Positivism typically recognizes that there are multiple causes of behavior. Deviance may be the result of a single factor, multiple causes, or a series of events or situations occurring over a period of time. The same deviant act committed by different people may be the outcome of totally different causes. The fact that there is no single cause of crime requires examining each individual case for reasons behind that behavior. The approach used by Positivists to identify causes follows a **medical model** or uses a medical analogy.

Using a medical model, the scientist approaches deviance the same way that a doctor approaches a sickness. Just like a doctor considers coughs and fevers as symptoms of other problems, the Positivist views deviant acts, like burglary and rape, as symptoms of other underlying causes or conditions. The Positivist attempts to identify what causes an individual to commit a deviant act and prescribes a tailored response to the person and circumstances. The emphasis in Positivism is not on the offense. The emphasis is on the offender, the unique situation, and the various factors causing the individual to be an offender.

Positivism believes in rehabilitation and treatment. Instead of punishing an individual for his or her actions, the key is to remove the root causes of the deviant behavior. The proper rehabilitation or treatment strategies may be as diverse as the number of clients. For example, one burglar committed the offense to get money to feed his family, while another burglar committed the crime out of anger toward the victim. The first individual needs financial help. The second offender may need counseling and anger management. Treatment and rehabilitation need to be tailored to the circumstances of the individual.

Positivism emerged from the 1800s as the dominant school of thought. Advances in medicine, psychology, and sociology presaged a more scientific approach to explaining and understanding deviance. The emerging juvenile justice system focused on identifying the causes of delinquency and sought ways to correct the inadequacies that led to delinquency. While the criminal justice system retained vestiges of Classicism and deterrence, the juvenile justice system and the emerging field of criminology embraced the ideas of Positivism.

Neoclassicism and a Summary

The juvenile justice system shifted back to a more Classical viewpoint over the past 30 years, with mandatory punishments, deterrence, and the waiver of youths to the adult system. While Positivism has not totally disappeared, the dominant approach better fits a label of **Neoclassicism**. Neoclassicism takes the position that an individual exercises some degree of free will. The choices, however, are limited by factors both within and outside of the individual. Sometimes referred to as **soft determinism**, an individual can make decisions only based on the available choices. The available options determine the extent to which the person can exercise his or her free will. This compromise gives both the Classicist and Positivist a stake in the criminal and juvenile justice systems.

The balance of this chapter, as well as the next chapter, discusses a wide range of theories. The biological and psychological theories appearing in this chapter are primarily Positivistic in orientation. For the most part, they approach deviance as the outcome of forces beyond the control of the individual. The sociological theories appearing in Chapter 4, however, more often incorporate elements of free will in their arguments.

BIOLOGICAL AND SOCIOBIOLOGICAL THEORIES

Explanations of deviance based on biological factors are among the earliest and the most recent theories in criminology. Medical advances, particularly in the 1800s, led to explanations of behavior that focused on the biological makeup of the individual. The underlying assumption made by the early biological theorists was that if the biological makeup of the individual dictated his or her physical capabilities, these characteristics could also contribute to the type of behavior exhibited by the person.

Physical Appearance

Early biological explanations focused heavily on observable physical features of offenders. The basic argument was that offenders could be identified by their appearance, which often was described in terms that suggested an ape-like appearance. Among the earliest of these approaches were **physiognomy** (the study of facial features) and **phrenology** (the study of the shape of a person's skull) (see Box 3.1).

Atavism

Cesare Lombroso, who is considered the father of modern criminology, based his ideas on Charles Darwin's theory of the survival of the species, and viewed criminals as throwbacks to an earlier state of human existence. These individuals were not as physically or mentally advanced as the rest of society.

BOX 3.1 PHYSICAL TRAIT EXPLANATIONS

KEY IDEA: an individual's physical features can indicate/identify who is or will be a criminal

Physiognomy	Focus on facial features
Phrenology	Considers the shape of the skull
Lombroso	Atavism: idea that offenders are throwbacks to an earlier stage of human development; ape-like
Sheldon	Somatotypes: considers different body types and related temperaments as explanations for deviant activity

A phrenology model of the locations of the "various organs of mind" in the human head, c. 1890. (Hand-colored woodcut of a nineteenth-century illustration.)

CREDIT: North Wind Picture Archives via AP Images

Lombroso (1876) identified a number of **atavistic**, or ape-like, qualities that generally reflected the physical features of the apes from whom man was a descendant. Typical features noted by Lombroso included a protruding jaw, a high forehead, deep/close-set eyes, and excessively long arms and legs. In a study of incarcerated offenders, Lombroso identified four categories of criminals: born criminals, insane criminals, criminaloids or occasional criminals, and criminals of passion (Wolfgang, 1961). *Born criminals* comprised more than 40 percent of the criminals, had five or more atavistic traits, and were a direct result of the lack of evolutionary progression found in the person. *Insane criminals* included imbeciles, idiots, and epileptics who acted in deranged ways. *Criminaloids* had innate traits similar to born criminals and also responded to opportunities to commit crimes (Vold & Bernard, 1986). The final group, *criminals of passion*, responded to emotional factors like anger, honor, or love.

Lombroso's work led to a great deal of controversy. His failure to include a control group of noncriminals meant that he was unable to state whether the results would be different if he studied people in the general public. Goring (1913) found only minor differences in the physical makeup of convicts and a control group of noncriminal citizens. Subsequent research by Lombroso, including control groups, revealed great physical similarities between offenders and nonoffenders, leading Lombroso to consider nonphysical atavistic qualities, as well as environmental and social factors for explaining deviance.

Somatotypes

Despite the criticisms of Lombroso and his contemporaries, the relation between physical appearance and deviance has appeared in twentieth-century research as **somatotypes**, or body types. Sheldon (1949) identified three basic somatotypes and related temperaments (see Table 3.2). Based on his observations of delinquents in a residential facility, Sheldon (1949) found that mesomorphic characteristics were most prevalent and ectomorphic features were the least common. He concluded that mesomorphic individuals were more likely to commit delinquent acts than were other youths. Support for the relationship between mesomorphy and delinquency is also found in the studies of Sheldon Glueck and Eleanor Glueck (1956) and Juan Cortes (1972).

Not unexpectedly, somatotype studies share similar methodological problems. First, much of the research is based on subjective determinations of body type, often by simply looking at photographs of the youths. Second, the researchers do not consider changes in body type as the youths grow older. Third, the researchers ignore the possibility that mesomorphic youths are more often recruited into delinquency because of their physical build, rather than having a

TABLE 3.2 Sheldon's Physiques and Temperaments

Physique	Temperament
Endomorph Short, fat, round, soft	**Viscerotonic** Soft, easygoing, extrovert
Mesomorph Muscular, large, barrel-chested, thick, hard	**Somotonic** Dynamic, active, athletic, aggressive, talkative
Ectomorph Bony, thin, skinny, small, delicate	**Cerebrotonic** Nervous, complainer, introvert

Source: Constructed by authors from Sheldon (1949).

natural propensity to commit delinquent acts. Fourth, considering delinquents as only incarcerated youths may bias the results if mesomorphic delinquents are institutionalized more often because they are perceived as greater threats than are smaller youths. Finally, the determination that mesomorphs were somotonic (aggressive, active, etc.) rests on the fact that many delinquents are mesomorphs and delinquent behavior is considered aggressive. Based on these problems, physical type theories have fallen out of favor and are rarely addressed in contemporary juvenile justice.

Biosocial Factors

Modern biological explanations of behavior involve what is known as bio-social approaches (see Box 3.2). **Biosociology, or sociobiology,** refers to the idea that the biological makeup of the organism and the surrounding environment are intimately related. The environment plays a part in shaping the organism, and the organism, through its daily activity and interpretation of the world, shapes the environment. Owen (2012) points out that genes impact the structure of the brain, but the environment has the ability to change the functioning of the brain. Biosociology sees deviance occurring when specific biological conditions coincide with appropriate sociological or environmental

BOX 3.2 BIOSOCIAL EXPLANATIONS

KEY IDEA: the interaction of an individual's biological makeup and the environment plays a role in behavior

Behavioral genetics	Examines the genetic influences in tandem with the environment. Assumes genetic similarity manifests similar behavior. Key topics: twin studies; adoption studies
Molecular genetics	The identification of specific genes and their impact on behavior. Key topics: DNA; ADHD; MAOA; epigenetics
Biological factors	Physiological impacts on behavior. Key topics: hormonal influences; orthomolecular factors; resting heart rate
Neurological mechanisms	Examination of organ functioning and behavior. Key topics: neurotransmitters; CNS; traumatic brain injury

factors. Barnes, Boutwell, and Beaver (2016) offer five domains of biosocial criminology: evolutionary biology, biological criminology, behavioral genetics, molecular genetics, and neurocriminology. We will discuss all of these except evolutionary biology (which addresses the biological contributions to long-term evolution and is beyond the scope of this book).

Behavioral Genetics

Biological explanations often assume a strong genetic contribution to behavior. The fact that physical features are clearly passed on from generation to generation has led some to extend that same propensity to nonphysical factors, such as behavioral tendencies. Two basic methods for inspecting this possibility are comparing the behavior of twins and comparing the behavior of offspring to their biological parents. In both sets of studies, it is not the criminal behavior that is considered to be inherited. Rather, it is factors such as low self-control, sensation-seeking, and temperament that are inherited, which lead to criminality (Eysenck & Gudjonsson, 1989; Mednick & Christiansen, 1977; Rowe, 2002).

Twin Studies. Studying twins for the genetic propensity to be deviant requires knowing whether the siblings are monozygotic (MZ) (identical) or dizygotic (DZ) (fraternal) twins. MZ twins are the product of a single fertilized egg that separates into two individuals with an identical genetic makeup. DZ twins are the result of two separate eggs fertilized by separate sperm. While genetically similar, the two offspring will not be genetically identical and are no more genetically similar than any two siblings born at different points in time. An examination of the genetic propensity for deviant behavior rests on finding greater **concordance**, or similarity, in behavior for MZ twins than for DZ twins or common siblings.

Several studies of twins find a genetic component to behavior. Newman, Freeman, and Holzinger (1937), for example, reported much higher concordance in behavior for MZ twins than DZ twins. Similarly, using a registry of 6,000 pairs of twins in Denmark, Christiansen (1974) uncovered three times as much concordance between MZ twins than between DZ twins when criminal records were inspected. Lyons (1996), in a large-scale analysis of subjects from a registry of Vietnam-era veterans born between 1939 and 1957, reported higher concordance in adult criminality for MZ twins than DZ twins. Each of these studies suggests that genetic factors have an influence on the actions of the individuals.

Adoption Studies. While the twin studies suggest a genetic component, they are unable to control for environmental influences that may be at work (Katz & Chamblis, 1995; Reiss & Roth, 1993). The concordance may be due to similarity in rearing, imitation between siblings, or other non-genetic factors. Studies of behavior and adoption implicitly add environment to the investigations by comparing the behavior of adopted offspring and their biological parents. Adoption studies assume that any similarity between the adopted offspring and the biological parent must be due to the genetic similarity between the subjects because the child has been raised in a different environment from the parent.

Various adoption studies find a genetic link to behavior. Hutchings and Mednick (1977) reported that 49 percent of criminal boys have criminal biological fathers while only 31 percent of noncriminal boys have criminal biological fathers. Whether the adoptive father is or is not criminal does not eliminate this relationship, although it does temper the results. Brennan, Mednick, and Jacobsen (1996) report a strong genetic component in their adoption study, but it is only true when considering property crimes. Similarly, in a study of Swedish adoptees, Cloninger, Sigvardsson, Bohman, and von Knorring (1982) report greater concordance in behavior when looking at petty criminality. Beaver, Rowland, Schwartz, and Nedelec (2011) uncover a relationship between adoptees' psychopathology and their biological father's criminality.

Several large reviews of the research find a genetic component to behavior. Walters (1992) undertook a meta-analysis of 38 twin and adoption projects dating from 1930 to 1989. In a **meta-analysis**, the researcher uses the reported data from past studies and computes a common statistic for all studies, thereby allowing a direct comparison of the different results. Walters (1992) reported that there is a "low–moderate" correlation between heredity and crime. Ellis and Walsh (2000), reviewing 72 studies, note that 93 percent provide strong support for a genetic contribution to behavior. In another meta-analysis, Rhee and Waldman (2012) find that more than 40 percent of the behaviors in twin and adoption studies are due to heritability, and the relationship is strongest in property offending. In all of these reviews, the authors note that the behavior itself is not inherited, only a propensity to criminality is inherited.

Molecular Genetics

The search for genetic influences on behavior has not been limited to adoption and twin studies. Barnes et al. (2016) point out that the ability to identify the known genome allows researchers to distinguish gene sequences that may be related to different behaviors. Owen (2012) points out that genetics impact a person's brain structure, how it functions, and how it reacts to social and environmental inputs. At the same time, DNA can be altered by the environment. The study of how this occurs is known as **epigenetics**.

Barnes et al. (2016) review a number of studies of different genes and their relation to behavior. Among these were genes influencing the processing of information in the brain. These are called **transporter genes**. They find that these genes are strongly related with antisocial activity. Watts and McNulty (2015) report similar results in an analysis of **monoamine oxidase A (MAOA)**, an enzyme that has the ability to facilitate or inhibit the transfer of information from neuron to neuron, thus altering possible reactions to inputs. Caspi et al. (2002) report that low MAOA activity is associated with antisocial activity. A meta-analysis by Kim-Cohen et al. (2006) uncovered a clear association between MAOA and delinquency/criminality.

Another example of a genetic influence on behavior involves **Attention Deficit Hyperactivity Disorder (ADHD)**. Anderson (2007) and Barnes et al. (2016) note there is a strong genetic basis for ADHD as demonstrated in a number of studies. Children suffering from this disorder are persistently disruptive, act impulsively, are easily frustrated, experience wide mood swings, and act inappropriately (Fishbein, Miller, Winn, & Dakof, 2009; Ward, 2000). To the extent that ADHD is related to deviant and criminal behavior, it can be argued that there is a genetic contribution to criminality (Anderson, 2007).

Research on molecular genetics and deviant behavior is still in its infancy. Future advances may reveal stronger contributors to a wide range of behaviors. The problem of separating the environmental influences from a genetic component, however, remains a major stumbling block in the research.

Biological Factors

Hormones. Among the normal functions of the body is the production and secretion of various **hormones**. These natural chemicals control many of the basic bodily functions, including growth, reproduction, and functioning of the central nervous system. In terms of deviant behavior, most attention has focused on reproductive hormones (Shah & Roth, 1974).

Androgen, the male sex hormone present in testosterone, has received a great deal of attention. It has been found to be related to aggressive behavior, particularly in animal studies. Studies on human subjects have found a relation between higher testosterone levels and aggression and more serious offending (Barnes et al., 2016; Booth & Osgood, 1993; Dabbs, Carr, Frady, & Riad, 1995; Ehrenkranz, Bliss, & Sheard, 1974; Kreuz & Rose, 1972; Rada, Laws, & Kellner, 1976; Soler, Vinayak, & Quadagno, 2000). While such studies suggest that testosterone leads to greater levels of aggression, the evidence is not totally convincing. Among the problems are the facts that testosterone levels vary over even short time periods; testosterone is affected by diet, stress, exercise, and social factors (Booth & Osgood, 1993; Katz & Chamblis, 1995; Nassi & Abramowitz, 1976; Reiss & Roth, 1993); and aggressive behavior may cause testosterone levels to increase, rather than the other way around (Harris, 1999).

Two other hormones that receive attention are **epinephrine** and **norepinephrine**. Both of these are responsible for the fight or flight reactions in humans (Owen, 2012). Increases in norepinephrine lead to increased heart rates and energy levels. Increases in epinephrine mean an increase in adrenaline. Changes in either may result in fear, greater activity, and/or aggressive responses to external stimuli (Mezzacappa, 1999). The external stimulus is typically some form of stress (Owen, 2012). While epinephrine, norepinephrine, and other hormones are involved in behavior, they are triggered by the environment and are not necessary or sufficient for deviance.

Orthomolecular Factors. **Orthomolecular factors** refer to chemicals that are introduced to the body or altered through diet or other influences. There is a wide array of such chemicals, including alcohol, drugs, lead, and sugar.

Alcohol and illegal drugs are commonly linked to deviant behavior. That alcohol and other drugs correlate with delinquency and criminality is indisputable. There is evidence that alcoholism has a genetic component (see Bohman, 1996). Reiss and Roth (1993) suggest a biological connection in which alcohol alters the processing of information and, depending on the dosage, may prompt aggression and irritability, or more passivity and sluggishness. From a **psychopharmacological perspective**, drugs have a direct causal impact on crime. Violence and aggression have been found to be related to long-term opiate, PCP, and amphetamine use (Reiss & Roth, 1993). Whether the drugs–crime relationship is psychopharmacological may be a function of the type of drug and related factors (its addictive properties, its cost, etc.).

Lead toxicity impacts the individuals in a variety of ways. Muller et al. (2018) and Wright (2011) note that lead exposure and toxicity is tied to aggression, antisocial behavior, academic deficits, and other problems. The recognition of lead as problematic has resulted in a range of policies for lead abatement in communities and the environment.

The role of sugar in aggression has been explored for a number of years. **Hypoglycemia** is the term most often used in these discussions. However, hypoglycemia, a condition of low blood sugar, manifests itself in a lack of energy, lethargy, nervousness, and, in the extreme, a coma. It is difficult to imagine hypoglycemic individuals taking aggressive, deviant actions against anyone. The proper term for the relationship between blood sugar levels and criminal activity is **reactive hypoglycemia**, which refers to changes in the blood sugar level, both higher and lower, as a result of dietary intake.

While various researchers claim to have found support for a relationship between hypoglycemia and crime (Bonnett & Pfeiffer, 1978; Geary, 1983; Hippchen, 1978, 1981; Podolsky, 1964; Schauss, 1980), their conclusions rest upon suspect research methodology (Gray & Gray, 1983). Much of the support comes from anecdotal accounts of physicians and psychologists who simply compare a person's diet to his or her behavior without establishing the different bodily needs or processes of the different individuals; or from the Oral Glucose Tolerance Test, which is not a definitive measure of blood sugar (Gray & Gray, 1983). When more accurate measures are used, the studies fail to support reactive hypoglycemia as an explanation for deviance. Given the state of the evidence, reactive hypoglycemia is considered a minor cause of deviance (American Dietetics Association, 1984; Gray & Gray, 1983).

Neurological Mechanisms

The functioning of the brain is a key to the impact of many sociobiological factors on behavior (Moffitt, Ross, & Raine, 2011; Raine, 2008, 2013). Brain functioning can be affected both in terms of factors impacting the ability to process information and in terms of the brain structure and injuries to the brain.

Neurotransmitters. The ability of the body to process information can be greatly impacted by **neurotransmitters**, which are chemicals involved in the transmission of electrical impulses through the nervous system (Anderson,

2007). These chemicals are capable of altering an individual's behavior. Among the neurotransmitters that have been investigated are serotonin and dopamine. Three common neurotransmitters that have been explored in relation to behavior are serotonin, dopamine, and norepinephrine.

Serotonin is an inhibitor of behavior, particularly aggressive and impulsive behaviors (Anderson, 2007). Low levels of serotonin have been found to be related to low self-control (Wright & Beaver, 2005) and aggression (Moffitt et al., 1998). Similarly, Virkkunen, Goldman, and Linnoila (1996) note that serotonin levels influence impulse control, hyperactivity, and other behavior related to deviance. **Dopamine** and norepinephrine act in the opposite way from serotonin. Specifically, higher dopamine and norepinephrine levels result in greater action and pleasure-seeking behaviors as well as heightened aggression (Anderson, 2007; Raine, 2013).

Research has shown that it is possible to alter various neurotransmitters. This can be done purposefully with drugs and inadvertently through the use of alcohol and other substances. While still in its early stages, this research suggests that there is a relationship between different neurotransmitters and deviance (Anderson, 2007; Brennan, Mednick, & Volavka, 1995; Raine, 2013; Reiss & Roth, 1993).

Structural Factors

Recognition that different parts of the brain are related to different behaviors has led some researchers to look at brain abnormalities, functioning, and deviance. Areas of the brain that have been related to criminal behavior include the amygdala, the hippocampus, and the prefrontal cortex (Chen et al., 2016; Raine, 2013). Advances in techniques for examining the brain and brain functions, such as magnetic resonance imaging (MRI), positron emission tomography (PET scans), and electroencephalography (EEG), have greatly increased the ability to study neurological influences on behavior. An MRI can show the physical makeup of the brain and reveal any physical problems (Rowe, 2002). A PET scan reveals differing levels of brain activity when faced with varying stimuli (Rowe, 2002). An EEG measures a person's electrical brain waves, which can be compared to those of other individuals (Rowe, 2002). Based on these technologies, there is clear evidence relating brain functioning, especially frontal and temporal lobe problems, to deviant activity (Raine, 2013; Raine, Venables, & Williams, 1995). The impact of these factors relative to other variables, such as the environment, however, is not clear.

Brain functioning is also impacted by outside forces. Traumatic brain injuries (TBIs) are strongly correlated with criminality, with criminals displaying more TBIs than the general population (Chen et al., 2016). TBI was found to be prevalent among both male (50.4 percent) and female (38 percent) inmates in four Canadian prisons (Colantonio et al., 2014). Recidivism has also been related to TBI among releasees from prison (Ray & Richardson, 2017). Fishbein et al. (2016a) report that TBI is related to earlier onset of substance abuse and to aggressive behavior. Research on neurotransmitters, brain functioning, and TBI suggest a clear relationship with antisocial behavior.

Summary

Biosocial explanations are receiving growing attention but remain outside the mainstream of criminological explanations for a variety of reasons. First, the identification of correlations is often touted as clear evidence of a causal relationship. The research has yet to establish a clear causal relationship in many cases. Second, the ability to generalize results of studies based on animals to human beings is questionable. Finally, the studies often fail to consider other spurious factors, such as social status, diet, and the environment, in the consideration of biosocial influences. It is possible that these other factors are influencing both deviance and neurological functioning.

Walsh (2009) outlines five typical objections lodged by mainstream criminologists against biosocial theories (see Table 3.3). These objections reflect two underlying problems. First, most criminologists are trained in the social science tradition. As a result, there is a fundamental lack of understanding and ignorance about biological issues. Even among those who study sociobiological topics, there is a lack of consensus on the relative strength of heritability and environment (see Barnes et al., 2014; Burt and Simons, 2014; Wright et al., 2015). Second, there is an assumption that biological explanations are being promoted as an alternative to sociological and psychological theories. Those making this objection are ignoring the fact that what is being promoted is "biosociology" or "sociobiology," which posits looking at the interaction between biological and traditional social science factors in causing crime and

---

TABLE 3.3 Common Objections to Biologically Based Explanations

Biological Theories are Deterministic and Socially Dangerous
- Ignores the fact that those espousing biology recognize the interplay of biology and the environment
- Does not assume single cause

Because Crime is Socially Constructed, There Cannot Be any Genes for Crime
- No claim of a gene for crime but genes do play a role in traits and subsequent behavior

If a Problem is Considered Biological, Therapeutic Nihilism will Ensue
- You can alter and influence biological factors that contribute to behavior
- Biological treatments are not enough in themselves

Crime Cannot Have a Biological Basis Because Crime Rates Change Rapidly While Changes in Genes Require Many Generations
- Of course environment influences change in rate, but individual factors influence when and who will start and stop offending

Biological Theories Tend to be Insensitive to People's Feelings
- If we find results that suggest one group or condition is more predisposed to certain behavior, should we ignore it just to be politically correct?

Source: Compiled by authors from Walsh (2009).

From left, seen clockwise, are the drugs Depo-Provera, Zoladex, and Lupron-Depot, photographed at Atascadero State Hospital. Some experts believe that sex offenders can control and manage their deviant sexual urges with a combination of drugs and psychotherapy.

CREDIT: AP Photo/Ben Margot

deviance. Indeed, biosocial theorists recognize that the biological factors often play a minor role in behavior and that the environment is a key factor in understanding crime and delinquency (Walsh, 2009).

Biological Implications for the Justice System

The modern biosocial approaches have engendered interest in biological influences on behavior. Conditions that have a genetic component on behaviors related to hormonal or orthomolecular problems can be altered or modified by changes in diet or drug therapy. For example, both chemical and surgical castrations have been employed to reduce testosterone levels in convicted sex offenders. Depo-Provera is a drug that inhibits the production of testosterone. As biosocial research progresses, additional practical uses for curbing deviance will emerge.

The degree to which biological development and functioning can be influenced early in an individual's existence suggests that early interventions may be useful. Olds et al. (1998) and Lipsey and Wilson (1998) note that interventions as early as prenatal and during infancy can alter later behavior, including delinquency. The avoidance of early trauma can avoid later antisocial activities. As Brennan and associates note: "Understanding of the interaction of genetic and environmental factors in the causes of crime may lead to the improvement of treatment and prevention. Several genetically based conditions are treated very successfully by environmental intervention" (Brennan et al., 1995:90). At the same time, caution must be taken when implementing programs based on biosocial research. These activities may also bring about more harm than good. For example, altering a diet to do away with "problem" foods may inadvertently damage an otherwise good diet. The most prudent direction for biosocial advocates to pursue at the present time would be expanded research.

PSYCHOLOGICAL EXPLANATIONS

A second general area of explanations for delinquency entails psychological theories. As with other types of theories, psychological explanations take a variety of forms and include a wide range of factors. The early base for psychological theories was biological/physical factors. Indeed, psychiatry, which is usually seen as a part of the general psychological field, is distinguished by its strong commitment to finding physiological bases for aberrant behavior. Psychiatrists are medical doctors who have specialized in the general area of mental disorders.

Many psychological explanations, however, do not look for a physical explanation. Instead, the psychological theories typically have the following distinctive characteristics:

- They generally view problems as arising out of early life experiences. Deviance is seen as a result of problems and flaws that were not recognized and corrected during the adolescent years.
- They are highly individualistic. While many individuals may display the same or similar behavior, different explanations or factors (such as incomplete socialization or poor personality development) may be at work for each person.
- They lend themselves to a treatment orientation. Rather than focus on who will become deviant, the emphasis is on working with individuals who are already having problems and assisting them to overcome the problem.

Psychoanalytic Explanations

Perhaps one of the most widely recognized names in psychology is Sigmund Freud (1856–1939). Freud pioneered the psychoanalytic approach to understanding human behavior. The major premise of **psychoanalysis** is that unconscious, and perhaps instinctual, factors account for much of the behavior displayed by individuals. In particular, deviance is the result of unconscious desires and drives being manifested in behavior. The goal of psychoanalysis is to identify the unconscious, precipitating factors, and then develop conscious methods for dealing with them.

Freudian psychoanalysis outlines three distinct parts to the personality that are involved in behavior (see Table 3.4). The **id** reflects the unconscious desires, drives, and instincts within the individual. In simple terms, the id can be seen as the selfish, "I want" part of the individual. The **superego** entails learned values that form the moral character of the individual and help dictate what the person considers acceptable or unacceptable behavior. The superego is a result of early moral training. Where the id looks for satisfaction of desires, the superego responds with either a "can't have" orientation or a "must do" response. That is, the superego helps orient the individual's behavior away from simple desires and toward the value system that the person has incorporated. The actions of the superego may be both conscious and unconscious. The final part of the personality, the **ego**, is the social identity that is exhibited through behavior. It is often the manifestation of the conflict between the id and the

TABLE 3.4 **The Freudian Personality**	
Id	Unconscious desires, drives, instincts
Superego	Learned values, behaviors; moral character of the individual; outlines the acceptable and unacceptable; may be conscious or unconscious
Ego	Social identity of individual; actual behavior; conscious activity

TABLE 3.5 Psychoanalytic Defense Mechanisms

REPRESSION

An active attempt to push desires and thoughts out of one's consciousness or to keep material from reaching consciousness. Example: You forget that you owned a pet that was run over by a car when you were a child.

DISPLACEMENT

A change in the primary object of a feeling or desire to a secondary one that is less threatening. Example: You are angry at your boss but you yell at your husband or wife instead.

SUBLIMATION

Here the displacement is more long-term and the object chosen is socially acceptable. Example: You want to hit and hurt your father, but you become a professional boxer or football player.

DENIAL

The truth of certain facts or experiences is denied, rather than forgotten as in repression. Example: Your daughter dies but you act as if she is alive, keeping a bed made up for her.

REACTION FORMATION

A desire is changed or transformed into the opposite feeling or desire. Example: You hate or deeply resent your father, but you tell everyone how much you love him and act toward him in a loving manner.

PROJECTION

You have an unconscious desire or thought, but you attribute it to someone else instead of acknowledging it in yourself. Example: You no longer love someone, but instead accuse him or her of no longer loving you.

RATIONALIZATION

The process of finding an acceptable reason for doing something unacceptable. Example: You punish your child harshly, but say "I'm doing this for your own good."

REGRESSION

You replace your desires or thoughts with those from an earlier stage of your development. Example: You are under stress and get angry at someone who works for you, so you throw a temper tantrum.

Source: Van Voorhis et al. (2007:44).

superego. The ego is the conscious attempt to satisfy the needs of the id while continuing to abide by the mandates of the superego. This aspect is always conscious because it is the solution to the question of whether the individual follows his or her drives or the morally correct line of activity.

Psychoanalysis seeks to uncover the causes of behavior by bringing the unconscious conflict between the id and the superego to consciousness. Often, psychoanalysis is only undertaken when an individual develops criminally deviant behavior. The conflict between the id and the superego may be resolved in various ways (see Table 3.5). One response can involve simply repressing the desires or thoughts and keeping them from being manifested in inappropriate behavior. The opposite can also occur and the individual simply acts in accord with the id, which may be deviant (such as stealing an item because you want it). Another response could be denying the id and replacing it (displacement) with another action that could also be deviance (such as hitting your spouse because you are mad at what happened at work). The individual could also sublimate the drive finding an acceptable long-term substitute. It is the goal of psychoanalysis to uncover why the individual acts as he or she does.

Despite the development of a large body of literature, the psychoanalytic approach is subjected to strong criticism. First, it is very hard to undertake empirical tests of the theory because there is no clear method for measuring the id, ego, or superego. A second major criticism involves the fact that psychoanalysis is totally retrospective. That is, it is useful only for looking at what has already happened. It is geared toward uncovering why something happened and working to correct problems. A third criticism is that psychoanalysis emphasizes early childhood and assumes that little change occurs after adolescence. Adult behavior is viewed only as a result of poor childhood socialization and not from factors appearing in adult life. Finally, psychoanalysis is criticized for ignoring social-structural factors in the determination of behavior. Indeed, with the heavy emphasis on the unconscious, psychoanalysis examines the social setting of the individual only to the extent that it failed to provide the necessary moral atmosphere during early adolescence.

Developmental Approaches

A number of writers identify the source of deviance in interrupted or arrested development (see Box 3.3). The basic assumption is that individuals develop through a number of stages. Each stage provides an integral part of the knowledge and understanding that a person needs to operate in society. The failure of an individual to complete any one of these stages or steps successfully may lead to some form of socially unacceptable behavior. This basic argument can be seen in Freud's psychoanalytic explanation in which the failure to develop appropriate superego and ego responses to the id takes place in early childhood. The child is born with the id but must learn and internalize the moral dictates of society as he or she grows.

Interpersonal Maturity

One of the most well-known developmental approaches in delinquency research is the **Interpersonal Maturity Levels (I-levels)**. The I-levels represent a continuum from the most basic stage of development through the most advanced stage (see Table 3.6). The interruption of any stage makes the attainment of later stages difficult, if not impossible.

BOX 3.3 DEVELOPMENTAL EXPLANATIONS

KEY IDEA: everyone develops through stages; deviance is the result of interrupted development

I-levels	Interpersonal Maturity Levels; deviance committed by those stuck in early levels that focus on individual needs
Kohlberg's Moral Development	Six stages of moral development; failure to develop to the stage of recognizing the needs of society/others allows for deviant behavior
Tremblay's Pre-Adolescent Development	Aggression is a natural outgrowth of early childhood; need to develop non-aggressive behaviors

TABLE 3.6 **Interpersonal Maturity Levels**	
Level 1	The individual learns to discriminate between themselves and others.
Level 2	The individual starts to separate things into persons and objects, partly on the basis of their own needs and what they can control.
Level 3	At this level the individual begins to learn rules and can start to manipulate the environment for their own benefit.
Level 4	The individual begins to perceive things from the standpoint of others. He/she sees conflicts between expectations of others and their own needs.
Level 5	Here the individual becomes aware of patterns of behavior and relationships. There becomes an awareness of distinctions made between events, objects, and roles in society.
Level 6	The individual is able to distinguish between himself/herself and the roles they play. These are not one and the same and can accommodate one another.
Level 7	At this level, the individual begins to perceive a variety of methods for dealing with the world and makes choices based on his/her and others' past experiences and for the benefit of everyone.

Source: Compiled by authors from Sullivan, Grant, and Grant (1957).

Most delinquency and deviance occurs in Levels 2, 3, and 4. Level 2 individuals operate primarily on the basis of their own need and use others only as a source of enjoyment or fulfillment. While Level 3 individuals begin to integrate rules, they are still oriented toward their own needs. As a result, they may realize what they are doing is wrong but cannot justify the rules with their desires. Finally, persons in Level 4 may resort to delinquent behavior as a means of striking out against what they perceive as contradictory demands. The inability to cope with competing demands may result in choosing delinquent activity. Individuals operating at lower maturity levels, however, tend to act in ways counter to societal demands.

Moral Development

A second well-known developmental approach is Kohlberg's (1981) **moral development**. Kohlberg's model notes that individuals progress through six stages of "moral development," which are arranged into three levels (Table 3.7). The Preconventional Level is characteristic of young children, while most adults fall into the Conventional Level. Only a small proportion of adults reach the Postconventional or Principled Level. Deviant individuals typically fail to display the same level of moral development as noncriminals with the same or similar characteristics. As in the I-level classification scheme, Kohlberg views deviance as a result of interrupted or incomplete development. For example, an individual at Stage 2 sees his or her own needs and feels that he or she does not get enough in return for what they do or want. As a result, that person may turn to deviance to "balance" the exchange.

TABLE 3.7 **Kohlberg's Moral Development**

Level I. Preconventional Level

Stage 1	Right is obedience to authority and rules, and avoiding punishment. There is clear concern for one's own physical well-being.
Stage 2	Right corresponds to seeing one's own needs, taking responsibility for one's self, and allowing others to do the same. At issue is a fair exchange with others.

Level II. Conventional Level

Stage 3	Right is avoiding the disapproval of others, having good intentions and motives, and being concerned for others. Individuals are aware of others and their needs.
Stage 4	Right is doing one's duty to society and others, and upholding the social order. The individual is capable of looking at things from society's viewpoint.

Level III. Postconventional or Principled Level

Stage 5	Right is based on upholding the rules and values agreed upon by society. The individual feels obligated to society. There is a recognized social contract between the individual and society that outlines acceptable behavior.
Stage 6	Right is a reflection of universal ethical principles. The individual recognizes the moral rightness of behavior and acts accordingly.

Source: Compiled by authors from Kohlberg (1981).

Tremblay's Pre-Adolescent Development

Tremblay (2007) advanced a slightly different take on the developmental process when he argued that aggression does not emerge during the adolescent years as many studies promote. He claims that these findings are actually the result of societal reaction to the aggression of adolescents due to their age and perceived threat level. The aggressive behavior does not develop during adolescence. Rather, Tremblay (2007) argues that the aggression develops during early childhood and can be seen as early as age two.

Early evidence of aggression appears in the behavior of children due to genetic and environmental factors (Tremblay, 2007). Very young children get into conflict over such things as toys and other objects that attract their attention. Their desire to hold and manipulate attractive objects leads to conflicts and the behavior continues over time. While most children will learn that these actions are not acceptable from their parents and/or the consequences of their disputes with others, some children continue this behavior. The environment in which the child matures will help dictate acceptance or rejection of aggressive behavior (Tremblay, 2007).

The basic premise of Tremblay's (2007) development approach is that aggression is a natural outcome of childhood. The child needs to learn the skills and abilities to utilize non-aggressive means of solving disputes. Rather than trying to restart the normal development that was interrupted in the

I-levels and Kohlberg's moral development approaches, Tremblay's approach suggests that the developmental patterns that were started in early childhood need to be interrupted and replaced with alternative behaviors and habits that are not aggressive in nature. In essence, children and adolescents need to learn new behavioral pathways.

Learning Theories

Implicit in developmental discussions is the idea that people learn right from wrong, and learning takes place over a long period of time. There is a cumulative nature to learning. In learning theories, the emphasis is on how an individual learns and what factors are effective in promoting learning. The failure of an individual to complete a developmental stage successfully, therefore, may be due to a problem in the learning process (see Box 3.4).

Modeling is perhaps the simplest form of learning. According to Bandura and Walters (1963), children learn by copying the behavior of others. Most modeling follows the behavior of significant others, particularly parents, siblings, peers, and other individuals close to the child. Modeling, however, is not limited to the people around the youth. Children also can learn from characters, both real and fictional. If the child continuously sees deviance, either real or fictional, the child may begin to copy that behavior. The child may not know whether it is right or wrong. He or she only knows that this is how people act. (Further discussion of modeling and identification will be taken up in Chapter 4.)

A more classical psychological learning theory is that of operant conditioning. Operant conditioning deals with the reinforcement of behavior through a complex system of rewards. Skinner (1953) and others view subsequent behavior as a consequence of past responses to behavior. Specifically, an individual repeats (or does not repeat) a behavior based on what happened when the behavior in question appeared in the past. For example, a child who does as he or she is told by his or her parents is given a treat for being good. The treat becomes a reinforcer for future good behavior. In operant conditioning the reinforcement comes after the behavior or action of the individual. Actions that result in a pleasurable response (positive reinforcer) or that eliminate painful or unpleasant situations (negative reinforcer) will be repeated. Learning, therefore, becomes an ongoing process, with every choice made by the individual

---

BOX 3.4 PSYCHOLOGICAL LEARNING EXPLANATIONS

KEY IDEA: behavior is learned over a long period of time

Modeling	Basic form of learning where individuals, particularly children, copy what they see
Operant Conditioning	Behavior is molded through a complex system of rewards and punishments applied to past behavior

resulting in some form of response. Future actions are based on the reinforcement, or lack thereof, of past behavior.

Bandura and Walters (1963) have combined conditioning and modeling in a general discussion of learning. They note that the degree to which a child models his or her behavior is mitigated by the level of reward or punishment that the model receives. For example, a child observing an act of aggression by another person or a fictional character is more likely to copy that act if the aggressive person is rewarded or not punished. Therefore, the process of learning through operant conditioning can take a vicarious route through observation of the experiences of others. Two key concerns have been raised in relation to psychological learning theories. First, while modeling and operant conditioning make intuitive sense and receive support from anecdotal evidence and case studies, most of the supportive studies rely on correlational analyses and contain serious methodological flaws. A second problem is that modeling and operant conditioning approaches ignore the potential contribution of the individual to behavior. The basic assumption is that the individual is a product of the environment and has little influence over his or her choice of activity.

Personality and Delinquency

Various researchers have proposed that deviants display certain personality characteristics that can be used to explain deviant and criminal behavior (see Box 3.5). Psychologists have developed a wide array of personality classifications and measures for uncovering personality traits.

One of the early attempts to distinguish delinquents from nondelinquents using personality factors was conducted by Sheldon and Eleanor Glueck (1956). Comparing 500 delinquents to 500 matched nondelinquents, Glueck and Glueck claimed that:

> delinquents are more extroverted, vivacious, impulsive, … less self-controlled … are more hostile, resentful, defiant, suspicious, … destructive … and are less fearful of failure or defeat than the nondelinquents. They are less concerned about meeting conventional expectations and are more

BOX 3.5 PERSONALITY EXPLANATIONS

KEY IDEA: certain personality characteristics can be used to explain deviant and criminal behavior

The Gluecks	Identified a delinquent personality by comparing delinquent and nondelinquent youths; delinquents are extroverted, impulsive, resentful, defiant, destructive
Antisocial Personality Disorder	A mental health condition where individuals manipulate and exploit others for their own personal benefit; outlined in the DSM-5
MMPI	Minnesota Multiphasic Personality Inventory; standardized test of personality; based largely on incarcerated individuals

ambivalent toward or far less submissive to authority. They are, as a group, more socially assertive. (Glueck & Glueck, 1956:275)

This picture of the delinquent was meant to summarize their overall personality pattern and indicate differences from conventional youths.

While the work of Glueck and Glueck still draws attention today, several concerns have been raised about the findings. First, not all the traits associated with the delinquents are undesirable. For example, being extroverted, assertive, less fearful of failure, and less submissive are traits that many individuals would find valuable. Second, the authors assume that the individuals had these traits before they exhibited delinquent behavior. It could be argued, however, that the delinquents were hostile, resentful, defiant, and ambivalent to authority due to their contact with the justice system. Finally, the individuals who evaluated the youths were aware of which youths were delinquent and which were not delinquent. Knowing an individual is delinquent and in an institution may prompt an evaluator to expect the subject to be more assertive, more hostile, or have less self-control.

One commonly referenced personality disorder is **Antisocial Personality Disorder (APD)**, which appears in the *Diagnostic and Statistical Manual of Mental Disorders* (5th ed.), known as the DSM-5, of the American Psychiatric Association. The National Center for Biotechnology Information (2010) defines APD as "a mental health condition in which a person has a long-term pattern of manipulating, exploiting, or violating the rights of others." This behavior may be criminal or noncriminal. The actual cause of APD is not clear, but a combination of genetic and environmental factors probably contribute to the condition (Mayo Clinic, 2010). Assessing the presence of APD requires psychological testing and identifying criteria listed in the DSM-5. Treatment is considered very difficult and involves mainly psychotherapy. Unfortunately for juvenile justice, APD typically is not identified until early adulthood and, thus, is most useful in the adult criminal justice system.

A major change in personality research has been to try to develop standardized measures of personality. The **Minnesota Multiphasic Personality Inventory (MMPI)** is one standardized method for uncovering personality traits in individuals. The MMPI is an inventory of over 500 true/false questions that are designed to tap 10 personality dimensions identified in past clinical analyses (Megargee & Bohn, 1979) without the need for extended clinical observation. The MMPI assumes that everyone answers some questions in a deviant manner. Therefore, no single question is associated with deviant behavior. Instead, deviance is considered more likely as the individual answers in a deviant fashion on a number of questions. While the MMPI has been used extensively, it has been challenged on a number of grounds. First, to the extent that the prior clinical evaluations are in error, poorly conceived, or invalid, the MMPI results are also questionable. The results are only as good and useful as the underlying clinical factors. Second, the

WEB ACTIVITY

You can read more about the DSM-5 at www.psychiatry.org/psychiatrists/practice/dsm/about-dsm.

MMPI is useful primarily in the treatment of offenders, and not for predicting or explaining deviance prior to its occurrence. Finally, because the MMPI has been refined using institutionalized subjects, it is possible that it reflects factors related to institutional life and experiences, rather than a deviant personality. The inventory has been subjected to relatively few tests outside of the institutional setting.

Mental Deficiency and Delinquency

Since the late 1800s, low intelligence has been offered as a prime cause of deviant behavior (see Box 3.6). The scientific interest in the relation between intelligence and deviance can be traced to the development of IQ testing. IQ, or intelligence quotient, was developed by Alfred Binet in the early 1900s as a numerical representation of the mental ability of the individual. The formula for IQ is rather simple:

IQ = (mental age/chronological age) × 100

The mental age of an individual is determined by performance on a standardized test. The test consists of questions geared toward different-aged individuals. For example, persons age 10 and up are expected to be able to answer a certain level of questioning and all those from the easier levels. More difficult questions are assumed to be beyond the ability of the average 10-year-old. Once an individual's mental age is determined, the researcher simply divides that figure by the respondent's actual age and multiplies by the base of 100.

Since the development of the IQ test, many researchers have attempted to show that delinquency and deviance are related to low intelligence. The assumption that IQ is related to crime is not a surprising one given the knowledge that most incarcerated offenders tend to be less educated and display below-average scores on academic achievement tests. The major source of debate concerning IQ revolves around the question of whether IQ is due to nature or nurture.

The **nature–nurture controversy** refers to the question of whether intelligence is inherited (nature) or whether it is an outcome of environmental influences (nurture). The nature argument views IQ as set at birth and not subject to outside influences, such as the social and physical environment, including education. Conversely, the nurture side of the debate proposes that an individual's IQ is the outcome of complex interactions between the genetic makeup of the person and the environment to which the individual is exposed. This view

BOX 3.6 MENTAL DEFICIENCY EXPLANATIONS

KEY IDEA: examination of a person's intelligence as a cause of deviance

IQ	Intelligence quotient; numerical measure of the mental ability of an individual; attempts to show that delinquency and deviance are related to low intelligence
Nature vs. nurture	Debate over whether intelligence is inherited (nature) or an outcome of environmental influences (nurture)

suggests that IQ can be altered through education and other environmental interventions.

The view that intelligence is genetically determined received a great deal of early support in the United States, where low IQ scores were used as a means of denying immigrants entry to the country. Goddard (1920) argued that most criminals were "feebleminded" (IQ of less than 75) and the government took the position that excluding such individuals was in the best interests of the country. Unfortunately, Goddard (1920) examined only incarcerated "criminals" and had no way of knowing whether they were more or less "intelligent" than anyone else. Wilson and Herrnstein (1985) and Herrnstein and Murray (1994) also have argued that IQ is substantially due to genetics and that IQ is a strong predictor of criminal activity. Hirschi and Hindelang (1977) provide the most widely cited argument in the IQ-delinquency literature. The authors argue that IQ is at least as important in predicting delinquency as social class or race and is related to delinquency regardless of the race or social class of the individual. Their opinion is that IQ is an indirect cause of delinquency. Specifically, low IQ, through genetics and/or environment, leads to poor school performance, which prompts a lack of concern for education, a rebellious attitude toward the school and societal demands, and, eventually, a heightened chance of deviant behavior. To the extent that environment has a role, individuals with a low IQ who can be encouraged to stay in school, receive special help, or otherwise enhance their abilities may not experience the problems and frustrations that precipitate deviant activity.

Implications of Psychological Theories for Juvenile Justice

Before addressing the impact of psychological theories, it is important to point out some of the criticisms leveled at these explanations. As has been noted throughout the above discussions, psychologically oriented explanations are not particularly good for the prediction of behavior. Many are formulated after the fact and seek, primarily, to explain the observed behavior retrospectively. The emphasis is on why something happened and not predicting what will happen in the future. A second concern with psychological studies is the reliance on subjective interpretations. Most psychological endeavors rest on the opinion of individuals who have been trained in the field of psychology. Unfortunately, there is no single orientation or perspective that drives the entire field, or even subfields, of psychology. The subjective nature of psychology, therefore, often leads to conflicting opinions, even when individuals are looking at the exact same information.

Some commentators criticize what they see as the individualistic nature of psychological explanations. Indeed, many psychological endeavors examine individual subjects, and the precise explanation for deviance could vary from subject to subject. This criticism may be shortsighted, however, given the fact that these individualistic approaches form the basis of other, more general theories. For example, operant conditioning is a key component of differential association-reinforcement theory, and hedonism is at the heart of Gottfredson and Hirschi's general theory of crime (see Chapter 4 for discussions of both of these theories).

Psychological explanations have their greatest impact on the correctional end of the juvenile justice system. Psychology's emphasis on identifying the cause of an individual's behavior fits the general treatment orientation of juvenile justice. As a result, juvenile corrections place heavy emphasis on counseling, education, and other rehabilitative methods. Techniques such as I-level classifications and the MMPI are used to gain insight into a juvenile's problems and subsequently design a response to those problems. Additionally, behavior modification techniques are used to set up token economies in detention centers and training schools. Psychology will more than likely remain primarily a correctional tool in juvenile justice until such time that more precise methods of evaluation are generated or the predictive ability of psychological findings are enhanced.

SUMMARY

The biological and psychological explanations discussed in this chapter represent theories and perspectives developed over many decades. While some have been discounted because of their lack of rigor and relevance, they have engendered discussions that may lead to more applicable and useful theories. Psychological explanations have found a clear place in the juvenile justice system. This is particularly true in the juvenile court and in the correctional phase of processing. Biological explanations have not fared so well. This is due mainly to the poor quality of the early explanations and the current lack of expertise in the physical sciences held by criminologists and criminal justicians. The next chapter turns to a discussion of sociological explanations that hold the dominant position in modern discussions of delinquency and criminality.

DISCUSSION QUESTIONS

1. Compare and contrast the Classical and Positivist schools of thought. What are the basic assumptions each hold about the individual and behavior? What implications do each have for the juvenile justice system?

2. There is a movement to incorporate a stronger biosocial emphasis in the juvenile justice system to explain delinquency. Point out and explain what you see as the more promising biosocial approaches. In addition, project the problems or shortcomings that will result if the emphasis is shifted to biosocial explanations (that is, what are the problems with the biosocial approach?).

3. Identifying a "criminal or delinquent personality" has proven to be quite difficult. Outline some of the more well-known methods for isolating this personality and what problems exist in these approaches. Which method would you use if you had to pick one and why?

4. Psychological theories are common in correctional practice. Pick specific psychological approaches and illustrate their usefulness and shortcomings for use in correcting juvenile delinquents (i.e., critique the approaches).

CHAPTER 4

Sociological Explanations of Delinquency

WHAT YOU NEED TO KNOW

- Shaw and McKay found that crime and delinquency were concentrated in the center of cities, where lower-SES individuals and immigrants or African Americans lived. The reason they offer for this finding was "social disorganization," meaning the residents did not exert control, thus allowing crime to flourish.

- Differential association argues that deviance is learned just as other behavior is learned. Modifications of differential association include differential identification (which adds the idea of learning from images in the media) and differential reinforcement (which argues we learn from the results of our actions).

- Subcultural theories suggest that youths often act in accordance with a different set of values and beliefs that invariably conflict with the dictates of the larger society, thus leading them to be considered deviant.

- The techniques of neutralization presented by Sykes and Matza allow youths to violate the law while maintaining a positive self-image as a conforming member of society.

- Routine activities theory argues that a criminal act requires a motivated offender and a suitable target to coincide where there is an absence of capable guardianship.

- Strain theory suggests that crime is a logical outcome of the disjunction between the socially prescribed goals and the means available for achieving those goals.

- General strain theory offers a view that strain can come from a wide array of sources besides simply economic strain and inequality.

- Hirschi's social control theory states that "delinquent acts result when an individual's bond to society is weak or broken." The bond is composed of attachment, commitment, involvement, and belief.

- Self-control theory argues that behavior is controlled by factors an individual internalizes early in life. Good self-control keeps an individual from violating the law.

KEY TERMS

anomie

bond to society

Chicago School

collective efficacy

containment theory

culture conflict

developmental theories

differential association

differential identification

differential reinforcement

drift

ecological fallacy

ecological perspective

elaboration model

external pressures

external pulls

focal concerns

general strain theory

inner containment

internal pushes

labeling

life-course theories

looking-glass self

mentalistic construct

modes of adaptation

DOI: 10.4324/9781003167112-4

■ The labeling perspective proposes that involvement in the juvenile justice system leads to more deviant behavior by labeling the individual as a deviant and forcing him or her to act in accordance with that label.

■ Attempts to integrate theories into more unified, coherent explanations of deviance have met only limited success in advancing sociological theory.

INTRODUCTION

The most prevalent explanations of delinquent behavior are sociologically oriented theories. Indeed, criminology, criminal justice, and juvenile justice have grown around sociological perspectives. The reasons for this are understandable. First, the great changes in society during and after the industrial revolution were accompanied by increased levels of deviant behavior. This behavior, however, was more prevalent in the cities. This led to a natural view that deviant behavior was an outgrowth of social relationships, especially those in urban areas. Second, sociological theories hold a great deal of intuitive appeal. Many of the ideas, as will be seen, are based on common sense and do not require a great deal of education or training for simple understanding. A third reason behind the dominance of sociological explanations entails the ability to test such theories. While tests of biologically oriented theories provide correlational support, and psychological theories often defy empirical testing or are restricted to only individuals, most sociological explanations are accompanied by attempts at empirical research and often find some degree of support.

Sociological theories and perspectives reflect elements of both Classicism and Positivism. From the Positivistic view, sociological theories consider a wide array of social and environmental factors as potential determinants of deviant behavior. Delinquency is caused by the neighborhood in which an individual grows up, one's peers, the views of others, social and moral training, the organization of society, economic conditions, and the effect of being processed in the criminal justice system, among many other factors. Classical elements appear in discussions of deterrence, control, and routine activities theories where the individual is presumed to have some degree of choice in his or her behavior. This chapter attempts to outline the major points of each theory or view and draw out similarities and differences in the sociological explanations for deviance.

THE ECOLOGICAL PERSPECTIVE

Perhaps the earliest sociological explanation to gain importance in criminology, the ecological perspective (or "Chicago School," so named because of the research done using the city of Chicago as a focus) sought to explain

BOX 4.1 ECOLOGICAL EXPLANATIONS

KEY IDEA: looks at the influence of the environment on where deviance occurs

Concentric zones	Community grows from the original city center, with the inner zone being poor and subsequent zones being more affluent and stable; Burgess
Social disorganization	Areas in which residents do not concern themselves with real improvement and fail to take control of behavior in the area; Shaw and McKay
Collective efficacy	The ability of the neighborhood to regulate or control behavior through both formal and informal means
Sources of control	Private, parochial, and public; Bursik and Grasmick

deviance as a natural outgrowth of the location in which it occurs, particularly large cities and places within large cities. Research in the early twentieth century recognized the great growth in the number and size of large cities. European immigrants and Southern blacks were flocking to the industrial cities of the north and northeast. These new residents typically moved to the central city areas, where the housing was more affordable and closer to the factories, and jobs were available to lower-skilled and educated individuals. These areas were densely populated, with many of the new residents unable to speak English. The cities could be viewed as a series of concentric circles, or zones, moving out from the original central business district of the community, through areas of growing industry with poor housing, to more affluent areas as the distance from the center increased (Burgess, 1925). Along with the great influx of people came increases in various social problems—including criminal activity (see Box 4.1).

Shaw and McKay: Social Disorganization

Clifford Shaw and Henry McKay (1942) analyzed where delinquency occurred in Chicago. The researchers identified the location of every recorded delinquent act in the city for two different time periods roughly 20 years apart. Based on where it occurred, Shaw and McKay (1942) reported that crime and delinquency was highest:

- in and around the central business district,
- in poor areas of the city, and
- in areas dominated by immigrants and African Americans.

All three conclusions pointed to the same physical location in the city, specifically the city center, where economic conditions were poorest and new arrivals were able to find affordable housing.

The stability of the delinquency levels in the same areas over time led Shaw and McKay (1942) to examine what it was about these areas that could explain the findings. What they uncovered was that these areas were undergoing constant change. Poor immigrants would settle in the central city

WEB ACTIVITY

Go to www.routledge.com/cw/whitehead to see how early researchers saw the layout of the city.

areas due to the availability of cheap housing and the proximity to factory jobs. Over time the new residents gained employment, were assimilated into American society, and they would leave the inner city for the more desirable neighborhoods outside the central city. They were replaced by new immigrants, thus establishing a constant turnover of residents. The delinquency problem was a result of this turnover. The turnover caused a problem referred to as **social disorganization** (Shaw & McKay, 1942). Social disorganization referred to the fact that the people in these core areas did not concern themselves with improving the area, getting to know one another, or taking control of conditions. They were primarily interested in bettering themselves and getting out as soon as possible. There was a lack of social organization that could bring about improvements. The residents were unable to exert control over the behavior of those living there.

Collective Efficacy

More recent discussions of the ability or inability of residents to control their neighborhoods and their conditions reference the degree of collective efficacy of the area. **Collective efficacy** refers to the willingness and ability of the neighborhood to regulate or control behavior through both formal and informal means (Sampson, Raudenbush, & Earls, 1997). Areas with stronger collective efficacy experience less crime. The level of collective efficacy is impacted by concentrated disadvantage, which Sampson (2012) measured by levels of public assistance, poverty, unemployment, and related factors.

Bursik and Grasmick (1993) identify three primary sources of control. These are private, parochial, and public control (see Table 4.1). Unfortunately, marshaling this control is not equal across neighborhoods. Lower-class, transient, high-crime neighborhoods have particular trouble developing these sources of control. Areas undergoing a great deal of change will have an unstable base for private and parochial control mechanisms. Even stable neighborhoods with strong private and parochial networks may not be able to marshal the public support needed for effective delinquency control (Bursik & Grasmick, 1993). Hope (1997) refers to this as a problem of **vertical integration**. That is, some neighborhoods are unable to marshal support from those in power, such as city/government agencies or social service providers.

Critique of the Ecological Approach

While the ecological approach shifted attention away from the biological views of Lombroso to a more sociological orientation, these new ideas also suffered from problems. First, the measurement of key terms is often hard to do. For example, "social disorganization" is typically measured by the presence of deviance and problems it is supposed to explain. That is, social disorganization explained the problems, and the existence of the problems was used as proof of social disorganization. This is a **tautological**, or circular, explanation. Second, many researchers fell into the trap of attributing results to individuals that are based on grouped data. This is known as the **ecological fallacy**. Just because delinquency may be highest in areas of low income, low average

TABLE 4.1	Sources of Neighborhood Control
Private	Interpersonal relationships: family, friends, and close associates
Parochial	Neighborhood networks and institutions: schools, churches, businesses, social organizations/groups
Public	Agencies and institutions of the city, state, or other governmental unit

Source: See Hunter (1985:230–242); and Bursik and Grasmick (1993).

education, and high density does not mean that an uneducated individual from a poor family living in a two-bedroom home with nine people would be delinquent. Indeed, many delinquents in poor inner-city areas may exhibit the exact opposite traits. Knowledge about an area tells little about a specific individual.

Despite problems with the ecological approach, this early work brought crime and delinquency theory squarely into the sociological tradition. For the most part, these early sociological explanations provided a clean break from the biological work of Lombroso and his followers. The ecological studies also provided much of the framework for subsequent theoretical advances.

LEARNING THEORY

Many sociological theorists see deviance as a result of learning. A variety of factors contribute to the learning process, including with whom an individual has contact, what the individual observes, and the consequences of one's behavior. The most prominent of the social learning theories is differential association, which forms the basis of other learning theories (see Box 4.2).

Sutherland: Differential Association

Edwin Sutherland's (1939) differential association views learning as the culmination of various social inputs faced by individuals throughout their lives. Sutherland observed that delinquency was concentrated in the inner-city areas where juveniles came into daily contact with both deviant and conventional

---

BOX 4.2 SOCIAL LEARNING EXPLANATIONS

KEY IDEA: deviance, like all behavior, is learned

Differential association	Learning comes from interaction with other people; different interactions have differential impact on an individual; Sutherland
Differential identification	Personal association is not necessary for learning; learning results from taking on a role seen in the media; Glaser
Akers' Social Learning	Learning involves interaction, imitation, and operant conditioning (differential reinforcement)

TABLE 4.2 Sutherland's Differential Association Theory

1.	Criminal behavior is learned.
2.	Criminal behavior is learned in interaction with other persons in a process of communication.
3.	The principal part of the learning of criminal behavior occurs within intimate personal groups.
4.	When criminal behavior is learned, the learning includes (a) techniques of the crime, which are sometimes very complicated, sometimes very simple; (b) the specification of motives, drives, rationalizations, and attitudes.
5.	The specific direction of motives and drives is learned from definitions of the legal codes as favorable or unfavorable.
6.	A person becomes delinquent because of an excess of definitions favorable to violation of law over definitions unfavorable to violation of law.
7.	Differential associations may vary in frequency, duration, priority, and intensity.
8.	The process of learning criminal behavior by association with criminal and anticriminal patterns involves all of the mechanisms that are involved in any other learning.
9.	While criminal behavior is an expression of general needs and values, it is not explained by those general needs and values, because noncriminal behavior is an expression of the same needs and values.

Source: Compiled by authors from Sutherland and Cressey (1974:75–76).

ideas. As a result, children could just as easily learn to accept deviance as they could conventional behavior.

In explaining his views, Sutherland proposed nine specific points to differential association (see Table 4.2). Underlying these nine points is the idea that deviance is learned in the same fashion as conforming behavior. The major sources of that learning are the people with whom an individual comes into contact, particularly family, peers, and religious institutions. Everyone is exposed to both deviant and conforming information. The individual's choice of behavior depends on the relative amount of influence favoring either deviant or conventional activity.

Differential association has been criticized from a variety of perspectives. One of the criticisms revolves around Sutherland's failure to define or operationalize many of his terms. The common definitions of frequency (number of contacts), duration (length of a contact), priority (temporal order of the contacts), and intensity (significance of the contact) have been supplied by other researchers. Sutherland also failed to explicitly define "an excess of definitions." Second, although there have been a large number of studies focusing on differential association (e.g., Adams, 1974; DeFleur & Quinney, 1966; Reiss & Rhodes, 1961; Short, 1960), most of the empirical support is indirect and highly qualified. Third, Sutherland explicitly discounted the influence of factors other than social, face-to-face contacts in differential association. This was probably due to the fact that during the early 1900s television did not exist, movies were silent, and radio and newspapers were the primary form of mass communication.

Differential Identification

Changes in the modern world prompted researchers to modify and extend the original ideas of differential association. Glaser's (1956) **differential identification** proposes that real and fictional presentations on television and in other mass media provide information concerning acceptable behavior, especially to children. The basic idea is that as an individual observes the activity of a character, he begins to imitate or model that behavior. Another term for this is **role-taking**. The child assumes the role that is portrayed. This is especially problematic because many children fail to realize that the media portrayals are in themselves roles and not the actual behavior of the actor. A youth might observe a glorified version of crime from a desirable fictional character and, thus, act in accordance with that portrayal.

Edwin Sutherland (1883–1950) proposed the theory of differential association, a learning theory of delinquency. Sutherland's theory can be considered the first truly sociological effort to explain crime.

CREDIT: Indiana University Archives

Akers' Social Learning

Ronald Akers (1985, 2001) expanded the basic principles of differential association to include input beyond face-to-face interaction (similar to differential identification), modeling, and operant conditioning. The definitions a person holds can be both general and specific (Akers, 2001). General definitions reflect broad attitudes and views about behaviors as acceptable or unacceptable and may be based on morality, religion, or ethical beliefs. Specific definitions address views of different types of behavior, such as acceptance of minor criminal acts (e.g., theft) but rejection of more serious acts (e.g., homicide, rape). The addition of modeling pays heed to the psychological learning approach of imitation under which an individual mimics the behavior of others.

An important third addition is Akers' (2001) discussion of **differential reinforcement**. Differential reinforcement proposes that an individual can learn from a variety of sources besides just social factors. Differential reinforcement has its basis in operant conditioning and the rewards and punishments that may accrue from behavior. If the behavior results in a pleasurable payoff (e.g., useful stolen goods), the behavior will be repeated. The absence of an acceptable return on the behavior may prompt the person to abandon the activity. Experiencing an undesirable outcome (e.g., being caught and imprisoned) would prompt a person to cease the activity or avoid the behavior in the future. While most reinforcement is based on social inputs, non-social reinforcement it also important (Akers, 2001).

STRAIN THEORIES

Strain theory views deviance as a direct result of a social structure that stresses achievement but fails to provide adequate legitimate means of succeeding. Unlike many other theories, strain places the onus for deviance on society. Unacceptable behavior by an individual is seen as a natural (and expected) response to the problems posed by the social structure (see Box 4.3).

Anomie

An understanding of strain theory begins with an examination of two basic facts. First, man is inherently egoistic (Durkheim, 1933). Happiness is the result of realizing one's expectations. Second, society does not provide equal access to the means of reaching one's wishes and desires. Modern society does not provide everyone with the education and training they need to succeed. It also requires people to fill different roles in society, meaning that some individuals receive more than others despite the fact that everyone aspires to reach the top. The mismatch between the expectations or goals of the individual and the available means to achieve those goals is called anomie. Loosely translated, anomie refers to a state of normlessness or inadequate regulation. More specifically, it is the inability of the individual to regulate his or her expectations in accordance with the societal structure. Anomie may result in various forms of deviant behavior, including crime.

Merton: Modes of Adaptation

Robert Merton took the basic ideas of anomie and expanded the discussion to what is known as **strain theory**. Merton (1938) saw anomie as the lack of correspondence between culturally accepted *goals* and socially institutionalized *means* to achieve those goals. The problem is that American society presents everyone with the goals of achieving material success and reaching the top. At the same time, society limits access to the means for achieving those goals. The disjuncture between goals and means is a property of the social structure.

BOX 4.3 STRAIN EXPLANATIONS

KEY IDEA: the social structure provides differential access to success which can lead to deviance

Anomie	A state of normlessness or inadequate regulation; the inability of the individual to regulate his or her expectations in accordance with the societal structure
Modes of adaptation	Each mode of adaptation reflects an individual's acceptance or rejection of culturally prescribed goals and socially institutionalized means of achieving those goals; some result in deviance/delinquency, others in conformity; Merton
General strain	Strain can arise from many things besides just blocked means to achieve goals; removal of pleasure; presentation of negative stimuli; Agnew

TABLE 4.3 Merton's Modes of Adaptation

Mode of Adaptation	Cultural Goals	Institutionalized Means
Conformity	+	+
Innovation	+	−
Ritualism	−	+
Retreatism	−	−
Rebellion	±	±

Note: + means acceptance, − means rejection, ± means rejection and substitution.

Source: Merton (1938).

Individuals can respond to the disjuncture between goals and means in various ways. Merton (1938) outlines five modes of adaptation (see Table 4.3). Each mode of adaptation reflects an individual's acceptance or rejection of culturally prescribed goals and socially institutionalized means of achieving those goals.

Conformity represents the acceptance of both the goals and means, regardless of whether he or she succeeds. *Innovation* reflects acceptance of the prescribed goals but, when faced with an inability to succeed via acceptable means, the individual resorts to unacceptable or illegitimate methods of achieving success. In *ritualism*, the exact opposite occurs. While the individual gives up on achieving the goals, he or she continues to act in a socially acceptable fashion. A *retreatist* rejects both the goals and the means. This individual retreats from society through such means as alcohol or other drug use, vagrancy, or psychological withdrawal. The final mode of adaptation, *rebellion*, reflects an attempt to replace the existing societal goals and means with a new set that provides more opportunity for everyone in society.

The choice of adaptation varies from individual to individual. The most common response is conformity (Merton, 1938). Conformity presents the individual with the least resistance and does not add the problems of deviance to the problem of not succeeding. In the remaining modes, individuals can be considered deviant either in their outlook or in their actions. Delinquency appears in innovation, retreatism, and rebellion, where accepted modes of behavior (means) are replaced by unacceptable actions. While the root problem of anomie is structurally determined, the choice of adaptation can be understood only in light of individual circumstances.

General Strain Theory

Critics of strain theory have argued that not everyone aspires to the societally prescribed goals underlying Merton's discussion. Rather than focus only on the inability to achieve the societally prescribed goals, Agnew (1992, 2006a, 2006b) has proposed a general strain theory that suggests that strain can arise from varying sources, some of which have a greater tendency to lead to crime and delinquency. Agnew (2006b) offers three groups of strains:

- Failure to achieve goals, such as economic stability and status.
- Loss of positive stimuli, such as possessions and valued relationships.
- Introduction of negative stimuli by others, such as abuse and interpersonal conflict.

The strain may prompt individuals to respond with delinquent or criminal behavior. Agnew (2016:213) notes that strains "lead to negative emotions, such as anger and frustration. These emotions create pressure for corrective action, and crime is one possible response." Crime and delinquency are more likely when the strain is seen as unjust, magnified, and it creates pressure in the absence of social control (Agnew, 2001).

WEB ACTIVITY

For another list of strains related to crime, go to www.routledge.com/cw/whitehead.

Assessing Strain Theory

The practical implication of strain theory would appear to be alleviating the causes of and conditions leading to strain. In the broadest, Mertonian sense, this would mean changing the structural barriers to success that underlie deviant activity. In a broader sense, it is important to address the myriad inputs that lead to and cause strain for an individual. The social structure and the misalignment of goals and means is not the only cause of strain. Agnew's general strain theory opens the discussion of strain to include many more factors. General strain theory has been subjected to numerous empirical tests. Analyses using both self-report and official data have found strong support for the theory.

SUBCULTURAL THEORIES

Subcultural explanations owe a great deal to the same research that prompted the early ecological, social learning, and strain theories. It was the diversity of people in the cities that prompted the idea of social disorganization and provided different inputs to the learning process. The strain felt by individuals leads to making choices to achieve success and status that may not adhere to accepted social norms. Subcultural theorists took these ideas and focused directly on the fact of diversity in the population (see Box 4.4).

Defining subculture is not an easy task. In the simplest sense, a subculture is a smaller part of a larger culture. While it must vary to some degree from the larger culture, it is not totally different. The subculture exists within and is part of the larger culture. More detailed definitions typically refer to differences in values, beliefs, ideas, views, and/or meanings that a group of individuals hold from those of the larger culture.

From a subcultural perspective, delinquency and criminality are the result of individuals attempting to act in ways that bring success and status that is in accord with subcultural norms. This can occur in several ways. First, an individual acts according to subcultural mandates that, unfortunately, may be considered deviant by the larger society. This problem could be common for

---

BOX 4.4 SUBCULTURAL EXPLANATIONS

KEY IDEA: there are variations in values and beliefs; conforming to one set results in violating those of another; culture conflict

Lower-class gang delinquency	Lower-class gangs are malicious, negativistic, and nonutilitarian; the lower classes cannot compete in a middle-class world; Cohen
Lower-class focal concerns	Lower class has a distinctive set of focal concerns (values); acting in concert with the focal concerns leads to conflict with middle-class norms; Miller
Techniques of neutralization	Methods used by individuals that allow an individual to accommodate deviant behavior while maintaining a self-image as a conformist; Sykes and Matza

---

new immigrants who have traditionally acted according to one set of cultural proscriptions and are now faced with a different set of expectations in a new cultural setting. Second, deviance may result from the inability to join or be assimilated into a new culture. Consequently, the individual may strike out against society because of the frustration faced in attempting to live according to the new cultural expectations. Third, many activities that bring acceptance, success, or status may conform to subcultural standards rather than the standards of the larger culture.

Lower-Class Gang Delinquency

Albert Cohen (1955), recognizing the concentration of delinquency among lower-class boys, argued there was a lower-class gang subculture. Lower-class youths feel ill-equipped to compete in and cannot succeed in a middle-class society. This is compounded by the fact that they are expected to follow the goals and aspirations of the middle class. All youths are measured against a middle-class measuring rod that they cannot meet. The failure to succeed in terms of middle-class values leads to feelings of failure and diminished self-worth among the lower-class youths. As a result, these boys join together in groups and act in concert with the group (subcultural) norms instead of with the mandates of the larger culture. While this provides the youths with some degree of self-worth, status, and success, it also leads to culture conflict. That is, by following one set of cultural (or subcultural) values, beliefs, and behaviors, the individual is violating the proscriptions of the dominant culture. In Cohen's study, adherence to the subcultural group's mandates means violating the laws of middle-class society.

Cohen (1955) identifies three aspects of the emergent "lower-class gang delinquency." He claims that the subculture is malicious, negativistic, and nonutilitarian. In support of this contention, Cohen points out that the youths often steal items, with the intent of causing trouble and harm for another person, not because they want the item. He sees much of the deviant activity as a means of tormenting others. The behavior brings about an immediate "hedonistic" pleasure instead of supplying any long-term need or solution to a problem. In general, there appears to be little point in the behavior besides causing trouble for the larger middle-class culture.

Lower-Class Focal Concerns

Walter Miller's (1958) subcultural explanation goes beyond the behavior of juveniles to include all lower-class males. Miller views the lower class as operating under a distinct set of cultural values, or **focal concerns** (see Table 4.4). These are: trouble, toughness, smartness, excitement, fate, and autonomy. Adherence to these lower-class focal concerns or values provides status, acceptance, and feelings of belonging for the lower-class individual (Miller, 1958).

At the same time that these values provide positive reinforcement in the lower-class world, they bring about a natural conflict with middle-class values. The goal of the lower-class individual is not to violate the law or the middle-class norms. Instead, the goal is to follow the focal concerns of their class and peers. Deviant behavior, therefore, is a by-product of following the subcultural focal concerns (Miller, 1958). Where Cohen (1955) saw deviance as a conscious reaction of lower-class youths striking out against the middle-class society and value system, Miller (1958) views the focal concerns as an integral part of the lower class.

Sykes and Matza: Techniques of Neutralization

Throughout the discussion of subcultural explanations there is a subtle failure to address the fact that no individual operates exclusively in the subculture.

TABLE 4.4 **Miller's Lower-Class Focal Concerns**	
Trouble	Refers to the fact that lower-class males spend a large amount of time preoccupied with getting into and out of trouble. Trouble may bring about desired outcomes such as attention and prestige.
Toughness	Emphasis on physical prowess, athletic skill, masculinity, and bravery. Partly a response of lower-class males raised in [single] female-headed households.
Smartness	Basically the idea of being "streetwise." The concern is on how to manipulate the environment and others to your own benefit without being subjected to sanctions of any kind.
Excitement	Refers to the idea that lower-class individuals are oriented around short-term hedonistic desires. Activities, such as gambling and drug use, are undertaken for the immediate excitement or gratification that is generated.
Fate	The belief that, in the long run, individuals have little control over their lives. Luck and fortune dictate the outcome of behavior. Whatever is supposed to happen will happen regardless of the individual's wishes. This allows for a wide latitude in behavior.
Autonomy	While the individual believes in fate, there is a strong desire to resist outside control imposed by other persons. Individuals want total control over themselves until fate intervenes.

TABLE 4.5 Sykes and Matza's Techniques of Neutralization	
Denial of Responsibility	The youth may claim that the action was an accident or, more likely, assert that he or she was forced into the action by circumstances beyond his or her control.
Denial of Injury	Focuses on the amount of harm caused regardless of violating the law. The absence of harm to an individual may involve pointing to a lack of physical injury, the action was a prank, or the person or business could afford the loss.
Denial of the Victim	The juvenile can deny the existence of a victim by claiming self-defense or retaliation, the absence of a victim (such as involving a business and not a person), and/or that characteristics of the victim brought the harm on himself or herself (such as hazing a homosexual).
Condemnation of the Condemnors	The youth turns the tables on those individuals who condemn his or her behavior by pointing out that the condemnors are no better than he or she. In essence, the condemnors are also deviant.
Appeal to Higher Loyalties	Conflict between the dictates of two groups will be resolved through adherence to the ideas of one group. The juvenile may see greater reward and more loyalty to the subcultural group on some issues which, in turn, lead to deviant behavior.

Source: Constructed by authors from Sykes and Matza (1957).

Rather, every individual must deal with both the subcultural and the larger cultural expectations. Indeed, many individuals attempt to abide by both sets of values. Juveniles, in particular, often act in accordance with one set of values or rules and still maintain a positive self-image in which they believe they fit into the acceptable behavior of the larger culture. Juveniles who commit delinquent acts often see themselves as no better and no worse than anyone else, despite recognizing their deviant activity.

Gresham Sykes and David Matza (1957) outlined five **techniques of neutralization** that allow the juvenile to accommodate the deviant behavior while maintaining a self-image as a conformist (see Table 4.5). Each technique requires the individual to admit to the behavior under question. The individual invokes one of the techniques in order to justify his or her behavior in light of confrontation with conventional cultural values. While an exact understanding of how, when, and by whom neutralization techniques are used is not known, evidence shows that such techniques are used in various settings (Agnew, 1994; Agnew & Peters, 1986; Minor, 1981; Thurman, 1984).

Critique of the Subcultural Approach

The attempt to explain deviance through the use of subcultures faces a number of problems. The greatest problem entails identifying a subculture. Since a subculture means there is a difference in values, beliefs, and norms from those held by the larger culture, it is necessary to measure those factors and show how they differ from the larger culture. Unfortunately, research typically identifies subcultures through the behavior of those in the subculture. The behavior indicates that a subculture exists, and the subculture is used to explain why the behavior occurs. This is a tautological (or circular) argument. A related second issue is that this definitional approach results in substituting behaviors for values. It is questionable to what extent you can impute values from behaviors. It is possible that different activities may reflect the same basic values. For example, in order to feed their families (basic value), one individual takes a low-paying job while another robs the local grocery store (different behaviors).

A third concern with subcultural explanations involves a possible middle-class bias. As already noted, many authors, including Cohen and Miller, construct their arguments by observing the behavior of lower-class individuals. Then, these middle-class researchers impute values and beliefs from the behaviors. From a middle-class point of view, the behaviors could appear to be malicious, negativistic, and nonutilitarian (à la Cohen), or indicators of trouble, toughness, or similar traits (à la Miller). The lower-class individuals, however, may be acting as they do for entirely different reasons from those assumed by the researchers. The imputed values are determined by the observers, not the individuals being observed.

ROUTINE ACTIVITIES AND RATIONAL CHOICE

Yet another theoretical area with ties to the ecological perspective is that dealing with routine activities and rational choice (see Box 4.5). Both of these approaches address the issue of opportunities for delinquency and crime, and the ability/choice of individuals to avail themselves of those opportunities. Two basic assumptions underlie these approaches. First, the movement of offenders and victims over space and time places them in situations in which criminal opportunities will be more or less possible. Second, within these different situations, individuals make choices about what to do and what not to do (see Clarke & Felson, 1993). Routine activities and rational choice arguments, therefore, rest in the arena of Neoclassicism, in which there is an element of choice.

Routine Activities

Routine activities theory assumes that the normal behavior of individuals contributes to deviant events. Cohen and Felson (1979) outline three criteria

---

BOX 4.5 ROUTINE ACTIVITIES/RATIONAL CHOICE EXPLANATIONS

KEY IDEA: crime and delinquency are largely a result of opportunities and the choice to act on those opportunities

Routine activities	Crime requires a suitable target, motivated offender, and an absence of guardians; Cohen and Felson
Rational choice	The individual chooses if, when, and where to commit a crime based on the opportunities that are presented to him or her; Cornish and Clarke

necessary for the commission of a crime: (1) the presence of a suitable target; (2) a motivated offender; and (3) an absence of guardians. The possibility for deviance is enhanced when these three elements coincide. Changes in family life offer one example of how routine activities may impact delinquency. The increase in the number of two-earner households means that many youths are unsupervised after school and at other times. This situation results in a lack of guardianship, while also offering suitable targets (such as other unsupervised youths or unoccupied homes) for potential offenders. Another example appears in schools, particularly large secondary schools, where motivated offenders and suitable targets (both students) are required to be in close proximity with relatively few teachers or staff (guardians) available to oversee what takes place. Research has shown that the routine activities of individuals are related to a wide array of both personal and property offenses (Belknap, 1987; Kennedy & Forde, 1990; Miethe, Stafford, & Long, 1987; Roncek & Maier, 1991).

Rational Choice

Closely tied to routine activities is rational choice theory. Rational choice theory assumes that potential offenders make choices based on various factors in the physical and social environments. The individual chooses if, when, and where to commit a crime based on the opportunities that are presented to him or her. Among the factors influencing choices are the payoff, effort, support, and risks involved in the potential behavior (Cornish & Clarke, 1986). There is ample evidence that offenders make choices, but this does not mean that offenders plan their behavior in detail. Rather, unplanned, spontaneous behavior may rest on past observations, experiences, and routine activities that lay the foundation for unconscious decision making.

The support for rational choice, however, is not without qualification. The factors identified as important in decision making can vary greatly from situation to situation. Rational choice theory is also criticized for its apparent inability to explain impulsive acts and actions that clearly take place in high-risk settings. It is possible, however, that individuals make immediate or split-second decisions based on prior knowledge or experiences. Rational choice does not require conscious or active thought at the time of the action.

Rational choice poses an interesting conundrum for juvenile justice. If one assumes that youths do not have the capacity to make truly informed decisions, to what extent can it be claimed that they are making rational choices? The traditional view of the juvenile justice system is that youths cannot form the requisite intent to be held accountable for their actions. Thus, they are not rational. Instead, their behavior is determined by other factors. At the same time, it is naive to assume no rationality by youths. Coupled with routine activities, rational choice may be helpful for explaining increased delinquency during after-school hours (when there are fewer targets but less supervision) or why theft is more common than robbery.

SOCIAL CONTROL THEORY

Where most theories look to identify factors that lead or push a juvenile into delinquency, **social control theories** seek to find factors that keep an individual from becoming deviant (see Box 4.6). Control theorists ask why many people refrain from violating the law even though they are hedonistic and presented with ample opportunity to commit crimes. Reckless (1967) views the main issue as explaining why one individual becomes deviant and another does not when both are faced with the same situations.

Containment Theory

One of the earliest control explanations was Walter Reckless's (1962) **containment theory**. Containment theory proposes that there are factors that promote conformity as well as forces promoting deviance. At the same time, the individual may have some control over his or her own behavior. Reckless (1962) outlines two types of containment: **outer containment** and **inner containment**. Outer containment offers direct control over the individual from outside sources. These include family members, friends, teachers, and others who provide supervision, training, and pressure to conform. Conversely, inner containment involves internalized moral codes, tolerance of frustration, and other factors that help the individual refrain from deviance. These play a role when an individual is not under the direct control of outer containment. The combination of these two factors should provide an effective means of avoiding deviant behavior. The factors that promote deviant behavior include **internal pushes** (restlessness, discontent, anxiety), **external pressures** (poverty, unemployment, inequality), and **external pulls** (deviant peers, subcultures, media) (Reckless, 1962). Each of these influences an individual's activity. These factors may lead or push people into deviant activity as a viable form of behavioral response and make deviance an acceptable alternative, while inner and outer containment work to offset their influence.

BOX 4.6 SOCIAL CONTROL EXPLANATIONS

KEY IDEA: considers what keeps an individual from being delinquent, rather than what causes or leads to deviance

Containment theory	Inner containment (internalized moral codes and factors); outer containment (family, friends, teachers, etc.); internal pushes (discontent, anxiety); external pressures (poverty, unemployment); external pulls (peers, media); Reckless
Hirschi's control theory	Deviance results from weak or broken bond to society; attachment, commitment, involvement and beliefs influence behavior
Self-control theory	Control internalized early in life; mainly parental influence; Gottfredson and Hirschi
Social support theory	Social support reduces antisocial behavior; support comes from parents, families, peers, society; Cullen
Social concern theory	Individuals who have concern about the welfare of others less likely to violate the law; concern from socialization, biology, evolution; Agnew

Hirschi's Control Theory

Travis Hirschi's (1969) control theory is perhaps the most well-known control theory and states that "delinquent acts result when an individual's bond to society is weak or broken" (p. 16). The underlying assumption is that the individual's behavior is controlled by the connections the person has to conventional social order. Deviance shows up when a person's **bond to society** is weak or broken. According to Hirschi (1969), the bond is developed through socialization during early childhood and consists of four elements: attachment, commitment, involvement, and belief (see Table 4.6). The failure of an individual to care about what others think about his or her behavior and views (attachment), to work toward acceptable goals (commitment), to use one's energies and time in socially acceptable behaviors (involvement), and/or to accept the common value system in society (belief) opens the door for deviant and delinquent behavior. A weak or broken bond does not *cause* deviance. Rather, *it allows for* deviance. In other words, a weak or broken bond could be viewed as necessary for deviance, but not sufficient. An individual with a weak bond may or may not choose to commit deviant acts.

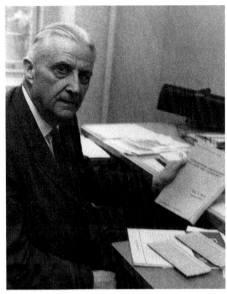

Walter Reckless (1899–1988) championed containment theory. One of the earliest control explanations, the theory proposes that there are factors that promote conformity as well as forces promoting deviance.

CREDIT: AP Photo

Numerous tests of Hirschi's social control theory have been undertaken. Hirschi (1969) tested his theory by surveying more than 4,000 high-school-aged boys

TABLE 4.6 **Elements of Hirschi's Bond**	
Attachment	"Sensitivity to the opinion of others" (p. 16)
	The more an individual cares about what others think of himself/herself, the less likely he/she will choose behavior that brings about negative input.
Commitment	A "person invests time, energy, himself, in a certain line of activity" (p. 20)
	As a person builds an investment in conventional endeavors, any choice of deviant behavior will place that investment at risk.
Involvement	"Engrossment in conventional activities" (p. 22)
	Because time and energy are limited, once they are used in the pursuit of conventional activities, there is no time or energy left for deviant behavior.
Belief	"The existence of a common value system within the society or group" (p. 23)
	As a person is socialized into and accepts the common belief system, he/she will be less likely to violate those beliefs through deviant activity.

Source: Constructed by authors from Hirschi (1969).

about their delinquent activity and elements of bond. Consistent with the theory, he found that delinquency was related to weaker attachment to parents, education, and school; lower aspirations (i.e., lacking commitment); more time spent "joy riding" in cars or being bored (involvement); and less respect for the police and the law (belief). Similar support has been found by other researchers (Hindelang, 1973; Krohn & Massey, 1980; Poole & Regoli, 1979; Wiatrowski, Griswold, & Roberts, 1981).

Despite support for the theory, there are a number of problematic issues. First, the theory tries to explain why individuals are deviant and not how a bond becomes weak or broken. Second, the relative impact of the four elements of a bond is left unresolved. For example, if attachment is strong and commitment is moderate but involvement and belief are weak, will this permit deviance or not? As a result of this problem, the theory cannot directly offer suggestions on how to avoid the weakening of a bond or how to repair a bond. Third, many youths **drift** between delinquent and conventional behavior. The theory does not explain the vacillation in choices over time and place. Finally, the theory assumes that all bonding is to conventional, nondeviant lifestyles. It may be possible that a juvenile is raised in a household in which the parents are deviant and espouse nontraditional behaviors. A juvenile in these circumstances should be bonded to deviance.

Self-Control Theory

Control theory has undergone its greatest change with the introduction of **self-control theory**. Rather than assume that behavior is controlled by outside forces throughout an individual's life, Gottfredson and Hirschi (1990) argue that self-control, internalized early in life, can serve to keep a person from involvement in deviant behavior. Self-control serves as a restraint from choosing the short-term gratification endemic to most criminal behavior. Low self-control is related to crime and deviance, and has six elements:

- a desire for immediate gratification
- a desire for easy or simple gratification of desires
- a desire for exciting, risky, or thrilling activity
- a lack of commitment to long-term pursuits, such as job, marriage, and family
- a desire to pursue activities that require little skill or planning
- a focus on personal satisfaction and lack of concern for pain or discomfort in others.

(Gottfredson & Hirschi, 1990:89)

Poor self-control is the result of ineffective child-rearing practices by the parents (Gottfredson & Hirschi, 1990). Good parenting requires exhibiting concern for the child, consistent monitoring of the child's behavior, the ability to identify problematic behaviors, appropriate reactions to inappropriate behavior, and the time and energy to carry through with parental responsibilities. Should the parents fail to build self-control, other social institutions, such as schools, may influence its formation but are typically poor substitutes for the family

(Gottfredson & Hirschi, 1990). Once self-control is internalized, it serves to modify an individual's behavior throughout his or her life.

Self-control theory has received both support and criticism. A number of studies have found evidence that a lack of self-control is related to deviant behavior (Grasmick, Tittle, Bursik, & Arneklev, 1993; Piquero, MacIntosh, & Hickman, 2000; Piquero, Langton, & Schoepfer, 2008; Pratt & Cullen, 2000; Wood, Pfefferbaum, & Arneklev, 1993). At the same time, the theory has been criticized for its inability to explain significant changes in behavior later in life and to consider the basic social structure as a contributor to parenting and self-control (Lilly, Cullen, & Ball, 1995). There are also concerns over how to measure self-control and the relative impact of the different components of self-control (Britt & Racque, 2016).

Social Support Theory

Another variation of control theory is Francis Cullen's (1994) social support theory. The premise of the theory is that social support reduces antisocial and criminal/delinquent behavior. This support can come from a variety of sources, including parents, families, peers, the criminal justice system, and society. Lilly et al. (2019:132) identify three primary propositions at the core of social support theory:

- social support reduces crime
- social support makes control more effective
- social support reduces crime by increasing prosocial and reducing anti-social influences.

Social support contributes to many of the core ideas of control theory. It builds relationships and bonds to others and to society. A supportive environment mitigates the negative consequences of system contact and builds more pro-social behaviors.

Social Concern Theory

Robert Agnew's (2014) social concern theory rests on four elements that can impact on crime. Those elements are:

- a concern about the welfare of others
- the desire to build ties to others
- following moral intuitions about what is right and wrong
- conforming to the views of others and social norms.

When considering these elements there are clear connections with Hirschi's bond and self-control ideas.

Agnew (2014) argues that people who incorporate the elements of social concern into their outlook, perspectives, and beliefs would be unable to violate the law. Their behavior would be more involved with prosocial and conforming activities that would keep them away from situations and settings conducive to crime and delinquency. Agnew (2014) notes that not all individuals have the same level of social concern. Such concern is the result of various inputs, including socialization. At the same time, social concern may come from biological/evolutionary inputs.

THE LABELING PERSPECTIVE

Another approach that places the blame for deviance on society is the **labeling perspective** (see Box 4.7). The basic assumption of labeling is that being labeled as deviant by social control agents forces the person to act according to the label. Further deviance is a result of being contacted and sanctioned by the system and being labeled a "delinquent." This label may lead to exclusion from participation in conforming activities and may prompt further deviant behavior. Continued deviance is a response to the actions of society.

The Construction of Self-Image

The labeling perspective owes much to the ideas of **symbolic interactionism**. Symbolic interactionism proposes that every individual develops his or her self-image through a process of interaction with the surrounding world (Mead, 1934). How an individual sees himself or herself is determined by how that person thinks others see him or her. That is, a person's self-concept comes out of interaction with other people and the environment. If an individual perceives a positive image of himself or herself from others, the person will hold a positive self-image. A simple way of viewing this process is through what Cooley (1902) calls the **looking-glass self**. The idea is that individuals view themselves in the way other people look at them.

Labeling takes these ideas and proposes that individuals mold their behavior in accordance with the perceptions of others. Frank Tannenbaum (1938) saw the sanctioning of deviant behavior as a step in altering a juvenile's self-image from that of a normal, conventional youth to that of being a delinquent. System processing identifies a youth as delinquent, emphasizes the label, and

---

BOX 4.7 LABELING EXPLANATIONS

KEY IDEA: people act in accordance with labels placed on them; system intervention causes further offending

Symbolic interactionism	Every individual develops his or her self-image through a process of interaction with the surrounding world; looking-glass self; Mead; Cooley
Transfer of evil	When an individual is sanctioned, the evil is often transferred from the act to the actor; Tannenbaum
Primary and secondary deviance	Primary deviance rationalized as part of being normal—no labeling; secondary deviance is acts committed in accordance with accepting the label; Lemert
Reintegrative shaming	Use sanctions in such a way as to shame the individual for the action but to simultaneously reintegrate him to society; no labeling; Braithwaite

ultimately segregates the youth from normal juvenile behavior. Juveniles begin to view themselves as deviant, which leads to actions consistent with the self-image. Basically, the process of labeling entails a transfer of evil from the act to the actor (Tannenbaum, 1938). Instead of viewing the act as deviant and bad, the actor becomes bad and the focus for social action.

Primary and Secondary Deviance

Edwin Lemert (1951) distinguished between two types of deviance—primary and secondary. **Primary deviance** comprises those actions that "are rationalized or otherwise dealt with as functions of a socially acceptable role" (Lemert, 1951). These deviant acts are common and garner minimal attention and mild sanctions. As a result, the individual is not labeled, and his or her self-image is not altered. **Secondary deviance**, however, occurs when an individual "begins to employ his deviant behavior or a role based upon it as a means of defense, attack, or adjustment to the overt and covert problems created by the consequent societal reaction to him" (Lemert, 1951). This means that society has successfully labeled the individual. The individual now views himself or herself as different and/or deviant, and acts accordingly.

It is important to note that primary and secondary deviant acts entail the same types of behavior. What distinguishes secondary from primary deviance is the reason behind the action. The behavior is secondary if the act cannot be rationalized as the outcome of a nondeviant social role *and* is committed as an attack or defense against societal reaction. Secondary deviance, therefore, is a **mentalistic construct**. That is, it relies on the mindset and attitude of the individual involved.

The reasons for conforming to the label are simple. First, a deviant label makes participation in conventional activity difficult. Societal members expect deviance and react to the individual as a deviant, regardless of whether specific behavior is deviant or conforming. Second, by accepting the label, the individual blunts the impact of any negative feedback provided by society. For example, young children cry when told they are bad because the information is counter to their beliefs. Children would not be affected, however, if they saw themselves as bad. Negative input would simply point out what they already knew and accepted. Finally, individuals conform to labels as a means of striking out against those who are condemning them. Using a kind of "if that is what you think" attitude, individuals decide to show society just how bad they can really be if that is what society wants.

The process by which an individual assumes a negative label is not simple. A single deviant act generally will not lead to the successful application of a label. Lemert (1951) proposes an outline of repeated primary deviant acts followed by increasingly stronger social reactions that eventually culminate in the imposition and acceptance of a deviant label. Lemert notes that this process is not set with any definite number of steps or particular sequence of events. Rather, the process varies by type of offense, offender, and societal response.

Reintegrative Shaming

Where labeling assumes that system intervention and societal reaction to offending invariably lead to a label and further deviance, it is possible to intervene without the imposition of a negative label. Braithwaite (1989) argues that shame can be used in a positive fashion to bring an offender back into society. Under reintegrative shaming, society needs to express disapproval of the delinquent activity while forgiving the offender for the action if the offender is willing to learn from the event and make reparations. The key is on "reintegration," thus the label does not carry the negatives outlined in labeling theory. The focus shifts from the negative action of the delinquent to the needs of the victim, the community, and the offender, and a shared response to make things better (Harris, 2003). This type of shaming does not lead to further delinquency, as does shaming aimed at excluding and stigmatizing the delinquent.

INTEGRATIVE EXPLANATIONS

The recognition that no one theory has been shown to adequately explain deviant behavior has led to attempts to integrate different theories into more unified, coherent explanations of deviance. A number of authors have experimented with linking different explanations into an integrated theory. This process is sometimes referred to as an elaboration model and attempts to take components of various theories to construct an explanation that incorporates parts of the individual theories into a coherent explanation.

One well-known attempt at integrating theories used strain, social control, and social learning theories. Elliott et al. (1979, 1985), working with extensive longitudinal data, provided a rough sequential process leading to deviant behavior. Strain, brought about by family and school experiences, led to a weaker bond to conventional society. In turn, the youths have increased bonds to deviant peers, which results in deviant activity. Mediating this entire process is the influence of learning.

Life-course theories generally reflect efforts that incorporate ideas from several theories and perspectives. Sampson and Laub's (1993) life-course perspective incorporates a number of theoretical factors to explain criminality over time. These authors point to structural conditions as key variables in establishing a base for behavior. Social bonds are an important contributor to actions in response to negative structural factors. In their age-graded control explanation, Sampson and Laub (2003) point to various events, or turning points, in life that will alter or impact the level of social control. Post-education, getting married, or joining the military will change the social settings in which a person operates. Getting a job or losing employment can shift the informal controls an individual experiences. Simply relocating, especially to new cities, will sever existing controls and introduce new control networks. All of these events (and many others) have the potential of eliminating existing sources of informal control and/or introducing new informal controls. Consequently, these changes can enhance or impede deviant behavior.

Using a broader set of potential factors, developmental theories may include biological, psychological, and sociological inputs to behavior. Using primarily sociological factors, Catalano and Hawkins (1996; also Catalano et al., 2005) look at social development to explain behavior. Their explanation incorporates social bonding and learning theories, with changes in bond to different persons opening opportunities to learn both prosocial and antisocial behavior. Individual behavior develops over time.

Conger and Simons (1997) point out that biological factors, both prenatal and neonatal, play a role in cognitive ability. Cognition impacts on how family, friends, and schools may treat a person, which may then impact on an individual's success in school or in making choices. Throughout this process, the individual faces different demands and opportunities, for which he or she may or may not be adequately prepared.

Another developmental explanation that incorporates biological factors is Thornberry and Krohn's interactional theory (2005). Biological and neuropsychological factors are especially important for young children, as are poverty and socioeconomic factors that impact opportunity. As children age, they are impacted more by family, and then by school and peers, which alters opportunities. Youthful deviant activities elicit responses ranging from family discipline to school, societal, and social disapproval and ostracism. This may further isolate the youth and prompt more deviant behavior. Thornberry and Krohn (2005) also suggest that cognitive deficits are related to delinquent and criminal behavior. All of these relationships with deviant behavior are aggravated or mitigated by the responses the individuals face from family, schools, peers, and others. This is an interactive process with a variety of inputs.

Many of these "new" integrated theories are still undergoing rigorous testing. No definitive relationships have yet emerged. This is partly due to the complexity of the proposed theoretical models and the lack of appropriate data for testing the full explanation. These tests require extensive longitudinal data with measures of a wide array of variables. McGee and Farrington (2016) note that interest in developmental and life-course theories only dates back to the late 1980s. The data are only now becoming more available for testing. The advantages of the elaboration/integration approach appear in the attempt to draw together long theoretical traditions, each of which has demonstrated some empirical support. The fact that no single theory has adequately explained deviance suggests that this new direction should be continued.

THE IMPACT OF THEORIES ON JUVENILE JUSTICE

While a good deal of theorizing has been devoted to the causes of delinquent activity, the extent to which these explanations have an impact on the daily operations of the juvenile justice system is highly variable. Court dispositions and correctional treatments display the closest relationships between the theories and justice system action. As noted in Chapter 2, the rhetoric of the juvenile court has consistently emphasized the importance of learning and benevolent care of youths. Social learning theory lends support to interventions that focus on providing proper role models and environments conducive to conforming behavior. Trends toward deinstitutionalization, community corrections, and less restrictive interventions rely on the arguments of labeling theory as well as learning principles. Recent movements toward incarceration and deterrence of juveniles clearly rely on Classical and Neoclassical assumptions of free will and hedonistic choice.

On a larger scale, various theoretical perspectives have helped influence general social movements. The Great Society reforms that began in the mid-1960s attempted to address the social inequities that lead to deviance. Educational programs, economic assistance, vocational training, physical improvement of inner cities, and other efforts can be traced to strain, subcultural, learning, and ecological explanations of social ills. In many of these social actions, delinquency and criminality were only two of many social problems being addressed. The impact of these specific programs is a matter of debate. The consistency in crime, delinquency, and recidivism rates suggests that there was little impact on these problems, but why they did not have an impact is not clear. Some authors argue that the interventions were too short-lived to alter long-standing social problems. Others claim that the implementation of the programs was incomplete or inappropriate. Still others deny the adequacy of the theoretical explanation being utilized. Regardless of past failures, the various theories continue to find their way into the policies and procedures of the juvenile justice system.

SUMMARY

Explanations of delinquent and criminal behavior, whether biological, psychological, or sociological in nature, provide some insight into the reasons for deviance. The diversity in perspectives, however, illustrates the lack of understanding that still exists. Indeed, the search for a single theory that explains all—or almost all—deviance appears to be an effort in futility. The most reasonable consideration is to view deviance as multifaceted. The explanation, therefore, must consider a wide range of variables and influences. Juvenile justice must not ignore theory simply because until this point in time it has failed to arrive at a totally adequate explanation. Rather, the system must take care to select, implement, and evaluate ideas in light of expanding knowledge and research. While the remainder of the text deals with various interventions and system actions, theory forms an implicit base for all discussions.

DISCUSSION QUESTIONS

1. Sociological explanations for deviance are currently the most well known. Pick any sociological theory, outline the argument, and translate those ideas into practical applications for dealing with juveniles.

2. The President has called for a study that will set the tone for future directions in juvenile justice. As a member of the Commission, you have the opportunity to advocate an underlying theory. Which sociological theory will you fight for, and why is it the best possible approach for guiding the juvenile justice system? Present strengths and weaknesses of your choice.

3. A recent trend in delinquency explanations is integration explanations. Discuss the similarities and differences in the elaboration model, life-course theories, and developmental theories. Provide specific examples. What do these new explanations provide that any single theory cannot?

CHAPTER 5

Gang Delinquency

WHAT YOU NEED TO KNOW

- Many studies note that delinquency is often committed in groups, and that such offending is more recognized by agents of social control.

- There is no one accepted definition of a gang, although common elements of most definitions include persistence over time, congregating in public, self-identifying as a gang, claims over turf, and participation in illegal activity.

- Thrasher provided one of the earliest studies on gangs and viewed them as mainly "spontaneous play groups" in lower-class areas of town.

- Measuring the extent of gang membership is not easy and generally is reliant on reports from police or other social control agencies.

- Most gang members are young, male, and Hispanic.

- Despite the frequent concern that gangs are migrating from the large cities to other locations, there is little evidence of any planned migration, and most movement is actually due to chance or relocation of gang members for non-gang reasons.

- Youths join gangs primarily for a sense of belonging, status, success, self-esteem, and cohesion.

- While most portrayals show gangs as violent and very criminal, actual gang behavior is mainly social and noncriminal. Criminal activity, however, is an important part of gang membership.

- Most gang violence is isolated and between gang members rather than directed at the general public.

- Among intervention strategies with gangs, suppression is the most used but considered the least effective, while opportunities provision is the least used but considered the most effective.

- Law enforcement/deterrent efforts to address ganging, such as the Boston Gun Project and civil injunctions, can be highly successful, but that success may last only as long as the project operates.

KEY TERMS

Boston Gun Project

civil abatement

civil gang injunctions

Community-Wide Approach to Gang Prevention, Intervention, and Suppression Program

detached worker programs

enhancement model

foray

gang

ganging

Gang Resistance Education and Training (G.R.E.A.T.) Program

group hazard hypothesis

hybrid gangs

internet banging

interstitial areas

near group

Operation Ceasefire

Project TOUGH

pulling levers

rumble

selection model

social facilitation model

STEP Act

DOI: 10.4324/9781003167112-5

> ■ Classroom-based anti-gang programs such as G.R.E.A.T. are showing promise in limiting gang membership and altering youthful views of gang behavior, although the impact on delinquency and criminality appears limited.

INTRODUCTION

For many individuals, agencies, and communities, the problem of youthful misbehavior is most notably gang delinquency. This is particularly true in large cities, where gangs are responsible for 25 percent or more of all homicides (Los Angeles, for instance, attributes half of its homicides to gangs [Howell, Egley, Tita, & Griffiths, 2011]). Law enforcement agencies consistently report that gangs and gang members are involved in violent crime, especially homicides (Egley, Howell, & Harris, 2014). A great deal of early research shows that juveniles commit more deviant acts while in the company of other youths than when they are alone (see, e.g., Erickson, 1971; Hindelang, 1971).

The existence of street gangs in the United States can be traced back to the very beginnings of the country. As early as 1783, youthful gangs emerged in New York City (Sante, 1991), with major ganging appearing in the 1820s (Adamson, 1998). The growth of gangs was largely related to the growth of major U.S. cities and the immigration of Eastern Europeans and Southern blacks to the industrial northeast and mid-west (Howell et al., 2011). Research on group delinquency dates back to the early twentieth century and the work of Thrasher (1936), Sutherland (1939), and Shaw, Zorbaugh, McKay, and Cottrell (1929).

Early delinquency research often focused on the idea that youthful misconduct was a result of peer influences. Differential association theory (Sutherland, 1939) proposed that much delinquent activity was the result of learning that took place in interactions between youths. Shaw and associates (Shaw et al., 1929; Shaw & McKay, 1942) focused heavily on the idea that juvenile misbehavior took place in groups. This theme of group behavior has persisted throughout the study of delinquency.

While studies claim a propensity for juveniles to act in groups, it is possible that much of the group dimension in offending is due to differential responses by society (Erickson, 1973; Feyerherm, 1980). The **group hazard hypothesis** proposes that delinquency committed in groups has a greater chance of being detected and acted upon by the juvenile and criminal justice systems (Erickson, 1973). In a study of 336 youths, Erickson (1973) reports that the group hazard hypothesis holds for select types of delinquent acts, especially more serious offenses. Group behavior simply may make recognition of a problem easier, thus more youths involved in group delinquency become involved with the juvenile justice system. The finding of high levels of group behavior in self-report surveys, however, suggests that the group hazard hypothesis is not a complete explanation of the group nature of delinquent activity.

Interest in gangs has waxed and waned over the years. From the 1950s to the early 1960s there was a great deal of attention paid to gang delinquency. This interest subsided in the late 1960s, possibly due to the shift in attention to broader concerns over the social order, such as the Vietnam War, the economy, and racial unrest (Bookin-Weiner & Horowitz, 1983). New theoretical orientations also shifted interest from the offenders to the structure of society and its systems of social control. As a result, gang problems did not retain their priority as research issues. Not until the late 1980s did we see a renewed interest in gangs and gang behavior. Gang researchers attribute the renewed interest to the escalation of gang violence and the belief that gangs are the driving force behind growing drug problems, particularly crack cocaine.

GANGS DEFINED

While there has been a great deal of interest and research in gang activity, no single definition of a gang has developed. In general, the term **gang** has referred to groups that exhibit characteristics setting them apart from other affiliations of juveniles.

> ### WEB ACTIVITY
>
> The National Gang Center has a wealth of information on defining and identifying gangs, as well as data on gang behavior. It is available at www.nationalgangcenter.gov.

Research Definitions

Various researchers have proposed different definitions of a gang. In one of the earliest gang definitions, Thrasher (1936:57) defined a gang as:

> an interstitial group originally formed spontaneously, and then integrated through conflict. It is characterized by the following types of behavior: meeting face to face, milling, movement through space as a unit, conflict, and planning. The result of this collective behavior is the development of tradition, unreflective internal structure, esprit de corps, solidarity, morale, group awareness, and attachment to a local territory.

This definition introduced a number of key ideas. First, a gang was a specific form of a group. Second, what made these groups different from others was a system of activity and behavior that included conflict and mutual support of members. Finally, gangs were found in those areas of a city that were deteriorating and in a state of disorganization (**interstitial areas**). Gangs, therefore, were seen by Thrasher as a unique phenomenon of the poor, inner-city, immigrant areas of the early twentieth century.

Today, one leading group of researchers and practitioners from Europe and the United States, the Eurogang Project, has defined a street gang as "a street gang (or troublesome youth group corresponding to a street gang elsewhere) is any durable, street-oriented youth group whose involvement in illegal activity is part of its group identity" (Weerman et al., 2009, p. 20). This definition may be overly broad and classify youth groups as gangs when the youths themselves do not consider their association as a gang (Esbensen, Brick, & Melde, 2008).

TABLE 5.1 Elements of a "Gang" Definition	
Group	Five or more members
Shared Identity	Name, colors, clothes, and symbols which serve to indicate membership
Identification	Members see themselves as a gang and are recognized by others as a gang
Permanence	Gang members have continuing contact and the group persists over time (at least several months)
Crime	Elevated levels of crime/delinquency compared to other youths

Source: Compiled by authors from Howell and Griffiths (2019).

Many definitions set forth different criteria for delineating a group as a gang. Howell and Griffiths (2019) present one such list of factors (see Table 5.1). Being a group is perhaps the easiest of the elements to understand. Howell and Griffiths (2019) use five or more as the criteria, which is greater than that found in many state statutes (which typically rely on three or more). A shared identity among the gang members includes a name, colors, identifiable clothing, and symbols. These elements provide both members and outsiders the ability to distinguish the members of the gang. Symbols may be used in communication between and among gangs, their members, and others (Curry & Decker, 1998). Beyond the shared identity, Howell and Griffiths (2019) note that both the members and others identify them as a gang. There is also an element of permanence to gangs with ongoing regular contact. The final element, crime, is the most important, because it pertains to group involvement in criminal activities. This is key to distinguishing a gang from other groups of people who may be identified as a group with names, symbols, and self-recognition. College fraternities, the Boy Scouts, sports clubs, and other groups are examples of these other groups. Curry and Decker (1998) offer a similar list of gang elements.

WEB ACTIVITY

The NGC maintains a website which provides a wealth of information on statutory definitions that can be searched at www.nationalgangcenter.gov/legislation. Review this material and see where your state stands and compares to other states.

Statutory Definitions

Beyond definitions used by researchers in studying gangs, many jurisdictions have passed laws specifically dealing with gangs and gang behavior. According to the National Gang Center (NGC, 2021), 43 states and the District of Columbia have statutes defining a gang, and 15 states define a "gang member." Interestingly, this means that seven states have no statutes specifically addressing gangs, and 35 fail to define a "gang member." Beyond this, 31 states statutorily define "gang crime." These statutory definitions include many of the same elements. In terms of "gangs," all statutes require some form of criminal activity or behavior. Most state statutes require gangs to have three or more individuals, while the federal government sets five or more as the minimum number of members. Statutory definitions of "gang members" typically include lists of criteria to use in determining whether an individual is or is not a gang member.

That a single definition of a gang has not been agreed upon by either researchers or legislators should be clear to the reader. The term "gang" has different meanings to different individuals, in different locations, at different times. What is common about gangs is the perception that they pose some form of threat to the safety of others.

EARLY GANG RESEARCH

Interest in gangs formed a good portion of the empirical and theoretical research prior to the mid-1960s. Much of the early research on gangs focused on describing the gangs and examining the daily workings of these groups. The research relied to a great extent on participant observation techniques. This research approach involved going out and observing the gangs on a daily basis. Such analysis provided a firsthand look at the structure and behavior of the gangs under study.

Thrasher's Gangs

Perhaps the most noted of the early studies of gangs was that of Frederick Thrasher. Thrasher (1936) studied 1,313 gangs with roughly 25,000 members in Chicago. He noted that the beginnings of gangs were within the interstitial areas of town that were characterized by a large amount of transience, great numbers of immigrant youths, poor living conditions, and a state of social disorganization. These ideas were simple extensions of the early work of Shaw et al. (1929), Shaw and McKay (1942), and the Chicago School.

Thrasher also viewed gangs as an outgrowth of innocent, everyday behavior among adolescents. The gangs supplied needed interaction and social contact for the youths, which were not supplied by families or other social institutions. Spontaneous play groups provided the basis and possibility for conflict. The groups provided a feeling of belonging and togetherness for the participants. The development of leadership, cohesion, and conflict served to strengthen the spontaneous groups and the establishment of a gang.

Gang activity very often centered on conflict within the individual gang and between different gangs. Conflict helped build esprit de corps and unity among the gang's members (Thrasher, 1936). Within-group disputes settled through conflict provided a basis for common values, loyalty, and cohesion among the membership. Successful conflict also provided the individual group member with prestige and status. Conflict with other gangs brought about increased cohesion among group members and helped to draw the gang into a more formal, organized, and long-term system of interaction.

Thrasher (1936) did not see gangs as a stable or permanent entity. The development of gangs, or **ganging**, was a continuous process. Gangs were composed mostly of juveniles between the ages of 11 and 17, and few members remained in gangs past young adulthood. Change in gangs was due to the maturing of individual members, the movement of members out of the immediate community, and marriage or employment of the member. While the specific makeup of the gang changed, many gangs would survive by replacing old members with new recruits. The recruits would come from those youths residing in the territory controlled by the gang.

Bloch and Niederhoffer: Gangs as a Natural Response

Twenty years after Thrasher's (1936) monumental work, Bloch and Niederhoffer (1958) expanded on many of his ideas. Where Thrasher viewed gangs as primarily a lower-class juvenile phenomenon, Bloch and Niederhoffer proposed that gangs were different from other juvenile groups simply by a matter of degree. The gang provided its members with status, success, and feelings of belonging that larger society was not providing (Bloch & Niederhoffer, 1958). Lower-class youths, who made up most gangs, were simply striving to succeed in the same sense as middle- and upper-class youths. Their social position, however, led them into situations that made gang behavior an acceptable alternative.

The organization of the gang was not greatly different from that portrayed by Thrasher (1936). Gangs developed leadership, cohesion, loyalty, and support through their daily activities. Bloch and Niederhoffer (1958), however, saw gangs as somewhat more fragile in terms of their longevity. The loss of a leader was seen as bringing about the dissolution of the gang. The gang was viewed as having less permanence than those studied by Thrasher. Despite this departure in views, both studies saw the gang as providing needed social support and status for participating youths.

Yablonsky: Near Groups

A different view of gangs is found in Yablonsky's (1962) explanation of gang formation and participation. First, he concentrates mainly on violent gangs whose activity focuses on violence and aggression. The violent gang strives for emotional gratification through hostile actions toward gang members and nonmembers. It also provides a sense of power for the participating individuals. Second, Yablonsky repudiates the idea that a gang is a well-organized group. Instead, he sees the violent gang as a **near group**, characterized by a relatively short lifetime, little formal organization, a lack of consensus between members, a small core of continuous participants, self-appointed leadership (as opposed to group-approved), and limited cohesion. Most "members" of the gang participate on the fringe and become involved only when individual or group violence is indicated. Self-aggrandizement, not group issues, is the major concern for gang members. This near-group view is restricted only to the violent gangs in Yablonsky's (1962) discussion. Other gangs may reflect the more classic portrayal found in other writings, although Yablonsky would argue that the violent "near group" is the dominant form of gang in society.

THE EXTENT OF GANG MEMBERSHIP

Measuring gang delinquency and/or gang involvement is not an easy task. A number of problems arise when attempting to assess the extent of gang membership. First, there is no single, accepted definition of what constitutes a gang. Any attempt to measure gang membership across jurisdictions, therefore, runs the risk of collecting data that reflect different problems or groups. This problem persists even when a survey (such as the National Youth Gang Survey [NYGS]) provides a definition for agencies to use, because the agency records typically reflect a local definition and the information is not reclassified to correspond to the desired definition before it is submitted. Second, many agencies classify individuals as gang members only if the individual self-identifies as such (Egley, Howell, & Major, 2004). Many youths may not claim gang membership, even if they fit a legal or other definition of a gang member.

Third, many jurisdictions may actively deny the existence of gangs and not collect any data on gangs, thus any count would be an undercount. Similarly, jurisdictions may fail to respond to surveys because they do not collect data (even if they recognize they have a problem) or do not keep special enumerations of "gang crime" separate from general crime. Despite these and other problems/issues, many attempts have been made to assess the extent of gangs and gang membership.

Estimates of gang membership typically rely on surveys of key informants, most often criminal justice system personnel. The earliest of these surveys, which was conducted by Miller (1975) and looked at only six cities, found a low estimate of 700 gangs with roughly 28,000 members. The most recent national data comes from the 2012 NYGS. The NGC conducted annual surveys to gauge the extent of gang behavior and responses to that activity from 1996 to 2012. The NGC surveyed the police departments of all cities with a population over 50,000, sheriff and police departments of all suburban counties in the United States, and randomly selected police and sheriff's departments serving small towns (between 2,500 and 24,999 population) and rural counties. More than 2,500 law enforcement agencies were surveyed each year (NGC, 2021). Unfortunately, the NYGS ended in 2012, and no further national data has been collected since that time. (The National Institute of Justice contracted with the Rand Corporation to conduct a new NYGS in 2021 but that project has not been completed at the time of this writing.)

Based on the 2012 NYGS, roughly 30 percent of the U.S. jurisdictions experience youth gang problems (Egley et al., 2014). This represents approximately 3,100 jurisdictions. The gang problem is much more common in cities having a population of 50,000 or more, where more than 8 out of 10 report gang problems (see Figure 5.1). On the other hand, fewer than 2 out of 10 rural counties report gang problems (NYGC, 2014).

In 2012, is was estimated that there were over 30,000 active gangs (NGC, 2021). This was 50 percent more than in 2003 and roughly the same level as in 1996. There were an estimated 850,000 gang members in the U.S. The number of gangs and gang members vary greatly from area to area (see Figure 5.2), but they appear in virtually all areas of the country. Figures based on the maximum number of reported gangs and gang members in different-size jurisdictions in the 2006–2012 NYGS reveal that larger cities hold the greatest proportion of

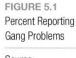

FIGURE 5.1
Percent Reporting
Gang Problems

Source:
Constructed by
authors from
National Gang
Center (2021).

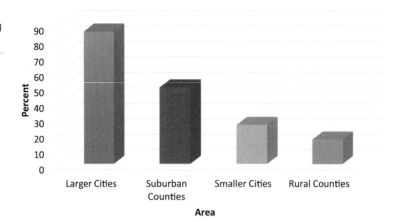

FIGURE 5.2
Distribution
of Gangs and
Members

Source:
Constructed
by authors
from National
Gang Center
(2021) data.

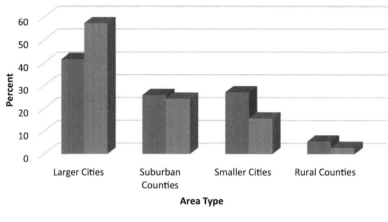

gangs and gang members, followed by suburban counties and smaller cities (with similar levels of gangs) and rural counties. Ten percent of large cities report having between 1,000 and 2,500 gang members, and 8.6 percent report over 2,500 members (NGC, 2021).

Klein and Maxson (2006) suggest that a better means of measuring gang participation is to survey youths. An important factor to consider in using surveys to gauge gang membership is whether the survey is conducted in areas with higher-than-typical concentrations of gangs and gang members. The use of nationally representative samples would provide more meaningful estimates, although most surveys are conducted using city-wide or county-wide samples. Based on their review of survey studies since 1990, Klein and Maxson (2006) find 33 different gang prevalence rates, ranging from roughly 5 percent to 20 percent reporting gang membership. Many of the higher figures relate to "ever" belonging to

WEB ACTIVITY

A great deal of information on gangs can be found online from the NGC. Explore the information at www. nationalgangcenter.gov/survey-analysis.

a gang, and the smaller figures reflect respondents reporting membership "in the past year."

Three clear results emerge from attempts to measure gang participation. First, gangs are found throughout the United States, in both large and small cities, and both urban and rural areas. Second, the scope of the gang problem is large. Finally, the majority of youths do not belong to gangs and probably never will. While the proportion claiming membership varies from one site to another, a small but significant percentage of youths do claim gang membership.

CHARACTERISTICS OF GANGS

Research has provided a great deal of information on gangs. Unfortunately, there is as much disagreement as agreement on many issues. As with the definition of a gang, questions still exist concerning characteristics of gang membership, gang organizational structure, and gang migration. The following pages attempt to synthesize the diverse literature and provide a general view of gangs in today's society.

AGE

Most early research portrayed the typical gang member as a teenage adolescent (Cooper, 1967; Kanter & Bennett, 1968; Klein, 1971; Miller, 1975; Robin, 1967; Short & Strodbeck, 1965). Miller's (1975) national survey showed that the peak age years tend to fall in the mid-teen age group. Gangs often use schools as recruiting grounds (Hutchinson & Kyle, 1993). Surveys show that the peak ages for participation are 14 and 15 (Klein & Maxson, 2006). Based on the 1997 National Longitudinal Survey of Youth, Pyrooz (2014) reports that the average age of onset for youthful gang participants is 15.11 years, with an average time in the gang of roughly two years. Indeed, only one-quarter of the youths report maintaining gang membership for three years or more. Various studies show that gang membership is a transient status and typically lasts for less than two years, with many individuals only remaining for less than a year (Bjerregaard, 2010; Gordon et al., 2004; Krohn & Thornberry, 2008; Melde, 2015; Pyrooz, 2014). This fact is reflected in the Eurogang definition of a street gang, in which the term "durable" is operationalized as three months or more.

Gangs are not limited to youthful members. Research since the mid-1980s (see, e.g., Hagedorn, 1988; Horowitz, 1983; Howell, 1997; Klein & Maxson, 1989; Moore, 1993; Spergel et al., 1990; Toy, 1992) shows that the age range of gang members has expanded, particularly at the older end. In 2011, the NYGS found that individuals age 18 or older make up 65 percent of all gang members (NGC, 2021). This suggests that gangs are retaining their members into young adulthood. The lack of meaningful employment opportunities, coupled with potentially lucrative gang behavior, is one reason for individuals to retain their gang membership into their twenties and thirties (Moore, 1991). The aging of gang membership is also partly a result of older gang members being released from incarceration and returning to their communities and gang roots (Egley & Howell, 2011).

TABLE 5.2 Gang Membership Onset and Tenure			
Type	Age of Onset	Tenure in Gang	Tenure Beyond 3 Years
Adolescence Limited	13.85	2.04 years	14%
Late Adolescence	16.84	1.78 years	9%
Adult Onset	20.15	1.62 years	5%
Early Adolescence	11.61	1.39 years	1%

Source: Constructed by authors from Pyrooz (2014).

Beyond consideration of the global age breakdown, it is possible to consider subgroup differences in the age of onset and tenure for gang membership. Pyrooz (2014) identifies four types or trajectories of gang membership based on age (see Table 5.2). In three of these, individuals commence gang participation in their adolescence. One represents commencing gang participation as a young adult (Adult Onset). Perhaps the most important factor to note is that the average tenure in a gang is two years or less in all four types. Only a small percentage of each group maintains membership beyond three years. These figures demonstrate that most youth gang participation is relatively transient.

Race and Ethnicity

Gangs do not appear to be reserved for any particular ethnic or racial groups. Virtually all races and ethnic groups have provided gang delinquents over the years, although different racial/ethnic groups have dominated at different points in time. Thrasher's (1936) gangs consisted mainly of white youths of European descent. Evaluations in the 1950s and 1960s tended to report greater numbers of black gangs. Figure 5.3 presents data from the NYGS on the racial/ethnic breakdown of gang membership as reported by police respondents. The statistics show that Hispanic/Latino youths comprise about 46 percent of all gang members, with blacks/African Americans contributing another 35 percent. Whites make up 11.5 percent of the gang population (NGC, 2021). These relative rates are consistent across area types except for rural counties where Hispanics/Latinos and blacks/African Americans switch places.

Traditionally, gangs tended to be homogeneous in terms of race and ethnicity (Klein, 1971; Short & Strodbeck, 1965; Spergel, 1966; Thrasher, 1936). That is, there were relatively few gangs that had white, black, Hispanic, and Asian members all in the same gang. Today, there is a developing trend toward hybrid gangs. The term hybrid gangs generally refers to gangs that are mixed racially or ethnically, but these gangs also can be characterized in other ways. For example, members may belong to more than one gang, or different gangs may cooperate with one another in some endeavor (Starbuck, Howell, & Lindquist, 2001). These gangs also may not fit the traditional definition of a gang and may not claim turf or utilize colors, signs, or other symbols typically considered important in recognizing gang behavior. While most gangs remain racially and ethnically homogeneous, Starbuck et al. (2001) note that

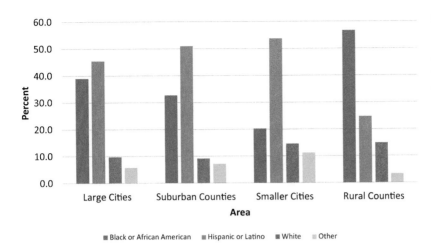

FIGURE 5.3
Race/Ethnicity of Gang
Members by Area Type

Source: Constructed by
authors from National Gang
Center (2021).

roughly one-third of the gangs identified in the 1998 NYGS fit the definition
of a hybrid gang.

Social Class

Most studies find that the vast majority of gangs are found in lower-class areas
and are composed of lower-class juveniles. The lower-class nature of gangs
finds a great deal of support in the early examinations and explanations of
ganging behavior. Thrasher's (1936) definition of gangs relies heavily on the
physical location of the groups in the lower-class, deteriorating areas of the
city. Subsequent analyses paint a similar picture of gang membership being
more common within lower SES areas, particularly when using official data
measures. More recent studies and those using self-report data suggest that
gang delinquency is no longer restricted to the inner city (Huizinga & Elliott,
1987; Johnstone, 1981; Spergel, 1984). The growth of gangs in suburban and
rural areas provides further evidence that gang behavior is not restricted to
lower-class, inner-city areas.

Females and Gangs

Traditional research on gangs has been devoted almost exclusively to the role
of males. This is due primarily to the failure of females to contribute to any
large extent to gang membership or activity. Thrasher's (1936) pathbreaking
study of 1,313 gangs found only five or six female gangs over the course of his
study. Surveys of youths uncover the same basic results, with roughly 10 percent of females reporting gang membership (Klein & Maxson, 2006). The 2010
NYGS reports that only 7.5 percent of all gang members are female (NGC,
2017). Interestingly, the number of gangs with female gang members is notably different by population area (see Figure 5.4), with gangs in rural counties
having female members while less than one-quarter of those in large cities
have female members.

The overwhelming dominance of male gangs found in law enforcement data
(such as the NYGS) is not mirrored in other sources of information. Research

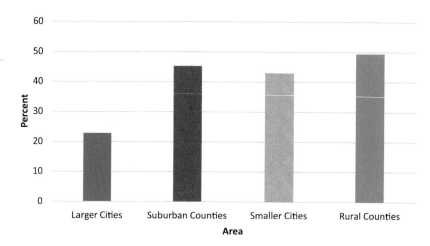

FIGURE 5.4
Gangs with
Female Members

Source:
Constructed by
authors from
National Gang
Center (2021).

shows that there is a great presence of females in gangs. Self-report data shows that between 25 percent and 33 percent of female respondents claim gang membership (Bjerregaard, 2002; Bjerregaard & Smith, 1993; Esbensen & Carson, 2012; Esbensen & Osgood, 1997; Gottfredson & Gottfredson, 2001; Maxson & Whitlock, 2002; Sickmund & Puzzanchera, 2014). Data from cities with gang problems reveals higher proportions of females claiming gang membership in line with male figures (Esbensen et al., 2008).

Traditionally, females were seen as part of auxiliary groups and responded to the mandates and activities of their male counterparts (Campbell, 1984, 1990; Monti, 1993). This auxiliary status of female gangs was most clearly seen in the adoption of similar names to the dominant male gangs (e.g., Disciples and Lady Disciples). Today, there are indications that many groups incorporate females into the main gang, although most gangs are still dominated by males (Miller, 2001; NGC, 2021). There are also more autonomous female gangs with their own leadership and separate meetings, which operate independently from the male gang in many instances (Batchelor, 2009; Campbell, 1990; Fishman, 1988; Moore, 1991). Female gang members tend to participate in many of the same forms of deviance as males, including drug use and violence (Bjerregaard & Smith, 1993; Campbell, 1990; Decker & Van Winkle, 1994; Fishman, 1988).

Organization and Size

Gangs tend to have some type of internal organization that affects the activities of its members, the status of those members, and the decision-making processes of the group (Bloch & Niederhoffer, 1958; Curry & Decker, 1998; Thrasher, 1936; Yablonsky, 1962). The degree of formality and control exercised by the gang varies greatly from gang to gang. Gangs that are more entrepreneurial tend to have a more formal hierarchical structure. Territorial gangs are more loosely organized and have an informal structure (see, e.g., Sanders, 1994). Klein and Maxson (2006) outline five gang types (see Table 5.3). These types indicate that gangs are not all mirror images of one another, and they can be diverse in size, structure, and activity. The most common gang form is the compressed type, followed by the neotraditional (Klein & Maxson, 2006). Several other typologies have been presented in the literature (see, for example, Knox, 1991; Taylor, 1990; Valdez, 2003). Howell and Griffiths (2019) point out that the value and applicability of the typologies will vary according to the specifics of the community and its needs.

U.S. Marshals deputies transport a suspected member of an Azusa, California, gang, following an early-morning raid in Irwindale, California.

CREDIT: AP Photo/Jason Redmond

At the heart of most gangs is a single core of devoted members. This core may vary in size but is always much smaller than the purported size of the entire gang. The majority of the gang usually reflects a body of fringe members who rarely take part in decision making and participate in gang activities only at selected times. Gangs that claim memberships of 100 and greater are probably counting a large number of fringe members. The core of the gang provides the leadership and decision-making body of the group.

Not all gangs have the same leadership structure (Kelling, 1975). In some groups, leadership is provided by a single individual determined according to the talents of the core members. Physical prowess often, but not always, determines who becomes the leader of the gang. Other gangs have highly differentiated leadership roles in which different talents call for different leadership. Fights and violence will call on the best fighter. Criminal activity for profit may require youths who know more about committing the crime and

TABLE 5.3 **Klein and Maxson's Gang Types**	
Traditional	Very large (over 100 members) with various subgroups; have been in existence for 20+ years; wide range of ages among members; territorial-based; wide range of criminal activity.
Neotraditional	Similar to traditional but not as old; typically 50–100 members; territorial; subgroups.
Compressed	Small gang with no subgroups (less than 50 members); members are close in age; short history; not necessarily territorial.
Collective	Like the compressed but larger (50+); wider age range of members, 10–15 years old; not necessarily territorial.
Specialty	Small gang with no subgroups; narrow age range; short history; very territorial; specializes in few types of crimes.

Source: Constructed by authors from Klein and Maxson (2006).

fencing the goods. Internal conflict may necessitate the efforts of someone who can negotiate and come up with alternative solutions. The extent of such specialization is determined by the abilities of the core members and the needs of the group.

Besides the core group, many gangs include a range of different subgroups (Miller, Gertz, & Cutter, 1961). This is especially true in recent years as we see gang members from different age groups, as well as more intergenerational gangs (Hutchinson & Kyle, 1993; Moore, 1991, 1993). Often, the subgroups are based on the age of the gang members. A simple form of organization may have only three membership groups—young "wannabes," the core of the gang, and "old guard" members. The different subgroups of a gang may be identified by various names or labels such as PeeWees, Juniors, Seniors, or Old Heads. It is important to note that this tripartite view of a gang is only a simple presentation. Various gangs may have a more complicated system of subgroups, including female auxiliaries or affiliations with gang chapters in other areas of a city. The actual organization varies greatly from gang to gang and place to place.

Gang Migration

One of the oft-mentioned "facts" about recent gang behavior is that of gangs migrating from place to place. Typically, this discussion centers around the idea that gangs are deliberately moving and setting up chapters in other places for the purpose of selling drugs. Support for this assertion is most often anecdotal and relies on the simple observation of the same or similar gang names, colors, graffiti, or behavior from place to place. Solid proof of gang migration, however, is not available.

For the most part, gang problems are typically "homegrown" and not imported (NYGC, 2014). The apparent migration is more accidental than planned. Skolnick, Bluthenthal, and Correl (1993) note that most gang travel and migration begins with non-gang, non-crime-related activities. Klein and Maxson (2006) note that visits to family members in other places or the relocation of a family are typical means by which gang members find themselves in a new environment. In essence, the gang migration is an unintended consequence of normal family behavior. The connection between gangs in different cities, usually considered a result of planned migration, is more illusory than real (Huff, 1993; Spergel et al., 1990; Valdez, 2000). According to the NYGS, almost half of all migration is related to social factors, while moving to secure illegal opportunities occurs in less than one-quarter of the moves (see Figure 5.5). The appearance of established gangs, such as the Crips and Bloods, in cities with no history of gang problems can often be attributed to the arrival of a single gang member who is displaced through family migration.

That there may be gang "chapters" in different cities cannot be totally discounted. Indeed, as competition for drug territory has increased, some gangs have attempted to establish operations in new areas. This movement, however, is typically limited and does not indicate state-wide or country-wide

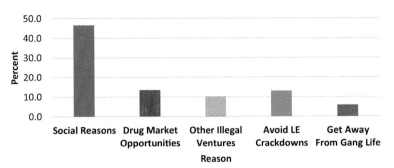

FIGURE 5.5
Factors Influencing Gang Member Migration

Source: Constructed by authors from National Gang Center (2021).

organizations of juvenile gangs (Klein & Maxson, 2006). One possible, and plausible, explanation for the apparent "franchising" of gangs in different cities is that more sophisticated drug dealers and organizations recruit youths and emerging gangs as local "employees" in the drug trade. Migration for drug selling, therefore, is more an illusion than a reality. Indeed, low migration levels result in relatively small impacts on a city's existing drug problems (Maxson, Woods, & Klein, 1996). For the most part, juvenile gangs are not as entrepreneurial as the public likes to think.

Summary

We must recognize that gangs, like any other collective of individuals, take on different characteristics based on the desires of the members and the underlying goal of the group. Some gangs may be highly structured with many members, clear leadership, and set agendas. Other gangs may be loose confederations of a few individuals who interact on a sporadic basis. Names, colors, territory, leadership, and other components of gangs are in themselves only potential indicators of ganging. Just as the general characteristics of gangs vary, so do the behavioral tendencies of these groups.

WHY DO YOUTHS JOIN GANGS?

The reasons behind gang behavior and violence are varied and, to some degree, mirror the reasons for youth participation in almost any group. Many features of a gang demonstrate that it provides something of value to its members. A sense of belonging, status, feelings of success, and financial gain are examples of what a gang can give its members. The cohesiveness and importance of the gang to the individual can be seen in the names, territory, and other identifiers associated with different gangs.

The fact that gangs are more prominent in lower SES areas suggests that youths join gangs in response to their inability to succeed through acceptable channels. The youths often face problems with success in schools and other social situations. Gang behavior is seen as an alternative to the lack of success and status faced by youths. Lower-class youths, regardless of ethnic or racial background, spend a good deal of time on the streets where they meet and interact with other youths. Turf or territory provides a sense of ownership and control, which often is denied the gang youths (Vigil, 1993). Overcrowded living conditions, frequent movement from place to place, lack of finances to purchase personal property, and other factors lead youths to feel a lack of control. The turf is a means of exerting control and ownership. While it is not ownership in the legal sense of the term, such control helps provide the feelings of status desired by the gang youths. Attacks on the turf are seen as an attack on the property, honor, and status of the individual gang members, and violence is used to protect the turf (Hutchinson & Kyle, 1993). The lower-class youths find support and unity with others facing similar problems, and gang activity can offer status and a sense of success not available elsewhere. The gang serves to provide a means of gaining status. Gang members can prove themselves on the street and are accepted for their contributions to the gang. They can gain honor through their allegiance to other gang members. They are provided with a sense of family and belonging that does not come from the broken, female-headed household.

The extent to which the gang is entrepreneurial may provide the members with an income (possibly significant) that is otherwise not available. Financial gain is another major reason for gang membership and activity. Faced with a lack of legitimate job opportunities, the gang can provide training in criminal activity (such as robbery and burglary), the opportunity for such criminal actions, and support for this behavior. Trafficking in illegal drugs is a lucrative activity for some gangs. It also brings about contact and opportunities with organized crime and a means of increasing status in the gang and community. At the same time that the drug trade has opened new doors for the gang members, it has also added to the stakes in control of turf and the level of violence between gangs.

While the outward appearance of gang behavior is different from socially acceptable activity, the reasons for the behavior are not much different from those of most other persons. The gang youths value status, belonging, ownership, control, and financial gain. These are major reasons behind the behavior of nondeviant youths and adults. The gang has simply supplied alternative methods for achieving its ends.

Another way to consider the question of why youths join gangs is to look at potential risk factors (Decker, Melde, & Pyrooz, 2013; Maxson, 2011). Table 5.4 presents five categories of risk factors. These are individual factors, family factors, school factors, peer group factors, and community factors. Explanations for female ganging follow the same logic found for male gangs and the risk factors are very similar.

WEB ACTIVITY

More extensive information on risk factors can be found on the NGC website (www.nationalgangcenter.gov/SPT/Risk-Factors). The Center lists a range of risk factors for different age groups from 0–2 years to 12–17 years.

The increased intergenerational nature of gang membership also contributes to the growth and construction of gangs. Younger members are often siblings or offspring of current or past gang members. "Apprenticeship" periods for "wannabes" and initiation rituals help build the sense of belonging. The gang provides its members with things they do not get at home, school, or elsewhere.

GANG BEHAVIOR

The media portrays gangs in constant violent confrontation with one another and with the general public. Contrary to this portrayal, gangs participate in a variety of different behaviors. While gang fights and drive-by shootings do occur, such violent confrontations are rare relative to other gang behavior. Indeed, gangs are involved in many nonviolent activities, including leisure activities, drinking and drug use, partying, gambling, and companionship. When gang aggression does occur, it is not necessarily physical in nature. Miller et al. (1961) note that roughly 94 percent of the aggression is verbal, and most does not contain anger.

While physical aggression may not dominate gang behavior, gangs are involved in significant numbers of crimes. Estimates of gang crime from law enforcement data reveal that gangs were responsible for more than 580,000 offenses in 122 cities and 8 counties in 1992 (Curry, Ball, & Decker, 1996). Most law enforcement agencies do not note whether offenses, with the exception of homicide, are gang-related or not (Egley et al., 2014). Based on various reporting programs, the National Gang Intelligence Center (2015) reports that street gangs are involved in assaults (43 percent of jurisdictions), street drug sales (59 percent), threats and intimidation (36 percent), robbery (35 percent), and a range of other behaviors. In 2012, the NYGS noted there were almost 2,400 gang-related homicides (Egley et al., 2014), accounting for roughly 16 percent of all homicides in the United States. Clearly, criminal behavior by gangs and gang members is evident in data supplied by law enforcement agencies.

The extent of criminal behavior by gang members also can be addressed through self-report surveys. Thornberry (1998) reported on gang crime as uncovered in the Rochester, Pittsburgh, and Denver youth studies. In every case, gang members accounted for at least 8 out of every 10 violent crimes and 7 out of 10 drug offenses. Gang members do not confine their offending to serious violent crime. They also participate in a large portion of all property crime (Thornberry, 1998). Similarly, Spergel et al. (1990) pointed out that gang members are more criminally active than nonmembers and commit three times the level of violence.

TABLE 5.4 Risk Factors for Gang Membership

Individual Factors
- Antisocial behavior
- Substance use
- Mental health problems
- Victimization
- Negative life events

Family Factors
- Poverty
- Weak family structure
- Lack of education
- Gang involvement

School Factors
- Poor academic performance
- Poor school climate
- Feelings of being unsafe at school

Peer Group Factors
- Peer gang involvement
- Aggressive peers

Community Factors
- High-crime neighborhoods
- Disadvantaged neighborhoods
- Poor neighborhood collective efficacy

Source: Compiled by authors from Howell (2010).

WEB ACTIVITY

The NAGIA and NGC offer information on dealing with gangs. Among these are links to individual state organizations and news reports concerning gangs from across the country. Available at www.nagia.org and www.fbi.gov/resources/library/gang-reports.

Drug Activity

Drug activity is a major topic of discussion in relation to gang behavior. The National Gang Intelligence Center (NGIC) notes that gangs are a major contributor to drug distribution throughout the United States (NGIC, 2015). There is no doubt that many gang members use and sell drugs, and that drug sales are an integral part of some organized gangs. The degree to which gangs are involved in drugs, however, is highly variable. For example, drug sales in one gang may involve sales only among its own members, while another gang may be deeply involved in the drug trade throughout the community. Reports from law enforcement reveal that 6 out of 10 agencies report street gangs are involved in street-level drug distribution and almost one-third participate in large-scale drug distribution. It is important to note that the NGIC report does not distinguish between youth gangs and adult gangs and the data reflect a composite for gang activity. Despite this fact, there is no doubt that youthful street gangs are involved in illegal drug-related activity. Fagan (1990), in a survey of Los Angeles, San Diego, and Chicago gang members, found that roughly 28 percent are rarely involved in drug use, while 35 percent are seriously involved in both use and sales. Research also shows that, while there is a great deal of drug use among youth gangs, the sale of drugs for profit by local gangs varies greatly from gang to gang (Decker & Van Winkle, 1994; Hagedorn, 1994; Mays, Fuller, & Winfree, 1994; Padilla, 1993).

Gang Violence

Gangs typically evoke images of violence and aggression, and it is with good cause. The level of violence and physical aggression has clearly changed and increased over time. Where much of the early research attempted to dispel the dominant myth of the centrality of violence in gangs, more recent studies note that violence is common. Decker et al. (2013) and Franzese, Covey, and Menard (2016) point out that gangs are disproportionately contributing to community violence. The NGIC (2015) notes that gangs are "driven by violence and will continue to compromise the safety of the communities they inhabit" (p. 48). Research suggests that the bulk of violence is aimed at other gang members.

The seriousness of the violence is high, as demonstrated by the number of gang-related killings. The NYGS estimates that gang-related homicides account for roughly 13 percent of homicides every year (NGC, 2021). Figure 5.6 presents 2012 data on gang-related homicides as reported in the NYGS. In large cities of more than 100,000 population, there were 1,587 gang-related homicides, accounting for over two-thirds of all gang-related homicides in the country. At the other end, "smaller areas" experienced 113 (or 4.8 percent) of the gang-related homicides (NGC, 2021). These figures are low estimates due to the fact that they reflect only those homicides occurring in jurisdictions that participate in the NYGS.

Modern gang violence differs from the earlier portrayals in a number of ways. Gang violence no longer conforms to the typical image of a **rumble** or gang fight. Rather, most violence appears as forays. A **foray** typically entails an attack

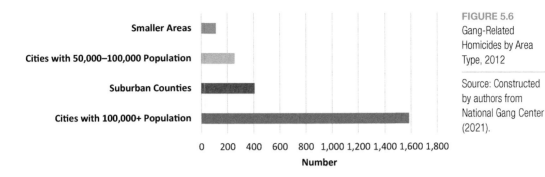

FIGURE 5.6
Gang-Related
Homicides by Area
Type, 2012

Source: Constructed
by authors from
National Gang Center
(2021).

by two or three youths upon a single member (or possibly a few members) of a rival gang. A typical form of attack is a "drive-by" shooting. For example, three members of the Bloods drive around a corner, where a member of the Crips lives, they shoot from the car, and then speed away from the scene. A similar retaliatory foray by the Crips is the consequence of the Bloods' action. The foray becomes a self-perpetuating activity. Indeed, gang homicides typically take place on the street and involve both firearms and motor vehicles (Klein & Maxson, 2006). Forays make violence appear to be more random, partly due to the use of automobiles and the willingness to attack when innocent bystanders are present. The violence also occurs more frequently through constant small forays rather than in the occasional large rumble. The hit-and-run tactics of the foray make the violence appear more impersonal. Non-gang peers and other individuals who become victims may often be injured as a result of a foray that occurs on the street. Today, gangs use lethal weapons, particularly firearms, more often (Decker, Pennel, & Caldwell, 1997), and recruit youths who already own guns, and they are more likely to carry guns than are non-gang youths (Bjerregaard & Lizotte, 1995).

Social Media and Gangs

The growth of social media use of youths has not been missed by those in gangs. The National Gang Intelligence Center (NGIC) noted that gangs use Facebook, YouTube, Twitter, and a range of other social media. Patton, Eschmann, and Butler (2013) refer to the use of violent threats and insults online as **internet banging**. The 2015 NAGIA survey found that almost 100 percent of the law enforcement respondents reported a gang using Facebook, almost 80 percent reported YouTube use, and more than 60 percent reported gang use of Instagram and Twitter (NGIC, 2015). The key question is: What is the purpose of gang members' use of social media?

Gangs and gang members use social media for various reasons, including recruitment, conversation, promotion, and planning of crimes/events. Table 5.5 lists five prominent purposes identified for why gangs use internet banging. Gangs post pictures and videos online, often as a substitute for graffiti (Womer & Bunker, 2010). This type of behavior can be a means of taunting other gangs and can provoke other gangs to retaliate (Patton, Eschmann, Elsaesser, & Bocanegra, 2016). Many of these actions could lead to arrest and sanctions.

TABLE 5.5 **Purposes of Internet Banging**
1. Promote gang affiliation and/or communicate interest in gang activity
2. Gain notoriety by reporting participation in a violent act of communicating an impending threat
3. Share information about rival gangs or network with gang members across the country
4. Coordinate or conduct criminal networks
5. Recruit new members

Source: Compiled by authors from Patton et al. (2013) and Howell and Griffiths (2019).

Pyrooz, Decker, and Moule (2015), interviewing almost 600 respondents in five cities, report that gangs use social media to coordinate assaults and plan drug sales, as well as other deviant activities. This behavior is especially noteworthy among active gang members. The same interviews did not find evidence of gang recruitment or actions furthering the gang organization (Pyrooz et al., 2015).

While social media can be used by gangs and gang members in furtherance of their efforts, it can also be used by agents of social control to fight gangs. Patton et al. (2016) note that social control agents can use social media posts to identify planned crime and to interview those involved in those actions. Social media, particularly photos, can assist law enforcement in identifying gang members, offenders, and problem locations, before, during, and after gang activity. Behrman (2015) points out that social control and social service agencies use social media as data and evidence for interventions and legal action. Indeed, more than half of all law enforcement agencies reporting to the National Gang Reporting Survey note their agency's use of social media in gang investigations (NGIC, 2015).

Gang Behavior and Types of Gangs

Not all gangs participate in the same types of deviant behavior. Indeed, research shows that some gangs tend to specialize their criminal activity. That same research even suggests that a few gangs exist primarily as a forum for criminal behavior, as opposed to a forum for more generalized group behavior. The identification of specific types of offending by gangs, however, is as elusive as identifying a single gang definition. Each gang may do something slightly different from every other gang.

Asian gangs exemplify the type of gang that appears to serve a definitive purpose for its members. A number of studies (Chin, Fagan, & Kelly, 1992; Huff, 1993; Toy, 1992) report that Asian gangs appear to be very profit-oriented and tend to restrict their deviant activities to those that bring a monetary return. Both Huff (1993) and Chin et al. (1992) claim that these gangs often have strong ties to organized crime, which directs both the financial dealings and the use of violence in the Asian communities.

Analyses of Chicano youths suggest they are strongly territorial-based (Moore, 1991; Sanders, 1994; Vigil, 1993, 1997), which provides the gang with a delineated area for which it has almost exclusive rights to gang recruitment. Besides the territorial nature of Chicano gangs, these groups tend to be more heavily involved in drug use (Moore, 1991, 1993) and general deviance (Vigil, 1993).

Skinhead gangs advocate white supremacy and are portrayed as very violent and racist, although this is not true of all skinheads. They also often take an anti-government stance and advocate withdrawal from the dictates of the government, including taxes and all regulatory laws. Skinheads use violence primarily against those who are perceived as a threat to white supremacy (Wooden & Blazak, 2001).

At another extreme are tagger gangs, whose members often view themselves as urban artists. These youths try to have their art seen by as many people as possible, and do not view the graffiti as vandalism, denoting ownership of turf, or harmful to others. It is solely an expression of individuality and a means of gaining status (Wooden & Blazak, 2001).

DO GANGS CAUSE DELINQUENCY?

Based on the level of gang member delinquency, one could argue that the elimination of gangs would significantly reduce the level of youthful deviance. An alternative possibility, however, is that gangs simply attract already delinquent youths, rather than causing increased deviance. The delinquency, therefore, is independent of gang membership. Following this argument, Thornberry, Krohn, Lizotte, and Chard-Wierschem (1993) identify three possible models of the delinquency–gang relationship: selection, social facilitation, and enhancement. The **selection model** maintains that gangs recruit or attract already delinquent youths. In this model, the level of delinquency would be independent of gang status. Under the **social facilitation model**, belonging to a gang is the cause of increased deviance. Periods of gang membership, therefore, will result in delinquent activity not found during nonmembership. Finally, the **enhancement model** strikes a middle ground in which gangs recruit delinquency-prone youths and enhance their deviance.

Several studies have sought to test these models of gang influence directly. Using panel data from the Denver Youth Survey, Esbensen and Huizinga (1993) report that gang members are indeed more delinquent while they are actively involved in the gang. At the same time, however, these youths also report higher levels of offending both before and after active gang participation. Melde and Esbensen (2011) investigate the three models in terms of gang membership being a turning point in one's life. Based on survey data for almost 1,400 youths, the authors find that joining a gang reduces informal social controls and increases delinquent behavior, in accord with the facilitation model. At the same time, at-risk youths are more likely to join gangs (Melde & Esbensen, 2011), reflecting selection factors. The fact that both sets of factors appear to be at work suggests an enhancement model.

Decker et al. (2013) argue that enhancement is the most important model. Gangs recruit youths experiencing problems and promote the violent behavior. Melde and Esbensen (2013), using data from seven cities and more than 3,700 youths, report that gang membership increases the odds of violent activity by 21 percent. This is a statistically significant increase in the level of violence. These studies suggest that the gang is not necessarily the cause of delinquent behavior. Rather, gang membership appears to add to an already established level of deviance by participating youths. Thus, while all three models have some support, the enhancement model is the most viable of the three.

INTERVENTION WITH GANGS

Responding to gangs and gang problems is an area in which much work remains to be done. Unfortunately, the first response by many cities to an emerging gang problem is one of denial (Hagedorn, 1988). Cities often do not want to admit that they have gangs. The outcome of such denial is the emergence of a full-blown problem before the authorities are prepared to deal with it. Once the problem is identified, a number of different responses have been used to address the problem.

Spergel and Curry (1993), in the NYGS, identified five common intervention strategies (see Table 5.6). Most respondents (44 percent) use suppression (the use of arrest, prosecution, incarceration, and other criminal justice system procedures) as their primary form of response. The intervention ranked second in primacy is social interventions (31.5 percent), followed by organizational change and development (10.9 percent), and community organization (8.9 percent). Opportunities provision is utilized the least by responding agencies.

TABLE 5.6 Gang Intervention Strategies

Suppression	Includes any form of social control in which the criminal justice system (police, courts, or corrections) or society attempt to impose formal or informal limits on behavior
Social Intervention	Basically a social work approach to working with gangs in the neighborhoods (such as detached worker programs)
Organizational Change and Development	Deals with altering the organization(s) that respond(s) to gang problems, such as through the establishment of gang units or specialized training of its personnel
Community Organization	Efforts aimed at mobilizing the community toward self-improvement and change, including both physical and social alterations
Opportunities Provision	Recognizing the lack of meaningful jobs and the training needed to succeed, and taking steps to change the problems; education, vocational training, and job placement are elements

Source: Spergel and Curry (1993).

Traditional criminal justice system responses to gangs are the most common responses, while efforts to alter the social conditions that cause ganging are addressed the least. Interestingly, in an analysis of the perceived effectiveness of the five types of intervention strategies, Spergel and Curry (1993) report that opportunities provision is viewed as the most effective/promising approach, while suppression is seen as the least effective.

Vigil (2010) argues that effectively responding to gangs and gang problems requires a balanced strategy incorporating elements of prevention, intervention, and law enforcement. It is important to consider the varying inputs to ganging and address all of them. This means creating solutions that address the economies of the area, the sociocultural factors surrounding the youths, and the sociopsychological marginality of the youths (Vigil, 2010). The role of law enforcement has got to include the traditional police functions as well as "soft suppression" interventions, such as youth programs, sports programs, and educational interventions (Vigil, 2010). The following pages will address a number of approaches to gang problems that reflect different elements suggested by Vigil, including detached worker programs, statutory changes, deterrence strategies, the G.R.E.A.T. program, and recent comprehensive initiatives.

Detached Worker Programs

Detached workers have been an integral part of many programs dealing with youths over the years. **Detached worker programs** place gang workers into the community and free the workers from heavy paperwork and administrative requirements (Klein, 1969). The workers are expected to spend considerable time in the neighborhoods, maintain consistent contact with the gangs, and provide immediate assistance and input to the youths. Many programs rely on past gang members for workers although there has been considerable opposition to the use of these individuals from many sources (Vigil, 2010). Klein (1971) notes that the strength of the program includes the ability to reach youths who normally are not contacted, the flexibility of workers to handle situations in unique ways, and the ability to establish confidential relationships with youths.

The impact of detached workers on gangs has been mixed. Klein (1969), in perhaps the most noted evaluation of such programs, claimed that the detached workers in Los Angeles organized 113 sporting events, 90 outings, 16 service projects, and 14 self-help programs. Unfortunately, greater contact between the gangs and a worker led to gangs becoming closer and more unified, and the gangs were more successful at recruiting new members. Additionally, these groups participated in greater numbers of delinquent acts after the intervention of the detached workers (Klein, 1969).

More recent proposals for intervention with gangs typically include a heavy detached worker component, although they may not use that terminology. Spergel's (1984, 1986), Fox's (1985), and Vigil's (2010) discussions of gang interventions reveal a striking similarity with detached worker programs. Emphasis is placed on intimate contact with gang members, providing alternative lines of behavior, and serving as a resource for gangs. Based on Klein's earlier work, it could be argued that this approach is ill-fated.

Statutory Changes

Increased concern about gangs has prompted the passage of new legislation as means of combating gang problems. Many states have passed legislation making gang affiliation a crime, or increasing penalties for gang-related criminal behavior. California's **STEP Act** (Street Terrorism Enforcement and Prevention) of 1988 effectively criminalizes membership in a street gang. Under STEP, the police can invoke civil penalties against gang members for associating with one another in public, promoting their gang, displaying gang symbols, and being involved in other similar gang behavior. As noted earlier in this chapter, many states have passed laws defining gangs and setting penalties for gang-related crimes. Statutes such as those in Florida (Florida Statutes 874.01) and Georgia (Georgia Code 16-16-3) require harsher penalties for gang-related crimes.

In support of such statutes, many police departments, particularly in large cities, have established specialized gang crime units (Curry, Fox, Ball, & Stone, 1993). Katz and Webb (2003) report on units in Albuquerque (NM), Las Vegas (NV), Phoenix (AZ), and Inglewood (CA). Weisel and Shelley (2004) consider units in San Diego and Indianapolis. In all locations the formation of the units was in response to political pressure, and the operations of the units were generally separate from the rest of the police activities. Katz and Webb (2003) find the units rely mostly on routine police responses and receive little training specific to gangs and gang problems. In both analyses, activities to prevent the formation of gangs is lacking. Rather, most attention seems to be directed at intelligence gathering and investigations aimed at crimes committed by gangs. In general, in neither analysis is there evidence of the units having any significant impact on gangs, gang formation, or gang crime.

Another innovative use of legal codes to fight gangs is to employ civil, rather than criminal, codes. **Civil abatement** procedures can be used to control or eliminate locations that gang members frequent or own (Cristall & Forman-Echols, 2009). **Project TOUGH** (Taking Out Urban Gang Headquarters) in Los Angeles is one such program. When an address is identified as a gang headquarters or hang out, the police and civil authorities, including health departments and building code enforcement, will bring lawsuits in civil court against the owners that can result in eviction and/or property forfeiture. Injunctions against gang members can also be used to order them to stay away from the property. The use of civil suits is in some ways easier than invoking the criminal code because the burden of proof is "preponderance of evidence" rather than "proof beyond a reasonable doubt," and there is no right to a jury trial (Cristall & Forman-Echols, 2009). This use of civil abatement is akin to the successful drug abatement projects in Oakland, California (see Mazerolle, Roehl, & Kadleck, 1998).

In a similar fashion, **civil gang injunctions** involve court orders that prohibit certain behaviors linked to criminal activity. These orders may prohibit gang

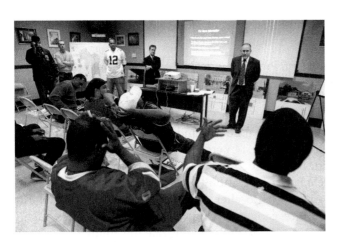

Los Angeles City attorneys present a gang injunction removal petition review process to gang intervention activists in Los Angeles. People subject to an injunction often can challenge the decision in court or file a petition asking for it to be removed.

CREDIT: AP Photo/Damian Dovarganes

members from associating in public, marking territory, trespassing, loitering, or other similar activities (Los Angeles City Attorney's Office, 2009). These injunctions are typically aimed at specific gangs/gang members, locations, and activities (Hennigan & Sloane, 2013). Violations can result in arrest and fines. Research on civil gang injunctions shows generally positive results in terms of reduced crime and fear in the target areas (Grogger, 2002; Maxson, Hennigan, Sloane, & Kolnick, 2004), although Hennigan and Sloane (2013) note that attacking the gang has the potential to build stronger ties among the members if individual attention to gang member needs is not included.

Deterrence Strategies

One approach that has received a great deal of attention in recent years is to have the police strictly enforce any and all codes and regulations (basically a suppression approach) in an attempt to deter gang members and criminal gang behavior. While deterrence is a cornerstone of the interventions, most projects include a strong social service component to later individual and gang activity (Engel, Tillyer, & Corsaro, 2013). Perhaps the most notable deterrence project is the **Boston Gun Project**, which targeted firearms use by gangs. Also known as **Operation Ceasefire**, the project used an approach referred to as **pulling levers**, as well as social service to assist gang members to move out of gangs. In terms of deterrence, pulling levers takes a zero-tolerance stance with regard to any transgressions (Cook, Moore, & Braga, 2002). For example, if a single gang member commits an offense with a firearm, the police inform the entire gang that they are subject to increased attention from police and the criminal justice system. Officers and other system personnel will enforce trespassing laws and curfews, frequently stop and question gang members, enforce vagrancy and loitering ordinances, check on and enforce probation and parole rules, seize illegal goods obtained through illegal activities, restrict plea bargaining, and impose the highest penalties possible for even the most minor transgressions (Kennedy, 1998). All of this represents a form of "legal harassment" that is meant to influence gangs and gang members to avoid the use of firearms. Evaluation of the Boston Gun Project reveals significant decreases in several offenses, including a 63 percent reduction in homicides, 25 percent reduction in assaults with firearms, and a 32 percent reduction in the number of shots fired (Braga, Kennedy, Piehl, & Waring, 2001).

The success of the Boston Gun Project has prompted several other jurisdictions to adopt similar programs. The Indianapolis Violence Reduction Partnership resulted in a 34 percent drop in homicides (McGarrell, Chermak, Wilson, & Corsaro, 2006). Operation Peacekeeper in Stockton, CA, saw a 35 percent reduction in gun homicides (Braga, 2008), and Project Safe Neighborhoods in Lowell, MA, uncovered a similar 44 percent drop in assaults with a firearm (Braga, Pierce, McDevitt, Bond, & Cronin, 2008). The Cincinnati Initiative to Reduce Violence, modeled after Operation Ceasefire, relied on focused deterrence, social services, and efforts to alter community views of violence. The program was able to reduce gang-member-involved homicides by roughly 40 percent (Engel et al., 2013). These results illustrate the ability of the criminal justice system to deter gang violence.

The G.R.E.A.T. Program

The **Gang Resistance Education and Training (G.R.E.A.T.) program** is the most recognizable prevention program targeting gangs. The program began in 1991 and was modeled on the Drug Abuse Resistance Education (D.A.R.E.) program. The original G.R.E.A.T. program consisted of nine one-hour lessons taught by local police officers in middle schools. The mission of the program is to: "Prevent Youth Crime, Violence, and Gang Involvement" (G.R.E.A.T., 2021).

A longitudinal evaluation of the original G.R.E.A.T. programs showed positive outcomes. Esbensen, Peterson, Taylor, Freng, and Osgood (2004), using data for four years following program participation, reported less victimization, less risk-taking behavior, improved attitudes toward the police, increased numbers of prosocial peers, and more negative views about gangs among those youths receiving the G.R.E.A.T. lessons. Unfortunately, the evaluation failed to find any impact on the more important target of the project—reduced gang participation. While disappointing, the promising results led the sponsors of the G.R.E.A.T. program to undertake a revision of the curriculum, which resulted in the current 13-lesson middle-school scheme (see Box 5.1).

WEB ACTIVITY

More information on G.R.E.A.T., including materials on the elementary, families, and summer components, can be found at the program's website: www.great-online.org.

The thrust of the program is to provide youths with the necessary skills for identifying high-risk situations and resisting the pressure/allure of taking part in gangs and gang activity. Beyond targeting just ganging, program curricula are geared toward increasing self-esteem, changing attitudes, and eliminating participation in violent behavior. A key component of G.R.E.A.T. is to teach nonviolent conflict-resolution techniques to the youths. The program has been adopted by schools throughout the United States.

The revised curriculum has been the subject of a rigorous national evaluation. A total of 195 classrooms in 31 schools in seven cities were included in the analysis, with a total of more than 3,800 students. In total, 130 classrooms

BOX 5.1 G.R.E.A.T. MIDDLE SCHOOL CURRICULUM

1. **Welcome to G.R.E.A.T.: A Gang and Violence Prevention Program**
   - *Lesson Goal*: Students will identify the relationship among crime, violence, drug abuse, and gangs.

2. **What's the Real Deal? The Real Deal on Gangs and Violence**
   - *Lesson Goal*: Students will analyze information sources and identify realistic, normative beliefs about gangs and violence.

3. **It's About Us: Being Part of the Community**
   - *Lesson Goal*: Students will define their roles and responsibilities in the family, school, and community.

4. **Where Do We Go From Here? How to Set Goals**
   - *Lesson Goal*: Students will write realistic and achievable goals.

5. **Decisions, Decisions, Decisions: Making the Right Choice**
   - *Lesson Goal*: Students will practice decision-making skills.

6. **Do You Hear What I Am Saying? How to Communicate Effectively**
   - *Lesson Goal*: Students will practice effective communication skills.

7. **Walk in Someone Else's Shoes: Thinking of Others**
   - *Lesson Goal*: Students will identify active-listening skills, how to recognize the emotional state of others, and how to demonstrate empathy toward victims of crime and violence.

8. **Say It Like You Mean It: Some Ways of Refusing**
   - *Lesson Goal*: Students will practice effective refusal skills.

9. **Getting Along Without Going Along: Dealing With Peers**
   - *Lesson Goal*: Students will practice effective refusal skills (continued).

10. **Keeping Your Cool: Managing Your Anger**
    - *Lesson Goal*: Students will practice anger-management skills.
    - Practice Cooling Off.

11. **Keeping It Together: How to Calm Others**
    - *Lesson Goal*: Students will identify how anger-management skills help prevent violence and conflicts.

12. **Working It Out: How to Solve Conflicts**
    - *Lesson Goal*: Students will practice conflict-resolution techniques.

13. **G.R.E.A.T. Days Ahead: Applying Your G.R.E.A.T. Skills**
    - *Lesson Goal*: Students will explain how their G.R.E.A.T. Project helped them develop a feeling of commitment and ownership of their school and their community.

Source: G.R.E.A.T. (2021). Available at https://great-online.org/Home/About/Middle-School-Component.

received the G.R.E.A.T. training and 93 classrooms served as the controls. Data were gathered over a five-year period, including four years post-program participation (Esbensen et al., 2011). Preliminary results based on the first year of follow-up data reveal overall positive results. Results show that participants are more positive about the police, are less positive about gangs, more often use refusal skills they have been taught, are better able to resist peer pressure, and are less involved in gangs (Esbensen, Osgood, Peterson, Taylor, & Carson, 2013). Most importantly, the data reveal 39 percent less gang membership among G.R.E.A.T. participants (Esbensen et al., 2013). These positive results are also sustained at four years post-participation. G.R.E.A.T. participants are still 24 percent less likely to be gang members and they maintain positive attitudes toward police, use of refusal skills, and hold more negative attitudes toward gangs (Esbensen et al., 2013). All of these results are significant.

Despite these positive results, the evaluation shows no impact on criminal and violent activity (Esbensen et al., 2013; Pyrooz, 2013). This may be due to the fact that G.R.E.A.T. targets entire classrooms, which include youths who are both low risk and high risk for gang membership. As a result, G.R.E.A.T. may influence a youth's self-identification as a gang member, but it may have little impact on the level of attachment to gangs and criminal gang activity among those who join (Pyrooz, 2013). While G.R.E.A.T. is a promising program, its full impact on behavior is not known.

A Planned Comprehensive Response to Gangs

Where most gang intervention programs focus on a single or limited approach, some efforts have attempted a broader-based set of strategies. In the mid-1990s, the Office of Juvenile Justice and Delinquency Prevention (OJJDP) initiated the **Community-Wide Approach to Gang Prevention, Intervention, and Suppression Program**. In essence, the program aimed to initiate a comprehensive set of strategies mirroring the five strategies outlined by Spergel and Curry (1993) (see Table 5.6). OJJDP funded program implementation and evaluation in five cities (Bloomington-Normal, IL; Mesa, AZ; Riverside, CA; Tucson, AZ; and San Antonio, TX).

Several factors emerged across the evaluations. First, in San Antonio the program was never fully implemented (Spergel, Wa, & Sosa, 2004a). Second, suppression remains the primary response in at least three cities (Spergel et al., 2001, 2002, 2003, 2004b). Third, several cities struggled with building programs that included grassroots community organizations. Most of the participants remained official criminal justice agencies and other social service providers (Spergel et al., 2001, 2002, 2004a, 2004b). Finally, the more successful programs offered a wider array of activities that could be considered opportunities provision and social interventions, such as counseling, referrals, and job training.

WEB ACTIVITY

The NGC website includes a great deal of information on effective and promising programs for combating gangs and gang-related behavior. Over 70 programs are reviewed and the material includes targeted risk factors and references for each program. Explore these programs at www.nationalgangcenter.gov/spt.

The program's impact on gang membership and crime is also mixed. The evaluations of the Bloomington-Normal, Mesa, and Riverside programs report reduced offending and reduced arrests among youths in the experimental neighborhoods (Spergel et al., 2001, 2002, 2003). While the Bloomington-Normal program appears to have reduced the level of gang participation (Spergel et al., 2001), there was no apparent impact in Riverside, Tucson, or San Antonio (Spergel et al., 2003, 2004a, 2004b). Despite the mixed results of the programs, the evidence suggests that a successfully implemented program that targets a wider array of interventions than just suppression activities has the ability to impact positively on the level of gang crime and gang membership.

Overview of Interventions

Evidence concerning the effectiveness of dealing with gangs mirrors the research concerning interventions with individual offenders. The basic conclusion is that many methods of intervention have had little impact on deviant activity. Indeed, some evaluations suggest that intervention exacerbates the problem. A large part of past failures may be due to what Klein (1995) refers to as "conceptually misguided, poorly implemented, half-heartedly pursued" responses and programs. Huey, Lewine, and Rubenson (2016) present the results of a meta-analysis of 38 controlled gang interventions, either prevention- or treatment-oriented. The results of the analysis show no positive effect on antisocial behavior and only mild effects on gang involvement. Huey et al. (2016) note that most program evaluations do not address gang involvement. In addition, many interventions do not address the major underlying cause of ganging and gang behavior—the lack of social opportunities. Despite the recognition that opportunity provision has the most promise, there are few programs that target this area. The lack of education, training, and jobs receives little attention in most gang interventions. Rather, arrest, prosecution, and incarceration remain the mainstay of society's response. Many authors (see, e.g., Cummings & Monti, 1993; Goldstein, 1993; Hagedorn, 1988; Huff, 1990, 1993; Moore, 1991) claim that until major changes are made in the basic social structure, gangs will persist and thrive.

SUMMARY

Interest in gang activity has a long history in juvenile justice and appears to have engendered renewed interest in recent years. The research efforts to date provide striking similarities to one another. The form and explanations for ganging have changed little since Thrasher's (1936) early work. The clearest difference in recent work has been the finding of more serious violence directed against a wider range of victims. Despite the persistent and increasingly dangerous problem, there do not appear to be any clearly successful methods for dealing with gangs.

DISCUSSION QUESTIONS

1. Gang delinquency is apparently on the rise and you are called on to explain to the public about gangs and gang behavior. How would you define a gang? What is the typical gang like? How much danger do gangs pose to the average citizen?

2. Gangs are typically accused of dominating violence and drug use/sales. What can you tell about gang involvement in these actions? How does this compare to the general impression about gangs?

3. Due to the apparent increase in gang violence, the police are called on to do something about the problem. As a member of the police department, what programs, interventions, or actions would you suggest for dealing with gangs and/or the public's perception? Be as specific as possible. If past programs form the basis of your suggestions, provide information on the strengths and weaknesses of those programs and how you would improve on them.

CHAPTER 6

Drugs and Delinquency

WHAT YOU NEED TO KNOW

- The Monitoring the Future project surveys 8th-, 10th-, and 12th-grade students every year to measure drug use. The results show that drug use is a major concern and a complex phenomenon that varies by drug.

- Trend data for drug use over time had been showing fairly consistent reductions in use, then some increase in use, but significant decreases for many drugs in data for 2021. Vaping, however, is a current concern.

- The relationship between drug use and delinquency is not entirely clear, with some studies showing that use precedes delinquency and others showing that delinquency precedes drug use. The actual relationship is probably a reciprocal one, with each behavior contributing to the other.

- No one type of drug treatment is effective for every individual or every drug. Treatment needs to vary by the individual circumstances.

- Gauging the effectiveness of drug treatment is very difficult due to the fact that most clients drop out before completion of treatment. What is clear is that treatment can be effective at reducing the need for and abuse of drugs.

- The "Just Say No" approach to prevention is shortsighted and has failed to show any impact on drug use.

- One positive approach is life skills training, which focuses on developing resistance skills for individuals. Evaluations show that this approach can be effective at curbing drug use.

- The popular D.A.R.E. program has failed to have any impact on drug use or abuse. The program has been revised to focus on multiple problem behaviors.

- Drug courts represent one of the more recent movements for addressing drug use and crime. These courts couple formal court action and intervention with individualized treatment plans involving the offender and his or her family.

KEY TERMS

affective interventions

Breaking the Cycle (BTC) program

detoxification

Drug Abuse Resistance Education (D.A.R.E.) program

drug court

incidence

"Just Say No"

Keepin' It REAL

knowledge approach

life skills training

maintenance programs

Monitoring the Future (MTF) Project

Multi-Dimensional Family Therapy (MDFT)

National Survey on Drug Use and Health

net-widening

outpatient drug-free programs

prevalence

psychopharmacological explanations

reciprocal relationship

DOI: 10.4324/9781003167112-6

INTRODUCTION

spurious
relationship

systemic
violence

therapeutic
communities

use, abuse, and
addiction

Youthful drug use continues to be a societal concern. Beyond the fact that drug use itself is a crime, such behavior is often associated with other criminal actions, including violence and property crime. As noted in the previous chapter, drug use and distribution are related to ganging and gang behavior. There is a continuing perception that drug use is problematic in the United States, especially among youths. The authors of Monitoring the Future (Johnston et al., 2021) note that current teen drug usage is a complex phenomenon that varies by drug and that is a major concern.

There is ample evidence that many youths are under the influence of alcohol or other drugs at the time they commit delinquent acts, or that they recently used alcohol or other drugs. Substance abuse is even more extensive among serious/chronic offenders (Beck, Kline, & Greenfield, 1988; Mulvey, Schubert, & Chassin, 2010). While the causal relationship between drugs and delinquency is the matter of some debate, the indisputable correlation between the two (Bennett, Holloway, & Farrington, 2008; Walters, 2017) raises a variety of issues for the juvenile justice system. This chapter will examine the various issues involved in the drugs–delinquency connection—the extent of drug use, the evidence on the causal relationship, and ways to combat the problem. Before examining these topics, however, it is necessary to define some key terms involved in drug research.

Three common terms used in any discussion of the drug problem are **use, abuse, and addiction**. While definitions for these ideas vary from source to source, we can identify some uniform components in most definitions. Use and abuse are considered to be synonymous by most authors when juveniles are considered. This is true due to the fact that juveniles are legally barred from the recreational use of any drug, including alcohol. Indeed, even medically prescribed drugs are supposed to be administered by an adult following strict guidelines. Abuse generally refers to the use of any drug beyond that legally prescribed for a medical condition. For juveniles, therefore, any use constitutes abuse. Addiction refers to chronic use of a drug to the point at which the individual develops a need to continue use of the drug, increases the amount used over time, and develops a psychological or physical dependence on the drug (World Health Organization, 1964).

GAUGING THE EXTENT OF DRUG USE

Measuring the extent of drug use is somewhat difficult due to the private nature of the behavior. The only individual involved is the user. There is no victim who calls the police and files a complaint. In essence, the victim and offender are the same person. Consequently, the primary source of information on drug use (the extent of it and changes in it) are individual self-reports of behavior. Such self-report surveys have been conducted on both the general population and groups of known offenders. Data from both sources are considered below.

Drug Use among Adolescents

Drug use by juveniles has been measured on a yearly basis since the 1970s by the Monitoring the Future (MTF) project carried out by Johnston and associates at the University of Michigan. The MTF Project surveys 8th-, 10th-, and 12th-grade students every spring (as well as college students and young adults) (Johnston et al., 2021; Miech et al., 2020). The project gathers information on a wide variety of behaviors, including levels and types of drug use. In addition, MTF presents drug use information for different time frames, ranging from "ever" using a drug to "daily use" in the past 30 days.

Table 6.1 presents information on the lifetime, annual, past month, and daily prevalence of drug use for high school seniors graduating in 2020. Prevalence indicates how many respondents used the drug during the year, as opposed to how many times (incidence) the drug was used. A number of key observations can be made from this information. First, drug use varies greatly by type of drug. Second, only a small fraction of respondents uses any drug other than alcohol or tobacco on a regular basis. This table clearly supports arguments that much drug use—other than marijuana, alcohol, or cigarettes—is experimental.

TABLE 6.1 Lifetime, Annual, Past Month, and Daily Drug Use by 12th Graders, 2020

Drug	Lifetime	Annual	Past Month	Daily Use
Any illicit drug	46.6	36.8	22.2	
Marijuana	43.7	35.2	21.1	6.9
Any illicit drug besides marijuana	17.5	11.4	4.8	
Inhalants	3.8	1.1	0.7	
Cocaine	4.1	2.9	0.8	
Crack	1.6	1.2	0.4	
Heroin	0.4	0.3	0.3	
Hallucinogens	7.5	5.3	1.8	
Amphetamines	7.3	4.3	1.7	
Methamphetamine	1.7	1.4	0.8	
Barbiturates	4.4	2.4	1.2	
Alcohol	61.5	55.3	33.6	2.7
Cigarettes	24.0		7.5	3.1
Any Vaping	47.2	39.0	28.2	
Vaping Nicotine	44.3	34.5	24.7	5.2
Vaping Marijuana	27.9	22.1	12.2	1.6

Source: Compiled by the authors from Johnston et al. (2021).

An important finding from the data on daily use is that usage varies considerably by drug. Only 6.9 percent claim daily use of marijuana, and about 3 percent claim daily alcohol use. Concerning past month usage, 22 percent reported use of any illicit drug but only about 5 percent (4.8 percent) reported use of a drug other than marijuana. About 21 percent reported use of marijuana and 33.6 percent reported use of alcohol. Three percent of seniors reported past month use of any prescription drug (not in Table 6.1), showing a continuing decrease from 8.6 percent in 2005. Under 2 percent reported past month use of amphetamines. For other drugs, past month use was roughly 1 percent. It is only when annual or lifetime figures are considered that drug use begins to appear to be a serious problem, with several categories of drugs being used by 5 percent or more of the high school senior respondents. Note that only 7.5 percent of 12th graders reported having smoked cigarettes in the last month, down from 36.5 percent in 1997 (not in Table 6.1).

The authors of Monitoring the Future (Johnston et al., 2021) conclude that adolescent use of most illicit drugs remained steady in 2020. Second, use of most psychotherapeutic drugs (amphetamines, tranquilizers, or narcotics other than heroin) declined. Cigarette smoking has been on a very substantial decline since the mid-1990s, but there was no further decline in 2020. "Alcohol remains the substance most widely used by today's teenagers" (Johnston et al., 2021). A positive sign was that vaping of nicotine and marijuana leveled and even reversed some in 2020, compared to dramatic increases in 2018 and 2019. The authors conclude that illicit drug use continues to be a "major concern" and that "[s]moking, drinking, and illicit drug use are leading causes of morbidity and mortality during adolescence as well as later in life" (Johnston et al., 2021:5). Marijuana use is associated with negative psychosocial outcomes and may adversely affect cognitive development (Paige & Colder, 2020). One specific reason for the danger of illicit drugs is that the makers and sellers of illicit drugs "seem to be totally unconcerned with adverse consequences for their users" (Johnston et al., 2021:5).

These self-report figures, however, must be considered cautiously due to the question of respondent representativeness in the MTF. Specifically, MTF data represent the responses from individuals who were attending school at the time of the survey. This ignores the fact that many youths drop out of school. Dropping out is especially great in the inner city, where the drug trade appears to be most concentrated. Johnston, O'Malley, and Bachman (1987) point out that roughly 15–20 percent of students drop out and are not included in the senior survey each year; moreover, they contend that dropouts tend to use drugs more often than those who remain in school. This suggests that the data underreport the level of drug use in the population. Given this caveat, the MTF data are useful from the point of view that the survey is conducted annually and provides a standardized set of data that can be compared over time.

TABLE 6.2 Drug Use by 12–17-Year-Olds, 2019

Drug	Ever Used	Past Year	Past Month
Any illicit drug	24.5	17.2	8.7
Marijuana/hashish	15.8	13.2	7.4
Cocaine	0.6	0.4	0.1
Inhalants	8.8	3.0	0.9
Hallucinogens	2.5	1.8	0.6
Psychotherapeutics	Not reported	4.3	1.3
Cigarettes	9.0	5.4	2.3
Alcohol	26.7	21.2	9.4

Source: Compiled by authors from Center for Behavioral Health Statistics and Quality: SAMHSA (2020). Available at www.samhsa.gov.

Another source of self-report data on youthful drug use is the **National Survey on Drug Use and Health**, which is conducted by the Substance Abuse and Mental Health Services Administration (SAMHSA). The figures from the survey reflect drug use among a sample of youths age 12 to 17, as compared to the data on students in individual grades in the MTF Project. The SAMHSA survey, therefore, includes a larger number of younger respondents. Table 6.2 presents ever used, past year, and past month use data for the 2019 household survey. The pattern in the results is similar to the MTF data in terms of both use in different time frames and drug categories. Alcohol is the most commonly used substance, followed by marijuana and cigarettes. In addition, use is greater when longer time frames are considered. The figures are smaller in most categories compared to the MTF data for high school respondents. The data in these tables, particularly those reflecting lifetime or annual use (and to some extent monthly use), often form the basis for claims of a drug problem or epidemic in the country. Use in the past year should not be used as an indicator of a drug "problem" because such use may simply reflect experimentation. When attention is focused on a more accurate indicator of serious abuse (such as daily use within the last 30 days, instead of on any use within the last year or even 30 days), the percentages of adolescents reporting frequent use are much lower.

Trend data for monthly drug use by 12th graders (see Table 6.3) suggest similar conclusions from the preceding discussion. First, past month use of any illicit drug has been a little over 20 percent since 1995. Much of this statistic is driven by marijuana usage, as use of drugs other than marijuana has decreased from 10 percent in 1995 to less than 5 percent in 2020. Use of drugs such as cocaine and heroin has been relatively rare and has remained low throughout the years. Only minor fluctuations in use appear in the data over time. Alcohol, tobacco, and marijuana have traditionally dominated the

WEB ACTIVITY

The SAMHSA data can be investigated further at www.samhsa.gov (search for "Detailed Tables").

TABLE 6.3 **Trends in Past Month Prevalence of Use of Selected Drugs for 12th Graders, Selected Years**

	Year					
	1995	2000	2005	2010	2015	2020
Any illicit drug	23.8	24.9	23.1	23.8	23.6	22.2
Any illicit drug other than marijuana	10.0	10.4	10.3	8.6	7.6	4.8
Marijuana/hashish	21.2	21.6	19.8	21.4	21.3	21.1
Cocaine	1.8	2.1	2.3	1.3	1.1	0.8
Crack	1.0	1.0	1.0	0.7	0.6	0.4
Heroin	0.6	0.7	0.5	0.4	0.3	0.3
Alcohol	51.3	50.0	47.0	41.2	35.3	33.6
Cigarettes	33.5	31.4	23.2	19.2	11.4	7.5
Vaping Nicotine						24.7
Vaping Marijuana						12.2

Source: Compiled by the authors from Johnston et al. (2021).

drug use data. Of particular note is that the most prevalently used substance (alcohol) has seen a significant decrease in use over the past 30 years (from a high of 72 percent in 1980 to a much lower figure of 33.6 percent in 2020). Use of marijuana/hashish, the second most commonly used substance, has been approximately 20 percent since 1995. Again, recent marijuana law changes may affect teen use in the next few years, although most 12th graders recently reported that they would be little affected by legalization (Miech et al., 2020). Cigarette smoking is down, but vaping nicotine is now a concern.

One major concern with the use of the MTF or the SAMHSA data is over the representativeness of the results. Various researchers argue that the level of drug use is much greater than appears in these sources. They claim that if more representative samples of youths and samples of inner-city residents were used, the figures would be substantially higher. In other words, in certain neighborhoods significant numbers of students who use drugs may be absent on the day of the survey or may have dropped out of school. On the other hand, surveys of dropouts could be biased toward portraying drug use in its most negative light.

Self-report figures, even those based on samples from high-crime areas, suggest that the drug problem can be blown out of proportion. The data show that the use of illicit drugs is not rampant in society. Relatively few individuals use illicit drugs with even a gross measure of regularity (within 30 days). Figures for daily use fall to almost zero for most illicit drugs. Nevertheless, use of alcohol, marijuana, and cigarettes (and vaping) does present cause for concern.

Concern over drugs is also justified in light of the availability of drugs. Besides asking about drug use, the MTF Project also asks students about the

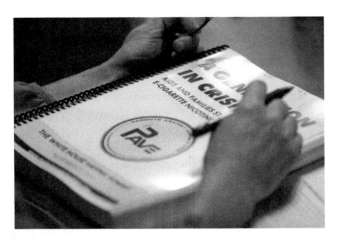

A member of Parents Against Vaping E-Cigarettes (PAVe) holds papers during a meeting on youth vaping in the Cabinet Room at the White House in November 2019.

CREDIT: Yuri Gripas/Abaca/Sipa USA (Sipa via AP Images)

TABLE 6.4 Percent Reporting Drugs Very Easy or Fairly Easy to Get, 2019*			
Drug	**8th Graders**	**10th Graders**	**12th Graders**
Marijuana	32.0	59.4	78
LSD	7.9	16.7	28.2
PCP	5.6	9.5	11
Cocaine Powder	8.6	12.9	19.9
Crack	8.3	11.2	16.9
Heroin	6.4	10.5	16.1
Other Narcotics	9.3	17.1	31.0
Amphetamines	12.4	21.4	39.0
Barbiturates	10.8	16.6	23.6
Tranquilizers	10.9	18.1	14.7
Alcohol	46.1	64.8	84.4
Cigarettes	39.4	55.0	71.0
E-liquid with Nicotine (for Vaping)	39.3	64.1	79.3
E-liquid for Marijuana Vaping	24.2**	47.7**	58.2**

Note: * Monitoring the Future presents some but not all statistics for 2020 due to small samples sizes. Accordingly, this Table uses mostly 2019 statistics. ** These are 2020 statistics.

Source: Compiled by the authors from Johnston et al. (2021).

ease of availability of different drugs (see Table 6.4). The figures are lowest for 8th-grade respondents and highest for 12th graders. Alcohol, cigarettes, and marijuana are the easiest drugs to obtain. Disturbing percentages of 12th graders report that cocaine powder (19.9 percent), heroin (16 percent), amphetamines (39 percent), and barbiturates (23.6 percent) are easy, very easy, or fairly easy to obtain. A recent development is that almost 80 percent of 12th graders report that E-liquid with nicotine for vaping is very easy or fairly easy to obtain, compared to 58 percent who say the same for E-liquid for marijuana vaping.

To summarize, the conclusion of the authors of Monitoring the Future that adolescent drug is a "major concern" and that "[s]moking, drinking, and illicit drug use are leading causes of morbidity and mortality during adolescence as well as later in life" (Johnston et al., 2021:5) merits repeating. As will be discussed in the next section, another concern is that substance use is often associated with delinquent behavior. A final note is that the availability of marijuana, alcohol, and prescription pain relievers is an important contributing factor to adolescent drug use.

Drug Use among Offenders

While information on the general population suggests that drug use is a problem but that relatively few youths use drugs on a regular basis, data based on offenders present a different picture. Various data sources suggest that drug use is a critical problem for offenders, including adolescents.

One source for information on drug use among offenders is official data. In 2019, more than 75,000 juveniles were arrested for drug abuse, liquor law, or drunkenness violations in the United States. Juveniles made up about 5 percent of persons arrested for drug abuse violations, 1 percent for drunkenness, and 15 percent for liquor law violations (FBI, 2020). According to juvenile court statistics, approximately 47,400 cases resulted in petitions to juvenile court for drug law violations in 2018. About 7 percent of the cases resulting in out-of-home placement involved drugs as the most serious offense (Hockenberry & Puzzanchera, 2020). Self-report data on incarcerated youths also can provide information on the use of illicit drugs. The most recent Survey of Youth in Residential Placement indicated that 44 percent of the youths surveyed said that they were or were accused of being under the influence of drugs or alcohol or both at the time of the offense leading to their placement. Sixty-one percent of the youths with drug offenses reported being under the influence (Sedlak & Bruce, 2016). Thus, arrest, court, and correctional data provide support for the argument that youthful drug use is highly related to contact with the juvenile justice system.

Youths in custody clearly use alcohol and other drugs at higher rates than youths in the general population. Specifically, almost 75 percent of youths in custody report having tried alcohol compared to 56 percent of youths in the general population. Similarly, 84 percent of youths in custody report using marijuana compared to 30 percent in the general population. Finally, half of youths in custody admit trying illegal drugs other than marijuana, compared to 27 percent of peers in the general population (Sedlak & McPherson, 2010b).

It must be remembered that statistics on youths involved in the juvenile court and institutions represent a worst-case scenario. These youths are not indicative of the majority of juveniles in the population and, therefore, the drug use figures are not applicable to youths not involved in the juvenile justice system. Indeed, this information reflects only those individuals who are caught by the system. It is possible that the use of drugs increases the risk of apprehension. Despite this fact, drug use is integrally related to juvenile justice system involvement.

A Summary of Youthful Drug Use

The fact that relatively few youths use drugs, particularly on a regular basis, does not mean that adolescent drug use is not a problem. At the same time, high levels of drug use by offending youths do not mean that use is a rampant problem in society. Rather, these figures point out that drugs are used by a small but significant number of youths, particularly by offenders, and that the problem needs to be addressed. To repeat the current assessment in the Monitoring the Future report, drug use is a complex phenomenon and varies by drug and is "a major concern for the nation" (Johnston et al., 2021:5). (For updates on use, see periodic reports issued by NIDA [National Institute on Drug Abuse, 2021].) Use becomes a greater issue if it engenders further delinquent behavior. The degree to which drug use causes delinquency, however, has been the subject of much debate.

THE DRUGS–DELINQUENCY CONNECTION

Statistics showing drug use among delinquent youths (particularly incarcerated individuals) are often pointed to as proof that drug use causes delinquency. The evidence on the drugs–delinquency connection, however, is unclear. A variety of studies note that there is a high degree of correspondence between drug use and delinquent/criminal behavior (see, e.g., Phillips, 2012, 2017; Rocca, Verde, & Gatti, 2019; Walters, 2014). What is not clear is which one causes which, or whether they are both the result of something else.

Possible Relationships

The actual relationship between drug use and delinquency can take a variety of forms (see Figure 6.1). White (1990) outlines four possible relationships (see also Bennett, Holloway, & Farrington, 2008). First, drug use may cause delinquent activity. This argument typically focuses on the high cost of drugs and the need for youths to commit property crimes in order to secure the funds needed to buy drugs. Indeed, various authors point out that drug users are often involved in property offenses (Chaiken & Chaiken, 1982; Johnson et al., 1985). Such an "economic need" argument, however, is only one reason that drug use would cause other forms of deviance. Goldstein (1989) suggests that drugs also may cause crime through their psychopharmacological effects and through systemic violence inherent in the drug market. **Psychopharmacological explanations** suggest that drugs have a direct effect on the user, either physically or psychologically, that impel him or her to act in a certain way. **Systemic violence** refers to violence due to factors such as competition between dealers, retaliation for the sale of bad drugs, the simple need to obtain a drug, or other factors related to the sale and marketing of drugs.

FIGURE 6.1
Possible
Relationships
between Drug Use
and Delinquency

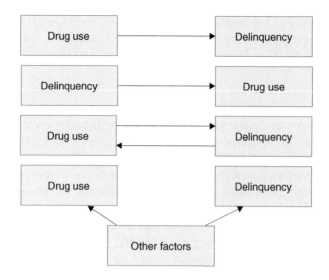

A second approach to the drugs–delinquency relationship is the view that delinquent activity causes drug use (White, 1990). This line of reasoning argues that delinquency leads to association with deviant peers and that it is within these peer groups that drug use appears (Akers, Krohn, Lonza-Kaduce, & Radosevich, 1979; Johnston, O'Malley, & Eveland, 1978). This explanation views drug use as a form of deviance just like other delinquent acts. As youths associate with others who are involved in deviant behavior, they will participate in the same activities as the other youths. If the group is using drugs, the individual will be more prone to use drugs.

A third possible relationship views drug use and delinquency as feeding one another in a **reciprocal relationship**. This approach is a combination of the first two. The final possibility is that there is a **spurious relationship** involving drug use and delinquency. Under this assumption there would be other factors that cause both drug use and delinquency. In essence, the theoretical explanations for why a youth becomes involved in delinquency would also apply to the reasons for drug use. Drug use and delinquency are simply two manifestations of the same basic problems, such as a broader deviant lifestyle (Bennett et al., 2008). Identifying which of the four possible relationships between drug use and delinquency is correct is not an easy task. Most attempts have focused on uncovering the time order between the two variables. That is, which came first, drug use or delinquency?

Walters (2014; 2017) has made an important contribution to this discussion by coining the term the "worst of both worlds hypothesis." This means that substance misuse and crime/delinquency together ("comorbid") are more harmful to future adjustment than either substance misuse or delinquency involvement alone. Youths with both problems as early adolescents were more likely to engage in future substance abuse and crime in late adolescence and early adulthood and were more likely to show such problems as moral disengagement, impulse control, and suppression of aggression.

RESEARCH ON THE DRUGS–DELINQUENCY RELATIONSHIP

Delinquency Causes Drug Use

Research on the temporal (time) order of drug use and delinquency reveals a complex relationship. As noted, there is consensus that there is a clear relationship between drugs and crime. In general, the odds of offending are between 2.8 and 3.8 times greater for drug users than nonusers. Odds vary by drug, with crack users and heroin users having much higher odds of offending than marijuana users (Bennett et al., 2008). A variety of studies suggest that the dominant direction in the relationship is from delinquent activity to drug use. In a study using longitudinal data on almost 2,000 high school graduates, Johnston et al. (1978) claim that general delinquency predates most drug use. They argue that youthful drug use is an extension of other deviant behavior. This same pattern of drug use following delinquency is uncovered by Inciardi, Horowitz, and Pottieger (1993) in a study of the behavior of serious inner-city delinquents. They claim that drug use most often appears after youths have become involved in minor delinquency. Other authors (Huba & Bentler, 1983; Kandel, Simcha-Fagan, & Davies, 1986; Speckart & Anglin, 1985) also note that delinquent behavior predates actual drug use. That is, the youths commit delinquent acts, join up with other delinquent peers, and enter into drug use along with their peers. Some of the reasoning about crime or delinquency leading to drug use is that criminals and delinquents use drugs as "chemical recreation" (partying) after successful crime commission (Bennett et al., 2008).

Data from the National Youth Survey (NYS) support this basic argument. The NYS collected data on delinquency, drug use, and demographic factors on a yearly basis from a representative sample of youths. The use of a panel design allows for the inspection of changes in behavior over time and the identification of the temporal order in the data. Elliott, Huizinga, and Ageton (1985) note that minor delinquency and tobacco use typically precede the use of alcohol and other drugs. Similarly, Huizinga, Menard, and Elliott (1989) show a general progression from minor delinquency to alcohol use, Index offending, marijuana use, and polydrug use, in that order. With the exception of alcohol, the data show that drug use temporally follows more general delinquent behavior. From these studies, drug use is a product and not a cause of deviant behavior.

Drug Use Causes Delinquency

Other studies lend support to the argument that the relationship is in the opposite direction—that drug use precedes and causes delinquency or crime. Ball, Shaffer, and Nurco (1983) report that heroin addicts commit four to six times as many offenses when they are actively using drugs than when not using drugs. Based on subjects in public drug treatment programs, Collins, Hubbard, and Rachal (1985) point out that daily heroin/cocaine users tend to commit substantially more property offenses than nonusers or weekly users. Anglin and Hser (1987) and Anglin and Speckart (1988) note that both official and self-reported criminal activity, particularly property offenses and drug possession/sales, increase with narcotics use. Other studies report a similar trend of elevated criminality during periods of heavy drug use (Nurco, Kinlock, Hanlon, & Ball, 1988; Watts & Wright, 1990). Stevens, May, Rice, and Jarjoura (2011) agree that some youths begin drug use for the immediate internal gratification, but that then involvement in peer groups influences continued use of hard drugs.

Rocca et al. (2019) argue that cannabis use and binge drinking together, that is, more problematic forms of substance abuse, increase the odds of being involved in more serious delinquency. Phillips (2017) notes that using and selling drugs is a combination most likely to be associated with criminal activity. DeLisi, Angton, Behnken, and Kusow (2015) conclude that juvenile drug use is significantly related to criminal careers but that property-related delinquent offenses are the strongest predictors of a habitual criminal career.

Reciprocity and Spuriousness

The fact that no consensus has emerged on the correct causal direction between drug use and delinquency suggests that the more plausible explanation is that the relationship is reciprocal. That is, criminal activity leads to drug use, and drug use leads to criminal activity. Support for a reciprocal relationship can be found in many of the same studies presented above. A number of authors note that increased drug use by already delinquent or criminal individuals leads to higher delinquency levels or more serious offending, not to a first offense (Anglin & Hser, 1987; Huizinga, Loeber, & Thornberry, 1995; Inciardi et al., 1993; Nurco et al., 1988). Similarly, Huizinga et al. (1989) point out that while delinquency precedes drug use, polydrug use is a typical precursor of serious persistent delinquency. Van Kammen and Loeber's (1994) analysis of the Pittsburgh youth study data reports that property offending predicted the onset of drug use. At the same time, however, the initiation of drug use was related to escalating participation in personal offenses. From these studies, it would appear that, regardless of which came first, drug use and delinquency contribute to each other. It appears that drug use leads to crime, and crime leads to drug use.

Recent research on serious juvenile offenders also points to a reciprocal relationship. A follow-up study of more than 1,300 serious juvenile offenders over seven years showed that "substance use and serious offending fluctuate in similar patterns over time, suggesting a reciprocal or sequential relationship" (Mulvey et al., 2010).

Similar to the argument for a reciprocal relationship is the view that posits a spurious relationship between drug use and delinquency. This simply means that drug use and crime are contemporaneous—they exist at the same time and vary in a similar fashion, and neither is the ultimate cause of the other. Rather, they are caused by either the same common factors or by different factors. Various authors (Kandel, Simcha-Fagan, & Davies, 1986; Passini, 2012; White, Pandina, & LaGrange, 1987) argue that there are common causal factors, such as peer and school influences, that underlie both delinquency and drug use. Some call explanations like this *common cause explanations* (Bennett et al., 2008). Carpenter, Glassner, Johnson, and Loughlin (1988) claim that the spurious nature of the drugs–delinquency relationship is evident in the fact that few youths routinely use drugs and commit delinquent acts. They further note that the majority of drug use and delinquent actions occur in the absence of the other behavior. The more plausible argument, therefore, is for a spurious relationship. Similarly, the same analysis of the NYS data that points out a sequence of behavior beginning with minor offending and ending with poly drug use (Huizinga et al., 1989) concludes that the actual cause of the behaviors probably lies with a common set of spurious influences. Other research leads to the same conclusion (Fagan & Weis, 1990; Fagan et al., 1990; White, 1990). One causal factor is involvement in drug dealing (Seffrin & Domahidi, 2014).

Summarizing the Relationship

The fact that drug use is related to delinquency cannot be disputed. While the causal relationship is unclear, a strong correlation between the two behaviors means that drug use can be used as a predictor of other delinquent behavior (Bennett et al., 2008; Mulvey et al., 2010). The research also suggests that each behavior contributes to the other, thereby providing insight for intervention and treatment. It may be possible to attack delinquency by attacking drug use. Drug use in itself is a delinquent act that can bring about action by the juvenile justice system. By acting on it the system is intervening in the lives of youths who are at a higher risk of participating in other delinquent activities. Finally, it is evident that other factors, such as low self-control, contribute to both drug use and delinquency (Bennett et al., 2008).

INTERVENTIONS

Interventions aimed at drug use and abuse can take a variety of forms and fall under the general categories of treatment and prevention. Treatment programs typically are aimed at those individuals who already have established a pattern of continued drug use. In essence, treatment programs are geared toward addicted individuals and can take a variety of forms, including maintenance programs, detoxification programs, therapeutic/residential communities, and outpatient programs. Prevention programs are geared more at keeping individuals from initial involvement with drugs or, at the least, keeping casual users from more frequent and varied drug use. Drug prevention programs for juveniles often include a variety of approaches, such as information dissemination, affective education, and resistance and social skills training. Each of the various treatment and prevention approaches will be examined below.

WEB ACTIVITY

NIDA provides a great deal of information on drug treatment, including materials on specific programs and drugs. These can be accessed at www.drugabuse.gov.

Treatment Approaches

What is known about the impact of drug treatment programs comes mainly from the study of programs focusing primarily on adults. This is because there have been relatively few studies of treatment programs for youths and because most juvenile interventions take a more preventive approach. The increased concern over drug use and related problem behavior (such as violence) has resulted in greater attention to treatment programs for juveniles. While programs may have a different emphasis, many similarities and common features appear across programs. For example, counseling and therapy of one sort or another appear in virtually all of the programs. The following discussion offers examples of the more well-known or effective treatment approaches. Other programs appear elsewhere in this book.

Research on treatment programs has led NIDA to list 13 principles of effective treatment (see Box 6.1). Rather than attempt to offer a prescriptive set of activities for an "ideal" program, NIDA's principles address more generalized issues that can be implemented in different ways. Indeed, the second principle notes that no one program is effective for all individuals or situations. In general terms, the principles argue that treatment must be responsive to the multiple needs of each individual.

BOX 6.1 NIDA'S 13 PRINCIPLES OF EFFECTIVE TREATMENT FOR DRUG ABUSE

1. Addiction is a complex but treatable disease that affects brain function and behavior.

2. No single treatment is right for everyone.

3. People need to have quick access to treatment.

4. Effective treatment addresses all of the patient's needs, not just his or her drug use.

5. Remaining in treatment for an adequate period of time is critical.

6. Behavioral therapies—including individual, family, or group counseling—are the most commonly used forms of drug treatment.

7. Medications are an important element of treatment, especially when combined with counseling and other behavioral therapies.

8. An individual's treatment and services plan must be assessed continually and modified as necessary to ensure that it meets his or her changing needs.

9. Many drug-addicted individuals also have other mental disorders.

10. Medically assisted detoxification is only the first stage of addiction treatment and by itself does little to change long-term drug abuse.

11. Treatment does not need to be voluntary to be effective.

12. Drug use during treatment must be monitored continuously, as lapses during treatment do occur.

13. Treatment programs should test patients for the presence of HIV/AIDS, hepatitis B and C, tuberculosis, and other infectious diseases, as well as provide targeted risk-reduction counseling, linking patients to treatment if necessary.

Source: NIDA (2018).

There appears to be consensus that there are effective drug abuse treatment programs for adolescents in general and for juvenile offenders in particular (see, e.g., Drug Strategies, 2005; Engle & MacGowan, 2009; Henderson et al., 2007; Pealer, 2017). NIDA (2018) lists the following approaches as evidence-based approaches: cognitive–behavioral therapy, contingency management interventions, community reinforcement approaches, motivational enhancement therapy, family behavioral therapy, and behavioral therapies primarily for adolescents. Cognitive–behavioral approaches, among other things, address thinking errors, learning self-control such as anger management, and identifying one's problems and goals (Latessa, Johnson, & Koetzle, 2020). Elements of effective treatment programs include developmentally appropriate treatment, qualified staff, use of standardized assessment tools, comprehensive services, family involvement in treatment, the need to address co-occurring disorders, continuing care, and the assessment of treatment outcomes. A program using Motivational Enhancement Therapy/Cognitive Behavioral Therapy-5 resulted in about half of the treated youths meeting recovery criteria, including abstinence from all substances and reporting no substance problems (Hunter et al., 2012). Unfortunately, juvenile offenders with drug problems are often treated in fragmented ways by systems of care that lack the resources to use evidence-based practices (Henderson et al., 2007). A positive note is that effective programs exist and can produce cost savings. For example, the FIT (Family Integrated Transitions for Probation Youth) Program in Washington State produced approximately $46,000 in benefits per youth served (Barnoski, 2009). Also, there is promising evidence that mentoring may contribute to reducing marijuana and illicit drug use by youths (Erdem & Kaufman, 2020). (For resources on specific evidence-based practices, see Stephens, 2011. For an in-depth examination of one therapeutic community for juveniles, see Pealer, Terry, & Adams, 2017.)

Maintenance and Detoxification Programs

Maintenance programs, a common intervention for addicted individuals, seek to establish a steady state in which the individual does not experience withdrawal symptoms when the drug begins to wear off. Consequently, the user will be able to function more normally and participate in everyday activities without the constant need for the drug (Stephens, 1987). The most common maintenance program involves the use of methadone, an oral substitute for heroin. Besides periodic checks (usually urinalysis) to establish abstinence from other drugs, maintenance programs rely heavily on individual and group counseling and the establishment of behavioral guidelines (Anglin & Hser, 1990). Some programs also include incentives/rewards given to clients who test negative for drug use (NIDA, 1999). Evaluations of maintenance programs generally report reduced drug usage and the commission of fewer crimes by patients when they are in the program (Hser, Anglin, & Chou, 1988; Olive et al., 2010). However, maintenance programs in correctional institutions reduced drug use but not recidivism (MacKenzie & Farrington, 2015). Unfortunately, the impact of these programs tends to disappear after program participation, and patients return to pre-program levels of drug use and criminal activity when they leave the program (Anglin, Speckart, Booth, & Ryan, 1989).

Often closely aligned with maintenance programs are programs that empha-size **detoxification**. This approach attempts to remove an individual from an addiction by weaning him or her off drugs. Drugs are used over the short term to minimize the pain and discomfort of withdrawal. Detoxification programs target a wide range of drugs, from alcohol to heroin, and can be found in many hospitals and facilities throughout the country. Anglin and Hser (1990) point out that while short-term follow-ups show that detoxification is successful at eliminating drug use, detoxification has not been adequately evaluated over the long term. Unfortunately, some drug users rely on detoxification to reduce the need for massive amounts of drugs to get high. They then return to more normal drug use until they again reach a point at which small amounts are no longer sufficient to serve their needs (Bellis, 1981).

Evaluations of both maintenance and detoxification programs are somewhat mixed. Sells and Simpson (1979) note that they are effective at lowering arrests and illegal activities among juvenile drug abusers. Other positive support is found in the fact that criminal activity is lower among drug users in treatment than among those receiving no intervention (Wish, Toborg, & Bellassai, 1988). NIDA (2018), in its list of effective principles for treatment, notes that the use of medications is an important part of treatment for some individuals (see Principle #7). Critics, however, allege that they are crutches that do not solve the problem, but instead lead to a nonproductive lifestyle of methadone, alcohol, other drugs, and petty crime (Stephens, 1987). An additional problem is that many maintenance drugs become simple substitutes for the original drug. A prime example of this is the fact that heroin was developed to solve morphine addiction. Today, instead of curing heroin addiction, methadone addiction has itself become an issue.

Therapeutic/Residential Communities and Outpatient Programs

Another major form of treatment, **therapeutic communities**, emphasizes the provision of a supportive, highly structured, family-like atmosphere within which individuals can be helped to alter their personality and develop social relationships conducive to conforming behavior (Anglin & Hser, 1990). Group sessions, called "games," often involve attention on one member because he or she is a new member of the therapeutic community, is suspected of violating a house rule, or is suspected of using drugs. Pressure is exerted to induce the person to admit the particular problem and the need for support from the group (Stephens, 1987). Group counseling is used to explore the reasons for drug use and to suggest alternative methods for dealing with the factors that lead to substance abuse. Therapeutic communities, such as Synanon, Daytop Village, and Phoenix House, boast positive results—including lower levels of drug use and criminal activity (Anglin & Hser, 1990; DeLeon & Rosenthal, 1989). The KEY/CREST program combines a residential therapeutic community with post-release assistance in the community. Along with the therapeutic community, clients participate in educational activities, HIV education, a 12-step alcohol program, and other activities aimed at preparing the clients for success out-side the institution. The New Vision Therapeutic Community program rests primarily on services while the clients are in prison, with an initial aftercare period upon release. Like the KEY/CREST program, clients undergo individual and group counseling, as well as educational activities.

A recent evaluation of a therapeutic community for juveniles did not produce a statistically significant decrease in recidivism. However, there were some problems in the treatment provided to the residents, and there was no aftercare supervision (Pealer, 2017).

A systematic review of drug treatment in correctional facilities showed some effectiveness. Specifically, therapeutic communities resulted in reduced recidivism and a trend toward reduction of relapse abuse. Group counseling reduced recidivism but not substance abuse relapse. Narcotics maintenance programs (e.g., methadone maintenance) reduced drug use but not recidivism (MacKenzie & Farrington, 2015). Therapeutic communities and methadone maintenance can also be cost-effective (Aos & Drake, 2013; WSIPP, 2016). One problem with drug treatment, however, is failure to complete the program. In one California program, for example, only 28 percent of the offenders completed the program.

The final treatment modality, **outpatient drug-free programs**, often follows similar approaches to those in therapeutic communities or residential settings. The greatest difference is the lack of a residential component. Individual and group counseling form the cornerstone of these programs. Programs such as Alcoholics Anonymous bring together current and former addicts to help one another stay off drugs. At meetings, members recount their drug histories and how the group is supporting them in their efforts to abstain from drug use. Other components of outpatient programs may include social skills training, vocational programming, social interaction, referral to other sources of assistance, and possibly short-term drug maintenance (Anglin & Hser, 1990). Several outpatient drug-free programs exist for youthful offenders. **Multi-Dimensional Family Therapy (MDFT)** is centered on the family, peers, and community influences around the youths. Similarly, Multisystemic Therapy addresses the multiple sources of inputs to youthful behavior, including the family, schools, peers, and neighborhoods (NIDA, 1999). The programs assess the needs of the youths and the youths' families, and provide intensive services to the youths within the different social contexts in which they operate. The intent of the programs is to ensure that youths and their needs do not go unaddressed. Each of these programs has been successful at reducing recidivism and drug use (Filges, Rasmussen, Andersen, & Jorgensen, 2015; NIDA, 1999; Office of Justice Programs, 2000).

Treatment Summary

There are several problems with the various treatment approaches. First, it is often difficult to motivate addicts and abusers to enter a treatment program. Convincing addicts that they have a problem is often half the battle against the problem. Besides getting drug users into programs, it is also difficult to retain them. Studies of therapeutic communities, for example, have indicated that up to 70 percent of those entering such communities drop out before completing the program (Stephens, 1987; see also Lipton, 1995). One solution to the participation problem may entail mandatory participation as an outcome of either criminal or civil litigation. Although some research has shown coerced treatment to be effective (Collins, Cuddy, & Martin, 2017), a recent systematic review found little evidence that compulsory drug treatment reduces drug use or criminal recidivism (Werb et al., 2016).

Despite various qualifications, treatment appears to be effective at reducing the use of and need for drugs (Fareed et al., 2011). In one summary evaluation of drug treatment, Simpson and Sells (1982) report lower drug use, lower criminal behavior, and improved employment status for clients as long as six years after the end of treatment. Non-treatment control clients fared significantly worse. MacKenzie's review concludes that "overall, drug treatment is effective in reducing the recidivism of drug-involved offenders" (2006:264; see also MacKenzie & Freeland, 2012). Conversely, Stephens (1987) suggests that maturing out of the addiction cycle may be the most frequent way out of the drug problem. As addicts age, it is simply harder physically to be a drug addict. As a result, some addicts find it easier to give up drugs than to continue addiction. Walker notes that there are not enough treatment programs available for all the persons who need services and that relapse into use is frequent. He adds that individual commitment to stop using drugs is critical, but that treatment programs cannot produce that commitment to quit. So his overall conclusion is that the evidence about the effectiveness of treatment programs is "mixed" (Walker, 2015:355).

Prevention Approaches

The National Institute on Drug Abuse offers 16 principles of effective drug prevention (see Box 6.2). These include a focus on protective factors; reducing risk factors; including families, peers, and communities in the interventions; dealing with social competence; coupling multiple approaches; and recognizing the long-term needs of the clients (NIDA, 2011). Many prevention programs incorporate more than one approach and rely on input from a variety of sources, such as the schools, families, and the community. These approaches can be seen in several of the prevention programs discussed below.

WEB ACTIVITY

As with treatment information, NIDA has a wealth of materials available on drug prevention. See www.drugabuse.gov.

The "Just Say No" Approach

Perhaps the most direct and simplest prevention programs are those that encourage youths to simply say "no" and resist drug use. During the 1980s, the federal government pushed "Just Say No" as the cornerstone of its prevention activities. This approach assumes that juvenile drug use develops out of peer interaction and that use occurs mainly in group situations. Children, therefore, are encouraged to make a personal decision in the face of peer influences to refuse any offer to use illicit drugs. Included in this approach is the basic message that drugs are harmful. The emphasis is on total avoidance of drugs.

BOX 6.2 NIDA'S 16 PRINCIPLES OF EFFECTIVE PREVENTION FOR DRUG ABUSE

1. Prevention programs should enhance protective factors and reverse or reduce risk factors.

2. Prevention programs should address all forms of drug abuse, alone or in combination, including underage use of legal drugs; the use of illegal drugs; and the inappropriate use of legally obtained substances, prescription medications, or over-the-counter drugs.

3. Prevention programs should address the type of drug abuse problem in the local community, target modifiable risk factors, and strengthen identified protective factors.

4. Prevention programs should be tailored to address risks specific to population or audience characteristics, such as age, gender, and ethnicity, to improve program effectiveness.

5. Family-based prevention programs should enhance family bonding and relationships and include parenting skills; practice in developing, discussing, and enforcing family policies on substance abuse; and training in drug education and information.

6. Prevention programs can be designed to intervene as early as preschool to address risk factors for drug abuse, such as aggressive behavior, poor social skills, and academic difficulties.

7. Prevention programs for elementary school children should target improving academic and social-emotional learning to address risk factors for drug abuse.

8. Prevention programs for middle or junior high and high school students should increase academic and social competence.

9. Prevention programs aimed at general populations at key transition points, such as the transition to middle school, can produce beneficial effects even among high-risk families and children.

10. Community prevention programs that combine two or more effective programs can be more effective than a single program alone.

11. Community prevention programs reaching populations in multiple settings are most effective when they present consistent, community-wide messages in each setting.

12. When communities adapt programs to match their needs, community norms, or differing cultural requirements, they should retain core elements of the original research-based intervention.

13. Prevention programs should be long-term with repeated interventions to reinforce the original prevention goals.

14. Prevention programs should include teacher training on good classroom management practices such as rewarding appropriate student behavior.

15. Prevention programs are most effective when they employ interactive techniques, such as peer discussion and parent role-playing, that allow for active involvement in learning about drug abuse and reinforcing skills.

16. Research-based prevention programs can be cost-effective.

Source: NIDA (2014).

The total avoidance of illegal drugs in light of peer pressure through a simple "no" response, however, is somewhat shortsighted. Trebach (1987) compares such a prevention approach to related efforts to tell kids to abstain from any premarital sexual activity. As some children are going to use drugs or engage in sex no matter what adult society says, there is an unrealistic naiveté involved in "Just Say No" and similar campaigns. In addition, there may be a certain amount of hypocrisy associated with a total abstinence crusade. Youths recognize drug use by adults and are influenced by the advertising that is aimed at adults. Some "Just Say No" advocates recognize that youths will use drugs anyway but justify the approach as a way to convey a message against drugs.

Knowledge/Education Programs

A related approach to "Just Say No" programs is the provision of factual knowledge about drugs and their effects. The **knowledge approach** entails providing youths with information on different types of drugs, such as the physical and psychological effects of the drugs, as well as the extent, impact, and possible legal consequences of drug use. In many instances these programs are offered as a part of the normal school curriculum. The basic assumption is that such knowledge will allow the individual to make an informed choice about drug use. It is further assumed that informed youths will opt against using drugs.

Interestingly, evaluations of knowledge/education approaches often suggest that the programs increase drug use by participants. What appears to be happening is that the increased knowledge leads to enhanced curiosity and experimentation by youths in a kind of "I want to find out for myself" attitude (Abadinsky, 1989; Botvin, 1990; Botvin & Dusenbury, 1989). Based on information from 143 prevention programs, Tobler (1986) concluded that knowledge programs fail to show any reductions in drug use behavior. The single point on which these programs can demonstrate success is in their ability to increase a subject's knowledge about drugs (Botvin, 1990).

On the other hand, there is evidence that school-based programs that go beyond simply imparting factual knowledge can be effective. Emmers, Bekkering, and Hannes (2015) looked at systematic reviews of studies on school prevention programs and found small but consistent effects for such programs. Factors related to preventing alcohol and other drug misuse were whether the programs were affective-based (see next section), comprehensive (combining knowledge with social skills), and based on various learning models. Similarly, a review of multiple studies of knowledge-based and social skills-based programs found some evidence for effectiveness when the emphasis was on building decision-making skills, self-esteem, and resistance to peer pressure (Faggiano et al., 2005).

Affective Approaches

Rather than provide information about different substances and issues related directly to drug use, **affective interventions** focus attention on the individual. The assumption is that by building self-esteem, self-awareness, and feelings of self-worth, the youth will be able to make wise choices and resist pressures to use drugs. Few programs, however, rely solely on affective education elements. Programs such as Here's Looking at You 2000, which purports to use an affective approach, typically also include drug information and social skills training. Consequently, it becomes difficult to isolate the impact of affective elements such as self-esteem on subsequent drug involvement.

One well-known program that incorporates a heavy affective component is the Big Brothers/Big Sisters program. This program matches adult mentors with at-risk children in the community. The goal of the program is to provide positive role models to the youths, help build self-esteem, promote healthy attitudes and behaviors, and prepare the youths for daily living. A key component is helping youths feel good about themselves. The Big Brothers/Big Sisters program can be found in all 50 states. Evaluations of the initiative show success at reducing drug use, reducing arrests, increasing educational success, and improving the overall quality of life for youths (Office of Justice Programs, 2000). These results are in contrast to other evaluations of affective programs where the interventions have failed to find any significant impact on substance use (Kim, 1988; Kim, McLeod, & Shantzis, 1993; Tobler, 1986). It is possible that this failure is due to attempts to look at affective interventions separated from other preventive elements, such as those found in Big Brothers/Big Sisters and similar programs.

Life Skills Training Approaches

Perhaps the failure of affective approaches to have an impact on drug use is the failure to include other elements along with building self-esteem. **Life skills training** often includes affective interventions along with a variety of elements, ranging from basic personal and social skills development (which deal with general life situations and how to cope with them) to the provision of specific resistance skills aimed directly at substance-abuse issues. This approach assumes that individuals who use drugs are poorly prepared to address the issues and pressures involved in daily decision making. For example, individuals who find themselves left out of the societal mainstream due to lack of education and/or job training need to be taught the skills necessary to obtain a job and succeed in an acceptable manner. Individuals who get into trouble because they simply follow the group need to be taught how to be independent, make decisions for themselves, and resist following others into unwise situations. The key resistance skills taught include how to recognize a problematic situation and what alternatives are available to the individual, how to resist outside pressures (such as peers or advertising), how to identify help, how to cope with stress, and how to make wise choices.

Research on life skills or resistance skills training has shown positive results. Perhaps the best example of this impact comes from a series of studies dealing with tobacco, alcohol, and marijuana use by Botvin and associates (see, e.g., Botvin & Dusenbury, 1989; Botvin, Epstein, Baker, Diaz, & Ifill-Williams, 1997; Botvin, Griffin, Paul, & Macaulay, 2003). In these studies, "life skills training" was successful at reducing the number of youths using drugs. Positive results also appear in evaluations of other programs that focus on life skills, social competence, and related topics (see, e.g., Eisen, Zellman, Massett, & Murray, 2002; Hawkins, Catalano, Kosterman, Abbott, & Hill, 1999). While most of the analyses focus on relatively short-term effects, positive outcomes do appear in longer follow-up assessments.

The D.A.R.E. Program

Perhaps the best-known drug prevention program in existence today is the **Drug Abuse Resistance Education (D.A.R.E.)** program, which incorporates elements of all the previously discussed approaches to prevention. D.A.R.E. is a police-taught, school-based program that began in the Los Angeles United School District in 1983. The program is aimed primarily at elementary students in the fifth or sixth grade, although there are companion programs for younger and older youths as well as for the parents of participating students. The D.A.R.E. curriculum is taught by police officers who have been trained by the program, and it is offered as part of the normal school experience. The topics covered in the program have recently been revised; the current curriculum reflects aspects of affective training, "Just Say No" approaches, peer resistance, and social skills training. The primary focus of the program is on enhancing the social skills of the individual.

Based on its widespread adoption by schools in every state, one would assume that the program has proven successful at combating youthful substance use. Interestingly, this is not the case; the program does not prevent drug use. Based on multiple studies over many years, Rosenbaum recommends policymakers to "Just Say No to D.A.R.E. In light of consistent evidence of ineffectiveness from multiple studies with high validity, public funding of the core D.A.R.E. program should be eliminated or greatly reduced" (Rosenbaum, 2007:815).

As noted in Chapter 12, in response to the research findings of lack of effectiveness, D.A.R.E. has been reimaged as **"Keepin' It REAL."** Police officers teach a 10-session curriculum to children and adolescents in schools. The focus of the program has shifted from drug prevention to teaching resistance skills. REAL stands for Refuse, Explain, Avoid, and Leave, and the program provides skills for youths to address situations, events, and people who promote or encourage them to use drugs or participate in other problem behaviors. Evaluations of the new program (Hecht et al., 2003; Hecht, Graham, & Elek, 2006; Kulis, Nieri, Yabiku, Stromwall, & Marsiglia, 2007) report reduced drug usage, altered attitudes, and increased use of resistance strategies.

A police officer teaches a D.A.R.E. class to 5th-grade students at Eads Elementary School in 2013. Though widely adopted by schools in every state, there is consistent evidence of the program's ineffectiveness from multiple studies with high validity.

CREDIT: AP Photo/ *The Times*, John Luke

BOX 6.3 911 GOOD SAMARITAN LAW

Forty-seven states and the District of Columbia have passed Good Samaritan Overdose Laws. A typical law provides protection against arrest and prosecution for small amounts of drugs for those who call 911 in an overdose emergency situation. Those in possession of large amounts or who are selling drugs would not receive protection. The objective is to encourage reporting of overdoses to prevent loss of life. Proponents argue that no one should fear going to jail if he or she is trying to save a life. Research indicates that the laws may result in lower rates of overdose deaths and increased reporting where citizens are aware of the law, but that awareness varies. On the other hand, if a state's law requires the caller to get treatment for herself, that may lower a person's willingness to call the police. Also, the law may not protect the caller from probation/parole violations, immigration enforcement, or child welfare consequences.

What do you think? How much protection against arrest and prosecution should there be for someone who reports an overdose?

Sources: U.S. Government Accountability Office (GAO) (2021); Drug Policy Alliance (2021).

A final note is that D.A.R.E. is another example of the panacea phenomenon (Finckenauer, 1982) in which common sense seems to say that a program is exactly what is needed for a particular problem, but evaluation research proves that it is not effective. (For a different law enforcement issue, namely a proposal about reporting drugs to the police, see Box 6.3.)

Prevention Summary

The evidence on prevention programs suggests that drug use can be impacted by certain types of programs. Resistance/life skills training appears to be the most promising at reducing the level of drug use, although more rigorous and extensive testing needs to be completed. On the other hand, programs based simply on knowledge provision may result in increased curiosity and experimentation with illicit drugs. Programs that stress self-esteem, self-awareness, and interpersonal growth in the absence of other strategies for dealing with life situations, including drugs (typically referred to as affective education programs), also fail to exhibit any strong influence on drug use (Botvin, 1990; Schaps, Moskowitz, Malvin, & Schaeffer, 1986; Tobler, 1986). Interactive programs are more effective than noninteractive programs (Tobler, 1997). In general, while many prevention programs exist and show promise, most still need to be evaluated with longer follow-up periods and better research designs (particularly using adequate comparison groups). Note that web-based programs have been developed, such as eCHECKUP TO GO, a personalized feedback intervention (Doumas, Esp, Turrisi, Bond, & Flay, 2020). (For an inventory of programs for the prevention and treatment of youth cannabis use, including level of evidence and benefit–cost percentage, see Washington State Institute for Public Policy, 2017.)

ALTERNATIVE RESPONSES TO DRUG USE

Responses to drug use do not always reflect pure treatment or prevention. The persistence of drug use in society over time, particularly coupled with the failure or modest impact of most prevention and treatment approaches, has prompted various alternate responses. Among the responses are increased enforcement of drug laws, the development of comprehensive programs that combine legal responses with treatment and prevention, and controversial responses, such as the legalization or decriminalization of drugs.

Increased Enforcement

The typical response in the United States is to invoke the legal process. Aggressive police tactics, strict prosecution, and mandatory sentencing are the norm in most communities. Examples of this include police crackdowns on drug markets, drug interdiction at borders, civil abatement procedures in court, and mandatory prison terms for drug possession or sale. This kind of "get tough" orientation has permeated the national drug policy in the past. Given the current turmoil surrounding policing, it is uncertain what direction both the federal government and local law enforcement agencies will pursue regarding drug enforcement in the next few years.

An approach that is part "get tough" and part treatment is the problem-solving, pulling levers approach. It involves tough enforcement and prosecution but also offers carrots such as treatment. An evaluation of such a police initiative in Rockford, Illinois, found that it did reduce drug crimes in the target area. The authors noted that this was consistent with similar positive outcomes for problem-oriented approaches in other cities (Corsaro, Brunson, & McGarrell, 2009).

Critics of the law enforcement approach to drugs argue that it is both ineffective and expensive. For example, the American Civil Liberties Union notes that in 2010 almost half of all drug arrests were arrests for possession of marijuana, and the cost was approximately $1.7 billion. Despite similar rates of use by blacks and whites, arrests have disproportionately involved black suspects. Further excessive costs include the costs of prosecuting drug cases and imprisoning many convicted of drug crimes; the estimated total cost of enforcement is $3.6 billion dollars a year. Thus, the ACLU advocates for legalization or decriminalization, having police departments de-emphasize drug enforcement, and ending any racial discrimination in enforcement (ACLU, 2013). Similarly, Human Rights Watch notes that criminalizing drugs has not reduced drug use; has harmed many persons with criminal records, imprisonment, and/or fees and fines; and can prevent people from getting health services. Human Rights Watch concludes that "[c]riminalizing drugs is not an effective public policy" (Human Rights Watch, 2016:11). See Box 6.4 for elements of the National Drug Control Strategy.

Enforcement Coupled with Treatment

The fact that many offenders use drugs and come to the juvenile justice system with an established pattern of substance use/abuse places the system in the position of needing to respond to the individual as both an offender and someone who needs help. As a result, both the adult and juvenile justice systems have developed processes that couple enforcement with treatment. Two examples of this are drug courts and the Breaking the Cycle program.

BOX 6.4 NATIONAL DRUG CONTROL STRATEGY

- Preventing drug use in our communities

- Seeking early intervention opportunities in health care

- Integrating treatment for substance use disorders into health care and supporting recovery

- Breaking the cycle of drug use, crime, and incarceration

- Disrupting domestic drug trafficking and production

- Strengthening international partnerships

- Improving information systems to better address drug use and its consequences

Source: The White House (2016).

Drug Courts

The drug court movement began in 1989, with the first juvenile **drug court** appearing in 1995. Based on the most recent national statistics, there are more than 300 juvenile drug courts and well over 1,000 adult drug courts in operation (National Drug Court Resource Center, 2017). The underlying philosophy for drug courts is to use the court's authority to promote participation in and successful completion of treatment aimed at reducing drug use and related criminal behavior. The courts represent a coalition of prosecutors, police, probation, judges, treatment professionals, social service agencies, and other community groups working together to get the offenders off drugs and keep them off drugs (Drug Courts Program Office, 2000). While the drug court process varies from location to location, there is a set of common core strategies that are found throughout most programs (see Box 6.5). Among the common elements are frequent appearances before the court, regular drug testing, treatment assessment, participation in treatment programs, focusing on families, working with schools, aftercare, and providing interventions that are tailored to the individual.

Advocates of drug courts point to a number of potential advantages resulting from the programs. One key advantage is providing treatment to offenders. While most correctional intervention programs, whether residential or nonresidential, offer the opportunity for some types of treatment component, their primary concern with suppression and control often means that treatment is not always available or appropriate. Drug courts, however, are premised upon the need to match offenders with appropriate treatments. The offenders who are admitted to the drug court program are guaranteed to receive some type of treatment. A second advantage is keeping the offender in the community and using community resources to address the offender's needs. The youths are not cut off from their family and community support groups, which are crucial for long-term success.

WEB ACTIVITY

The popularity of drug courts has resulted in a wealth of information on the approach. One good starting point is the National Drug Court Resource Center at www.ndcrc.org.

BOX 6.5 JUVENILE DRUG COURT STRATEGIES

1. Collaborative Planning—Engage all stakeholders in creating an interdisciplinary, coordinated, and systemic approach to working with youth and their families.

2. Teamwork—Develop and maintain an interdisciplinary, nonadversarial work team.

3. Clearly Defined Target Population and Eligibility Criteria—Define a target population and eligibility criteria that are aligned with the program's goals and objectives.

4. Judicial Involvement and Supervision—Schedule frequent judicial reviews and be sensitive to the effect that court proceedings can have on youth and their families.

5. Monitoring and Evaluation—Establish a system for program monitoring and evaluation to maintain quality of service, assess program impact, and contribute to knowledge in the field.

6. Community Partnerships—Build partnerships with community organizations to expand the range of opportunities available to youth and their families.

7. Comprehensive Treatment Planning—Tailor interventions to the complex and varied needs of youth and their families.

8. Developmentally Appropriate Services—Tailor treatment to the developmental needs of adolescents.

9. Gender-Appropriate Services—Design treatment to address the unique needs of each gender.

10. Cultural Competence—Create policies and procedures that are responsive to cultural differences and train personnel to be culturally competent.

11. Focus on Strengths—Maintain a focus on the strengths of youth and their families during program planning and in every interaction between the court and those it serves.

12. Family Engagement—Recognize and engage the family as a valued partner in all components of the program.

13. Educational Linkages—Coordinate with the school system to ensure that each participant enrolls in and attends an educational program that is appropriate to his or her needs.

14. Drug Testing—Design drug testing to be frequent, random, and observed. Document testing policies and procedures in writing.

15. Goal-Oriented Incentives and Sanctions—Respond to compliance and noncompliance with incentives and sanctions that are designed to reinforce or modify the behavior of youth and their families.

16. Confidentiality—Establish a confidentiality policy and procedures that guard the privacy of the youth while allowing the drug court team to access key information.

Source: Bureau of Justice Assistance (2003).

On the negative side, some critics argue that drug courts can be too quick to intervene with juveniles with no serious drug problems and limited delinquency histories. The critics worry about possible negative effects of court processing instead of allowing them to grow up without the harmful consequences of formalized processing. They also note that many drug courts are small and may only serve a very small number of youths annually (Butts, Roman, & Lynn-Whaley, 2012).

Earlier research on the effectiveness of drug courts did show reduced recidivism (e.g., Brewster, 2001; Spohn, Piper, Martin, & Frenzel, 2001). The earlier research even showed cost benefits of more than $11,000 per offender (Aos & Drake, 2013).

Now that a number of research studies have been conducted, several recent reports have synthesized the research. A recent meta-analysis of drug courts found that adult drug courts were more effective than juvenile drug courts. Whereas adult drug courts reduced overall recidivism from 50 percent to 38 percent, juvenile drug courts only reduced overall recidivism from 50 percent to 43.5 percent, an effect the authors describe as "small" (Mitchell, Wilson, Eggers, & MacKenzie, 2012). An Office of Juvenile Justice and Delinquency Prevention-sponsored study of drug courts in nine sites found almost no support for juvenile drug courts. Most of the sites saw higher recidivism for drug court youths, compared to matched youths on probation. The authors speculate that the drug court model may be more appropriate for adults than for adolescents due to such factors as the ability of youths to weigh costs and benefits (Blair, Sullivan, Latessa, & Sullivan, 2015). A review and meta-analysis of 46 studies found "no clear evidence" of the effectiveness of juvenile drug courts in reducing general recidivism, drug recidivism, or drug use compared to traditional juvenile court processing (Tanner-Smith, Lipsey, & Wilson, 2016). However, their analysis allowed for the possibility "that there are some configurations of juvenile drug courts that are effective" (Tanner-Smith et al., 2016:509). These authors also noted that much youth drug use is experimental, and thus many of the youths sent to juvenile drug courts may not actually have a substance-abuse disorder. In summary, these reviews of the research indicated that juvenile drug courts have not been very effective and perhaps drug courts are not the best approach for adolescents. Nevertheless, Latessa and his colleagues (2020) recommend that existing juvenile drug courts use assessment processes to identify appropriate individuals for treatment and cognitive–behavioral approaches.

Breaking the Cycle

The **Breaking the Cycle (BTC) program** takes a similar approach to that found in drug courts. The program seeks to identify offenders with substance-abuse problems early in their system processing, assess the appropriate treatment needs of the offender, and establish an integrated set of interventions (sanction, treatment, and rewards) for the individual. The key to the BTC program is coordinating services offered by law enforcement, the courts, corrections, families, schools, social service agencies, communities, and substance-abuse treatment providers. The court is a pivotal participant because it can provide sanctions if youths fail to comply with the program. The BTC program has been used in several sites with adult offenders.

Lattimore, Krebs, Graham, and Cowell (2005) reported on an evaluation of a juvenile BTC program in Lane County, Oregon. The evaluation of the juvenile BTC program provides mixed results (Lattimore et al., 2005). Comparing program youths to a nonequivalent comparison group, the researchers reported greater access to and use of drug treatment interventions by experimental subjects. Participants also reported reductions in marijuana use, although there were no reductions in any other drug use, including alcohol use. In addition, while there was little impact on subsequent arrest immediately after program participation, there were clear reductions between 6 and 12 months after participation (Lattimore et al., 2005).

Evidence from both juvenile drug courts and the juvenile BTC project shows that one issue is that adolescent drug use is different from adult use. In addition, adolescents may not have reached a point where they are receptive to treatment compared to adults who may have reached a more critical point in drug abuse.

Ready Availability of Drugs

A proposal at the other end of the political spectrum from those discussed elsewhere in this chapter is the call for the free (or inexpensive) availability of psychoactive drugs. This is a call to legalize, or to decriminalize at least, the possession of drugs such as heroin and marijuana. Nadelmann (2004), for example, argues that he sees no difference between responsible use of alcohol and responsible use of other drugs.

In the last decade, a number of states have either legalized or decriminalized marijuana. For example, both Colorado and Washington State have legalized marijuana for recreational use (with stores actually opening in 2014). (For current information on state laws, consult periodic reports from the National Conference of State Legislatures: www.ncsl.org).) An interesting note is that Washington State is allocating some of the revenues generated from drug sales to fund programs to prevent and treat youthful marijuana use (Washington State Institute for Public Policy, 2017). Research on the effects on use are contradictory. For example, one study found that after legalization in Denver and Seattle, use increased for adults but not for youths, and that the increased use for adults began prior to the change in the law (Maxwell & Mendelson, 2016). Another study found an increase in use for some youths in Washington State but no increase in Colorado (Cerda, Wall, & Feng, 2016). A study in Oregon found that an increase in the number of registered marijuana patients and growers was associated with a higher prevalence of marijuana use among youths from 2006 to 2015 (Paschall, Grube, & Biglan, 2017). A study of Washington State found no impact on adolescent use (Midgette & Reuter, 2020). Raw vehicle crash risk seemed to increase for drivers who tested positive for illegal drugs and for THC, but adjusting for risk factors such as age, gender, race, and ethnicity erased any significant differences (Lacey et al., 2016; National Highway Traffic Safety Administration [NHTSA], 2017). Fatal crashes for drivers age 15 to 24 declined in cities where marijuana had been legalized but increased in some cities where it had been decriminalized (Cook, Leung, & Smith, 2020). Concerning effects on crime, Maier, Mannes, and Koppenhofer (2017) found that both property and violent crime rates were higher in states where marijuana remained illegal, but these differences were not statistically significant. A study in Colorado found no association between the presence of marijuana outlets and violent crime but did find a relationship between outlets and higher rates of property crime in spatially adjacent areas (Freisthler, Gaidus, Tam, Ponicki, & Gruenewald, 2017). Two recent studies of spillover effects of legalization in Colorado and Washington State on neighboring states showed some decreases in crime (Wu, Boateng, & Lange, 2020; Lu et al., 2021). A study of police officers in states bordering on Colorado found that most but not all officers perceived that adolescent use increased in their states (Ward, Lucas, & Murphy, 2019). Legalization is still fairly new so it may take more time before researchers can come to definitive conclusions about the long-term effects of legalizing or decriminalizing marijuana. For the moment, however, it appears that legalization has not produced immediate, dramatic negative effects. (For a more thorough discussion, see Maier et al., 2017, and Paschall et al., 2017).

Although legalization may be practical for marijuana and in fact has been enacted in quite a few states, it does not seem to be a realistic possibility for many other psychoactive substances. Current attitudes simply do not favor such a liberal approach. For example, even among high school seniors, 97 percent disapprove of taking heroin occasionally, and 89 percent disapprove of trying cocaine once or twice. In fact, despite legalization in some states, 63 percent disapprove of smoking marijuana regularly (Johnston et al., 2021). Thus, "our value system, rooted in the Protestant ethic, simply will not permit lawmakers to make freely available such powerful mind-altering and euphoria-producing drugs" (Stephens, 1987:120). (For a debate on the legalization or decriminalization of heroin, see Husak [2003] and Sher [2003].)

SUMMARY: THE RESPONSE OF THE JUVENILE JUSTICE SYSTEM

The juvenile justice system must face several issues concerning drugs and juvenile offenders. First, many of the delinquents committing the worst crimes and the most frequent crimes have drug problems. Statistics clearly demonstrate that offenders tend to have drug problems. It is unclear whether drug use leads to delinquency, delinquency causes drug use, or something else causes both drug use and delinquency. What is clear is that something needs to be done.

The literature on drug treatment and prevention does offer some suggestions for action. As noted earlier, interactive prevention programs fare better than noninteractive programs. Therapeutic communities have had some success in prison settings, especially when followed by aftercare. Multi-dimensional, comprehensive initiatives appear to hold more promise than single-modality programs. Finally, research shows principles of effective intervention that can and should be implemented for juvenile offenders with drug abuse problems (Drug Strategies, 2005; Latessa et al., 2020).

The juvenile justice system often attempts to deal with less serious drug users by diverting those youths to other programs. The problem with diverting users of alcohol and other drugs to voluntary programs is that such actions may lead to **net-widening**. That is, more youths are sent to private programs than really need to be sent. In reaction to this problem, some states, such as Washington, simply opt to divest the juvenile court of its jurisdiction over users of alcohol and other drugs. Unfortunately, such a decision can result in complaints "from disgruntled parents who believed that social control—mandated by the court—was essential for straightening out their children" (Schneider, 1988:123–124).

Beyond the problems directly faced by the juvenile justice system, there is the fact that American society has failed to take a consistent approach toward drug use. For example, while many drugs are illegal, they are still used by both youths and adults. The most recent change in this area is legalization of recreational marijuana use and medical marijuana use in some states. This puts parents and drug counselors in a bind. Warnings to avoid drugs completely may fall on unreceptive ears. As noted above, however, high percentages of high school seniors express disapproval of drug use, including smoking marijuana on a regular basis.

Efforts to label some drugs as dangerous and criminal and others as socially acceptable lead to problems. Adults can buy and use alcohol and tobacco—and marijuana in some states—with little or no restraint but have to break the law to obtain even extremely small amounts of controlled substances. This societal "schizophrenia" (Hills, 1980) leads to conflicts in attitudes and hypocrisy in enforcement. The "war on drugs" has led to mass imprisonment, no clear evidence of effectiveness, and charges of discriminatory, if not racist, enforcement. Many interventions focus on certain drugs (such as heroin, cocaine, and marijuana) and ignore the serious problems of alcohol and tobacco abuse. Such slighting occurs even though alcohol and tobacco cause harm to more people than any of the so-called dangerous drugs. It will be important to watch how legalization of marijuana in some states affects overall drug use and drug enforcement.

It is important to recall the concerns of Johnston and his colleagues (2021) at the Institute for Social Research at the University of Michigan who prepare the annual Monitoring the Future study. Recall that they caution everyone that illicit drug use is "a major concern" and that cigarettes, alcohol, and illicit drugs are major causes of morbidity and mortality during adolescence and beyond.

In summary, there are no easy answers to the question of how the juvenile justice system should deal with drug offenders. On the one hand, adolescents grow up in a culture that embraces alcoholic beverages and now legalizes marijuana. On the other hand, many want all teens to "just say no" to drugs. For society to expect adolescents to completely avoid drugs, perhaps the first step is for adults to admit their shortcomings and to lead by example. Clear, Clear, and Braga (1997) argue that the criminal and juvenile justice systems must be realistic in their efforts. They take the position that any search for a completely drug-free society is unrealistic. A more realistic vision is to limit drug use as much as possible.

DISCUSSION QUESTIONS

1. How would you characterize youths' drug use? Is it an epidemic, a problem, or simply part of teenage experimentation? Offer statistics to support your position.

2. You are asked whether drug use causes delinquency. Discuss the possible relationships between drug use and delinquency and take a position on which one is correct. Justify your position.

3. The state legislature has just appointed you to oversee all treatment and prevention programs dealing with drug use. What programs will you keep or institute to fight the drug problem? Why have you selected these programs?

4. Legislation has been proposed to decriminalize or legalize drug use in your state. To date, it appears that effects on crime and use are minimal, if any. Would you favor or oppose such legislation? Why?

5. The local police department seeks to start a drug prevention program for teens. Having just completed a degree in criminal justice, you are called upon for advice. What advice would you offer about this issue?

6. Critics of the police war on drugs (especially the war on marijuana) argue that it is ineffective, costly, and discriminatory—even racist. Do you favor or oppose a police war on marijuana? Discuss your choice and the reasons for your choice.

CHAPTER 7

Policing and Juveniles

WHAT YOU NEED TO KNOW

- In 2019, police arrested 696,620 persons under age 18. The majority of these (over 70 percent) were referred to juvenile court jurisdiction, other police departments, adult court, or another agency. The police used their discretion to handle and release 26 percent of youths taken into custody.

- A new view of the police role is one of community or problem-solving policing. This view tries to include the community as a partner in defining and solving crime and disorder problems.

- "Broken windows" policing places emphasis on policing disorder such as loitering and vagrants because this model sees disorder as a factor associated with street crime. The theory is that if police can reduce disorder, crime will also decrease.

- Research indicates that some departments using traditional police strategies refer to it as community or problem-solving policing. So not all departments are actually following the directions of innovators.

- African Americans generally hold less-positive views of the police than whites. Many youths appear to be either indifferent or less than overwhelming in their support of police.

- Racial issues have been at the center of media and political attention in the last five years. Particular concern has arisen over police shootings and practices such as Stop, Question, and Frisk.

- Disproportionate minority contact refers to the overrepresentation of any racial group in arrest and court statistics compared to the proportion of that group in the population.

- Research indicates that juvenile curfew laws are not effective in reducing crime.

KEY TERMS

"broken windows" policing

community policing

deadly force

disproportionate minority contact (DMC)

gatekeeper role

juvenile curfew laws

mission distortion

police effectiveness

police use of excessive force

problem-oriented policing

professional policing

restorative justice conferences

school resource officers (SROs)

school-to-prison pipeline

DOI: 10.4324/9781003167112-7

INTRODUCTION

Policing brings to mind images of arresting suspects, shooting at criminals, writing traffic tickets, testifying in court, driving on patrol, and interrogating murder suspects in the detective bureau. Police still do these things, but they also engage in activities that many people are not aware of. For instance, today police also lead community meetings to discuss the extent and causes of neighborhood crime and disorder. Together with community members, they are searching for solutions to urban problems. Police go to homes of juveniles who are on probation to assist probation officers in making curfew checks and try to determine what can be done to help juvenile probationers stay out of trouble and adjust. Police also facilitate **restorative justice conferences**, in which, for instance, a burglary victim meets a juvenile burglar and explains precisely how the burglary impacted the victim. Supporters for both sides are present and, with the help of the police officer leader, they work out an agreement on how the youth can make amends for what he or she did.

So policing today means much more than it did 35 years ago. Back then police were wondering how they could adjust car patrol to reduce crime. They were wondering if more cars would reduce crime or if faster response time would reduce crime. Today police are raising questions about the definition of policing. What is policing? What role do the police have in a democratic society? These questions and the solutions raised so far are having important effects on how police interact with juveniles.

Policing today is all too often in the public eye. Critics argue that the police are too quick to use excessive force, exhibit implicit or explicit bias against people of color, and even shoot suspects without sufficient reason to do so. Defenders of the police worry that critics go too far and that calls to defund the police are a mistake.

In this chapter we will look at police and juveniles. We will discuss the changing police role, particularly as it involves contact with youths. We will also look at attitudes and the police, including both citizen attitudes toward the police and police attitudes toward citizens, some recent developments in policing, the effectiveness of policing, and improper use of police force. Finally, we will examine current controversies such as the issue of race and policing and the issue of police shootings.

STATISTICS ON POLICE WORK WITH JUVENILES

The *OJJDP Statistical Briefing Book* presents the basic picture of what police do with juvenile offenders. Other than traffic and neglect cases, in 2019, police arrested fewer than 700,000 juveniles (696,620) persons under age 18 (Puzzanchera, 2021). (Note: The FBI Uniform Crime Reports and NIBRS may give different numbers, based on several factors. Charles Puzzanchera presents a yearly in-depth report published by the Office of Juvenile Justice and Delinquency Prevention.) About 30 percent (29 percent) were referred to juvenile court jurisdiction. Twenty-six percent were handled within the police department and released. Two percent were referred to criminal or adult court, and the rest were referred to a welfare agency, another police agency, or another authority (FBI, 2020).

Two points are noteworthy. First, the percentage of offenders that police refer to juvenile court (approximately 30 percent) is lower than prior years. Second, the fact that 26 percent of the juveniles taken into custody are simply handled and released shows the discretion that police have with juveniles. Such discretion can have critical consequences for youths. A youth released in this manner does not have to worry that if he or she commits a new delinquent act a year later the first one will be held against him or her and he or she will be treated as someone with a prior record. The juvenile may be treated as someone without any record. If police impose any racial or other biases into their decisions, those racial biases can have serious effects on later decisions by police, prosecutors, and judges. Much of this discretion is hidden and thus difficult to discover.

A highlight of the arrest statistics on juveniles is that in 2019 there were an estimated 860 arrests of juveniles for murder (Puzzanchera, 2021). This is a 15 percent decrease compared to 2010. In addition, the 2019 number is down considerably from the peak year of 1993, when there were approximately 3,800 juvenile arrests for murder. In 2019, juvenile arrests for all crimes were down almost 60 percent from 2010. Violent crime arrests were down 40 percent; property crime arrests were down 67 percent; drug abuse violations were down 52 percent. Total arrests of juveniles were the lowest in nearly four decades (Puzzanchera, 2021).

WEB ACTIVITY

One source of information about juvenile arrest statistics is the *OJJDP Statistical Briefing Book*, available at www.ojjdp. gov/ojstatbb. Arrest statistics can also be found in the FBI's *Uniform Crime Reports*, available at www.fbi.gov. See especially Table 68, Police Disposition: Juvenile Offenders Taken into Custody, 2019.

The overall crime decline that started in the 1990s has yet to be fully explained. Some credit the crime decrease to changes in policing that involved targeting disorder based on a belief that loitering, panhandling, and other types of disorder cause crime (Braga & Bond, 2008). Some credit the decrease to the increase in imprisonment that has been going on for more than 20 years. Others argue that broader trends seem to be at work. Zimring (2007, 2012), for example, argues that crime also decreased in Canada even though that country did not use the police tactics that New York City used. In the next section we will discuss the police role in general and also devote more attention to the effectiveness of police efforts to reduce disorder as a strategy to reduce crime and delinquency.

PROFESSIONAL POLICING AND JUVENILES

For much of the twentieth century, police tried to be professional crime fighters. This often translated into police driving in one- or two-officer patrol cars until they saw something suspicious or received a radio call to respond to a crime or a call for service. The rationale was that quick response to calls would enable the police to apprehend suspects or deal quickly with problems that citizens reported to central dispatch. Many called this the **professional policing** model. Others have called it "911 policing" because 911 is the emergency phone number used to contact police.

There were several problems with this professional or 911 policing model. One was that increased professionalism did not reduce crime. Studies showed, for example, that simply increasing the extent of patrol in a given sector did not reduce crime. In addition, research showed that quicker response time did not have dramatic effects on crime (Walker, 2011), and that much of a police officer's shift did not even involve crime. Citizens call the police for all types of problems that are not directly crime-related. Some of the actions prompting those calls could escalate into crime, but many of the calls occur because people regard the police as government workers who are available seven days a week, 24 hours a day, and thus should be able to deal with their problems.

Another problem with the professional model is that it built barriers between the police and citizens. When officers sit in one- or two-person cars, they do not have the opportunity to interact with citizens. Interaction can have positive consequences. It can alert police to problems in the neighborhood, or it can produce tips about who might be engaged in either criminal activity or disorder. The old-fashioned foot patrol officer could get to know both neighborhood problems and tips about who might be causing the problems by having opportunities to meet with shopkeepers, pedestrians, and people sitting or standing near corners or other gathering places. Professional policing decreased the number of foot patrol officers and put the police car as a barrier between the officer and citizens. Unintentionally, professional policing may be one reason for some of the problems facing police today.

Custody Rules with Youths

Police action in relation to detaining youths has been an interesting problem since the inception of the juvenile court. Under the *parens patriae* doctrine, the use of arrest tactics typically invoked by police in relation to adult offenders would normally be avoided with youths. Fingerprinting, photographing, and incarcerating youths were all either forbidden or severely restricted. The shift to a more punitive orientation in recent years, including mandatory sentencing and more liberal waiver procedures, has resulted in major changes to police procedure and practice with youths.

Perhaps the clearest rules for police handling of youths involve holding juveniles in secure facilities. When a youth is taken into custody there are clear guidelines that must be followed in terms of the custody facility. Youths must be segregated from adults. This segregation has to be physical, visual, and aural (sound) separation. These requirements pose special problems for many police departments. Those that are very small, especially in rural, isolated areas, typically have very small jails where it is often impossible to separate the youths from adults. The choice facing the police, therefore, is either violating the laws on conditions of holding youths in custody or releasing the youths outright.

The rules governing fingerprinting and taking photographs of youths vary from state to state and have changed a great deal over the past several decades. The traditional prohibition against these practices has been replaced with rules outlining who and under what circumstances photos and fingerprints can be gathered, as well as the use and disposition of those records. The state of Ohio, for example, requires judicial consent before fingerprinting and photographing of juveniles is undertaken (Ohio Revised Code [ORC], §2151.313). The law allows the police to obtain these records without judicial consent if the arrest involves a felony or an act besides a traffic offense or minor misdemeanor. The police must immediately inform the juvenile court that this action has been taken and provide details on the youths and number of fingerprints and photos taken. Further, these materials are to be destroyed within 30 days unless the youth is adjudicated delinquent for an act that is a violent misdemeanor or felony, at which time the judge will set parameters for the retention and/or destruction of the records (ORC, §2151.313). These rules illustrate an attempt to balance protection of the child with the needs of the juvenile and criminal justice systems.

Other states take a more liberal approach to allowing fingerprinting and photographing of youths. Florida, for example, lists a number of specific crimes for which these actions should be taken (Florida Statutes, §985.11). At the same time, fingerprints and photographs can be taken of any child in custody, regardless of the offense, at the sole discretion of the agency. These records are considered confidential but can be shared with other agencies and are part of the youth's permanent record that is accessible by the adult court (Florida Statutes, §985.11).

Most states allow some form of fingerprinting and photographing of youths. These requirements, however, vary from state to state and from what are permissible with adults taken into custody. This is one example of how policing youthful misbehavior raises new and unique challenges for the professional police model.

Interrogation Tactics with Juvenile Suspects

As we will see in Chapter 9, the Supreme Court has held that a juvenile suspect can waive the privilege against self-incrimination and the right to consult with an attorney and go ahead and agree to be interrogated. Then a court will judge the voluntariness of any confession by looking at all the circumstances of the interrogation and confession. However, the Court did note in 2011 that police should consider the age of the child as one of the custody factors. In other words, a youth may feel less free in an interrogation situation, and this factor affects how a judge assesses the voluntariness of any apparent waiver (*J.D.B. v. North Carolina*, 2011).

A study by Barry Feld examined the transcripts of 66 police interrogations of juvenile suspects in Minneapolis, Minnesota. Eighty percent of the juveniles waived their *Miranda* rights and agreed to interrogation. On the positive side, police immediately stopped questioning those youths who invoked their rights. On the negative side, police questioned juvenile suspects in much the same manner as they questioned adults. The police often suggested that talking would be beneficial to the suspect, or they phrased the warnings as if they were just a bureaucratic formality instead of a serious constitutional issue with important consequences for the suspect (Feld, 2006). Feld also concluded that the behavior of 16- and 17-year-olds parallels the behavior of most adult suspects; the adult waiver rate is also about 80 percent. So he thinks that 16- and 17-year-olds are about as psychologically mature as adults and understand their rights to the same extent as adults.

In a second study, Feld (2013a) analyzed the interrogation files (including transcripts) of 307 juvenile suspects in four Minnesota counties. As in his 2006 article, Feld noted that 16- and 17-year-olds are similar to adults but that younger youths "lack ability to understand and competence to exercise rights" (Feld, 2013a:24). So he recommends that youths age 15 and younger be required to consult with an attorney prior to waiving constitutional rights. Based on his research, he also recommends that interrogations not be allowed to take longer than four hours and that all interrogations be recorded.

In a study of 57 recorded interrogation sessions from 17 police agencies, no attorneys were present for any of the interrogations. The author concludes that this total absence of attorneys "suggests the widespread occurrence that juvenile suspects are making interrogation decisions without the knowledge or advice of counsel" (Cleary, 2013).

An important concern is the danger of false confessions. More than one-third of proven false confessions come from suspects under 18 years of age. In a recent study of 193 14- to 17-year-olds incarcerated for serious offenses, Malloy, Shulman, and Cauffman (2014) found that 17 percent of the youths stated they had made a false confession to police, 81 percent reported having been threatened, and 21 percent experienced force. Feld thinks that 16- and 17-year-olds are similar to adults, but that younger suspects do need greater protection. He argues for recording all confessions as a safeguard (Feld, 2006).

An intriguing issue about police interrogation techniques is that although the police think they are very good at detecting deception in suspects, research indicates that they are not. Although interrogation experts claim 85 percent accuracy, research puts police accuracy at about 50 percent. What is particularly disturbing about juvenile suspects, moreover, is that juveniles often exhibit behaviors that the interrogation experts claim are deceptive, such as slouching and not making eye contact with the interrogator. Therefore, when a youth is just "being youthful," an interrogator will interpret that behavior as evidence that the youth is lying. Another problem is suggestibility. The desire to please or the tendency to trust authority figures, for example, can influence youths to confess falsely (Meyer & Reppucci, 2007).

In their study of more than 300 police investigators in Baltimore, Meyer and Reppucci (2007) found that police used the same interrogation techniques with children under age 14, youths ages 14–17, and adults (age 18 and older).

Police believed that children and youths outside the context of interrogation do not understand some words used by adults but then stated that they thought that children, youths, and adults all understand their rights in the interrogation session and the purpose of interrogation. The researchers found that 83 percent of their sample used body language as an indicator of deception despite the problem noted previously that youths are likely to slouch and avoid eye contact. Finally, the Baltimore police also reported using coercive and deceptive interrogation techniques with suspects, regardless of age, even though there is greater likelihood of getting inaccurate reports from youthful suspects (Meyer & Reppucci, 2007). In summary, many juveniles waive their rights, and consent to interrogation. Despite age-related problems with interrogating youthful suspects, many police investigators use techniques, including threats and force, that can lead to inaccurate statements and even false confessions from juvenile suspects.

THE POLICE AND JUVENILES

A long record of research on the role of police in controlling juveniles has described that role as one of "gatekeeper" to the juvenile justice system. This means that police officers exercise considerable discretion with juveniles; officers are often the ones who decide whether a juvenile is processed in the juvenile justice system. Police also experience conflicting feelings toward juveniles. Police want to prevent and control crime, but they also feel a duty to prevent harm to the juvenile and prevent delinquency. These conflicts can result in police taking different actions with juveniles than they would with adults (Brown, Novak, & Frank, 2009).

An observational study of 20 nonurban police departments in southwestern Ohio confirmed the gatekeeper role. Field observation resulted in 195 encounters between police and juveniles ages 13–17 years. In cases involving juveniles initially assuming the role of a suspect or a disputant, only 23 (16 percent) of those 138 juveniles were actually arrested. In cases in which a juvenile actually committed a crime, only 42 percent of those cases ended in an arrest. As previous research found: "the deviant behavior of juveniles will more often than not involve less serious offenses, and nonurban police appear to be just as inclined as urban cops to act as 'gatekeepers' by resolving juvenile encounters informally without an arrest" (Liederbach, 2007:119). In traditional terminology, much police work with juveniles involves order maintenance rather than crime fighting, as well as discretion (see, e.g., Hurst, Frank, & Browning, 2000; Walker, 1992).

An interesting side note from this Ohio study is that the most frequent police encounters with juveniles were traffic-related offenses, including speeding, accidents, violations, and others. Part of the reason for this may be that it was a study of suburban police departments and the automobile is a central feature of suburban life. So, while older studies involved police on foot making contact with juveniles, many of the police contacts with juveniles now involve traffic-related problems (Liederbach, 2007). The importance of traffic stops is also seen in an analysis of contacts between the police and the public (age 16 and older) in 2018. Over 18 million people—30 percent of all contacts that year—reported that their most recent contact with the police was as a driver in a traffic stop, most frequently for speeding (Harrell & Davis, 2020). Clearly, we are a nation of drivers, and this affects contacts with police for both juveniles and adults.

Prior research indicated that gender (being male) and demeanor are important correlates of police officers' decisions to take a youth into custody (see, e.g., Lundman 1994; Morash 1984). Most of that research was based on observational study of police. One study took a different approach. Allen (2005) surveyed more than 400 police officers in Cleveland, Ohio, and found that disrespect on the part of a youth, being out late at night, being male, and indicators of suspicious behavior, such as clothing and hair style, were factors influencing the police officers to conclude that the youth should be taken into custody or at least stopped and questioned. Allen (2005) commented that clothing and hairstyle could result in more black youths being stopped or taken into custody but also noted that there are more black police officers today, which should reduce discrimination against black youths.

Brown et al. (2009) conducted systematic social observation of street-level police officers in Cincinnati, Ohio, from 1997 to 1998. They found that police are more likely to arrest juveniles than adults and more likely to arrest juveniles in distressed communities. A number of factors influenced police to arrest both adults and juveniles, namely offense seriousness, quantity of evidence, commission of a crime in the officer's presence, race (white), and intoxication. Interestingly, disrespect on the part of an adult suspect but not a juvenile suspect also influenced officers to make an arrest (Brown et al., 2009).

In summary, the police continue to operate as gatekeepers to the juvenile justice system. They exercise considerable discretion in their encounters with juveniles. It is critical that police have guidelines to ensure that such discretion is not abused.

Police Use of Force, Including Excessive Force (Brutality)

Police use of excessive force is a sensitive topic and thus it is difficult to gain accurate information about its extent. Like any profession, police will not just open up and reveal professional secrets. They will not readily disclose how frequently and under what circumstances they may use excessive force. So researchers often survey citizens to derive estimates of police use of force.

It is unclear exactly how frequently police use force, proper or improper. According to the Police-Public Contact Survey, between 2 and 4 percent of those 16 and older who had contact with the police in 2018 experienced the threat of force or actual force. The percentage for 16- and 17-year-olds was 3.4 percent. A disturbing note is that most of the 16- to 17-year-olds who experienced force (62 percent) said the force was excessive (Harrell & Davis, 2020). On the other hand, interviews with 324 juvenile arrestees in Arizona showed that half (50.3 percent) of the youths reported some type of force, ranging from kicking or grabbing the youth all the way up to the threat or use of a gun (Morrow, Nuno, & Mulvey, 2018). Similarly, a study in Hartford, Connecticut, found that the 132 youths interviewed reported approximately 400 negative experiences (Borrero, 2001). Thirty-nine percent involved physical encounters (force, hitting, injury), 24 percent involved verbal harassment, and 34 percent were categorized as "other." Worden (1996) thinks the use of improper force is infrequent, a conclusion supported by the national survey. The hopeful conclusion is that Worden and the national survey are correct. A more pessimistic conclusion is that force is more frequent, especially against minority youths, and that efforts are required to reduce any use of force as much as possible. (For a discussion of possible use of force in schools, see Box 7.1.)

An extreme example of the use of excessive force is the use of **deadly force**. Between January 1, 2015 and June 10, 2021, police officers shot and killed over 6,300 Americans, including 113 persons under 18 years of age (*Washington Post*, 2021). Police deadly force is extremely rare, as there are more than 40 million police contacts with citizens each year. A recent study found that "most civilians killed by police were armed with a deadly weapon or were actively attacking officers. Less than 10 percent ($N = 93$) of civilians shot and killed by police in 2015 were unarmed" (Nix, Campbell, Byers, & Alpert, 2017:327–328). Another study found that: "officers involved in shootings tend to be younger [w]hite males at the rank of officer and possess a high school diploma. Moreover, officers who have experienced one shooting are more likely to become involved in a future shooting" (McElvain & Kposowa, 2008:519). As will be discussed later in this chapter, the issue of race and police shootings has become a critical one in the last few years.

The primary test case on the use of deadly force involved the shooting of a 15-year-old youth in Memphis, Tennessee. A Memphis police officer shot and killed Edward Garner, a 15-year-old 8th-grade student, under that state's common law "fleeing felon" rule, which authorized police to shoot any fleeing felon—even nondangerous ones. Garner had been prowling inside an empty house and refused to halt in the yard when the police officer warned him to stop. Consequently, the officer shot the youth as he tried to climb a fence to escape. In *Tennessee v. Garner et al.* (1985), the United States Supreme Court ruled that police may not institute a policy to shoot any and all fleeing suspects;

BOX 7.1 BAN ON POLICE USE OF TASERS IN SCHOOLS?

When a student tried to break up a fight in a Texas high school, an officer shot the 17-year-old youth to the floor. His head hit the concrete floor so hard that he suffered a severe brain hemorrhage and spent 52 days in a medically induced coma. His parents are suing. Several groups have urged the Texas Education Agency to end the use of tasers and pepper spray.

Police report that a review of the case showed that the officer followed use of force policy and guidelines. A grand jury declined to indict the officer.

What do you think? Is there a need for such devices in schools? Are they also necessary in elementary schools?

Source: Werner (2014).

rather, they may shoot only those escaping felons who pose a threat to the officer or to others. A subsequent Supreme Court decision, *Graham v. Connor* (1989), set the stage for many of the controversial police shootings in the last few years by offering greater room for officer judgment in the heat of the moment. Specifically, in *Graham v. Connor*, the Court stated that the standard for deadly force is what a reasonable police office would do when "forced to make split-second judgments—in circumstances that are tense, uncertain, and rapidly evolving." While the police focus on the need to make split-second decisions, critics argue that decisions leading up to the decision to shoot, such as the decision to stop a pedestrian or a motorist, are not split-second decisions and may have been the product of overt racial bias or implicit racial bias (Sherman, 2020).

One disturbing aspect of several highly publicized police shootings or related incidents is the fact that the reason police were called to the scene was not a life-threatening situation but, in retrospect, a fairly mundane matter. In Ferguson, Missouri, Michael Brown was initially accused of shoplifting and shoving a clerk who tried to stop him. In New York City, Eric Garner was accused of selling cigarettes without taxes. In Minneapolis, Minnesota, George Floyd was accused of passing a counterfeit $20 bill. Also in Minneapolis, Daunte Wright was stopped for an expired license tab. One possible lesson is for police to refrain from drastic actions if the initial reason for intervention is not a serious or violent crime situation.

A critical problem with police shootings is that many black citizens think that race is a factor in the decision to shoot. For example, a recent survey found that 73 percent of black citizens think that the police are too quick to use lethal force, compared to only 35 percent of white citizens (Ekins, 2016). Many blacks have joined the Black Lives Matter movement to protest what they feel

BOX 7.2 THE U.S. SUPREME COURT ON DEADLY FORCE

In *Tennessee v. Garner et al.*, the U.S. Supreme Court set down guidelines for the constitutional use of deadly force by police officers. Here are some excerpts from the majority opinion by Justice White:

> The use of deadly force to prevent the escape of all felony suspects, whatever the circumstances, is constitutionally unreasonable. It is not better that all felony suspects die than that they escape. Where the suspect poses no immediate threat to the officer and no threat to others, the harm resulting from failing to apprehend him does not justify the use of deadly force to do so. It is no doubt unfortunate when a suspect who is in sight escapes, but the fact that the police arrive a little late or are a little slower afoot does not always justify killing the suspect. A police officer may not seize an unarmed, nondangerous suspect by shooting him dead …
>
> Where the officer has probable cause to believe that the suspect poses a threat of serious physical harm, either to the officer or to others, it is not constitutionally unreasonable to prevent escape by using deadly force. Thus, if the suspect threatens the officer with a weapon or there is probable cause to believe that he has committed a crime involving the infliction or threatened infliction of serious physical harm, deadly force may be used if necessary to prevent escape, and if, where feasible, some warning has been given.

Source: *Tennessee v. Garner et al.* (1985).

are instances of improper police shootings of black citizens. On the other hand, some have criticized the Black Lives Matter movement for racializing relations between police and citizens and for charges of insufficient respect for the flag.

One issue is the so-called "Ferguson effect," which states that police may become reluctant to intervene in situations in order to avoid charges of improper behavior, especially improper shootings. For example, one poll found that 72 percent of the officers surveyed thought that officers in their department are now less likely to stop and question suspicious persons (Morin, Parker, Stepler, & Mercer, 2017). Part of a Ferguson effect would be an increase in crime as police take fewer actions to prevent crime (so-called de-policing). A study of crime rates for the 12 months before and after Ferguson (August 2014) found no nationwide effect overall on crime rates. However, robbery rates did increase, and homicide rates increased in some cities (Pyrooz, Decker, Wolfe, & Shjarback, 2016).

In recent years, a number of recommendations have been made and implemented in an effort to reduce police shootings: adoption of body-worn cameras, de-escalation training, implicit bias training, early intervention systems, and civilian oversight. Unfortunately, a review of the evidence does not show that any of these reform initiatives are effective (Engel et al., 2020). Siegel (2020) argues that structural factors such as segregated neighborhoods and racial gaps in economic resources and employment are related to police shootings of black individuals. He argues that solutions include bias training, integrating neighborhoods, and increasing economic resources.

Several cautions about police shootings are in order. First, each shooting incident needs to be examined thoroughly. For example, an investigation of the shooting of Michael Brown in Ferguson, Missouri, concluded that the police officer did *not* act improperly (U.S. Department of Justice, 2015). The shooting of Laquan McDonald in Chicago, on the other hand, resulted in the officer being charged and convicted of murder. As this edition is being written, Derek Chauvin was convicted for the killing (although not a shooting) of George Floyd, and the guilty verdict has held him accountable for his actions. Second, official findings such as the Department of Justice finding in Ferguson do not automatically calm citizen concerns. Some citizens continue to think that a shooting may have been improper despite the findings of an official investigation. Third, the information we have about police shootings nationwide is incomplete. It appears that most victims of police shootings in 2015 were armed or were actively attacking officers. On the other hand, there is some indication of implicit bias (Nix et al., 2017). Fourth, the issue of shootings must be placed in broader context. For example, police decisions to engage in a war on drugs and to engage in aggressive stop-and-frisk actions in cities such as New York and Chicago often are interpreted by minority citizens as discriminatory. As a result, many blacks agree with civil rights advocate Michelle Alexander that the criminal justice system in general is racist. Specifically, Alexander calls the criminal justice system "the New Jim Crow," which sees that "black people, especially black men, are criminals" (Alexander, 2012:197).

This file image from video shows former Minneapolis police officer Derek Chauvin, center, being taken into custody after the guilty verdicts were read at his April 2021 trial for the murder of George Floyd. In June 2021, Chauvin was sentenced to 22.5 years in prison for the second-degree murder.

CREDIT: Court TV via AP, Pool, File

Likewise, the American Civil Liberties Union states that "the war on marijuana has largely been a war on people of color" (ACLU, 2013:9).

It is important to note that police do face the possibility of being shot at and killed. One study found that from 2014 to 2019, an average of 245 officers a year were shot at and an average of 42 a year were killed (Sierra-Arevalo & Nix, 2020). Threat of such firearm assaults on officers is part of each officer's mindset when confronting suspects.

The issue of race and police shootings is a real and disturbing crisis. Black citizens suspect the police of differential treatment if not racism. Police want to be able to defend themselves if they are in danger and are concerned that they might be second-guessed for what they thought were reasonable decisions in often split-second judgments. In Chapter 14, we note several suggestions for police reform. A later section of this chapter discusses the more general issue of race and policing juveniles (see below).

COMMUNITY OR PROBLEM-SOLVING POLICING

One response to the shortcomings of the professional policing model is **community policing**, which is also called problem-solving or **problem-oriented policing**. Community policing does not necessarily mean exactly the same thing to everyone who subscribes to it. Some key features do emerge, however, as critical common elements.

One critical factor is problem-solving. As Herman Goldstein (1990) has noted, police can and should be problem solvers in the community. Problem-solving involves an effort to deal with conditions or factors that lead to crime or disorder. If the police can solve the problem, then they prevent crime from happening. A simple example with juveniles is police in one community leading the community to transform a vacant lot into a skateboard park. This solved the disorder problem of kids skating in the street and on sidewalks (Chaiken, 2004). Another critical element of community policing is community building (Novak, Frank, Smith, & Engel, 2002). An important part of community policing is to strengthen the community and its ability to solve problems and prevent and minimize crime, disorder, and other difficulties. In essence, this involves establishing partnerships between the police and the public (Schnebly, 2008). Police departments need to engage community members both to identify problems and implement solutions. Police cannot act alone; they must work with neighborhood residents "to coproduce public safety" (President's Task Force on 21st Century Policing, 2015:3).

In **"broken windows" policing,** the police also broaden their concerns and actions, compared to traditional 911 policing. Instead of focusing only on crime, the police pay attention to both crime and disorder. Based on the "broken windows" hypothesis, police consider disorder—for example, rowdy teens hanging out on street corners, "squeegee men" offering to wash car windows for cash "contributions," prostitutes plying their trade, youths or adults trying to jump turnstiles to avoid paying subway fare, "winos" urinating on the street or sleeping in public places like subway stations, and so on—as a serious problem that leads to street crime.

Disorder demoralizes communities, undermines commerce, leads to the abandonment of public spaces, and undermines public confidence in the ability of government to solve problems; fear drives citizens further from each other and paralyzes their normal, order-sustaining responses, compounding the impact of disorder (Kelling & Coles, 1996:242).

"Broken windows" theory holds that disorder creates fear in citizens, causing them to stay off the streets. The more citizens avoid streets, the more deserted the streets get, and the more citizens avoid them. This affects urban trafficking, both auto and pedestrian, hurts business, and can contribute to crime. Some of the strategies used as part of "broken windows" policing are opportunity reduction, problem-solving, and crime prevention through environmental design (Kelling & Coles, 1996). Some cities (e.g., Indianapolis, IN) have focused on the "broken windows" model of community policing, while other cities (e.g., St. Petersburg, FL) have focused more on police–community cooperation and problem-solving (Paoline, Myers, & Worden, 2000).

In New York City, police focused "broken windows" order maintenance activities on stop, question, and frisk actions hoping to catch serious offenders engaging in public marijuana smoking or drinking. Critics see unjustified racial imbalances and constitutional violations that make the strategy "misguided" (Geller & Fagan, 2010). Police argue that proactive police strategies have taken guns off the streets and saved more than 7,000 lives (Kelly, 2013).

Problem-solving, community building, and addressing "broken windows" can directly target youthful problems and concerns. For example, citizens might complain that a particular street corner or bus stop is a center for gang-related activity. After problem identification, police and citizens together explore possible solutions. In Chicago, citizens decided to conduct marches in gang-related areas to discourage gang activity there. Together with police, Chicago citizens also worked with the bus company to relocate a particular bus stop where school children were being harassed. Citizens and police also sought the help of city housing inspectors and housing courts to close down buildings where drug dealers were conducting business.

In another Chicago neighborhood, citizens found that the local juvenile court was so busy that it was ignoring minor offenders. In response to this problem, the community started an alternative-consequence program. This was a program that gave out community service orders for juveniles accused of misdemeanors such as underage drinking, graffiti, vandalism, shoplifting, and bicycle theft. Youthful offenders usually performed between 8 and 100 hours of community service, usually in beautification projects (Skogan & Hartnett, 1997).

In Indianapolis, police act as facilitators at restorative justice conferences. (For a complete discussion of restorative justice, see Chapter 12.) This program is intended for first-time offenders, age 14 and younger, charged with battery, trespass, mischief, conversion, or felony D theft. If the youth is willing to participate, supporters from both sides (offender and victim) meet in a conference. The facilitator tries to get the group to understand what happened. For example, the facilitator asks the youth about the effects of his or her behavior on the victim and asks the victim how the crime affected him or her. After a thorough exploration of the event, the group tries to work out an agreement to repair the harm that was done. Restitution and community service are key elements of agreements. In Indianapolis, police and others (e.g., neighborhood prosecutors, civilian volunteers) have coordinated restorative justice conferences, which have taken place in police stations, schools, libraries, and community centers (McGarrell, Olivares, Crawford, & Kroovand, 2000).

More than 90 percent of victims in conference cases report being satisfied with the way the case was handled. Ninety-eight percent said they would recommend the conference approach. At six months after the initial incident, only 20 percent of the youths who went through restorative justice conferences recidivated, compared to 34 percent in the control group. One year after the initial incident, 31 percent of the restorative justice conference youths had been rearrested, compared to 41 percent of the control group. Both differences were statistically significant (McGarrell et al., 2000).

In Houston, Texas, community police officers provide a "Knock and Talk" service for truants; they visit truants and talk to them about their truancy problems. In Tacoma, Washington, community police officers deliver truants to a community truancy center (Baker, Sigmon, & Nugent, 2001). In Cleveland, Ohio, police converted houses used as crack houses into police substations. In these so-called "RAPP houses" (named for the Residential Area Policing Program) youths could come in and talk to police officers who were there around the clock (Dunworth, 2000). All of these examples are efforts to both solve problems related to crime and disorder and to enhance the ability of the community to participate in policing itself.

Boston police have taken an approach considerably different from the restorative justice approach used in Indianapolis, but it is still considered to be a problem-solving approach. The problem targeted was violence, specifically homicide. In the Boston Gun Project's Operation Ceasefire, police targeted gangs engaged in violent behavior and used a strategy called "pulling levers," which entailed delivering a message to violent gangs that violence will not be tolerated. In Operation Ceasefire, police hold forums with gang members to announce their intent to apply whatever sanctions they can. Police then arrest gang members for trespassing, public drinking, overt drug use, disorder offenses, probation violations, and outstanding warrants. Evaluators report that Operation Ceasefire

> was associated with a 63 percent decrease in youth homicides per month, a 32 percent decrease in shots-fired calls for service per month, a 25 percent decrease in gun assaults per month, and a 44 percent decrease in the number of youth gun assaults per month in the highest risk district. (Braga et al., 2001:3)

It should be noted, however, that other research indicates that youth gun homicides had begun to decline in 1995 and that they declined 75 percent in other Massachusetts cities during this period (Fagan, 2002).

The Office of Juvenile Justice and Delinquency Prevention has supported the development of comprehensive, community-wide approaches to gang prevention. These programs involve both suppression and services. Suppression means that police—and often probation—work together in surveillance and information sharing. Service means efforts to provide academic, economic, and social opportunities for gang members. One program targeted older members (17–24 years old) of two of the most violent gangs in the Little Village neighborhood of Chicago. Results were favorable, including reduced serious gang violence among the targeted gang members, compared to gang members in a comparison group. Specifically, the program resulted in reduced arrests for serious gang crimes (especially aggravated batteries and assaults) among the targeted youths (Howell, 2000).

In summary, community or problem-solving policing tries to solve or prevent problems that contribute to crime and delinquency. Community policing has resulted in a number of innovative strategies in the last 25 years. A recent review of research found that hot spots policing efforts (focusing on high-crime locations) with a problem-solving emphasis are effective in crime prevention (Braga, Papachristos, & Hureau, 2014).

CITIZEN ATTITUDES TOWARD POLICE

Police shootings have demonstrated the racial divide in citizen attitudes toward the police. For example, 84 percent of black adults say that in general in our country these days, blacks are treated less fairly than whites in dealing with the police. Also, 44 percent of blacks but only 9 percent of whites say that they have been unfairly stopped by police. Further, only 33 percent of blacks, but 75 percent of whites, say that the police in their community do an excellent job when it comes to using the right amount of force for each situation (DeSilver, Lipka, & Fahmy, 2020).

On the one hand, many citizens overall hold positive attitudes. For example, a recent poll reported that 73 percent of those polled rated the honesty and ethical standards of police either very high or high (Gilberstadt, 2020). Police ranked sixth in the list of professions, only below nurses, pharmacists, doctors, engineers, and dentists and above college teachers, clergy, and lawyers (Reinart, 2020).

Citizens vary considerably, however, in their approval of the police. For example, in the survey just noted, 78 percent of whites but only 52 percent of blacks and 66 percent of Hispanics rated the honesty and ethical standards of police as high or very high. Similarly, 84 percent of whites but only 56 percent of blacks reported at least a fair amount of confidence in the police. Younger respondents (ages 18–39) report lower confidence at 70 percent, compared to 87 percent confidence for those 55 and older. Republicans report higher confidence (87 percent) than Democrats (71 percent) (Gilberstadt, 2020). Less than half (49 percent) of blacks ages 18–39, compared to 75 percent of whites in that age group, report at least a fair amount of confidence in the police (Gilberstadt, 2020). Gallup points out that "[o]n the surface, Americans' confidence in the police appears strong and steady but [a] closer look [examining subgroup differences] reveals a troubling loss of confidence among key groups in U.S. society" (Gallup, 2017).

One attitude in particular has received considerable attention in the last few years: police legitimacy. Tyler (2006, 2017) contends that if citizens see the police as legitimate—if they have the attitude that police have legitimate authority to tell citizens what they can and cannot do—then citizens will be less likely to break any laws. He further argues that when police treat citizens with procedural justice, that causes citizens to see the police as legitimate. In a review of the evidence allegedly showing that procedural justice increases perceptions of legitimacy, Nagin and Telep (2020) failed to find that relationship. Instead, they found that "there is no evidence that procedurally just treatment of citizens increases their compliance with the law" (Nagin & Telep, 2020:779). These authors assert, however, that procedural justice is a legitimate goal by itself.

A recent study shows how this issue affects youths. Brunson and Wade (2019) interviewed 50 young black males in Brooklyn and the Bronx and found considerable legal cynicism. In other words, due to negative encounters with police and believing that police engage in both under-policing and over-policing, black youths did not trust police or the criminal justice system. As a result, youths would not cooperate with police even in investigations of violent crime but instead armed themselves as a means of protection. In short, the respondents "reported lack of faith in police effectiveness and questioned whether there was a genuine commitment to keeping them safe. Consequently, legal cynicism contributed to young men's decisions to seek justice through retaliation" (Brunson & Wade, 2019:643). A classic study had similar findings.

Anderson (1994) argued that lower-class youths have little faith in the police and subscribe to a street code whereby the "police are most often seen as representing the dominant white society and not caring to protect inner-city residents" (Anderson, 1994:82). As a result of the perception and/or the reality that police do not respond when called, the inner-city youth often relies on self-protection: "taking care of himself" (Anderson, 1994:82) is a critical part of this street code.

WEB ACTIVITY

Gallup conducts polling on numerous attitudes, including attitudes about criminal justice. Consult the Gallup website (www.gallup.com) for up-to-date polling results.

Results from a study in St. Louis, Missouri, confirm Anderson's argument. This was a qualitative study that used a purposive sample of 75 African-American youths, a number of whom were highly active in delinquency. High percentages of the youths in St. Louis had been harassed or mistreated by the police. About half of both male and female respondents agreed that the police engage in frequent harassment or mistreatment of people. In summary, young men

> described being stopped on a regular basis and treated as suspects. They said officers routinely used disrespectful language, engaged in physically intrusive actions such as strip searches and cavity probes, and assumed young men "got lucky" rather than were innocent when no evidence of criminal wrongdoing was discovered. (Brunson & Miller, 2006:548)

Several of the young men reported that if police lacked enough evidence to arrest them, the officers would drive them to another area, let them out, and make them walk home (Brunson, 2007). Simply being a young black male in a disadvantaged neighborhood put these males at risk of police suspicion of criminal activity (Cobbina, Miller, & Brunson, 2008).

One study offers a suggestion for getting beyond the issue of race and attitudes toward the police. A study of four dimensions of trust in the police found that youths, whether white, black, or Latino, who had less commitment to school and who had seen police stop other youths and treat those other youths with disrespect had significantly less trust in the police. The lesson for police is that their behavior with the public can affect not only those with whom they are interacting but will also affect any witnesses (Flexon, Lurigio, & Greenleaf, 2009). Even delinquent youths who reported that they felt police treated citizens more fairly rated the police higher on legitimacy (Lee, Steinberg, & Piquero, 2010).

A study of more than 5,000 8th-grade students found that youths were "indifferent" toward the police—that is, they were neither positive nor negative (Taylor, Turner, Esbensen, & Winfree, 2001). Part of the reason for youths' indifference or negative attitudes toward the police is that youths often have negative experiences with the police. A study in Hartford, Connecticut, for example, found that the 132 youths interviewed reported approximately 400 negative experiences. Thirty-nine percent involved physical encounters (force, hitting, injury), 24 percent involved verbal harassment, and 34 percent were categorized as "other." For example, a 15-year-old Hispanic female reported being thrown against the ground and then against a wall when she was hanging out on the street with friends. A black youth suspected of dealing drugs when he was talking to a friend on the street was grabbed, thrown up against the car, and hit with billy clubs. (He admitted possessing but not dealing drugs.) Another youth was driving and was signaled to pull over. The officer smashed his car window and several officers grabbed, beat, and injured the youth (Borrero, 2001).

A national survey of 1,289 youths in middle and high schools found that youths who had been arrested had significantly less-positive attitudes toward the police than youths who had not been arrested or who had other types of contact with police. There were no gender differences in attitudes toward the police, but black youths had less favorable attitudes. Based on these findings, the authors suggest that police officers need to be aware of the troubled history between blacks and the police, and "efforts are made to become more inclusive of [b]lack perspectives" (Brick, Taylor, & Esbensen, 2009:493).

These variations in attitudes toward the police help to explain the paradox that police often hold negative or cynical views of citizens while citizen attitudes toward the police are actually rather positive. Part of the explanation for this apparent contradiction is that the police are much more likely to come in contact with citizens with less positive views—minority and younger citizens—than with older citizens who hold more positive views. A second explanation for the paradox is that the police often come into contact with citizens at inopportune times—in instances in which citizens have broken the law (even if only a traffic law), been victimized, or witnessed a crime. At such times, citizens are likely to be under stress. They may react with frustration at receiving a speeding ticket or at hearing an officer say that there is little hope of recovering their stolen property. Citizens may lash out at the available target (i.e., the police officer), much like a frustrated customer reacts to a customer service representative who is not responsible for the problem but has the unpleasant job of trying to rectify it. Repeated contacts with citizens in times of crisis can also lead the police to job burnout (Maslach & Jackson, 1979), cynicism (Niederhoffer, 1967), suspicion (Skolnick, 1966), and/or stress (Crank & Caldero, 1991; Kroes, Margolis, & Hurrell, 1974). In addition, dissatisfaction with a specific police contact leads to lower evaluations of police services in general (Huebner, Schafer, & Bynum, 2004).

By the time you read this chapter, Derek Chauvin will have been sentenced for killing George Floyd in Minneapolis and the case against the police officer who killed Daunte Wright will likely be resolved. Unfortunately, it is possible that even more cases of police killing unarmed black citizens will occur and attract media attention. At this point in time, police use of deadly force against black citizens is the major factor influencing the attitudes of black citizens, including black youths, toward the police. Thus, citizen attitudes toward the police will depend greatly on what reforms, if any, are pursued to decrease any improper police use of deadly force.

Implications of the Attitudinal Research

The most critical conclusion which can be drawn from this discussion of police attitudes toward citizens and citizen attitudes toward the police at this point in time is that police legitimacy is in serious question for many black citizens. Highly publicized shootings in the last few years have made blacks suspicious of police and have led to demonstrations, even calls from some to defund the police. Related to this, police are concerned that their decisions and actions are subject to scrutiny. It seems clear that reforms are necessary. Chapter 14 includes police reform as one of the reforms that legislators and the police themselves need to address to improve the future of juvenile justice. This crisis of legitimacy simply overshadows all other aspects of citizen and police attitudes toward each side at this time.

One possible suggestion comes from recent emphasis on the police as problem solvers. Some police experts think that traditional policing can do little more than take reports for many problems. If policing were restructured, however, perhaps more could be done about many of the concerns that citizens, black and white, have. If police spent less time running from call to call and more time exploring the causes and solutions of various problems, then the police could be more effective and have greater impact (see, e.g., Trojanowicz, Kappeler, Gaines, & Bucqueroux, 1998).

RECENT ISSUES IN POLICING CONCERNING JUVENILES

Police work with juveniles has undergone various changes over the past several decades. Among these initiatives are the introduction of police in schools, the problem of racial profiling and disproportionate minority contact, enforcement of curfew laws, participation in intensive supervision of probationers, and policing of underage drinking.

Police in Schools

Since the early 1990s, police presence in schools has grown considerably. In 2005–2006, 42 percent of schools reported one or more security staff (either security guards, security staff, or school resource officers [SROs]). That increased to 61 percent in 2017–2018. Specifically, for the 2017–2018 school year, 51 percent of primary schools, 80 percent of middle schools, and 84 percent of high schools had one or more security staff (either security guards, security staff, or SROs) present at least once a week (Wang, Chen, Zhang, & Oudekerk, 2020) (for more details on security in schools, see Table 7.1). Much of this growth is due to a number of highly publicized shootings in schools such as Columbine, Colorado, and Newtown, Connecticut, which attracted attention and action. Violent crime, drug violations, weapons violations, and bullying have also aroused concern and calls for increased police officer presence in schools (Booth, Van Hasselt, & Vecchi, 2011). One article claimed that both school police and surveillance cameras are in "widespread" use in urban, suburban, and rural schools (Hirschfield & Celinska, 2011). Specifically,

TABLE 7.1 Percentage of Schools with One or More Security Staff Present at Least Once a Week by Selected School Characteristics: School Year 2017–18	
School Characteristic	
School level	
Primary	51.4%
Middle	80.3
High School	84.3
Enrollment	
Less than 300	44.7%
300 to 499	51.5
500 to 999	69.0
1,000 or more	94.3
Locale	
City	63.3%
Suburban	63.3
Town	68.9
Rural	53.7
Percent of children eligible for free or reduced-price lunch	
0 to 25 percent	53.6%
26 to 50 percent	64.7
51 to 75 percent	61.6
76 to 100 percent	63.4

Source: Constructed by authors from Wang et al. (2020).

95 percent of schools now control access to school buildings, and 84 percent of schools use security cameras to monitor school buildings (Wang et al., 2020).

Student reports of security measures at school demonstrate the dramatic changes since 2001. In 2001, only 39 percent of students reported one or more security cameras at school, compared to 84 percent in 2017. In 2001, only 49 percent of students reported that exit doors were locked during the day, compared to 79 percent in 2017 (Wang et al., 2020).

Most police in schools were involved in traditional police functions, including patrolling, making arrests, and providing security (see Table 7.2). At the same time, many police officers in schools, particularly those in an SRO capacity, provided counseling, mentoring, and referrals as well as training to teachers and parents; taught programs such as Drug Abuse Resistance Education (D.A.R.E.); and chaperoned school events (Travis & Coon, 2005). (For discussion of the effectiveness of D.A.R.E., see Chapter 6.)

The introduction of police to schools has not been without controversy. Some observers argue that SROs try to balance their roles as law enforcers and mentors/instructors/problem solvers. Others contend that the widespread introduction of police into the school setting criminalizes school discipline.

At the same time as police have been introduced to school, there has been an introduction of zero-tolerance policies whereby students are suspended or expelled for certain behaviors such as bringing a weapon to school. Critics contend that the introduction of police resource officers and zero-tolerance policies are signs of criminalization in schools. In other words, instead of seeing discipline problems as requiring solutions by teachers and principals, these practices treat students as quasi-criminals and mandate quasi-criminal justice solutions and thereby label youths as criminals. Critics see this as part of a more general trend to ignore problems of poverty and deindustrialization. For example, "the transfer of disciplinary responsibilities from school professionals to the police also supports this purpose given that police are ill-equipped to recognize and address the psychological and social roots of school misconduct" (Hirschfield & Celinska, 2011:7).

This emphasis on police in schools and zero-tolerance policies are part of what is called the **school-to-prison pipeline** (Kim, Losen, & Hewitt, 2010). This refers to a combination of factors that appear to criminalize much youthful behavior and facilitate the eventual placement of youths in our nation's prisons. Kupchik (2014) argues that educational approaches such as tutoring, improved classroom management techniques, and increasing staff diversity are steps that schools could take to reduce problems.

TABLE 7.2 Activities of Law Enforcement Officers in Schools

- Law enforcement patrol
- Operate metal detectors
- Conduct safety inspections
- Respond to crime/disorder reports
- Make arrests
- Write reports
- Perform drug sweeps
- Advise/mentor staff
- Mediate disputes
- Advise students
- Work with parent-teacher groups
- Advise athletic teams
- Mentor students
- Chaperone events
- Present awards
- Teach D.A.R.E.
- Anti-gang classes
- Anti-hate classes
- Law-related education
- Firearm safety
- Crime awareness and prevention
- Conflict resolution
- Problem-solving

Source: Travis and Coon (2005).

A school resource officer (SRO) speaks with an 8th grader at Lewis and Clark Middle School in Billings, Montana.

CREDIT: AP Photo/Matthew Brown

A dramatic example of the school-to-prison pipeline is the Texas practice of handling truancy cases in adult court: 113,000 such cases in 2012. Part of the reason for this is that fines pay for more than half of the operating costs of truancy courts in Dallas County. Dallas County collected $2.9 million in such fines in 2012 (National School Boards Association, 2013). A complaint has been filed with the U.S. Department of Justice to investigate the practice.

One study found that arrest is related to a 20 percent increase in dropping out of high school and thus "hinders the transition to adulthood" (Kirk & Sampson, 2013:54). As a response to the more general problem, Connecticut probation officers are now reviewing each summons to avoid criminalizing "school incidents that are in keeping with normal adolescent behavior" (Bracey et al., 2013:428). More generally, the Council of State Governments Justice Center has recommended that police should not be involved in routine classroom management and minor offenses at school should not be referred to the courts (Morgan, Salomon, Plotkin, & Cohen, 2014).

Gottfredson and colleagues (2020) found that the presence of SROs in school does not reduce school crime and actually results in increases in weapon- and drug-related school crimes. The use of SROs in schools also increases the use of exclusionary responses (suspensions and expulsions) to disciplinary problems in schools. As a result, Gottfredson and her colleagues (2020) recommend that police only be regularly assigned to schools with extremely high levels of violence. Most schools just need an assigned officer who can respond when necessary but is not at the school on a regular basis.

As in other areas of juvenile justice, diversion programs have been instituted to offer another way to deal with school problems. One program in Florida had misdemeanor school offenders perform community service instead of being processed in juvenile court. The referred students completed 96 percent of the community service hours that they had been ordered to perform and a preliminary analysis of recidivism was promising (Sullivan, Dollard, Sellers, & Mayo, 2010). These positive findings indicate that there are at least some youths who do not need harsh punishment for school infractions but who will respond positively to programs that use more of a problem-solving approach.

Evaluations of effective school–police partnerships also indicate that more is needed than simply placing police officers in schools. First, many schools have problems such as overcrowding, lower attendance rates, larger minority populations, and lower funding than other schools. Second, evaluations of effective partnerships show the need for both parent cooperation and supplementing law enforcement presence "with intensive monitoring, counseling, and other related services that strengthen cooperation and collaboration with other community-based groups having a vested interest in the social justice needs of students attending schools in the community" (Brady, Balmer, & Phenix, 2007). This is congruent with research on Scared Straight (see Chapter 11). Simple solutions such as prison confrontation programs and putting police in schools are not cure-alls for complex problems such as delinquency.

Instead of measures such as zero tolerance of rule violations via expulsions from school and spending more dollars on measures such as increased police presence (SROs) and metal detectors, threat assessment seeks to identify troubled youth who may be at risk of committing school violence. Then a team of school officials such as counselors works to reduce any risk of violence by identifying what problems may be troubling the student and then trying to resolve those problems. Although clear evidence of effectiveness in preventing school violence cannot be claimed at present, experience in Virginia does show that "hundreds of threats to shoot others … have been resolved without violence" (Cornell, 2020:249). Such positive preliminary evidence stands in contrast to findings that "show no support for security measures to prevent shootings or reduce crime generally in schools" (Cornell, 2020:248). Another reason for adopting threat assessment is evidence that many adolescents contemplating an attack at school often leak out their intent to attack ahead of time (Silver, 2020). A threat assessment team could encourage students to report such leakages of intent and then try to address the situation before any violence occurred.

Race and Policing

The issue of police shootings (discussed above) raises the broader question of the effect of race on police decisions to arrest and juvenile court decisions to detain, petition, and sentence. The outcome of differential decision making is often called **disproportionate minority contact** (see Chapter 8 for more on disproportionate minority contact in juvenile court decisions). While black youths made up 15 percent of the U.S. population under juvenile court jurisdiction in 2018, they made up half of arrests for violent crime and 42 percent of arrests for property crime (Puzzanchera, 2020), 35 percent of delinquency cases in juvenile court, 40 percent of detention cases, and had a higher rate out-of-home placement than white youths (Hockenberry & Puzzanchera, 2020). A recent report noted that despite few differences in offending, black youths are "2.3 times as likely to be arrested as white youth for all delinquent offenses" (Rovner, 2016b:7). Arrest differences continue throughout the system: Black youths are more likely to get transferred to adult court and 19 percent more likely to be committed to an institution (Rovner, 2016a). This disproportionate contact raises the question of possible unfair police action.

A study by Pope and Snyder addressed this question. Using police data from the National Incident-Based Reporting System (NIBRS), they found that in the 17 jurisdictions analyzed there was "no evidence to support the hypothesis that police are more likely to arrest nonwhite juvenile offenders than white juvenile offenders, once other incident attributes are taken into consideration" (Pope & Snyder, 2003:6). Overall, victims identified 69.2 percent of offenders to be white, and 72.7 percent of juvenile offenders arrested were white. The only indication of bias was indirect: "Nonwhite juveniles … are more likely to be arrested when the victim is white than when the victim is nonwhite" (Pope & Snyder, 2003:6).

In a report on disproportionate minority contact in Pittsburgh, Rochester, and Seattle, evidence of such contact was found at all three sites. Huizinga et al. (2007) did not find evidence that differences in offending behavior explained the disproportionate contact. In other words, it is not the case that minorities clearly commit more delinquency and that this explains why police arrest more minorities. Risk factors such as type of neighborhood, family economic status, and youth education problems did substantially reduce the disproportionate minority contact. These findings do not necessarily prove police bias but are consistent with bias if bias does in fact exist (Huizinga et al., 2007). See Box 7.3 dealing with the race of the officer.

In an analysis of disproportionate minority contact in general, Bishop (2005) noted some of the subtler ways that race can enter into the policing of juveniles. First, police views of neighborhoods as dangerous or having suspicious persons are related to considerations of race and class. Related to this are high crime rates in urban underclass neighborhoods. A result is that police devote more surveillance to such neighborhoods, which leads to more encounters with juveniles and more arrests. Second, race can have an indirect effect via demeanor in police encounters with juveniles. For example, police can interpret a hostile or less cooperative demeanor as a sign of criminal propensity. Complainant preference can also have an effect. Complainants more often press for arrest of African-American suspects. Bishop thus concludes:

> In sum, the literature indicates that, for a number of reasons, minority youths are more likely than whites to be arrested, referred to court, and detained by police … The overrepresentation of minorities in police arrest data, especially for violent offenses, reinforces racist expectancies. (Bishop, 2005:45)

In an attempt to come up with a definitive answer on this question, Kochel, Wilson, and Mastrofski (2011:498) conducted a meta-analysis of 40 research reports and conclude "more definitively than prior nonsystematic reviews that racial minority suspects experience a higher probability of arrest than do Whites." Specifically, a minority suspect's probability of arrest is 30 percent higher than that of a white suspect (Kochel et al., 2011).

BOX 7.3 DOES THE OFFICER'S RACE MATTER?

In an observational study of Cincinnati, Ohio, police officers, Brown and Frank found that white officers are more likely to arrest suspects in general than black officers. The suspect's race had no effect on white officers' decisions to arrest, but it did have an impact on black officers' decisions. With situational circumstances being equal, the probability that a white officer would arrest a black suspect was 93 percent; the probability that a black officer would arrest a black suspect was 98 percent.

Source: Brown and Frank (2006).

The clear lesson is that race is a factor that needs close attention. Police need to be aware of how race can affect decisions to stop, to arrest, and to shoot. They also need to be clear that factors such as a youth's neighborhood and demeanor can bring in race as an indirect influence on those critical decisions. Moreover, police officials need to consider the racial impact of organizational decisions about which crimes to focus on, which neighborhoods to devote attention to, which policies (e.g., stop and frisk, any police war on drugs) to emphasize or de-emphasize, and hiring policies. Police officials need to make sound decisions about such issues as mandating body cameras, hiring minority officers, and providing effective training and oversight. Citizens, however, need to be aware of the pressures on police officers to make decisions in situations presenting danger to citizens and danger to the officer. As writers such as Rovner (2016b) stress, police are the gatekeepers of the system. Decisions police make have ripple effects throughout.

A further note is that a significant part of the problem and of any solution to the problem of race and policing is the war on drugs. Many argue that this war needs to be stopped or at least scaled down. As noted above, Alexander (2012) calls for the end of the war on drugs. Like Alexander, the Sentencing Project states: "Reforms should be enacted that scale back the use of prison for low-level drug crimes and instead redirect resources to prevention and drug intervention programs" (Nellis, 2016). The American Civil Liberties Union (2013) calls for an end to the war on marijuana.

Juvenile Curfew Laws

Juvenile curfew laws have been enacted in numerous cities across the country in an effort to reduce victimization of and by juveniles. The curfew law in Charlotte, North Carolina, included such objectives and also strove to "reinforce and promote the role of parents in raising and guiding children" (City of Charlotte Code, cited in Hirschel, Dean, & Dumond, 2001). To accomplish these goals, children under 16 years of age were prohibited from being on the streets from 11:00 P.M. to 6:00 A.M. during the week and from midnight to 6:00 A.M. on Friday and Saturday nights. Other cities with curfews may have different age or time stipulations. Vernon, Connecticut, for example, enacted a curfew for juveniles under 18 and prohibited them being on the streets from 11:00 P.M. to 6:00 A.M. every night of the week (Males, 2000). In one California city, the curfew applied from 11:00 P.M. to 5:00 A.M. on weeknights and from 1:00 A.M. to 5:00 A.M. on weekends. Exceptions involved standing in front of their own homes, returning home within one hour of attending certain activities, working, or being in the company of a parent (Sutphen & Ford, 2001).

Research on the effectiveness of curfews indicates that curfew laws do not reduce crime or victimization. For example, after the implementation of the curfew law in Vernon, Connecticut, Part I crimes did decrease, but the decrease "was similar to or less than the crime declines experienced in similar cities and the state as a whole" (Males, 2000:259). A time-series analysis of victimizations in New Orleans showed that the law was "ineffective for reducing victimizations, victimizations of juveniles, and juvenile arrests" (Reynolds,

Seydlitz, & Jenkins, 2000:219). A study of a curfew law in Washington, DC, that included a sophisticated replication design showed that it did not reduce juvenile crime (Cole, 2003). In addition, the laws do not appear to reduce subsequent offending by juveniles who are cited for curfew violations. In Charlotte, for example, 40 percent of the youths cited for curfew violations were arrested for an offense following their first curfew violation (Hirschel et al., 2001). A national evaluation of 52 counties showed that curfew laws only affected significant decreases in 3 of 12 crimes (burglaries, larcenies, and simple assaults). The authors concluded that their research "provides, at best extremely weak support for the hypothesis that curfews reduce juvenile crime rates" and that the "results do not encourage the idea that curfews help prevent juvenile crime" (McDowall, Loftin, & Wiersema, 2000:88).

In a review of studies of teen curfews, Adams (2003) identified 10 empirical studies of juvenile curfews. Adams concluded that the weight of the evidence from these 10 studies overall "fails to support the argument that curfews reduce crime and victimization" (Adams, 2003:155). Adams also questions the fairness of curfew law enforcement, arguing that curfew enforcement relies heavily on officer discretion. Adams worries that curfew enforcement will "fall most heavily on low-income and minority areas" (Adams, 2007:666). Two recent reviews failed to find support for curfews. One review found that the limited quality and number of research studies prevents drawing conclusions about the effectiveness of curfew laws (Grossman & Miller, 2015). Likewise, finding problems with the available research, a Campbell Systematic Review noted (not conclusively) that the "evidence suggests that juvenile curfews are ineffective at reducing crime or victimization" (Wilson et al., 2016:8).

One reason for the ineffectiveness of curfews is that the hours covered by the laws may not be times evidencing high victimization. In Vernon, Connecticut, for example, it was found that juvenile crime was much more likely to occur in the afternoon (Males, 2000). Nationally, it appears that violent offenses and gang crimes peak at approximately 3:00 P.M. (Sickmund, Snyder, & Poe-Yamagata, 1997). One response to this issue is to have daytime curfews for those youths who are not under the jurisdiction of truancy laws. One survey found that 10 percent of the responding jurisdictions had daytime curfews. In fact, some were so restrictive that even a youngster cutting class and not being in the place he was supposed to be in was technically in violation of that city's daytime curfew law (Bannister, Carter, & Schafer, 2001).

It appears that curfew laws may be on the way out. In the last few years, several Texas cities (Austin, San Antonio, and Waco) have voted down or repealed curfews, and other cities have backed off from enforcing curfews (Shane, 2019). The Austin Police Department found that other approaches could be used and that there were concerns that the curfew ordinance was applied disproportionately against minority youths (Cordner, 2020). On the other hand, Tennessee recently passed a curfew law that applies even to 18-year-olds, who are actually adults (McKeehan, 2017). For a list of cities that have a juvenile curfew, go to the website of the National Youth Rights Association (www.youthrights.org).

Assistance with Intensive Supervision of Probationers

Another way the police have enhanced their activity with juveniles is through their participation in probation. Anchorage, Alaska, has tried using police officers to enhance probation officer supervision of juvenile offenders. Anchorage used police officers to turn regular supervision into intensive supervision. This means that the juvenile probationers received additional contacts, contacts with their probation officers, and contacts with police officers. Like many previous intensive supervision programs, there was no reduction in criminal recidivism; there was no significant difference in the percentage of offenders under intensive supervision who committed any new offense or the percentage of offenders under regular supervision who committed any new offense. However, about 30 percent of the intensive supervision offenders had a probation violation, compared to 17 percent of the regular offenders. Thus, increased supervision translates into increased monitoring and detection of technical violations.

It is interesting that Anchorage tried an intensive supervision effort using police when so much prior research on intensive supervision has not been promising. What is promising is a program such as Operation Eiger in Baton Rouge, Louisiana. Here police also help probation officers conduct unscheduled evening visits six times per month, but the program involves addressing needs as well as enforcing probation conditions. Services are provided to deal with substance abuse, anger management, academic difficulties, and employment needs (Lizotte & Sheppard, 2001). Hopefully, this combination of intensive supervision and treatment will have greater success than the program in Alaska using intensive supervision alone.

San Bernardino, California, is another example of a police–probation partnership. There, a police officer and a probation officer together make a home visit to all new juvenile probationers. They explain the rules of probation and also search the probationer's residence for weapons and drugs. The program has had some effect in reducing serious crimes in the city, but one concern is **mission distortion** for probation. In other words, probation officers may no longer see themselves as service providers or social workers but may instead over-identify with a law enforcement role (Worrall & Gaines, 2006). (See also Chapter 11.)

A survey in Texas showed that most police agencies did not have formal partnerships with juvenile probation agencies. However, 71 percent did report a formal or informal information-sharing partnership with juvenile probation (Kim, Matz, Gerber, Beto, & Lambert, 2013). This suggests that police–probation partnerships are rather limited at this point in time.

Policing Underage Drinking

The National Minimum Drinking Age Act standardized the legal drinking age at 21 in 1984. Police bear responsibility to enforce this act. Studies show that youths under age 21 are able to purchase alcohol despite the law. Studies in the 1990s using either actual underage buyers or decoy buyers (individuals over 21 who looked younger than 21) showed that purchase rates ranged from 45 percent to 88 percent. A study in a large Midwestern area had an overall sales rate to pseudo-underage buyers of 26 percent (Britt, Toomey, Dunsmuir, & Wagenaar, 2006). The authors concluded that there has been progress in reducing such sales over the last decade and believed that improved training could result in even lower sales. Roodbeen and his colleagues contend that research has "documented the benefits of enhanced enforcement in reducing alcohol sales to minors, drinking behavior, and associated harm" (Roodbeen et al., 2020:722).

Police tend to use compliance checks or "Cops in Shops" programs to combat such underage alcohol purchases. Compliance checks are similar to the research just noted: police use underage decoys to try to purchase liquor. Cops in Shops programs put undercover officers in establishments to detect and cite youths who try to purchase alcohol illegally. Police agencies are twice as likely to use compliance checks as Cops in Shops programs (Montgomery, Foley, & Wolfson, 2006). (For further discussion of the issue of the legal drinking age, see Chapter 9.)

POLICE EFFECTIVENESS WITH JUVENILE CRIME

In examining **police effectiveness**, it is clear that the police are making a variety of efforts to combat juvenile crime. As noted earlier, police are staffing RAPP houses in Cleveland, working in schools in a variety of capacities, facilitating restorative justice conferences in Indianapolis, going to community meetings in Chicago, enforcing curfews all over the country, and participating in demonstration projects such as Operation Ceasefire in Boston.

Overall, how effective are the police in their new efforts against crime and delinquency? For many of these programs, we have already noted specific outcome results. Here a summary is in order.

First, some things simply do not work. Juvenile curfew laws, for example, have been tried in numerous cities. Most evaluations indicate that they are not very effective in the fight against juvenile crime. Related to this, most police encounters with juveniles are for matters such as "hanging out" that are not easily resolved. Even if the police do resolve them, they do not consider that much of an accomplishment. Youths, on the other hand, often see police reprimands as harassment (Watkins & Maume, 2012).

Second, a possible reason that some interventions do not work is that they are simplistic and contrary to what we know. Both the juvenile curfew laws and the Anchorage intensive supervision program, for example, stem from a Scared Straight panacea phenomenon that looks for simple answers: pass a law to keep juveniles off the street or ask a police officer to stop in at a juvenile's house. Human behavior is more complicated than this.

Third, research has indicated what is effective, such as problem-solving approaches, pulling levers strategies, and hot spots policing (Braga et al., 2014;

Braga, 2015). For example, a number of studies have shown that a problem-solving/pulling levers strategy reduces youth violence (Corsaro et al., 2009). Concerning hot spots, a Seattle analysis revealed that 50 percent of juvenile arrests took place in less than 1 percent of street segments. In general, much juvenile crime occurs on pathways to school or in areas where kids "hang out," such as playgrounds and malls. Accordingly, one author suggests that school officials be present on walk routes to school, that business owners keep an eye on nearby vacant lots, and that police and communities work to provide safe areas where youths can socialize (Roth, 2013).

Fourth, it is critical to avoid unrealistic expectations. In their study of community policing in Chicago, for example, Skogan and Hartnett (1997) found that some neighborhood conditions improved. Every neighborhood had at least one improvement. Victimization declined in two areas, street crime dropped in two others, drug and gang problems declined in two, and graffiti declined in another. Overall, compared to comparison areas, there were positive changes in 27 of the 51 outcomes that the evaluation measured, an overall success rate of 53 percent (Skogan & Hartnett, 1997:244). Skogan and Hartnett emphasize that communities should have realistic expectations from community policing. A success rate of 50 percent appears to be realistic. Expectations of 95 percent or even 75 percent success rates are fanciful.

Fifth, the police are only part of the picture. Eck and Maguire (2000), for example, contend that the decrease in crime in the last 10 years is the result of communities and the nation mobilizing to fight crime. Such mobilization involves police initiatives such as community policing, increased use of prison, demographic trends (the aging of the population and the decrease in the proportion of young males), and the decline of retail drug markets. A realistic perspective on the police impact on crime can be summarized as follows:

> There is one thing that is a myth: The police have a substantial, broad, and independent impact on the nation's crime rate. Rather than think of the police as an isolated institution that has a distinctive impact on crime, perhaps we should think of the police as part of a network of institutions, some of them formal (e.g., courts and schools) and some of them informal (e.g., families and churches), that respond to crime … When considered in isolation, the effectiveness of any one element of this diverse array of people and organizations may be slight. But collectively, the response might be more dramatic. (Eck & Maguire, 2000:247–248)

SUMMARY

Unfortunately, in the last few years attention has focused on several highly publicized incidents of police shootings. As noted above, there have been charges of racial bias and also concerns that police might refrain from responding to crime situations out of fear of being called racist. Police shootings have resulted in the Black Lives Matter Movement as a vehicle to protest perceived discriminatory policing. Some think the protests have gone too far and may cause police to refrain from proper law enforcement efforts.

In order to prevent problems, police are taking some specific steps, such as mandating body cameras. Several observers say that policing is in crisis (e.g., Walker, Spohn, & Delone, 2018; White & Fradella, 2016). It is clear that reform is necessary so that citizens feel safe and fairly treated and so that police feel they can do their job without unfair criticism. (See Chapter 14 for police reform suggestions.)

An important point to remember in any consideration of the police is that policing is only part of the effort to prevent, reduce, or control crime. When crime increases, much of society reacts, and many institutions and actors try to mobilize against crime. It is erroneous to think that the police alone can reduce crime. It is erroneous to think that SROs and zero-tolerance policies will be a magical solution to problems in schools. So instead of focusing only on the police, we should think of them as part of an interrelated network of responders.

> When violent crime grows into a serious social concern, it is not just the police that focus more attention on the problem. Schools, community groups, businesses, health officials, and many other organizations and individuals also respond to crime ... In summary, as the police mobilize to address crime more effectively, so do many other institutions. (Eck & Maguire, 2000:249–250)

So we will repeat our citation of Eck and Maguire at the end of the section on police effectiveness: It is a myth that the "police have a substantial, broad, and independent impact on the nation's crime rate" (Eck & Maguire, 2000:247), but a realistic review of the research shows evidence "for focused policing strategies contributing to the drop in violent crime" (Eck & Maguire, 2000:245). It is also important to note that "[s]ome of the policing strategies that have received the most attention (for example, CompStat and zero-tolerance policing in New York City) are the least plausible candidates for contributing to the reduction in violent crime" (Eck & Maguire, 2000:245).

We need to be realistic in our expectations of the police. On the one hand, citizens clearly have a right to expect unbiased policing. On the other hand, although the police play a role in combating delinquency, to expect the police to be the only factor—or even the most important factor—is unrealistic. Many factors contribute to delinquency and crime. All the institutions of society must play a part in addressing the problem.

DISCUSSION QUESTIONS

1. Community policing is based on the assumption that the job of the police is to solve the problems that lead to crime. Do you agree or disagree with this assumption? To what extent can society hold the police responsible for the problems that cause crime?

2. Police are trying new types of policing such as community or problem-solving policing, and "broken windows" policing. Which approach do you favor? Discuss. Note any possible problems with the various approaches.

3. What do we know about police attitudes toward citizens? About citizen attitudes toward the police? What can be done to improve attitudes on both sides?

4. What do curfew laws seek to accomplish? Are they effective?

5. What do we know about police use of force with juveniles? What can be done to minimize any improper use of force by police?

6. Schools are adopting school resource officers and zero-tolerance policies. Some argue that schools should devote more attention to improving classroom teaching and management. The most drastic issue in this area is the so-called school-to-prison pipeline. What can be done to minimize the criminalization of school misbehavior and avoid referring troublesome youths to court?

7. What can be done to improve policing in response to race-related issues such as police shootings, the war on drugs, and disproportionate minority contact? Some call for defunding the police and spending more money on mental health services or other approaches to delinquency prevention. Is there any reason to defund the police?

8. Policing is changing. Would you want to be a police officer in light of all the change that is taking place in policing? Are protests preventing any significant number of people from becoming police officers? Would any of the problems involving police make you hesitate about choosing a career in policing?

CHAPTER 8

The Juvenile Court Process

WHAT YOU NEED TO KNOW

- In 2018, juvenile courts processed almost 745,000 delinquency cases and about 98,000 petitioned status offense cases. Approximately 3,600 delinquency cases were transferred (waived) to adult court.

- The detention decision concerns whether to keep a juvenile in custody or to allow the youth to go home with his or her parents while awaiting further court action. Two options are secure detention and nonsecure detention.

- When an intake officer does not file a petition against a youth but tries to resolve the matter, that is called informal adjustment.

- Two avenues for youths not petitioned to court are teen court and drug court.

- The prosecutor's role in juvenile court may include approving petitions, deciding to prosecute some juveniles in adult courts, and prosecuting juveniles in juvenile court.

- There are several means for youths to be sent to adult court. The most traditional is transfer or waiver, in which the juvenile court judge makes the decision after a hearing.

- Statutory exclusion means that the state legislature rules that certain offenses automatically go to adult court.

- Prosecutorial waiver gives juvenile and adult court concurrent jurisdiction over certain cases. The prosecutor decides which court to use.

- Research on transfer indicates higher recidivism for youths who were transferred to adult criminal court.

- Adjudication and disposition in juvenile courts are the equivalent of conviction and sentencing in adult courts.

- There are several problems concerning attorney representation of juveniles: many youths waive their right to counsel, many attorneys have high caseloads and are poorly paid, and many defense attorneys are unsure whether they should follow the zealous advocate model of defense with juveniles.

KEY TERMS

adjudication

blended sentencing

concerned adult role

day–evening centers

detention decision

disposition

drug courts

home detention

informal adjustment

intake decision

justice by geography

legislative waiver

nonsecure detention

"once an adult, always an adult" provisions

petition

plea bargaining

prosecutorial waiver

reverse waiver

secure detention

statutory exclusion

teen courts

token economy programs

training schools

transfer (waiver)

zealous advocate role

DOI: 10.4324/9781003167112-8

■ In the late 1990s and early 2000s, the trend in juvenile court was one of increasing punitiveness, but a more recent trend is to consider the research from developmental psychology that teens are still in the process of maturing. One example has been legislation to return to age 18 as the initial age of adult criminal court jurisdiction. A second example is legislation in some states making changes in transfer provisions.

INTRODUCTION

Once a police officer takes a youth into custody, the police have several options. In 2019, 29 percent of the youths taken into custody were referred to juvenile court, and 2 percent were sent directly to adult criminal court. The other arrests were either handled within the police department and released (approximately 26 percent) or referred to a social welfare agency, another police agency, or another authority (about 43 percent) (FBI, 2020).

When police refer a youth to juvenile court, the court personnel must then make one or more critical decisions: whether to detain (jail) the youth, whether to actually file a **petition** (charges) against the youth, whether to find (adjudicate) the youth a delinquent, and how to dispose of the petition. These decisions correspond to the adult court decisions of bail versus jail, formal charge versus dismissal, determination of guilt by plea or by trial, and sentencing. An additional decision is whether to prosecute the youth as an adult in criminal court or retain jurisdiction in juvenile court. Several juvenile court actors—probation officers, defense attorneys, prosecutors, and judges—are involved in these important decisions. While the judge is often the primary decision-maker, other court personnel play important roles in deciding the fate of juvenile suspects.

This chapter will examine the critical decision points in the juvenile court process: detention, intake, file, transfer (waiver), adjudication, and disposition. We will look at the roles the various court personnel play and should play in the court process. We will describe what happens when a juvenile suspect goes through the juvenile court process and will compare the ideal with the reality. Finally, we will examine some of the controversial issues facing juvenile court today, such as the question of the impact of race on decision making and whether juveniles should have the right to a jury trial.

In 2018 (the latest year for which complete figures are available), juvenile courts processed almost three-quarters of a million (about 744,500) delinquency cases (see Figure 8.1). More than half (57 percent) of the delinquency cases were petitioned, and approximately 3,600 cases were transferred to adult court via judicial waiver (1 percent of all delinquency cases). An estimated 220,000 cases were adjudicated delinquent in juvenile court. Juvenile courts also processed an estimated 97,800 petitioned status offense cases.

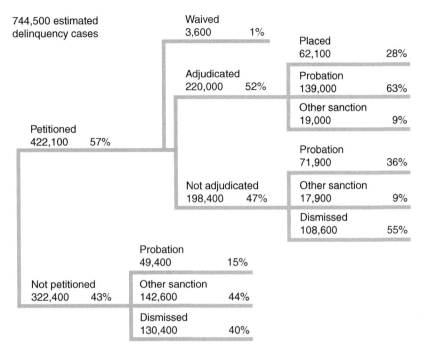

FIGURE 8.1
Juvenile Court Processing
of Delinquency
Cases, 2018

Source: Hockenberry
and Puzzanchera (2020).
Reprinted with permission.

744,500 estimated delinquency cases

Petitioned 422,100 57%

Waived 3,600 1%

Adjudicated 220,000 52%

Placed 62,100 28%

Probation 139,000 63%

Other sanction 19,000 9%

Not adjudicated 198,400 47%

Probation 71,900 36%

Other sanction 17,900 9%

Dismissed 108,600 55%

Not petitioned 322,400 43%

Probation 49,400 15%

Other sanction 142,600 44%

Dismissed 130,400 40%

Thirty-five percent of these were adjudicated a status offender (see Figure 8.2) (Hockenberry & Puzzanchera, 2020). Finally, several thousand youths were processed in adult court as a result of direct file by prosecutors or by statutory exclusion (see below for additional details). (For the latest statistics, go to "Easy Access to Juvenile Court Statistics," available at www.ojjdp.gov.)

As the figures show, over 60 percent of the adjudicated delinquency cases and almost 60 percent of the adjudicated status offense cases were placed on probation. Some non-adjudicated cases also were placed on probation. Significant proportions of adjudicated delinquency and status offense cases (28 percent and 7 percent, respectively) were ordered into residential placement (Hockenberry & Puzzanchera, 2020).

DETENTION

The first decision that juvenile court personnel must make is the **detention decision**. It must be decided whether to keep a juvenile in custody or to allow the youth to go home with his or her parents while awaiting further court action. The detention decision is the juvenile court counterpart of the bail decision in adult court. It is very important because it concerns the freedom of the child and, therefore, resembles the disposition decision. In fact, children sent to detention may stay there for an extensive period of time—perhaps even for a longer time than children sent to state **training schools** (i.e., youth prisons for juveniles determined to be delinquent). In 2018, approximately 202,900 delinquency cases involved detention. This number represents approximately 26 percent of delinquency cases, slightly above 2005 (25 percent). The offense

FIGURE 8.2
Juvenile Court Processing of Petitioned Status Offense Cases, 2018

Source: Hockenberry and Puzzanchera (2020). Reprinted with permission.

profile of detained delinquency offense cases was 36 percent person offense cases, 29 percent property cases, 8 percent drug cases, and 27 percent public order cases (Hockenberry & Puzzanchera, 2020). It should be noted that detention can also be used in some states as a disposition for a brief period of incarceration and as a sanction for violations of probation conditions (Griffin & King, 2006).

For status offense cases, in 2018, detention was used in 5 percent of cases, down from 10 percent in 2005. This percentage was similar for whites and blacks. The offense profile of detained status offense cases was 20 percent runaway, 33 percent truancy, 6 percent curfew, 14 percent ungovernability, 18 percent liquor law, and 10 percent miscellaneous. It should be noted that the number of status offense cases involving detention decreased 78 percent from 2005 to 2018 (from 20,000 to 4,500) (Hockenberry & Puzzanchera, 2020).

Black youths made up a disproportionate share of the detention caseload. They made up 35 percent of the total delinquency caseload and 40 percent of the detention caseload (Hockenberry & Puzzanchera, 2020). In one study, the average IQ score of detainees was 82.5, well below average (Viljoen, Klaver, & Roesch, 2005).

Several years ago it was estimated that it cost about $116 to keep one child in detention for one day in 2005, and just over $200 a day in 2006 (Cohen &

Pfeifer, 2011). Crowding is often a problem; 20 percent of public detention facilities were over capacity in 2002 (Snyder & Sickmund, 2006).

Detention workers or probation officers usually make the initial detention decision. State law may stipulate that a detention hearing be held within a specified period of time so that a judge can rule on the continued need for detention. The Model Juvenile Delinquency Act, a guideline for state codes, stipulates that the detention hearing be held within 36 hours and that certain criteria be used to decide whether to detain a particular youngster (Rossum, Koller, & Manfredi, 1987; see Box 8.1 for the relevant section of the Model Juvenile Delinquency Act).

A troubling feature of detention hearings is that often they are the first opportunity for the juvenile to meet with an attorney. In one study, more than half of the public defenders did not meet their clients prior to the detention hearing. In one site, an unsupervised law student with no background investigations on the youths represented youths at detention hearings (Puritz, Burrell, Schwartz, Soler, & Warboys, 1995). In Pennsylvania, a study found that at detention hearings attorneys did not have much opportunity to confer with their juvenile clients and were not familiar with alternatives to detention (Miller-Wilson & Puritz, 2003).

As noted in Chapter 10, many youths in the juvenile justice system have a mental health disorder (see Skowyra & Cocozza, 2006). A study of almost 2,000 juvenile detainees in Chicago found approximately 10 percent had thought about committing suicide in the six months prior to being interviewed, and 10 percent had attempted suicide in the past. Cutting and drug overdose were the most common methods used in recent suicide attempts (Abram, Paskar, Washburn, & Teplin, 2008). For youths with mental health problems, barriers to receiving mental health services can exist. More than half of such detainees believed that their problem would go away or they could solve it on their own, and about one-third were not sure where to get help (Abram et al., 2008). In

---

BOX 8.1 MODEL JUVENILE DELINQUENCY ACT

Section 26. [Grounds for Pre-Hearing Detention]
A youth taken into custody may be detained if there is probable cause to believe that:

- The juvenile is a fugitive from justice;

- The juvenile has committed a felony while another case was pending;

- The juvenile has committed a delinquent act and

- The juvenile will likely fail to appear for further proceedings;

- Detention is required to protect the juvenile from himself or herself;

- The juvenile is a threat to the person or property of others;

- The juvenile will intimidate witnesses or otherwise unlawfully interfere with the administration of justice; or

- There is no person available or capable of caring for the juvenile.

Source: Rossum et al. (1987:33).

addition, more than 90 percent of the detainees had experienced trauma and 11 percent had experienced post-traumatic stress disorder (PTSD) in the previous year (Abram et al., 2013).

Substance use and abuse are also problems. More than three-quarters of detained male juveniles in Cook County (Chicago, Illinois) reported marijuana use in the previous six months, and 4 percent reported cocaine use. Three-quarters of female detainees reported marijuana use, and 10 percent reported cocaine use (McClelland, Teplin, & Abram, 2004). These findings indicate some of the treatment needs in detention facilities. Fortunately, most detention centers do screen for substance abuse, mental health needs, and suicide risk (Snyder & Sickmund, 2006; for details on California, see Cohen & Pfeifer, 2011).

Physical health concerns also need attention. For example, testing at the Harris County (Houston, Texas) juvenile detention center in 2006 and 2007 showed that about 10 percent of the boys and about 25 percent of the girls tested positive for a sexually transmitted disease. More positively, only two boys and no girls tested positive for HIV (Schneider, 2008).

Detention Options

Court personnel have several options at the detention decision point. Releasing a child to his or her parents is the most frequently used option; this is the preferred decision in most states (e.g., Alabama Code 12-15-59). Secure detention—placing a child in the juvenile equivalent of a local jail—is another alternative. It involves placement in a locked facility of 10, 20, or more youths who are awaiting further court action or are awaiting transfer to a state correctional facility. In some places, nonsecure detention is another option for youths involved in less serious crimes and for those who do not pose much threat to the community or themselves. Such youths may be placed in small group homes that are not locked or not locked as comprehensively as a secure detention facility—hence the term "nonsecure." Youths housed in nonsecure detention centers might even go to regular public school classes during the day. Alternatives to detention, such as home detention, will be discussed later in this chapter.

Detention Decision Making

As noted above, in 2018, black youths made up a disproportionate share of the detention caseload. Research confirms that minority youths are more likely to be detained than white youths (Bishop, 2005; Piquero, 2008). One reason for this is structural disadvantage, that is, living in disadvantaged areas (Rodriguez, 2010). Many courts are now using risk assessment instruments to base the detention decision on proven risk factors and reduce possible bias. For an example of a risk assessment instrument, see Box 8.2.

Amendments in 1992 to the Juvenile Justice and Delinquency Prevention Act were intended to reduce disproportionate minority contact (DMC) in general. The Juvenile Detention Alternatives Initiative (JDAI) was funded by a

BOX 8.2 EXAMPLE OF A RISK ASSESSMENT INSTRUMENT

New York State calculates a Risk Score for a youth's Detention Recommendation based on four factors (one point for each positive answer):

1. A prior delinquency petition;

2. A prior status offense petition;

3. An outstanding delinquency or status offense warrant;

4. The current arrest charges include burglary, grand larceny, autostripping, or motor vehicle theft.

A score of two to four calls for detention. A score of zero calls for release without restrictions and a score of one calls for release with restrictions. There is also a list of reasons for not following the risk-score recommendation.

Source: Website of the New York State Office of Children and Family Services. Available at www.ocfs.state.ny.us/main/rehab/drai.

private foundation in the early 1990s to reduce secure detention and increase the use of community alternatives to detention. It has both reduced the use of detention by as much as 50 percent and also helped to reduce racial disparities in detention in several jurisdictions (Barton, 2012). For example, a study of decision making in a Virginia court that has been implementing the JDAI found that race was not a significant predictor of detention decisions, apparently due to the use of a risk assessment instrument to help caseworkers make decisions based on relevant criteria. Girls, however, continued to benefit from a degree of leniency as they were less likely to receive secure detention than boys (Maggard, Higgins, & Chappell, 2013). Race, however, did affect override decisions, that is, decisions to go against the outcome determined by one's score on a risk assessment instrument. Thus, policymakers need to review and possibly change instruments if workers believe that numerous override decisions are appropriate (Chappell, Maggard, & Higgins, 2012).

WEB ACTIVITY

If you Google "detention risk assessment instrument," you will be able to see a number of instruments in use in various states. Or go to the website of the Annie E. Casey Foundation (www.aecf.org) to get details on their Juvenile Detention Alternatives Initiative efforts.

Detention Programming

The psychological technique of behavior modification has inspired many detention centers to use token economy programs. With this approach, staff members use points or dollar values to reward detained youths for appropriate behavior and withhold or subtract points for inappropriate behavior. Youths earn credits when they follow the rules and they lose credits when they disobey the rules. If they have more credits than losses, they can "purchase" rewards such as snacks, table games, and room privacy at the end of the day and/or on the weekend. (See Box 8.3 for examples of rewards, punishments, and costs.) This type of program is based on psychological principles of conditioning that contend that human behavior is learned through reinforcements.

BOX 8.3 DETENTION REWARDS AND FINES

How Dollars May Be Earned:

1.	School attendance	$10
2.	YMCA activities	$10
3.	Cleaning room (make beds, sweep, mop, etc.)	$5
4.	Extra work (per hour)	$5
5.	Good hygiene	$5
6.	Attending church, etc.	$5
7.	Cleaning unit	$10
8.	Good behavior	$5

Fines for Inappropriate Behaviors:

1.	Body contact (slapping, etc.)	$20
2.	Disrespect (sarcastic or abusive speech, not following rules)	$30
3.	Profanity	$10
4.	Instigating (influencing others to break rules)	$30
5.	Arguing (other youth or staff)	$30
6.	Lying	$40
7.	Complaining (irritating staff with complaints about program, food, other staff, dollars, etc.)	$25
8.	Contraband	$50
9.	Fighting (another resident)	$100
10.	Attempted escape	$150

Source: Constructed by authors from *Handbook of Procedures, Rules, and Regulations* (Jefferson County Detention Center, Birmingham, Alabama). Items have been renumbered by authors.

Given the unique needs of girls in detention, it is critical that detention centers develop gender-specific programs for girls. One issue is that about 70 percent of girls in the juvenile justice system have histories of physical abuse compared to only about 20 percent of the boys (Lederman & Brown, 2000). Programming should also include attention to alcohol, drug, and mental disorders. As noted above, significant proportions of detained juveniles have one or more of these problems.

Positive Programs

Research has found that education should be the cornerstone of detention programming. It is important for detention centers to teach basic academic skills, general education development (GED) test preparation, and also special education, employment readiness training, and programs about social, cognitive, and life skills such as problem-solving and moral reasoning (Stephens & Arnette, 2000). For example, in Jackson, Mississippi, the detention center is actually an extension of the district public school alternative school. In addition to academic programming, the school also offers vocational training and parent training (an "effective parenting" course) (Stephens & Arnette, 2000).

Arizona has been using character education in its detention and correctional facilities since 2001. Based on programs in regular schools, the "Character Counts!" program teaches character traits that philosophers and religious leaders of all denominations can agree on: trustworthiness, respect, responsibility, fairness, caring, and citizenship. An independent evaluation found an increase in positive behaviors such as taking responsibility and not making excuses (Martinez, 2008).

Often the best programming is to find an alternative to detention. The Juvenile Detention Alternatives Initiative has been operating for some 25 years. Participating sites have reduced the annual number of days in detention by about 1.4 million days, cut annual admissions by 49 percent, and documented juvenile crime decreasing by more than 40 percent on the indicators evaluated (Annie E. Casey Foundation, 2017).

The survey of youth in residential placement (a survey of youths in various types of placement) gives some indication of what juveniles think about their experiences. The survey showed some problem areas. One-quarter (25 percent) of the detained youths reported being afraid of being attacked by another resident, and more than 20 percent (22 percent) reported being afraid of being attacked by a staff member. About one-quarter reported problems with dirty sheets, towels, or clothes, and one-third reported dirty bathrooms. On the positive side, however, one-third of the youths in detention surveyed reported a good recreational program, and 42 percent reported a good school (Sedlak & McPherson, 2010a).

A disturbing issue is that about 33 percent of detained youths have experienced solitary confinement (Rubin, 2013). In addition, a recent investigation found that few detention centers met minimal standards of health care, with wide variability according to race and geography (Barton, 2012).

DETENTION ALTERNATIVES

Because of criticisms of detention programming and because of the high costs of detaining youngsters in secure detention facilities, many jurisdictions have sought alternatives to traditional detention facilities. For example, years ago, New York City found that at the time secure detention cost about $58,000 per year per child and that nonsecure detention (foster care and boarding homes) cost about $20,000 per year. Hence, they began using converted stores or lofts as **day–evening centers**. In such centers, mornings involved formal educational programs, early afternoons were devoted to remedial and tutorial work, and late afternoons were reserved for recreational programs (e.g., weekly swimming at YMCA facilities). Two of the four New York City centers also offered evening hours twice a week for children considered to need extra supervision and for those on a waiting list for admission into the day program (Lindner, 1981). In Washington, DC, evening report centers have had 90 percent of youths report for all court dates and no rearrests pending court processing (Muhammad, 2019).

Home Detention

Another popular alternative to traditional detention is home detention. This is the juvenile court counterpart of supervised pretrial release for adult criminal defendants. In home detention, the youth awaiting further juvenile court action is allowed to live at home but is also under the supervision of a detention worker who ensures that the youth is attending school (or working on a job) and maintaining a curfew. The detention worker, often a paraprofessional, may check on the home detention youngster up to four times a day if the worker suspects that the child is getting into new trouble (delinquency). Studies show that 70–90 percent of home detention youths do not reoffend and appear in court (Austin, Johnson, & Weitzer, 2005). Similarly, Dallas is now using electronic monitoring for truants instead of detention (Kovach, 2008).

Bail

Bail is not universally available in juvenile court (Rossum et al., 1987:109), but bail for juveniles appears to be an option that is receiving greater attention. New Mexico, for example, authorized bail for serious youthful offenders detained before trial in an adult facility (National Conference of State Legislatures, 1993). This is a reflection of the changing philosophy of the juvenile court, from *parens patriae* to punishment. Bail is considered inappropriate in the traditional juvenile court, in which the judge acts like a concerned parent in deciding to detain or release juveniles awaiting further court action. With the changing views of juvenile crime and juvenile court, however, states are beginning to see bail as a reasonable option. The current view that the juvenile is a responsible criminal rather than an immature youth in need of help is consistent with the use of bail as a means to guarantee continued appearance for court hearings.

THE INTAKE DECISION

The second major decision point in juvenile court is the intake decision, analogous to the filing decision in adult court. At intake, a court official—either a probation officer or a prosecutor (or both)—decides whether to file a court petition of delinquency, status offense, neglect, abuse, or dependency in a particular case. Traditionally, a probation officer has made the intake decision. The *parens patriae* philosophy of the court dictated this approach because its treatment orientation indicated that the probation officer (ideally a trained social worker) should consider the best interests of the child as well as the legal aspects of the case (as an adult court prosecutor might). That is, an intake probation officer is supposed to resolve every case in light of the considerations of the welfare of the child and the legal demands of the police and victim. This tradition is changing; a number of states even allow prosecutors to make the decision to file certain cases directly in adult criminal court and thereby completely bypass the juvenile court.

Informal Adjustment

One frequent decision of the intake officer is not to file a petition alleging delinquency or a status offense, but instead to try to resolve the matter without resorting to a formal petition against the child. As noted above, almost half (43 percent) of the estimated 744,500 delinquency cases coming to juvenile court in 2018 were not petitioned (Hockenberry & Puzzanchera, 2020). (Statistics on the number of status offense cases not petitioned are not available.) Many (4 out of 10) of the nonpetitioned cases were dismissed; others were handled informally. Informal handling is usually called adjustment at intake or **informal adjustment**. Examples would include requiring a first-time shoplifter to pay restitution to the store or ordering a vandal to paint the public building he or she has defaced. Similarly, intake probation officers often try to counsel troubled family members on a short-term basis or to refer them to counseling services in the community. As a result, a youth involved in runaway behavior, chronic disobedience ("incorrigibility"), or repeated truancy will not be immediately petitioned to court as a status offender. Instead, the youth receives help in dealing with the problem that brought him or her to the attention of court officials.

It is important to note that such informal adjustment practices occur as frequently as 25 percent of the time (Butts, 1994; McCarthy, 1987) and have been part of juvenile court since its inception. With the emphasis on diversion in the 1970s, informal adjustment practices by intake officers took on added dimensions.

Teen Courts

One diversion option to the traditional juvenile court is the use of **teen courts** (sometimes called youth courts). Here the philosophy is based on restorative justice, and youths act as judge, attorney (prosecutor and defense attorney), and jury in cases involving status offenses, misdemeanors, and occasionally a low-level felony. (About one-half of teen courts use adult judges.) The most common penalty is community service. Other sentences include teen court jury duty, writing essays about offending, writing apologies to victims, and monetary restitution. As of 2017, it was estimated that there were more than 1,050 teen court programs in operation handling more than 100,000 cases per year, making them a primary diversion option (National Association of Youth Courts, 2020).

Two studies of the effectiveness of teen courts found no difference between teen courts and comparisons, but three studies found lower recidivism rates in teen court cases than for comparison youths. A study of an Illinois teen court found that most of the offenses handled were low-level infractions such as shoplifting (43 percent of the cases processed), curfew violation, possession of marijuana, disorderly conduct, and so on. Recidivism was only 12 percent after one year and 19 percent after two years (Rasmussen, 2004).

A multi-site study of teen courts in Alaska, Arizona, Maryland, and Missouri found statistically less recidivism for teen court youths in two of the four sites. In Alaska, 6 percent of teen court youths recidivated, compared to 23 percent of non-teen court youths; in Missouri, 9 percent of teen court youths recidivated, compared to 28 percent of non-teen court youths. The authors of the study concluded that "teen courts represent a promising alternative for the juvenile justice system" (Butts, Buck, & Coggeshall, 2002:34). A recent review of teen courts examined results from 22 experimental or quasi-experimental studies of teen courts. For the 15 studies reporting statistically significant findings, 10 found no difference, one found traditional juvenile court more effective, and only four found teen courts more effective (Gase, Schooley, DeFosset, Stoll, & Kuo, 2015). The lead author later did a study of Los Angeles teen courts and found modest support for the positive effects of that teen court system (Gase, Kuo, Lai, Stoll, & Pone, 2016). In response to some issues in the Gase et al. research, Bouchard and Wong (2017) did a further statistical analysis of available evaluations of teen courts but still found that teen court is no more effective at reducing recidivism than formal juvenile court handling or diversion programming.

Teen court is not intended to deal with serious delinquency, but it appears to be an alternative method for dealing with status offenses, minor delinquent acts such as shoplifting, or problems with alcohol or marijuana. As one author put it, teen court may be a "partial solution to the juvenile justice system's failure to give anything more than a 'slap on the wrist' to first-time offenders" (Rasmussen, 2004:615) but at present the results are mixed (Gase et al., 2016).

Drug Courts

Another diversion option is juvenile **drug courts** in which the judge, prosecutor, and defense attorney collaborate as a team with drug treatment specialists. Like adult drug courts, juvenile drug courts attempt to intervene in both the criminal activity and the drug usage of clients. The courts use treatment, coordination, and extensive monitoring. The youths must appear in court frequently so that judges can monitor progress and offer encouragement and admonishment to the juveniles. There is frequent drug testing, and there are penalties for failing to test negative. Sanctions for youths that are not following the rules can range from a warning, an order to write a book report or paper or to do household chores, to fines, community service hours, or even detention. There also are incentives such as the dismissal of charges and termination of probation requirements upon graduation. Other rewards include verbal praise and such incentives as gift certificates and tickets to local events. Drug courts usually celebrate completion with a graduation ceremony in court that may include additional features, such as a gift of athletic shoes (Rossman, Butts, Roman, DeStefano, & White, 2004).

As noted in Chapter 6, there is mixed evidence on the effectiveness of juvenile drug courts. Earlier studies found some positive results. However, recent studies have been discouraging. A recent meta-analysis of drug courts found that adult drug courts were more effective than juvenile drug courts. Whereas adult drug courts reduced overall recidivism from 50 to 38 percent, juvenile drug courts only reduced overall recidivism from 50 to 43.5 percent, an effect the authors describe as "small" (Mitchell et al., 2012). An Office of Juvenile Justice and Delinquency Prevention-sponsored study of drug courts in nine sites found almost no support for juvenile drug courts. Most of the sites saw higher recidivism for drug court youths compared to matched youths on probation. The authors speculate that the drug court model may be more appropriate for adults rather than adolescents due to such factors as the ability of youths to weigh costs and benefits (Blair et al., 2015) and differences in youthful drug use compared to adult use (Sullivan, Blair, Latessa, & Sullivan, 2016). A review and meta-analysis of 46 studies found "no clear evidence" of the effectiveness of juvenile drug courts in reducing general recidivism, drug recidivism, or drug use compared to traditional juvenile court processing (Tanner-Smith et al., 2016). However, their analysis allowed for the possibility "that there are some configurations of juvenile drug courts that are effective" (Tanner-Smith et al., 2016:509). These authors also noted that much youth drug use is experimental and thus many of the youths sent to juvenile drug courts may not actually have a substance-abuse disorder. In summary, these reviews of the research indicated that juvenile drug courts have not been very effective and perhaps drugs courts are not the best approach for adolescents. It is also important to note that not completing drug treatment has been a persistent problem for persons in various types of treatment (Stein, Deberard, & Homan, 2013).

Thus, one possible problem with drug courts is that they may be reaching the wrong population. If drug courts are actually intended for drug-dependent or addicted youths, they are not capturing many such youths with severe drug problems.

> If, on the other hand, juvenile drug courts are designed to deliver prevention services for a broad cross-section of youth involved with alcohol and other drugs, then their current mode of operating may be appropriate, but such a broad mission would raise other questions about the risks of labeling, net-widening, and iatrogenic effects (i.e., the cure may be worse than the disease). (Butts, Zweig, & Mamalian, 2004:142)

Much like the "war" on drugs in general, drug courts often paint a wide stroke that takes in more than is necessary. We worry so much about adolescent drug use that we overreact and do too much.

A related reform is juvenile mental health courts. Recent information indicates that there are more than 300 mental health courts nationwide but does not specify how many of these are juvenile mental health courts (Council of State Governments Justice Center, 2017). Research on the effectiveness of mental health courts is inconclusive, with program completion being a critical factor

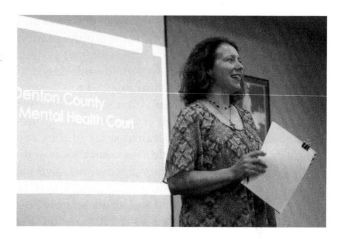

Judge Kimberly McCary gives a presentation on a juvenile mental health court called SOAR at the Emily Fowler Library in Denton, Texas.

CREDIT: Daniel Burgess/*The Denton Record-Chronicle* via AP

in any success (Lim & Day, 2014). However, one study found positive personal effects beyond the usual focus on recidivism. Specifically, Canada and Ray (2016) found that clients reported reduced psychiatric symptoms, increased periods of sobriety, improved personal relationships, and more positive engagement in life.

The Prosecutor's Role

If an intake probation officer decides to file a petition against a child, often that decision requires the approval of an attorney, normally the prosecutor. The prosecutor's approval of the probation officer's decision to file a petition ensures that a legally trained official has reviewed the legal criteria for a properly authorized petition. The prosecutor checks the legal wording of the petition, determines that enough evidence is available for establishing the petition (finding the delinquent or status offender "guilty"), and makes sure that the offense occurred in the court's jurisdiction and that the child was of proper age at the time of the offense.

Because of the importance of such legal criteria, and because of the emphasis on more punitive juvenile models, some jurisdictions have turned away from the traditional probation-officer model of intake toward models in which the prosecutor is either the first or the sole intake decision-maker. Such models are more consistent with more legalistic views of juvenile court in which the state has abandoned the traditional *parens patriae* philosophy. For example, the state of Washington has switched responsibility for the intake decision to the prosecutor for all felony charges and most misdemeanors. There prosecutors make such decisions on the basis of explicit criteria: offense seriousness, prior record, and the age of the youth. Furthermore, informal adjustments are no longer permitted at intake, although police agencies can still "exercise their traditional discretion regarding whether to refer or adjust incidents involving juveniles" (Schneider & Schram, 1986:214). In place of informal adjustments at intake, minor offenses are supposed to be diverted to restitution programs. This action by Washington represents a radical break with traditional juvenile court thinking and practice and is a close approximation of adult processing

---

BOX 8.4 THE INTAKE PROCESS

Traditional Intake	Prosecutorial Model (e.g., Washington State)
• Police, parents, school officials, or victims bring youths to attention of Intake	• Police, parents, school officials, or victims bring youths to attention of Intake
• Intake officer files petition OR makes an informal adjustment OR diverts to a treatment program	• Prosecutor files a petition OR declines to file a petition OR diverts to a restitution program
• Juvenile court hearing	• Juvenile court hearing

---

with its retributive emphasis. (For a diagrammatic comparison of traditional intake and the Washington State practice, see Box 8.4.) Like the legislation in the state of Washington, the Model Juvenile Delinquency Act also stipulates that the prosecutor shall "[d]irectly supervise all matters relating to intake," although the probation officer may continue to make the file-divert decision in misdemeanor cases if the prosecutor so delegates (Rossum et al., 1987:40). Similarly, the National District Attorneys' Association stipulates a very active role for the prosecutor (Shine & Price, 1992), and Louisiana has given the prosecutor greater authority over the intake process (National Conference of State Legislatures, 1993).

A development in the early 2000s was that the prosecutor was taking on increased responsibility in juvenile cases as more states were allowing prosecutors to file cases directly in adult criminal court. In addition to traditional waiver (transfer), several mechanisms allow prosecutors to proceed against juveniles in criminal court: concurrent jurisdiction, statutory exclusion, presumptive waiver, reverse waiver, and "once an adult/always an adult" statutes. (These prosecutor options will be discussed in greater depth later in this chapter.)

Research on Intake Decision Making

As was the case with police discretion (see Chapter 7), many researchers and analysts have been concerned about the discretion of intake decision-makers either to file or not file petitions. Of particular concern has been the question of whether race is an important factor in the intake decision and whether racial discrimination occurs at intake. This issue has been termed the issue of disproportionate minority contact or DMC.

Several conclusions can be drawn from the studies that have been conducted on intake decision making. First, seriousness of the alleged offense clearly influences the decision to file a petition, though it is not necessarily the prime factor. Thus, youths accused of more serious offenses are more likely to be petitioned to court than youths accused of less serious offenses (Bishop & Leiber, 2012; McCarthy & Smith, 1986; Minor, Hartmann, & Terry, 1997). Second, prior record is a factor. Youths with prior records are more likely to be referred (Fenwick, 1982; McCarthy & Smith, 1986). Third, demeanor often has an effect; uncooperative youths are more likely to be petitioned than cooperative youths (Bell & Lang, 1985; Fenwick, 1982). However, demeanor often is not measured in studies because many researchers rely on official records that do not include any record of the attitude of the child when he or she is interviewed by the court official making the intake decision. Finally, variables such as age, race, class, and gender have produced mixed results. As a result, there is considerable controversy surrounding the impact of each of these variables on the intake decision (for a review and analysis, see Bishop, 2005; Bishop & Leiber, 2012). (For further discussion of DMC, see the section on Dispositional Decision Making below.)

PROCESSING JUVENILES IN ADULT CRIMINAL COURT

Many juvenile offenders are now being handled in adult criminal court rather than juvenile court. This is a crucial decision because processing a youth in adult court makes the juvenile subject to adult penalties such as lengthy incarceration in an adult prison as opposed to a relatively short period of incarceration in a juvenile training school. Such a decision also results in the creation of an adult criminal record, which is public and may hinder future opportunities for employment in certain occupations. A juvenile court record, on the other hand, is usually confidential and, therefore, should not harm the child in any way.

There are several methods that states use to place juveniles into adult court jurisdiction: **transfer or waiver**, statutory exclusion, prosecutorial waiver, and lowering the age of juvenile court jurisdiction. Traditionally, waiver or transfer was the primary method of placing juveniles into adult criminal court. Most states (46) have statutes allowing judicial waiver (Hockenberry, 2021).

In 2018, approximately 3,600 juvenile cases were waived to adult criminal court (Hockenberry & Puzzanchera, 2020). This is 73 percent below the peak number of 13,300 cases waived in 1994. The offense profile of waived cases in 2018 was 56 percent person cases, 26 percent property cases, 10 percent drug cases, and 8 percent public order cases (Hockenberry & Puzzanchera, 2020).

Juvenile courts are waiving or transferring fewer cases to adult court because the states have been using other means (statutory exclusion and prosecutorial waiver) to prosecute juveniles in adult criminal court. One estimate was that states use legislative exclusion, prosecutorial discretion, and judicial transfer (waiver) to transfer more than 10,000 youths a year to adult criminal court, and that about 84,000 16- and 17-year-old youths are processed in adult court due to their state's jurisdictional age limits (Butts & Roman, 2014). However, this number will probably decrease since more states have returned to age 18 as the initial age of criminal court jurisdiction (see Chapter 14).

Statutory exclusion, also called **legislative waiver**, means that state legislatures rule that certain offenses, such as murder and other serious offenses against persons, automatically go to adult court. By 2018, 28 states had exclusion laws (Hockenberry, 2021). Several states (including Georgia, Illinois, and New York)

BOX 8.5 AUTOMATIC TRANSFER (DIRECT FILE): ONE STATE'S EXPERIENCE

The Juvenile Justice Initiative examined three years of data on 257 youths prosecuted and sentenced in adult court in Illinois from January 2010 to December 2012 under the state's automatic transfer (direct file) law. More than half of the cases ended up with convictions for lesser offenses—offenses that could not have triggered transfer. In this group of youths there was only one white youth. Many of the youths could have received longer sentences in juvenile court. Specifically, 18 percent of the transferred youths received a prison sentence of five years or less. A juvenile court sentence for a 15- or 16-year-old would be to age 21, a sentence of five to six years. The report recommended ending automatic transfer and returning to judicial waiver hearings to produce more positive outcomes.

What do you think? Is judicial waiver more appropriate than automatic waiver? Why might it be more appropriate to allow judges to conduct waiver hearings before any youth is transferred to adult criminal court?

Source: Ishida, Clarke, and Reed (2014).

exclude youths as young as 13. For a critique of the Illinois law in effect at that time, see Box 8.5.

An evaluation of the statutory exclusion law in Washington State (called "direct decline" in that state) found that a sample of youths processed under the law had higher recidivism rates, although not significantly so, than the comparison group on three measures: total recidivism, violent felonies, and all felony convictions. The cost of the policy was estimated to be over $72,000 per youth, although benefits could not be calculated (Drake, 2013).

Prosecutorial waiver/discretion (direct file/concurrent jurisdiction) is another method for placing juveniles into adult criminal court. State law gives juvenile and adult court concurrent jurisdiction over certain cases. Depending on the offense, the age of the offender, and/or the youth's prior record, the prosecutor decides whether to file the case in juvenile or adult court. By 2018, prosecutorial waiver/discretion (concurrent jurisdiction)

Zachary Neagle, age 14, makes his first appearance in court in Caldwell, Idaho, where he was charged as an adult with the first-degree murder of his father. Due to a plea agreement, he was later given a blended sentence.

CREDIT: AP Photo/*Idaho Press-Tribune*, Mike Vogt

was available in 14 states and the District of Columbia (Hockenberry. 2021). Many states limit this option to violent or repeat offenses involving firearms or other weapons. A report on Florida's experience with its direct file statute indicates serious problems. First, prosecutors have unfettered discretion to choose adult court; there are no criteria to guide the decision, whereas judges have to consider eight statutory factors at a transfer hearing. Second, there is no hearing to allow any challenge of the decision. Third, Human Rights Watch found wide variation in decisions by court district. Others have labeled this "justice by geography" (Feld, 2012). Fourth, there is racial disparity. In one district, 8.8 percent of white youths arrested for drug felonies were processed as adults versus 30.1 percent of black juveniles arrested for drug felonies. Human Rights Watch (2014a) thus recommends repeal of the direct file law.

Another way to direct juveniles to adult court is for state legislatures to lower the maximum age of juvenile court jurisdiction. The most recent trend has been for states (for example, New York and North Carolina) to go back to age 18 as the beginning age of criminal court jurisdiction. This reform is based on developmental research, which indicates that maturation actually continues into the late teens and early twenties. (See Chapter 14 for further discussion.)

It should be noted that 28 states allow for **reverse waiver** (Hockenberry, 2021). This means that the criminal courts can return certain cases that they received due to mandatory judicial waiver, legislative exclusion, or prosecutorial waiver back to juvenile court. It is also important to note that 36 states have **"once an adult, always an adult" provisions** (OJJDP, 2017). This means that all or certain categories of youths placed in criminal courts must automatically be processed in adult court for any subsequent offenses (Bishop, 2000).

The waiver decision is made at a hearing that is analogous to the preliminary hearing in adult court. At a waiver hearing, the prosecutor must only show probable cause that an offense occurred and that the juvenile committed the offense. The prosecutor does not have to prove guilt beyond a reasonable doubt. Proof of guilt is reserved for the trial in adult court (if waiver is successful) or for the adjudication stage in juvenile court (if the waiver motion fails). The juvenile transfer hearing differs from an adult court preliminary hearing in that the prosecutor must go further and establish that the juvenile is not amenable to juvenile court intervention or that the juvenile is a threat to public safety. An example of nonamenability would be the case of a youth who is already on parole from a state training school for an earlier delinquent act who then commits another serious offense (e.g., armed robbery). If probable cause were established that the youth committed the robbery, then the judge would have to find that the juvenile court had a history of contacts with the boy dating back several years and that one more juvenile court effort to deal with the boy's problems—either through probation or a training school placement—would be futile. An example of a case involving a threat to public safety would be a murder case or an offender with a history of violent offenses.

Recent Changes to Transfer Laws: Keeping More Juveniles in Juvenile Court

The laws on transfer and direct file discussed in this chapter appear to be changing. For changes, consult the website of the Office of Juvenile Justice and Delinquency Prevention (www.ojjdp.gov) or the website of the National Conference of State Legislatures (www.ncsl.org). A number of states have made changes moving away from the punitive, "get tough" stance of the late 1990s and early 2000s. For example, a number of states have amended their transfer laws limiting waiver criteria, reserving adult court for only the most serious offenders. California, Maryland, and Nebraska have legislated that juvenile court judges consider age, health, and the possibility of rehabilitation when making transfer rulings. Illinois has eliminated automatic transfer of 15-year-olds, Connecticut has raised the age of transfer to 15, New Jersey and Virginia have raised the age to 16 (National Conference of State Legislatures, 2015, 2021). Similarly, a number of states have returned to age 18 as the initial age of criminal court jurisdiction (see Chapter 14 for further discussion of the age issue). Vermont has gone further and now processes most 18-year-olds in juvenile court (except for 12 serious offenses) and will do the same for 19-year-olds by July 2022 (National Conference of State Legislatures, 2021). Also, as of 2021, 28 states now have blended sentencing provisions that allow adult criminal courts to impose juvenile dispositions (Hockenberry, 2021).

The Effectiveness of Transfer and Other Methods of Adult Court Processing

Research on transfer and other methods of placing youths into adult court has raised several issues. One concern is what influences the transfer decision; another is that transferred juveniles are receiving harsher sentences than they should. For information on the tragic result of one youth transferred to adult court and sentenced to adult prison, see Box 8.6.

One review of the research on transfer concluded that there is need for more research but that "the bulk of the empirical evidence suggests that transfer laws, as currently implemented, probably have little or no general deterrent effect on would-be juvenile offenders" (Redding, 2010:8). Similarly, Steiner and Wright (2006) did a time-series analysis of passing direct file waiver laws in 14 states. They found that there was no effect on juvenile homicides and no effect on violent juvenile crime except in one state. Research on specific deterrence, on the other hand, is stronger and has clearer implications. Based on six large-scale studies in five jurisdictions, the results are consistent:

> All of the studies found higher recidivism rates among offenders who had been transferred to criminal court, compared with those who were retained in the juvenile system … Thus, the extant research provides

---

BOX 8.6 THE RESULTS OF ONE TRANSFER DECISION: RAPE AND DEATH

Rodney Hulin was convicted of arson at age 16 in Texas and sentenced to adult prison. Within a week of arriving at the Clemens Unit in Brazoria County, Texas, he was raped. During the following months, he was repeatedly beaten, robbed, and forced to perform oral sex. After he was denied protective custody, he became depressed and attempted suicide. After being in a coma for several months, he died. Rodney was small: 5'2" tall and 125lb.

Rodney's parents sued. The case was settled out of court. How serious a crime must be committed for a youth to be transferred to adult court? How serious must the crime be for a youth to be sentenced to an adult prison, where assaults and rapes can occur, especially if the youth is not that strong or not that inclined to defend himself or herself? Based on all the information in the chapter about transfer, is it a positive option?

Source: Adapted from Human Rights Watch (2001).

sound evidence that transferring juvenile offenders to the criminal court does not engender community protection by reducing recidivism. On the contrary, transfer substantially increases recidivism. (Redding, 2010:3)

Jordan and Myers (2011) agree that the research usually shows either no effect on recidivism (no effect was also found in a recent study of 193 transferred youths in Arizona [Mulvey & Schubert, 2012]), or that transferred youth have higher recidivism than nontransferred youths. Additionally, their study of transfer in Pennsylvania found that it only promoted additional punishment severity, not certainty or swiftness (Jordan & Myers, 2011).

A recent review and meta-analysis of the research on transfer found that transfer to adult court "leads to a small but statistically nonsignificant increase in future offending" (Zane, Welsh, & Mears, 2016:915). The authors claim that because they focused on rigorous evaluations of waiver, their finding of a nonsignificant effect "lends greater credence to the consensus in the extant literature that transfer does not have a specific deterrent effect" (Zane et al., 2016:915).

In another study, Zane (2016) found that legislative waiver is more likely to result in noncriminal outcomes (lower recidivism). Because it simply considers the offense and not the offender, legislative waiver is an ineffective way to determine which juveniles need to be sent to adult court.

In a study of transferred youths in Florida, Lehman, Chiricos, and Bales (2018) found that transferred youths were less likely to be sentenced to prison. On the other hand, if sentenced to prison, transferred youths were more likely to get a longer sentence term than adults sentenced to prison.

Based on this research, and on research that shows that youths are developmentally different from adults, the American Bar Association (ABA) does not favor prosecuting juveniles as adults. The ABA opposes, in principle, the trend toward processing more and younger youths as adults in the criminal justice system and urges policymakers at all levels to take the previously mentioned principles into account in developing and implementing policies involving youth under the age of 18 (cited by Mathis, 2007:S1).

Feld and Bishop (2012) argue that the processing of juveniles in adult courts ignores critical developmental differences between youths and adults and that such processing should be extremely rare. Waiver should be used only after a juvenile court waiver hearing with clear criteria and subject to rigorous appellate review. Similarly, based on the accumulating research on developmental differences between teenagers and young adults versus older adults (at least 21, if not 25), the Sentencing Project recommends eliminating prosecutorial discretion/direct file and automatic waiver. It also recommends that states eliminate low-level charges, such as drug offenses, from adult courts altogether (Rovner, 2016a). A positive note is that many states have changed or are considering changing their transfer laws to limit transfer (Rovner, 2016a).

For a historical note on "passive" transfer in the first juvenile court, see Box 8.7.

BOX 8.7 TRANSFER IN THE FIRST JUVENILE COURT: COOK COUNTY, ILLINOIS

In the first juvenile court in Cook County, Illinois, there was some confusion about the jurisdiction of the court over older teens. There was also some concern that perhaps it was unconstitutional not to give older teens full due process rights. So the juvenile court judges exercised what is called "passive" transfer. This meant that they did not exercise their jurisdiction over older teens who committed serious crimes while on probation in juvenile court. They simply allowed these teens to be treated as adults in criminal court. They hoped that this strategy would prevent either the state legislature or the Illinois Supreme Court from overruling the law authorizing the juvenile court. The strategy worked; the Illinois Supreme Court did not interfere with the operations of the juvenile court.

Source: Tanehaus (2004).

Youth and Worker Attitudes

Research on both youth and worker attitudes toward adult court processing indicates that there are some problems with moving juveniles to adult court jurisdiction.

In interviews with 95 serious and chronic adolescent male offenders in Florida (49 of whom had been transferred to criminal court), Bishop found that almost all described juvenile courts favorably but had criticisms of adult court. Most transferred youths believed that criminal court judges did not show interest in them, saw the proceedings as rushed, and, most importantly, had difficulty understanding everything that took place in criminal court. The transferred youths also perceived the criminal courts to be involved in game playing and felt that the public defenders were more interested in talking the youths into accepting pleas. The youths also perceived the courts to be clearly focused on punishment, based not so much on what they had done but on judgments that "they were depraved or irredeemable" (Bishop, 2000:137).

Research also indicates that transferred youths sentenced to adult prisons are more susceptible to abuse in prison and commit more misconduct violations. They may commit misconducts to avoid certain situations or to protect themselves in other ways. The authors conclude that the adult "prison environment does not meet the developmental needs of young people" (Kolivoski & Shook, 2016:1255).

In a study of 100 juvenile court personnel in three courts, workers—especially defense attorneys and probation officers—expressed prime concern for rehabilitation. Forty-seven percent of judges, 65 percent of public defenders, 80 percent of private attorneys, and 70 percent of probation officers said that rehabilitation was the paramount concern of judges. However, 40 percent of judges and 64 percent of prosecutors rated balancing the interests of child and society as the paramount concern (Sanborn, 2001). In other words, although the public and politicians may favor transfer as a way to "get tough" on juvenile crime, not all youths and workers agree that this is the best course of action.

ADJUDICATION AND DISPOSITION

For children not sent to adult criminal court, the next steps after the filing of a petition are adjudication and disposition. In these decisions, a judge determines whether there is enough evidence to establish the petition and then decides what to do if there is enough evidence. These decisions are comparable to the plea, trial, and sentencing decisions in adult court. Refer back to Figures 8.1 and 8.2 for statistics on adjudication and disposition in juvenile court.

Ideally, the determination of the truth of the petition occurs in a rational fashion, with the prosecutor, defense attorney, and judge using their abilities and training to seek justice. In reality, juvenile court sessions often are hectic and hurried, and may reflect the self-interests of the parties involved rather than justice or the best interests of the child. For example, Peter Prescott has described one day in the operations of the Bronx (NY) Family Court as a:

> flow of incompetence and indifference. One court officer perpetually frowns, shaking his head in mute consternation at so much exposure to human fallibility. The court clerk, arrogant and disdainful, speaks as little as possible as if in fear of contamination. When he must speak, his tone is dry and contemptuous, his words chopped short: the burden of dealing with these people and their problems! "I've been here two years," a court officer remarks. "Two years too long. But once you're assigned to Family Court, you're stuck because no one wants to come here." (Prescott, 1981:85–86)

An account of the Los Angeles juvenile court system (Humes, 1996) indicates that numerous problems continue to plague juvenile court, an institution marked by both frustration and heroism.

Attorneys in Juvenile Court

There are several problems concerning attorneys in juvenile court. First, many juveniles do not have attorneys. Many juveniles waive their right to an attorney, often because they do not fully understand their rights, especially the importance of the right to an attorney (see, e.g., Feld, 2012; Henning, 2010). A second critical problem is large caseloads for public defenders in juvenile court. Depending on the state, the caseload for the average public defender can range from 360 to 1,000 cases per defender (Jones, 2004). With attorneys being so overworked, many juvenile defendants get the clear impression that "their attorneys do not care about them" (Puritz et al., 1995:47).

Additional problems with public defender systems may include insufficient funding, lack of training, high turnover, low prestige, and low salaries (Feld, 1999; Feld & Schaefer, 2010; Feld & Moriearty, 2020). Starting salaries for public defenders in Ohio, for example, were as low as $35,000, and hourly rates for appointed counsel in several counties paid only $50 an hour for in-court work and $40 an hour for out-of-court work (Brooks & Kamine, 2003). Similarly, Georgia only pays appointed attorneys $60 per hour for in-court work, and one county has a cap of $300. Maine pays $50 per hour with a cap of $315. In Louisiana, the state only pays public defenders from $22,000 to $30,000 per year (Jones, 2004).

In actual practice, most youths do not get a public defender but a private attorney appointed by the court. Unfortunately, these attorneys lack the resources of a fully funded public defender's office such as investigators, paralegals, clerks, technology staff, and social workers (National Juvenile Defender Center, 2020). The fact that such private attorneys defend many juveniles may be one reason that there is a "lawyer penalty"; several studies have found that youths represented by defense attorneys are more likely to be removed from their homes and placed in an institution (see, e.g., Burruss, Peck, & Cameron, 2020).

Many attorneys in juvenile court, both public defenders and private attorneys, are reluctant to utilize the **zealous advocate role** that is (at least theoretically) the norm in adult criminal court. Attorneys in adult criminal courts justify such zealous advocacy (where the attorney fights as hard as possible for all defendants, even defendants who have admitted that they are factually guilty) on the grounds that the system is adversarial and that the adversarial process is best for bringing out the truth. In juvenile court, some attorneys, parents, and judges feel that the adult criminal court norm of zealous advocacy is inappropriate.

They may worry that strong advocacy can result in an outcome by which a child who "needs help" will not get it because failure to establish the petition leaves the court with no jurisdiction over the child. As a result, at least some attorneys assume a **concerned adult role** rather than a zealous advocate role, encouraging youths to admit to petitions in cases in which an adversarial approach may have resulted in a dismissal of the petition. Additional problems are that juvenile court is not considered prestigious (it is called "kiddie court") and that judges may pressure attorneys into cooperating rather than being adversarial (Feld, 1999). (For a look at what can happen to a youth without an attorney, see Box 8.8.)

A qualitative study indicated that attorneys expressed considerable concern for their youthful clients but that the attorneys were not always sure of the correct course of action. Specifically, interviews with 10 attorneys and 10 clients showed that many of the juveniles did not always understand what was going

---

BOX 8.8 ONE YOUTH WITHOUT AN ATTORNEY

The National Juvenile Defender Center describes what happened to one youth who faced police interrogation without an attorney. Anthony was a 17-year-old youth in Illinois suspected of committing armed robbery. Police questioned him for two hours without informing him of his right to an attorney or his right to remain silent. He asserted his innocence 35 times. His IQ was 60, equivalent to the functioning of a 9- or 10-year-old. He confessed and was sentenced to 45 years in prison. Nine months later, a court viewed videotapes of Anthony's confession and dropped the charges against him.

Source: National Juvenile Defender Center (2017).

on either during police interrogation or in court—often they "just didn't get it" (Tobey, Grisso, & Schwartz, 2000:230). For example, one youth waived his *Miranda* rights and talked to the police because he did not understand his right to remain silent. Many of the youths just wanted to "get it over with" (Tobey et al., 2000:234). Attorneys, in turn, felt that their youthful clients were often passive about decisions such as pleading guilty and thus attorneys "spoke of walking an ethical tightrope regarding who, in fact, was making the decision about such matters" (Tobey et al., 2000:237).

Buss (2000) agrees that many juveniles do not understand the role of the attorney as zealous advocate. Youths usually see adults as in control, not as advocates willing to listen to their wishes. Lawyers, in turn, may reinforce inaccurate images. Large caseloads prevent lawyers from devoting sufficient attention to juveniles. In addition, attorney hesitation to embrace the role of zealous advocate instead of concerned parent can influence attorneys to be paternalistic toward youthful clients. The result of any misunderstanding of the lawyer's role is that juveniles often are not fully honest with their attorneys. One way to help juvenile defendants to see their attorneys as zealous advocates is to honor confidentiality, especially by respecting confidentiality in relation to parents. If the attorney shows the youth that he or she will not divulge confidences to the youth's parents, that will demonstrate the attorney's undivided loyalty to the youthful defendant. Another important matter is simply to spend more time with youthful clients to counteract any impression that the youth does not matter (Buss, 2000).

Plea Bargaining

As in adult criminal court, the vast majority of cases in juvenile court are resolved by plea bargains (Feld, 2012). Because of the pressure on youths to plead guilty (admit the allegations in the petition) and because of the problems with **plea bargaining** (see, e.g., Newman, 1986), the ABA has recommended that plea bargaining either be made visible or eliminated entirely (Institute of Judicial Administration–American Bar Association [IJA–ABA], 1980). The ABA maintains that if plea bargaining is retained, the judge should not participate in the process. However, the judge "should require disclosure of the agreement reached and explicitly indicate the conditions under which he or she is willing to honor it" (IJA–ABA, 1980:39). If the judge will not accept the plea agreement, he or she should give the juvenile a chance to withdraw his or her plea. Finally, the judge should consult with the juvenile's parents before accepting a plea (IJA–ABA, 1980:47). These regulations (or alternatively, the abolition of plea bargaining) would eliminate many of the traditional abuses of the practice.

The issue of plea bargaining may take on increasing importance. Texas, for example, recently revised its laws to allow more determinate sentencing in juvenile court as an alternative to waiving some youths to adult court. Youths subject to this provision can get longer prison sentences and may complete their sentences, when they turn 21, in the adult system. Mears (2000) found that such increased sentencing options gave prosecutors greater leverage in pressuring juveniles to accept plea bargains.

Attorney Effectiveness

Research has shown some disturbing results concerning the effectiveness of defense attorneys in juvenile court. As we will explain, many of the studies show several problems with attorney representation of juvenile clients.

In a study of more than 500 juvenile felony court cases in Missouri, Burruss and Kempf-Leonard (2002) found an adverse effect of attorneys. In other words, "out-of-home placement was more likely to occur if a youth had an attorney, even when other relevant legal and individual factors were the same" (Burruss & Kempf-Leonard, 2002:60). To be more specific, concerning youths charged with felonies in three Missouri courts (one urban, one suburban, and one rural), suburban youths with counsel were almost three times more likely to be removed from home, and rural youths were two and a half times more likely to get out-of-home placement than youths without attorneys. All the urban youths had counsel (Burruss & Kempf-Leonard, 2002). This negative effect of attorney representation raises an interesting point: Would kids be better off without attorneys? Burruss and Kempf-Leonard think not. They think that the negative impact of attorneys in juvenile court may be due to high caseloads, retaining counsel too late in the process, or other court personnel co-opting the attorneys out of an adversarial role.

An ABA investigation of Ohio juvenile courts produced several disturbing findings. First, "large numbers of poor youth throughout Ohio go unrepresented, even during some of the most critical proceedings that affect their liberty interest" (Brooks & Kamine, 2003:25). In many counties, investigators noted that waiver of counsel was common, with as many as 80 percent of juveniles going without counsel. Second, many attorneys (slightly over 40 percent) saw their role as representing the "best interest" of the youth rather than being the youth's advocate. In some counties this view of the attorney role was so strong that it did not seem important to have an attorney represent the youth. Third, for many youths who did have attorney representation, the quality of that representation was questionable. The report found that many Ohio youths "receive ineffective assistance of counsel from attorneys who are ill-prepared, insufficiently trained, and/or overwhelmed by high caseloads, insufficient resources and low pay" (Brooks & Kamine, 2003:29). Thus, most cases are handled informally or by plea bargaining, and attorneys had little impact at disposition. One specific problem was low compensation. Starting annual salaries for public defenders were as low as $35,000, and hourly rates for appointed counsel in several counties paid only $50 an hour for in-court work and $40 an hour for out-of-court work. Such low rates do not help to attract or retain competent attorneys (Brooks & Kamine, 2003).

An ABA study in Pennsylvania showed similar problems. Significant numbers of youths did not have representation, and many others had ineffective counsel due to lack of preparation or training. At detention hearings attorneys often had little chance to confer with their juvenile clients and were not familiar with alternatives to detention. Most cases were resolved by pleas, and attorneys saw many courts simply interested in dispensing treatment or punishment.

Probation officers made disposition recommendations with little challenge from attorneys. At disposition, many attorneys simply were not acting as advocates for their juvenile clients. The investigators found that probation officers were very influential in the juvenile justice system, to the extent that "the system's over-dependence on [probation's] role has tipped the scales toward a 'best interest' system in delinquency cases in lieu of a system that demands the Commonwealth [of Pennsylvania] prove its case" (Miller-Wilson & Puritz, 2003:59).

A report by the National Juvenile Defender Center clarifies why many juveniles do not have an attorney. First, many simply cannot afford one. Many children must pay to have an attorney. Thirty-six states allow children to be charged fees for a "free" lawyer. The fee is $275 in New Hampshire and $300 in Massachusetts. Another reason is that 43 states allow children to waive their right to an attorney without first consulting with an attorney, despite research showing that many youths do not understand their right to an attorney (National Juvenile Defender Center, 2017).

A recent meta-analysis of 17 studies showed a strong lawyer penalty effect: having an attorney increased the odds of receiving an out-of-home placement at disposition by 200 percent. The authors do not think that this was due to the seriousness of the crimes the youths committed but rather to factors such as lack of training, being overworked, the lawyer thinking that placement was best for the youth, and judges punishing youths for asserting their due process rights (Burruss et al., 2020). The National Juvenile Defender Center (2020) thinks that the problem is that too many indigent youths are represented by appointed attorneys instead of being represented by adequately funded public defender offices. These youths do not benefit from a well-funded, well-managed, well-trained, and well-supported public defender office.

Thus, the situation in America's juvenile courts appears to be such that some attorneys are adversarial, some are still traditional and act as concerned adults, and some are in between the two extremes. Furthermore, in some states, many juveniles are not represented by attorneys (National Juvenile Defender Center, 2017). Even a new law mandating attorneys in felony and serious misdemeanor cases in Minnesota did not essentially change the rate of representation by counsel (Feld & Schaefer, 2010). One frequent problem is simply that many juveniles waive their right to an attorney (Feld, 2012; Jones, 2004). In some states, unreasonable criteria for indigency result in many youths being denied appointed counsel. For example, Florida disqualified youths for appointed counsel if their parents had as little as $5 in the bank (Henning, 2010). This state of affairs raises the issue of which is the best approach: zealous advocate, concerned adult, or some compromise between the two alternatives? The chief advantage of the zealous advocate model is that it is probably the best insurance that only truly guilty youths will come under court jurisdiction. Because the attorney does not pressure the child to admit to the petition (plead guilty), there is less danger that the court will attempt some type of intervention program with youths who are not actually guilty. An added advantage is that this approach may well generate the most respect from juveniles for the court system. Fewer youths will feel that they have been betrayed or tricked into something that some adult thought was best for them, despite their own wishes.

The biggest danger of the zealous advocate approach is that it may contribute to what Fabricant (1983) calls the contemporary version of benign neglect. That is, because many youths appearing in juvenile court come from families racked with problems, such as low income, public assistance, and/or broken homes, they do need assistance. An adversarial approach may prevent these children from being railroaded into juvenile prisons or other types of intervention due to insufficient legal defense. That adversarial approach, however, does nothing about the real problems faced by these children in their homes and their neighborhoods:

> It must be presumed that these youngsters' fundamental problems will neither be addressed nor resolved through a faithful adherence to process. Just as important, their troubles are likely to be compounded by social indifference. Therefore, a policy of calculated nonintervention may, over time, cause severer and/or increased antisocial behavior from troubled youths who initially are ignored by the court or state. (Fabricant, 1983:140)

The advantage of the concerned adult model is that it seeks to address the problems of the child that presumably led the child into delinquency. The problem is that this helping philosophy has been the rationale of the juvenile court since 1899 and, as David Rothman has so aptly phrased it, the rhetoric of individualized attention has always far outstripped the reality of ineffective if not abusive programs (Rothman, 1980).

Jury Trials for Juveniles

Because the U.S. Supreme Court has not mandated the right to a jury trial for all juveniles (see Chapter 9), only 10 states generally allow jury trials as a right for juveniles and another 11 states allow jury trials in special circumstances (Szymanski, 2002). On the other hand, if a juvenile is transferred to adult court, she may get a jury trial there. Some contend that it is critical for juveniles to have the right to a jury trial. For example, Rosenberg (2008) notes that judges find guilt about 25 percent more often than juries do. Feld (2012) argues that juries can serve as a check on abuses by both prosecutors and judges and thereby enhance procedural safeguards which "may be even more critical in low-visibility juvenile courts that deal with vulnerable, dependent youths" (Feld, 2012:679; see also, Feld, 2018). The ABA agrees that judges may be biased, and further states:

> A jury trial gives enhanced visibility to the adjudicative process. A jury trial requires the trial court judge to articulate his or her views of the applicable law in the case through jury instructions, thereby facilitating appellate court review of the legal issues involved. Without the focus on legal issues that such an exercise entails, the danger is great

that the applicable law may be misperceived or misapplied and that the error will go uncorrected on appeal. (IJA–ABA, 1980:53)

Having the right to a jury trial, however, may not make that much difference in juvenile court. In her study of a suburban juvenile court, Mahoney (1985) found that only 7 cases out of the 650 actually went to trial. For those 7 youths, and for 87 other youths who initially requested a jury trial but later settled without a jury trial, there was no impact of setting (scheduling) a case for trial on outcomes. Thus,

> in a handful of serious cases in which a child denies charges, it [a jury trial] may be essential to the cause of justice, but it is unclear how much a jury trial benefits a youth or the community in the great majority of cases. (Mahoney, 1985:564)

Similarly, relatively recent research in Ohio showed that most attorneys reported that 10 percent or less of cases went to trial and trials were almost nonexistent in some counties (Brooks & Kamine, 2003). In a study of mock jurors, Najdowski and Weintraub (2020) found that overall juror gender did not affect verdicts but that where there were differences; women jurors were less empathetic than male jurors. (For a note on jury trials and life without parole sentencing, see Chapter 9.)

The Emphasis on Punitiveness: Late 1990s to the Present

Traditionally, the disposition stage of juvenile court has been the epitome of the *parens patriae* philosophy. With the advice of probation officers, social workers, psychologists, and psychiatrists, the judge has tried to act in the best interests of the child. About 20 years ago, however, disposition (sentencing) in juvenile justice took on an increasingly punitive character.

One indicator of this increasingly explicit focus on punishment was the revision of the purpose clauses of state juvenile codes. In the past, states emphasized prevention, diversion, and treatment. As of 2005, at least six states emphasized "community protection, offender accountability, crime reduction through deterrence, or outright punishment, either predominantly or exclusively," and only four states had traditional child welfare emphases (Griffin & King, 2006). Sixteen states used the language of balanced and restorative justice, emphasizing public safety, individual accountability to both victims and the community, and offender skill development. Nine states modeled their statutes on the Standard Juvenile Court Act, and six states had a multi-part purpose clause based on the Legislative Guide for Drafting Family and Juvenile Court Acts (Griffin & King, 2006).

A prime indicator of the trend toward punitiveness was the move by many states to expand provisions for processing juveniles in adult criminal court rather than juvenile court. Between 1998 and 2002, 31 states changed their laws governing the prosecution and sentencing of juveniles in adult criminal courts. For example, 18 states expanded their transfer laws, including the addition of new offenses eligible for transfer. Three states (Illinois, Maryland, and

North Carolina) legislated "once an adult, always an adult" laws in which processing in criminal court automatically excludes the juvenile from any juvenile court jurisdiction after that (Griffin, 2005). The overall result is that it is easier to process juveniles as adults in criminal court.

Still another development in this direction was blended sentencing. In blended sentencing, either the juvenile court or the adult court imposes a sentence that can involve either the juvenile or the adult correctional system or both systems. The adult sentence may be suspended pending either a violation or the commission of a new crime. Fourteen states had juvenile blended sentencing schemes (the juvenile court imposes sentence) and 18 states had criminal blended sentencing laws (the criminal court imposes sentence) by 2010 (OJJDP, 2011). Twenty-eight states have blended sentencing provisions (Hockenberry, 2021).

Still another sign of increasing punitiveness was the passing of statutes concerning the confidentiality of juvenile court records and proceedings. Traditionally, such records and court proceedings were closed to the public. The *parens patriae* rationale dictated that this would protect the juvenile from publicity so that a delinquent act would not stigmatize him or her permanently. In the punitive era, however, critics called for publicity to assure community protection, and legislatures have responded. At the end of 2004, 14 states allowed the public to be present for some cases (e.g., cases of older youths charged with a felony) (Snyder & Sickmund, 2006).

A consequence of these punitive developments was that the involved states created two ways of processing juveniles. If a youth is older, commits a serious offense, and/or has a prior record, he or she will be treated as an adult or similar to an adult. If a younger youth commits a less serious offense and lacks a prior record, he or she will be handled in a traditional juvenile court. Much of the rationale behind this division of juveniles into quasi-adults and children is the belief that youths have changed. Youths who commit what appear to be willful violent crimes are considered mature and responsible adults who should be held accountable for their actions. Younger youths who commit less serious offenses are still looked on as wayward youths who can be salvaged by the traditional *parens patriae* juvenile court.

As noted above, a new trend has taken place that recognizes the implications of psychological research on development that shows that youths continue to develop in their late teen years and even into their early twenties. As a result, a number of states have made comprehensive reforms of their juvenile justice system to reduce detention, incorporate evidence-based programming, utilize risk and needs assessment, invest in community-based programming, and limit institutionalization to only the most serious offenders. (For details on several state reform measures, see Crime and Justice Institute, 2017.) More specifically, a number of states have limited transfer and given more discretion to juvenile court judges. Second, several states have added blending sentencing provisions which allow adult criminal court judges to impost a juvenile disposition (Hockenberry, 2021). Third, a number of states such as New York have returned the age of criminal court jurisdiction to age 18. In fact, in 2020 Vermont began to process most 18-year-olds in juvenile court and will do so with most 19-year-olds by July 2022 (Teigen, 2021). Another sign of change is the fact that as of 2016 five states moved away from a punishment emphasis in their purpose clauses to an emphasis on a developmental approach that takes into account the psychological development of juveniles (National Center for Juvenile Justice, 2017). Thus, what Bishop and Feld (2012) discerned a few years ago as the beginnings of a rebalancing of punishment and treatment concerns in juvenile court has continued to unfold. (See Chapter 14 for further discussion.)

Dispositional Decision Making

A major issue in juvenile justice is the question of which factors influence judges in their dispositional (sentencing) decisions. Research indicates several general conclusions. Legal variables such as seriousness of the offense and prior record have a strong influence on dispositions (e.g., Bishop & Leiber, 2012; Clarke & Koch, 1980; Dannefer & Schutt, 1982; McCarthy & Smith, 1986). The impact of prior record on dispositions, however, may reflect bias amplification (Dannefer & Schutt, 1982; Sampson, 1986). In other words, prior record may mask the influence of race or social class in police decision making. The impact of offender characteristics such as age, race, social class, and gender has mixed results (for reviews of prior research in this area, especially prior research on the impact of race, see Bishop & Leiber, 2012; Leiber, 2013). Usually, the impact of these variables is weaker than the impact of legal variables. One study, however, indicated that "measures of social class and race become increasingly important as direct influences on the final disposition as youths are selected into the system for further processing" (McCarthy & Smith, 1986:58). Another way to put this is that racial bias at early decision points such as detention hearings can have a cumulative effect at disposition such as being sentenced to residential placement (Guevara, Spohn, & Herz, 2004; Rodriguez, 2010).

A number of studies report that females receive more severe dispositions than males for minor offenses, especially status offenses, stemming from traditional sex-role expectations. Other studies find leniency for females following the chivalry hypothesis, a paternalistic attitude toward female misbehavior compared to an excusing of boys "sowing their wild oats" (Chesney-Lind, 1977; Chesney-Lind & Shelden, 1992; Cohen & Kluegel, 1979). On the other hand, some studies show no gender bias after controlling for offense type or severity (see Leiber & Mack, 2003).

Prior case processing decisions exert some influence on dispositions. For example, detained youths receive harsher dispositions or are more likely to be formally processed (see Rodriguez, 2010, for a discussion) than youths who are not detained. Moreover, prior case dispositions can affect subsequent dispositions (Henretta, Frazier, & Bishop, 1985, 1986; Thornberry & Christenson, 1984). Finally, some authors report that dispositions vary from one jurisdiction to the next (e.g., Belknap, 1984; Dannefer & Schutt, 1982), while others fail to find such differences (e.g., Staples, 1987).

Summarizing the research on the impact of race (disproportionate minority contact—DMC) on dispositions in juvenile court, Bishop and Leiber (2012) argue that race affects police, intake, and detention decisions. Police make decisions to police underclass neighborhoods more extensively, which places minorities at higher risk of arrest; and police also more often perceive minority juveniles to be insolent and uncooperative. Minority juveniles are not diverted as often as whites, but instead more often are referred for formal processing. One reason may be that intake officers make assessments of parental control and supervision. Another may be to opt for court processing to make youths eligible for treatment at state expense. Still another factor is stereotypes of minority offenders as threatening and dangerous. The result is that research shows that "legal variables have the strongest effects on court processing from intake through final disposition, [but] they are contaminated to an unknown degree" (Bishop & Leiber, 2012:471). For example, race may affect the detention decision, which then affects the disposition (see Bishop & Leiber, 2012 for a thorough review and analysis of the impact of race).

Where race is still a factor in juvenile court dispositions, it may be that more is needed than simply addressing the problems of juvenile court. Krisberg and Austin (1993), for example, argue that problems in juvenile court dispositions, especially any findings of possible racial disproportionality, cannot be resolved in isolation but are "tied inextricably to the pursuit of social justice. Reforms will continue to fail, as they have in the past, if they do not address the maldistribution of wealth, power, and resources throughout society" (Krisberg & Austin, 1993:110; see also, Currie, 2020).

Several conclusions can be drawn about the impact of race on juvenile court processing. First, there is disparity; blacks often receive unfavorable decisions compared to white youths: "An extensive body of research shows that non-Whites are disproportionately arrested, adjudicated, detained, and disposed to out-of-home placements relative to their representation in the general population" (Donnelly, 2019: 288; see also: Leiber & Fix, 2019; Lowery & Smith, 2020; Piquero, 2008). Second, offense severity and prior record are important factors that affect decisions. Third, even after controlling for offense and prior record, race is still a factor. Fourth, disparities are more likely at earlier stages of system processing (arrest, intake, detention) than at adjudication, disposition, and placement in secure confinement (Shannon & Hauer, 2018). More specifically, disparity occurs most frequently at the detention decision and is quite rare at adjudication, as this stage relies on the facts of the case and on legal rules of procedure (Spinney et al., 2018). Race can also increase the likelihood of a prison sentence and the length of that sentence for transferred juveniles (Lehman, Chiricos, & Bales, 2017). Fifth, disparity is complex. Blacks are often disadvantaged, but at many decision points whites are disadvantaged. Some but not all efforts to reduce DMC have been successful (Mallett, 2018).

In the last 10 years, there have been several formal efforts to reduce DMC. Leiber and Fix (2019) argue that these efforts have only achieved, at best, mixed results. They state that there has not been much effort to improve disadvantaged communities but that most efforts have focused on trying to change the individual

BOX 8.9 SUGGESTIONS FOR REDUCING THE EFFECT OF RACE ON COURT DISPOSITIONS

Bishop and Leiber (2012) offer several suggestions for the problem of minority overrepresentation in the juvenile justice system. First, since delinquency is related to family, school, and neighborhood factors, juvenile court reforms alone are not enough. Issues such as poverty, unemployment, family disruption, schools, and access to health care all need to be addressed. Second, stereotypes of minority youths, families, and neighborhoods as threatening need to be addressed. A specific recommendation in this area is training criminal justice officials in cultural awareness. Third, to prevent the use of court processing as a method of providing services for minority youths, Bishop and Leiber suggest alternatives such as vouchers for mental health and other services in the community. Finally, they suggest government attention to such inner-city problems as job creation, efforts to improve schools, and efforts at community organization. They conclude: "In the final analysis, reducing minority offending and disparities in the processing of minority offenders will require nothing less than elevating the problems faced by impoverished inner-city families to a national priority" (Bishop & Leiber, 2012:475–476). (For a related discussion, see Chapter 14 concerning Elliott Currie's (2020) reform proposal.)

offender. Donnelly (2019), on the other hand, examined efforts to reduce DMC in three areas of the country and concluded that "this study demonstrates that DMC intervention can transform the decision processes for secure detention and placement" (Donnelly, 2019:303). For a discussion of changes intended to improve juvenile court dispositions, see Box 8.9.

A final note about dispositions in juvenile court is the issue of justice by geography. Apart from the issue of whether courts in some locations disproportionately sentence black youths differently than white youths, the broader issue is that urban courts often lack the mechanisms for informal social control found in rural courts. Urban courts tend to be more formal, focus more on due process, place more youths in detention, appoint attorneys more often, and hand out more severe sentences than either suburban or rural courts. So youths in cities receive harsher sentences than their counterparts in suburban or rural courts, hence the term "justice by geography."

SUMMARY

This chapter has examined the critical decision points in juvenile court: intake, detention, waiver, and other means of getting youths to adult court, adjudication, and disposition. This review has shown that the ideal of a beneficent court system has not always been reached. Sometimes, for example, detention facilities have been deteriorating physical facilities concealing punitive practices. Even though almost 50 years have elapsed since the *In re Gault* decision established due process protections for juveniles (*In re Gault*, 1967), attorneys in juvenile court may be confused about their role and often have high caseloads that prevent effective representation of juveniles. Worse, many juveniles do not even have attorney representation. Despite the history of civil rights legislation and concern, race—disproportionate minority contact (DMC)—appears to be a factor in juvenile court decision making. About 20 years ago, critics became concerned about juvenile crime and the adequacy of the juvenile justice system to handle the serious offender. Thus, increased use of waiver, legislative exclusion, and prosecutorial waiver, and of other more punitive measures such as blended sentencing, began to characterize many juvenile court systems. Elements of this trend may continue, but a counter trend exists that is following the psychological research on adolescent development and is pushing back against more punitive approaches.

In light of the ferment in juvenile court, concern for the due process rights of juvenile offenders is more critical than ever. In the next chapter, we will discuss due process issues and the rights of juveniles in general.

DISCUSSION QUESTIONS

1. H. Ted Rubin argues that token economies and other detention programs are violations of juvenile detainees' rights because most of the youths have not been adjudicated delinquent. Do you agree, or do you feel that such programs can be justified because they establish order and thereby protect the detainees? Are such practices similar to what "free" youngsters experience every day in a typical school setting?

2. Much of the research described in this chapter concerns the decisions to detain, petition, and dispose of alleged delinquents. One of the basic issues in all of these decisions is whether the decision makers should or should not consider social factors in their decision making. For example, should the attitude of the youth or the quality of parental care influence whether he or she is formally processed or allowed to go home with a warning or a much less severe consequence? Do such social factors have a place in these decisions, or are such social factors so liable to ethnic bias that the decisions should be based solely on legal factors?

3. Do you favor the use of bail in juvenile court? If so, for what sorts of offenders and under what circumstances?

4. Would you consider a career in juvenile detention as an administrator, counselor, teacher, or attendant (guard)?

5. Consider the following: A juvenile is accused of raping a 24-year-old high school teacher. You are a defense attorney and the defendant has asked you to represent him. You are convinced that you could "get the juvenile off" on a technicality. However, several members of your extended family are teachers and feel very strongly about this case. Would you accept the case? Would you pursue the technical defense that would exonerate the defendant, or would you encourage the youth to plead guilty and accept the psychiatric help that an expert feels is needed for the young man?

6. What do you think about the trend of a decade ago toward increased punitiveness (increased criminal court processing of youths, blended sentences, changes in purpose clauses to include punishment and incapacitation as juvenile court objectives, and changes in confidentiality)? Do you favor that trend, or does it represent an abandoning of the ideals of juvenile court? Do you approve

of the more recent trend of moderating the "get tough" movement of a few years ago, based on the accumulating research on the delayed development of adolescent maturity into the early twenties?

7. Suppose that a 13-year-old youth became extremely agitated and angry. He went to his parents' bedroom and got a pistol that was kept there in case an intruder broke in. He then murdered a family member. If this youth had no prior record but also no evidence of psychiatric disturbance, would you favor or oppose processing this youth as an adult in criminal court? How would the factor of a prior record influence your decision? What details of a prior record would most affect your decision? What are your reasons for your position?

8. The use of blended sentences and the processing of juveniles in adult court results in youths being incarcerated in adult prisons or in new youthful offender prisons instead of traditional training schools. What might be some positive and negative consequences of this? How can we prevent a tragedy such as a young man sent to adult prison where he is raped and eventually dies (see Box 8.6)?

CHAPTER 9

Due Process and Juveniles

WHAT YOU NEED TO KNOW

- The U.S. Supreme Court clarified the rights of juvenile defendants in several landmark cases.

- For example, the *Gault* decision ruled that juveniles have the privilege against self-incrimination and the right to the assistance of counsel in cases with the possibility of a decision to put the juvenile in confinement in a locked facility.

- In *McKeiver v. Pennsylvania*, the Supreme Court ruled that juveniles do not have the right to trial by jury.

- Reasonable corporal punishment is permissible in schools.

- Students do have limited free speech rights at school, but school officials can exercise broad editorial control over student publications.

- School officials can search students when they have reasonable suspicion to do so.

- Carefully drawn curfew laws have been upheld as constitutional. Excessively vague laws have not been upheld.

- Raising the legal drinking age has had positive effects on both traffic fatalities and protecting youths from long-term negative outcomes.

KEY TERMS

consent search

corporal punishment

freedom of speech

graduated licensing

legal drinking age

preventive detention

reasonable doubt standard

school prayer

search and seizure

student search

DOI: 10.4324/9781003167112-9

INTRODUCTION

Juveniles share some—but not all—of the same constitutional rights as adults. While a comprehensive analysis of juvenile rights would require an entire book and is, therefore, beyond the scope of this text, it is important to examine some of the rights pertaining to juveniles. This chapter will first examine the landmark juvenile Supreme Court cases of the 1960s and 1970s (such as *In re Gault*) because those cases fundamentally altered the contours of the juvenile justice system. Then we will examine the Fourth Amendment rights of juveniles in terms of search and seizure by the police. Finally, we will analyze some other important rights of juveniles such as rights in school and rights at home.

THE LANDMARK SUPREME COURT CASES

Between the founding of the juvenile court in 1899 and the *Kent v. United States* case in 1966, the United States Supreme Court basically left the juvenile court alone. In other words, the Supreme Court respected the intentions of juvenile court officials to seek the best interests of the child by allowing juvenile court judges and related personnel a great deal of discretion in attempting to achieve those objectives. In the mid-1960s, however, the Supreme Court was confronted with several cases that indicated that such a hands-off approach was no longer appropriate.

Kent v. Unites States

In *Kent v. United States* (1966), the Supreme Court was faced with a waiver case appeal wherein a 16-year-old, Morris Kent, had been waived (transferred) to adult criminal court without a hearing, without the assistance of counsel, and without any statement of the reasons for the judge's decision to transfer the matter to the adult court. A judge had decided to transfer Kent, who had been charged with rape, simply on the basis of a review of the youth's social service and probation files. The judge did not allow Kent's privately retained attorney to review any of the files, nor did the judge conduct any hearing on the matter or state the reasons that convinced him to transfer the case. Thus, the waiver decision, a very critical decision that results in the possibility of an adult criminal record and adult penalties, had been made by the judge acting alone, without any concern for Morris Kent's rights.

The Supreme Court Justices decided that due process of law entitles a defendant like Morris Kent to certain minimum safeguards, including a hearing, the right to the assistance of an attorney, and a statement of the reasons for transfer if the judge decides to transfer the case to adult court. The Supreme Court reasoned that the juvenile court judge denied Kent his right to the assistance of an attorney. Without a hearing, Kent's attorney had no opportunity to represent the youth. The denial of the assistance of counsel, a Sixth Amendment right, was compounded by the judge's denial of access to the case files. That denial prevented the attorney from raising any challenges to possible errors in social service or probation staff reports about the defendant.

The *Kent* case is important not so much because it corrected the wrongs done to one individual or because it put some order into the waiver (transfer) procedure, but because it marks the Supreme Court's first major examination of juvenile court processing. This examination found serious shortcomings of both the particular juvenile court that had handled Morris Kent and of juvenile courts in general:

> While there can be no doubt of the original laudable purpose of juvenile courts, studies and critiques in recent years raise serious questions as to whether actual performance measures well enough against theoretical purpose to make tolerable the immunity of the process from the reach of constitutional guaranties applicable to adults. There is much evidence that some juvenile courts, including that of the District of Columbia, lack the personnel, facilities and techniques to perform adequately as representatives of the State in a *parens patriae* capacity, at least with respect to children charged with law violation. There is evidence, in fact, that there may be grounds for concern that the child receives the worst of both worlds: that he gets neither the protections accorded to adults nor the solicitous care and regenerative treatment postulated for children. (*Kent v. United States*, 1966)

A final comment on the *Kent* case is that many states are now resorting to prosecutor direct file and statutory exclusion (see Chapter 8 for more details) instead of transfer or waiver to prosecute juveniles as adults in criminal courts. Reliance on these other methods means that the affected juveniles do not get the waiver hearing and protections that *Kent* was intended to guarantee.

In re Gault

The case of *In re Gault* (1967) was even more significant. Gerald Gault was a 15-year-old Arizona youth who was arrested for allegedly making obscene phone calls to an adult woman. He was adjudicated a delinquent in a court proceeding that resembled a kangaroo court or a dictatorial tribunal rather than a court of law and was sentenced to the state training school for a possible six-year sentence. The maximum penalty for an adult committing the exact same offense was a $50 fine and two months in jail.

Gault, after being accused, was taken into police custody and detained. Within about a week, he was adjudicated a delinquent and committed to the state training school until he was discharged or turned 21 years of age, whichever came first. All of this occurred without the complainant (the target of the obscene phone calls) ever appearing in court to testify, without any detailed and specific charges being filed (Gault was simply accused of being a "delinquent"), without the assistance of an attorney for Gault (his probation officer "represented" him), and without any transcript of the proceedings. The end result was the possibility of a six-year sentence for what was at worst a nuisance offense.

In reviewing the case, Supreme Court Justice Abe Fortas traced the history of the juvenile court and of the *parens patriae* philosophy and found some fundamental problems. Supposedly, due process guarantees such as the assistance of an attorney were to be relaxed in juvenile court so that youths would receive the treatment benefits promised by both the founders and current advocates of the juvenile court. Instead, as the Court observed in the *Kent* case, the child often received the worst of both worlds: lack of procedural fairness and substandard treatment.

Interestingly, the Supreme Court did not go on to discard the juvenile court philosophy of *parens patriae*. Instead, Justice Fortas observed that due process rights would not hinder juvenile court judges from seeking the best interests of the child but actually would assist them in that effort:

> But recent studies … suggest that the appearance as well as the actuality of fairness, impartiality, and orderliness—in short, the essentials of due process—may be a more impressive and more therapeutic attitude so far as the juvenile is concerned. (*In re Gault*, 1967)

Judge Fortas went on to rule that juveniles do have certain due process rights in delinquency proceedings in which there is the possibility of confinement in a locked facility. Specifically, such juveniles have the Fifth Amendment privilege against self-incrimination (the right to remain silent) and Sixth Amendment rights to adequate notice of the charges against them, to confront and cross-examine their accusers, and to the assistance of counsel.

As noted in Chapter 8, unfortunately providing juveniles with defense attorneys has not always improved their outcomes in court (Burruss et al., 2020). Also, Feld and Moriearty (2020) argue that providing attorneys to juveniles may have inadvertently hindered progress in achieving racial justice for black youths in juvenile court. They argue that guaranteeing procedural justice rights such as the right to an attorney may have deflected attention and efforts from societal actions that needed to be taken to address racial injustice in policing and in the rest of the juvenile justice system (see again Chapter 8 for more information).

In re Winship

In 1970, the Supreme Court went a step further. In the case of *In re Winship*, an appeal of a New York case involving a 12-year-old boy who had stolen $112 from a woman's purse from a locker, the Supreme Court turned its attention to the issue of the standard of proof (how strong a case must be to prove delinquency) in juvenile court. The Court made two rulings. First, the Court ruled that the U.S. Constitution requires that adult criminals be convicted only by the standard of "guilty beyond a reasonable doubt" (the **reasonable doubt standard** of proof). This had been standard practice in adult courts; the Court simply stated that the Constitution mandated what the states had been doing all along. Second, the Court extended the reasonable doubt standard of proof to juvenile delinquency proceedings in which there was the possibility of commitment to a locked facility. As was the case in *In re Gault*, the Court reasoned that this safeguard of the reasonable doubt standard would not detract in any way from the noble intentions of the *parens patriae* philosophy.

It also suggested that, rhetoric aside, juvenile training schools were the functional equivalents of adult prisons because both resulted in deprivation of liberty—and any such deprivation of liberty requires due process protections. Finally, the Supreme Court noted that New York State's standard of proof in juvenile proceedings (i.e., guilty by a preponderance of the evidence) was open to inaccurate findings. There was a real possibility that youths could be found delinquent when in fact there was insufficient evidence for such findings.

McKeiver v. Pennsylvania

A year later, in 1971, the Supreme Court took up the issue of a juvenile's right to a jury trial in the case of *McKeiver v. Pennsylvania* (1971). In *McKeiver*, the Supreme Court declined to go so far in extending adult rights as to grant juveniles the right to trial by jury. The Supreme Court decided not to grant juveniles the right to jury trials for several reasons. First, the Court did not want to turn the juvenile court process into a fully adversarial process and end "the idealistic prospect of an intimate, informal protective proceeding" (*McKeiver v. Pennsylvania*, 1971). Second, the Court noted that because bench trials (trials decided by a judge rather than by a jury) for adults often result in accurate determinations of guilt, jury trials are not an absolute necessity for accurate determinations of delinquency. The Court also indicated that it was reluctant to impose a federal requirement of a jury trial because such a mandate could prevent individual states from experimenting with different methods. Finally, the Court noted that it had not reached such total disillusionment with the juvenile justice system to warrant abandoning it.

Barry Feld (2012) contends that the denial of the right of a jury trial to juveniles was an important decision because judges and juries view cases differently. The result of the denial of the right to a jury trial is that it is "easier to convict a youth in a juvenile court bench trial than to convict a younger person in a criminal proceeding when the state presents similar evidence to a jury" (Feld, 2012:682). In other words, Feld believes that judges need less evidence to convict than do juries and that delinquents would fare better before juries.

These cases of *Kent*, *Gault*, *Winship*, and *McKeiver* constituted a philosophical revolution in juvenile court. Together, they forced juvenile courts to at least pay lip service to the notion that juveniles deserve many of the due process safeguards available to adults. Although the *McKeiver* case ruled against extending the right of trial by jury to juveniles, even this case indicated that the Supreme Court would not tolerate the wholesale denial of rights to juveniles. The *McKeiver* case implied that if accurate fact-finding were not available to juveniles, then the Supreme Court might have to impose additional limits on juvenile court discretion.

Still, it must be remembered that a philosophical revolution is not always a revolution in practice. Just because the Supreme Court has ruled that juveniles should be entitled to certain rights, such a pronouncement alone does not guarantee the actual provision of those rights. There is evidence that many children waive their right to counsel and that high caseloads prevent many lawyers representing juveniles from being effective (Miller-Wilson & Puritz, 2003; see also Feld & Schaefer, 2010). Thus, court practices and lack of resources can prevent juveniles from actually benefiting from Supreme Court rulings.

ADDITIONAL SUPREME COURT RULINGS

Since the landmark cases just discussed, the U.S. Supreme Court has decided several cases concerning delinquency proceedings in juvenile court.

Roper v. Simmons: A Ruling on the Death Penalty

In 2005, in *Roper v. Simmons*, the Supreme Court ruled that the death penalty is unconstitutional for juveniles. This case is discussed in detail in Chapter 14.

Three Rulings on Life without Parole

In *Graham v. Florida* (2010), the Supreme Court ruled that a Life Without Parole (LWOP) sentence is unconstitutional for a juvenile offender who did not commit homicide. This case applied most directly to Florida, which had 77 such offenders in prison at the time of the ruling. It is important to note that the Supreme Court is not ordering states like Florida to release all juvenile offenders. The Court simply has ordered the states to allow such offenders some way to demonstrate sufficient maturity and rehabilitation to justify their release. States may determine that an offender is irredeemable and should not be released. The Court is simply telling the states that they cannot make the decision to keep a juvenile offender in prison for life at the time of sentencing and then deny the offender any opportunity in the future to demonstrate fitness for release. It is important to note that LWOP is constitutional for a juvenile offender who commits murder. In *Miller v. Alabama* (2012), the Court banned the mandatory imposition of LWOP for juveniles. In other words, states can still impose an LWOP sentence on a juvenile, but only after individualized consideration of the juvenile and the juvenile's offense. Some, but not all, states interpreted *Miller v. Alabama* to apply retroactively to juveniles previously sentenced to LWOP. As a result, in *Montgomery v. Louisiana* (2016), the Supreme Court ruled that *Miller* does apply retroactively. In its most recent ruling on juvenile LWOP, *Jones v. Mississippi* (2021), the Supreme Court ruled that a judge does not have to find a youth "permanently incorrigible" before it can sentence him to juvenile LWOP. The judge simply has to have the discretion to consider a defendant's youth in sentencing.

The Supreme Court decisions on life without parole may be a pyrrhic victory; that is, critics of LWOP may have won a battle but lost the war. A recent report indicates that about 8,600 persons who committed their crimes as minors are serving Life With Parole or virtual life sentences (Nellis, 2021). (See Chapter 14 for a complete discussion of life sentences for juveniles.)

In light of the *McKeiver* ruling against jury trials for juveniles, one author raises a critical issue. A number of Supreme Court cases, such as *Blakely v. Washington* (2004), appear to require that a jury find certain facts before a judge can give a sentence that goes beyond the jury's verdict. If the Supreme Court were to apply this rule to juvenile LWOP, then states would have to provide jury trials

Anthony Shamont Jones, left, age 55, was re-sentenced in Kalamazoo County Circuit Court in 2017, making him eligible for parole for his involvement in the 1979 shooting death of grocery store owner Ronald Hermanns. Kimberly Thomas, right, represented Jones during the hearing. Jones was 17 when he was sentenced to life without chance of parole.

CREDIT: Mark Bugnaski/*Kalamazoo Gazette*-MLive Media Group via AP

for any juvenile facing LWOP. The author concludes that this is an unresolved issue (Russell, 2015). Thomas and Stich (2019) contend that juries are better at decision making than judges because judges can be biased.

Breed v. Jones: A Ruling on Waiver

In *Breed v. Jones* (1975), the Court made the waiver process more explicit by ruling that states cannot first adjudicate a juvenile a delinquent and then waive or transfer the youth to adult court. The Court ruled that by doing this in a particular case, the state of California violated the youth's Sixth Amendment protection against double jeopardy (being tried twice for the same crime). The state of California had claimed that double jeopardy was not at issue because the juvenile was only punished once, but the Supreme Court ruled that being tried both in juvenile court and then again in adult court did indeed constitute a violation of the double jeopardy provision.

In a sense, the case of *Breed v. Jones* was not much of a victory for juvenile rights. Prior to the case, juveniles were tried in juvenile court, adjudicated delinquent, and then transferred to adult criminal court where they were tried as adults and sentenced. All that the U.S. Supreme Court ruling accomplished was a procedural change by which the juvenile court would now conduct a waiver or transfer hearing to determine if there was probable cause to believe that the juvenile committed the delinquent act. If the juvenile court finds probable cause and also determines that the juvenile is not amenable to juvenile system intervention (for example, the youth is getting too old for juvenile programs or has been in juvenile programs previously without much success), the juvenile court simply transfers the juvenile to the adult system without any final deter-mination of the charge. A few years ago, one of the authors of this text observed such a waiver hearing, which equaled a full trial on the delinquency petition in every respect except that the judge declared a finding of "probable cause" rather than "delinquent" at the end of the hearing. The practical result of such waivers (transfers) to adult criminal court is the same as if the child had been adjudicated a delinquent. *Breed v. Jones* may be more a case of window dressing rather than an influential juvenile justice case.

J.D.B. v. North Carolina and *Fare v. Michael C.*: **Rulings on Interrogation**

In *J.D.B. v. North Carolina* (2011), the issue was an interrogation of a 13-year-old burglary suspect in a school conference room by police and school administrators. The Court ruled that courts should consider age as a factor in the custody analysis when the child's age was known to the officer or would have been objectively apparent to a reasonable officer. The majority noted that a child may feel pressure to submit to questioning when an adult would feel free to leave the interrogation because children in general are less mature and responsible than adults. The dissent objected that the majority was making the determination of custody too difficult whereas it should be clear and straight-forward. The dissent also objected that this could open the door to the Court demanding that police could consider other factors such as intelligence, cultural background, and education. The result of this decision is that police will have to consider age as a possible factor that could affect whether trial and appellate courts will rule on whether a youthful suspect is considered in custody or not for *Miranda* purposes.

As noted above, two of the provisions of the *Gault* case were its explicit endorsements of the Fifth Amendment privilege against self-incrimination and the Sixth Amendment right to the assistance of counsel for juveniles. *Gault* applied to juvenile delinquency suspects the *Miranda* rights granted to adult criminal suspects. Like adults, juveniles may waive these two rights and consent to police interrogation without any attorney being present. A voluntary confession can then be used against the juvenile in court.

Gault left it unclear whether a juvenile could waive these so-called *Miranda* rights without first speaking with at least one parent or an attorney. The American Bar Association (ABA) has gone so far as to recommend mandatory consultation with an attorney prior to any confession to the police (Institute of Judicial Administration–American Bar Association [IJA–ABA], 1982). Most states, however, simply stipulate that the police give *Miranda* warnings in language that is understandable to juveniles (see Holtz, 1987).

The Supreme Court clarified this issue in the case of *Fare v. Michael C.* (1979). In this case, a juvenile murder suspect consented to an interrogation after he was denied the opportunity to consult with his probation officer. The Court ruled that there is no constitutional mandate to allow a suspect to speak with his or her probation officer. The rationale of the Court was that the Sixth Amendment specifies the right to the assistance of counsel, while a probation officer is basically on the side of the police in seeking to prosecute any juvenile who has violated his probation. More importantly, the Court ruled that the child can voluntarily waive his or her privilege against self-incrimination without first speaking to his or her parents and without first consulting an attorney. In such a situation the trial court judge must evaluate the voluntariness of any confession based on the totality of the circumstances rather than on any ironclad rule (called a *per se* rule) mandating the police to bring in at least one parent or an attorney to advise the child about the wisdom of waiving his or her rights. In evaluating the totality of the circumstances of the waiver, the trial court must consider such factors as the age, maturity, experience, and intelligence of the youth. Thus, judges might allow as admissible the waiver of rights by a 17-year-old high school student with a prior record but probably not the waiver of rights by a 13-year-old first offender of below-average intelligence.

It is important to note that there is some controversy about the Supreme Court's wisdom in not requiring more explicit or extensive warnings for juvenile suspects prior to interrogation. First, some research indicates that not all juveniles clearly understand their rights when arrested (Huang, 2001). In one study, about one-third of a sample of institutionalized delinquents thought (erroneously) that they were required to talk to the police (Robin, 1982). Other research has indicated that more than one-half of the youths tested lacked full understanding of all the *Miranda* warnings, and only about one-fifth adequately understood all of the warnings (Holtz, 1987:550; see also Grisso & Schwartz, 2000). Recent neurobiological research confirms difficulties for minors in understanding and asserting their *Miranda* rights (Feld, 2012). Second, parents tend not to be the best protectors of juvenile rights. One study showed that about one-third of parents would advise their own children to confess criminal involvement to the police (Robin, 1982). Due to considerations such as these, some model juvenile law codes stipulate that police must have juvenile suspects consult with an attorney prior to police interrogation (IJA–ABA, 1982).

Most states follow the "totality of the circumstances" approach outlined in the *Fare* case. A few states put in so-called *per se* rules requiring that juveniles have the opportunity to confer with a parent, guardian, attorney, or other interested adult. Unfortunately, a number of states (Georgia, Louisiana, and Pennsylvania) overturned their *per se* rules as part of the "get tough" movement (Huang, 2001). However, appellate courts in three states—Alaska, Minnesota, and Wisconsin—have ordered that police electronically record all juvenile interrogations in order to assure the voluntariness of confessions and prevent police coercion (Ziemer, 2005). The Pennsylvania Supreme Court ruled that a juvenile can waive his or her right to counsel only after a judge questions the juvenile to determine if the juvenile understands the allegations and that a lawyer can be helpful (Burke, 2005).

In *Yarborough, Warden v. Alvarado* (2004), the U.S. Supreme Court ruled that age was not a factor in determining that a juvenile was not in custody for purposes of police questioning. The case involved a two-hour police interview of a 17-year-old murder suspect in a police station without giving the *Miranda* warnings or allowing the boy's parents to be present in the interview room. Based on his statements to the police, the youth was convicted of murder. The court ruled that the lower court made a correct ruling on the noncustodial status of Alvarado based on objective factors such as: (1) the police did not transport the juvenile to the station; (2) his parents were in the lobby; and (3) at the end of the interview the youth went home. The dissent argued, among other factors, that age is an objective factor that the police and courts should consider in determining custody status.

Feld (2012) observes that, as a whole, Supreme Court rulings on the interrogation of juveniles have excluded statements from youths 15 or younger but admitted statements of 16- and 17-year-olds. He adds that this follows the developmental research that youths 15 and younger face clear and substantial disabilities in exercising competence in exercising their *Miranda* rights, while 16- and 17-year-olds can function about the same as adults.

Schall v. Martin: A Ruling on Preventive Detention

In *Schall v. Martin* (1984), the U.S. Supreme Court ruled that a juvenile who is awaiting court action can be held in **preventive detention** if there is adequate concern that the juvenile would commit additional crimes while the primary case is pending further court action. The juvenile, however, does have the right to a hearing on the preventive detention decision and a statement of the reasons for which he or she is being detained. The Court justified its decision on the basis that every state permits such preventive detention for juveniles and on the rationale that such detention protects "both the juvenile and society from the hazards of pretrial crime" (*Schall v. Martin*, 1984). Furthermore, the Court majority reasoned that "juveniles, unlike adults, are always in some form of custody" (*Schall v. Martin*, 1984). The three dissenting Justices, on the other hand, noted the impossibility of predicting which juveniles will engage in future crime (this is often labeled the "false positive issue") and considered the punitive nature of many detention facilities.

SEARCH AND SEIZURE

Consideration of these landmark U.S. Supreme Court cases demonstrates that juveniles do indeed have basic rights at important stages of the juvenile justice process, especially the waiver (transfer) hearing and the adjudication (trial) stage. Very important are the Fourth Amendment rights of juveniles during investigation or arrest.

The issue of **search and seizure** is a complex one involving a myriad of U.S. Supreme Court interpretations of the Fourth Amendment. This amendment reads:

> The right of the people to be secure in their persons, houses, papers, and effects, against unreasonable searches and seizures, shall not be violated, and no Warrants shall issue, but upon probable cause, supported by Oath or affirmation, and particularly describing the place to be searched, and the persons or things to be seized.

The Fourth Amendment indicates a preference for warrants before the police can search or arrest suspects, but this preference for warrants is riddled with numerous exceptions. This is not the place to describe those exceptions (but see, for example, O'Brien, 1997). Here it is important to examine one question that does affect juveniles: the **consent search** in which a defendant voluntarily allows the police to search someone's effects without a search warrant. Since *Schneckloth v. Bustamonte* (1973), the U.S. Supreme Court's ruling on adult consent searches has been that the police may simply ask a person for consent to search the person or his or her house, car, or effects. Unlike the *Miranda* situation, in which the police must advise a person of the right to refuse interrogation, the police do not have to specifically advise an adult suspect that he or she has the right to refuse a search. The police may simply ask an adult, "Do you mind if we take a look around your house?" If the person agrees, then—aware of it or not—the individual has agreed to a consent search. This would be a reasonable search in terms of Fourth Amendment guarantees.

In the case of juveniles, the issue arises whether a juvenile is mature enough to withstand police pressure and intelligent enough to understand his or her rights. The ABA has recommended that juveniles be advised of their right to refuse a consent search and that they also be advised of the opportunity to consult an attorney (IJA–ABA, 1982). The ABA felt that these two safeguards would compensate for any youthful susceptibility to police coercion and any lack of sophistication needed to understand fully one's rights. Another set of standards, the American Law Institute Model Code of Pre-arraignment Procedure, stipulates that if a person about to be asked to consent to a search is under 16 years of age, then a parent should be the one who gives consent. The Model Code further advocates that in any consent search situation involving juveniles or adults, the police should advise the individual that he or she "is under no obligation to give such consent and that anything found may be taken and used in evidence" (Wadlington, Whitebread, & Davis, 1983:301). In other words, the Model Code drafters advocated warnings for consent searches that were similar to the *Miranda* warnings used in interrogation situations. They felt that it should not be assumed that juvenile offenders are aware of their right to refuse a consent search without a clear warning of their right to do so.

A Supreme Court case from 2002 suggests that today's courts are probably inclined to rule on the side of law enforcement rather than to extend offender rights. In *United States v. Mark James Knights* (2002), the Court ruled that a warrantless search of a probationer, supported by reasonable suspicion and authorized by a probation condition, satisfied the Fourth Amendment. This follows *In re Tyrell* (1994), in which a California court ruled that a search of a juvenile on probation (which found marijuana in his pants) did not violate the Fourth Amendment. Police made a pat-down search of the youth when they saw a knife on one of two other youths with him. Even though the police did not have probable cause to conduct the search and even though the youth did not consent to the search, the Court felt the police did not violate the juvenile's expectation of privacy because the boy had been placed on probation, which stipulated the condition that he submit to searches by police, probation officers, or school officials. This probation condition erased any reasonable expectation of privacy (Juvenile Justice Update, 1995).

RIGHTS IN SCHOOL

Because juveniles spend much of their time in school, many questions about juvenile rights have arisen within the context of school policies and procedures.

Corporal Punishment

In *Ingraham v. Wright* (1977), the U.S. Supreme Court ruled that **corporal punishment** (e.g., paddling) of students is permissible so long as it is reasonable. The reasonableness decision depends on: "the seriousness of the offense, the attitude and past behavior of the child, the nature and severity of the punishment, the age and strength of the child, and the availability of less severe but equally effective means of discipline" (*Ingraham v. Wright*, 1977).

The Court noted that corporal punishment could be abused but observed that common-law remedies were effective deterrents to any such abuse of the practice. The Court reasoned that students and their parents could sue school officials or charge them with criminal assault if they went too far in paddling any particular student.

As is often the case, dissenting opinions in Supreme Court cases raise very interesting issues. In fact, dissents sometimes are more noteworthy than the majority or plurality opinions of the Justices. Box 9.1 presents excerpts from the dissenting opinion of Justice White in the case of *Ingraham v. Wright*. These show that there are other sides to the issue of the constitutionality of corporal punishment in schools. The ABA has followed Justice White's dissent and has recommended that "[c]orporal punishment should not be inflicted upon a student" (IJA–ABA, 1982:136). Finally, a review of the research on corporal punishment concluded that it should be banned because children who receive corporal punishment are more prone as adults to various deviant acts. Among the later problems are depression, suicide, physical abuse of children and spouses, commission of violent crime, drinking problems, attraction to masochistic sex, and problems attaining a prestigious occupation (Straus, 1994). Despite such research findings and despite calls by professional medical and legal associations (AMA, American Academy of Pediatrics, ABA) to end the practice, as of 2021, 19 states allow corporal punishment (Kennedy, 2021). In some districts, parental consent is required. In a Ninth Circuit case, the judges ruled that "no reasonable principal could think it constitutional to intentionally punch, slap, grab, and slam students into lockers" (*P.B. v. Koch*, 1996). (For a note on excessive discipline in schools, see Box 9.2.)

Freedom of Speech for Students

Another school rights issue is the First Amendment right to **freedom of speech**. Here the U.S. Supreme Court has upheld the basic principle that students have at least some degree of constitutional protection in that they do not "shed their constitutional rights to freedom of speech or expression at the schoolhouse gate" (*Tinker v. Des Moines Independent Community School District*, 1969). This does not mean that students can say or express anything they wish in whatever manner they wish. What it means is that the right of free speech is to be balanced with the school's interest in education and discipline. Students are entitled to express themselves as long as their expression does not materially and substantially interfere with school discipline or the educational process.

BOX 9.1 EXCERPTS FROM JUSTICE WHITE'S DISSENT IN *INGRAHAM V. WRIGHT*

If there are some punishments that are so barbaric that they may not be imposed for the commission of crimes, designated by our social system as the most thoroughly reprehensible acts an individual can commit, then, a fortiori, similar punishments may not be imposed on persons for less culpable acts, such as breaches of school discipline. Thus, if it is constitutionally impermissible to cut off someone's ear for the commission of murder, it must be unconstitutional to cut off a child's ear for being late to class. Although there were no ears cut off in this case, the record reveals beatings so severe that if they were inflicted on a hardened criminal for the commission of a serious crime, they might not pass constitutional muster.

The essence of the majority's argument is that school children do not need Eighth Amendment protection because corporal punishment is less subject to abuse in public schools than it is in the prison system. However, it cannot be reasonably suggested that just because cruel and unusual punishments may occur less frequently under public scrutiny, they will not occur at all. The mere fact that a public flogging or a public execution would be available for all to see would not render the punishment constitutional if it were otherwise impermissible. Similarly, the majority would not suggest that a prisoner who is placed in a minimum-security prison and permitted to go home to his family on the weekends should be any less entitled to Eighth Amendment protections than his counterpart in a maximum-security prison. In short, if a punishment is so barbaric and inhumane that it goes beyond the tolerance of a civilized society, its openness to public scrutiny should have nothing to do with its constitutionality.

By holding that the Eighth Amendment protects only criminals, the majority adopts the view that one is entitled to the protections afforded by the Eighth Amendment only if he is punished for acts that are sufficiently opprobrious for society to make them "criminal." This is a curious holding in view of the fact that the more culpable the offender the more likely it is that the punishment will not be disproportionate to the offense, consequently, the less likely it is that the punishment will be cruel and unusual. Conversely, a public school student who is spanked for a mere breach of discipline may sometimes have a strong argument that the punishment does not fit the offense, depending upon the severity of the beating, and therefore that it is cruel and unusual. Yet the majority would afford the student no protection no matter how inhumane and barbaric the punishment inflicted on him might be.

This tort action (student lawsuits against teachers who abuse corporal punishment) is utterly inadequate to protect against erroneous infliction of punishment for two reasons. First, under Florida law, a student punished for an act he did not commit cannot recover damages from a teacher "proceeding in utmost good faith … on the reports and advice of others"; the student has no remedy at all for punishment imposed on the basis of mistaken facts, at least as long as the punishment was reasonable from the point of view of the disciplinarian, uninformed by any prior hearing. The "traditional common-law remedies" on which the majority relies, thus do nothing to protect the student from the danger that concerned the Court in *Goss* [*v. Lopez*]—the risk of reasonable, good-faith mistakes in the school disciplinary process.

Source: *Ingraham v. Wright* (1977).

In the *Tinker* case, for example, at issue was the wearing of black armbands by students to protest U.S. involvement in the Vietnam conflict. The students doing so were suspended and sent home. When the case reached the U.S. Supreme Court, the majority of the Justices ruled that the students' First Amendment rights had been violated, noting that the students had expressed themselves without creating any disturbance or interfering with school discipline.

BOX 9.2 EXCESSIVE DISCIPLINE/CRUEL AND UNUSUAL PUNISHMENT

Cruel and unusual punishment is an issue in prisons. The parallel issue in schools is excessive discipline. For example, recently a teacher ordered a 10-year-old student to clean a toilet. She had mistakenly concluded that the student intentionally put too much toilet paper in the toilet in order to clog the toilet. She made the boy put his hands in the toilet and pull out the paper. He washed his hands and returned to class.

The case made it to the Tenth Circuit. Judges used the "shock the conscience" test. The judges concluded that the teacher had not acted with malice and so her actions were not deliberate, conscience-shocking actions.

The general lesson from cases such as this is that appeals courts use the standard of shock the conscience. But they interpret:

a very high threshold, and that school personnel's conduct must truly be outrageous. Finally, it is of considerable import that both courts focused primarily on the intent of the school personnel to do harm. Therefore, it is important to ask the question: What inspired the school personnel's action? Unless it was malice or sadism or the injury is substantially severe, there is a strong likelihood the school and its personnel will prevail. (Colwell, 2002:3)

What do you think? Did this teacher's actions "shock the conscience"? If not, what would she have to do to shock the conscience?

Source: Colwell (2002).

Furthermore, the school system had been inconsistent in that it had allowed some students to wear political campaign buttons and others to wear the traditional symbol of Nazism (the swastika). Writing for the majority, Justice Fortas took serious issue with school system prohibition of student expression of only one particular type:

> In our system, state-operated schools may not be enclaves of totalitarianism. School officials do not possess absolute authority over their students. Students in school as well as out of school are "persons" under our Constitution. They are possessed of fundamental rights which the State must respect, just as they themselves must respect their obligations to the State. In our system, students may not be regarded as closed-circuit recipients of only that which the State chooses to communicate. They may not be confined to the expression of those sentiments that are officially approved. In the absence of a specific showing of constitutionally valid reasons to regulate their speech, students are entitled to freedom of expression of their views. (*Tinker v. Des Moines Independent Community School District*, 1969)

This case can be misinterpreted as an outstanding victory for children's rights if some cautions are not noted. First, the Court was probably more concerned with the issue of free speech in general rather than with free speech for children. That is, the ruling in favor of the pupils can probably be traced to the Supreme Court's "long tradition of zealous protection of First Amendment rights" (Davis & Schwartz, 1987:58). Second, the case may be interpreted not so much as a children's rights case as a parents' rights case, because the children in this case shared the same views as their parents on governmental involvement in Vietnam (Davis & Schwartz, 1987). If the views of the students and their parents had not been the same, the ruling may have been otherwise. Finally,

BOX 9.3 FREE SPEECH IN SCHOOLS: POSTING A WEBSITE

A Pennsylvania middle-school student created a website that had negative comments and pictures about his algebra teacher and school principal. Pictures on the site showed the teacher's head dripping with blood and her face changing into Adolf Hitler. The site also offered money for a hit man to kill the teacher.

In a unanimous decision, the Pennsylvania Supreme Court ruled that school officials could punish the student because the website created a substantial disruption of school activities. The Court reasoned that there was a nexus between the website and the school so that the speech could be considered as occurring on-campus. Following the *Fraser and Tinker* cases (see text), the Court concluded that "the website created disorder and significantly and adversely impacted the delivery of instruction" (see www.firstamendmentschools.org).

What do you think? Does the school have the legal authority to punish a student for the contents of a website that the student creates in his or her own home? Should a student be able to create a website and put highly negative content about teachers on that website? Should a student be able to devise a website that criticizes the teaching ability of his or her teachers but does not go so far as to compare the teachers to Hitler or mention anything such as hiring a hit man? What are the limits of free speech for students on websites?

In a recent case, a judge upheld a school disciplining a student for posting a notice on Facebook about a bomb in the school. The judge noted that school officials had a legitimate concern "in the interest of safety" (*R.L. v. Cent. York School*, 183 F. Supp.3d 625 [2016]).

the case distinguished between passive expression and disruptive expression of views. Passive speech (for example, wearing armbands) is less disruptive than disturbances or other types of expression. The Court is more likely to uphold such passive speech than more rowdy forms of speech. (For a case about free speech by students on the World Wide Web, see Box 9.3.)

More recently the Court addressed the issue of student speech at a school-supervised event that took place off-campus. Specifically, in *Deborah Morse, et al., v. Joseph Frederick* (2007), the Court addressed the issue of student speech at an Olympic Torch Rally in Juneau, Alaska, that passed through the street in front of a high school while school was in session. The principal permitted students to watch the relay from the other side of the street and one student unfurled a 14-foot banner reading "BONG HiTS4JESUS." The principal interpreted this message as endorsing drug use and confiscated the banner after the student refused to take it down. Justice Roberts ruled that "schools may take steps to safeguard those entrusted to their care from speech that can reasonably be regarded as encouraging illegal drug use" (Majority Opinion, *Deborah Morse, et al., v. Joseph Frederick*). In his dissent, Justice Stevens argued that the banner did not infringe on anyone's rights and did not interfere with any of the school's educational programs.

In other First Amendment cases, the Supreme Court has addressed the issue of whether school officials can discipline a student for giving a lascivious speech and who holds editorial control over student publications. In *Bethel School District No. 403 v. Fraser* (1986), the Court addressed the issue of "whether the First Amendment prevents a school district from disciplining a high school student for giving a lewd speech at a school assembly." Matthew Fraser nominated a fellow student for a student office by using "an elaborate, graphic, and sexual

BOX 9.4 LEWD SPEECHES IN SCHOOL

In *Bethel School District No. 403 v. Fraser* (1986), the U.S. Supreme Court argued that students do not have an absolute right to free speech under the First Amendment. They refused to equate lewd language given as part of a political statement with the wearing of protest armbands in the *Tinker* case. The Justices distinguished the *Fraser* case from *Tinker* in that, in the *Tinker* case, the speech involved political expression and therefore it merited greater protection; whereas:

> the penalties imposed in this case were unrelated to any political viewpoint. The First Amendment does not prevent the school officials from determining that to permit a vulgar and lewd speech such as respondent's would undermine the school's basic educational mission. A high school assembly or classroom is no place for a sexually explicit monologue directed towards an unsuspecting audience of teenage students. Accordingly, it was perfectly appropriate for the school to disassociate itself to make the point to the pupils that vulgar speech and lewd conduct is wholly inconsistent with the "fundamental values" of public education. (*Bethel School District No. 403 v. Fraser*, 1986)

Further, the Court noted that schools play an important role in preparing students for adult citizenship:

The process of educating our youth for citizenship in public schools is not confined to books, the curriculum, and the civics class; schools must teach by example the shared values of a civilized social order. Consciously or otherwise, teachers—and indeed the older students—demonstrate the appropriate form of civil discourse and political expression by their conduct and deportment in and out of class. Inescapably, like parents, they are role models. The schools, as instruments of the state, may determine that the essential lessons of civil, mature conduct cannot be conveyed in a school that tolerates lewd, indecent, or offensive speech and conduct such as that indulged in by this confused boy.

The pervasive sexual innuendo in Fraser's speech was plainly offensive to both teachers and students—indeed to any mature person. By glorifying male sexuality, and in its verbal content, the speech was acutely insulting to teenage girl students. The speech could well be seriously damaging to its less mature audience, many of whom were only 14 years old and on the threshold of awareness of human sexuality. Some students were reported as bewildered by the speech and the reaction of mimicry it provoked. (*Bethel School District No. 403 v. Fraser*, 1986)

metaphor." His obscene language violated a school rule, so he was suspended from school for two days. Both the District Court and the Court of Appeals ruled that the school had violated Fraser's First Amendment right to free speech. They reasoned that the speech was basically the same sort of action as the wearing of the protest armbands in the *Tinker* case. The U.S. Supreme Court, however, reversed the lower courts' decision and determined that the school does have a right to ban sexually explicit language, even if it is couched within a political speech, because it is counter to the basic educational mission of the school (see Box 9.4). The Court also limited the degree of freedom students have in expressing themselves in student publications, again pointing out the educational mission of the schools for justification (see Box 9.5).

In November of 1995, the U.S. Supreme Court declined to hear a case (denied certiorari) involving the right of a Tennessee junior high school teacher to refuse a research paper on the life of Jesus. In 1991, Brittany Settle, a junior high school student in Dickson County, submitted an outline on the life of Jesus for her research paper assignment. The original assignment noted that the topic must be "interesting, research-able, and decent." The teacher rejected Brittany's outline because, among other factors, she failed to get permission for

BOX 9.5 CENSORSHIP OF STUDENT PUBLICATIONS

In an important First Amendment school case, the Supreme Court ruled that school officials can exercise broad editorial control over student publications:

> Instead, we hold that educators do not offend the First Amendment by exercising editorial control over the style and content of student speech in school-sponsored expressive activities so long as their actions are reasonably related to legitimate pedagogical concerns. (*Hazelwood School District v. Kuhlmeier*, 1988)

The case involved a principal's censorship of a high school newspaper. The principal prevented publication of an article describing three students' experiences during pregnancy and of another article describing student reactions to parental divorce. Writing for the majority, Justice White distinguished the *Tinker* case type of speech as "a student's personal expression that happens to occur on the school premises" from "school-sponsored publications, theatrical productions, and other expressive activities" that are "part of the school curriculum" and "are supervised by faculty members and designed to impart particular knowledge or skills" (*Hazelwood School District v. Kuhlmeier*, 1988). For educational reasons, schools have "greater control" over the latter type of speech.

In his dissent, Justice Brennan castigated the majority viewpoint as approving "thought police" and the violation of "the First Amendment's prohibitions against censorship of any student expression that neither disrupts classwork nor invades the rights of others, and against any censorship that is not narrowly tailored to serve its purpose" (*Hazelwood School District v. Kuhlmeier*, 1988). Justice Brennan concluded that "[t]he mere fact of school sponsorship does not … license such thought control in the high school, whether through school suppression of disfavored viewpoints or through official assessment of topic sensitivity" (*Hazelwood School District v. Kuhlmeier*, 1988).

the topic, the teacher thought that Brittany's strong belief would interfere with objectivity in a research assignment, and the assignment required four sources but Brittany used only one source: the Bible. In the U.S. District Court case, Brittany relied on *Tinker* for the right of free speech. The Court, however, relied on *Hazelwood School District v. Kuhlmeier*:

> The free speech rights of students in the classroom must be limited because effective education depends not only on controlling bois-terous conduct, but also on maintaining the focus of the class on the assignment in question … Teachers therefore must be given broad dis-cretion to give grades and conduct class discussion based on the con-tent of speech. (*Settle v. Dickson County School Board*, 1995)

In June 2021, the Supreme Court issued a ruling on off-campus student speech. After not making the varsity cheerleading squad, a high school stu-dent (B.L.) in Pennsylvania posted a vulgar criticism of the school—"F— school f—softball f—cheer f everything"—on social media. The school suspended her from the junior varsity cheerleading squad which she claimed violated her free speech rights. When the case got to the Supreme Court, the Court ruled that B.L. had a First Amendment right to criticize the school and that her post did not constitute a substantial disruption or interference with the school's efforts to maintain school order or cohesion on the cheer-leading squad. On the other hand, the Court noted that schools do have some rights to regulate off-campus speech, but refrained from giving specific guidelines (*Mahanoy Area School District v. B.L., A Minor, by and through her Father, Levy, et al.*, 2021).

Larry Levy, left, and Brandi Levy, right, review the U.S. Supreme Court ruling in *Mahanoy Area School District v. B.L.*, which was decided in their favor on June 23, 2021. The Court voted 8–1 in favor of Brandi, who was a 14-year-old high school freshman when she expressed her disappointment over not making the varsity cheerleading team on Snapchat with a string of curse words and a raised middle finger.

CREDIT: David McKeown/*Republican-Herald* via AP

BOX 9.6 CYBERBULLYING AND SCHOOLS

Cyberbullying—online bullying via text messages, Facebook, and other online communications—raises contemporary free speech issues. In traditional bullying, only a few people witness the act and the bully's offensive speech only lasts as long as spoken. Now cyberbullying can have the audience of the World Wide Web and last forever. In 2017, 20 percent of students age 12–18 reported being bullied at school during the school year. Of those bullied, 15.3 percent reported being bullied online or by text. Over a quarter of the bullied students reported that being bullied at school had somewhat or a lot of negative effect on them (Wang et al., 2020). Cyberbullying can even lead to victims committing suicide, as happened with one 15-year-old when teasing at school escalated into daily online taunts of "fat," "ugly," and worse (Araujo, 2012).

Araujo argues that courts have relied too much on the *Tinker* case standard of "substantial disruption" of school activities, and thereby actually have protected

bullies. Instead, Araujo argues, later decisions suggest that a better standard would be that off-campus cyberspeech is protected by the First Amendment, unless it is "(1) directed at an identifiable member of the school; (2) unwanted or uninvited; and (3) lewd, cruel, embarrassing, harassing, or threatening" (Araujo, 2012:371). As noted above, the Supreme Court has included severe bullying as one legitimate interest of schools in addressing and possibly limiting off-campus speech.

What do you think? If a student uses his computer or phone away from school to bully another student by calling him or her offensive names, do you agree with Araujo that such embarrassing or harassing language can and should be subject to school regulation? Or do you think that school officials should only be permitted to step in if the speech substantially disrupts school activities (following the *Tinker* standard and the 2021 *Levy* case)?

Source: Araujo (2012).

For discussion of cyberbullying, see Box 9.6. Box 9.7 includes Justice Breyer's note that the Court will not give specific examples of off-campus speech that might allow regulation and reasons why Levy's speech deserved First Amendment protection, including the finding that it was not obscene.

Two additional areas in which freedom of speech in schools has been questioned involve compulsory community service and school prayer. At first glance, the issue of compulsory community service would not appear to be a First Amendment issue. With the advent of programs that require service for high school graduation in several places (such as Dodge City, Kansas;

BOX 9.7 EXCERPTS FROM JUSTICE BREYER'S MAJORITY OPINION IN *MAHANOY AREA SCHOOL DISTRICT V. B.L.* (2021)

The school's regulatory interests remain significant in some off-campus circumstances.

[…]

Thus, we do not now set forth a broad, highly general First Amendment rule stating just what counts as "off campus" speech and whether or how ordinary First Amendment standards must give way off campus to a school's special need to prevent, e.g., substantial disruption of learning-related activities or the protection of those who make up a school community.

[…]

Putting aside the vulgar language, the listener would hear criticism, of the team, the team's coaches, and the school—in a word or two, criticism of the rules of a community of which

B.L. forms a part. This criticism did not involve features that would place it outside the First Amendment's ordinary protection. B.L.'s posts, while crude, did not amount to fighting words. See *Chaplinsky v. New Hampshire*, 315 U.S. 568 (1942). And while B.L. used vulgarity, her speech was not obscene as this Court has understood that term. See *Cohen v. California*, 403 U.S. 15, 19–20 (1971). To the contrary, B.L. uttered the kind of pure speech to which, were she an adult, the First Amendment would provide strong protection.

Do you agree with Justice Breyer? Or did the student go too far in her use of vulgarity to criticize the school? Second, should severe off-campus bullying justify school regulation? You can find the full Opinion at www.supremecourt.gov.

Boston; and the state of Maryland), opponents have argued that such service forces a student to engage in "expressive conduct." That is, the activity serves as an expression of support for the agency receiving the service. For example, a student might object that doing community service at the Girl Scouts sends the message that the student believes in what the Girl Scouts organization represents. This issue was argued in *Steirer v. Bethlehem Area School District* (1994). On appeal the Supreme Court denied certiorari (i.e., the Court declined to consider the case, letting the lower court ruling stand). The Court stated that there was no First Amendment free speech issue because expressive conduct was not clearly at stake. The Court noted that engaging in community service is not the same thing as wearing a black armband or burning a draft card, acts that clearly do express a viewpoint. Despite this ruling, Charters (1994) argues that community service can be seen as fostering an ideological viewpoint and that "students have no civic duty to perform acts of altruism and self-sacrifice the omission of which would justify a school district's withholding a student's diploma" (Charters, 1994:613).

School prayer has become a topic of much debate in recent years. The key to the debate is the issue of whether school prayer represents the promotion of religion by the school. The Supreme Court, in *Lee v. Weisman* (1992), ruled that school officials erred in providing guidelines and permitting prayer at a high school graduation ceremony. However, the U.S. Fifth Circuit Court upheld the right of students to plan and lead prayer at school functions (*Jones v. Clear Creek Independent School District*, 1992). The degree to which prayer in school will be permitted has yet to be determined. Box 9.8 provides some insight into this issue.

BOX 9.8 PRAYER AT GRADUATION AND AT FOOTBALL GAMES

God of the Free, Hope of the Brave:

> For the legacy of America where diversity is celebrated and the rights of minorities are protected, we thank You. May these young men and women grow up to enrich it.
>
> For the liberty of America, we thank You. May these new graduates grow up to guard it.
>
> For the political process of America in which all its citizens may participate, for its court system where all may seek justice we thank You. May those we honor this morning always turn to it in trust.
>
> For the destiny of America we thank You. May the graduates of Nathan Bishop Middle School so live that they might help to share it.
>
> May our aspirations for our country and for these young people, who are our hope for the future, be richly fulfilled. (*Lee v. Weisman*, 1992:2652–2653)

A rabbi gave this invocation at graduation for a middle school and a high school in Providence, Rhode Island, in June of 1989. The middle school principal had given the rabbi a guideline for nonsectarian prayers at civic ceremonies and recommended that the invocation and benediction be nonsectarian. The father of one of the students unsuccessfully attempted to get a restraining order prohibiting any invocation or benediction. The District Court held that the actions of the school violated the Establishment Clause of the First Amendment banning governmental advancement of religion. The United States Court of Appeals for the First Circuit affirmed the judgment of the District Court. The case was then appealed to the Supreme Court. Judge Kennedy's opinion for the court affirmed the lower court decision against the school's actions. Justice Kennedy was concerned about the principal's participation in the composition of the prayer: "our precedents do not permit school officials to assist in composing prayers as an incident to a formal exercise for their students" (*Lee v. Weisman*, 1992:2657). He was also concerned "with protecting freedom of conscience from subtle coercive pressure in the elementary and secondary public schools" (*Lee v. Weisman*, 1992:2658). He distinguished a graduation ceremony from prayer at the opening of a legislative session "where adults are free to enter and leave with little comment" (*Lee v. Weisman*, 1992:2660). He concluded that

> the prayer exercises in this case are especially improper because the State has in every practical sense compelled attendance and participation in an explicit religious exercise at an event of singular importance to every student, one the objecting student had no real alternative to avoid. (*Lee v. Weisman*, 1992:2661).

Thus, "the State, in a school setting, in effect required participation in a religious exercise" (*Lee v. Weisman*, 1992:2659).

Writing for the dissent, Justice Scalia argued that standing silently during a prayer does not automatically imply that the person is joining in the prayer but may simply signify "respect for the prayers of others." Justice Scalia ridiculed the argument of subtle coercion, noting that the opinion treats students "as though they were first-graders" instead of individuals "old enough to vote" (*Lee v. Weisman*, 1992:2682). Theoretically, Justice Scalia lambasted the decision as "the bulldozer of its social engineering" for ignoring historical precedent and laying "waste a tradition that is as old as public-school graduation ceremonies themselves, and that is a component of an even more longstanding American tradition of nonsectarian prayer to God at public celebrations generally" (*Lee v. Weisman*, 1992:2679). Justice Scalia's reading of history showed that the "history and tradition of our Nation are replete with public ceremonies featuring prayers of thanksgiving and petition" (*Lee v. Weisman*, 1992:2679).

Shortly after the Supreme Court decision, the Fifth Circuit Court ruled that a graduation prayer did not violate the First Amendment because students voted on the prayer, participation was voluntary, and students themselves, rather than a religious official, led the prayer (*Jones v. Clear Creek Independent School District*, 1992). Shortly thereafter, several state legislatures introduced bills authorizing student-initiated prayer in the schools (Rossow & Parkinson, 1994). In the spring of 1994, Congress passed an education act that would prevent funds from going to schools adopting "policies designed to prevent students from engaging in constitutionally protected prayer or silent reflection" (cited in Underwood, 1994:1040).

BOX 9.8 *continued*

Similarly, the Santa Fe School District allowed a student to deliver a "non-sectarian, nonproselytizing" prayer over the public address system before each football game. Writing for the majority in *Santa Fe Independent School District v. Doe* (2000), Justice Stevens noted that the invocations were authorized by a government policy and took place on government property at a government-sponsored event. In addition, the process of selecting the student to deliver the invocation focused on the majority and denied voicing of minority voices. Justice Stevens ruled that the invocation policy and practice was unconstitutional because:

> the realities of the situation plainly reveal that its policy involves both perceived and actual endorsement of religion. In this case, as we found in Lee, the "degree of school involvement" makes it clear that the pregame prayers bear "the imprint of the State" and thus put school-age children who objected in an untenable position. (*Santa Fe Independent School District v. Doe*, 2000:590)

What do you think? Should prayers such as the one above be permitted at graduation ceremonies? Is such a prayer at graduation improper governmental intrusion into religion? If you were an atheist or a member of a nonmainstream religion, how would you feel during a nonsectarian invocation before a football game? Would it make a difference if each week different students—atheists, Buddhists, Hindus, and so forth—got up to deliver these invocations?

Is it appropriate for students and teachers to wish each other "Merry Christmas" in school? Does such a greeting involve an intrusion of religion into the school setting? Legal scholars see no problem with wishing one another "Merry Christmas," contrary to some television talk show hosts who have declared that there has been a "war on Christmas."

In May of 1997, the United States Court of Appeals for the Eleventh Circuit affirmed the decision of a federal District Court that upheld a 1994 Georgia statute authorizing a "moment of quiet reflection" to begin the school day. The statute noted that this moment of quiet reflection "shall not be conducted as a religious service or exercise but shall be considered as an opportunity for a moment of silent reflection on the anticipated activities of the day" (O.C.G.A. 20-2-1050, 1996). The judges noted that there was no coercion in the statute: "All that students must do under this Act is remain silent for 60 seconds; they are not encouraged to pray or forced to remain silent while listening to others' prayers" (*Brown v. Gwinnett County School District*, 1997:1464). The court also noted that there was no endorsement of religion in the law and no authorization of any prayer. (For a Supreme Court ruling on permitting a religious club to conduct meetings on school premises after school hours, see Box 9.9.)

In 2003, the Secretary of Education issued a directive about constitutionally protected prayer in public elementary and secondary schools. The guidelines address such issues as prayer during non-instructional time, moments of silence, graduation ceremonies, and organized prayer groups. For example, the directive noted that if a school has a "minute of silence" or other quiet times during the school day, then "[t]eachers and other school employees may neither encourage nor discourage students from praying during such time periods" (p. 4 of Directive). Education law attorneys warn that schools should not follow the guidelines blindly because the guidelines are not necessarily an accurate rendering of case law (Colwell, 2003). Opinion poll research, however, shows that the overwhelming majority of students favor at least some form of prayer being allowed in schools, especially a moment of silence but not necessarily a prayer that mentions Jesus Christ (Ott, 2005). Opinion polls

BOX 9.9 IS THE GOOD NEWS CLUB GOOD FOR SCHOOL?

The Milford Central School allowed the Good News Club, a private Christian organization for children ages 6–12, to hold weekly meetings in the school cafeteria after school. The club sang songs, heard Bible lessons, memorized scripture, and prayed. Proponents claimed the First Amendment right of free speech. Opponents were concerned about a violation of the Establishment Clause versus the separation of church and state.

The majority concluded that in denying the club the right to meet, the school board denied the Good News Club its right to free speech. Justice Thomas saw this as viewpoint discrimination and argued that no Establishment Clause interpretation justified that restriction. Justice Thomas wrote that there was no indication that the school board was endorsing religion or creed. Justice Thomas saw the club as similar to organizations like the Boy Scouts that rely on "the invocation of teamwork, loyalty, or patriotism … to provide a foundation for their lessons" (Good News Club v. Milford Central School, 2001).

In their dissent, Justices Souter and Ginsberg cited a sample lesson about how "the Bible tells us how we can have our sins forgiven by receiving the Lord Jesus Christ" and "to trust the Lord Jesus to be your savior from sin." Such content led the dissenting Justices to conclude that:

> It is beyond question that Good News intends to use the public school premises not for the mere discussion of subjects from a particular, Christian point of view, but for an evangelical service of worship calling children to commit themselves in an act of Christian conversion. (Good News Club v. Milford Central School, 2001)

According to a Gallup Poll, 77 percent of Americans favor allowing the use of school facilities for religious groups, 61 percent favor daily prayer in the classroom, and 75 percent favor graduation speech prayers (Riffkin, 2014). What do you think? Should religious clubs be allowed to meet on school premises after school hours? Is a club that invites children "to trust the Lord Jesus to be your savior from sin" simply another club that fosters "teamwork" and "loyalty" (in Justice Thomas's terminology)? Or, in the words of the dissent, does opening the school for the Good News Club in effect open the school "for use as a church, synagogue, or mosque"?

of adults show some decline in Catholic and mainline Protestant support for school prayer, but evangelical Protestant support has remained relatively stable (Schwadel, 2013). The choice of a new Secretary of Education may start a new direction.

In 2020, President Trump's Administration issued Guidelines on School Prayer. One section of the Guidelines states that students may pray during non-instructional times such as recess and lunch and may read their Bibles or Korans. Concerning prayer at graduation, school officials "may not mandate or organize prayer at graduation or select speakers for such events in a manner that favors religious speech such as prayer," but they can select speakers based on neutral criteria who may include prayer in their speech (U.S. Department of Education, 2020). Teachers can pray or engage in Bible study with other teachers during lunch and before and after school. For a possible effect of such activity by teachers, see Box 9.10.

Student Searches

Another issue involving students is the right of school officials to conduct searches of students versus students' right of privacy. This issue was highlighted in the Supreme Court case of New Jersey v. T.L.O. (1985), which involved the search of a student's purse by an assistant vice-principal based on a teacher's

BOX 9.10 MIGHT TEACHERS ENGAGING IN PRAYER OR BIBLE STUDY HAVE AN IMPACT ON STUDENTS?

The White House Guidelines on teachers and prayer (U.S. Department of Education, 2020) stipulate that teachers may meet with other teachers for prayer or Bible study before school or during lunch.

If teachers follow this guideline and students are aware of their teachers participating in prayer or Bible study groups before school begins or during lunch, might that have any impact on students? Consider, for example, a student who is an atheist, an agnostic, or just a questioning individual. Might the knowledge that her teacher is religious enough to join a prayer group or Bible study group prevent her from expressing her opinions on religion on written assignments or on tests? Might this discourage the student from expressing opinions in class? Might she fear that her teacher's public embracing of religion means that her teacher would grade any opinions that question religion more negatively than positive opinions on religion? Might a non-Christian student (e.g., a Jewish student or a Muslim student) have similar reservations about her teacher participating in a Christian Bible study group?

suspicion that the student had been smoking in the lavatory in violation of school rules. The Court ruled that such a student search was legitimate if it was reasonable in its justification and its extent. By this, the Court meant that:

> Under ordinary circumstances, a search of a student by a teacher or other school official will be "justified at its inception" when there are reasonable grounds for suspecting that the search will turn up evidence that the student has violated or is violating either the law or the rules of the school. Such a search will be permissible in its scope when the measures adopted are reasonably related to the objectives of the search and not excessively intrusive in light of the age and sex of the student and the nature of the infraction. (*New Jersey v. T.L.O.*, 1985)

It is important to realize that the Supreme Court explicitly noted that it was not ruling about a student's right to privacy in lockers or desks, about whether it would make a difference if the school was acting in cooperation with or at the suggestion of a police department, or about whether "individualized suspicion" is such an essential element of the reasonableness standard for school searches so as to preclude general searches of students or lockers (*New Jersey v. T.L.O.*, 1985). Thus, the U.S. Supreme Court left open many of the troubling issues surrounding searches on school premises, but it did grant school officials considerable latitude to conduct warrantless searches of students. It gave school officials greater authority to search students than other governmental officials have to search adults. In the case of *New Jersey v. T.L.O.*, Justices Brennan and Marshall concurred in part but also dissented in part. Box 9.11 indicates some of their concerns about the majority opinion.

A 1981 action of the Supreme Court sheds additional light on the Court's attitude toward student searches. Specifically, the Court (*Doe v. Renfrow*, 1981) that year refused to consider an Indiana case in which school officials and police used dogs to sniff students and their possessions for marijuana, searched pockets and purses, and even went so far as to conduct nude body searches of a few students. By refusing to hear the case, the Supreme Court let stand the

BOX 9.11 EXCERPTS FROM THE BRENNAN–MARSHALL PARTIAL CONCURRENCE–PARTIAL DISSENT IN *NEW JERSEY V. T.L.O.*

In this case, Mr. Choplick (the assistant vice-principal who conducted the search) overreacted to what appeared to be nothing more than a minor infraction—a rule prohibiting smoking in the bathroom of the freshmen's and sophomores' building. It is, of course, true that he actually found evidence of serious wrongdoing by T.L.O., but no one claims that the prior search may be justified by his unexpected discovery. As far as the smoking infraction is concerned, the search for cigarettes merely tended to corroborate a teacher's eyewitness account of T.L.O.'s violation of a minor regulation designed to channel student smoking behavior into designated locations. Because this conduct was neither unlawful nor significantly disruptive of school order or the educational process, the invasion of privacy associated with the forcible opening of T.L.O.'s purse was entirely unjustified at its inception.

The schoolroom is the first opportunity most citizens have to experience the power of government. Through it passes every citizen and public official, from schoolteachers to policemen and prison guards. The values they learn there, they take with them in life. One of our most cherished ideals is the one contained in the Fourth Amendment: that the Government may not intrude on the personal privacy of its citizens without a warrant or compelling circumstance. The Court's decision today is a curious moral for the Nation's youth. Although the search of T.L.O.'s purse does not trouble today's majority, I submit that we are not dealing with "matters relatively trivial to the welfare of the Nation. There are village tyrants as well as village Hampdens, but none who acts under color of law is beyond the reach of the Constitution."

Source: *New Jersey v. T.L.O.* (1985).

lower court ruling that the school could use a canine team to conduct a general search of classrooms and could legally search pockets and purses, but went too far in requiring nude body searches (*Doe v. Renfrow*, 1981).

In *Safford Unified School District, V. Redding* (2009), the Supreme Court directly addressed the issue of strip searches. A 13-year-old girl had brought forbidden prescription and over-the-counter drugs to school and her underwear was searched. Delivering the opinion of the Court, Justice David Souter ruled that a strip search, due to its intrusiveness, is permitted but only if there is reasonable suspicion of danger or that the drugs are hidden in the student's underwear. In this case the majority did not see evidence of danger to other students or evidence that the girl was in fact carrying pills in her underwear. Thus, the search of this girl was not reasonable.

Nelson (2011) notes that the Supreme Court has not ruled on strip searches in detention centers. She argues that, following *Safford*, courts should consider the reasonableness of a strip search in a detention center based on the seriousness of the offense and the intrusiveness of the search considering the age and sex of the juvenile. Greater leeway to strip search should be given in cases of serious crimes.

The stretching of the right to search students has continued to advance. In 1995, the Supreme Court ruled that public schools could make student athletes undergo random drug testing as a condition for playing on school sports teams (*Vernonia School District v. Acton*, 1995). In *Todd v. Rush County Schools* (1998), the Seventh Circuit relied on *Vernonia* to uphold the actions of an Indiana school district that required students to undergo random, unannounced drug tests (urinalysis) before participating in any extracurricular programs or being able to drive to and from school. In a November 1997 case, the U.S. Court of Appeals for the Seventh Circuit upheld a "medical assessment" of a high school student suspected of having smoked marijuana. The "assessment" involved a school nurse taking the student's blood pressure and pulse. In 1996, the Eighth Circuit upheld a search of all male 6th through 12th graders. The students had to remove their jackets, shoes, and socks; empty their pockets; and be given a metal detector test after a school bus driver informed the principal that there were fresh cuts on the seats of her bus (*Thompson v. Carthage School District*, 1996). Rossow and Parkinson (1994) had argued that such a ruling would be welcomed by schools using metal detectors at school entrances.

In *Board of Education of Independent School District No. 92 of Pottawatomie County et al. v. Lindsay Earls et al.* (2002), the Supreme Court ruled that random drug tests of students participating in extracurricular activities such as band or Future Farmers of America are not a violation of the Fourth Amendment. The court noted that schools were concerned about the health risks to students from drug use and made note of the voluntary character of participation in such extracurricular activities. Dissenting Justice Ginsburg, however, argued that such drug testing violates the reasonable subjective expectation of privacy that students have about being forced to submit to urine tests. Justice Ginsburg also noted that participation in extracurricular activities is not completely voluntary but rather "a key component of school life, essential in reality for students applying to college, and, for all participants, a significant contributor to the breadth and quality of the educational experience" (*Board of Education of Independent School District No. 92 of Pottawatomie County et al. v. Lindsay Earls et al.*, 2002).

In a 2013 case (*G.C. v. Owensboro Public Schools*, 2013) the Sixth Circuit Court of Appeals ruled that a school had gone too far in searching a student's cell phone. A teacher seized the phone when the student was caught texting in class. Previously, the student had disclosed that he used drugs and was depressed, even thinking about suicide. The Court ruled, however, that since the school had no specific reason to believe that he was now engaging in unlawful activity or contemplating harm to himself or others, but merely violating a school rule against texting in class, the search was illegal.

RIGHTS AT HOME AND IN THE COMMUNITY

Not all questions of juvenile rights have emerged in the context of school. Several issues and cases have arisen in the home and community.

The Constitutionality of Curfews

Curfew laws have mushroomed in the United States. Cities have enacted curfews to decrease juvenile crime and to protect juveniles from victimization (Davis, Scott, Wadlington, & Whitebread, 1997). Courts have upheld some curfew laws and struck down others. The recent trend seems to be to uphold the laws if they are narrowly drawn and if they provide exceptions for reasonable activities.

A case involving a curfew law that was challenged and ruled to be constitutional is *Qutb v. Strauss*. This was a 1993 case that concerned the Dallas, Texas, curfew law. That ordinance prohibited juveniles under age 17 from being on the streets from 11:00 P.M. until 6:00 A.M. on weeknights and from midnight until 6:00 A.M. on weekends. Exceptions included being accompanied by a parent, doing an errand for a parent, or attending school, religious, or civic activities. The ordinance also allowed interstate travel or playing on one's own or a neighbor's sidewalk.

The United States Court of Appeals ruled that the law did not violate either equal protection or free association grounds and therefore was not unconstitutional. The Court ruled that the law did serve a compelling state interest, namely, "to reduce juvenile crime and victimization, while promoting juvenile safety and well-being" (*Qutb v. Strauss*, 1993). Here the Court noted that the City of Dallas presented statistics on juvenile crime and victimization during the hours covered by the curfew to substantiate the argument of reducing crime and victimization. Concerning a juvenile's right to free association (a First Amendment right), the Court noted that the law had sufficient exceptions in it so that impositions on association were minor. For example, contrary to arguments that the law prohibited playing midnight basketball, the Court noted that the juvenile could play in such a game as long as it was sponsored by some organization or as long as a parent accompanied the youth to the game.

Similarly drawn curfew laws have stood appeals court challenges, while overly broad laws without exceptions have been struck down. For example, a 1981 case, *Johnson v. City of Opelousas* (1981), was struck down because its only exception was for "emergency errands." Here the judges noted that there was no exception for such associational activities "as religious or school meetings, organized dances, and theater and sporting events, when reasonable and direct travel to or from these activities has to be made during the curfew period" (*Johnson v. City of Opelousas*, 1981).

Thus, clearly drawn curfew laws are withstanding constitutional challenge as long as they allow reasonable exceptions. On the other hand, some think that in failing to rule on curfews, the U.S. Supreme Court has failed to give needed clear direction (Stoddard, Steiner, Rohrbach, Hemmens, & Bennett, 2015). In a related matter, the Supreme Court struck down Chicago's anti-loitering ordinance as vague. The law prohibited two or more people from loitering for "no apparent purpose." The Court said that the law was too vague to give the public adequate notice of the conduct that is prohibited (*Chicago v. Morales*, 1999).

Research indicates that curfew laws do not reduce juvenile crime or victimization (Wilson, Gill, Olaghere, & McClure, 2016) nor underage drinking (Grossman, Jernigan, & Miller, 2016). Another problem is that they are inefficient because they take up a great deal of police time (Adams, 2007).

The Legal Drinking Age

An important children's rights issue is the question of the appropriate age for adolescents to drink alcoholic beverages. In fact, because of the actions of groups such as Mothers Against Drunk Driving (MADD) and because of the threat of reduced federal highway funds, all states prohibit the purchase of alcohol by persons under 21 years of age.

Interestingly, raising the legal drinking age to 21 is the flip side of the previous historical trend to lower the drinking age. Not too many years ago, lowering the drinking age was very much the norm, and it was part of a more general trend in both the United States and Canada of lowering the age of privilege-responsibility, including lowering the voting age to 18. In Canada the rationale behind this movement was that because "youths paid taxes, could quit school and work, join the military, vote federally, and drive cars, it was felt that they should be allowed to drink" (Vingilis & DeGenova, 1984:163). In the United States, the military draft provided the added argument that if "boys were old enough to be sent to Viet Nam, … they were old enough to drink" (Vingilis & DeGenova, 1984:163). Finally, there was some feeling that if "youth had to use substances, alcohol was society's preferred drug" (Vingilis & DeGenova, 1984:163).

Proponents of a high minimum drinking age argue that it reduces automobile accidents and fatalities, especially for adolescents themselves. They reason that teens need to be protected from their immaturity and impulsiveness because they are inexperienced at both driving and drinking alcohol.

It appears that these arguments make good sense because the research suggests that lowering the drinking age is indeed associated with increases in alcohol-related collisions and with higher fatality rates for night-time and single-vehicle crashes involving young drivers. Conversely, raising the drinking age is associated with a reduced number of collisions (Vingilis & DeGenova, 1984:166–169). Specifically, the Department of Transportation estimates that raising the legal age for drinking to 21 has saved hundreds of lives a year due to reduced alcohol-related traffic fatalities among underage drivers, or a total of 31,959 between 1975 and 2017 (NHTSA, 2020). In related research, it appears that states with the most restrictive graduated driver licensing laws have lower rates of heavy drinking among drivers ages 15 to 17 than states with the least restrictive laws but that there is no comparable difference in binge drinking (SAMHSA, 2004). (For a summary of research on the positive effects of underage drinking in general, see Hingson & White, 2014.) An important note is that related laws and policies such as suspending a driver's license for underage drinking, social host liability laws, and graduated driver licensing with night driving restrictions have also contributed to crash reductions (Hingson & White, 2014).

In a review of research between 2006 and 2013, DeJong and Blanchette (2014) argue that the case in favor of 21 as the minimum drinking age is now closed:

> the current law has served the nation well by reducing alcohol-related traffic crashes and alcohol consumption among youths while also

protecting drinkers from long-term negative outcomes they might experience in adulthood, including alcohol and other drug dependence, adverse birth outcomes, and suicide and homicide … lowering the legal drinking age would lead to a substantial increase in injuries, deaths, and other negative health-related consequences. (DeJong & Blanchette, 2014:113)

The issue, however, received attention in 2008 when some college presidents asked for public debate on the minimum legal drinking age. Arguments were made that improvements in car safety were the real reason for fewer traffic deaths and that the age-21 law was forcing college students to drink at private parties with less regulation of drinking than in bars (Wechsler & Nelson, 2010). It now appears that this attention was short-lived. For example, 2014 polling indicated that 74 percent of Americans opposed lowering the drinking age back to 18 (Gallup, 2014). One survey in Boston, however, found that almost 40 percent of the respondents favored lowering the age back to 18 in Massachusetts (MacNeill, 2020). In addition, research indicates that heavy drinking among college students continues to be problematic (Marzell, Bavarian, Paschall, Mair, & Saltz, 2015).

A problem with raising the drinking age is the question of fairness. That is, the specific issue of raising the drinking age raises the more general issue of the fairness of prohibiting 18-, 19-, and 20-year-olds from drinking, thereby, in effect, treating them as children when the law treats them as adults for other purposes. We have seen, for example, that all states consider 18-year-olds as adults in terms of their responsibility for criminal actions. In fact, one trend in juvenile justice is toward more liberal waiver and related provisions that allow younger and younger juveniles to be tried as adult criminal suspects (subjecting them to the possibility of imprisonment in adult facilities and even capital punishment). The question arises whether it is fair to subject teens to adult criminal court sanctions while at the same time treating them as immature children in terms of their legal ability to drink alcohol. Additional arguments against a high minimum drinking age include the "forbidden fruit" argument, which maintains that it increases the attraction of alcohol, and the "teach-them-to-do-it-right" argument, which contends that parents can use a lower minimum age as an educational device.

Franklin Zimring (1982) argues that it is fair to prohibit 18-year-olds from drinking, but he does not necessarily agree that it is fair to submit adolescents to criminal court sanctions, especially the death penalty. He states several reasons for his view that age 21 is a fair minimum drinking age. First, he believes that 18-year-olds are not mature but that they are in the process of becoming mature adults. Recall that recent Supreme Court decisions

WEB ACTIVITY

For fact sheets on the legal drinking age issue, see the website of the Centers for Disease Control and Prevention, available at www.cdc.gov/alcohol/fact-sheets/mlda.htm. For statistics on lives saved by minimum drinking age laws and teen fatalities, consult NHTSA's website at www.nhtsa.gov, including reports such as *Young Drivers* (NHTSA, 2020).

For an online brief in favor of retaining the age of 21, see the website of the Council on Addictions of New York State, available at www.canys.net.

on the death penalty and LWOP for juveniles relied heavily on research that adolescents are not fully developed. Second, he is opposed to a low minimum drinking age because of the leakage problem. Leakage means, for example, that if 18-year-olds can legally purchase alcoholic beverages, then their 16-year-old dates may also drink and be subject to auto accidents and fatalities. Finally, he argues that there are three different aspects to adulthood: liberty, entitlement, and responsibility. Liberty refers to the freedom of choice that adults possess in matters such as making decisions about medical care. An entitlement is a benefit or program offered by government such as the Job Corps, which provides free job training for young persons. Responsibility means "paying the full price for misdeeds and being responsible, as are adults, for self support" (Zimring, 1982:111). It is Zimring's position that it is better to keep the ages for these three aspects of adulthood separate rather than to lump them together. Thus, he sees no inconsistency in permitting adolescents to drive at 16, vote and be drafted at 18, and be able to purchase alcoholic beverages at 21.

Zimring also raises the intriguing issue of raising the drinking age to 25. Based on evidence that single male drivers under 25—not just under 21—are a serious driving risk, he contends that these actuarial facts and logic would argue for an even higher drinking age than 21 to prevent many accidents and fatalities. He notes that there is some precedent for this in that the Constitution does require senators and the president to be older than 21 years of age. However, Zimring rejects raising the minimum drinking age to 25 because:

> That kind of law is not merely politically implausible and socially div-isive, it is also unjust. I have argued elsewhere that our current deferral of liberties can be justified because adolescence merely seems like for-ever. But using age-grading to defer common liberty into the mid-20s is exploitation in almost every case. Adding four or seven years onto an already long wait is simply too much of a burden. The twenty-first birthday has a long history of serving as the outer boundary for legal disability based on age. There is no good reason to risk the legal inco-herence and social division that pushing beyond this limit imposes. (Zimring, 1982:124)

Zimring was writing just before the more recent push to waive increasingly younger juveniles to adult court, so he did not explicitly address the issues of the age of criminal responsibility and the appropriate age for capital punishment. There are strong indications, however, that he would not favor such actions. For example, he clearly believes that even 19- and 20-year-olds are not fully mature and may need some protection from their youthful mistakes. Thus, Zimring is convinced that our legal policy should be one that "preserves the life chances for those who make serious mistakes, as well as preserving choices for their more fortunate (and more virtuous) contemporaries" (Zimring, 1982:91–92).

Zimring's position is worth considering. Contrary to many contemporary voices, he does not advocate a policy that on the one hand would prohibit drinking until 21, but on the other hand would allow waiver to criminal court at 14. Instead, he takes the more consistent view that persons under 21 are not fully mature and responsible, but that certain aspects of adulthood may be more appropriately begun at 18.

In connection with this issue, Barnum (1987) argues that it is false to justify the existence of a separate juvenile court system on the claim that children are less mature and less responsible for their behavior than adults. Rather, "normal intrinsic cognitive development is sufficient for this capacity [to appreciate what they are doing or what effect it will have] by age two or three" (Barnum, 1987:72). Nevertheless, many think there are developmental differences between children and adults that do justify a separate court for juveniles: "children are less able to be responsible for themselves, ... adolescents normally experience transient irresponsibility, and ... even poorly socialized children may have a better prognosis for rehabilitation than do poorly socialized adults" (Barnum, 1987:78). In other words, most children do know right from wrong, just as do most adults. However, there are other differences between children and adults that may justify a separate juvenile court system. (For a discussion of the privacy rights of teen drivers versus parental efforts to track teen driving habits, see Box 9.12.)

Perhaps a fitting conclusion to this discussion is Davis and Schwartz's observation that there is a fundamental tension in the law between paternalism (protecting children) and autonomy (granting them responsibility) that will not disappear:

> The law is protective of children, for example, in the areas of contracts, employment, and to a great extent, medical decision making in life-threatening cases. The law grants a measure of autonomy to children or their parents in other areas—for example, abortion decision making (but only to a limited extent), torts (but more as a result of a policy favoring compensation of victims than of a desire to grant children greater responsibility), non-life-threatening medical decision making, and emancipation decision making. These disparate results stem from an inherent conflict in the law—a kind of schizophrenia—between the desire to accord children a greater degree of control over their lives and

BOX 9.12 PARENTAL TRACKING OF TEEN DRIVING

Some parents are installing black boxes in cars that monitor the driving habits of their teenage sons and daughters. The devices record such behaviors as seat belt use and speed of the car. The devices also make a noise when the driver exceeds safety thresholds while driving. AAA's On Board device allows a parent to set speed alerts to notify the parent when the set speed limit is exceeded. Parents can also view their teen's trip history to see date, time, and starting and ending locations of trips.

One teen rights advocate argued that these boxes are an "invasion of privacy" (Davis & O'Donnell, 2005). What do you think? Are automobile black boxes an invasion of privacy or is this simply a reasonable attempt by parents to monitor the driving behavior of teens? Is it legitimate for 16- and 17-year-olds but not for youths 18 or older? Is there any difference between monitoring driving speeds and trip history?

Source: Davis and O'Donnell (2005).

freedom of choice, and the need, on the other hand, to protect them from others, their surroundings, and, sometimes, from their own folly. (Davis & Schwartz, 1987:201)

It is interesting that at present society is lowering the age of criminal responsibility but at the same time insists on making 21 the age of eligibility to purchase alcohol and is pushing for graduated licensing. Davis and Schwartz's description of this as "a kind of schizophrenia" seems most fitting.

Recent developments in juvenile justice—such as some states returning to age 18 as the beginning age of criminal court jurisdiction (see Chapter 14 for further discussion of this development), and the emphasis on incomplete adolescent development, even at 18, affecting Supreme Court decisions about juveniles—indicate a narrowing of what Davis and Schwartz called "a kind of schizophrenia." It appears that society is becoming more consistent in its view of juvenile maturity issues.

SUMMARY

This chapter has examined the landmark U.S. Supreme Court cases involving juveniles. The Fourth Amendment rights of juveniles and some of the controversial rights issues in school and in the home were examined. There is no perfectly consistent treatment of juveniles and their rights. Sometimes the law treats them as children, and sometimes it treats them as adults. As Zimring (1982) has pointed out, however, because the issue of juveniles' rights is so complex, perhaps a refusal to come up with one magical age for all children's rights issues is the best solution. Finally, as was noted in the discussion of the landmark Supreme Court cases, the mere stipulation of a right by the Court does not guarantee that police or courts will actually or fully protect that right. Practice is not always the same as philosophy.

DISCUSSION QUESTIONS

1. Has the Supreme Court gone too far or not far enough in protecting the rights of juvenile delinquency suspects? If you were on the Supreme Court, what would you seek to change concerning those rights?

2. Your 15-year-old brother has been arrested for the robbery of a convenience store. He is of average intelligence but is immature and impulsive. This is his first arrest. Do you think that he should be allowed to waive his privilege against self-incrimination and his right to confer with an attorney, or do you feel that state law should mandate that an attorney be brought in before the police can conduct any interrogation?

3. Assume that you are the editor of the high school newspaper and that one of your best reporters has just completed a lengthy article on drug use in your school. No names are mentioned in the article; in fact, your reporter has gone to great lengths to protect confidentiality. The principal has read the article and

has said that she does not want it published in the school paper. What would you do?

4. Do you agree with the Supreme Court's position that corporal punishment is permissible as a school discipline technique? If you became a teacher or principal, would you use corporal punishment? If so, when and under what circumstances? More generally, how would you feel about your children being subjected to corporal punishment?

5. If you were a high school principal, what would your policy on student searches be? The Supreme Court ruled that drug testing of students in bands and clubs is permissible. Would you follow the direction of the Supreme Court and initiate testing of band members and the Future Farmers of America?

6. What is your opinion about compulsory community service? Do you think high schools should be allowed to force students to perform community service as a condition for graduation? Why or why not?

7. What is your opinion about school prayer? Should a school be allowed to invite a priest, minister, rabbi, or other religious leader to graduation to offer a nonsectarian invocation? Should the students be allowed to compose and lead their own invocation at graduation? What do you think about a moment of silence to begin (or end) the school day? Should prayer be permissible at athletic events? Is there any problem with White House Guidelines that allow teachers to engage in prayer groups or Bible study groups on-campus either before or after school or during their lunch hours? What effect might teacher participation in such groups have on students?

8. What do you think should be the response of a school to cyberbullying? If the bullying does not disrupt school activity, should the school stay out of the controversy? Or do you agree with one expert who thinks that school authorities should have more leeway to intervene and protect students?

9. What age do you favor as the minimum legal drinking age? How would you feel about the age being set at 25? What do you think about graduated licensing laws? Do you favor or oppose them?

CHAPTER 10

Institutional/Residential Interventions

WHAT YOU NEED TO KNOW

- Approximately 36,500 juvenile offenders were in public, private, or tribal residential placement on the date of the most recent census. In addition, 653 juveniles were in adult prisons, according to recent data.

- Boot camps can be cost-effective and result in academic progress. They do not reduce recidivism, however, despite the common-sense belief that military-type discipline is beneficial.

- Recent statistics indicate that 70–80 percent of juveniles released from state facilities are rearrested. On the other hand, effective programs can reduce recidivism significantly.

- The most prevalent problem in the juvenile justice system is the presence of mental disorders. Studies show that more than two-thirds of juveniles in the juvenile justice system experience mental disorders.

- Estimates of victimization, including sexual victimization, in juvenile facilities vary; some estimates indicate that almost two-thirds of youths are victimized. In a recent government survey, 7.1 percent of youths in state juvenile facilities and large private facilities reported one or more incidents of sexual victimization in the previous year or since their admission to the facility.

- Racial tension has been a problem in juvenile facilities. In 2019, minorities constituted 67 percent of youths in residential placement.

- Deinstitutionalization or stopping involuntary placements of status offenders continues; in 2017, only 1,690 committed status offenders were in residential placement, a decline of 60 percent from 1997 (Hockenberry, 2020).

- Many wilderness programs have not been effective, but a recent evaluation showed that such programs with treatment enhancements can reduce recidivism.

KEY TERMS

behavior modification

boot camps

common-sense corrections

cottage system

deinstitutionalization

institutional life

program effectiveness

racial tension

shock incarceration

state training schools

victimization

wilderness programs

DOI: 10.4324/9781003167112-10

INTRODUCTION

This chapter will examine juvenile institutional correctional interventions, both public and private. Although more youths are in community correctional programs, residential programs are a critical component of juvenile corrections.

INSTITUTIONAL CORRECTIONS FOR JUVENILES

On the latest one-day count of juveniles in residential placement in 2019, 36,479 juvenile offenders were in detention, correctional, or shelter facilities (OJJDP, 2021). Most of these were delinquency offenders. Seventy-four percent of the youths were in public facilities, and 26 percent were in private facilities. Sixty-three percent of these youths were committed (after being tried in court), and 37 percent were being detained prior to a court hearing, adjudication, disposition, or placement elsewhere. About 4 percent of the youths in placement were status offenders. The juvenile custody population dropped 65 percent from 1997 to 2019, and this represents the lowest number since 1975 (OJJDP, 2021). The 2017 facility census showed a population of 43,580 which dropped to 37,529 juveniles in 2018 (Hockenberry, 2020; Hockenberry & Sladky, 2020). (Note: The latest complete OJJDP report covers 2017 but the OJJDP website gives more recent statistics on select issues.) The latest information available indicates that the average length of stay was approximately four months (Mendel, 2011). Many juvenile facilities are outdated, built in the 1970s at best (Roush & McMillen, 2000).

WEB ACTIVITY

For the latest available statistics on juveniles in custody, see the Office of Juvenile Justice and Delinquency Prevention's (OJJDP's) *Statistical Briefing Book* at www.ojjdp.gov. For comprehensive reports on juveniles in custody, see periodic reports from OJJDP such as Hockenberry (2020), available at www.ojjdp.gov.

According to the most recent statistics, at year end 2019, there were 653 prisoners 17 or younger in state and federal (adult) prisons. This number represents a decrease of 11 percent from 2018 (Carson, 2020). In 2019, six states (Arizona, Connecticut, Florida, New York, North Carolina, and Texas) held more than half of all juveniles in state prisons (Carson, 2020). Although probation handles many more youths, institutions involve a significant minority of the offenders who go through the juvenile justice system. They are the costliest part of the system. One estimate put the average daily cost of incarcerating one juvenile offender at $241 a day or about $88,000 for one year. In California, the cost to confine one youth for a year is about $250,000 (Mendel, 2011). For more information on costs, see Box 10.1.

In 2019, the residential population was 85 percent male and 15 percent female. The racial composition of juvenile offenders in custody was 33 percent white, 41 percent black, and 20 percent Hispanic (the remainder were categorized as "other") (OJJDP, 2021). Thus, blacks are overrepresented in juvenile institutions, one part of the more general problem of disproportionate minority contact.

BOX 10.1 ESTIMATED LONG-TERM COSTS FOR CONFINEMENT OF YOUTHS

As noted, the direct costs of confining one youth for one year can go as high as $80,000. A report from the Justice Policy Institute notes that there are additional costs. For example, when a released youth offends again (recidivates), there are costs to victims and to taxpayers. Incarceration can also have short- and long-term effects on the future earnings of formerly incarcerated juveniles. The report also estimated the cost of sexual assault during confinement. Adding up all these costs, the report estimated that long-term costs of confinement, over and above the direct expenses of confining youths, can range from $7.9 to $21.47 billion.

Source: Justice Policy Institute (2014), available at www.justicepolicy.org.

Correctional managers contend that juvenile correctional facilities seek to serve the "best interests of the child," which means that they attempt to provide educational, therapeutic, and recreational programs staffed by concerned care givers. Critics argue that, at best, the facilities are warehouses or holding tanks where little, if any, positive change takes place. Both past and more recent critics have contended that juvenile facilities harbor as many horror stories as they do children: tales of neglect, abuse, and even death (Human Rights Watch, 2006; Wooden, 1976).

This chapter examines various types of institutional and residential interventions with juveniles, including state training schools, youth camps, private placements, and group homes. After describing these various placements, we will examine some of the current issues about their operation, such as the determination of appropriate targets for intervention, effectiveness in reducing recidivism, and client and worker adaptations to the pressures of institutional life. The chapter concludes with information on innovative trends in this area, such as deinstitutionalization and wilderness programs.

STATE TRAINING SCHOOLS

State training schools are the juvenile justice system's equivalent of the adult prison; they house those delinquents whom juvenile court judges consider unfit for probation or some other lesser punishment. Some training schools resemble adult prisons in terms of their architecture: high walls or fences, locked cell blocks, self-sufficiency (they have their own laundry, hospital, and maintenance facility), and solitary confinement for persistent rule breakers. Other training schools have the so-called cottage system of architectural design. Unfortunately, the cottage system is often a far cry from the homelike atmosphere intended by its founders. Cottages are often deteriorating dormitories with decrepit plumbing, heating, and lighting, and an accompanying host of social-cultural problems as well.

Missouri, on the other hand, has developed what many consider a model program. In fact, by emphasizing individual and group treatment in small group dormitory settings, such as a converted school building in St. Louis, the state of Missouri has been awarded an Innovations in American Government Award by Harvard University's Ash Institute (Ash Institute, 2008; McGarvey, 2005).

Training School Programs for Residents

The programming at state training schools is often a combination of academic and vocational education and **behavior modification**. Residents attend school much of the day just like their noninstitutionalized counterparts, but the school run by the prison teaches youths who have significant problems. About one in three residents need or are receiving special education, over half have reading and math skills below grade level, and more than half had been suspended or expelled from their school in the community (Council of State Governments Justice Center, 2015). In addition, youths in custody report spending less time in school each day than their free-world counterparts and only 51 percent of youths in custody consider their school program to be a good program (Sedlak & McPherson, 2010a). Further evidence of educational problems is the fact that more than one-half of youths in custody reported skipping classes and having been suspended from school in the year prior to entering custody, and 26 percent reported having repeated a grade (Sedlak & Bruce, 2010). (For a list

---

BOX 10.2 EXPECTED BEHAVIOR PER THE TEXAS JUVENILE JUSTICE DEPARTMENT YOUTH HANDBOOK

Rules:

Be in the right place at the right time.

    Example: Be on time for routine events and activities in assigned area; follow movement procedures, etc.

Follow directions.

    Example: Do what is asked by staff, follow code of conduct, attend to standard hygiene, chore, and dress code requirements

Participate in activities.

    Example: Attend and participate in all required or assigned education, group, recreation, activities, etc.

Respect others.

    Example: Demonstrate social skills such as asking permission, greeting others, taking turns, and being courteous

Accept consequences.

    Example: Address and work to understand own behavior through check-ins, admits mistakes, and attempt to make amends, etc.

Major rule violations include:

1. Assault, defined as "unauthorized physical contact with staff or another youth" (no injury)

2. Assault causing bodily injury to staff or another youth

3. Attempted escape

4. "Chunking" bodily fluids, defined as "throwing your blood, seminal, or vaginal fluid, spit, urine, or feces at someone to harass them"

5. Distribution of prohibited substances

6. Escape

Minor rule violations include:

1. Breaching group confidentiality

2. Disruption of program

3. Failure to abide by dress code

4. Failure to do proper housekeeping

Source: Texas Juvenile Justice Department Youth Handbook, January 2016. Available at www.tjjd.texas.gov.

BOX 10.3 TYPICAL WEEKDAY DAILY SCHEDULE AT A RESIDENTIAL PLACEMENT FOR DELINQUENTS

6:30 A.M.	Wake up: dress and clean room
7:00 A.M.	Calisthenics
7:30 A.M.	Hygiene (showers, etc.)
8:00 A.M.	Clean dormitories
8:30 A.M.	Breakfast
9:00 A.M.	Start school
10:30 A.M.	"Rap" half-hour
11:00 A.M.	Return to school
12:00 A.M.	Lunch
12:30 P.M.	"Rap" half-hour
1:00 P.M.	School
3:30 P.M.	Group therapy
5:00 P.M.	Dinner
5:30 P.M.	Work details (kitchen clean-up and dormitory clean-up)
6:00–7:00 P.M.	TV news
7:00–9:00 P.M.	Activities (vary by day; e.g., Values Clarification, Occupational Therapy, Recreational Therapy, etc.)
9:00 P.M.	Bedtime for Phase 1 (9:30 P.M. in the summertime)
10:00 P.M.	Bedtime for Phase 2 and above

Note: In this context, to "rap" is to talk freely and frankly.
Source: Manual from a Midwestern residential facility.

of the school rules in one state, see Box 10.2; for a typical daily schedule, see Box 10.3.)

In addition to standard academic subjects, educational programs may include life skills development, remedial reading and writing, conflict resolution skills development, computer literacy, and learning skills assessment. Additional programming may include groups on anger management and substance abuse resistance and recreation such as sports, crafts, board games, reading, and computer games (Roush & McMillen, 2000).

The behavior modification system usually involves the grading of children at one of several levels. The system includes the daily awarding of points for almost every possible action of the child's day, from getting up on time to getting to bed quietly and on time. The points earned each day can be spent on various privileges, ranging from games, television time, and telephone calls home to off-campus group outings and visits home. The higher the child's level, the more extensive the privileges available. (Box 10.4 gives an actual list

BOX 10.4 TYPICAL INSTITUTIONAL POINT

	Responsibilities	Points	
1.	Get self up on time (6:00 A.M.)	+25	−50
2.	Locker neat, orderly, clean room or area with bed made	+50	−100
3.	Appropriately dressed	+25	−50
4.	Brush teeth and comb hair	+25	−50
5.	Daily bath and use deodorant	+25	−100
6.	Exercise	+25	−50
7.	Acts appropriately:		
	a. Breakfast	+10	−20
	b. Lunch	+10	−20
	c. Dinner	+10	−20
8.	School (per hour)	+40	
9.	Study hour or watching news (per hour)	+25	
10.	Daily chores	+50	−100
11.	Volunteer work (per hour) (120 maximum per day)	+60	
12.	See counselor (per hour)	+25	
13.	Attend group (per hour)	+50	−100
14.	Attend church or Sunday school services	+25	
15.	Bonus points (+100 maximum per day)		

Note: A +25 indicates that a resident can earn up to 25 points for performing the specified behavior. A −100 indicates that a resident can have as many as 100 points deducted if the behavior is not performed or not performed properly.

Spending Opportunities

1.	Swimming	25 points
2.	Recreation room	25 points
3.	Parlor games (checkers, cards, etc.)	25 points
4.	Telephone calls	20 points
5.	Use of television room	25 points
6.	Play outside	25 points
7.	Group outing off-campus	300 points
8.	Group outing on-campus	200 points
9.	Living room	25 points
10.	Movies in dorm	100 points
11.	Home pass	350 points

Source: Student manual from a Southeastern training school.

of opportunities for earning and spending points at a Southeastern training school.) In addition to qualifying for daily privileges, such as television, the points earned also count toward movement from one level to another with additional privilege possibilities. One training school employee characterized the point system as working both as a behavioral control device and as a device to monitor progress within the institution.

Youths in placement report watching an average of 2.9 hours of television on a typical weekday. Youths in everyday society average 2.5 hours. Fifty percent of youths in residential treatment rated the school program as good and 40 percent rated the recreational program as good, but only 38 percent rated the food as good. Sixteen percent of the youths reported having been offered contraband (alcohol and other drugs, or weapons) since arrival at placement. Nearly one-third profess gang affiliation. Punishments range from removal of privileges, such as television, or being ordered to do extra chores to confinement to one's room or solitary confinement (Sedlak & McPherson, 2010a).

Concern for the victim and for crime control has translated into some new programs in juvenile institutions. In California, for example, the Impact of Crime on Victims program combines an educational curriculum with presentations by victims and victims' advocates. In Texas, juvenile murderers receive group psychotherapy and role-playing sessions to help them learn responsibility for their crimes and to imagine what they put their victims through (Bilchik, 1998).

OTHER PLACEMENTS

Traditional training schools are not the only means that states use for housing delinquents. Many youths are held in long-term open facilities that allow greater freedom for residents within the facilities and more contacts with the community. The open facilities category of placements includes shelters, halfway houses, group homes, and a few ranches. Group homes are residential facilities for relatively small numbers of youths (perhaps one or two dozen youngsters). The residents often attend regular public schools but participate in group counseling sessions and recreational activities at the group home.

Juvenile court judges also have been known to commit juvenile delinquents to detention centers for a short period of time. Youths are placed on probation, and one condition of probation is a short stay in the local detention facility.

States also utilize private residential placements to house delinquents and some status offenders. In 2019, private facilities held 27 percent of all juveniles in placement (OJJDP, 2021). Private facilities, like state facilities, range from relatively large institutions to small group homes and even wilderness programs where juveniles camp out. Many were originally started by churches as charitable institutions but have evolved into nonsectarian operations that charge the state thousands of dollars each year for each child they handle.

Critics of private placements allege that pressure to turn a profit can too easily influence administrators to cut back on services to juveniles in residence. As Butts and Pfaff (2019) point out, however, publicly run institutions also face cost constraints; state legislators do not just allocate unlimited dollars to public facilities. Furthermore, the answer to ensuring that private placements do provide the services they are supposed to provide is capable monitoring of the contracts that states sign with the private companies that operate private institutions and offering contract incentives for providing both safety and rehabilitation.

Boot Camps

A declining trend is the use of **boot camps** (also called **shock incarceration**). Boot camps are short-term (90-day/120-day/6-month) facilities that are intended to resemble basic training facilities for the military. There is considerable emphasis on discipline and physical training such as marching, running, calisthenics, and other types of conditioning. Usually a "drill instructor" is assigned to each group of offenders. Many boot camp programs also involve aftercare supervision for program graduates.

The rationale behind boot camps is multifaceted. It is claimed that boot camps can protect the public, reduce prison crowding, reduce costs, punish offenders, hold offenders accountable, deter additional crime, and rehabilitate (through counseling and education) (Cronin, 1994).

DeMuro (2008) notes first that actual and potential abuse are both problems at boot camps, ranging from in-your-face yelling in imitation of military boot camps to physical abuse. Abuses are one reason that a number of states have abandoned boot camp prisons. Furthermore, since boot camps exist "without any empirical evidence that … [they] work," he supports calls for the closing of boot camps and the re-direction of funding to effective interventions.

The effectiveness of boot camps for both adult and juvenile offenders is mixed. There is some indication that boot camps can reduce state correctional costs and that participants rate their experience in camp as positive, but the evidence shows that boot camps have little or no effect on recidivism (Cronin, 1994; Parent, 2003). Based on multiple studies, it is clear that boot camps do not reduce recidivism (Aos, Miller, & Drake, 2006; Lipsey, 2009; Meade & Steiner, 2010; MacKenzie & Freeland, 2012). Ironically, even though many politicians like boot camps because they appear to be "tough," it appears that the educational and rehabilitative programming is what helps the offenders.

Boot camps are part of a trend in society to "get tough" on crime that started decades ago. One author (Clear, 1994) calls this trend the "penal harm movement"; another team of authors calls it "the punishment paradigm" (Cullen & Wright, 1995). These authors contend that since 1980 the United States has operated on the premise that more punishment is needed to deter crime and incapacitate offenders. Boot camps are one component of the movement, which includes increased use of prisons and jails, lengthier

Youths at the Department of Youth Services juvenile boot camp in Prattville, Alabama, wait to go outside for physical training.

CREDIT: AP Photo/Rob Carr

sentences, determinate sentences, career criminal sentencing provisions, increased use of capital punishment, and harsher community sanctions (intensive supervision, house arrest, and electronic monitoring). For juveniles the punishment paradigm translated into greater prosecution of juveniles in adult court and blended sentences involving the adult correctional system. Thus, boot camps are not an isolated phenomenon but are part of a broader trend in criminal justice focusing on retribution, deterrence, and incapacitation. As noted in Chapter 14, the "smart on juvenile justice reform" movement indicates some softening of the "get tough" era.

A final word on boot camps comes from Cullen, Blevins, Trager, and Gendreau (2005), who see the boot camp phenomenon as a clear-cut example of the dangers of "common-sense thinking" in corrections and criminal justice. What they mean is that based on the common-sense thinking that military boot camps "made men out of boys" for the army, many individuals were convinced that correctional boot camps would do the same for juvenile offenders. The research on the lack of success of boot camps, however, shows the dangers of relying on such common-sense thinking: "It is dangerous precisely because it seems so correct, leaves our biases unchallenged, and requires virtually no effort to activate" (Cullen et al., 2005:66). Elsewhere, Cullen argues that boot camp interventions fail because they "are based on a limited theory of crime (rational choice) and do not target the known proximate risk factors for reoffending" (Cullen, 2007:720).

PROGRAM EFFECTIVENESS

One of the most critical issues facing residential interventions is the effectiveness issue: Do the interventions have any impact on the criminal behavior of their charges? Although much of what follows pertains most directly to publicly run placements (especially state training schools), the problems also affect private placements.

Reviews of Multiple Studies

In the last decade, a number of states have reported recidivism rates for youths released from state juvenile correctional facilities. When rearrest is the measure, on average, 70–80 percent of released youths recidivate in two to three years. That figure drops to 40–70 percent failure when the measure is reconviction or re-adjudication. With reincarceration as the measure, the failure rate drops to between 20 and 60 percent (Mendel, 2011). These statistics give no information on what sort or what quality of rehabilitation programs took place in these states.

While much of the **program effectiveness** research has focused on specific programs, some researchers have tried to summarize individual program research into a global conclusion on effectiveness. Most of these studies have used the technique of meta-analysis. Meta-analysis is a technique that allows researchers to re-analyze individual studies and arrive at a summary statistic of effectiveness for each individual study that can then be compared to the summary statistics from the other studies.

Lipsey (2009) conducted a meta-analysis of 548 study samples and found that there were many instances of programs that had positive effects. The most effective treatment types had an impact on recidivism that was equivalent to reducing a control group baseline recidivism rate of 50 percent to 37–39 percent. If the recidivism rate for these juveniles would have been 50 percent without treatment, the most effective programs reduced it by approximately 25 percent. Successful interventions included counseling, multiple services, skill building, and restorative programs. More specifically, cognitive–behavioral therapy, mentoring, and group counseling programs were found to be effective intervention strategies. Deterrence and discipline programs actually made recidivism worse (Lipsey, 2009). (For other reviews of effective correctional interventions, see Greenwood, 2008; MacKenzie & Farrington, 2015; and see also Chapter 11.) As noted in Chapter 11, successful programs follow the risk-need-responsivity principles (for a complete discussion see Latessa et al., 2020).

Because youths in custody report higher drug usage and problems related to substance abuse than youths in the general population, correctional programs need to include substance abuse counseling. For example, 84 percent of youths in custody report having used marijuana at some point in their lives, compared to only 30 percent of youths in the general population. Thirty percent of youths in custody report having used cocaine or crack, compared to only 6 percent of youths in the general population. More than half of the youths in custody report that they were drunk or high on drugs several times a week or more in the months prior to being taken into custody (Sedlak & McPherson, 2010b).

Conclusions about Program Effectiveness

First, it is clear that certain efforts are not effective. Ineffective programs are those with no theoretical basis or those based on deterrence and control. Second, there are effective programs. Effective programs range from so-called brand name programs such as Multisystemic Therapy (MST) to programs that incorporate proven principles and approaches such as cognitive–behavioral approaches that address transformation in thinking and attitudes (see Chapter 11 for a discussion of those principles; for reviews of effective programs, see Lipsey, 2009; MacKenzie, 2006; MacKenzie & Freeland, 2012). Third, in addition to reducing recidivism, effective programs can also reduce costs (Aos & Drake, 2013; Washington State Institute for Public Policy, 2016). Fourth, unfortunately, often youths simply do not receive the treatment interventions they need, whether during confinement in a residential program or on after-care status (Schubert & Mulvey, 2014). Fifth, programs that target high-risk delinquents are more effective than those that target low-risk delinquents (for further discussion, see MacKenzie & Freeland, 2012).

Before proceeding to discuss other current issues in juvenile institutions, it is important to note that the measurement of the effectiveness of treatment programs in such settings assumes that the programs are in fact carried out as originally intended. Some call this treatment integrity. Unfortunately, that is not always true. Although Wooden did his research years ago, his observations on this matter apply today. Specifically, Wooden contended that institutions were using behavior modification techniques "to manipulate and control the child for the convenience of the custodians" (Wooden, 1976:101). In a New York facility, "education" actually meant watching movies on the VCR, especially on Friday (Singer, 1996). According to another report, in a facility referred to as "Cottage Blue," staff were chosen to put together notebooks with lesson plans for each week. These staff members simply pulled pages from the internet and from workbooks. Notebooks were so badly photocopied that it was impossible to read them (Inderbitzin, 2006a). In what was intended to be a new model facility in Arizona, treatment quickly deteriorated. Staff appeared inconsistent and capricious in such matters as scoring youths' behaviors, staff were disrespectful and interrupted youths in group meetings, a few staff made racially insensitive remarks, and youths were shackled when transported to receive medical treatment. A key educational program did not accomplish its objectives and substance-abuse treatment was not provided. In short, there was a "repeated and systematic violation of the program's fundamental principles and spirit" (Bortner & Williams, 1997:112). Therefore, impressive terms such as "behavior modification," "model program," and "education" do not necessarily translate into humane and progressive interventions. If such interventions are implemented in such negative ways, it is hardly possible to know what results an evaluation study will find or what sort of confidence can be placed in the results. It is critical to have treatment integrity in order to carry out the intervention as intended.

INSTITUTIONAL LIFE

An important concern in juvenile justice is the effect of institutional life on youths. The theory of institutional placements is that they will provide a caring and nurturing environment that will allow the delinquents to change to pro-social behavior in the institution. This will then carry over into future behavior after release. As we shall see, however, the practice often falls far short of the theoretical ideal.

Mental and Substance Disorders

Research shows that the most prevalent problem in the juvenile justice system is mental disorders. Studies show that more than two-thirds of juveniles in the juvenile justice system experience mental disorders. In fact, a study that looked at more than 1,400 youths in three states found that 70 percent of youths in the system met the criteria for at least one mental health disorder. The most common disorders found were disruptive disorders such as conduct disorders, then substance-abuse disorders such as alcohol abuse, then anxiety disorders (e.g., obsessive-compulsive disorder), and then mood disorders (e.g., depression) (Shufelt & Cocozza, 2006). A study of juvenile offenders in Florida found that race affected diagnoses of conditions such as conduct disorder (Baglivio, Wolff, Piquero, Greenwald, & Epps, 2017). Even a sample of first-time offenders found high rates of mental health problems (Burke, Mulvey, & Schubert, 2015). Importantly, mental health problems increase the likelihood of being sentenced to confinement in a correctional facility, and the effect is even greater for black youths (White, 2016).

High rates of disorder persist even if conduct and substance-abuse disorders are removed from the equation. If conduct disorders were removed, 66 percent of youths still met the criteria for a mental health disorder. If both disorders were removed, almost one-half (45.5 percent) of youths still met the criteria for having a mental health disorder (Shufelt & Cocozza, 2006). Another problem is trauma, with high percentages of youths in custody experiencing trauma such as anxiety, post-traumatic stress, or depression. Such trauma stems from factors such as neglect or abuse, parental criminal history, and an unstable living environment (Calleja, 2020).

Youths themselves report problems. More than 60 percent of youths in custody report anger problems and more than 50 percent report feelings of depression and anxiety such as worry and loneliness. About one-fifth report suicidal feelings and past suicide attempts. Despite these problems, about one-quarter of youths are in facilities that do not screen every child for suicide risk and fewer than half are in facilities that conduct mental health evaluations or appraisals for all youths (Sedlak & McPherson, 2010b). An encouraging note is that more recent research showed that almost three-quarters (73 percent) of clinical staff in juvenile correctional facilities stated that services in their facility were adequate for meeting the mental health needs of the residents (Swank & Gagnon, 2016).

Girls involved in the juvenile justice system have higher rates of mental disorder than boys. More than 80 percent of girls met the criteria for at least one mental health disorder compared to 67 percent of boys. Girls were more likely to exhibit internalizing disorders such as anxiety and mood disorders (Shufelt & Cocozza, 2006).

Most importantly, 27 percent of boys and girls in the juvenile justice system had a disorder serious enough to require "significant and immediate treatment" (Shufelt & Cocozza, 2006:4). In short, many juvenile offenders are suffering from mental health disorders, many need immediate attention, and many others need some type of treatment. On the other hand, a recent study found that a substance-abuse disorder (but not mental health problems) was associated with rearrest in a sample of over 1,300 serious youthful offenders. A critical issue was whether youths had criminogenic risk factors. The authors conclude that mental health treatment services for young offenders may be justified on ethical grounds, but may not be justified on claims of a means to reduce recidivism (Schubert & Mulvey, 2014). An additional concern is that in one state black male offenders were 32 percent less likely to receive treatment than white male juvenile offenders (Baglivio et al., 2017).

It is not surprising that many juvenile offenders experience mental health problems, since many have suffered Adverse Childhood Experiences (ACEs). For example, a study of high-risk juveniles with a history of arrests showed that 50 percent or more of both white and black youths had experienced such adverse experiences as emotional, physical, or sexual abuse, neglect, family violence, separation or divorce of their parents, or incarceration of a family member (Baglivio & Epps, 2016). Related to this, many juveniles in placement report that at the time of their arrest they were in less-than-ideal home situations. Specifically, 45 percent were living with just one parent, usually the mother, and another quarter were living with someone other than a parent, often a grandparent (Sedlak & Bruce, 2016).

Although mental disorders are a serious problem for incarcerated juveniles, it is interesting that a study of youths incarcerated in a smaller Midwestern system found that the youths surveyed had complex views, many of which echoed the opinions of experts. For example, the youths strongly supported rehabilitation and disapproved of the "tough love" options of boot camps and Scared Straight-type programs. As experts have found that incarceration by itself does not reduce recidivism, only 19 percent of the youths agreed that incarceration should be the purpose of the juvenile justice system. Finally, youths did agree that they should make amends to victims for the injuries they received (Pealer et al., 2017).

Educational Problems

Youths in placement also often have a history of problems in school. A quarter (24 percent) report that they were not enrolled in school at the time that they entered placement. Over half (57 percent) report that they had been suspended at some point in the year prior to placement. Half (53 percent) reported having skipped classes, 28 percent said they had been expelled, and 25 precent had repeated a grade (Sedlak & Bruce, 2016).

Victimization

As is true of adult prisons, probably the most dramatic example of a negative effect of the institution on incarcerated youths is the problem of victimization, which ranges from creating feelings of lack of security to sexual victimization to even homicide. The following paragraphs offer information on victimization, but it is important to note that some victimization is not reported.

According to a Survey of Youth in Residential Placement, more than one-third of youths (38 percent) fear attack by someone, including 25 percent who fear attack by another resident and 22 percent who fear physical attack by a staff member (Sedlak & McPherson, 2010a). In an English study, 47 percent of juvenile prisoners reported overall fear of victimization, and 27 percent reported fear of physical victimization (Chan & Ireland, 2009). Bullying is also a problem. In interviews with 190 young offenders (ages 16 to 19) in Ontario, Canada, 37 percent reported being verbally bullied, 30 percent physically bullied, 11 percent robbed, 7.6 percent beaten up, and 1 percent (two youths) sexually bullied (Connell, Farrington, & Ireland, 2016). It is clear that the institutionalized youngster is deprived of the security that teenagers in positive home environments take for granted.

The Prison Rape Elimination Act (PREA) of 2003 requires facilities to report statistics on sexual violence in both adult and juvenile correctional facilities to the federal Bureau of Justice Statistics. In 2012, juvenile facilities reported 1,478 allegations of sexual violence. Almost 60 percent (55 percent) involved charges of youth-on-youth violence, and the rest (45 percent) were staff-on-youth incidents. More than half (58 percent) of these incidents occurred in state-operated facilities, and about 42 percent took place in local or privately operated facilities. The overall rate of sexual violence was 23 incidents per 1,000 youths (Beck & Rantala, 2016). It must be emphasized that these numbers are based on what officials reported to the federal government.

According to the Survey of Youth in Residential Placement, 46 percent of youths surveyed in 2003 reported personal property having been stolen and 10 percent reported that someone used force or the threat of force to steal their personal property. Almost 30 percent (29 percent) reported having been beaten up or threatened with being beaten. Four percent reported having been forced to engage in sexual activity in their current facility. About half of the perpetrators were staff and about half another resident (Sedlak, McPherson, & Basena, 2013). Thirty percent of youths in training schools or other correctional facilities feared physical attack by another resident, and 28 percent feared physical attack by a staff member (Sedlak, 2016).

In another survey, the National Survey of Youth in Custody, 7.1 percent of youths in custody reported one or more incidents of sexual victimization by another youth or staff member in the previous year. Approximately 1.9 percent reported victimization by another resident; 5.8 percent reported victimization by a staff member. The majority of staff sexual misconduct involved the touching or penetrating of body parts. Male youths were more likely to report such misconduct than female youths (Smith & Stroop, 2019). It should be noted that sexual minority youths are more likely to report sexual assault victimization than straight youths (Wilson et al., 2017).

Small percentages of youths in adult prisons (due to transfer) experience sexual assault. About 1 percent are assaulted by other inmates, and about 1 percent are assaulted by staff. Risk factors include a history of prior sexual assault and moderate to severe mental health issues. The surest way to prevent such assaults would be to eliminate waiver (Ahlin & Hummer, 2019).

The federal government also reports on the number of deaths of juveniles in custody. Between October 1, 2017, and September 30, 2018, eight juveniles died in custody; six deaths were suicides, one was from illness/natural causes, and one was an accident. Four deaths occurred in public facilities and four occurred in private facilities (Hockenberry & Sladky, 2020). From 2001 to 2016, 21 prisoners age 17 or younger died in state and federal prisons; 11 committed suicide (Carson & Cowhig, 2020). As the next paragraph shows, however, there are many more acts of suicidal behavior than actual suicides.

Recent lawsuits and newspaper stories offer further evidence of problems in correctional institutions. According to the Annie E. Casey Foundation, over the last 40 years, 57 lawsuits in 33 states plus the District of Columbia have resulted in court-ordered remedies for physical or sexual abuse, excessive use of isola-tion or restraint, or failure to provide services such as education and health care. More specifically, the Associated Press noted that 13,000 claims of abuse were reported between 2004 and 2007, and more than 1,300 of these claims had been confirmed (Mendel, 2011). In a 2015 update to its 2011 report, the Casey Foundation concluded that youth prisons "are inherently prone to abuse" and thus "children should be removed from home only rarely" (Mendel, 2015:29). Such abuses have led one authority to summarize the current status of juvenile corrections as "deeply troubled" (Krisberg, 2012a:766). A study of juvenile sui-cide in confinement found 110 such suicides between 1995 and 1999. Of the suicides analyzed, 42 percent occurred in training schools or secure facilities, 37 percent in detention facilities, 15 percent in residential treatment centers, and 6 percent in reception/diagnostic centers. Seventy percent of the victims had a history of suicidal behavior with prior suicide attempts as the most fre-quent type of history. Almost all of the suicides were by hanging and more than 70 percent of the victims used their bedding materials to commit suicide. The study recommended that youth facilities have a detailed written suicide prevention policy and effective training programs (Hayes, 2004). For further discussion of living conditions in juvenile prison, see Boxes 10.5 and 10.6.

Despite apparent increases in staff victimization, a study of correctional officers in two juvenile detention facilities in Virginia showed low levels of fear of vic-timization and perceived risk of victimization. In addition, it did not matter whether the guard was working in a therapeutically oriented detention center or a more traditional detention center (Gordon, Moriarty, & Grant, 2003).

A study of 500 juveniles in institutions (about half were in traditional institutions such as training schools and about half were in boot camps) focused on the psychological states and perceived environments of the residents. First, juveniles perceived their institutional environments to have high levels of both activity and justice. So the juveniles felt that they had things to do and were being treated fairly but they also perceived the environments to be restrictive and controlled. Levels of anxiety and depression both decreased over time. Childhood maltreatment (e.g., coming from an abusive home) increased the

BOX 10.5 CONDITIONS AT COTTAGE BLUE: MUCH ADO ABOUT NOTHING, OR SOMETHING?

Gresham Sykes coined the phrase "deprivations of imprisonment" to refer to the losses or the pains that prisoners suffer because of incarceration. He listed these deprivations or pains as deprivation or loss of freedom, autonomy, goods and services, security, and heterosexual sexual activity (he was writing of adult prisoners, not juveniles) (Sykes & Matza, 1957).

Inderbitzin's (2006b) study of Cottage Blue points out some of the deprivations, losses, or pains of imprisonment for contemporary juvenile offenders at one facility.

The youths noted deprivation of autonomy in that they had to ask permission to shave or shower, to make a phone call, to send a letter, or to get paper and pencil. So they felt like helpless children. They also suffered loss of privacy; they complained about irritating roommates who smelled or wet the bed or were just plain annoying by talking all the time or asking questions all the time. Part of the problem was having to live with youths of different races or different ages.

Concerning what Sykes would call loss of possessions (goods and services), the youths complained of "inferior" products such as cheap soap or inferior pizza on Friday nights. More generally, they complained of bland food and too much starch in their meals. Another complaint was boredom. So they often asked staff to rent movies or video games for them or to bring them magazines and books.

What do you think of these complaints? How serious are complaints about cheap soap, bland food, or not enough video games? How much attention should staff and administrators in these facilities give to such concerns? Are these complaints trivial, or is it important to make juvenile facilities as positive as possible?

Source: Adapted by authors from Inderbitzin (2006b).

BOX 10.6 HUMAN RIGHTS WATCH: GIRLS IN CUSTODY IN NEW YORK

In addition to physical abuse, Human Rights Watch documented three cases in the five years prior to their report of staff having sexual intercourse with girls. The investigation also found less serious sexual abuse, including verbal innuendo, male staff observing girls in different states of undress, and unwanted touching. Some staff also made humiliating comments about the past sexual history of girls or the fact that they had a sexually transmitted disease. Some also harassed girls who were lesbians or did not conform to stereotypes. Staff also used frequent strip searches and inspected girls' genitals. Human Rights Watch concluded that the facilities were often failing to serve or even protect the incarcerated girls. Staff and administrative failure to provide meaningful oversight and lack of outside monitoring meant that the girls had no way to seek assistance to stop the abuses.

What needs to be done to protect girls in custody? What must be done to protect girls from sexual abuse, in any form, by male staff members? Is it necessary to have an independent monitor or inspector visit such facilities on a periodic basis, or can facility administrators ensure the safety of the girls?

Source: Adapted by authors from Human Rights Watch (2006).

levels of depression and anxiety. Therefore, it appears that institutional staffs should target therapeutic programming for youths with histories of child mal-treatment (Gover & MacKenzie, 2003).

Because some juveniles are transferred to adult court and/or subjected to blended sentencing, a number of youths under 18 are being imprisoned in adult facilities. As noted previously, there were almost 4,000 such juvenile inmates in state prisons in 2000, but only 653 at year end 2019 (Carson, 2020). On a typical day in 2018, there were about 3,400 juveniles being held in local jails, about 80 percent of whom had been tried or were awaiting trial as adults (OJJDP, 2021). There is evidence that these young prisoners are at heightened risk of assault, including sexual assault. One reason is that young prisoners often lack the coping skills of older prisoners. One study found that juveniles in adult prisons were 21 times as likely to be assaulted or injured as teens in the juvenile system (see Benekos & Merlo, 2008). Suicide risk is also higher for such juveniles (Mumola, 2005). One way juveniles in adult prisons cope and also defend themselves is resorting to misconduct (Kolivoski & Shook, 2016).

Girls may face special problems. They report more mental–emotional problems and traumatic experiences than boys (Sedlak & McPherson, 2010b). For example, girls have undergone strip searches and cavity searches in the presence of male guards. This tends to reinforce the belief that they do not have control over their own bodies. Some facilities have not given girls clean clothes and clean towels and washcloths, and some have provided limited hygiene supplies. These abuses and deprivations can be especially important to adolescent girls as they make the transition to womanhood (Acoca, 1998).

A Human Rights Watch investigation found evidence of staff physical abuse of girls in two New York State residential facilities. The investigation alleged that staff frequently applied a technique called "restraint" to girls. Staff would grab a girl from behind, push her on to the floor, push her arms up behind her, and hold or handcuff her. This was used in many situations that did not involve danger or threats—such as talking back or "mouthing off" or not making one's bed correctly. Sometimes the girls got "rug burns" on their faces or all over their bodies. The report noted that excessive force may be especially harmful to girls because past experiences of physical or sexual abuse can lead to intense emotions for them (Human Rights Watch, 2006).

The same investigation also found staff sexual abuse of the residents, ranging from observation of girls in states of undress by male staff, to unwanted touching, all the way to sexual intercourse. Staff abuse also included publicly humiliating comments revealing girls' past sexual histories or their experiences of domestic abuse (Human Rights Watch, 2006).

A study of 22 girls in a large women's prison in the Midwest indicated several problem areas for juvenile girls who had been sentenced to adult women's prisons. One problem was lack of recreation time and equipment. Recreation equipment had been ordered for the under-21 unit but had not arrived by the time of the research. No girl reported having been "raped" by an older woman, but some had experienced either name-calling or more serious sexual comments. Four girls indicated that they were in a sexual relationship with an older woman prisoner but that it was consensual. GED education and even college education (an associate degree program in Social Services) were available. Most programs were designed for adult women, but anger management, a Girl Scouts program, and a gang awareness program were specifically targeted at the young prisoners. The authors concluded that their research "raises critical

Female detainees take a test at the Green Oaks Juvenile Detention Center in Monroe, Louisiana. Studies show that girls in institutions may face special problems compared to boys.

CREDIT: AP Photo/*The News-Star*, Terrance Armstard

questions about the quality of care given to girls in adult prisons, particularly in programming areas such as education, life skills, recreation, and work training" (Gaarder & Belknap, 2004:75). The authors call for improvements in all these areas but they add the cautionary note that their ideal solution is to not put any girls or women in women's prisons because "[w]omen's prisons mirror the regulatory mechanisms and treatment of women in society at large, and we seek to dismantle both" (Gaarder & Belknap, 2004:77).

Schaffner (2006) did qualitative research on girls in California detention centers. She argues that many workers, including probation officers, hold inappropriate notions about contemporary girls and even subtly racist attitudes. She argues that juvenile justice needs to implement more gender-specific programming and also address the needs of girls and women who are gay or other in their sexual orientation. Kempf-Leonard (2012) echoes these concerns about lack of services and lack of gender-appropriate services for girls, and states that the time to address the needs of girls in placement is "past due" (Kempf-Leonard, 2012:515).

Racial Tension

The statistics on victimization also suggest that **racial tension** is a problem in juvenile institutions. For example, Bartollas and Sieverdes found African-American youths to be both more dominant and more aggressive than white inmates: "Twice as many black as white residents were classified by staff members as highly aggressive toward others; over 40 percent of whites were defined by staff as passive" (Bartollas & Sieverdes, 1981:538). Bartollas and Sieverdes attributed this situation to role reversal in the institution, where white Southern youths found themselves in the novel position of being in the minority. White inmates were outnumbered by black inmates (about 60 percent of the inmates were black) and about half of the staff members were black. The white youths felt threatened because they were in an environment very different from "the southern culture, [where] whites are used to a position of greater superiority in the free society relative to minority groups than are youth elsewhere in the United States" (Bartollas & Sieverdes, 1981:541). Even a model youth prison in Arizona experienced some racial tensions. It was reported that one staff member called a youth a "taco bender" and another staff member called an African-American youth "colored" (Bortner & Williams, 1997).

The fact that training schools continue to be places with significant proportions of several ethnic groups suggests that racial/ethnic tensions will continue into the foreseeable future. As noted at the beginning of this chapter, in 2019 minorities constituted 67 percent of the juveniles in residential placement.

Blacks made up 41 percent of those in placement and Hispanics accounted for 20 percent of those in placement (OJJDP, 2021). For the United States as a whole, black youths were more than four times as likely to be committed to secure placements as white juveniles (Rovner, 2021a). Rovner attributes this to both differences in offending and unequal policing.

The federal government, through legislation, research, training, and technical assistance, has been attempting to reduce disproportionate minority confinement. One strategy to reduce such disproportionate confinement is using standardized risk assessments at decision points in the juvenile justice system. Such risk assessment structures decision making and thus has the potential to reduce racial bias by court officials (Hsia, Bridges, & McHale, 2004). Another strategy is staff training to make staff more aware of possibly unconscious factors that contribute to disproportionate minority confinement (Bishop, 2005). Rovner (2021a) suggests both community investment and racial impact statements for new laws and policies. (For more on the issue of race, see Chapter 14.)

Inmate Misconduct

Inmate misconduct has been studied more extensively in adult prisons than in juvenile institutions. Recent research, however, has addressed this topic. A study of 4,686 youths released from a large Southern juvenile correctional system showed that on average each delinquent committed about 53 misconduct incidents while incarcerated. This number was the same for males and females but a higher percentage of males (58 percent) were considered institutional dangers during their placement than females (35 percent). One promising note was that risk-score classification was a good predictor of misconduct, suggesting that higher-risk youths can be identified and given more attention (Trulson, 2007).

A study that focused on 2,520 serious and violent male delinquents sentenced between 1987 and 2004 in a large Southern youth correctional system under a blended sentencing statute found that, overall, the delinquents committed an average of 7.64 major misconduct violations during their incarceration for a total of almost 19,000 major violations. On the one hand, 71 percent of the sample was involved in at least one ward assault. On the other hand, 57 percent of the sample had only between zero and four violations and most types of major misconduct were committed by less than one-third of the residents. Variables associated with misconduct included younger age at commitment, number of previous adjudications, substance abuse, gang membership, and a chaotic home environment prior to commitment (Trulson, DeLisi, Caudill, Belshaw, & Marquart, 2010).

A study of juvenile offenders who were serving a blended sentence showed that almost two-thirds (63.3 percent) were "abstainers" who committed no rule infractions. On the other hand, 20 percent began committing misconduct at a high rate from the start and continued to break rules. Juveniles incarcerated for robbery, homicide, and assaultive offenses tended to commit serious institutional violations and therefore need special attention and programming (Reidy, Sorensen, & Cihan, 2018).

As might be expected, research indicates that organizational structure affects the norms and behaviors of youthful prisoners. In other words, "[t]he more custodial and punitive settings had inmate cultures that were more violent, more hostile, and more oppositional than those in the treatment-oriented settings" (Feld, 1981:336). This finding on the impact of organizational structure on inmate culture suggests that it is possible for administrators to reduce the negative environments in juvenile prisons by opting for an organizational structure that emphasizes treatment over custody. One specific option that administrators can take is to limit the size of juvenile residential placements. Larger populations are more susceptible to custodial climates than smaller populations. Another option is to facilitate communication between treatment staff and custodial staff so that staff members do not exacerbate potential treatment–custody conflicts.

One final note relates to the issue of placing juveniles in adult prisons. A study of the misconduct of juvenile inmates in an adult prison system (Florida) shows that juveniles are overrepresented in prison misconduct and violence. For example, 16 percent of juveniles threatened a correctional officer compared to 7 percent of adult inmates; 24 percent were charged with fighting compared to 10 percent of the adult inmates; and 21 percent committed assault compared to 5 percent of the adult inmates. Juveniles committed misconduct most frequently in their second year of incarceration (Kuanliang, Sorensen, & Cunningham, 2008).

One possible explanation for misconduct committed by juvenile offenders in adult prisons is that they are more prone to suffering abuse and engage in misconduct to avoid certain situations or to protect themselves from abuse. Another factor is the presence of mental health issues (Kolivoski & Shook, 2016). Because of the high rate of mental health issues among transferred juveniles and the lack of enough mental health treatment services, Kolivoski and Shook (2016) assert that these two factors are additional arguments against placing juveniles in adult prisons.

Deprivation of Heterosexual Contact

Another negative effect of institutions is that incarcerated youths are deprived of heterosexual relationships at a time when such relationships are critical in helping the teenager to define himself or herself as a mature sexual adult. Although written about incarcerated girls, Giallombardo's (1974) comments on this matter apply equally well (with the appropriate adjustments) to imprisoned boys:

> They are developing images of themselves as adult women, and they are beset with many anxieties concerning their sexuality and acceptance by males. The exclusion of males in their own age group is a source of confusion for adolescent girls … Their confusion is compounded by

virtue of the fact that during incarceration they are socialized to view other women as legitimate sex objects. (Giallombardo, 1974:244)

In response to this deprivation, many of the girls adjust by participating in kinship role systems and/or homosexual alliances. In the training schools Giallombardo (1974) studied, for example, the girls had affectionate nicknames for one another, wrote love letters to other girls, picked their own special songs, "went steady," and even got married in formal ceremonies (out of staff view). Another study reported that only about 17 percent of the institutionalized girls reported at least one homosexual experience (ranging from kissing to intimate sexual contact) but about half of the girls reported taking a "make-believe family" role (Propper, 1982). Such behavior was clearly not intended by the authorities and has been labeled a "secondary adjustment" (Goffman, 1961:199). The problem with secondary adjustments is that they divert the youths' attention away from the main aspects of the supposedly rehabilitative programs, such as education and counseling, and direct that attention to making life within the training school as pleasant as possible.

As noted above, Schaffner (2006) claims that concern for deprivation of heterosexual contact needs updating. She argues that some girls are gay, transgender, or questioning of their sexual orientation. If juvenile correctional programs are not aware of this, they are missing a critical component of the lives of the offenders they are trying to help. She also thinks that many correctional workers are not aware of contemporary social habits, even of heterosexual girls, and thus can be overly judgmental of behaviors or remarks that should be seen as nothing out of the ordinary for the contemporary culture.

Other problems faced by incarcerated youths include loss of liberty, deprivation of personal possessions, and boredom. Particularly important in terms of possessions is the loss of clothing articles. This is important because it entails a loss of the opportunity to explore various clothing styles. According to Giallombardo (1974), such exploratory behavior is directly related to a girl's sense of identity as well as her popularity.

In one training school, youths had several complaints: loss of autonomy; they felt like helpless children who had to ask permission to shower or get paper and pencil; loss of privacy; they had roommates who smelled bad or talked all the time; loss of desirable possessions; low-quality soap or toothpaste; and bland food. They hoped staff would rent movies or video games for them or bring them books or magazines to break the boredom (Inderbitzin, 2006b).

An important national study on living conditions in juvenile facilities found "substantial and widespread deficiencies" in four matters: living space, security, control of suicidal behavior, and health care (Abt Associates, 1994). The most recent Survey of Youth in Residential Placement notes that 25 percent of youths report no positive feature about their facility. More specifically, 11 percent of youths in residential treatment report dirty sheets, towels, or clothes; 44 percent report insects or bugs; and 28 percent report dirty bathrooms (Sedlak & McPherson, 2010a).

Many institutions experience problems concerning crowding, safety, prevention of escapes, suicidal behavior, and health screening. That same Survey of Youth in Residential Placement report also advocated collecting systematic data on confined youths' educational and treatment needs. Further evidence of problems in juvenile institutions is the fact that, over the last 40 years, 57 lawsuits in 33 states and the District of Columbia have resulted in court-sanctioned remedies for either abuse or unconstitutional conditions in juvenile facilities (Mendel, 2011). Further, a 2008 newspaper investigation found that 13,000 claims of abuse had been reported between 2004 and 2007 (Mendel, 2011). Mendel concludes that the "case against America's youth prisons and correctional training schools can be neatly summarized in six words: dangerous, ineffective, unnecessary, obsolete, wasteful, and inadequate" (Mendel, 2011:5). A 2015 update reinforces his 2011 conclusion (Mendel, 2015).

NEW DIRECTIONS IN INSTITUTIONAL INTERVENTIONS

Deinstitutionalization of Status Offenders

Since the mid-1970s, there has been a movement away from placing status offenders and delinquents in the same state-operated institutions. It is felt that any mixing of status offenders and delinquents can have harmful consequences on the status offenders. In fact, much of this movement has been one of **deinstitutionalization**: Trying to avoid any involuntary placements of status offenders (the practice of some states to deinstitutionalize delinquents as well as status offenders will be discussed in the next section). The strength of this movement is indicated by the fact that only 1,690 committed status offenders were in placement in 2017 and fewer in 2019. This is a 60 percent decrease from 1997 (Hockenberry, 2020; OJJDP, 2021).

Deinstitutionalization (Closing Training Schools)

Several states, including Massachusetts, Maryland, Pennsylvania, and Utah, have decreased dramatically their use of training schools by closing some of these facilities. In Massachusetts, for example, only about 15 percent of the approximately 800 youths committed to the State Department of Youth services each year are first placed in a locked treatment program. The other 85 percent of the committed youths are placed in community-based programs such as group homes, forestry camps, day treatment programs, outreach-tracking programs, or foster care. Most of the programs have been privatized; private agencies run the programs on a contract basis with the state. In addition, the residential programs are small in size, with no more than 30 youths housed in a facility (Krisberg & Austin, 1993). What this means for most youths is that they spend only about four weeks in secure placement and then are placed in nonsecure treatment programs. In states with heavy reliance on traditional training schools, most youths spend several months in secure confinement and then are placed on aftercare (parole).

The National Council on Crime and Delinquency evaluated the Massachusetts reform and found it to be successful. Compared to other states still relying on traditional training schools, Massachusetts had similar recidivism results, and the effort was cost-effective. More specifically, depending on how long Massachusetts would incarcerate youths in traditional training schools, it would have to spend $10 million to $16.8 million more per year than it was spending in its deinstitutionalization mode (Krisberg, Austin, & Steele, 1989).

An evaluation of the closing of one institution in Maryland, however, found contrary results. Almost three-quarters (72 percent) of the youths committed to the State Department of Juvenile Services after the institution's closing were rearrested during the one-year follow-up period, whereas only about 45 percent of the youths who had been institutionalized at the training school prior to its closing were rearrested. In a two-and-one-half year follow-up period, 83 percent of the post-closing group were rearrested compared to 66 percent and 69 percent of the two groups that had been incarcerated at the training school under study. The authors concluded that "the alternatives available when Montrose [the state training school] was closed were less effective in reducing crime than institutionalization would have been" (Gottfredson & Barton, 1993:604). The authors suggest that their findings support the conclusion that "neither institutional nor community-based programs are uniformly effective or ineffective. The *design* of the intervention rather than its location appears important" (Gottfredson & Barton, 1993:605 [emphasis in original]). In other words, simply closing traditional training schools is only half of the strategy. The other half is to devise effective programs for the youths that would have been committed to the training schools. It appears that Massachusetts was able to devise such effective alternative programming for its delinquent commitments. Maryland apparently did not come up with effective alternative programming so the recidivism rates for the group not sent to the training school were disappointing.

Another state that has tried to reduce its institutional population is Missouri. It closed its only training school in 1983 and has tried to keep newer institutions at 50 beds or fewer with an average population of 20 youths. To accomplish the goal of reduced placements, Missouri uses such strategies as day treatment programs and trackers. Day treatment is intended for youths released from residential confinement; it involves education, counseling, tutoring, and/or community service. Trackers are personnel, often college students completing a degree in social work or a related field, who monitor and support about 800 youths in community supervision. Trackers offer support, mentoring, and assistance. Missouri also uses nonsecure group homes. One benefit has been cost savings. In 2000, Missouri spent about $94 per youth age 10 to 17 in the state compared to $140 per youth in surrounding states. The state also reports that only about 11 percent of youths released from custody were rearrested or returned to juvenile custody within one year (Mendel, 2001). Mendel (2001) argues that much of the reason for the apparent success of Missouri's emphasis on community programming is the hiring of high-quality staff. At all times, youths are overseen by at least two educated and highly trained staff members compared to other states, in which less skilled officers supervise youths. An indication of the success of Missouri is the award it received for innovative programming in 2008 (Ash Institute, 2008). Unfortunately, however, there has not been a systematic evaluation of the Missouri model that might specify which aspects of the initiative are related to its apparent success (Bonnies, Johnson, Chemers, & Schuck, 2013).

As of the writing of this edition, California is slated to begin closing its three youth prisons and switch to county programs that are trauma responsive and culturally informed (Quarantana, 2021). Similarly, in recent years, Connecticut, Wisconsin, and South Dakota have closed youth prisons and switched to either smaller facilities or community programs (Teigen, 2018). Wayne County, Michigan (Detroit) has stopped sending youths to the state juvenile system and instead created local services. As a result, in 2010 the county only had two youths in state training schools (Muhammad, 2019).

As noted, the most recent census of juveniles in residential placement showed that there were fewer than 36,500 juveniles in public or private facilities in 2019, a drop of over 7,000 youths since 2017 and a drop of 65 percent since 1997 when over 105,000 youths were in placement (OJJDP, 2021; Hockenberry, 2020). This drop reflects the efforts of several states (see above) to follow the recommendations of experts to reduce placements (see, e.g., Feld, 2018).

Critics applaud this trend of decreasing institutional placement of youthful offenders, but some call for even greater decreases. The Annie E. Casey Foundation, for example, argues that the "case against juvenile corrections facilities is overwhelming. Countless studies and decades of experience show that these institutions are both dangerous and ineffective" (Mendel, 2011:28). Their report suggests more community-based interventions and placement of only very few delinquents in small facilities when considered necessary (Mendel, 2011). The 2015 update of this report repeats this criticism of institutional placement (Mendel, 2015). The National Research Council argues that "public safety can be well-served—indeed, better served—by abandoning a confinement-oriented correctional approach in favor of community-based services for the majority of juveniles who can be safely supervised in the community" (Bonnies et al., 2013).

Forces behind the decreasing numbers of youths in correctional facilities are the research and criticisms of problems in institutions, research on effective alternatives to incarceration, and calls by even conservatives to reduce spending on prisons (see, e.g., www.rightoncrime.com).

Blended Sentencing

The creation of blended sentencing allows either the juvenile court or the adult court to impose a sentence that can involve either the juvenile or the adult correctional system or both (see Chapter 8 for further discussion of blended sentencing). The adult sentence may be suspended pending either a violation or the commission of a new crime. Texas, for example, allowed juveniles convicted of certain violent crimes or of habitual offender status to be sentenced to terms of up to 20 years for a second-degree felony and up to 10 years for a third-degree felony (Feld, 1998). A positive sign is that at the end of 2014, 14 states had blended sentencing laws, down from 18 in 2011 (OJJDP, 2017).

A study on victimization among youthful inmates in adult prisons is important in light of the development of blended sentencing. Maitland and Sluder (1998) interviewed 111 inmates ages 17 to 25. They found that less than 1 percent reported that they had been forced to engage in sexual activity, 3 percent had been forced to give up their money, and 5.5 percent had had a weapon used on them. Less serious victimization experiences, however, were much more frequent. Fifty-nine percent had been verbally harassed, approximately 50 percent had had their property stolen, and 38 percent had been hit, kicked, punched, or slapped. The authors concluded that "young, medium-security prison inmates are most likely to be subjected to less serious forms of victimization by peers during their terms of incarceration" (Maitland & Sluder, 1998:68). Thus, any trend toward putting delinquents in adult prisons when they are 17 or 18 can be expected to produce such victimization results for the youthful offenders so incarcerated.

Another negative aspect of blended sentencing and putting juveniles into criminal court and adult institutions is that the youths may have negative perceptions of how they were processed. In research on criminal court processing of youths in Florida, it was found that the court message to the youths was that their behavior was bad and they were bad. Prison staff also communicated a similar negative message; the youthful prisoners heard that "they were lost causes who could never redeem themselves or return to normal personhood" (Bishop, 2000:153).

A study of 1,804 serious and violent male delinquents sentenced to incarceration under a blended sentencing law in a large Southeastern state found 64 percent of the youths were rearrested at least once post-release. Almost half (46 percent) were arrested on at least one felony. Parole supervision was not related to rearrest frequency but did increase the odds of rearrest for a felony offense arrest. Average exposure time was almost six years (Trulson, DeLisi, & Marquart, 2011). This study suggests that blended sentencing is not a simple or complete solution to the question of how to deal with serious and violent juvenile offenders.

Wilderness Programs

Another example of what Cullen and his colleagues (Cullen et al., 2005:66) call common-sense corrections is the use of various types of wilderness programs, ranging from relatively short stays in outdoor settings to rather long wagon train or ocean ship trips. Both private operators and some states have used this type of programming, which places delinquents in settings where they learn survival skills, limits, and self-esteem. The youths are put in natural settings where they must learn to cook, obtain shelter from the elements, tell directions (read a compass), start fires, and so forth. In the process of accomplishing such tasks, the youths learn to depend on both others and themselves. The thinking is that a successful survival experience in a natural setting will then transfer to the youth's normal environment and he or she will turn to more constructive activities than delinquency. The program, then, is based on common-sense notions (perhaps stemming from experience or familiarity with Boy Scouts and Girl Scouts) that outdoors know-how is beneficial.

A wilderness program in Georgia received attention when a 13-year-old boy died. Authorities fired several staff members due to the incident. It is alleged that camp counselors restrained the boy face down and denied him his inhaler (he was asthmatic) (Miller, 2005).

In earlier research, Lipsey and Wilson (1998) concluded that wilderness programs generally had weak effects or no effects on the recidivism rates of the youths who went through the programs compared to control groups. But in a more recent analysis of wilderness and challenge programs for juveniles, they found that programs with more intense physical activities or greater therapeutic enhancements reduced recidivism from 37 percent down to 29 percent (Wilson & Lipsey, 2003). A meta-analysis of wilderness therapy programs for paying participants (not juvenile offenders) found positive effects, but the majority of the studies reviewed did not use a control group (Bettman, Gillis, Speelman, Parry, & Case, 2016). Thus, the evidence is weak.

In conclusion, simply putting teens through a "survivor's" experience as depicted on television is not enough to reduce delinquency. It appears that the wilderness program must have a therapeutic aspect to be effective (Wilson & Lipsey, 2003). Once again, a common-sense belief such as "getting outdoors is what those kids need" is not always accurate (Cullen et al., 2005:66).

SUMMARY

This chapter has examined state and private residential placements, ranging from training schools to wilderness experience programs. An examination of the effectiveness of institutional placements indicates that many children do not really need to be in training schools. Instead, they can be handled in less restrictive settings without any increase in recidivism. This part of the chapter also examined several problematic factors in residential placements, such as victimization and racial tension. Unfortunately, residential placements often translate into horror stories for the children rather than therapeutic havens. Sexual assaults and racial tension have been well-documented components of placements in the past, and they are unlikely to disappear completely. As will be noted in Chapter 14, a number of states have reformed their juvenile justice systems in order to be "smart on juvenile justice." This includes relying on evidence-based interventions and trying to reduce placements in order to save state monies. One way to reduce placements is to reduce the number of placements due to violations of probation. In addition, a number of states have returned to determining age 18 as the beginning age for criminal court jurisdiction.

These developments are part of the explanation for the large drop in incarceration since 1997, as noted at the beginning of this chapter. Thus, while the 1990s and early 2000s witnessed a "get tough" era with more use of institutional placement, the number of youths placed in youth institutions and adult prisons has dropped dramatically since 1997 and appears to be continuing to drop significantly. One continuing concern is the problem of punishing juvenile murderers with life without parole or other life sentences, an issue discussed in Chapter 14.

Based on current trends, one prediction is that the number of juveniles in institutional confinement will continue to decrease. As noted, some call for the end of juvenile prisons or for as much reduction in confinement as possible. Hopeful predictions are that more youths will receive the interventions they need and that there will be continued efforts to make residential placements as safe as possible.

DISCUSSION QUESTIONS

1. While many are calling for minimal use of juvenile incarceration, there are still some who favor harsher punishment for juvenile offenders, especially violent juvenile offenders. Do you think that persons holding that position are aware of the information on victimization in juvenile training schools (prisons)? Would knowledge of victimization risks in juvenile prisons affect calls for tougher measures for juveniles?

2. Do juveniles deserve prisons that are quite different from adult offenders? Should we continue to model juvenile prisons after schools? Should we drop any pretense of lesser punishment for juveniles and make juvenile facilities very similar to adult prisons?

3. Would you consider a career in juvenile corrections, in either public or private facilities?

4. Should corrections for juveniles go back to its roots and try to emphasize rehabilitation, or should it attempt to incorporate more punitive dimensions? What would the ideal residential program for juveniles look like? How can states prevent some of the abuses noted in this chapter, especially sexual abuse of female inmates?

5. Common sense has led to correctional efforts such as boot camps and wilderness experience programs. Evaluation research often indicates that these common-sense solutions are not all that effective. Why is common sense often a poor guide to public policy?

6. How do you envision juvenile corrections in 10 years? What will juvenile prisons look like a decade from now? Do you agree with severe critics of juvenile institutions such as the Annie E. Casey Foundation that juvenile facilities are "both dangerous and ineffective" (Mendel, 2011:28) and "inherently prone to abuse" (Mendel, 2015:29), and that placement in such institutions should be cut back as much as possible?

CHAPTER 11

Juvenile Probation and Community Corrections

WHAT YOU NEED TO KNOW

- In 2018, probation handled more than 280,000 cases which were processed in some way for delinquency or a status offense by the juvenile court.

- In juvenile court, the probation presentence investigation may be called a social history investigation or a predisposition report.

- "Aftercare" is the juvenile court term for parole.

- One current approach in juvenile community corrections is the balanced approach, which attempts to balance offender accountability, competency development, and community safety.

- Police–probation partnerships, including searches of the offender's residence, are an example of a tough approach to juvenile probation.

- Other recent approaches in juvenile probation include restorative justice, peacemaking, and community justice.

- A number of treatment interventions are effective, including cognitive–behavioral and social learning programs.

- Some current concerns about juvenile probation include the problems of goal confusion and some aspects of both restitution and community service. Project HOPE, emphasizing swift and certain sanctions, has been tried with adult probationers, but it is questionable if such a deterrence model is suitable for juveniles on probation.

- Probation managers must attempt to implement programs that are effective in a variety of ways, including reducing recidivism, meeting offender needs, and satisfying the public.

KEY TERMS

aftercare

balanced approach

community/restorative justice

effectiveness

emphasis on status offenses

goal confusion

motivational interviewing

peacemaking

probation

Project HOPE

punitive directions in probation

reduced use of probation (Mendel)

restitution

restorative justice

social history investigation (predisposition report)

DOI: 10.4324/9781003167112-11

INTRODUCTION

Even before the founding of the first juvenile court in Illinois in 1899, community interventions had been a central weapon of those seeking to fight delinquency. This chapter will examine both traditional and nontraditional community interventions and focus on some of the problems with these approaches to the delinquency problem. The chapter will first describe probation and aftercare for juveniles, highlight some of the current trends in community interventions, and then look at some of the concerns in the field. One of the key issues examined in this chapter is the **effectiveness** issue: Do community interventions have any impact on recidivism? In other words, do community interventions help to reduce the number of offenses committed by the juveniles exposed to the programs, or are the programs ineffective in reducing delinquent activity?

PROBATION

Statistics demonstrate that **probation** continues to be a critical part of the juvenile justice system. In 2018 (the most recent year for which complete data are available), an estimated 139,000 cases adjudicated delinquent in juvenile court resulted in probation. This represents more than half (63 percent) of the 220,000 cases which were adjudicated delinquent. Another 71,900 cases not adjudicated delinquent resulted in some form of probation and another 49,400 cases not petitioned resulted in some form of voluntary probation. So probation handled approximately 260,300 delinquency cases altogether in 2018. For status offenses, 20,100 adjudicated cases resulted in probation, 59 percent of all status offense cases that were adjudicated in juvenile court. Probation was the most common disposition for adjudicated status offenders (Hockenberry & Puzzanchera, 2020). (Table 11.1 shows the offenses for which delinquents were placed on probation.) Thus, probation continues to be the workhorse of the juvenile court (Torbet, 1996).

Social History (Predisposition) Investigations

When a child has been adjudicated as either a delinquent or a status offender, usually a probation officer conducts a **social history investigation (predisposition report)** of the youngster and his or her family. Similar to the so-called presentence investigation report in adult courts, social history reports offer judges legal and social information. Legal information includes descriptive material about the delinquency or status offense, including the child's, the victim's, and the police officer's (if a delinquent act) version of the offense, and verified data on the child's prior contacts, if any, with the juvenile court and with the police department's juvenile bureau. Social history information includes verification of the child's age (a critical legal condition for court action) and information on the child's development, family, education, and possible problems such as alcohol or other drug abuse.

Probation officers gather such information by interviewing the youth; the youth's family, teachers, and other school personnel; the victim; and the

TABLE 11.1 Adjudication Offenses for Juvenile Delinquency and Status Offense Probation Cases (%)

Offense Profile of Cases Adjudicated Delinquent, Resulting in Probation

Most Serious Offense	2005	2018
Person	26	30
Property	36	31
Drugs	13	12
Public Order	26	26
Total	100	100

Offense Profile of Adjudicated Status Offense Cases Resulting in Probation

Most Serious Offense	2005	2018
Runaway	10	10
Truancy	32	54
Curfew	5	3
Ungovernability	17	14
Liquor Law	26	12
Miscellaneous	9	7
Total	100	100

Note: Details may not add to total because of rounding.

Source: Hockenberry and Puzzanchera (2020). Reprinted with permission.

police; and by checking various police, court, and school records. They usually collect information on previous arrests from police and court files. Likewise, they may obtain a copy of the child's cumulative school record which contains information on the child's grades, attendance, disciplinary history, and intelligence testing. If necessary, in probation departments that have the resources, the officer may also see to it that a psychologist and/or a psychiatrist examine the child for any suspected emotional problems and to determine the child's intelligence quotient (IQ) more accurately (by an individual IQ test rather than a group test). The probation officer then summarizes all of this information in a report that provides the judge with a more informed basis for the disposition decision.

Some adult courts are now omitting all the social history information. Determinate sentencing in many jurisdictions means that only information about the current charges and the prior record of the accused pertains to sentencing.

Racial disparity can enter into probation reports. An examination of more than 200 narrative reports

WEB ACTIVITY

For the latest available statistics on juveniles and probation, go to the website of the Office of Juvenile Justice and Delinquency Prevention and search for the latest report on juvenile court statistics. Consult the Office of Juvenile Justice and Delinquency Prevention's (2021) *Statistical Briefing Book* at: www.ojjdp.gov.

in a Western state indicated that probation officers were more likely to note negative personality factors in reports about black youths but were more likely to note negative environmental factors in reports about white youths. Officers were also more likely to assign a higher risk of reoffending to black youths than white youths. There were no racial differences in sentencing recommendations (Bridges & Steen, 1998). Bishop claims that this study "provides some of the most compelling evidence to date of racial stereotyping by juvenile justice officials and of the power of racial stereotypes to influence decision making" (Bishop, 2005:57).

Probation Supervision

Youths who are placed on formal probation supervision in court must follow various conditions such as reporting regularly to a probation officer, obeying the law, attending school, and remaining within the geographical jurisdiction of the court. Judges may also order specific conditions such as restitution to the victim(s) of the delinquent act or community service restitution (e.g., performing clean-up work at the local park or playground). Another special condition might be to attend counseling sessions with a social worker, psychologist, or psychiatrist, or require the parents to attend the counseling sessions.

A Project Service Achievement Work (SAW) Program coordinator with the Mojave County (Arizona) Probation Department supervises program participants as they install a railing on a museum exhibit. The program, which is for 16- and 17-year-old juveniles who are on probation and have dropped out of school, puts teens to work in the community.

CREDIT: AP Photo/*Kingman Daily Miner*, Linda Stelp

A judge might also order a short stay (about one month) in detention as a condition of probation (Schwartz, Fishman, Rawson Hatfield, Krisberg, & Eisikovits, 1987).

If a juvenile follows the conditions of the probation disposition and is adjusting favorably at home, in school, and in the community, then the probation officer can request an early discharge from supervision. If a youngster is not abiding by the conditions and is not adjusting well, then the probation officer may request that the judge order that the youth is in violation of the probation agreement. In that case, the judge can either order the probation to continue (perhaps with additional conditions such as more frequent reporting to the probation officer) or can terminate the probation and place the youth under the supervision of the state youth correctional authority for placement in a public facility or place the youth in a private residential setting.

AFTERCARE

Approximately 100,000 youths exit the juvenile justice system every year (Nellis, 2009). Many states have aftercare or parole programs for youths released from state training schools, group homes, or forestry camp placements. **Aftercare** supervision is very similar to probation supervision. In fact, in some states, probation officers also perform aftercare supervision duties. Just as with probation, youths on aftercare status must follow specific conditions and report on a regular basis to a parole officer. If they do not, parole can be revoked, and they can be sent back to an institutional placement. There are also privately operated aftercare programs that have government contracts to provide aftercare services (Dum & Fader, 2013).

As noted in Chapter 10, recidivism statistics for youths released from institutions cause concern; states are reporting that 70–80 percent of released youths are arrested for a new offense within two or three years (Mendel, 2011). A national evaluation of intensive juvenile aftercare proved disappointing. Approximately one-half of the youths were arrested for one or more new felonies and, if technical violations (breaking the rules of probation) were included, about 80 percent were rearrested for something. The most disturbing conclusion was that "no statistically significant or substantive differences were seen between IAP [intensive aftercare] and control youth on almost all the recidivism measures" (Wiebush, Wagner, McNulty, Wang, & Le, 2005:80). Recidivism measures included percent arrested, number of offenses, severity and frequency of offenses, and time to first arrest. There was some minor evidence that more treatment was associated with less recidivism, but this finding was significant in only one of the study sites. So even a program intended to improve post-release performance did not produce the desired results.

Similarly, a study of 1,804 serious and violent male delinquents sentenced to incarceration under a blended sentencing law in a large Southeastern state found 64 percent of the youths were rearrested at least once post-release. Almost half (46 percent) were arrested on at least one felony. Parole supervision was not related to rearrest frequency but did increase the odds of rearrest for a felony offense arrest. Average exposure time was almost six years (Trulson, DeLisi, & Marquart, 2011).

Studies on reentry programs and other interventions have not found a clear-cut or simple answer to what makes for successful reentry. However, the research does indicate some suggestions for success. First, mental health services can reduce recidivism. Second, mentoring is related to reduced recidivism, reductions in testing positive for drug usage, and more connections to educational and employment services and mental health treatment (Nellis, 2009).

One study of aftercare workers in a privately contracted program found that the workers were poorly paid, felt pressure to focus on paperwork, and experienced problems with clients such as clients not showing up for appointments or avoiding them. Despite these difficulties, a number of the aftercare workers tried to connect with youths and make a difference in their lives, to provide "proactive caregiving" (Dum & Fader, 2013). Another recent study found that about two-thirds (65 percent) of the 413 youths in the study had no aftercare services during the critical first six months after release from a juvenile residential setting (Schubert & Mulvey, 2014).

SUPERVISION AND COUNSELING

Probation and aftercare (parole) officers working with juveniles use various combinations of assistance and control (Glaser, 1964; Ward & Kupchik, 2010) to help youthful offenders avoid further trouble. Some officers act like social workers or counselors as they try to understand the youth and his or her problems and assist the youngster in gaining greater self-insight and self-esteem. Such officers also might attempt some family therapy to help parents better understand the family interaction patterns that have contributed to the child's misbehavior. Other officers assume a tougher role: a quasi-police officer who first threatens the youth with punishment and then monitors the compliance of the child to the court conditions. This "surveillance" (Studt, 1973) type of officer typically believes that deterrence and incapacitation are more important goals than rehabilitation. Based on in-depth interviews with 31 probation officers, Schwalbe (2012) found that officers integrate both care (therapeutic programming) and control into a participation process model. This model uses risk assessment, evidence-based practices, and mechanisms of motivation including parental support. A recent study of adult and juvenile probation officers in South Carolina found that juvenile officers in that state are more treatment- and assistance-oriented than officers who work with adult probationers (Bolin & Applegate, 2016).

Whether oriented toward assistance or control, probation and parole officers tend to use one of several counseling techniques including reality therapy, client-centered (nondirective) therapy, rational emotive therapy, or behaviorism. Assistance-oriented officers utilize these counseling techniques to a greater extent than control-oriented officers but even the latter use some of the basic principles of these approaches to interview probationers and to establish some rapport (for more information on counseling techniques, see Van Voorhis & Salisbury, 2016).

Both cognitive techniques (Chavaria, 1997) and behavior modification have proven effective in community interventions with juveniles (Lipsey, 2009; MacKenzie, 2006; MacKenzie & Farrington, 2015). Cognitive approaches address faulty thinking patterns such as "school is useless" or "I'll never amount to anything."

Recently, attention has also been focused on offender–agent interactions in the supervision process. Experts are suggesting that motivational interviewing can be effective in probation. **Motivational interviewing** refers to "a style of communication that makes it more likely that offenders will listen, will be engaged in the process, and will be more ready to make changes" (Walters, Clark, Gingerich, & Meltzer, 2007:10).

Motivational interviewing does not mean that officers are to become therapists. It simply recognizes the important role that officers play. It is unrealistic to think that officers can simply refer youthful probationers on their caseloads to therapists or programs, or that officers can simply say, "You need to go to counselor X or program X." If the juvenile offender is not motivated to change and is not motivated to go to the counselor or the program, he or she most likely will not go and will not change. In summary, motivational interviewing recognizes that officers interact with probationers and that those interactions can be crucial in the change process (Walters et al., 2007:10).

A study in Maryland evaluated an evidence-based supervision model that included features such as motivational interviewing and other cognitive–behavioral strategies. The program reduced arrest recidivism by 42 percent and technical violations by 20 percent but had no impact on positive drug tests (Taxman, 2008). Taxman's conclusion is that this new model of community supervision, which is a shared decision-making model that involves the offender in the process of determining goals and ways to achieve those goals, can be effective in probation and parole (Taxman, 2008).

A program that provided training in evidence-based practices including service-oriented supervision and motivational interviewing to probation case managers in one state reduced recidivism on two of four measures (Young, Farrell, & Taxman, 2013). A study of probation with heavy reliance on evidence-based practices versus residential placement in Connecticut showed lower likelihood of adjudication and conviction but no significant effect on referral to court or arrest (Ryon, Early, Hand, & Chapman, 2013). However, another study of training of probation officers using motivational interviewing found no impact on probationers although the officers became more empathetic. The authors of that study noted that system factors such as lack of time to spend with probationers, scarce resources, and high officer turnover might work against even a positive strategy such as motivational interviewing (Walters, Vader, Nguyen, Harris, & Eells, 2010). These studies offer support for the use of evidence-based practices versus practices not supported by research and versus probation supervision that is so lax that probationers quickly learn that they can ignore the rules (Kleiman, 2011). One factor to note is that if probation officers do not have the training, time, or resources themselves to provide an evidence-based intervention directly, one possibility is that probation personnel provide vouchers to juveniles and/or their families to purchase an intervention directly from a private service provider (see, e.g., Corbett, 2015).

One positive note is that a study of recidivism of first-time violent offenders found that probation worked better than two more restrictive settings, probation camps and group homes. Specifically, the likelihood of recidivism was 2.3 times higher for youths who had been placed in group homes and 1.29 times higher for youths who had been placed in probation camps. The authors concluded that probation is "in fact, a far more sensible and cost-effective approach to interrupting the criminal careers of first-time violent offenders as compared with more restrictive and disruptive setting[s], such as probation camps or group homes" (Ryan, Abrams, & Huang, 2014:15).

CURRENT TRENDS IN COMMUNITY SUPERVISION

Several developments are taking place in community corrections. Many are calling for tougher community corrections with greater attention to punishment and controlling offender risk. Other voices, however, continue to insist that probation and other community interventions need to be more than just strict punishment for crime.

The Balanced Approach

One current approach in juvenile corrections is the **balanced approach**. "This philosophy requires the system to provide balanced attention to the need for competency development, accountability, and community safety and requires efforts to restore, to the greatest extent possible, the victim and community to their precrime status" (Kurlychek, Torbet, & Bozynski, 1999:3). It is thought that restitution and community service send out a message that the offender is responsible for his or her crime and is being held accountable for it. It is considered important that the offender comes to realize the harm he or she has caused the victim(s). As of 2015, 40 states had legislated provisions focusing on the balanced approach. However, only 11 states specified restorative justice-oriented tasks in a state statute (Hsieh et al., 2016).

As you might guess, the balanced approach is actually a combination of traditional rehabilitation, restorative justice, and classical criminology. One example of the balanced approach is Utah's juvenile restitution program, which includes a restitution work fund. Juveniles without jobs or money can perform community service tasks and thereby earn money for their restitution orders. In Boston, Operation Night Light has police and probation officers together on street patrol checking to ensure that probationers are complying with their probation conditions. St. Louis uses deputy juvenile officers and police to make random home visits to check compliance with court-ordered curfews (Urban, St. Cyr, & Decker, 2003). A similar program in Maryland has the probation officers and police targeting selected crime "hot spots" (Kurlychek et al., 1999).

Pennsylvania has attempted to implement the balanced approach. In fact, the state legislature amended the juvenile law purpose clause in 1995 to include balanced and restorative justice principles. More specifically, the Mission Statement for Juvenile Justice in Pennsylvania lists three goals: community protection, victim restoration, and youth redemption. In other words, Pennsylvania seeks to promote public safety, repair of harm inflicted on victims, and rehabilitative change for youths (Blackburn, 2019). A report on outcome measures in 12 Pennsylvania counties for calendar year 2003 provides a snapshot of what the departments have been attempting to do and what they have achieved. Related to the objective of community protection, the counties report that 87 percent of probation cases had no new offenses and 87 percent also had no serious probation violations. Under the objective of accountability, more than 100,000 hours of community service were completed with 92 percent of probationers ordered to perform community service actually completing such orders. Almost one-half million dollars of restitution was paid ($479,587); 47 percent of the amount ordered. Eighty-four percent of the probationers ordered to pay restitution paid it in full. In summary, more than 75 percent of the juveniles on probation were attending school or GED classes or were working at case closing. Almost 80 percent were closed as "successful" and only 3 percent were closed as "unsuccessful" (Griffin & Thomas, 2004). A more recent report indicates that decision making in probation is partly guided by risk and needs assessment—as intended—but that officers are still drawing on both punitive and welfare-oriented concerns beyond what the assessment instruments call for (Miller & Palmer, 2020).

On the other hand, it is necessary to keep a certain caution about glowing outcome reports. A focus on outcome reporting can lead to attempts to make the statistics as positive as possible, even if those statistics hide deficiencies. Officers can be tempted to close cases as "successful" even where there is less than complete or desired success. The perfect evaluation would be a controlled or quasi-experiment in which probation is compared to a control group that gets supervision from a nonofficial agency or perhaps no supervision at all. This is especially important in analyzing juvenile probation because many of the youths are first-time offenders or less serious offenders and a good scare in court might well deter them from future delinquency.

A specific example of the need for caution is the information on community service. The report notes that in Allegheny County alone (Pittsburgh, PA), probationers completed almost 69,000 hours of community service in 2002, the equivalent of more than $350,000 in labor if the youths had been paid the minimum wage for all those hours. (They simply multiply the number of hours worked by the minimum wage to get this estimate of value.) This line of reasoning assumes that all the work the youths did was necessary and not simply "make work" projects. It also fails to mention the costs of setting up the community service and then supervising the youths as they perform the community service.

Punitive Directions in Probation

One concern about the balanced approach is whether it in fact "balances" the concerns for competency development, accountability, and community safety or simply places emphasis on accountability. If the balanced approach is not actually balanced, then it might be considered a punitive direction in probation. This philosophy is quite direct: The offender, even if a juvenile, deserves to be punished.

As mentioned in Chapter 7 on policing, one recent example of tough probation is police–probation partnerships, as in San Bernardino, California, where a police officer and a probation officer together make a home visit to all new juvenile probationers to explain the rules of probation and search the probationer's residence for weapons and drugs. Although the program has had some effect in reducing serious crimes in the city, one concern is mission distortion for probation—that probation officers may no longer see themselves as service providers or social workers but may instead over-identify with a law enforcement role (Worrall & Gaines, 2006). A study that interviewed probation officers working in partnerships in Washington State found that several officers desired to be more law enforcement-oriented (Murphy & Lutze, 2009).

However, a study in Pennsylvania found no evidence of mission distortion or role confusion (Alarid, Sims, & Ruiz, 2011).

Another recent development in this direction is Hawaii's Opportunity Probation with Enforcement (HOPE) Program for adult probationers considered to be at high risk of a probation violation. HOPE is based on a deterrence model, which emphasizes swift and certain sanctions (SAC, for short).

The thinking behind SAC is that historically probation and probation officers have not been swift enough or certain enough in responding to probation violations. When a probationer broke a rule, more often than not, he or she would not be sanctioned immediately or even at all. Rather it would take multiple rule violations or a more serious violation to get a probation officer to respond. The violations would be so numerous or so serious that the response would be revocation of probation and incarceration for years. In SAC, probation officers try to respond immediately if a probationer fails to report or tests positively for drug use. The probationer may have to spend 1–3 nights in jail. Swiftness and certainty of punishment are emphasized over severity.

Evaluations of HOPE-type programs have been mixed and controversial. Rehabilitation advocates Francis Cullen and his colleagues (2016, 2018) argue that a "gold standard" evaluation study has shown that HOPE programs are not effective and that there should be a moratorium on starting new ones. Instead, such programs have spread to 31 states, in part because the founding judge has worked to spread adoption of the program, using personal testimonials of worth instead of scientific proof (see Alm, 2016).

For the most part, SAC probation programs have been focused on adult offenders and often on adult drug offenders. It is not clear that HOPE-type programs are what juvenile probation needs. Do we really want to start putting youths who miss a probation meeting with their officer in jail or detention for one or more nights? Does the immaturity of youthful offenders suggest that probation not focus on deterrence principles but instead try to implement evidence-based interventions that are more developmentally appropriate? A critical question about getting tough/punitive directions is whether such tactics are effective in reducing recidivism. That issue is discussed in the next major section of this chapter. Another interesting question posed by this "get-tough" movement is whether it is appropriate to use supervision fees in probation. For a discussion of this issue, see Box 11.1.

Renewed Emphasis on Status Offenses

An emphasis on status offenses, such as truancy, is making a comeback in some circles. In 2018, an estimated 97,800 status offense cases were petitioned to juvenile court and about 20,000 cases were placed on probation for status offenses. About 2,300 status cases resulted in placement and another 11,600 petitioned status offense cases were given another sanction, such as an order to get counseling, to pay restitution or a fine, or do some sort of community service (Hockenberry & Puzzanchera, 2020). About 54 percent of the cases

BOX 11.1 SUPERVISION FEES: A NEW DIRECTION?

A number of states are now charging juveniles supervisions fees. For example, Georgia may charge an initial fee of $10 to $200, followed by a monthly fee of $2 to $30. Florida and New York can charge $30 a month. Some states grant waivers for financial hardship (Teigen, 2021). Since juveniles are normally in school, fees would have to be set up in relation to parental earnings or be limited to juveniles old enough to work. A problem is that many parents of juvenile probationers and juveniles who work earn minimum wage or a little above minimum wage. This could result in late or no fee payment and possible revocation hearings to deal with such problems.

One suggestion is to use community service as a sanction, since it does not create problems for adult probationers or parents of juvenile probationers who are struggling to earn enough money to pay for necessities. Another problem is that fee payment can easily become a major concern of probation officers, instead of paying attention to help juvenile probationers overcome their problems.

What do you think? Should parents who can afford it be required to pay supervision fees for their children on probation? Should juveniles old enough to work be charged fees? What are possible problems with such fees?

placed on probation involved truancy, about 14 percent ungovernability, about 12 percent a liquor law violation, and about 10 percent runaway behavior.

Restorative Justice

Bazemore and Maloney (1994) argue that restorative justice should be the theme in a new paradigm for criminal justice, juvenile justice in general, and probation in particular. In contrast to retributive justice, which focuses on vengeance, deterrence, and punishment, restorative justice "is concerned with repairing the damage or harm done to victims and the community through a process of negotiation, mediation, victim empowerment, and reparation" (Bazemore & Maloney, 1994:28). In addition to a focus on such repair, restorative justice also emphasizes involving victims, offenders, and community members in the process and rethinking the roles of government and community in trying to achieve justice (Bazemore & Schiff, 2005; see also Bazemore, 2012). As one commentator puts it, "restorative justice is about relationships—how relationships are harmed by crime and how they can be rebuilt to promote recovery and healing for people affected by crime" (Kurki, 2000:266).

As Chapter 12 also discusses restorative justice, we will end the discussion of restorative justice in probation at this point. We simply note that restorative justice programs can be quite positive. For example, an evaluation of the Community Justice Committee's restorative justice program in Maricopa County, Arizona, showed that youths in the program were 0.704 times less likely to have a petition filed against them than youths in the comparison group (Rodriguez, 2007). A program that attempted to combine the concept of graduated sanctions with restorative justice did reduce the victimization, but not the criminal activity, of the juvenile probationers, possibly due to the fact that they could not go out in the evening. The restorative justice element involved such features as ordering the youth to perform community service or writing a letter of apology if he or she violated curfew (Urban, 2008). Another impressive piece of evidence in support of restorative justice is a meta-analysis of 35 restorative justice programs that found them to be more effective than traditional programs in improving victim and offender satisfaction, increasing compliance with restitution, and reducing recidivism (Latimer, Dowden, & Muise, 2005). Finally, the Washington State Institute for Public Policy found that restorative justice programs for low-risk offenders reduced recidivism by 8.7 percent and produced cost savings of $7,000 per youth (Aos, Miller, & Drake, 2006).

Peacemaking

Like restorative justice, peacemaking is a positive philosophy that seeks to go beyond simply criticizing the status quo and beyond a simple focus on recidivism reduction. Peacemaking is a perspective that supports efforts of corrections workers, whether prison counselors or probation officers, to help offenders find greater meaning in their lives. Two proponents, Bo Lozoff and Michael Braswell (1989), contend that all great religions teach four classic virtues: honesty, courage, kindness, and a sense of humor. In this perspective, reductions in recidivism and programs like counseling or vocational training are still important, but they are more external. The deeper goal is internal personal change:

> The primary goal is to help build a happier, peaceful person right there in the prison [if working with prisoners], a person whose newfound self-honesty and courage can steer him or her to adjust to the biases and shortcomings of a society which does not feel comfortable with ex-offenders. (Lozoff & Braswell, 1989:2)

In a peacemaking perspective, both personal transformation and institutional change are critical but personal change is seen as the basis of social change. It is critical to begin with yourself. It is also a lifetime task that needs constant work (Braswell, Fuller, & Lozoff, 2001).

Community/Restorative Justice

Clear (2020) agrees with others that officers should have the responsibility to focus on change instead of compliance or control. He calls for a "community/restorative justice" model and asserts that the rationale of community corrections is not public safety for the community. Rather community corrections "should help improve the human potential of the person under supervision" (Clear, 2020:191). To do this, officers should focus on the strengths and human potential of probationers. Finally, probation should not focus only on probationers but also needs to focus on improving communities so that they are "healthy places for people to live, work, and raise families" (Clear, 2020:191).

Elliott Currie (2020) takes Clear's call to improve communities one step further. Currie argues that the violent crime problem is rooted in disadvantaged and segregated neighborhoods and the solution is to devote massive resources to improve such neighborhoods and create good paying jobs for youths, especially black youths (see Chapter 14 for a more complete discussion of Elliott's ideas.)

Reforming Probation

Several authors have noted current problems in probation and suggested ways to address these problems. Although these authors were addressing adult probation, some of what they say has direct implications for juvenile probation.

One problem is that many probationers are not succeeding on probation. In fact, they are failing and having their probation revoked. Probation revocations account for about 30 percent of admissions to prison. As such, probation revocations are part of the reason for the problem of extensive prison expansion—that is, the mass imprisonment problem. Similarly, on a typical day, about 5,000 youths are in out-of-home placement due to a technical violation of probation (W. Haywood Burns Institute, 2016).

One reason for probation failure is setting unrealistic conditions. One author gives the example of expecting a probationer to attend school full-time when that probationer clearly has limitations such as a history of school failure, a learning disability, or lack of family support. Klingele (2013) suggests that a short term of confinement would be a more fitting sanction. A related issue is setting up so many conditions for a probationer that the sheer number of conditions makes it possible that the probationer will slip one or more times and thus qualify for revocation. Solutions would be to minimize the number of conditions and to impose only those conditions that the probationer can realistically fulfill (W. Haywood Burns Institute, 2016).

Another reason for probation failure is that in at least some places probation has turned into a revenue generator rather than community supervision with the ability and intent to assist probationers with their needs. Numerous jurisdictions have turned probation officers into collectors of fees and fines in order to pay for court expenses or to beef up the general revenue of the city or county. One ironic result is placing indigent people on probation and then violating them for failure to pay fees and fines and placing them in jail, when jail costs far exceed what these indigent probationers could ever pay. (See again, Box 11.1.)

Corbett (2015) argues that still another reason for probation failure is the growth of poverty, including child poverty. He notes that one state reported that almost half (48 percent) of its probationers were unemployed at the time of arrest and 55 percent reported having financial problems. Corbett cites a study showing that one neighborhood in Philadelphia was a place where many of the youths could not find jobs and turned to drug dealing to survive economically. The suggested remedy is to recognize poverty as a significant problem for many probationers and to improve the job chances of probationers.

Both Klingele (2013) and Corbett (2015) suggest that regular probation is not providing the services (e.g., education, counseling, job training, job placement) that probationers need. They suggest that probation supervision be eliminated or cut back, and in its place, probationers be given vouchers to purchase the services they need. In terms of juvenile probation, this would mean that families would be given vouchers to purchase appropriate educational or counseling services for youths placed on probation. According to this thinking, juvenile probation departments need to shift gears from focusing on compliance to a focus on helping and supporting youths on probation (W. Haywood Burns Institute, 2016).

A related development is that a number of jurisdictions are reducing the time a youth serves on probation. Arizona cuts 20 days off a youth's probation sentence for every 30 days with no new crime or no probation violation. South Carolina cuts 10 days. Washington, DC now has a one-year maximum term for juvenile probation (Muhammad, 2019).

Mendel's Reform Proposals

Mendel (2018) offers several noteworthy suggestions. First, probation should be limited to youths who have committed a serious offense or are otherwise a risk to public safety. Diversion would be available for lesser offenses, and sometimes diversion would only involve a warning or an apology letter. Since fewer youths will be on probation, there can be smaller caseloads, perhaps eight to 12 juveniles per officer. This way officers can "[p]artner with families and communities to promote personal growth, positive behavior change and long-term success (as opposed to surveillance and compliance), as a means to protect public safety—and do so in ways that promote racial and ethnic equity" (Mendel, 2018:19). Instead of a long list of standard conditions for all offenders, officers should develop individualized treatment plans for each youth that utilize effective intervention programs, ones that improve critical thinking skills, address factors that cause delinquent conduct, hold youths accountable, and promote victim empathy and reparation. Another suggestion is to use positive incentives to encourage prosocial behavior such as paid jobs and internships, popular recreational activities, and reducing behavior restrictions and the duration of the probation order. Violations of probation should be a last resort used only after a set of calibrated responses to misbehavior have been exhausted. Schwartz (2018) presents almost the same set of changes for probation, including a call for probation officers to offer supervision that is as "parent-like as possible" (p. 51).

Mendel's suggestions to use effective interventions, hold youth accountable, and include victim mediation and restorative justice programs align with many others' suggestions for probation, such as the reform underway in Pennsylvania (Blackburn, 2019). His calls to dramatically reduce the use of probation and limit it to serious offenders at high risk of reoffending, to divert a high proportion of offenders, and to drastically reduce the number of youths facing violation of probation are more controversial. It is possible that these latter suggestions would face the objection that they would result in not holding many youths accountable for their delinquent acts and possibly endangering public safety. A positive note is that Lucas County (Ohio) Probation has diverted all misdemeanor youth from probation by establishing a Misdemeanor Services Unit (MSU) for both misdemeanants and low-risk youth charged with a first-time nonviolent felony (Esthappan, Lacoe, & Young, 2019). Another strategy—Remote Justice—aims to reduce the burden on probation officers and increase the time they can devote to youths who need services, see Box 11.2.

BOX 11.2 REMOTE JUSTICE

A number of adult probation departments are using kiosk reporting or remote justice, that is, web-based reporting for low-risk probationers so that officers can devote more time and assistance to higher-risk clients. Kiosk reporting means that the offender comes to the office and reports on a screen at the probation office. Remote justice allows an offender to use a home computer to report. Probationers update their status—home, work, and/or school, add anything they think relevant, and can ask questions. Officers can message probationers whenever they think it is necessary. In North Carolina, remote reporting has reduced violations of probation considerably (Saunders, Midgette, Taylor, & Faraji, 2021).

Do you think remote justice would be appropriate for juveniles? Or do youths need face-to-face meetings with a probation officer?

The positive news is that many politicians, both liberal and conservative, are recognizing the costs of incarceration of adults and institutional placement of juveniles. Thus "smart on crime" and "smart on juvenile justice" advocates question the fiscal wisdom of sending too many offenders, adult or juvenile, to a prison or a youth placement. As a result, a number of states have taken measures, for example, to limit the number of probationers that can be revoked and sent to prison. (See Chapter 14 for further discussion.)

It is difficult to predict where community corrections will go from here. One possible path is to continue down the "get tough" road. A grim reality is that further financial cutbacks will force probation to do less and less. In adult probation, financial pressures have led to dramatic increases in the use of both fees and fines to cover the costs of probation supervision. One study indicated that fees were being imposed in two-thirds of juvenile probation cases in one state (Haynes, Cares, & Ruback, 2014). Based on this development in Pennsylvania, it is possible that more and more jurisdictions pressed for revenue might consider assessing supervision fees that juveniles and parents of juveniles on probation would be forced to pay. (For more on probation fees, refer back to Box 11.1.)

Another path is to attempt to return probation to a more traditional focus on trying to rehabilitate offenders. Other departments may seek to implement the balanced approach, restorative justice, or community justice (or some combination of such programs). An important issue in deciding on which direction to take is the effectiveness of community corrections. The next two sections will discuss some important findings from the effectiveness literature. The first section will review major findings on the effectiveness of community sanctions such as probation. The second section will review the research on effective treatments. Together these findings give some assistance in thinking about the most appropriate direction for community corrections to take.

EFFECTIVENESS OF JUVENILE PROBATION AND RELATED SANCTIONS

Although national recidivism statistics on juvenile probationers are not readily available and although the research on juvenile probation has not been as extensive as the research on adult probation, there are considerable research findings available to illuminate the effectiveness issue for juvenile probation. Based on research on both juveniles and adults, several conclusions about the effectiveness of community correctional interventions for juveniles seem sound.

One implication of the research is that simply making probation tougher does not work (MacKenzie, 2006; MacKenzie & Farrington, 2015). The cumulative research on such "get-tough" measures as Scared Straight programs, boot camps, and intensive supervision has demonstrated that harsher measures, without any treatment elements, do not reduce recidivism. Experimental evaluations of such programs have shown that these tough measures do not reduce recidivism (new arrests or convictions) (Cullen, 2007; MacKenzie, 2006; MacKenzie & Farrington, 2015).

Related to this is the finding that often community supervision may be no worse than incarceration—that is, at least as effective as incarceration (see Krisberg & Howell, 1998). In fact, Lipsey and Wilson (1998) found that among programs that produced consistent evidence of positive effects for serious offenders, non-institutional programs showed greater reductions in recidivism than institutional programs. This is important. Although offenders released to community supervision commit some new crimes, the fact that they do no worse (and may do better) than offenders sentenced to training schools and then released on traditional aftercare suggests that society can use community supervision knowing that it is not more harmful than incarceration.

Still another lesson is that intensive supervision can lead to easier detection of technical violations (Petersilia, 1997). In other words, officers are more likely to detect intensive supervision offenders violating the rules of probation such as not reporting to the probation officer, leaving the jurisdiction without permission, breaking curfew, testing positive on a urine drug test, and skipping school. This explains why intensive supervision can be ineffective if the goal is to reduce prison or training school populations. Detection of technical violations often results in revocation of probation. Then the offender is incarcerated as punishment for breaking the conditions of probation. So a sanction (such as intensive supervision) intended to reduce the number of persons being institutionalized can in fact increase the number being institutionalized. This problem can be avoided, however, if a court and correctional agency put in place a system of graduated penalties for technical violations (Altschuler, 1998). A discouraging finding is that some studies have shown that simply being on probation supervision without any officer contacts sometimes is just as effective as being on probation and being seen by an officer (National Council on Crime and Delinquency, 1987). This finding questions whether probation officers have much impact on their clients. One explanation is that perhaps officers are not doing much for their clients. Support for this explanation comes from a study that found that 40 percent of the officers surveyed were *not* engaging in best practices—either control or treatment-oriented practices—but were doing the bare minimum (Viglione, Rudes, Nightingale, Watson, & Taxman, 2018). Another explanation is that some offenders are at low risk of recidivism

(Latessa et al., 2020) and do not need much supervision. Perhaps being caught and being placed on probation sent a clear message to these probationers and they have learned their lesson and will not reoffend.

An encouraging finding in recent research is that intensive supervision that includes treatment components can reduce recidivism by an average of more than 20 percent, but that surveillance-only programs have no impact on recidivism (Aos et al., 2006; Petersilia, 1997). This suggests that although being tough is not enough, addressing offender needs can make a difference. Recall also that a national evaluation of intensive juvenile aftercare did not show effectiveness but that in one of the study sites treatment was associated with less recidivism (Wiebush et al., 2005 [see discussion earlier in this chapter]). Contrary to this claim, one study of aftercare with treatment did not show any effectiveness. The study, however, involved a sample of all substance-abusing offenders (Sealock, Gottfredson, & Gallagher, 1997). Because research indicates that treatment is critical, the next section will review the treatment research to show which types of treatment appear to offer promise and which seem to be ineffective.

EFFECTIVE AND INEFFECTIVE TREATMENT INTERVENTIONS WITH OFFENDERS

Although many politicians and citizens favor "get-tough" approaches to crime and delinquency, there is considerable consensus that correctional interventions are effective and cost-effective. Lipsey (1999, 2009) has done extensive meta-analysis research on effective programming for juvenile offenders. Recall that meta-analysis is a research technique that studies the overall effects of interventions based on grouping together individual studies. If five studies have looked at the impact of individual counseling programs, for example, meta-analysis would convert the individual findings of each study into an overall effect size for all the studies combined. Using this technique, Lipsey has reported that, on average, counseling, skill building, and restorative interventions reduce recidivism by at least 10 percent. Specific interventions reduce recidivism by more than 20 percent. For example, cognitive–behavioral skill-building programs reduce recidivism by 26 percent and mentoring programs reduce recidivism by 21 percent (Lipsey, 2009). Similarly, an evaluation of an adult probation program called "Citizenship," which incorporated the principles of effective interventions, found that it reduced recidivism by 31 percent (Pearson, McDougall, Kanaan, Bowles, & Torgerson, 2011). (For details on the recidivism reductions of various interventions for noninstitutionalized offenders, see Table 11.2. For a summary of the research findings on successful intervention principles, see Box 11.3. This is only a brief summary of the effectiveness literature, but it gives an outline of effective intervention principles.)

Greenwood and Turner (2012) argue that the most successful programs focus on family interactions, since parents are the ones supervising and training juveniles. They specifically mention Functional Family Therapy (FFT) and

TABLE 11.2 Effective Types of Intervention and Estimated Effects on Recidivism

Intervention Philosophy (N)	Recidivism Reduction (%)	Treatment/Control Recidivism Contrast*
Counseling programs	13	0.43/0.50
Individual counseling (12)	5	0.48/0.50
Family counseling (29)	13	0.44/0.50
Mentoring (17)	21	0.39/0.50
Group counseling (24)	22	0.39/0.50
Skill building programs	12	0.44/0.50
Social skills (18)	13	0.43/0.50
Behavioral (30)	22	0.39/0.50
Cognitive–behavioral (30)	26	0.37/0.50

Note: Numbers in parentheses represent number of studies in that category. * For example, counseling programs produced an average recidivism rate of 43% versus 50% for the control groups; a reduction of 13% (after rounding).

Source: Lipsey (2009).

BOX 11.3 SUMMARY OF RESEARCH FINDINGS ABOUT SUCCESSFUL CORRECTIONAL INTERVENTIONS

Research indicates that correctional interventions should:

1. Concentrate on changing negative behaviors by requiring juveniles to recognize and understand thought processes that rationalize negative behaviors.

2. Promote healthy bonds with, and respect for, prosocial members within the juvenile's family, peers, school, and community network.

3. Have a comprehensible and predictable path for client progression and movement. Each program level should be directed toward and directly related to the next step.

4. Have consistent, clear, and graduated consequences for misbehavior and recognition for positive behavior.

5. Recognize that a reasonable degree of attrition must be expected with a delinquent population.

6. Provide an assortment of highly structured programming activities, including education and/or hands-on vocational training and skill development.

7. Facilitate discussions that promote family problem-solving.

8. Integrate delinquent and at-risk youths into generally prosocial groups to prevent the development of delinquent peer groups.

To update these principles, in her analysis of effective treatment interventions, Doris MacKenzie (2006) emphasizes that punishment and deterrence interventions are not effective. Individual change is critical, especially the offender's cognitive reasoning, antisocial attitudes, and attitudes toward drug use and vocational skills. Most importantly, "[t]here is sufficient evidence to reject the 'nothing works' mantra. Correctional programs do reduce recidivism. Specifically, effective programs provide human service treatment and focus on changing the individual."

Sources: Kurlychek et al. (1999); MacKenzie (2006:334–346).

Multisystemic Therapy (MST), both of which address effective parenting skills. Another recommended intervention is Aggression Replacement Therapy (ART), a form of cognitive–behavioral therapy that teaches anger control and moral reasoning skills. All three have produced both recidivism reductions and cost savings. For example, it is estimated that FFT for youths on probation can produce a net benefit of more than $27,000 per youth (Washington State Institute for Public Policy, 2017). (For a detailed list of both effective and ineffective interventions, see Greenwood & Turner, 2012.)

Gendreau and his colleagues have spearheaded much of the treatment research (Gendreau, Smith, & French, 2017). They have concluded that there are several principles of effective interventions. First, interventions need to be intensive and behavioral. Intensive means that the intervention takes up at least 40 percent of the offender's time and goes on for three to nine months. Behavioral interventions are based on the principles of operant conditioning, especially reinforcement. Simply, there must be rewards for desirable behaviors. Some examples are token economies, modeling, and cognitive–behavioral interventions such as problem-solving, reasoning, self-control, and self-instructional training. Successful programs target criminogenic needs such as antisocial attitudes, peer associations, substance-abuse problems, and self-control issues rather than noncriminogenic needs such as low self-esteem, anxiety, or depression. The responsivity principle means that attention needs to be paid to matching offenders, therapists, and programs. For example, offenders who prefer structure do better in a more structured program such as a token economy. More anxious offenders do better with therapists who show more interpersonal sensitivity. Programs need to enforce their rules in a firm but fair manner, and positive reinforcers should outnumber punishers by a ratio of at least four to one. Therapists need to be sensitive and adequately trained and supervised. Relapse prevention and advocacy and brokerage with other community agencies are also necessary (Gendreau, 1996; see also Andrews, 2006). (For a comprehensive discussion of effective vs. ineffective interventions, see Latessa et al., 2020.)

An additional principle is attention to risk; intensive programs should target high- or medium-risk youths rather than low-risk youths and should not mix high- and low-risk offenders (Andrews, 2006). Appropriate risk screening and use of intermediate sanctions for medium- and high-risk offenders with less serious offenses can divert offenders from prison (D'Amato, Silver, Newsome, & Latessa, 2021). An encouraging note, however, is that there are effective interventions for low-risk youths. For example, a program in Michigan targeted shoplifters. Although not a serious, violent crime, shoplifting accounts for about one-quarter of all property offense petitions in juvenile court. A diversion program using probation officers incorporated such restorative justice components as community service, restitution to charities, and victim apology letters, as well as other elements. The study used random assignment and a two-year follow-up period. Ten percent of the treatment group youths had new petitions filed versus 25 percent of the control group (Kelley, Kennedy, & Homant, 2003).

One caution about the risk principle is that some have alleged that the instruments used to assess risk can in some instances be racially biased. Larson, Mattu, Kirchner, and Anglin (2016) at ProPublica claim that in the data they analyzed, black defendants were more likely to be considered at higher risk of recidivism than white defendants. The Council of State Governments (2016) admits the possibility of mistaken assessments according to race, but argues that proper validation procedures and attention not to weight variables such as education, employment, and family resources too heavily, because they correlate with race and class, can minimize errors.

As noted earlier, Lipsey (2009) finds that mentoring programs can reduce recidivism by as much as 21 percent (see Table 11.2). It bears emphasizing that mentoring programs will not be extremely expensive because they rely on volunteers. On the other hand, it is critical that a successful mentoring program includes such factors as establishing goals for the relationship and providing training, supervision, and support for the mentors (Rhodes, 2008). So either a probation department or a community agency will need to provide proper oversight. Moreover, additional research on mentoring is needed to clarify which aspects of mentoring make it effective (Tolan, Henry, Schoeny, & Bass, 2008).

One balancing observation is that although the research shows that interventions that use evidence-based principles and practices are effective, there is no panacea or cure-all for delinquency. For example, as Table 11.2 shows, even a 22 percent reduction in recidivism means that 39 percent of the offenders who received the effective intervention recidivated compared to a higher base of 50 percent for the control group (50 – 39 = 11; 11 × 2 = 22 percent reduction). While there is reason for optimism, proponents of correctional interventions have to remind both politicians and the public that it is erroneous to think that even effective interventions will wipe out all delinquency. The warning of Finckenauer (1982) against expecting a panacea or cure-all for crime or delinquency is as true today as it was when he first noted the "panacea phenomenon."

A variation on the call for evidence-based rehabilitation is the Good Lives Model which emphasizes such basics as helping offenders overcome drug abuse but goes further. The "further" step is to contend that offenders seek more in life than simply to avoid criminal activity. Like all of us, offenders also seek a sense of purpose in their lives via meaningful work and fulfilling relationships (Ward, 2010). Probation based on the Good Lives Model might mean that probation officers would have to discuss what youths on probation are seeking in life, what values they embrace, and what they hope to accomplish in terms of career and relationships. (For further discussion of helping youths find purpose and meaning in their lives, see Chapter 14.)

In summary, there are effective interventions that can reduce recidivism. Second, effective interventions are also cost-effective; they save money. Third, many "get-tough" or deterrent approaches are not effective. Fourth, effective interventions can reduce recidivism, but they are not cure-alls or panaceas; they do not wipe out or prevent delinquency completely.

Additional Factors Related to Effectiveness

The effectiveness research is critical. It is imperative to know what works and what does not work. It is also important, however, to recall some additional factors about successful intervention with offenders.

One point to note is that often programs are simply not available for offenders. An assessment of the gap between needs and services provided in Texas found that only 57 percent of those juveniles with high mental health needs received any mental health services. Only one-third of those youths with high needs for substance-abuse services received substance-abuse treatment (Kelly, Macy, & Mears, 2005). A study of more than 1,300 serious youthful offenders found that many did not receive services while in placement, and only 35 percent reported receiving services during the first six months after release (Schubert & Mulvey, 2014). Although research indicates that resolving criminogenic needs such as substance-abuse problems is critical in changing offenders and reducing recidivism, the programs to change such offenders are not always readily available. Part of the problem is that the public and politicians are reluctant to increase government spending, even for worthy projects.

A second factor that probation officers need to consider is that youths on probation may have more serious or more prevalent problems than official records indicate. In a study of juvenile probationers in Southern Illinois, official records indicated that only 20 percent of the youths were truant and only 6 percent were involved in drug usage, whereas almost one-half of the youths themselves admitted to truancy and 43 percent admitted to drug usage (Cashel, 2003). This reflects the strong possibility that juvenile probationers have problems that are more extensive than officers know.

Another factor to consider is that interventions that would appear to offer benefits for offenders do not always do so. For example, many people assume that part-time employment for teens reduces their chances of committing delinquent acts. These people assume that having a job teaches important life lessons in responsibility. Some research, however, shows that employment is not always beneficial. Wright and his colleagues found that the "number of hours employed had an indirect effect in increasing delinquency across the sample" (Wright, Cullen, & Williams, 1997:215; see also, Staff, Osgood, Schulenberg, Bachman, & Messersmith, 2010). In fact, much of the delinquency of working teens is occupationally related (Wright & Cullen, 2000). It may not always be productive for probation officers to help teenage probationers get part-time jobs. Instead, it may be productive to provide teens with "modest" cash incentives to graduate. In one study such incentives prevented approximately the same amount of crime as a three-strikes law at one-tenth the cost (Wright et al., 1997).

This issue is complex, however. Several programs for older adolescents that included an emphasis on employment or advanced skills training had very positive effects. Thus, Krisberg, Currie, Onek, and Wiebush (1995) argue that such programs are effective for older teens.

Many also thought that alternative education programs that have distinct school schedules intended for students not doing well in traditional classrooms would be beneficial for delinquents. One meta-analysis of alternative schools found that they could have positive effects on school performance and attitude, but they did not reduce delinquent behavior (Cox, Davidson, & Bynum, 1995).

Recent budgetary problems may affect probation. As jurisdictions struggle with the effects of a struggling economy on budgets, many are reconsidering how many offenders they are sending to prisons and juvenile correctional centers. One possibility is that cost concerns may influence legislators and system officials to try to utilize more cost-effective interventions. As noted above, the state of Washington has been a leader in this direction and its policy research office has studied the costs and benefits of various interventions (Aos & Drake, 2013; Washington State Institute for Public Policy, 2016).

Goddard and Myers (2017) also call for addressing such issues as housing, education, and employment. They argue that the literature on risk assessment and evidence-based practices is misguided in the sense that it does not address the structural causes of delinquency and racial injustice. They contend that criminologists who emphasize evidence-based practices are reducing delinquency to an individual-level problem when society needs to address the root causes of crime such as poverty, unemployment, and discrimination, including racial disparities in policing and the courts. Without attention to structural problems, a focus on risk assessments and evidence-based programs can turn into efforts that only "'help' young people better tolerate unconscionable social conditions" (Goddard & Myers, 2017). (For a related section on reform via structural change, see the section on Elliott Currie in Chapter 14.)

CONTINUING CONCERNS IN COMMUNITY CORRECTIONS

As juvenile court and probation enter into their second century of formal existence since the historic founding of the Illinois juvenile court in 1899, several concerns continue. This section will discuss the concerns of goal confusion, restitution, and community service.

Goal Confusion

Goal confusion, also known as "mission distortion" (Worrall & Gaines, 2006), means that judges, probation and aftercare officers, probation directors, state legislators, and juvenile justice experts disagree about the purposes and objectives of juvenile court and community supervision. Part of the reason for such goal confusion is that we have conflicting images of juvenile offenders. At times we see them as "kids gone wrong"—as victims who are not completely evil. At other times we see them as "hostile predators" and "full-fledged" criminals (Morse, 1999). These conflicting images influence how we treat juveniles. Thus, what was once a rather clear institution for supplementing parental concern by means of adult advice and psychological/social work skill has become a matter of controversy. Some courts, officers, and experts still advocate a *parens patriae* and rehabilitation philosophy. In Glaser's (1964) terminology, the emphasis is on assistance to the probationer rather than on controlling the offender. As noted above, however, developments such as punitive probation, including police–probation partnerships, see the juvenile as a criminal to be patrolled and arrested rather than as a youth in need of assistance. They indicate that many no longer adhere to a pure assistance model. Moreover, advocates of restorative justice argue that it is time to go beyond the stale debates of the past, and place new attention on the concerns of the victim. Proponents of the balanced approach would second that suggestion and add that community safety should also be a prime concern. Parenthetically, a recent study of officers' attitudes found that juvenile probation officers were favoring treatment over punishment and welfare over just deserts. Thus, these officers were resisting the adultification of juvenile court and were continuing to "adhere to many of the beliefs of the original juvenile court" (Bolin & Applegate, 2016:332).

A trend that may reduce goal confusion is increasing emphasis on the use of evidence-based practices to achieve measurable outcomes. Probation, like other government agencies, is beginning to focus on practices that research evidence demonstrates are successful in achieving measurable outcomes such as reductions in drug usage and recidivism and increases in positive outcomes such as payment of restitution and fines and higher employment rates. The federal probation system has turned to such an outcome-based focus (Alexander & Vanbenschoten, 2008) and it is likely that many local and state probation agencies will do so in the near future. In fact, a number of states now mandate that juvenile correctional services use evidence-based practices (e.g., Tennessee).

Restitution

Restitution occurs when juvenile offenders pay for all or part of the damage inflicted on crime victims or property. Restitution can take the form of either the payment of money or the performance of work (chores) for the victim. Restitution may be part of victim–offender reconciliation in which the offender and victim meet to express their concerns and feelings. In some cases, probation officers or restitution officers help juveniles find jobs so they can afford to make restitution payments.

The costs of victimization show the importance of restitution to victims. For 2019, the FBI reported that the average dollar value loss per robbery was $1,797, per burglary was $2,661, and per larceny-theft (e.g., shoplifting) was $1,162. Thefts from motor vehicles made up 27 percent of all larceny thefts (FBI, 2020); see also, Lugo & Przybylski, 2018).

Although restitution has many positive features, especially concern for the victim, there are some problems. Some critics think that it is unfair to law-abiding juveniles to help law-breaking youths find jobs. From this viewpoint, job assistance seems like a reward for delinquency. Second, the claims made about the amounts of money paid back to victims are often exaggerated.

WEB ACTIVITY

For further details on the latest crime trends and costs (as well as additional reports), go to the FBI's Uniform Crime Reports, available at https://ucr.fbi.gov.

Victims may be told that all of their losses will be recouped but actual restitution often falls short. Third, restitution advocates often neglect to consider all of the costs involved in administering a restitution program such as the salaries of those who oversee the program.

On the other hand, there have been positive findings. A study in California found that approximately 15 percent of youths in an intensive program and control group youths completed their court-ordered restitution. For the intensive program juveniles, the mean restitution paid was $55 while the mean restitution ordered was $777; for the control group, the mean paid was $42 out of an average order of $321 (Lane et al., 2005). A review of a juvenile restitution program in Vermont showed that only about one-third of the youths were ordered to pay restitution, and enforcement of all conditions (not just restitution) was a problem (Karp, Bazemore, & Chesire, 2004). As noted above, almost one-half million dollars of restitution was paid ($479,587) in 12 counties in Pennsylvania in 2003, 47 percent of the amount ordered (Griffin & Thomas, 2004). More positively, in 2006, in Reading, Pennsylvania, almost all the restitution ordered for juvenile probationers ($204,720 or 94 percent of the $217,787 ordered) was paid (*Reading Eagle*, 2008). In addition, a meta-analysis of 35 restorative justice programs found them to be more effective in improving victim and offender satisfaction, increasing compliance with restitution, and reducing recidivism than traditional programs (Latimer et al., 2005).

A recent study of restitution in Pennsylvania found that restitution was being ordered in only 33 percent of restitution-eligible cases. On the other hand, fees such as court costs were imposed in 66 percent of cases, and the average fee was $538 (Haynes et al., 2014). The authors concluded that accountability to communities (imposing fees) was being emphasized over accountability to victims (failure to order restitution). Another finding was that some juveniles have been unable to pay restitution because they could not find jobs or because of family circumstances. As many as 40 percent of young offenders come from areas of low—if not the lowest—economic status (Walsh, 2014). One suggestion is to require community service but pay a stipend for it and then the juveniles would pay back victims out of that stipend (Haynes et al., 2014).

A more recent evaluation of restitution in Pennsylvania found that on average youthful probationers were only paying about half of the restitution ordered and youths ordered to pay restitution had a significantly higher likelihood of recidivism. Further, race was a factor as almost 30 percent of non-whites still owed fines, fees, or restitution at case closing compared to about 16 percent of white youths. This racial factor led the authors to question the appropriateness of restitution and financial penalties (fines and fees) (Piquero & Jennings, 2017).

Community Service

Community service is similar to restitution. It means that offenders perform unpaid work for government or private agencies as payment for crimes without personal victims (e.g., vandalism of public property). Community service could include cutting grass at local parks, doing volunteer work in hospitals, or painting the clubhouse of a Boys Club.

Advocates argue that community service helps delinquents realize the extent of the damage they have done and feel they have paid their debt to society. Proponents also argue that cost benefits result from the "free" labor of the youths. Critics argue that extensive use of community service could take away jobs from law-abiding citizens and that the actual cost benefits of community service are not as impressive as claimed. More specifically, critics contend that the work done is not always necessary (e.g., the clubhouse did not really need a new coat of paint) and that many of the hours of community service labor included such nonproductive activities as learning the job, work breaks, and dawdling if an adult supervisor is not in constant watch over the work. These criticisms do not mean that restitution or community service is worthless, but that claims about their worth should be realistic rather than exaggerated.

As noted in the earlier discussion of restorative justice, an important question is whether the community service is simply busy work or has some relationship to the delinquent's offense. If a delinquent can see the connection between his or her community service order and the harm he or she has done, or can see that the community service is a meaningful contribution to the community, he or she is then more likely to see the importance of such service. The offender is then more likely to learn something positive from the community service assignment rather than merely see it as a boring burden to finish as quickly as possible. Community service needs to be taken seriously by both the juvenile justice system and the juvenile so that it is a teaching tool and not just something to keep a youth busy for a few hours a week. One juvenile court in Washington State was able to avoid any appearance of just forcing youths to do busy work by putting youths to work in various community projects that included the youths working side by side with volunteers doing the same work (Wood, 2012).

Teenagers from the Cabell County Youth Reporting Center with the West Virginia Division of Juvenile Services participate in a community service gardening project called The Produce Peddlers, in which they grow vegetables in vacant city lots and deliver fresh vegetables to people in the community.

CREDIT: Toril Lavender/For *The Herald-Dispatch* via AP

SUMMARY

Probation is under scrutiny. One author has gone so far as to state that in the 1990s, probation faced a "crisis of legitimacy" (Corbett, 2002:175). By this, Corbett meant that in light of the alarming statistics on juvenile violence at that time, many were questioning whether probation could do anything to stem the tide. Like all government programs, probation is under pressure to show results. Two well-researched studies, one on intensive probation and one on aftercare, showed no differences in recidivism despite hopes that increased services in both programs would produce such differences. On the other hand, the research on Pennsylvania probation demonstrates that probation agencies can show that they are producing outcomes such as hours of community service, restitution dollars, and probationers who are engaged in meaningful activities such as education. More importantly, research on effective interventions (e.g., Greenwood & Turner, 2012; Lipsey, 2009; MacKenzie & Farrington, 2015) and on cost–benefit analyses of effective interventions (Washington State Institute for Public Policy, 2016) shows that probation programs and other programs that incorporate evidence-based principles and practices can both reduce recidivism and save money.

Mendel (2018) joins the chorus endorsing the use of evidence-based interventions but he also calls for drastically **reduced use of probation**, limiting it to serious or chronic offenders. Most youths would get diversion. He also calls for utilizing positive incentives such as paid jobs and internships, recreational activities, and shorter time periods on probation.

As noted above and also in Chapter 12, restorative justice programs have many positive features, such as paying attention to crime victims and involving the community in the justice process. Tough programs such as Boston's Operation Night Light and San Bernardino's Operation Nightlight offer statistics on homicide reduction and other street crimes that are at least compelling in a public relations sort of way, even if not scientifically compelling.

The future of probation will probably include increased reliance on the use of evidence-based practices and greater attention to cost-effectiveness. Constant concerns about state budgets would seem to indicate such a direction. (See Box 11.4 for a contemporary vision statement for probation.) One way to save money is to turn to web-based reporting. Although Clear (2011) has called for reducing spending on prisons so as to reinvest in communities, it is questionable that legislators will follow his advice. As we note in Chapter 14, there is "pervasive public antipathy" to helping the poor, disadvantaged, disproportionately minority youths who are often the clients of the juvenile justice system (Feld, 1999). A safer prediction is that legislators will be more willing to turn to evidence-based, cost-effective practices than to reinvest huge sums of money in low-income communities that do not receive the attention that they deserve. Although deterrence-based probation (e.g., **Project HOPE**) has been instituted in adult probation, it seems that this model is not well-suited for juveniles. It is hoped that juvenile probation will not turn to supervision fees and treatment fees to the extent that some adult probation departments have in order to raise

---

BOX 11.4 A CONTEMPORARY VISION STATEMENT FOR JUVENILE PROBATION

We envision the role of juvenile probation as that of a catalyst for developing safe communities and healthy youth and families. We believe we can fulfill this role by:

- Holding offenders accountable;

- Building and maintaining community-based partnerships;

- Implementing result-based and outcome-driven services and practices;

- Advocating for and addressing the needs of victims, offenders, families, and communities;

- Obtaining and sustaining sufficient resources; and

- Promoting growth and development of all juvenile probation professionals.

Source: Griffin and Torbet (2002).

---

revenues (see Human Rights Watch, 2014b). Adopting such fees in juvenile probation to the same extent would be devastating for many disadvantaged families. A more positive direction would be to do what at least some officers are currently doing; namely, trying to implement a positive approach that includes caring officers, the use of evidence-based approaches, and the encouragement of offender and parental participation (Schwalbe, 2012).

DISCUSSION QUESTIONS

1. Some call for harsh punishment for juvenile offenders, especially violent juvenile offenders. Do you think that community corrections can supervise such offenders and protect the public? Will the public support community corrections for violent juvenile offenders?

2. Would you consider a career in juvenile corrections, either training schools or community corrections?

3. What measures should community corrections take to best serve juveniles? Give specific suggestions. Is there any indication that new measures can also be cost-effective?

4. Should community corrections for juveniles go back to its roots and try to emphasize rehabilitation, or should it attempt to incorporate more punitive dimensions? Do advocates of restorative justice or the balanced approach have the answer to the question of how we can make juvenile probation better? Does the swift and certain deterrence model of HOPE offer any practical suggestions for juvenile probation? What would the ideal probation program for juveniles look like?

5. Probation is placing increasingly more emphasis on outcomes and outcomes assessment and research on effective interventions. What are the positive implications of this emphasis? Are there any possible problems with greater attention to outcomes, outcomes assessment, and effectiveness?

6. How important are considerations such as costs? Adult probation has moved to the use of fees and fines to pay for at least part of the cost of community corrections. Should juvenile probation departments start charging parents for the costs of supervising juveniles on probation? Or should probation make more use of web-based reporting to save money? Mendel (2018) suggests that probation offer jobs and paid internships to youths on probation. How can funds be generated to pay for these suggestions?

7. Where do you envision juvenile community corrections in 10 years? What will juvenile probation and aftercare look like a decade from now?

CHAPTER 12

Prevention in Juvenile Justice

WHAT YOU NEED TO KNOW

- Prevention programs need to target key risk factors for delinquency and criminality.

- Among the categories of risk factors are family factors, peer relationships, school factors, psychological/personality influences, and biological factors.

- Parent training programs have been shown to have significant impact on families and children. These programs address factors from prenatal nutrition to training teachers on classroom management and discipline.

- Schools play a crucial role in prevention by preparing youths for later education, working with families, and giving youths tools for resisting peer pressure and deviance.

- Skills training is an important contributor to prevention and can address general social interaction or specific behaviors, such as drug use and delinquency.

- Restorative justice seeks to repair the harm done to both the victim and the community, while simultaneously changing the behavior of the offender.

- Restorative justice takes four primary forms: victim–offender mediation, family group counseling, neighborhood reparative boards, and sentencing/peacemaking circles.

- Evaluations of restorative justice reveal a great deal of satisfaction among participants and some reduced recidivism, although a great deal of additional research is needed.

KEY TERMS

Big Brothers/Big Sisters (BB/BS)

bullying

dispute resolution

Drug Abuse Resistance Education (D.A.R.E.) program

Early Head Start (EHS)

Elmira Prenatal/Early Infancy Project

family group conferencing (FGC)

FRIENDS

Gang Resistance Education and Training (G.R.E.A.T.) program

Head Start

Incredible Years program

Keepin' It REAL

mentoring

neighborhood reparative boards (NRBs)

Olweus Bullying Prevention Program (OBPP)

DOI: 10.4324/9781003167112-12

peacemaking/
sentencing
circles

peer mediation

Perry Preschool
Project

Promoting
Alternative
Thinking
Strategies
(PATHS)

reintegrative
shaming

resistance skills
training

Resolving
Conflicts
Creatively
Program (RCCP)

restorative
justice

retributive
justice

risk factors

Seattle Social
Development
Project (SSDP)

Syracuse Family
Development
Research
Program

victim–offender
mediation (VOM)

INTRODUCTION

Throughout the previous chapters we have looked at the functioning of the juvenile justice system, primarily in terms of how the system and society responds to youthful misbehavior. Identifying the behavior and responding from the point of arrest through correctional intervention/punishment are typically the focus when one considers juvenile justice. This chapter takes a different tack and focuses on preventing youthful misbehavior before it initially occurs. At the same time, it is possible to look at efforts to prevent recidivism which is a cornerstone of the entire juvenile justice system. Given this fact, this chapter will also examine restorative justice.

RISK FACTORS AND PREVENTION

Any attempt to prevent delinquency is faced with a very broad spectrum of variables and issues that could be addressed. Virtually everything that occurs to youths and around youths as they grow and mature has a potential impact on their behavior. It is not feasible to try to address every possible factor. The more recent trend in identifying individuals and situations where offending will occur involves the identification of risk factors related to deviant behavior. In essence, the goal is to identify risk factors for misbehavior and implement programs to mitigate their impact.

Risk factors are indicators of who may become deviant in the future. The risk factors are indicators or flags that can signal the need for increased attention or possible preventive action. The identification of potential risk factors is not a new idea. Indeed, the idea of working with youths at risk of becoming delinquents or later adult criminals is a cornerstone of the juvenile justice system. The very premise of the juvenile court is to work with troubled at-risk youths. Implicit in this task is the idea of identifying the factors underlying the juvenile's behavior and working to alter those conditions.

The list of potential risk factors that have been identified for youthful misbehavior is extensive. Typical groups of factors found in the literature are community, family, peer, psychological/personality, and biological risk factors (see Table 12.1). While various authors may classify individual risk factors slightly differently, these categories are generally representative of those used in the literature. This is not an exhaustive list of risk factors. Rather, it offers some insight into some of the more recognized variables that have been discussed in the literature.

Community Influences on Behavior

One potential source of risk is the community within which an individual is raised and resides. Looking at the influence of the community dates back to the earliest days of criminology. Burgess, Shaw, McKay, and others viewed the community/neighborhood as a prime contributor to/explanation for deviant behavior. The interest in community has not waned since the early 1900s. Indeed, analyses continue to look to community problems, such as economic

TABLE 12.1 Common Risk Factors Found in the Research

Community	School
economic deprivation/poverty	suspension/expulsion
disorder/incivilities	truancy
availability of firearms/drugs	school attitude
socioeconomic status	academic failure
gang activity	school quality
area crime/violence	dropping out
Family	**Psychological/Personality**
parental criminality	hyperactivity
poor parental supervision	impulsivity
harsh discipline	inability to concentrate
inconsistent discipline	learning disabilities
abuse/maltreatment	low IQ
family bonding/relationships	anxiety
broken homes	aggressiveness
family size	**Biological**
socioeconomic status	prenatal complications
family conflict	perinatal complications
family functioning	low birth weight
Peers	drug use during pregnancy
gang membership	poor nutrition
peer deviance/criminality	neurotransmitter problems
sibling criminality	low at rest heart rate
community disorganization	neurological injuries

deprivation, low socioeconomic status, disorder/incivility, poor neighborhood integration, the presence of gangs, and similar factors, as contributors to youthful misbehavior (see, for example, Bursik & Grasmick, 1993; Sampson & Lauritsen, 1994; Shannon, 1991; Skogan, 1990). Each of these community factors contributes to the level of risk.

Family Factors

Family factors are primary targets when addressing delinquency. A wide range of family situations and factors influence both the immediate care of an individual as well as later behavior. Poor parental supervision and inconsistent and harsh discipline are key early risk factors for later misbehavior. Research has found a strong relationship between youthful offending, poor parental supervision, and harsh and inconsistent discipline (Capaldi & Patterson,

1996; Hawkins, Arthur, & Catalano, 1995; Loeber & Stouthamer-Loeber, 1986; McCord, 1979; Wells & Rankin, 1988). Exposure to violence and offending is also related to future misbehavior. Parental criminality, abuse, and maltreatment are all risk factors for youths. In perhaps the most recognized study on this topic, Widom (1989) finds that both physical abuse and neglect predict later participation in criminal activity. Other family factors that are considered in the literature include family relations (or bonding), family size, and broken homes. The most important observation to make based on this varied literature is that family functioning is an important contributor to the present and future behavior of youths. The identification of family risk factors offers an opportunity to develop appropriate interventions.

Peer Factors

The influence of peers is generally viewed as one of the most important factors involved in adolescent behavior (Elliott, 1994; Elliott & Menard, 1996; Lipsey & Derzon, 1998; Thornberry, Huizinga, & Loeber, 1995). "Peer pressure" is an oft-noted cause of youthful misbehavior. Of particular importance to adolescence is the presence and/or participation in youth gangs. Participation in gangs is related to higher levels of offending (Esbensen & Huizinga, 1993; Thornberry, 1998; Thornberry et al., 1993), as well as initiation into deviant activity (Elliott & Menard, 1996).

School Factors

Another set of factors that contribute to risk involves schools. While schools are a part of the community, they may contribute uniquely to risk. Hirschi (1969) points out that schools and academic participation are key factors in delinquent behavior. Poor academic performance and school failure are common factors related to current and later deviance. Various studies show that dropping out of school and low academic achievement are strong correlates of delinquency (Farrington, 1989; Gold & Mann, 1972; Maguin & Loeber, 1996; Thornberry, Moore, & Christiansen, 1985; West & Farrington, 1973).

Psychological/Personality Factors

An array of psychological and personality variables has been identified as risk factors for aggressive behavior. Brennan, Mednick, and Mednick (1993) and Loney, Whaley-Klahn, Kosier, and Conboy (1983) note that hyperactivity among preteens is significantly related to violent behavior during the young adult years. Impulsivity and problems with concentration also are related to higher levels of adolescent deviance (Farrington, 1989; Farrington & Loeber, 1998; Loney et al., 1983). Other factors often related to deviant behavior include learning disabilities, low IQ, and similar issues that may inhibit an individual's success in school and elsewhere (see, for example, Denno, 1990; Lipsey & Derzon, 1998; Loeber et al., 1993; Loeber, Green, Keenan, & Lahey, 1995; Maguin & Loeber, 1996).

Biological Risk Factors

A final set of risk factors, which do not receive the same degree of attention as other factors, are biological risk factors. The major reason for this state of affairs is the fact that criminology is dominated by social scientists who focus their attention on other variables. Among the possible biologically based risk factors are prenatal and perinatal complications (Brewer, Hawkins, Catalano, & Neckerman, 1995; Farrington, 1996; Kandel & Mednick, 1991; Reiss & Roth, 1993). Included here are low birth weights, complications with pregnancy, drug use while pregnant, and poor nutrition. Neurotransmitters, such as serotonin, which are bodily chemicals that transmit messages in the brain, are also possibly related to deviant behavior (Moffitt et al., 1997). Yet another biological factor shown to be related to violent delinquent behavior is a low resting heart rate (Farrington, 1997; Raine, 1993). Research on the impact of many of these factors on later behavior is still in its infancy, although support is found in various studies.

Summary of Risk Factors

Any risk factor can be a target for prevention. The following discussion will offer some notable programs/interventions that have emerged to try to address delinquency and later criminality. Some of these address delinquency and criminality in an indirect fashion. That is, they attempt to have more immediate impacts on the risk factors and in intermediate outcomes that appear between the risk factor and later behavior. An example of this would be an intervention that addresses parental supervision. The program analyzes change in parenting and a child's subsequent coping abilities. Any impact on delinquency or criminality may not be assessed in the initial evaluations.

ADDRESSING COMMUNITY RISK FACTORS

Community risk factors require broad-scale changes at the societal or broad community level. The Great Society Reforms of the Johnson Administration in the 1960s attacked many of the risk factors for deviance. Programs addressing education, training, jobs creation, community development, and others all targeted factors that have been implicated in deviant activity, such as inequality, low socioeconomic status, economic deprivation, and disorder/incivility. This is evident in an inspection of various theories of crime, including strain, control, social disorganization, subcultural, social disorganization, and conflict theories.

The impact of these interventions typically entails major social shifts over extended periods of time. The impact on delinquency will be seen at the macro level. That is, the changes will be seen in rates of offending in society. It will be difficult, if possible at all, to see changes at the individual or local level. While addressing community factors has the potential to have a major impact on society and delinquency/criminality, these efforts are beyond the scope of this book/chapter. Of more immediate concern are risk factors and prevention programs/interventions that rest at the micro and meso levels, which are considered in the balance of this chapter.

PARENT TRAINING

Concern over the preparation and ability of parents to provide an appropriate environment for children has prompted the development of various interventions. These interventions range from those targeting expectant mothers to those working with families of young children to those addressing families with school-age children. Among these programs are the Elmira Prenatal/Early Infancy Project, the Syracuse Family Development Program, and the Incredible Years program.

The **Elmira Prenatal/Early Infancy Project** targets the earliest stage of a child's development, specifically when the child is still in the womb. The program is aimed at young, poor, first-time, and often unmarried mothers. The centerpiece of the program is home visitation by nurses beginning during pregnancy and lasting through the child's second birthday (Olds et al., 1997, 1998). Mothers are visited an average of nine times during pregnancy and 23 times after the child's birth. The visits focus on health and health-related activities of the mother and child, providing appropriate care to the child, and developing social and personal skills for the mothers. Nurses also provide referrals, access, and transportation to other assistance (Olds et al., 1997). Evaluation of the program revealed a number of positive outcomes. First, program mothers experienced fewer arrests. Second, maternal abuse and neglect were significantly reduced. Finally, in a 15-year follow-up, the children reported significantly less running away, arrests, and substance abuse (Olds et al., 1997, 1998). The success of the project has led to its replication in other sites.

The **Syracuse Family Development Research Program** has many similar characteristics to the nurse home visitation program. Begun in 1969, the intervention targeted pregnant, young, single, African-American mothers. The project worked with the families from birth to age 8 and included home visitation by child development trainers; parent training in health, nutrition, and child rearing; and individualized day care for the children (Lally, Mangione, & Honig, 1988). The key element of the project was weekly visits to the subjects' homes. Children from the project have done better academically, demonstrate better self-control, and have fewer arrests than control youths (Honig, Lally, & Mathieson, 1982; Lally Mangione, & Honig, 1987, 1988).

Home visitations with families from birth onward have greatly expanded over the past 30 years, largely as a result of the early success of programs like those listed above. Since 2009, the Administration on Children and Families, a division of the U.S. Department of Health and Human Services, has monitored the effectiveness of home visitation programs. The Home Visitation Evidence of Effectiveness (HomVEE) report is produced annually and reviews the literature and evidence on any early home visitation initiatives that target birth through age 5. Using established criteria for selection of programs to review, the quality of the program design, the criteria for meta-analyses of the evidence, and other factors, the report provides a good assessment of the state of the evidence.

The 2019 HomVEE report (as well as earlier reports) offers a great deal of positive information. Programs have positive impacts on child health, maternal health, school readiness, reductions in child maltreatment, improved parenting practices, and other outcomes. Most evaluations and programs do not assess program impact on delinquency, crime, or family violence, but when they do there is evidence of positive success. This should not be surprising given that fact that the programs target youths up to age 5, before the years when documentation of delinquency and criminality would be made.

WEB ACTIVITY

The HomVEE program provides a wealth of information on early home visitation initiatives. Investigate the findings of the program at homevee.acf.hhs.gov.

Another program targeting parental training that has proven effective is the Incredible Years program. Rather than target expectant mothers, the program identified families for intervention that had youths displaying early conduct problems at ages 4–8 (Webster-Stratton & Hammond, 1997). The current program works with families of youths ages 2–12 (Incredible Years, 2012). Parents receive training in parenting skills, how to recognize and address their child's problem behaviors, how to set rules and use incentives, and other key components of child rearing. The program also helps children recognize emotions, deal with anger, choose appropriate responses to problem situations, and enhance educational skills. A teacher component trains them on classroom management, providing skills to youths, handling problem youths and behaviors, and disciplinary practices (Incredible Years, 2012). Evaluations of the program reveal consistent positive results, including improved parenting skills, less coercive and punitive punishments, fewer antisocial behaviors, improved interpersonal skills, and better preparation for school (SAMHSA, 2012; Webster-Stratton, 2001; Webster-Stratton & Hammond, 1997). The strength of the program and its consistent positive evaluations have led the Substance Abuse and Mental Health Services Administration to list the Incredible Years on its National Registry of Evidence-based Programs and Practices.

WEB ACTIVITY

A great deal of additional information on the Incredible Years program is available online, including specific program activities for parents, children, and teachers. Take a look at this material and see if you can find elements of the program in what you remember from school: www.incredibleyears.com/program/parent.asp.

Interest in and the growth of parent/child training interventions often does not consider impacts on problem behavior, basically due to the young age of the children under consideration. In one attempt to summarize the state of the evidence on disruptive behavior of children subsequent to parent/child training programs, Piquero, Farrington, Welsh, Tremblay, & Jennings (2009) conducted a meta-analysis of 55 studies. Based on data from self-reports of parents and teachers and some observational data, the authors found that these programs have a significant impact on youthful antisocial behavior and delinquency (Piquero et al., 2009).

PRESCHOOL PROGRAMS

One suggestion for addressing antisocial behavior involves early preparation of children for school. Indeed, an important component within the parent training programs is setting the stage for the children to be successful in school and elements of parental training are important in programs targeting educational success. Preschool programs are viewed as a means of establishing a level of competence that avoids early placement into differential ability tracts, building a positive attitude toward school, and providing basic social skills to youths who were not prepared to enter school. The expectation for preschools is that success in school will translate later to greater social success out of school and lower delinquency.

One of the earliest and best-known preschool programs is the **Head Start** program. Head Start was initiated in 1965 as part of President Lyndon Johnson's "War on Poverty." The premise of Head Start is that disadvantaged youths are not prepared to enter school without some form of early intervention targeted at social and intellectual skills (Gottfredson, 1987). Head Start is meant to provide youths with positive early experiences and, in turn, successful long-term academic careers. The reauthorization of Head Start in 1994 included the establishment of **Early Head Start (EHS)** which incorporates interventions with expectant parents, infants, and children prior to age three. EHS could employ both home-based and center-based programming and sought to improve both parenting and school readiness.

Evaluations of Head Start and EHS show generally positive results. Children are better prepared for kindergarten, exhibit better cognitive development, score better on social-emotional measures, and are more likely to graduate from high school and attend college (Aikens, Kopack Klein, Tarullo, & West, 2013; Love et al., 2002; Vogel, Xue, Moiduddin, Kisker, & Carlson, 2010; Zhai, Brooks-Gunn, & Waldfogel, 2011). Brooks-Gunn, Love, Raikes, and

A mother helps her son finish a puzzle before picking him up from the Community Action Partnership of Western Nebraska's Head Start program, July 2021, in Scottsbluff, Nebraska. Evaluations of Head Start programs show generally positive results.

CREDIT: Olivia Wieseler/*The Star-Herald* via AP

Chazan-Cohen (2013) note that program graduates have greater self-control and self-esteem, as well as demonstrate better parenting practices as adults. In terms of juvenile or criminal justice system involvement, there is evidence of reduced juvenile delinquency, adult criminality, arrests, family violence, child maltreatment, and childhood aggression (Aikens et al., 2013; Barr & Gibbs, 2017; Brooks-Gunn et al., 2013; Garces, Thomas, & Currie, 2002; Walsh & Mortenson, 2020).

One of the most extensively studied preschool programs is the **Perry Preschool Project**. The project seeks to provide students with a positive introduction to education. This is accomplished by involving the children in the planning of activities, a low child–teacher ratio, enhanced reinforcement of student achievement, and frequent home visits with parents. One evaluation of the program randomly assigned youths to either the program or a non-preschool control group. All study subjects were from low-income black families, typified by low parental education, unemployment, and single-parent households. All children were tracked throughout school and were periodically surveyed through age 19, with follow-up evaluations undertaken through age 40 (Berrueta-Clement, Schweinhart, Barnett, Epstein, & Weikart, 1984).

Evaluations of the Perry Preschool program reveal significant increases in academic performance, reduced need for special education and remedial work, increased positive attitudes toward school, enhanced high school graduation rates, and lower unemployment after graduation from high school (Berrueta-Clement et al., 1984). Schweinhart (1987) reported fewer serious offenses at both ages 15 and 19 for experimental subjects. Results through age 27 revealed that program participants were arrested at about half the rate of control group subjects (Schweinhart, Barnes, & Weikart, 1993), and data from a 50-year follow-up reveals lower criminal activity, increased earnings, and increased employment (Hechman & Karapakula, 2019).

Preschool projects generally report improved academic performance and less need for special education in the future. Unfortunately, many studies show that the results are short term and fade within the first two years of elementary school, although some show positive results in long-term follow-up (such as the 50-year follow-up of the Perry Preschool program). Most studies fail to address the program's impact on delinquency and criminality and mainly address educational outcomes.

SKILLS TRAINING

Another preventive approach seeks to provide youths with the skills to recognize and respond appropriately to problem situations. Many of these interventions appear in school settings and under various titles, including life skills training. These programs attempt to teach self-control, anger management, and how to recognize your feelings and emotions, as well as build a positive self-image, identify the needs and concerns of others, and how to solve problems. In essence, the skills to be learned are how to interact with others without resorting to aggression or antisocial behavior. To a large extent, the training seeks to provide youths with the skills to combat peer pressure and aggression from other youths.

Promoting Alternative Thinking Strategies (PATHS), which is taught in regular classrooms, is a five-year curriculum offered in preschools, kindergartens, and grades one to five. The curriculum is intended to reduce both behavioral and emotional problems, while building self-control and problem-solving abilities. The program has been used in more than 3,000 schools (Fishbein et al., 2016b) and is used across grades or as abbreviated versions in only certain grades. PATHS can be adopted for use with different populations and for implementation outside the school setting (Greenberg & Kusche, 1998). Evaluations of PATHS utilizing experimental and control groups of students revealed improved problem-solving ability, reduced hyperactivity, increased planning activity, reduced self-reported conduct problems, less peer aggression, and reduced teacher reports of conduct problems (Greenberg & Kusche, 1996; 1997; Greenberg, Kusche, Cook, & Quamma, 1995). Evaluations of PATHS on preschool and kindergarten students reveal increased prosocial behaviors, reduced aggression, reduced impulsivity, and enhanced social competence (Fishbein et al., 2016b; Gibson, Werner, Sweeney, 2015). Similar results appear in Crean and Johnson's (2013) evaluation of 3rd-grade students followed for two years post-program participation.

WEB ACTIVITY

You can investigate the PATHS Program further on the Blueprints for Healthy Youth Development website at www.blueprintsprograms.com/factsheet/promoting-alternative-thinking-strategies-paths.

A second developmental training program in this venue is the FRIENDS program. FRIENDS is a cognitive therapy intervention targeting anxiety and stress in youths (FRIENDS, 2015). The focus on stress is due to its relation to school failure and academic problems, as well as later substance abuse and unemployment. The program has several age-graded versions including FunFRIENDS for ages 4–7, FRIENDS for Life for ages 8–11, and the My FRIENDS Youth Program for ages 12–15. The training takes place primarily in schools over 10 class sessions. FRIENDS stands for:

F   feelings
R   relax
I   I can try
E   encourage
N   nurture
D   don't forget, be brave
S   stay happy

The program is typically taught in school classrooms over 10 weeks. Class sessions focus on emotional resilience, problem-solving, and self-confidence (FRIENDS, 2015). The program has been the subject of numerous evaluations in a variety of countries, including Australia, the United Kingdom, the United States, and others, and has been identified by the World Health Organization

(2004) as an effective program. Results generally show significant reductions in anxiety and
increases in self-esteem (Dadds, Spence, Holland,
Barrett, & Laurens, 1997; Lowrey-Webster, Barrett,
& Dadds, 2001; Rodgers & Dunsmuir, 2015;
Stallard et al., 2005). Barrett, Farrell, Ollendick, and
Dadds (2006) note that the program is effective
at lowering anxiety at 12-, 24-, and 36-month
follow-up points. In a meta-analysis of anxiety prevention measures, FRIENDS
emerges as the most effective program (Fisak, Richard, & Mann, 2011).

> ## WEB ACTIVITY
>
> Visit the FRIENDS Programs website to see
> the variations in the program for different
> age groups, available resources, and other
> materials at www.friendsresilience.org.

RESISTANCE SKILLS TRAINING

Other programs that focus on skills training are those considered resistance
skills training. This training comes under a variety of names, with the most
well known being the Drug Abuse Resistance Education (D.A.R.E.) program.
Resistance skills training involves a set of ideas dealing with recognizing problematic situations and issues, dealing with peer pressure, recognizing pressure
from media presentations, knowing proper responses to temptations, building
self-esteem and assertiveness, and knowing how and when to take a stand. The
implicit assumption in this type of prevention is that youthful misbehavior is
largely a function of situation and peer involvement, and that youths need to
learn how to recognize peer pressure and how to make proper decisions in the
face of that pressure.

The Drug Abuse Resistance Education (D.A.R.E.) program, begun in Los
Angeles in 1983, targets school youths through a police officer-taught curriculum. Various methodologically rigorous evaluations of the original
D.A.R.E. program failed to find any significant impact on drug use behavior.
Ringwalt, Ennett, and Holt (1991), Clayton, Cattarello, and Walden (1991),
and Rosenbaum, Flewelling, Bailey, Ringwalt, and Wilkinson (1994), looking
at schools from different jurisdictions, all reported no impact on substance
use. Rosenbaum and Hanson (1998) tracked D.A.R.E. participants and control youths for more than six years to assess the impact of the program.
The authors reported that D.A.R.E. had little impact on attitudes, beliefs,
or social skills directly addressed by the program. More importantly, the
program had no significant impact on any measure of drug use. Due partly
to these negative findings, D.A.R.E. has been reimaged as Keepin' It REAL.
The 10-session Keepin' It REAL curriculum is still taught to children and
adolescents in schools by law enforcement officers, but the focus of the
program has shifted from drugs to resistance skills. REAL stands for Refuse,
Explain, Avoid, and Leave, and the program provides skills for youths to
address situations, events, and people who promote or encourage them to
use drugs or participate in other problem behaviors. Evaluations of the new
program (Hecht et al., 2003; Hecht, Graham, & Elek, 2006; Kulis, Nieri,
Yabiku, Stromwall, & Marsiglia, 2007) report reduced drug usage, altered
attitudes, and increased use of resistance strategies.

WEB ACTIVITY

More details on G.R.E.A.T. and its individual components can be found at www.great-online.org/GREAT-Home.

Another resistance skills program taught by law enforcement officers is the **Gang Resistance Education and Training (G.R.E.A.T.)** program. This program targets peer pressure and the tendency for some youths to turn to gangs and gang behavior. The curriculum consists of 13 one-hour lessons and is presented in middle schools (see Chapter 5 for more details on the program). The thrust of the program is to provide youths with the necessary skills for identifying high-risk situations and resisting the pressure/allure of taking part in gangs and gang activity. Beyond targeting just ganging, program curricula are geared toward increasing self-esteem, changing attitudes, addressing peer pressure, and eliminating participation in violent behavior.

The G.R.E.A.T. program has undergone extensive evaluation. An early longitudinal evaluation of the original G.R.E.A.T. program showed less victimization, less risk-taking behavior, improved attitudes toward the police, increased numbers of prosocial peers, and more negative views about gangs four years following program participation among those youths receiving the G.R.E.A.T. lessons (Esbensen, Peterson, Taylor, Freng, & Osgood, 2004). Unfortunately, the evaluation failed to find any impact on actual gang participation. Based on these results, the sponsors of the G.R.E.A.T. program revised the curriculum to better address gang participation. The current 13-lesson program has been the subject of a rigorous national evaluation (discussed earlier in Chapter 5). As noted, results show positive outcomes on skills usage, attitudes, and gang participation by program subjects.

ANTI-BULLYING PREVENTION

The problem of bullying in schools and the workplace is a major topic today. **Bullying** behavior includes both physical and verbal aggression that is repeated over time and is meant to intentionally harm the victim (Olweus & Limber, 2000). Studies in Norwegian, Swedish, and U.S. schools find that at

4th graders at Scandia Elementary in Minnesota listen to their teacher speak about bullying and behavior expectations. The school tracks data on bullying by using a prevention strategy named for Dan Olweus, a pioneer of bullying research.

CREDIT: AP Photo/Minnesota Public Radio, Tom Weber

least 15 percent of the students report being either bullied or being a bullying offender (Melton et al., 1998, Olweus, 1993). Bullying prevention is identified as an exemplary program for attacking violence by youths (Elliott, 2000). The most notable anti-bullying program is that of Olweus and his colleagues (Olweus & Limber, 2000; Olweus, 1994; Olweus, 1995).

Developed in Norway, the Olweus Bullying Prevention Program (OBPP) is aimed at the entire school and relies on active student, teacher, and parent participation. The program attempts to raise awareness about the problem of bullying, establish rules and regulations governing behavior and responses to offending, train school staff on how to integrate bullying discussions into the curriculum, require meetings between parents and teachers, and hold meetings between bullies and their victims. Based on survey data gathered before the onset of the program and periodically over a two-year follow-up, Olweus (1994, 1995) reported significant reductions in bullying, classroom disruption, and general delinquency. Replicating the program in England, Whitney, Rivers, Smith, and Sharp (1994) reported similar positive results, particularly for students in younger grades. This suggests that the intervention should be targeted at young students before bullying behavior becomes ingrained in individuals. Melton et al. (1998), testing the program in South Carolina grade schools, found significant reductions in bullying, as well as vandalism, general delinquency, and school misbehavior. Finally, Limber, Olweus, Wang, Masiello, & Breivik (2018), in an evaluation in Pennsylvania schools, found significant reductions in bullying and being bullied, with the results being maintained over a period of three years. Based on these results, anti-bullying programs appear promising as a means to prevent both the initial aggression and subsequent offending and antisocial behavior.

WEB ACTIVITY

The Olweus Bullying Prevention Program has been recognized as a blueprint for violence prevention and has been adopted around the world based on its proven impact. Read more details on the program at www.blueprintsprograms.org/programs/11999999/olweus-bullying-prevention-program/.

MENTORING PROGRAMS

One major push in addressing problem youths in recent years has been matching youths with adult mentors. The cornerstone of mentoring initiatives is assisting the development of youths. Mentoring involves pairing adult volunteers with youths in need of friendship, emotional support, guidance, and advice. Youths are typically between the ages of 10 and 16 and are from single-parent homes. Mentors and mentees are expected to meet two to four times per month for three to four hours each time. Both the adult volunteers and the youths undergo initial training that outlines expectations and requirements for the programs (Grossman & Tierney, 1998). Many programs also involve regular contact with the parents. Mentoring programs specifically target academic failure, dropping out of school, truancy, and delinquency, among other things.

The most notable mentoring program is Big Brothers/Big Sisters (BB/BS), a nonprofit organization with the goal of helping children reach their potential through professionally supported, one-to-one relationships with volunteer mentors. BB/BS began in 1904 in New York City and currently boasts over 235 agencies across the U.S. and has served over 2,000,000 children over the last decade (Big Brothers Big Sisters of America, 2021). BB/BS also operates in 14 other countries. Beyond BB/BS, it is estimated that there are more than 5,000 other mentoring organizations in the United States (DuBois, Portillo, Rhodes, Silverthorn, & Valentine, 2011; Matz, 2014).

Research on BB/BS presents generally positive results. Grossman and Tierney (1998) evaluated BB/BS programs in eight locations using an experimental design with random assignment of roughly 1,000 youths to BB/BS and a nonmentored control group. They report that mentored youths are roughly 50 percent less likely to start illegal drug use, 25 percent less likely to start alcohol use, and 30 percent less likely to assault other youths. There are also positive impacts on academic performance and relationships with parents. DeWit, DuBois, Erdem, Larose, and Lipman (2016), evaluating BB/BS programs in Canada, report both significant short-term and long-term effects of the program. Participants have fewer behavioral problems, less depression and anxiety, and exhibit stronger coping skills. In another long-term follow-up, DuBois, Herrera, and Rivera (2018) find that program participants commit fewer offenses and those receiving high-quality mentoring experience fewer arrests, lower alcohol use, and improved social-emotional well-being roughly 20 years later.

WEB ACTIVITY

Visit the Big Brothers/Big Sisters website at www.bbbs.org and the MENTOR website at www.mentoring.org to learn more about mentoring.

Systematic reviews of the research on mentoring programs reveal positive outcomes. In a meta-analysis of 55 mentoring studies, DuBois, Holloway, Valentine, and Cooper (2002) uncovered favorable mentoring effects across different demographic groups of youths, especially disadvantaged youths. The greatest impact appears where the mentors and mentees establish strong relationships. The positive effects with disadvantaged mentees are reinforced by results showing that mentoring is more effective with high-risk youths (DuBois et al., 2011). Finally, Tolan et al. (2014) reported on a meta-analysis of 44 studies that included delinquency as a program outcome. The results revealed reductions in delinquency, aggression, and drug use, as well as higher academic achievement.

The evidence on mentoring suggests it is an important prevention approach. Additionally, the number of programs and youths involved demonstrate its level of acceptance in communities. The greatest obstacle in many programs and communities is the inability to recruit enough adult mentors to meet the mentee demand.

CONFLICT MANAGEMENT/RESOLUTION

Teaching youths how to handle conflict and make proper choices when faced with difficult situations (such as peer pressure to use drugs or commit a crime) is a popular intervention that takes a variety of forms. Conflict management/resolution is a common program in schools. These programs appear under a variety of names, including dispute resolution, dispute mediation, conflict resolution, and conflict management. The basic goal of these programs is to avoid and/or resolve conflicts before they escalate into serious problems (such as physical confrontations). A key component in many programs is **peer mediation**, in which students are trained to assist one another in resolving disputes in such a way that all parties to the dispute accept the resolution.

The **Resolving Conflict Creatively Program (RCCP)** in New York City includes student mediation as a core component of the intervention. This program mainly targets pre-kindergarten to grade eight but it includes programming in secondary and special education curricula as well as a separate parent program (DeJong, 1993). The curriculum consists of grade appropriate lessons emphasizing relationship building, identifying and managing feelings and emotions, developing empathy, and building social responsibility (Collaborative for Academic, Social and Emotional Learning, 2021). The program includes a heavy reliance on peer mediation and parental involvement. Ba and Hawkins (1996) list four program objectives:

- Reduce violence
- Promote caring and cooperative behavior
- Teach life skills and conflict resolution
- Promote a positive learning environment.

Evaluation of RCCP reveals positive results. DeJong (1993) reports that students successfully learn the lessons, are involved in fewer fights, and believe that they can handle problems better as a result of the program. Aber, Pedersen, Brown, Jones, and Gershof (2003) note that program participants display lower hostility, fewer conduct problems, declines in aggressive behavior, and improved problem-solving abilities and strategies. The impact of the program increases with the number of lessons and the quality of the teacher training (Samples & Aber, 1998).

The growth of conflict management/resolution programs in schools remains an important effort, despite the fact that many programs have not undergone rigorous evaluations. Many programs do not reach a large enough portion of the student body and the programs are not very well integrated into other school activities. School-based conflict management programs have expanded over the last 20–30 years and generally rely on the basic assumptions of social-emotional learning. While many evaluations rest on small samples, individual schools, and/or lack an independent evaluation, the emerging evidence is generally favorable.

MULTI-COMPONENT PROGRAMS

Multi-component programs often begin by targeting youths who have already displayed antisocial behavior and/or delinquency. At the core of the programs is a recognition of a need to address the causal factors leading to the deviant behavior and keep the youths from engaging in more problematic activities. Multi-component programs also share the common feature of utilizing a range of interventions rather than only one or two approaches. While it is possible to find multiple inputs in the programs discussed earlier, multi-component programs tend to be even more inclusive of different techniques.

The **Seattle Social Development Project (SSDP)**, started in 1981, is one well-known multi-component program. The primary setting for the program is classrooms, although there is a strong home/family component to the project as well. The project focuses on the social development of school-age children and identifying risk and protective factors for delinquency, substance abuse, and academic failure (Hawkins, Smith, Kosterman, & Catalano, 2007; Social Development Research Group [SDRG], 2012). The actual intervention has three main parts targeting teachers, parents, and students. Teachers receive training in appropriate classroom management techniques, the establishment of rules and consequences, teaching positive social skills, and motivating students. Parent training involves recognizing problematic behaviors, rewarding positive behavior, promoting academic success, and building a strong family bond to help avoid antisocial activities. Finally, children learn to recognize and cope with peer pressure, build communication skills, appropriately respond to aggression by others, and avoid problematic situations and people (Hawkins et al., 2007; Hill, Roberts, Grogger, Guryan, & Sixkiller, 2011; SDRG, 2012).

Interviews with parents and children have been conducted on a regular basis to assess the impact of the Seattle Social Development Project since its inception. Program evaluation reveals that youths who complete the program are more successful in school, have a higher graduation rate, commit fewer delinquent and criminal offenses, and have lower levels of substance abuse (Hawkins et al., 2007). The project has expanded to look into intergenerational relationships, especially in terms of the impact of drug use on child development. One of the most recent analyses tracked youths through age 39 (Catalano et al., 2021). Individuals in the program do better in school and on the job, graduate at higher rates, attend more post-secondary programs, display better emotional control, are less likely to consider suicide, tend not to initiate drug use, and are less delinquent and criminal across their lifetime, compared to control subjects. Overall, the project is successful at identifying early risk factors, developing training and interventions to address those factors and build protective factors, and having a positive impact on youthful behavior.

RESTORATIVE JUSTICE

Not all prevention efforts target initial antisocial behavior. Indeed, a great deal of what the juvenile justice and criminal justice systems do is aimed at preventing further offending. The earlier chapters in this book have examined delinquent and antisocial behavior and the formal response of society to those actions. The focus is on the offender and what can be done to or for the offender, largely to keep the individual from recidivating. The emergence of restorative justice over the past 30 years has introduced a new set of responses to violations that incorporate elements of prevention (of recidivism) within efforts to restore victims, the community, and the offender to the pre-offense state. The restorative justice approach is in contrast to that of retributive justice.

The concept of restorative (or reparative) justice seeks to use interventions that return the victim and offender to their pre-offense states. Restorative justice seeks to repair the harm that was done to both the victim and the community, while simultaneously changing the behavior of the offender. For offenders, it means assuring that the action will not be repeated. For victims, this means repairing the harm done. For the community, it means returning things to their state prior to the offensive behavior. In contrast, retributive justice generally focuses on the lawbreaker and the imposition of sanctions for the purposes of deterrence, vengeance, and/or punishment. Table 12.2 juxtaposes some of the basic assumptions underlying both retributive and restorative justice.

While restorative justice shifts the focus to include victims and the entire community, there is also a belief that the offender is in need of assistance in recognizing the impact of his or her actions and identifying what needs to change in order to avoid such behavior in the future. Restorative justice is accomplished by bringing together a range of interested parties in a nonconfrontational setting, including the victim and the offender as well as family members or friends, criminal justice system personnel, and members of the general community. The participants, as a group, seek to understand the actions that led to the criminal or antisocial behavior, reveal the feelings and concerns of all parties, negotiate or mediate a solution agreeable to everyone, and assist in implementing that solution (Bazemore & Maloney, 1994). Kurki (2000:266) notes that "restorative justice is about relationships—how relationships are harmed by crime and how they can be rebuilt to promote recovery and healing for people affected by crime."

Restorative justice is not a new idea. Braithwaite (1999:2) argues that: "Restorative justice has been the dominant model of criminal justice throughout most of human history for all the world's peoples." Throughout most of history, victims and their families were expected to take action themselves to address the problems and repair the harm from the offense. The development of formal justice systems, particularly the police and criminal courts, shifted the emphasis for taking redress from the victim to

WEB ACTIVITY

There are several organizations that offer information on restorative justice. Two of the leaders are the International Institute for Restorative Practices (www.restorativepractices.org) and the Restorative Justice Online Blog (www.restorativejustice.org).

TABLE 12.2 Assumptions of Retributive and Restorative Justice

Retributive Justice	Restorative Justice
Crime is an act against the State, a violation of a law, an abstract idea.	Crime is an act against another person or the community.
The criminal justice system controls crime.	Crime control lies primarily in the community.
Offender accountability defined as taking punishment.	Accountability defined as assuming responsibility and taking action to repair harm.
Crime is an individual act with individual responsibility.	Crime has both individual and social dimensions of responsibility.
Punishment is effective. a. Threat of punishment deters crime. b. Punishment changes behavior.	Punishment alone is not effective in changing behavior and is disruptive to community harmony and good relationships.
Victims are peripheral to the process.	Victims are central to the process of resolving crime.
The offender is defined by deficits.	The offender is defined by capacity to make reparations.
Focus on establishing blame, on guilt, on past (did he/she do it?).	Focus on problem-solving, on liabilities/obligations, on future (what should be done?).
Emphasis on adversarial relationship.	Emphasis on dialogue and negotiation.
Imposition of pain to punish and deter/prevent.	Restitution as a means of restoring both parties; goal of reconciliation/restoration.
Community on sideline, represented abstractly by State.	Community as facilitator in restorative process.
Response focused on offenders' past behavior.	Response focused on harmful consequences of offender's behavior; emphasis on the future.
Dependence upon proxy professionals.	Direct involvement by participants.

Source: Adapted from Bazemore and Umbreit (1994); Zehr (1990).

the state. It was at this point that the victim became little more than a witness for the state and the response to crime and delinquency became punishment and retribution. In many respects, it could be argued that the very bases for the development of a juvenile court and juvenile justice system are found in restorative justice principles. The *parens patriae* philosophy of the juvenile court focuses not on the offense but the offender and the actions needed to help the youth.

An immediate precursor to restorative justice is dispute resolution or dispute mediation. The basic idea behind **dispute resolution** is to bring the opposing parties together in an attempt to work out a mutually agreeable solution. These programs involve a third-party mediator who monitors participant interaction, keeps the discussion focused, and makes suggestions whenever the need arises. Typically, many disputants have known each other over a period of time and

Dane County, Wisconsin, Executive Joe Parisi introduces a pilot program to divert young people receiving municipal citations into restorative justice programs in Madison, Wisconsin.

CREDIT: Ed Treleven/*Wisconsin State Journal* via AP

are neighbors, friends, or family members. Most participants are referred to the program by a member of the criminal justice system. The prosecutor has often reviewed the case and decided that the interests of justice can be better served in a nontraditional manner. Programs typically require voluntary participation by disputants, and if either party declines to take part, the dispute moves back to formal legal action. Rules of evidence are not enforced, and attorneys are not permitted. Instead, the process relies on discussion rather than rigid fact-finding, and the mediator has a free hand to conduct each meeting as he or she sees fit. Dispute resolution in school settings often takes the form of peer mediation or conflict resolution (discussed earlier in this chapter).

The Theoretical Basis of Restorative Justice and Prevention

The underlying theoretical explanation for restorative justice that is most relevant to a prevention argument is Braithwaite's (1989) reintegrative shaming. **Reintegrative shaming** rests on the assumption that the typical processing of offenders through the criminal justice system serves to isolate the offender and stigmatize him or her. This action marginalizes the offender (even more than he or she may already be in society). In addition, it does nothing to correct the behavior or repair the harm done to the victim. Basically, typical system processing serves only to exact a punishment (retribution) for the criminal act.

The underlying premise of Braithwaite's (1989) theory is that shame can be used in a positive fashion to bring the offender back into society. Under reintegrative shaming, the system needs to express its disapproval of the criminal activity while simultaneously forgiving the offender for the action, if the offender is willing to learn from the event and make reparations to the victim and society. The key is "reintegration" rather than "stigmatization" (Braithwaite, 1989). The ability to employ reintegrative shaming effectively rests on shifting the sole focus of societal response from the offender to a shared focus on the offending behavior, social disapproval (often by family, friends, and significant others), the needs of the victim and community, and a shared response to make things better (Harris, 2003). This orientation fits well with the *parens patriae* philosophy where the emphasis is on correcting the youth and not just punishing them.

Types of Restorative Justice

Restorative justice takes a variety of different forms, although they all attend to the same basic tenets. The diversity in restorative programs can be seen in the extent to which they address the different goals of empowerment, restoration, reintegration, and emotional and social healing for the varied participants in the restorative process (Harris, 2003). *Empowerment* reflects the need for all interested parties to be involved in the process. This provides a sense of legitimacy for both the victim and the offender. *Restoration* simply refers to repairing the harm done to all participants. At the same time, retribution is disavowed as a legitimate response to the behavior. Restorative justice also seeks to *reintegrate* both the offender and the victim into the community without the stigma of being an offender or being different from the other community members. Finally, there is a clear need to address the *emotional harm* that accompanies the behavior. Restorative justice programs that can attend to all of these goals can be considered "fully restorative."

Four broad types of restorative conferencing are victim–offender mediation, family/community group conferencing, neighborhood reparative boards, and peacemaking/sentencing circles. Each of these approach restorative justice in slightly different ways using the involvement of different individuals and groups (see Table 12.3).

Victim–Offender Mediation

Victim–offender mediation (VOM), also referred to as victim–offender reconciliation programs (VORPs), is a direct outgrowth of dispute resolution/dispute mediation programs of the early 1970s and is considered the oldest form of restorative justice (Umbreit, 1999). VOM is typically a post-conviction process (although pre-conviction programs exist) in which the victim and the offender are brought together to discuss a wide range of issues. A trained mediator attends these meetings.

The basic premise of VOM is that the criminal incident and its consequences are complex and beyond the ability of the criminal code to address on its own (Nicholl, 1999). The VOM meetings identify for the offender the types and level of harm suffered by the victim as a result of the crime. The victim is given the opportunity to express his or her concerns about the crime and his or her loss. At the same time, the offender is given the chance to explain why he or she committed the act and the circumstances that may underlie the behavior. Among the potential tangible outcomes for the victim may be the offender making monetary restitution or providing service to repair the harm done. Perhaps of equal importance are changes in behavior and attitude on the part of the offender.

Participation in VOM is voluntary for the victim but the offender may be required by the court to participate as a part of the court process (Umbreit,

	Victim–offender Mediation	Family Group Conferencing	Neighborhood Board	Peacemaking Circles
Who normally participates	Mediator, victim, offender (family)	Facilitator, offender, family (victim)	Board chair, volunteers, offender, family (victim)	Keeper, offender, volunteers, family, victim and offender supporters
Common permanent structure/staffing	Program coordinator, volunteer mediators (some paid mediators)	Program coordinator, facilitator (volunteers)	Coordinator, volunteer board chair, volunteer board members	Coordinator, volunteer circle members
Facilitation and dominant process	Victims option to speak first; mediator facilitates open-ended dialogue with minimal interference	In most programs facilitator follows script or outline in which offender speaks first, followed by victim and other participants; seeks to move process through phases	Board chair initiates member deliberation after questioning offender and parents, though some variation emerging toward circle or family group conferencing process	Keeper opens session and closes session, person allowed to speak when talking piece is passed to them. Shared leadership and consensus decision-making
Dominant philosophy	Meeting victim and offender needs, healing dialogue as transformative	Family group as essential problem-solver; respectful, normative, disapproval with support; offender empathy and emotion key	Neighborhood social support and community norm affirmation; neighborhood problem-solving focus	Collective healing; community focus; broad problem-solving, community building focus beyond individual offense

TABLE 12.3 Restorative Conferencing Models Administration and Process

Source: Bazemore and Schiff (2005:38). Reprinted with permission.

1999). Additionally, VOM may be a part of the formal criminal justice system or may be run by other agencies that are not directly connected to the system. In some jurisdictions, mediation may be ordered by the judge in lieu of formal sentencing.

Family/Community Group Conferencing

Family group conferencing (FGC) finds its roots in indigenous practices of the Maori in New Zealand and came to prominence in 1989 when New Zealand, responding to the increasing number of Maori youths being handled in the formal justice system (Crawford & Newburn, 2003), mandated that all youths age 14–17 (with only a few exceptions for very serious offenders) be removed from formal court processing and diverted to FGC (Kurki, 2000). The basic ideas of FGC were adapted by the police in Wagga-Wagga, Australia, in 1991 into a process known as community group conferencing (CGC) (McCold, 2003).

FGC differs from VOM in several ways. First, FGC was developed and remains primarily an approach dealing with youthful misbehavior and issues. Second, FGC includes family members, close friends, other support groups, and community members in the conferences (McCold, 2003). There is also the possibility of including criminal justice system personnel, including social workers, police officers, and an offender's attorney (Van Ness & Strong, 2015). A third difference between FGC and VOM is the absence of a mediator. Instead, FGC is led by a trained facilitator who will make contact with all participants prior to the conference, explain the process and the role of each individual, and emphasize the fact that the conference should conclude with a resolution to which all parties are in agreement.

Once the conference begins, the facilitator leads the participants through a discussion of the facts of the case, the impact of the victimization on the parties, the feelings of all participants toward the action and the offender, and the development of a mutually agreed-upon resolution (Nicholl, 1999). The families and support persons are very important to this process. They are expected to voice their feelings about the harm that was committed, their concern for the victim of the crime, their disappointment with the offender's behavior, and their suggestions for how to resolve the problem. Of great importance is that the support groups are expected to take some responsibility in monitoring the offender and making certain that any agreements are carried out after the conference (Kurki, 2000). Conferences can be held either pretrial or posttrial, and have become a part of police and pretrial diversion programs in many countries (McGarrell et al. 2000; Moore & O'Connell, 1994). Fox (2018) and Dijkstra, Creemers, Asscher, Deković, and Stams (2016) point out that FGC has built a role within social work when addressing intra-family issues such as abuse/neglect, foster care, out-of-home placement, and other issues.

Neighborhood Reparative Boards

Neighborhood reparative boards (NRBs), or neighborhood accountability boards, have existed since the mid-1990s and typically deal with nonviolent youthful offenders. Cases are referred to the boards by the court, most often prior to formal adjudication.

There are several key differences between NRBs and other types of restorative conferencing. First, victims are not required to participate, and many early boards frowned upon victim participation (Strickland, 2004). Second, the conferences are often open to the public, but actual participation is limited by the board to those it wishes to interview. The board questions the offender and examines statements made by members of the offender's family and others knowledgeable about the event (Bazemore & Umbreit, 2001). Third, the boards are composed of a small group of citizens who have been specially trained in conducting hearings and constructing appropriate sanctions.

At the conclusion of the hearing, the board undertakes private deliberations and outlines a suggested set of actions to be followed by the offender. If the offender agrees with the plan, the board oversees the offender's compliance with the terms and reports to the court about the success or failure of the offender (Bazemore & Umbreit, 2001). Typical conditions of agreements include restitution, apologies, and community service (Karp, 2001).

Peacemaking/Sentencing Circles

The final type of restorative justice program, peacemaking/sentencing circles, are based on Canadian First Nation practices and began formal operation in the early 1990s. Circles invite members from across the community to participate in determining the appropriate sanctions for offenders (Van Ness & Strong, 2015). As a sentencing procedure, this process usually occurs after a case is concluded and the offender is found guilty in court. Participants in circles typically include all of the parties found in FGCs as well as general community members who wish to be included.

Most cases handled by sentencing circles involve minor offenses, although some programs will consider more serious crimes (Stuart, 1996). Because this process can include a wide array of participants, circles normally require a great deal of preparation before they actually convene (Kurki, 2000). A facilitator meets with all participants prior to the actual circle to explain the process, outline the facts of the case, answer any questions the parties may have, and make plans for the actual meeting. The extensive preparation may mean that the circles take place months after the crime occurred and the court case concluded. Every participant in the sentencing circle is given the opportunity to speak, express his or her feelings about the crime, and offer opinions about the potential outcome. The intended outcome of the circle is consensus on a plan of action.

Outcomes of the circles may include further meetings between the victim and offender, apologies by the offender, restitution, community service, treatment/rehabilitation programs (such as counseling or drug/alcohol treatment), and/or explicit sentencing recommendations to the trial judge (Nicholl, 1999; Van Ness & Strong, 2015), including possible jail or prison time (Stuart, 1996). The decision of the circles is often binding on the offender (and may be specifically incorporated into the official court record). Failure to adhere to the decision may result in further criminal justice system processing or being returned to the circle (Van Ness & Strong, 2015).

Summary of Types of Restorative Justice

While each of the forms of restorative justice take a slightly different approach to repairing the harm done by the criminal act, all are considered restorative because they seek to address the needs of the victim, the offender, and the community. The various approaches bring about restoration by attempting to build understanding between the parties, identifying the factors at work in the behavior, arriving at a plan of action that is agreed to by all parties, and preventing future problems. The form most closely aligned with juvenile justice is FGC, which was developed specifically with problem youths in mind.

The Impact of Restorative Justice

Restorative justice programs are intended to have a number of different possible outcomes, including rehabilitating the offender, preventing recidivism, and repairing the harm done to the victim. Assessing the impact of the interventions, however, is difficult to do. Most evaluations focus on victim and offender satisfaction with the process and the level of compliance or completion of the agreed-upon settlement. Less common are analyses of the impact of the programs on subsequent offending by the offender.

Satisfaction, Fairness, and Compliance

In terms of satisfaction, feelings of fairness by victims, and compliance with the agreements, with very few exceptions, restorative justice receives positive reviews. Participants express satisfaction with the restorative process in which they have participated (Braithwaite, 1999). Evaluations of VOM typically reveal that 75–100 percent of the participants express satisfaction with the mediation (Kurki, 2000). Similarly high levels of satisfaction arise from FGCs (Bazemore & Umbreit, 2001; Gal & Moyal, 2011; Moore & O'Connell, 1994; Umbreit, Vos, Coates, & Brown, 2003). Participants also feel the process is fair (McCold, 2003; McGarrell et al., 2000; McGarrell & Hipple, 2007; Umbreit, 1999; Umbreit & Coates, 1992; Umbreit et al., 2003).

There is also evidence that most meetings culminate in an agreement and most parties comply with the settlement (Braithwaite, 1999; Kurki, 2000; Schiff, 1999; Umbreit & Coates, 1992). Restitution is a common component of many agreements and evaluations reveal that 90 percent or more of the offenders in FGC comply with ordered restitution (Wachtel, 1995).

Recidivism

Reducing reoffending (recidivism) is an important restorative goal, particularly in a discussion of juvenile justice. Many evaluations of recidivism have appeared in relation to VOM programs. Umbreit and Coates (1992) uncovered significantly less recidivism on behalf of the youthful VOM sample. Umbreit, Coates, and Vos (2001) report that youths completing VOM projects in two Oregon counties reduced their offending by at least 68 percent in the year after program participation compared to the year before the intervention. Nugent, Umbreit, Wiinamaki, and Paddock (1999) note that both the level of reoffending and the seriousness of subsequent offenses is lower for youths who enter and complete VOM programs.

Positive results also appear in numerous evaluations of FGC. McGarrell et al. (2000), in an analysis of restorative justice conferences for youths in Indianapolis, report a 40 percent reduction in recidivism for the program youths compared to those undergoing normal system processing. Bonta, Wallace-Capretta, Rooney, and McAnoy (2002) report that youths in conferencing recidivate less than those in traditional processing, particularly when subjects are matched on risk. Jeong, McGarrell, and Hipple (2012) report that graduates of group conferencing exhibit lower recidivism for as long as 12 years post-intervention, although the statistical significance of the results wanes over time. Hipple, Gruenewald, and McGarrell (2014, 2015) note that the effectiveness of FGC is tied to the degree of program fidelity to restorative practices. Basically, a greater degree of restorativeness leads to greater reductions in reoffending. Bergseth and Bouffard (2012) note that youths participating in restorative justice stay offense-free longer than other youths, and this result holds more for younger youths, males, and first-time offenders. Numerous other studies (e.g., Daly, 2002; deBeus & Rodriguez, 2007; Hayes & Daly, 2004; McGarrell & Hipple, 2007; Rodriguez, 2005) find that conferencing and restorative justice program participants are less likely to reoffend than other youths.

A number of meta-analyses report positive results from restorative interventions. In a meta-analysis of 35 restorative justice programs, two-thirds of the effect sizes showed reductions in recidivism (Latimer et al., 2005). Sherman, Strang, Mayo-Wilson, Woods, and Ariel (2015) found reduced recidivism in an analysis of 10 studies (although nine of the studies addressed adult subjects). Focusing on studies of restorative justice with youths, Wong, Bouchard, Gravel, Bouchard, and Morselli (2016) note that restorative justice significantly lowered recidivism rates.

Summary of Restorative Justice

Restorative justice programs offer an alternative to traditional juvenile justice processing of problem youths. The intent of these programs is multifaceted. The programs attempt to repair the harm that has been done to both the victim and the larger community. Equally important is rehabilitating the offender so that he or she does not recidivate. There is also a desire to build the community's capacity to address social issues before or as they emerge.

SUMMARY

Ideally, preventing youthful misbehavior before it ever occurs should be the goal of the juvenile justice system, society, schools, and families. One premise of the juvenile justice system it to prevent delinquent youths from becoming adult offenders. Preventing delinquency requires identifying the risk factors underlying the behavior and implementing an effective intervention to address those precipitating causes. The list of risk factors is long, and the interventions range from major societal/community changes to family assistance to school programming to new restorative practices. Despite the positive evaluations of many prevention efforts, the juvenile justice system and society continue to emphasize responding to youths after delinquent acts. Perhaps greater attention needs to be paid to truly preventive programming.

DISCUSSION QUESTIONS

1. What are the different categories of risk factors? What specific factors/variables are in each category?

2. What are some of the most promising prevention programs? What risk factors are addressed by these programs? Discuss the research/evaluation of these programs/interventions.

3. Restorative justice programs are appearing throughout the United States. Do you think this approach is an appropriate direction for preventing youthful misbehavior? If so, what form of restorative justice practice should be emphasized (VOM, FGC, NRB, or peacemaking/sentencing circles)? If not, what should be done instead of restorative justice?

CHAPTER 13

The Victimization of Juveniles

WHAT YOU NEED TO KNOW

- Victimization of youths is a very common occurrence and a problem that needs to be addressed by the juvenile justice system.

- According to the NCVS, roughly 4 percent of all youths are victims of a violent crime each year, with a very large portion of that crime taking place at school.

- Counter to popular belief, the killing of students at school is an extremely rare event.

- Youths are also victimized within family settings. Child maltreatment, either as abuse or neglect, is a major problem.

- Youths may adopt an array of responses to victimization, ranging from fear, to avoidance, to carrying weapons and joining a gang.

- Formal agencies that respond to child maltreatment include child protective services, the juvenile court, family court, and the adult criminal justice system.

KEY TERMS

abuse
avoidance
bullying
child maltreatment
child protective services (CPS)
Children's Advocacy Center (CAC)
Court-Appointed Special Advocate (CASA)
cyberbullying
cycle of violence
domestic relations court
family courts
guardian *ad litem*
in camera testimony
intraindividual theories
lifestyle explanations
National Child Abuse and Neglect Data System (NCANDS)
National Crime Victimization Survey (NCVS)
neglect
routine activities theory
social learning approaches
sociocultural explanations

DOI: 10.4324/9781003167112-13

INTRODUCTION

The juvenile justice system does not deal exclusively with delinquent youths. As has already been seen, the juvenile court is tasked with handling noncriminal misbehavior by juveniles, typically considered as status offenders or unruly/ ungovernable. In many jurisdictions, it also has the responsibility of handling youths who are the victims of maltreatment. Beyond the fact that the juvenile justice system must deal with more than just juvenile offenders is the reality that most victims of juvenile offenders are themselves juveniles and these youths are also in need of assistance.

This chapter turns the orientation of the book on its head and focuses on youths as victims rather than offenders. Several topics are explored. First, the chapter presents evidence on the extent of juvenile victimization, as depicted in both victimization survey data and data on child abuse and neglect. The chapter also discusses explanations for the different forms of victimization. What will become apparent is that there is no single explanation for victimization just as there is no single explanation for delinquency. Individuals also respond to victimization in different ways and these methods are explored. Finally, the chapter addresses the roles of the juvenile and criminal justice systems in dealing with youthful victims.

THE EXTENT OF VICTIMIZATION

Gauging the extent of victimization can be accomplished through the use of various data collection techniques. Official records, such as the Uniform Crime Reports, provide some indication of the overall extent of victimization in society through counts of offenses brought to the attention of social control agencies. In discussions of victimization, however, most attention turns to surveys that ask respondents about their experiences as a victim of crime. Victim surveys are only about 50 years old and were developed in response to criticisms that official measures underreport the level of crime in society. Consequently, most victim surveys tend to address offenses similar to those found in the official statistics. Victim surveys, however, have been used to address crimes occurring in specific locations such as in schools and at work as well as other types of activities such as abuse and neglect. Beyond victim surveys, organizations such as the American Humane Association and various medical groups also collect information on specific types of victimization.

General Victimization in the Community

The most well-known source of victimization data is the National Crime Victimization Survey (NCVS). The current version of the NCVS is the direct descendant of early work in the 1960s and 1970s that explored both the extent of self-reported victimization and the best ways to survey the public. Among the earliest victimization surveys were those commissioned by the 1967 President's Commission on Law Enforcement and Administration of Justice. Those early surveys indicated that, on average, there was twice as much crime occurring as reflected in police records. The NCVS (originally called the National Crime

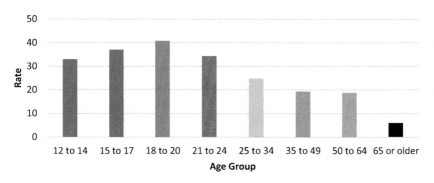

FIGURE 13.1
Estimated Total Violent
Victimization Rates for
Different Age Groups
(per 1,000), 2019

Source: Constructed
by authors from Bureau
of Justice Statistics
(2021) NCVS Victim
Analysis Tool.

TABLE 13.1 **Estimated Personal Crime Victimization Rates for Youthful Age Groups (per 1,000), 2019**

	White		Black		Other		Male		Female	
Age	**12–14**	**15–17**	**12–14**	**15–17**	**12–14**	**15–17**	**12–14**	**15–17**	**12–14**	**15–17**
Total Violence	34	40.2	31.4	28.7	29.9	27.7	42.4	35.6	23.7	38.9
Rape/Sexual Assault	1.1	6.2	1.1	1.4	12.5	8.4	0.5	0.6	1.6	9.1
Robbery	1.9	2.4	3.6	6.5	9.7	1.2	3.8	2.9	4.6	0.8
Aggravated Assault	2.5	10.9	0.6	7.9	0.8	7.6	2.6	16.1	1.4	1.7
Simple Assault	28.6	20.7	27.2	22.1	29.1	10.4	6.1	16.1	20.6	23.6

Source: Compiled by authors from Bureau of Justice Statistics (2021) NCVS Victim Analysis Tool.

Survey, which began in 1972) provides a great deal of information about the extent of victimization; characteristics of the victim; known information about the offender; data on the time, place, and circumstances of the offense; the economic and physical impact of the crimes; responses by victims; and contact with the criminal justice system.

One important piece of information provided by the NCVS is the breakdown of crimes by victim age and demographic characteristics. Figure 13.1 presents estimated 2019 victimization rates for youths ages 12–14 and 15–17. For these age groups, the estimated rate of all personal violent crime victimizations is 33 per 1,000 youths ages 12–14, and 37 per 1,000 youths ages 15–17. This represents almost 900,000 youths ages 12–17 who are victims of a violent crime in a single year. Note that all of these offenses entail physical confrontations with an assailant. Young adults (age 18–20) is the one group that displays notably more victimization (rate over 40). Compared to persons age 25 and older, youths are victimized at much higher rates. Violent crime victimization rates are 34.4 per 1,000 for persons 21–24 years of age, 25 for persons 25–34 years of age, 19.5 for persons 35–49 years of age, 18.9 for persons 50–64 years of age, and only 6 for those 65 and over (Bureau of Justice Statistics, 2021). What these data show are that youths contribute disproportionately to the ranks of crime victims.

Breakdowns by race and sex can be seen in Table 13.1. In terms of race, younger white juveniles are violent crime victims slightly more often than young blacks in overall crimes of violence but are less victimized in the 15–17 age category. White youths are victims of aggravated assault more than black youths while black youths are victimized more in terms of robbery. Black youths are victimized at lower rates in terms of aggravated assault. Comparisons of youthful victimization by males and females reveal some interesting results. Among the very young (age 12–14), males are more often victimized in terms of all crimes of violence and simple assault. For older youths (age 15–17), females are more victimized in the same categories.

WEB ACTIVITY

You can view additional information on victims of crimes on the Bureau of Justice Statistics website, where you can request a variety of analyses through the interactive analysis tool, available at www.bjs.gov/index.cfm?ty=nvat.

The NCVS figures demonstrate that a significant number of youths are victims of crimes. A number of other facts are also apparent from the NCVS. First, youths are more likely to be victimized by offenders of the same age, race, and sex as the victim. Second, youths also know the offender more often than do adults. Third, juveniles are less likely to report their victimization experience to the police. Many youths report the offense to someone other than the police.

Victimization in Schools

Whitaker and Bastian (1991) note that many youths are victimized at school. Because youths spend more than one-third of their waking hours at school, it should not be surprising that they experience victimization at school. Victimization at schools is not rare.

One major source of data from students is the NCVS. Data from the NCVS appear in Table 13.2. The data indicate that 33 out of every 1,000 youths ages 12 to 18 report being victimized at school. The highest rates of victimization across most demographic categories appear in violent offenses, followed by theft crimes. Breakdowns by gender, race/ethnicity, and age reveal some interesting results. First, the rate of violent victimization is higher for males, but it is similar in other categories. Second, victimization rates vary across racial/ethnic groups, with whites being the highest for total crimes and violent crimes, while Hispanic and "other" youths exhibit significantly lower rates for all categories of offenses.

Based on figures such as those seen here, some people have suggested that the problem of school crime is rather small. Indeed, relatively few students are ever the victim of any serious violent victimization, and the percent of property victimizations is also small. What can be lost in these figures, however, is the number of youths who are victimized. According to the NCVS, 836,100 students age 12 to 18 were victims of non-fatal crimes at school in 2018 (Wang et al., 2020). This figure translates into 225,600 thefts and 610,500 violent crimes. What these numbers show is that, despite the relatively low rate, the actual number of victims at school is significant. At the same time, the level of reported victimization at school declined significantly from 1992 to the present.

TABLE 13.2 Rate (per 1,000) of Student-Reported Victimization at School by Selected Characteristics, 2018[a]				
Student Characteristics	**Total**	**Theft**	**Violent[b]**	**Serious Violent[c]**
Gender				
Male	42.2	8.8	35.5	5.7
Female	23.1	9.0	14.1	6.4
Race/Ethnicity				
White	39.0	9.0	30.0	6.6
Black	32.5	6.0	26.5	12.6
Hispanic	24.7	9.9	14.8	3.4
Other	21.9	9.8	12.2	0.5
Age				
12–14	47.1	9.8	37.3	6.4
15–18	19.3	8.0	14.1	11.3
Total	32.9	8.9	24.0	6.0

Note: [a] Data for students age 12 to 18. [b] Violent crimes include rape, sexual assault, robbery, aggravated assault, and simple assault. [c] Serious violent crimes include the violent crimes except for simple assault.

Source: Adapted by authors from Wang et al. (2020).

One attention-grabbing form of victimization at school has been killings of students by other students. Concern over school shootings has been a major topic in the news and in society since the shootings at Columbine High School in 1999. The killings at Columbine, Jonesboro (Arkansas), Sandy Hook Elementary, Marjory Stoneman Douglas High School, and others attract a great deal of media attention and claims of "crises" facing schools. The reality, however, is that such events are rare. In 2018, there were 24 school shootings with a total of 79 injuries, 28 students killed, and 35 total deaths (Education Week, 2019). This was the largest number of school shootings, injuries, and deaths over the past 20 years. The majority of those deaths occurred in a single event at Marjorie Stoneman Douglas High School in Parkland, Florida on February 14. Looking at homicides of children age 5–18 at schools compared to those in the general population (see Figures 13.2 and 13.3), the rare nature of homicides at school is illustrated. Compared to homicides of youths age 5–18 outside of school, homicides in schools typically account for approximately 1 percent of all youthful homicides. During the 2016–2017 school year, there were 18 homicides at schools, compared to 1,587 homicides of youths age 5–18 in the United States. Youths are clearly more at risk of violent death outside the school building.

Figures 13.2 and 13.3 reveal that homicides of youths, both in school and away from school, have been on a downward trend, despite the "mass" shootings

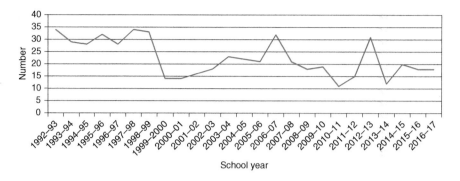

FIGURE 13.2
Number of
Homicides of
Youths Age 5–18
at School

Source:
Constructed by
authors from
Wang et al.
(2020).

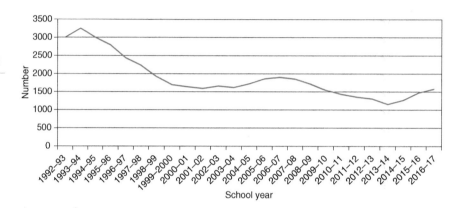

FIGURE 13.3
Total Number of
Homicides for
Youths Age 5–18

Source:
Constructed by
authors from
Wang et al.
(2020).

at schools over the years. With few exceptions, homicides in schools (which includes school shootings) have dropped from roughly 30 per year in the 1990s to fewer than 20 per year in recent years.

Shootings and homicides in schools form the basis of a great deal of fear among students, families, and the general citizenry. Dvorak (2018) notes that more than 220,000 students have been exposed to gun violence at school since 1999, and more than 4.1 million students participated in school lockdowns during the 2017–2018 academic year. The events underlying these figures often appear in national news reports that play repeatedly over many days. These reports lead to a great fear of crime and the belief that these events are inevitable. The figures on homicide and related reports, however, need to be placed into context.

WEB ACTIVITY

Extensive information on crime and victimization at school is compiled each year by the Departments of Education and Justice. Their findings appear in the annual Indicators of School Crime and Safety report that can be accessed at https://nces.ed.gov/programs/crimeind icators.

Victimization at school raises a number of perplexing problems. First, the schools are failing to protect the youths who are legally required to attend school. This raises potential issues of liability. Second, the level of victimization at school may have a direct impact on the quality of education received by the students. This may result from students missing days of school because of the offense or fear of being victimized. It also may occur because school officials must spend time trying to establish discipline and control or because the level of crime makes the staff feel that the students are not interested in receiving an education. Crime and victimization, therefore, may replace educating as the primary concern of the school. Consequently, victimization has both immediate and long-term impacts on students.

Bullying

A major topic of concern for many youths and their parents is the problem of bullying. The issue of bullying has received a great deal of attention over the past decade. This is partly due to events at schools where part of the blame/ explanation for violent behavior is attributed to past bullying. While most bullying does not lead to such levels of retaliatory violence, it clearly has an impact on the victim.

Bullying behavior can be classified into four types: verbal, physical, social, and cyberbullying. Too often it is assumed that bullying is primarily verbal, such as teasing and name-calling. It is important to note that many forms of bullying involve physical confrontations that are actually forms of criminal victimization. Included here are hitting, shoving, and punching. Starting rumors about someone or ostracizing them from participating in events are examples of social bullying. The final major form, **cyberbullying**, involves the use of the internet and other technologies to attack the victim and differs from the other forms in several ways. First, cyberbullying can take place through posts on social media (such as Facebook, TikTok, and other applications), texts, sexting, and unwanted internet contacts and can occur 24 hours a day, every day of the year. Second, it does not require the parties to be in the same place at the same time or ever come face to face. Third, the offender can remain anonymous. Finally, the messages or images may remain in public view for a very long time.

Information on the extent of bullying generally comes from survey data. According to the 2017 *NCVS: School Crime Supplement*, 20.2 percent of all students reported being bullied at school, with 41.4 percent reporting they expect to be bullied again (Wang et al., 2020). An inspection of the types of bullying reported in Table 13.3 shows that several categories are actually forms of criminal victimization, although the students report it as bullying. These figures show that bullying, with few exceptions, is more prevalent against

The issue of bullying continues to garner attention. Protesters hold signs at Hamilton Middle School in Cypress, Texas, to bring attention to the suicide of Asher Brown, an 8th grader who killed himself at home. His parents blamed his suicide on two years of bullying they say he had suffered at the school.

CREDIT: AP Photo/*Houston Chronicle*, Karen Warren

TABLE 13.3 Percent of Students Reporting Bullying, 2017

Type of Bullying	Total (%)	Male (%)	Female (%)
Made fun of, called names, or insulted	13.0	10.3	15.8
Subject of rumors	13.4	9.3	17.5
Threatened with harm	3.9	4.2	3.6
Pushed, shoved, tripped, or spit on	5.3	6.1	4.4
Tried to make do things did not want to do	1.9	1.9	1.9
Excluded from activities on purpose	5.2	3.5	6.9
Property destroyed on purpose	1.4	1.3	1.5
Cyberbullied (Electronically bullied*)	14.9	9.9	19.7
Total	20.8	16.7	23.8

Note: * Electronically bullied includes "being bullied through texting, Facebook, or other social media."

Source: Compiled by authors from Wang et al. (2020).

WEB ACTIVITY

A good resource for information on bullying is www.Stopbullying.gov.

females. Bullying reports are similar for whites and blacks, similar in public and private schools, and more prevalent among younger youths (data not shown).

Cyberbullying is a growing problem in recent years and is not restricted to one location or setting. Data from the Centers for Disease Control and Prevention reveal that, in 2015, 15.6 percent of school students reported being "electronically bullied" over a 12-month period of time. According to the 2017 *NCVS: School Crime Supplement*, a total of 15.3 percent of the student respondents reported being bullied online or by text. This is up from less than 4 percent in 2007. Different forms of cyberbullying reported by students include harmful information posted on the internet, the distribution of private information on the internet, and various forms of harassment.

Child Maltreatment

Victimization surveys and most official sources of crime data generally miss a major form of victimization against youths, namely child maltreatment. Child maltreatment is a term encompassing a variety of actions in which children are harmed, either intentionally or unintentionally. According to the Federal Child Abuse Prevention and Treatment Act of 2010 (CAPTA), child abuse and neglect is defined as:

> … any recent act or failure to act on the part of a parent or caretaker, which results in death, serious physical or emotional harm, sexual abuse or exploitation …, or an act or failure to act which presents imminent risk of serious harm. (42 U.S.C. 5101)

This definition incorporates a number of different actions, including physical abuse, neglect, sexual abuse, emotional abuse, abandonment, and substance

BOX 13.1 MAJOR TYPES OF CHILD ABUSE AND NEGLECT

Physical abuse is nonaccidental physical injury (ranging from minor bruises to severe fractures or death) as a result of punching, beating, kicking, biting, shaking, throwing, stabbing, choking, hitting (with a hand, stick, strap, or other object), burning, or otherwise harming a child, that is inflicted by a parent, caregiver, or other person who has responsibility for the child. Such injury is considered abuse regardless of whether the caregiver intended to hurt the child. Physical discipline, such as spanking or paddling, is not considered abuse as long as it is reasonable and causes no bodily injury to the child.

Neglect is the failure of a parent, guardian, or other caregiver to provide for a child's basic needs. Neglect may be:

- Physical (e.g., failure to provide necessary food or shelter, or lack of appropriate supervision)

- Medical (e.g., failure to provide necessary medical or mental health treatment)

- Educational (e.g., failure to educate a child or attend to special education needs)

- Emotional (e.g., inattention to a child's emotional needs, failure to provide psychological care, or permitting the child to use alcohol or other drugs).

Sexual abuse includes activities by a parent or caregiver such as fondling a child's genitals, penetration, incest, rape, sodomy, indecent exposure, and exploitation through prostitution or the production of pornographic materials.

Emotional abuse (or psychological abuse) is a pattern of behavior that impairs a child's emotional development or sense of self-worth. This may include constant criticism, threats, or rejection, as well as withholding love, support, or guidance. Emotional abuse is often difficult to prove and, therefore, child protective services may not be able to intervene without evidence of harm or mental injury to the child. Emotional abuse is almost always present when other forms are identified.

Abandonment is now defined in many states as a form of neglect. In general, a child is considered to be abandoned when the parent's identity or whereabouts are unknown, the child has been left alone in circumstances where the child suffers serious harm, or the parent has failed to maintain contact with the child or provide reasonable support for a specified period of time.

Substance abuse is an element of the definition of child abuse or neglect in many states. Circumstances that are considered abuse or neglect in some states include:

- Prenatal exposure of a child to harm due to the mother's use of an illegal drug or other substance

- Manufacture of methamphetamine in the presence of a child

- Selling, distributing, or giving illegal drugs or alcohol to a child

- Use of a controlled substance by a caregiver that impairs the caregiver's ability to adequately care for the child.

Source: Compiled by authors from Child Welfare Information Gateway (2019). Retrieved on June 12, 2021, from www.childwelfare.gov/pubs/factsheets/whatiscan.

abuse. Definitions of each of these can be found in Box 13.1. Broadly stated, **abuse** is the intentional commission of an act upon a child, while **neglect** refers to the omission of a caretaker to provide what a child needs. Neglect can be physical (e.g., failing to provide food or shelter), medical (i.e., failing to provide medical care), emotional, or educational.

What makes child maltreatment especially noteworthy is the fact that the offender is typically a parent or other relative. While not a new phenomenon, it is only since the 1960s that child abuse and neglect have been seen as a social problem. Prior to that time, these types of actions were primarily considered private problems that were best dealt with by the family.

Measuring child abuse and neglect is difficult due to the nature of the actions and the victim–offender relationship. First, abuse and neglect typically do not take place in public. Instead, they occur at home where there are no witnesses besides the victim, offender, and other family members. Second, in many cases the victim may not recognize the action by the parent as wrong. The child is either too immature to understand the nature of what is happening, cannot adequately verbalize the events, or does not know who to tell about the abuse or neglect. Third, despite the abuse, children often still express love and affection for the parent/relative and may not want to do something that will get the offender into trouble. As a result, the child will not report, and may even deny, the existence of maltreatment.

Due to these problems, no firm figures on abuse and neglect are available. What is known is that the problem is widespread. One source of data on child abuse and neglect is child protective services (CPS) agencies in each state. Data from these agencies are collected and compiled by the **National Child Abuse and Neglect Data System (NCANDS)**. In 2019, CPS agencies received 3.5 million referrals for child abuse or neglect. There was an estimated 656,000 child victims of abuse or neglect in the United States (see Figure 13.4) (Administration on Children, Youth, and Families, 2020). This is a rate of 8.9 per 1,000 children. Roughly two-thirds of the maltreated children experienced neglect. Sixteen percent experienced physical abuse, 10 percent experienced physical maltreatment, and 7 percent experienced sexual maltreatment (Administration on Children, Youth, and Families, 2020). Unfortunately, child maltreatment

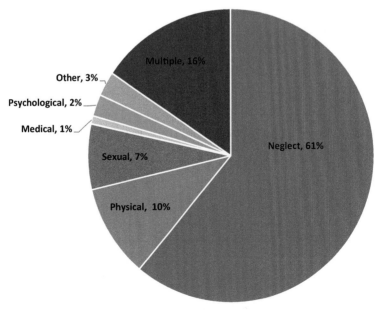

FIGURE 13.4
Types of Maltreatment Victims, 2019

Source: Constructed by authors from Administration on Children, Youth and Families (2021).

often leads to the death of the victim. According to NCANDS data, 1,840 children were killed in 2019 as a result of maltreatment for a rate of 2.5 per 100,000 children.

WEB ACTIVITY

More information on what constitutes child maltreatment and how you can identify potential maltreatment can be found at www.childwelfare.gov/pubs/factsheets/whatiscan.cfm.

The figures for the extent of abuse and neglect are only estimates. There is no accurate count for this type of victimization. The fact that most such acts occur behind closed doors between relatives means that we may never have a complete picture of the problem. What can be concluded is that these are baseline figures and that the real extent of abuse and neglect is probably much higher.

EXPLAINING JUVENILE VICTIMIZATION

Attempts to explain why an individual is a victim can take a variety of forms. Certainly, one way to explain victimization is to turn the equation over and focus on the offender. The various theories addressed earlier in this text (Chapters 3 and 4) follow this more traditional approach to understanding unacceptable behavior. Because the perpetrator is the one who has violated the law, it is natural to focus attention on that individual, rather than the victim. There must be something about the offender that led to the victimization.

The realm of victimology, however, does not rely exclusively on the theories already presented in this text. Rather, attempts to explain juvenile victimization range from those that focus on the lifestyle of victims to explanations that target specific forms of victimization.

Lifestyle

Early research on victims paid considerable attention to who the victims were and the circumstances surrounding the events. Throughout these works was an underlying theme that individuals became victims because of something they did, did not do, or could not do. For example, von Hentig (1941) outlined 13 categories of victims, including the young, females, the elderly, minorities, and mentally defective individuals. What made these people victims was the fact that they were somehow vulnerable. Some people cannot physically ward off an attack, others do not recognize they are being victimized, and others see themselves outside the societal mainstream and accept the victimization.

Lifestyle explanations and routine activities theory are commonly employed to show how individual behavior contributes to victimization. These theories argue that where individuals go, who they go with, and when they go all define their lifestyle and their chances of victimization (Cohen & Felson, 1979; Hindelang, Gottfredson, & Garofalo, 1978). If one's choices for behavior place a person in an area where crime is common, at a time when there is no one to provide protection, then the chances for victimization are enhanced. That person's lifestyle, therefore, contributes to becoming a victim.

Examples and support for a lifestyle explanation of juvenile victimization are plentiful. The fact that juveniles are disproportionately represented among offenders would suggest that juveniles would also be the victims for a variety of reasons. First, other youths are available to victimize—at school, out-of-doors in the neighborhood, in play groups, and as acquaintances. Second, juvenile offenders will view other youths as more physically vulnerable than most adults. Third, interaction with other youths provides knowledge and opportunities for offending. Fourth, individuals who engage in deviant behavior are themselves at higher risk of being a victim (Clark & Lab, 1995; Esbensen & Huizinga, 1991; Lauritsen, Sampson, & Laub, 1991). In essence, the juvenile lifestyle includes more youths to victimize than adults. As youths either find themselves or place themselves in situations in which delinquency is more likely, they will invariably be victimized.

Explanations of Child Abuse and Neglect

Where the lifestyle approach emphasizes the behavior and choices of the victim as contributors to victimization, explanations of child maltreatment focus exclusively on the offender and society. The victim is not considered culpable. In general, explanations for child maltreatment can be divided into three categories: intraindividual theories, sociocultural explanations, and social learning theories (Doerner & Lab, 2021). **Intraindividual theories** view child maltreatment as an internal flaw or defect of the abuser. Abusers are considered to exhibit some form of psychopathological condition (Steele & Pollock, 1974). Intraindividual theories have been used to absolve society of any responsibility for child abuse and lay the blame on a few "sick" individuals.

Sociocultural explanations shift the emphasis from the individual to society and the environment. The abuser may be stressed by any number of factors, such as unemployment, conflicts at work or home, family size, social isolation, and economic problems (Belsky, 1978; Garbarino & Gilliam, 1980; Gelles, 1980; Gil, 1971). This stress may lead the individual to strike out against a child who has neither the physical stature nor the social standing to resist maltreatment. A child, therefore, becomes the recipient of abuse as a proxy outlet for stress.

Social learning approaches to child maltreatment rest on the assumption that an individual has learned to be abusive by observing past abusive behavior. This observation includes the possibility that the abuser was himself or herself abused as a child. The idea that a child who is abused or who witnesses abuse will grow up to be an abuser is often referred to as the **cycle of violence** (Schwartz, 1989; Straus, 1983). Widom (1989, 1995), following abused/neglected youths and a control group into adulthood, reports a significant relationship between abuse/neglect as a child and deviant behavior later in life.

Explanations for child abuse and neglect are still in their infancy. Indeed, scholarly interest in this form of victimization is relatively new, with most work dating since the 1960s. Consequently, little consensus exists on the explanations for maltreatment or how to best attack the problem.

RESPONSES TO VICTIMIZATION

Victimization, whether direct or vicarious, has the potential of eliciting a number of responses from the victim. While victims may view the responses as beneficial, they are often debilitating and may lead the victims into criminal or delinquent behavior. Youthful responses can range from raised levels of fear of crime to various actions aimed at reducing the risk of initial or further victimization. Carrying weapons for protection or joining gangs may be responses chosen by youthful victims. In both cases, however, the response may be illegal and/or lead to more victimization.

Fear of Crime as a Response

Whether or not a victim takes an action at the time of an offense, there will probably be some changes in beliefs or behavior subsequent to the victimization experience. While many studies show that roughly 40–50 percent of the population is fearful of crime (Hindelang, 1975; Skogan & Maxfield, 1981; Toseland, 1982), there is relatively little research that assesses fear among juveniles. This is particularly interesting because youths are among the most victimized.

When research does look at youths, fear does not appear to be a minor concern. Lab and Clark (1994), in their study of junior and senior high school students, found that 30 percent of the students claimed to fear being attacked at school, independent of whether they had ever been victimized in the past. Similarly, the 2019 *NCVS: School Crime Supplement* reports 4.2 percent of youths are fearful of being attacked at school, and 2.7 percent are fearful of attack or harm away from school (Wang et al., 2020). These levels of fear are relatively stable across gender, race, and location.

Fear can be debilitating, regardless of whether it is a result of past victimization. Fear leads some people to avoid other persons and places. It makes others decide to carry a weapon for protection, and still others to join groups to fight crime. The very fact that fear can cause people to change their normal routine is evidence that it is something to be addressed. This is not to suggest that fear is always a bad thing. Indeed, to the extent that fear alters a person's behavior and chances of being victimized, fear is a useful tool.

Avoidance

A common reaction to actual or potential victimization and fear is **avoidance** of certain places or people. Avoidance is possibly the leading response to fear of victimization (Gates & Rohe, 1987; Skogan, 1981). Reasonable avoidance behavior for a youth may include staying away from a playground where gang members are known to hang out or refraining from walking alone at night in an area with a high crime rate.

For youths, avoidance is problematic when the school is the location of victimization. Victimization at school raises the option of staying home from school or avoiding certain places at school. Avoidance at school, however, means that

TABLE 13.4 Responses of Students to Victimization and Fear in School, 2017	
Avoidance Behavior	(%)
Any place at school	6.1
School activities	2.4
Avoided classes	0.8
Avoided places	4.9
Entrances	0.9
Hallways or stairs	2.2
School cafeteria	2.3
Restrooms	2.2
Other places	1.1
Carrying Weapons to School	3.8
Carrying Weapons Anywhere	15.7
Presence of Gangs	8.6

Source: Compiled by authors from Wang et al. (2020).

schoolwork is missed, the student is distracted from work while at school, and/or there is discomfort and inconvenience involved in avoiding important parts of the school (such as a restroom or the cafeteria). Table 13.4 displays avoidance behavior related to schools. The 2017 *NCVS: School Crime Supplement* reports that roughly 6 percent of students avoid school, school activities, and/or specific places at school due to fear of attack or harm (Wang et al., 2020). A variety of other studies have reported similar proportions of youths who skip school due to fear (Lab & Clark, 1996; Lab & Whitehead, 1994; Metropolitan Life, 1993; Ringwalt, Messerschmidt, Graham, & Collins, 1992). While the youths may be attending school, the quality of the education they receive is diminished. Some students may go hungry, suffer discomfort because they are afraid to use restrooms, arrive late for classes due to using only certain stairways or hallways, or refrain from taking part in enriching extracurricular activities. In essence, the school experience is far from an ideal nurturing atmosphere. The ultimate form of this avoidance is quitting school. Students who drop out are not included in surveys of students. Thus, the number of youths who report avoiding school due to fear in most studies is an undercount of who is taking this action.

Resorting to Weapons

Another form of response involves self-defense actions, particularly carrying weapons for protection. An inescapable fact about youths in recent years is their ability to obtain and use weapons. According to data from the 2017 Youth Risk Behavior Survey conducted by the Centers for Disease Control and Prevention (see Table 13.4), 3.8 percent of high school students reported carrying a weapon to school at least once in the past 30 days (Wang et al., 2020). Almost 16 percent carry weapons someplace in the past 30 days. Lab and Clark (1996) found that 24 percent of the respondents carried a weapon to school for protection at least once over a six-month time period. Even higher levels of weapon possession at school emerge in studies of inner-city schools (see, for example, Sheley, McGee, & Wright, 1995). Among the weapons carried for protection are guns, knives, brass knuckles, razor blades, spiked jewelry, and mace (Lab & Clark, 1996).

Unfortunately, while bringing a weapon to school may make a youth feel safer, such devices have the potential of causing more problems than they solve. One negative outcome is that being caught with a weapon can lead to expulsion, criminal prosecution, and other sanctions against the student who is trying to protect himself or herself. A second possibility is that if the student is attacked and does try to use the weapon, the level of violence and victimization may escalate. That is, a fistfight can become a shooting, or a theft can result in an aggravated assault. The victim may be more seriously harmed, or the victim may become the offender. Yet another consequence is that schools can become armed camps where the administration is forced to take progressively intrusive measures to keep weapons out of school.

Gangs as Protection

In times of crisis or turmoil, it is natural for people to seek out support from those around them. Most victims will turn to family members for such assistance. Another source of support is close friends and peers. For many youths, the friends and peers include gang members. This is particularly true for youths in large inner-city areas. The response to victimization, therefore, may entail joining a gang for protection. Some youths see joining a gang as a means of restoring a feeling of security. If a youth is victimized by gang members, either directly or by mistake, joining a gang further becomes a self-defense mechanism. The presence of gangs in schools opens the possibility of youths turning to gangs for protection. According to the 2017 *NCVS: School Crime Supplement*, almost 9 percent of youths report gangs are present at their schools during the school year (see Table 13.4), with over 11 percent of urban youths making this claim (Wang et al., 2020).

A student at Brainerd High School in Chattanooga, Tennessee, walks through a metal detector as she enters the building.

CREDIT: AP Photo/*Chattanooga Times Free Press*, Tim Barber

Joining gangs as a response to victimization, however, is a double-edged sword. While the gang may supply some sense of protection, it typically demands participation in illegal behavior and conflict with other gangs and individuals. These demands often result in further victimization of the individual rather than protection from victimization. At the same time that gang membership may alleviate victimization, joining a gang can also contribute to ongoing victimization, albeit as a member of a group and not just as an individual.

WEB ACTIVITY

The National School Safety Center (www.schoolsafety.us) addresses a wide range of victimization and safety issues for schools. What kinds of suggestions and materials can you find on its website for addressing school safety?

Summary of Victimization Responses

Juveniles can respond to victimization in a variety of ways. At the same time, many of the potential responses have negative aspects that can exacerbate problems for the youth. Fear, which may serve as a protective measure, can lead to withdrawal from other people and the community. It can also prompt a youth to stay home from school or avoid certain places at school. Still other victims may purchase and carry weapons for protection. Victimization also may drive a youth to join a gang as a means of feeling safe. While each of these may appear reasonable, they can lead to further victimization, more serious situations, and, certainly, a deterioration in the general quality of life.

THE ROLE OF FORMAL SOCIAL CONTROL AGENCIES

Various social control agencies can become involved in youthful victimization. Most social control agencies, however, focus on juvenile victims of abuse and neglect and ignore the victim status as it emerges from other forms of offending. Clearly, a juvenile who loses money due to a theft or is hurt from an assault tends to be considered a witness more so than a victim by the justice system. Assistance to these victims is relatively limited to mediation and similar programs already discussed. On the other hand, victims of abuse and neglect receive a great deal of attention by various formal control agencies, particularly CPS and the different court systems.

Perhaps the only agency that will have contact with all forms of youthful victims will be the police. This is because they are typically the ones called whenever someone is in need of help. The police, however, are geared toward identifying offenders, making arrests, and preparing cases for prosecution. Except for initial contacts, providing immediate protection, referrals to other sources of assistance, and work with prevention programs, law enforcement officers spend little time dealing with the victim. This is true whether the victim is an adult or a juvenile. Consequently, the balance of this section looks at how other system components deal with youthful victims.

Child Protective Services

An alternative point of system entry besides the police that has been established for the purposes of protecting youths is child protective services. **Child protective services (CPS)** are mandated in every state as a direct result of the Child Abuse Prevention and Treatment Act of 1974 (Wiehe, 1992). This federal act required states to set up rules for the reporting and handling of abused children. States not conforming to the Act would be denied various forms of federal funding. Because the exact nature of how a state would provide protective services was left to the state, these services appear under various state agencies such as Social Services and Departments of Human Services.

Child protective service agencies fill a variety of roles and have diverse powers. First, in virtually all jurisdictions, these agencies are responsible for accepting reports of abuse and neglect cases and undertaking or coordinating the investigation of such allegations. While many investigations are done by employees of the child protective service, others may be assigned to other agencies, such as the police or prosecutor's office. A second common function of CPS is the removal of children from suspected (or documented) abusive situations. This removal may last for only a short time or can last for an extended period, depending on the facts of the case. The protection of the child from further possible harm is the goal of any decision to remove a child from his or her parents. Child protective services often provide oversight to foster care, adoption, and other forms of custodial arrangements for the state.

Finally, CPS focus on the preservation of the family unit. Underlying this approach is the belief that the family setting is the most appropriate for raising a child. Stabilizing the family situation, removing the problematic elements in the home, and improving the quality of life for the child guide the decisions made by the agency. Given this preoccupation with family preservation, most child protective agencies do not need court orders or sanctions to work with families. Much like diversion programs or informal probation, CPS will work with families to solve problems without resorting to formal court procedures if all parties agree. In some cases the agency will actually provide the recommended intervention, and in others the agency may act as more of a referral source than service provider.

Child protective services reach a large number of victims and families each year. An estimated 7.9 million children were referred for preventive measures in 2019 (Administration on Children, Youth, and Families, 2021). Almost 55 percent of these referrals received post-investigative services, of which roughly 16 percent were victims of crimes (Administration on Children, Youth, and Families, 2021). Roughly 656,000 substantiated cases of abuse and neglect were identified in 2019, for a rate of 8.9 victims per 1,000 children. Seventy-five percent were victims of neglect, 17.5 percent were victims of physical abuse, and 9.3 percent were sexual abuse victims. Just over 142,000 youths were removed from their homes in 2019 as a result of abuse or neglect (Administration on Children, Youth, and Families, 2021). These figures reveal two things. First, CPS agencies reach a substantial number of abuse and neglect victims. Second, these agencies handle many youths for an array of problems beyond just victimization.

Child protective services personnel work very closely with different courts. While these agencies often generate cases for the criminal and juvenile courts, the courts also call on these services for assistance as cases work their way through the system. This referral from the courts to protective services can range from taking custody of children when parents are incarcerated for a crime to investigating allegations of abuse and neglect that emerge in the course of divorce proceedings.

Children's Advocacy Centers

A Children's Advocacy Center (CAC) is an umbrella organization, independent of the criminal justice system, that brings together CPS workers, law enforcement officers, the prosecutor's office, educators, mental health counselors, and medical personnel in an effort to provide a coordinated response and seamless service delivery to maltreated children. This multidisciplinary team approach is designed to keep children from being shuttled from one agency to the next, and to provide a variety of services under one roof. The first CAC opened its doors in 1985 in Huntsville, Alabama. Since then, the concept has expanded, and there are 900 CACs operating in the U.S. which served over 371,000 children in 2019 (National Children's Alliance, 2019).

The goals of a CAC are to minimize the trauma child victims undergo, and to provide a safe and comfortable atmosphere. One notable service CACs provide is videotaped forensic interviews. Among other things, videotaping reduces the number of interviews/interviewers, preserves testimony for later use, documents the tone of the session and the conditions under which the interview took place, and allows an assessment of the child's veracity (Chandler, 2000). In fact, an independent assessment of "best practices" specifically praised a multidisciplinary team approach, trained forensic interviewers, videotaping interviews, and the CAC model as being among the "best practices" to utilize when conducting child maltreatment investigations (Jones, Cross, Walsh, & Simone, 2005).

The Juvenile Court

The juvenile court deals with a wide variety of issues related to youths. Besides handling delinquents and status offenders, it faces cases of dependency, abuse, and neglect. In these cases, the court must consider the protection and needs of the juvenile victim, the needs of the entire family unit, and the possible sanctioning and needs of the (typically adult) offender.

Cases of abuse and neglect force the juvenile court to assume more of a conflict orientation than presumed under the *parens patriae* philosophy. Because of the diverse issues in abuse and neglect cases, many juvenile courts are affiliated with (or even part of) what are more generally known as **family courts**. Larger family courts may designate certain judges to handle delinquency matters and others to deal with abuse and neglect cases. These latter cases typically follow a more rigorous set of procedural guidelines, including evidentiary safeguards, the presence of attorneys, and formal examination and cross-examination of witnesses. This is required because of the due process rights of the accused.

In every case of abuse and neglect, the primary concern of the juvenile court is the well-being of the juvenile and the family unit. Other youths in the home also become a focal point along with the individual victim, based on the assumption that they are potential victims. Because abuse and neglect cases place the interests of the child in conflict with that of an accused parent, the court typically appoints someone to be an advocate for the needs and interests of the child. Two common names for such an advocate would be a **Court-Appointed Special Advocate (CASA)** or a **guardian ad litem**. The CASA program began in Seattle in 1977 and has since spread to 49 states and the District of Columbia (National CASA, 2017). According to National CASA (2021), there are over 948 local programs with almost 97,000 volunteers handling 276,809 children in the United States. These advocates usually serve in a voluntary capacity, although some courts provide office space, supplies, and

BOX 13.2 EXCERPTS FROM OHIO'S GUARDIAN *AD LITEM* STATUTE

2151.281 Guardian *ad litem*

(A) The court shall appoint a guardian *ad litem*... to protect the interest of a child in any proceeding concerning an alleged or adjudicated delinquent child or unruly child when either of the following applies:

 (1) The child has no parent, guardian, or legal custodian.

 (2) The court finds that there is a conflict of interest between the child and the child's parent, guardian, or legal custodian.

(B) (1)... the court shall appoint a guardian *ad litem*, subject to rules adopted by the supreme court, to protect the interest of a child in any proceeding concerning an alleged abused or neglected child ...

 (4) The guardian *ad litem* appointed for an alleged or adjudicated abused or neglected child may bring a civil action against any person who is required ... to file a report of child abuse or child neglect that is known or reasonably suspected or believed to have occurred if that person knows, or has reasonable cause to suspect or believe based on facts that would cause a reasonable person in a similar position to suspect or believe, as applicable, that the child ... is the subject of child abuse or child neglect and does not file the required report and if the child suffers any injury or harm as a result of the child abuse or child neglect that is known or reasonably suspected or believed to have occurred or suffers additional injury or harm after the failure to file the report.

(I) The guardian *ad litem* for an alleged or adjudicated abused, neglected, or dependent child shall perform whatever functions are necessary to protect the best interest of the child, including, but not limited to, investigation, mediation, monitoring court proceedings, and monitoring the services provided the child by the public children services agency or private child placing agency that has temporary or permanent custody of the child, and shall file any motions and other court papers that are in the best interest of the child ...

Source: Ohio Revised Code Section 2151.281 retrieved June 2, 2021, from http://codes.ohio.gov/orc/2151.281.

travel expenses. The exact role and responsibility of a CASA volunteer or a guardian *ad litem* varies across jurisdictions, although their general duty is to protect the interests of the child in virtually any legal proceeding (see Box 13.2). These individuals typically receive training in the functioning of the juvenile court, the needs of youths, the availability of resources, and how to investigate the circumstances of the case.

WEB ACTIVITY

Look up the statutory guidelines for a guardian *ad litem* in your state.

Court-appointed advocates often fulfill some of the same functions as other actors in the criminal and juvenile justice systems. These individuals, because of their focus on youths, can undertake a more thorough investigation of a case than can an overburdened police force. They can also spend the time to identify potential sources of treatment for the child, offender, and family that is not a role of law enforcement investigators. In some places these individuals also serve in the place of an attorney on the child's behalf. One key difference, however, between an attorney and a CASA volunteer or guardian *ad litem* involves their orientation toward the case. Whereas an attorney argues in accordance

TABLE 13.5 Outcomes of CASA Involvement

- Youths spend a longer time in foster care.
- Youths receive more case services.
- More cases are permanently closed before the youth reaches the age of majority.
- Higher likelihood of a successful "permanent plan" being implemented.
- Lower chance of family reunification—more adoptions.

Source: U.S. Department of Justice (2006).

WEB ACTIVITY

More information about the CASA program can be found at the national website at www.nationalcasa.org.

with the client's wishes, a court-appointed advocate is supposed to argue in the best interests of the child, even if that conflicts with the desires of the child (Sagatun & Edwards, 1995). These court volunteers provide a vital source of information and recommendations to the juvenile or family court.

CASA volunteers have had a big impact on abuse and neglect cases. An evaluation conducted by the U.S. Department of Justice's (2006) Inspector General noted that cases in which a CASA was involved tended to receive more and longer services and arrive at better position outcomes than cases without their intervention (see Table 13.5). The only surprise was the fact that cases involving CASAs had a lower rate of family reunification. This is probably due to the fact that the CASA program handles more complex and difficult cases.

The Criminal Court

The criminal court holds a difficult position when faced with youthful victims, particularly abuse and neglect victims. This is because of its orientation toward determining guilt or innocence of the accused and imposing sentences on the convicted. The victim in the criminal court holds no more stature than does any witness. It is the state that is the aggrieved party and the state that is pursuing the prosecution of the offender (Doerner & Lab, 2021). As a consequence of this situation, the criminal court focuses on providing the accused with his or her due process rights. Besides the victim's role as a witness, the court's only other concern for a victim is to protect him or her from further harm.

A juvenile victim in the criminal court is especially problematic due to his or her lack of maturity. The process can be very traumatic for a child, particularly if the accused is an abusive or neglectful parent. In the past, many cases never reached trial, or the prosecution was unsuccessful due to problems with youthful victims/witnesses. In recent years, however, criminal courts have started to make accommodations for youthful victims. For example, some jurisdictions provide victim counselors as a means of minimizing the trauma of a court appearance and assisting youths with recall problems (Burgess & Laszlo, 1976; Geiselman, Bornstein, & Saywitz, 1992). These counselors can serve in a fashion and capacity similar to CASA workers and guardians *ad litem*. Other courts have relaxed the hearsay rule (Levine & Battistoni, 1991) or allowed *in camera* testimony (Bjerregaard, 1989; Melton, 1980) as a means of entering testimony while protecting the victim. The relaxed hearsay rule allows third-party testimony, such as from a counselor or psychiatrist. *In camera* **testimony** entails testimony outside the courtroom, such as in a judge's chambers or by means of closed-circuit television or on tape. While these efforts are not allowed in all jurisdictions, they are gaining acceptance as a way to protect the youthful victim while still prosecuting the accused.

On a related note, both juvenile and adult victims hold few rights in the criminal court. As noted earlier, there have been some accommodations made for juveniles as witnesses. Other inroads to the court appear in legislation that provides victims with rights such as the right to be informed about court proceedings, the right to protection from intimidation, and the right to address the court at the time of sentencing (Doerner & Lab, 2021). Unfortunately, there is little discussion of youthful victims in any of the arguments for these changes or in the enacting legislation.

Domestic Relations Court

A final court in which juvenile victims may find themselves is a domestic relations court. These are civil courts devoted to the issues involved in divorce, child support, and related matters. As with juvenile courts, domestic relations may be configured as a special court within a larger family court setting in some jurisdictions. Youthful victims appear in these courts primarily in cases in which allegations of abuse or neglect are made by one parent against another. The child does not have a separate standing in the court, despite the possibility of abuse or neglect. When such allegations are made, the court will order an investigation (often by protective services agencies) for the purpose of making a determination with regard to the question before the court (e.g., divorce, support payments, etc.). It is possible that the court will provide a CASA worker or a guardian *ad litem* to the child when such allegations are made. If evidence of abuse or neglect is uncovered in the case, those issues are turned over to the criminal or juvenile courts for action. Therefore, while youthful victimization may emerge in domestic relations courts, those problems are outside of the court's jurisdiction and will be turned over to another court.

SUMMARY: THE NEED TO RECOGNIZE THE VICTIM

Addressing children as victims of crime has long been a component of the juvenile justice system and, to a minimal extent, other courts; but this fails to garner much attention in discussions of juvenile justice. This is unfortunate, because most youthful offenders prey on other youths and significant numbers of youths are victims of abuse and neglect. While the juvenile court has long standing in the areas of abuse and neglect, youthful victims have few coping mechanisms available for dealing with other forms of victimization. This is especially true outside the juvenile justice system. To what can this anonymity of juvenile victimization be attributed? One major source of blame has to be the fact that too often the emphasis on juvenile offenders ignores the other half of the offense dyad—the juvenile victim. We have attempted to begin to rectify this shortcoming in this chapter. It is also important, however, that more emphasis be placed on research and programming for juvenile victims. Without those efforts, juvenile victims will continue to receive little attention.

DISCUSSION QUESTIONS

1. You have recently been hired to work for an agency that deals with abused and neglected youths. Research your state statutes and report on the legal definitions of abuse and neglect, and what is mandated in terms of dealing with these victims (such as mandatory reporting, treatment, etc.). What gaps do you see in the statutes? What changes would you make?

2. You have been asked to draw up new legislation dealing with child abuse and neglect. Define the terms, outline the issues you would include in the legislation, and discuss the role you see for the juvenile court and how, if at all, it would alter the court's philosophy.

3. Discuss the responses youths make when victimized. What are the positive and negative consequences of the various responses? What types of services are available to handle victimized juveniles (not including abuse and neglect)? What services are in your town? What services would you like to see initiated?

4. Your local Parent Teacher Association (PTA) is clamoring for increased security measures at school. The PTA wants to prevent homicides and other violent crimes. What information should the PTA and the school be aware of in order to make reasonable choices?

CHAPTER 14

Future Directions in Juvenile Justice

WHAT YOU NEED TO KNOW

- Reform proposals for juvenile court include reemphasizing and reinvigorating the rehabilitative orientation of juvenile court, changing juvenile court into a scaled-down version of criminal court, and "smart on juvenile justice" proposals.

- Another model is to adopt a restorative justice model for juvenile court.

- Social issues that affect juveniles include race (disproportionate minority confinement and contacts), disadvantage, and segregated neighborhoods. Elliott Currie offers a bold reform plan to address these issues. There are also calls for police reform as a necessary step to improve juvenile justice.

- In *Roper v. Simmons* (2005), the U.S. Supreme Court ruled that the death penalty is unconstitutional for juveniles. Like the dissenting Justice Scalia, some would argue that the death penalty is appropriate for juveniles.

- The Supreme Court has ruled that life without parole sentences cannot be given to juveniles for a non-homicide offense (*Graham v. Florida* [2010]) and that mandatory life without parole sentences are unconstitutional for juveniles (*Miller v. Alabama* [2012]). Both rulings were based on the incomplete adolescent psychological development and impulsiveness of juveniles. Life with the possibility of parole and virtual life sentences (extremely long sentences) are also possible for youths who commit homicide.

- There is some confusion over the proper role of juvenile court concerning status offenders. Petitioned cases are decreasing, but many argue that they need to decrease even more.

- Although many would like an easy solution, that is not possible. The answer is to address the problems of youths who break the law. Police reform is also critical.

KEY TERMS

capital punishment

criminalized juvenile court

Currie's reform proposal

divestiture

harm reduction (Barry Feld)

jurisdiction over status offenders

restorative justice juvenile court

smart on juvenile justice/the fourth wave/new balance effort

spiritual dimension in corrections

DOI: 10.4324/9781003167112-14

INTRODUCTION

The juvenile court is at a turning point. It appears that the "get tough" movement is being joined with reforms that accept the psychological research on adolescent development and also attempt to reduce costs. One example of this is states returning to age 18 as the initial age of adult criminal court jurisdiction. Another example is that of states reforming their juvenile justice systems to incorporate risk assessment and evidence-based practices and measures to reduce incarceration.

This chapter will examine several proposals about the future of juvenile court. We will outline these proposals and assess them. This chapter will also look at some broader issues affecting the treatment of juvenile offenders. For example, we will look at the role of community and family in dealing with delinquency. We will question whether steps can be taken to improve the ways in which both community and family try to prevent delinquency.

PROPOSALS FOR REFORMING JUVENILE COURT

Rehabilitating the Rehabilitative *Parens Patriae* Court

One approach to the problems of the juvenile court is to try to return to the rehabilitative and *parens patriae* roots of the court. Reformers who support this option think that the failures of juvenile court are failures of implementation: The juvenile court has not delivered the rehabilitation that it initially promised. A major factor behind this failure of implementation is lack of funding. Legislators have not provided the money needed to help youths obtain education, individual counseling, family counseling, and vocational training.

If juvenile courts received adequate funding and if they followed the advice of the research on effective rehabilitation programs (see Chapters 10 and 11 for summaries of those findings), then juvenile court could be the ideal youth court envisioned by the Progressives at the beginning of the twentieth century. Juvenile court judges could act like concerned parents trying to help children.

A leader in the drive to get juvenile court to deliver rehabilitation is Lipsey (2009; also see Cullen, 2007). Lipsey has done meta-analysis research on effective interventions. He believes that such research shows that there are effective interventions for both institutionalized and noninstitutionalized offenders. The best programs have the capability to "reduce recidivism by 40–50 percent, that is, to cut recidivism rates to very nearly half of what they would be without such programming" (Lipsey, 1999:163). Furthermore, these programs "do not entail exceptional efforts or costs" (Lipsey, 1999:163); they are doable and affordable. (For recent reviews of effective correctional interventions for both juveniles and adults, see Lipsey, 2009; MacKenzie, 2006; MacKenzie & Farrington, 2015; Latessa et al., 2020.) Krisberg uses the term "redemption" and offers the moral argument that we need to be concerned about redeeming all children:

> Moreover, it is patently clear that most of us would seek a justice system that is founded on core principles of charity and redemption if it were our own children who were in trouble. This, of course, is the key issue. If we recognize the truth that all children are our children, the search for the juvenile justice ideal is our only moral choice. (Krisberg, 2005:196)

Corbett (2001) agrees with the call to implement the findings on effective interventions and adds that it is important to focus on early intervention instead of late intervention. Parent training, for example, has been shown to be effective. Another suggestion is to emphasize "the paying of just debts": "Restitution and community service programs repay and restore victims and harmed communities and counter the prevalent notion that juvenile offenders are immune from any real penalties" (Corbett, 2001:149). He also suggests that probation officers should act as moral educators who help juveniles build character. He maintains that setting an example is crucial:

> Every occasion where self-restraint is exercised in the face of a probationer's provocation, where kindness and courtesy is extended to a probationer's family in defiance of the juvenile's expectation, and every effort by the officer to insure fair treatment in dispositional and revocational proceedings are opportunities for character building and moral education. (Corbett, 2001:149)

His final suggestion is to attempt violence prevention through anger-management skills training and similar social skills education programs.

Bishop claims that many states have actually passed legislation to continue rehabilitation in juvenile court. Purpose clauses continue to include treatment as a primary purpose of the court. Three states have recently passed legislation to improve individualized treatment plans for youths in custody, four states have passed laws providing mental health assessment and treatment, and several states have passed laws to establish teen courts and other diversion programs. Still other states operate drug and/or mental health courts with a clear treatment focus. Mississippi ended its boot camp program, and Connecticut and other states raised the age of jurisdiction from 16 to 18. Bishop argues that such legislative actions are evidence that "the juvenile justice system is less punitive and more treatment-oriented than is commonly assumed" (Bishop, 2006:659).

None of these suggestions requires a radical reshaping of probation or the juvenile justice system. The suggestions build on the history and tradition of probation as caring individuals (probation officers in the tradition of probation founder John Augustus). What Corbett proposes is that today's officers utilize both social science findings (e.g., parent education and anger-management training) and common sense, such as setting a character-building example, to attempt to induce juveniles to become prosocial.

Another note in favor of a rehabilitative juvenile court is that public opinion supports it. For example, in a survey of 1,308 Florida residents, Mears and his colleagues Hay, Gertz, and Mancini found that more than 80 percent of the public disapproves of abolishing the juvenile justice system. In fact, even "many conservatives … view violent juvenile offenders as capable of being rehabilitated" (Mears et al., 2007:249). Similarly, Applegate, Davis, and Cullen (2009) found that more than three-quarters of their sample of Florida residents thought that having a juvenile justice system "makes good sense." Finally, a recent national poll found that Americans still favor rehabilitation as the main goal of juvenile justice (Bolin, Applegate, & Ouelette, 2021).

A final argument in favor of a rehabilitative juvenile court is that effective interventions can also be very cost-effective. A cost–benefit study has reported the following benefits per juvenile offender: Functional Family Therapy: $58,043; Multisystemic Therapy: $26,545; and Aggression Replacement Training: $55,821. Deterrence-based programs, however, such as surveillance-oriented parole and Scared Straight, result in additional costs per offender—for example, almost $13,000 for each youth in Scared Straight (Aos & Drake, 2013). Given current budget constraints on governments, such cost considerations are a powerful argument to use evidence-based treatment interventions with juvenile offenders.

A Criminalized Juvenile Court

A solution to the problems of juvenile court is to "criminalize" juvenile court: to attempt to make it a scaled-down version of adult criminal court. In order to do this, two things need to be done. First, a **criminalized juvenile court** would entail providing juveniles with all the procedural protections of criminal court. Thus, children would have the right to a jury trial and would have fully adversarial defense attorneys, not attorneys who often slip into the role of a concerned parent trading off zealous advocacy for promises of treatment. A second action that needs to be taken to transform juvenile court into a criminal court for youths would be to scale down penalties out of concern for the reduced culpability of children. Sentences would be shorter in such a juvenile court compared to adult criminal court. This reform was suggested about 30 years ago by the American Bar Association and the Institute of Judicial Administration. The suggestion was published in the Juvenile Justice Standards (IJA–ABA, 1982).

The major problem with the suggestion for a criminalized juvenile court is that it may not satisfy calls for a more punitive approach to juvenile offenders. Some critics of the current juvenile justice system do not want reduced penalties; they want adult penalties for what they perceive as adult offenses: "adult crime, adult time," in the words of one governor (see Vandervort & Ladd, 2001:229). Such critics contend that violent offenses indicate culpability and should be punished with lengthy prison terms, and that is not the vision of the Juvenile Justice Standards.

A New Balance/Smart on Crime/the Fourth Wave

A few years ago, Bishop and Feld (2012) argued that the current juvenile court was showing signs of rebalancing, or a new balance. They argued that the punitive strains of the "get tough" era of the 1980s and 1990s were softening and they saw "signs of a counterbalance to the repressive policies of the recent past" (Bishop & Feld, 2012:921). This comment turns out to have been prophetic, as this tendency has grown since then. The change has included states returning to age 18 as the initial age of criminal court jurisdiction and some states enacting sweeping reforms of their juvenile justice systems. Some call this movement "smart on juvenile justice"; others call it the "fourth wave of juvenile justice."

There are several factors behind this softening of the "get tough" era. First, the famous crime decline (see Chapter 7) of the 1990s has eased calls for harsh treatment of juveniles. Second, advances in both neuroscience and developmental psychology have provided scientific support for the proposition that youth are less mature and less responsible. Third, advocacy groups have worked to soften punitive demands of the "get tough" era.

A basic element of the rebalancing is a trend to return the lower bound of criminal court jurisdiction to age 18. Connecticut, Illinois, Massachusetts, and New York have done this. The push to influence states to do this was labeled the "Raise the Age" effort. (For a discussion of going even further than raising the age to 18, see Box 14.1.) Second, other states have restricted the offense or offender criteria for transfer, or have mitigated the possible sentences for transferred youth (for details, see Daugherty, 2013, and Crime and Justice Institute, 2017). The trend is not perfect, as "get-tough" provisions still exist. A third sign is that the Supreme Court ruled against life without parole sentences for youths convicted of non-homicide offenses (*Graham v. Florida*, 2010) and ruled against mandatory life without parole sentences for juveniles (*Miller v. Alabama*, 2012; *Montgomery v. Louisiana*, 2016). More important than the holdings, in these decisions the Court extended the *Roper* rationale that juveniles are not as culpable as adults. In addition, a number of states are giving greater protection to the right to counsel for juveniles by prohibiting or dissuading waivers of counsel.

The more extensive reach of this **smart on juvenile justice/the fourth wave/ new balance effort** is substantial revision of juvenile justice in several states. Specifically, a number of states—including Pennsylvania, Illinois, Louisiana, Washington, Georgia, Hawaii, and Kentucky—have reformed their juvenile justice systems as a result of cost pressures, concerns over disproportionate minority contact, research on effective interventions, and suggestions of experts. (For details on state reform legislation, see Crime and Justice Institute, 2017.) One name for this direction is getting "smart on juvenile justice." Another source calls the latest trend the "fourth wave" of juvenile justice (based on the premise that there have been three prior major movements in juvenile court thinking) (Weiss, 2013).

One common theme of this smart on juvenile justice reform is the implementation of research-grounded, evidence-based practices in juvenile court and juvenile corrections. From intake to aftercare supervision, research findings would be used to guide decisions. Another key element is risk assessment. At

BOX 14.1 RAISING THE AGE OF JUVENILE COURT TO 21 OR 25

Going beyond raising the age of criminal responsibility to 18, some argue that juvenile court jurisdiction should be extended to age 21 or even age 25 instead of the current 18 in most states. For example, in Massachusetts there is a movement to include 18- to 20-year-olds in juvenile court jurisdiction (www.raisetheagema.org). (Note: 18- to 20-year-old murderers would still be automatically processed in adult criminal court.) Vermont has now included 18-year-olds, except for the commission of certain serious offenses, as slated for juvenile court processing and will include most 19-year-olds by July 2022 (Teigen, 2021). As noted in the discussion of the *Roper* decision on the death penalty, the research in psychology and neurobiology shows that young adults are not fully developed and mature until their mid-twenties. In addition, some experts say that other factors that affect the maturation process have changed dramatically in the last few decades. Fewer young adults are married, and more are disconnected from work and are earning less today than decades ago. For example, less than 10 percent of young adults were married in 2010, compared to 45 percent in 1960. Marriage and work have been life-course events that influence youths to mature.

One option for recognizing that full maturity comes later would be to treat youths as juveniles until age 21 or age 25. A second option would be to have a third system for young adults age 18 to 21 or 18 to 25 in addition to juvenile court for those under 18 and adult criminal court for those 21 and above, or 25 and older (depending on the new age boundary). Another possibility is to offer sentencing discounts for youthful offenders. For example, Finland provides a two-thirds discount for youths age 15–17 and a one-third discount for youths age 18–20 (Barnert et al., 2017).

What do you think? Are young adults less mature today than in past decades due to changes in marriage patterns and in employment opportunities? Do you believe that those from generations who frequently married by age 21, and also could possibly get factory jobs fresh out of high school, were influenced to take on adult responsibilities and mature sooner than young adults of today? Should that make states change how they treat young adults who commit a crime? Or do you think that young adults are just looking for an excuse to escape responsibility for their decisions and actions?

several decision points, proven risk assessment instruments would be given to juveniles to determine their level of risk and their needs for intervention and treatment. Low-risk youths could be diverted or screened out of the system. Moderate- and high-risk youths could be given appropriate services and supervision. As can be seen from the chapters on both institutions and probation, this model relies on research that has identified a number of interventions that have been proven to reduce offending, such as several family interventions and cognitive–behavioral approaches (see Chapters 10 and 11 for further discussion). A major push in this model is to beef up community interventions so as to prevent and reduce placing youths in juvenile prisons. The reasoning is twofold: get youths appropriate services and also save money.

While many applaud the states that have tried to become "smart" on juvenile justice and embrace the so-called fourth wave of juvenile justice reform, Rovner (2016a) cautions that all is not well with current juvenile justice processing. Specifically, he argues that an important concern over current juvenile justice functioning is that in many states it is still much too easy to arrest, convict, and sanction (even imprison) kids as adults for even minor drug crimes. For example, in Indiana, 14-year-olds can be waived to adult court for manufacturing or distributing drugs. In Oregon, many drug crimes can result in transfer starting at age 15. Rovner claims that such transfer provisions are remnants of the tough-on-crime climate of the 1990s. His call for reform would involve

BOX 14.2 REFORM DOES NOT NECESSARILY MEAN WHAT YOU THINK

A case study of juvenile justice reform in Texas raises critical concerns. In 2007, Texas legislators passed what was hailed as a significant juvenile justice reform bill. On the positive side, the state has reduced its state juvenile correctional population from 4,700 in 2007 to about 1,500 in 2012. Reports characterized the reform as "a model for the nation."

A closer examination, however, reveals serious concerns about what Texas has actually accomplished. It appears that the state has switched from incarceration in state youth prisons to expansion of county control over juveniles, including detention facilities operated by private companies. Similarly, the state continues to make frequent use of solitary confinement and trying youths as adults. Overall capacity in secure facilities has grown, and the number of local detention officers has grown by more than 1,500. Similarly, the funds available for probation have increased, but a major expansion of juvenile probation has been for punitive programs such as electronic monitoring—from 103 programs in 1999 to 9,331 such programs in 2012. Cate (2016:579) characterizes all of this as "not a stark reversal of prior policies, but rather a continuation of the 'cheap and mean' punishment that Texas had always been committed to." The lesson is that simply calling a change "reform" can be misleading: It is imperative to examine actual changes to see if the change is really "reform" or is simply a modified way of doing the same things that have been the conventional routine.

completely removing direct file and automatic waiver and eliminating low-level crimes like drug offenses from adult courts altogether. Transfer would be available only via a transfer hearing and only for serious crimes (Rovner, 2016a). (Recall the discussion of transfer and related mechanisms in Chapter 8.) For a criticism of the Texas reform, see Box 14.2.

Harm Reduction: Barry Feld

Barry Feld (2018) has gone beyond the New Balance model. His latest reform proposal asserts that intervention is often harmful, especially for black youths. So he states that the first priority of juvenile justice should be harm reduction. This can be achieved through diversion and minimal sanctions, as many delinquents simply grow out of their misbehavior. He also calls for decriminalizing most criminal misdemeanors and violations of probation so that fewer youths will be placed out of home (Feld & Moriearty, 2020). Further ways to reduce harm are deinstitutionalization—adopted by states such as Massachusetts and Missouri—and delinquency prevention programs which would prevent many harms.

For youths who do get caught up in the juvenile court process, his first reform suggestion is mandatory provision of defense counsel, recording all interrogations, and limiting the time of interrogation on a sliding scale with younger youths subject to the least interrogation. Plea bargaining should be subjected to greater scrutiny, and all states should offer the right to a jury trial. Critically, waiver should be available only for youths whose serious and persistent offenses necessitate minimum periods of confinement that greatly exceed the maximum sanctions available in juvenile court. Feld would limit severe sanctions to youths charged with homicide, rape, robbery, or assault with a firearm or substantial injury. At sentencing, all youths would receive a substantial youth discount, with no mandatory LWOP, or de facto life sentences for young offenders. For example, a 16-year-old would only get a sentence that is 50 percent of the adult sentence. Feld also calls for maximum sentences of no more than 20 or 25 years. He also calls for raising the age of jurisdiction to 18 in every state and making 16 the minimum age for transfer. He even goes so far as to call for extending some protections to youths age 18 to 21, due to the psychological research on delayed development (Feld, 2018).

A Developmental Approach

The National Research Council of the National Academies of Science recently completed a comprehensive study on the implications of the research on adolescent development for the juvenile justice system. The resulting report recommended that juveniles be held accountable for offending, but that condemnation, control, and lengthy confinement are not necessary to do so. Instead, restorative justice programs and restitution are two examples of developmentally appropriate methods. A second focus should be to prevent reoffending by implementing evidence-based programs after appropriate risk/needs assessment. Intervention efforts should engage the youth's family and draw on neighborhood resources. A third emphasis is on procedural fairness, including attorney representation and reducing racial/ethnic disparities via reduced processing or structured decision making. Attention needs to be devoted to making sure that adolescents are competent to understand all proceedings and to ensure that juveniles perceive that they have been treated fairly. An interesting note to this report is that the report authors argued that juvenile court is based on seeing juveniles as children, while recent "get tough" measures see juveniles as adults. The research on adolescent development, however, sees juvenile offenders as between the two (Bonnies et al., 2013). (For additional voices focusing on the need to base policy on what we know about adolescent development, see Sullivan, Piquero, & Cullen, 2012; Zimring & Tanenhaus, 2014.)

The National Research Council report edited by Bonnies et al. (2013) is based on a wide range of research and is comprehensive. In contrast to the other reform proposals in this chapter, this set of suggestions has the added weight of being written by a panel of experts from a nationally recognized body of scientists. Thus, no one can claim that this report and its recommendations are simply one person's viewpoint.

A Restorative Justice Juvenile Court

For years, Gordon Bazemore (1999) has been arguing that states should adopt a restorative justice model in the juvenile justice system. (Recall the related discussion of restorative justice in Chapter 12.) A restorative justice focus emphasizes the victim and the community. The approach is "focused less on achieving public safety by incarcerating individual offenders and more on reducing fear, building youth–adult relationships, and increasing the capacity of community groups and institutions to prevent crime and safely monitor offenders in the community" (Bazemore, 1999:98; see also Takagi & Shank, 2004).

This represents a radical rethinking of the role of juvenile court. Instead of sanctioning and supervising offenders, the role of the **restorative justice** juvenile court would be to build community so that neighborhoods can better respond to—but also prevent—delinquency. Communities would be more involved in sentencing through community panels or conferences or dispute resolution programs. Communities would return to their role of being responsible for youths. Bazemore argues that the community must address socialization needs with "caring adults who spend time with young people not because they are paid to do so but because they share a commitment to the idea that youth development is a community responsibility" (Bazemore, 1999:101).

A positive feature of Bazemore's proposal is that it is not a hypothetical proposal; many restorative justice programs are already in place. As noted, numerous communities already are working at restorative justice. A major question, however, is how far restorative justice can go. How willing are citizens to assume the responsibilities that restorative justice would give them in deciding cases and monitoring sanctions such as community service? If people are not available to staff the restorative justice programs, they will not work. Proving that it is possible to implement such programs, Vermont has a system of 49 restorative justice boards with almost 300 volunteer board members in operation (Karp et al., 2004). These boards use 30- to 60-minute meetings to negotiate restorative justice contracts between victims and offenders, so it is possible to implement such programs.

On the one hand, restorative justice is a reality in many juvenile courts. As of a few years ago, Bazemore and Schiff (2005) noted that there were well over 700 restorative justice programs, some adult and some juvenile, in operation across the country. While most of these programs do address the core restorative justice principle of repairing harm, not all of the programs have addressed community and government role transformation. In other words, many operate within the traditional framework of government programs rather than trying to achieve community building. A probation department may start a restitution program or a community service program or even some type of victim–offender mediation, but it may not take the next step of involving community members to a much greater extent in seeking justice and making both victims and offenders whole once again (Bazemore & Schiff, 2005).

A concern about restorative justice is the reliance on communities to get involved in programs such as mediation and conferencing. Takagi and Shank (2004), for example, note that in Oakland, California, the black youth unemployment rate approaches 50 percent, more than half the people in homeless shelters are African American, and three black high schools in Oakland consistently rank at the bottom of the state in academic performance. What does community mean for the unemployed, the homeless, and the poorly educated? Is restorative justice possible if community is so fractured?

A recent comment of Bazemore's (2012) is that restorative justice is in danger of being perceived as being a "boutique" program or having the "Oprah" effect. What he means is that Oprah Winfrey has featured restorative conferences on her show, and Bazemore fears that restorative justice may be seen as something "often viewed as 'perfect for' just the right (unfortunately rare) case"

(Bazemore, 2012:713). So it is seen as "interesting" and fine for minor offenses, instead of being found useful for almost all delinquency cases, as it has been used in New Zealand.

Summary of Proposals for Reforming Juvenile Court

In the last decade, a number of states have legislated specific changes affecting juveniles, such as raising the age of criminal responsibility to 18. Other states have undertaken major reforms of their juvenile justice systems. These changes reflect the developmental research on adolescents that shows they are still maturing in terms of decision making by removing minor offenses from juvenile court processing and reserving the harshest handling for the most serious offenses. The next few years will show whether these changes do in fact result in clear differences or whether, as Cate (2016) has claimed about the Texas reforms, the changes mask a continued emphasis on getting tough and punishing juveniles.

BROADER ISSUES

Beyond the need to make changes in juvenile court, there are additional issues that need to be addressed if American society is to help juveniles grow into mature, responsible, law-abiding adults. We will note several such issues here and show how they relate to juvenile justice. We will consider the issues of race and juvenile court, the possible decline of community and social capital, the role and needs of American families, and the political economy.

Race and Juvenile Court

Several sources note that race is a problem in juvenile justice. The harshest criticism is that the entire criminal justice system—including juvenile court—is racist. Writers such as Alexander (2012) argue that the criminal justice system is simply a cover for societal racism in which criminal sanctions allow society to treat blacks, especially black men, as second-class citizens. A related but less direct criticism is that the public is not as concerned about disadvantaged children as about middle- and upper-class children (Feld, 1999; Krisberg, 2012b). The consensus is that the juvenile justice system has a problem of disproportionate minority contacts (see, e.g., Bishop, 2005; Piquero, 2008; Rovner, 2016b, 2021a). In response, the federal government, for example, has made the elimination of disproportionate minority confinement in juvenile correctional facilities a priority.

As noted in previous chapters, statistics indicate that there are racial disparities throughout the juvenile justice system. In 2016, black youths made up 15 percent of youths in the United States but constituted 35 percent of juvenile arrests and were 4.6 times more likely to be committed to an institution (Rovner, 2021a; Sentencing Project, 2018). In juvenile court, case rates for person, property, and public order offenses were higher for black youths than for youths of other races. Black youths accounted for 35 percent of delinquency cases despite making up 15 percent of the population under juvenile court jurisdiction (Hockenberry & Puzzanchera, 2020). Studies show that race effects persist even after controlling for legal variables such as offense seriousness, and that early decisions to arrest and detain contaminate decisions at later stages to an unknown degree (Bishop & Leiber, 2012). In other words, police decisions to focus on certain neighborhoods, police tendencies to react to the attitudes of minority suspects, and decisions to not divert and to detain that are affected by such factors as resources available to lower-class children, begin early in the process and have indirect effects later on. As Feld and Moriearty put it, "the primary sources of these [racial] disparities are the over-criminalization, over-policing, and over-punishment of juveniles of color, and the implicit racial biases that drive decision makers to rationalize their disparate treatment" (Feld & Moriearty, 2020:787).

Quite disturbing is Feld's (1999) assertion that there is pervasive public antipathy to the problems of disadvantaged and minority children. If society does not really care for poor minority children, then it may not matter all that much which court—juvenile rehabilitative, juvenile criminal, or adult criminal—is designated to process juvenile delinquency. Unless society is truly committed to the problems of all youths, and especially disadvantaged youths, then youth crime will persist. (See also Currie's reform proposal later in this chapter.)

An analysis of three major studies of delinquency in Pittsburgh, Rochester, and Seattle found clear evidence of greater contact/referral of minorities in the juvenile justice system. This differential minority contact cannot be accounted for by higher offending by minorities. However, the researchers could not conclude that differential minority contact proves racial bias (Huizinga et al., 2007). This report suggests that race continues to be an issue that merits concern in the juvenile justice system.

Similarly, recent reviews of the research on juvenile justice system processing conclude that race is still a factor in processing (Bishop, 2005; Piquero, 2008). One reason for the influence of race is at the very heart of the juvenile justice system. As noted in Chapter 2, juvenile court was founded to treat children with problems. This intent put discretion into the system. Because officials have discretion, they often focus on minority juveniles because they think that minority youths need the help that the juvenile justice system is supposed to offer. The positive intention of offering assistance to minority children has resulted in a disproportionate share of minority youths being subjected to juvenile court processing and dispositions such as placement. While the intent may have been positive, the result has been a disproportionate share of minorities at all stages of the juvenile justice system, starting with police and ending with custodial placements (Bishop, 2005).

Some make a very straightforward argument that the criminal justice system, the juvenile justice system, and U.S. society as a whole are all racist, and that drastic action needs to be taken to eliminate widespread, pervasive racism. Perhaps the most compelling case for this argument has been made by Michelle Alexander (2012). As noted, she claims that attacking "crime" and "criminals" is the new way to cover up racism:

In the era of colorblindness, it is no longer socially permissible to use race, explicitly, as a justification for discrimination, exclusion, and social contempt. So we don't. Rather than rely on race, we use our criminal justice system to label people of color "criminals" and then engage in all the practices we supposedly left behind. Today it is perfectly legal to discriminate against criminals in nearly all the ways it was once legal to discriminate against African Americans ... As a criminal you have scarcely more rights, and *arguably* less respect, than a black man living in Alabama at the height of Jim Crow. We have not ended racial caste in America; we have merely redesigned it. (Alexander, 2012:2)

To solve this pervasive and deep-seated problem, Alexander calls for drastic actions, especially ending the war on drugs (for a similar point of view, see Hinton, 2016). Similarly, Currie (2020) calls for massive public spending on jobs and improving disadvantaged neighborhoods (see below for further discussion of Currie).

Race and Police Reform

Events of the last several years have made it clear that the issue of race and policing is one of the most critical problems in both juvenile and criminal justice today. The names of too many victims of police shootings/killings—Michael Brown, Laquan McDonald, George Floyd, Daunte Wright—have become familiar to all Americans, black and white. A number of observers state that there is a crisis of legitimacy in policing (White & Fradella, 2016) or a national race crisis (Walker et al., 2018). In other words, many blacks do not trust the police to treat them fairly, believe that police may stop them for no reason, and are even skeptical that the police will respond to their calls for help.

One response is that publicized police shootings quickly trigger demonstrations. Unfortunately, some demonstrations following highly publicized police shootings have turned into vandalism and looting, such as what happened in Minnesota after the killing of George Floyd and the shooting of Daunte Wright. While black citizens protest what they perceive as injustice, many business owners fear damage to their shops, restaurants, or offices as a consequence of protests. Research on police attitudes before and after the Ferguson shooting reveals that demonstrations due to Ferguson have not demoralized the police and resulted in only minor reductions in police activity (slightly less foot patrol and writing fewer citations [Marier & Fridell, 2020]). If citizens react more vehemently in the future, however, that could change. Apart from public protests, police fear that responding to suspected crimes or calls for service can too easily escalate into actions that will be caught on camera and quickly subjected to criticism, if not outright condemnation, and possibly being fired or charged with a crime.

The term least likely to stir emotional debate is disparate minority contact—DMC. Blacks, including black youths, are more likely to be "contacted"—stopped, frisked, and arrested—by police officers (see also Chapter 7). The more emotionally charged label is racism, a term used by writers such as Alexander (2012) and Forman (2017).

In a nutshell, many blacks think that the police are, at worst, racist, and, at best, not doing all they can to make black neighborhoods as safe as possible. Police, on the other hand, feel under siege, feel that their every action is under scrutiny with many citizens quick to claim racism, brutality, or inappropriate use of deadly force.

Several steps seem reasonable at this point. First, police need to focus on procedural justice both because it is the right thing to do and because it may help increase police legitimacy. Specifically, police need to treat citizens with respect and to give citizens a voice in encounters and in setting policies and priorities (Mazerolle & Terrill, 2018). Second, police need to reduce the use of force. Two steps to reduce the use of force are recruiting officers who favor a "guardian" role over a "warrior" role and adopting a restrictive or even a least force policy (Terrill, 2020). Police need to take steps to prevent or minimize problems in a proactive way. For example, when a department such as Chicago is found guilty of clearly unreasonable use of force (U.S. Dept. of Justice Civil Rights Division & U.S. Attorney's Office, Northern District of Illinois, 2017), that finding indicates that the problem was not addressed proactively. Third, police departments need to review policies, practices, and training to ensure that officers are aware of and follow correct policies and procedures and that officers receive training and supervision that address possible racial bias. Fourth, citizens need to refrain from immediate judgments of police actions as being improper or racist even before any investigations are conducted. Like all citizens, police deserve the right to a fair investigation of their actions. Similarly, if a court finds that a police officer is innocent of wrongdoing, citizens need to respect that finding. Fifth, communities in particular, and the nation as a whole, need to address such issues as structural disadvantage and segregated neighborhoods. (For a thorough discussion of police reform, see Katz & Maguire, 2020.)

Some are calling for the police to do less. For example, the National Institute for Criminal Justice Reform (2021) is calling for the police to respond to serious violence but for new crisis response teams to respond to many of the calls that police currently handle. These teams would be trained in mental health and also de-escalation techniques. Police forces would be reduced as these crisis teams take up some of the work police normally do.

The current status quo is extremely volatile. Both black citizens, including black youths, and many police officers are primed to see problems where there may not be a problem. Reform is critical so that citizens can feel safe and fairly treated and so that police officers can feel that they will be able to do their job without fear that their decisions will snowball into either violence on the street or media headlines accusing them of racist actions. Both recent shootings and the aftermaths of those shootings make it painfully clear that changes are needed for there to be both justice and peace. The conviction of Officer Derek

WEB ACTIVITY

Search the web for details on police reform legislation in your state and at the federal level. Compare the reform bills from various states and the federal government.

Chauvin for killing George Floyd showed that the justice system can hold a white officer accountable for criminal behavior against a black suspect. One case, however, does not solve decades of problematic treatment of black citizens. A final note is that both state and federal legislators are working on police reform legislation in response to current controversies about the police.

Elliot Currie's Call for Reform

Elliott Currie (2020) focuses on the problem of violence, particularly as it affects black Americans, including black youths. He explains the extent of the problem, its causes, and remedies. Blacks, especially black males, experience significantly higher rates of violent victimization than whites. For example, young black males face 15 times the chances of dying from violence as their white counterparts. In 2018, 930 young white men died from homicide. If young white males faced the same rate of homicide victimization as young black men, the number of deaths of young white men would have been almost 14,000 deaths (Currie, 2020).

Currie's reform proposal argues that structural disadvantage and segregation are the principal causes of the disparity in violent victimization of blacks, including black youths. Youths experience "deep poverty, vanished opportunities, and absence of social support" (Currie, 2020:220), all of which also lead to very negative attitudes. In a nutshell, black youths disproportionately live in poor neighborhoods, live in one-parent families, attend substandard schools, and face employment obstacles, all of which are related to involvement in crime and delinquency. For example, in 2017, almost one million young black males and females, age 16 to 24, were "disconnected," meaning that they neither had a job nor were enrolled in school (Currie, 2020:182). In Chicago, 45 percent of young black males (age 20–24) were disconnected (Currie, 2020).

Currie dismisses the recent "get tough" policy on crime as a dismal failure. In its place he calls for a guarantee of meaningful employment for all Americans with wages that allow for a decent standard of living. One step that would help would be apprenticeship programs for both blue-collar and white-collar jobs. Another step would be spending on jobs. Second, he calls for massive public sector investment in schools, health care, and childcare. He also advocates prevention programs for youths and intensive help for the problems that caused youthful offenders to commit crime and delinquency. He notes, for example, that while nearly one in six children fall below the federal poverty level, that number jumps to nearly three in 10 for black children. Countries such as Denmark and Finland, in contrast, have child poverty rates below 4 percent (Currie, 2020).

Currie's analysis and reform proposals clearly link the problems of delinquency and crime, especially violent crime, with economic disadvantage and racial segregation. His solutions would address disadvantage in education, housing, health care, welfare, and employment. In short, Currie goes much further than many current proposals to use risk and needs assessment instruments and evidence-based practices such as cognitive–behavioral interventions (see, again, Chapters 10 and 11). Those proposals address real individual-level problems but ignore the structural problems of economic disadvantage, poor schools, and segregation as well as systemic problems such as over- and under-policing and racially biased policing. As Currie puts it: "The 2020 protests against abusive policing have driven home the reality that, since the Jim Crow era, police have not only failed to reliably protect black Americans against violence in their communities but, all too often, have contributed to it" (Currie, 2020:221). One other negative aspect of many traditional intervention efforts is that they often appear to be telling black youths that they should simply

> adapt to intolerable conditions—to accept uncomplainingly the prospect of lives that are dramatically different from those of more fortunate people, and that offer little hope of anything much better. The evidence tells us that that approach is more often futile than not. (Currie, 2020:220)

Perhaps the biggest question about Currie's proposals is how to get a majority of Americans to agree to support fundamental economic changes that would cost money and raise taxes. A related question is whether public opinion would see Currie's proposals as insufficiently punitive. A recent national poll found that Americans still favor rehabilitation as the main goal of juvenile justice. However, they also continue to support deterrence, incapacitation, and even retribution as important goals (Bolin, Applegate, & Ouelette, 2021). A disturbing note is that states that adopted reforms to address the problem of disproportionate minority contact in their juvenile justice systems tended to adopt weak reforms, the most common reform measure being legislation to conduct an exploratory study of racial distinctions in the state (Donnelly, 2017).

One way to generate support for Currie's proposals is to emphasize that poverty and disadvantage affect many children overall, not just black children. In 2018, 17 percent of all children in metropolitan areas were living in poverty, and 15 percent lived in households in areas classified as food insecure. Seventy-five percent suffered neglect, 18 percent physical maltreatment, and 9 percent sexual maltreatment (Federal Forum on Child and Family Statistics, 2020). On the positive side, research shows that "supportive programs—programs that invest in at-risk children and in at-risk families—work to reduce crime" (Cullen, Wright, & Chamlin, 1999:198–199). There is also clear evidence that early prevention programs such as preschool intellectual enrichment, home visitation and parent management training, and community-based mentoring programs can prevent delinquency and crime (Welsh & Farrington, 2007).

MacKenzie and Farrington (2015) raise the issue that research on providing opportunities has not reduced delinquency. They argue that faulty thinking patterns need to be changed first before enhancing opportunities will work to reduce delinquency. Currie (2020), however, points out that decades of blocked opportunities, racial discrimination, and segregation have affected

BOX 14.3   SHOULD THE GOVERNMENT AND PRIVATE FUNDING SOURCES FUND YOUTH GROUPS THAT SUPPORT EFFORTS THAT CRITICIZE POLICE

Goddard and Myers (2018) report on groups that are trying to improve juvenile justice in nontraditional ways. Like Currie, these groups see youth crime as a product of social injustice and thus they seek to transform both social and penal policies. As a result, they involve the youth they serve in both community improvement efforts and consciousness raising and public protests.

What do you think? Should efforts to reduce delinquency include consciousness raising and even protests about how police treat black youths? Is it desirable public policy to encourage disadvantaged youths to see how social and criminal justice policies affect them and then, in turn, protest perceived injustices? Or should delinquency prevention efforts avoid what might be perceived as political positions that can become controversial?

the attitudes of many young blacks. In other words, depressing conditions do produce negative attitudes. A classic study, Elliot Liebow's *Tally's Corner* (Liebow, 2003), made much the same point, namely, that many blacks are very aware that the deck is stacked against them, and a realistic assessment of their life chances is by necessity negative. Currie would push for changing the opportunity structure so as to produce more positive attitudes, while MacKenzie and Farrington argue that attitudes need to improve before opportunity enhancement can work.

The ideal course of action for the future would seem to be to incorporate many, if not all, of Currie's points and also address individual-level problems such as the educational needs of offenders, working with their families to increase parental guidance and support, and helping youthful offenders adopt positive attitudes. If reform can provide access to meaningful employment and attack segregated neighborhoods—as Currie rightly emphasizes— then the attention to individual-level needs could not be criticized as efforts to make black youths try to adjust to an unfair world, since a main focus of Currie is to make the American economy and society a fair—or at least a fairer—reality for all. On the other hand, if reformers only strive to get youthful offenders to adjust to what they perceive to be and what writers such as Currie say is an extremely unfair world, the delinquency problem will continue to be with us. (For a controversial aspect of calls for social justice, see Box 14.3.)

Reintroducing the Spiritual Dimension into Corrections

As noted in Chapter 11, the Good Lives Model states that offenders seek more than simply a job and avoiding crime. They also seek a sense of purpose in their lives via meaningful work and fulfilling relationships (Ward, 2010). *New York Times* writer and television commentator David Brooks (2015) calls for striving to follow your vocation, in other words, to seek out work "that is intrinsically compelling" so that "you will end up serving yourself and the community ..." (Brooks, 2015: 266).

John Whitehead and Michael Braswell (2000) agree with these writers and phrase the issue as the need to re-introduce the spiritual dimension in corrections. This would entail efforts of corrections workers, whether prison counselors, chaplains, or probation officers, to help offenders find greater meaning in their lives.

Both residential institutions and probation can try to address the spiritual needs of juvenile offenders. Prisons and jails have always had chaplains and religious services as part of their programming. That can and should continue, but institutions and probation/parole can take additional steps to incorporate the spiritual dimension into correctional practice.

First, correctional workers—correctional counselors, probation officers, parole officers, correctional officers—can all attempt to help offenders focus on the question of meaning in their lives. In group sessions and individual reporting, these workers can encourage offenders to think about the meaning of their lives.

Second, correctional workers have the simple but potentially profound example of their own lives. They can come to work each and every day showing a sense of purpose and meaning in their lives and in their interactions with prisoners that will influence those who come in contact with them. All of us can attest to persons who show by the example of their lives that there is something that energizes them and inspires them despite the difficulties they face. This is in stark contrast to workers who exert a negative influence in the prison or in the parole office. For example, in one women's prison, some guards came in and plopped down in front of the television set to watch hours of sports programming (Girshick, 1999), and in some Canadian correctional facilities, guard supervisors were found to create an environment rife with sexual harassment (McMahon, 1999). At the very least, workers need to refrain from abuse, harassment, and anything else that detracts from prison as a place where offenders can think about the meaning of their lives.

A concrete suggestion is to adopt an intervention strategy such as the "Making Life Choices" program, which is a participatory learning strategy that focuses "on creating contexts in which young people themselves can discover their own competence for influencing the direction of their lives" (Ferrer-Wreder et al., 2002:170). The goal is "accepting control and responsibility of one's life" (Ferrer-Wreder et al., 2002:171). More generally, Christian Hoff Sommers argues that parents and schools need to emphasize character education, that is, "habituating children to the exercise of self-control, temperance, honesty, courage" (Sommers, 2000:191).

A similar suggestion is to start faith-based training schools for juveniles. The state of Florida has started faith-based prisons for adult prisoners, and the federal government started some faith-based programming in 2002 (Camp, Klein-Saffran, Kwon, Daggett, & Joseph, 2006). A recent evidence-based assessment of faith-based programs found some evidence that the programs reduced recidivism. The authors noted that much of the research in this area is weak but concluded that it would be "premature to abandon faith-based programs" (Dodson, Cabage, & Klenowski, 2011:381). At this point it appears that definitive results are not yet available. One concern about faith-based prisons is that they could divert money away from important programs for all prisoners, such as education and vocational training (Jablecki, 2005).

One reason for raising the issue of introducing the spiritual dimension into corrections is that there is evidence that it matters. In a study of offenders ages 15 to 24, Benda (2002) found that religion was inversely related to carrying a weapon, violence, the use of illicit drugs, and the selling of illicit drugs. Religion was measured by church attendance, religious expressions, and forgiveness.

One task of corrections may be to help that segment of offenders who are open to asking and seeking answers to the perennial questions about life: Why am I here? What is the meaning of life? What is happiness? Should I just seek more money and prestige or are there other more important goals in life? Do I just consider myself or should I think about others? Am I making moral or immoral choices? As one thinker puts it, am I seeking "significance through engagement in the processes of reflection, creativity, compassion, and the gift of self to others" (Staples, 2000:33)? None of this should lead to proselytizing or to erasing the separation of church and state. No correctional worker should impose his or her religious beliefs on inmates or probationers.

Some may object that attempting to inject the spiritual into correctional practice is too ambitious a project. If corrections cannot accomplish the basic objective of keeping offenders crime-free, then how can it be expected to help offenders become better persons spiritually? However, this objection may have it backward. Perhaps one reason that corrections has had such an uninspiring record with recidivism is that it makes no effort to help offenders in a search for meaning and purpose in their lives. If the implicit objective of corrections is that offenders only need to buy into the American Dream, and if that dream is questionable and uninspiring and one that ignores the deeper potential of human living, then it may be no surprise that probation does little to improve recidivism.

A final note is that research has shown the importance of religion in delinquency causation. In a study of boot camp inmates, Benda (2002) found that religion was clearly correlated (inversely) with crimes against persons. In fact, religion was the fifth largest correlate in the model. So the more religious these inmates, the less likely they were to be involved in violence. Similarly, an analysis of the National Youth Survey found that religiosity affected adolescent use of illicit drugs (Jang & Johnson, 2001). These studies confirm the importance of religion and suggest its usefulness in preventing delinquency (see also, Dodson et al., 2011).

CAPITAL PUNISHMENT FOR JUVENILES

In 2019, there were an estimated 16,425 homicides in the United States, and an estimated 860 arrests of juveniles for homicide (Puzzanchera, 2021). This is dramatically lower than the approximately 3,800 arrests of juveniles for murder in 1993, the peak year for murders by juveniles (Puzzanchera, 2021). Despite this decrease, however, we will probably see continued media attention on juveniles who kill.

For adult murderers, **capital punishment** has been debated for years (see, e.g., van den Haag & Conrad, 1983; and Costanzo, 1997, for further discussion). The questions in the debate have been both philosophical and empirical. Some of the philosophical questions involve the moral issue of the state taking a human life and the morality of capital punishment in the face of the possibility of mistakes (i.e., executing someone who

WEB ACTIVITY

For extensive information on the death penalty, including current statistics, go to the website of the Death Penalty Information Center: www. deathpenaltyinfo.org.

has been mistakenly convicted). The empirical questions include the deterrent impact of capital punishment (does it prevent individuals from committing murder because they fear being sentenced to die?) and the issue of racial or class bias (is the death penalty more likely to be imposed on minorities than on whites?). These same issues apply to the question of the appropriateness of the death penalty for juveniles.

In 2005, the Supreme Court ruled that the death penalty is unconstitutional for juveniles. In *Roper v. Simmons* (2005), writing for the majority, Justice Arthur Kennedy wrote that "[t]he Eighth and Fourteenth Amendments forbid imposition of the death penalty on offenders who were under the age of 18 when their crimes were committed." The ruling came in a case in which Christopher Simmons, age 17, with two accomplices, broke and entered a home at 2:00 A.M., took a woman captive, drove away, and threw the woman from a railroad trestle into a river.

The majority opinion reasoned that the juvenile death penalty is rejected by the majority of the states and is used infrequently in states that authorize it. This suggests that today, American society views juveniles as less culpable than adults. The majority went on to cite scientific evidence that juveniles under 18 are less mature and responsible than adults, more susceptible to peer pressure, and have characters that are less well formed than those of adults. The majority recognizes that there is no perfect decision about the appropriate age for the death penalty, but that a line has to be drawn somewhere. They choose age 18. "The age of 18 is the point where society draws the line for many purposes between childhood and adulthood" (*Roper v. Simmons*, 2005). (See Box 14.4 for quotes from the majority opinion and from Justice Scalia's dissent.)

The Supreme Court's *Roper* decision has ended the debate over the juvenile death penalty for practical purposes. An unintended consequence of the decision was an increase in the number of juveniles serving life without parole and related sentences. The Supreme Court has issued rulings on life without parole. The next section discusses all life sentences for juveniles.

LIFE SENTENCES FOR JUVENILES WHO MURDER

As of 2020, there were 1,465 persons serving life without parole (LWOP) sentences who were under 18 when they committed their crimes; this is down 45 percent from the peak year of 2012 (Nellis, 2021). Advocates estimate that

BOX 14.4 MAJORITY AND DISSENTING OPINIONS IN THE *ROPER* CASE

Justice Kennedy's Majority Opinion:

The susceptibility of juveniles to immature and irresponsible behavior means "their irresponsible conduct is not as morally reprehensible as that of an adult." *Thompson*, supra, at 835 (plurality opinion). Their own vulnerability and comparative lack of control over their immediate surroundings mean juveniles have a greater claim than adults to be forgiven for failing to escape negative influences in their whole environment. See *Stanford*, 492 U.S., at 395 (Brennan, J. dissenting). The reality that juveniles still struggle to define their identity means it is less supportable to conclude that even a heinous crime committed by a juvenile is evidence of irretrievably depraved character. From a moral standpoint it would be misguided to equate the failings of a minor with those of an adult, for a greater possibility exists that a minor's character deficiencies will be reformed.

Justice Scalia's Dissent:

Murder, however, is more than just risky or antisocial behavior. It is entirely consistent to believe that young people often act impetuously and lack judgment, but, at the same time, to believe that those who commit premeditated murder are—at least sometimes—just as culpable as adults. Christopher Simmons, who was only seven months shy of his 18th birthday when he murdered Shirley Crook, described to his friends beforehand—"[i]n chilling, callous terms," … the murder he planned to commit. He then broke into the home of an innocent woman, bound her with duct tape and electrical wire, and threw her off a bridge alive and conscious.

What do you think? Is Justice Kennedy correct that minors are still immature and struggling with their identity? Is there greater chance that they can be reformed? Or is Justice Scalia correct that some individual juveniles are just as culpable as adults—that some youths commit heinous crimes and should be held fully accountable for them? Do you agree with Justice Kennedy that all youths should be ineligible for the death penalty, or do you agree with Justice Scalia that some youths may deserve the death penalty?

an additional 700 youths have had their LWOP sentences invalidated and are awaiting a new sentence. Further, about 8,600 persons who committed their crimes as minors are serving life with the possibility of parole or virtual life sentences. A virtual life sentence is a sentence of 50 years or more (Nellis, 2021). Of all three groups, the prisoners are almost all male (98 percent) and majority African American (55 percent) (Nellis, 2017).

As noted in Chapter 9, the Supreme Court has issued four recent decisions concerning juvenile LWOP. In *Graham v. Florida* (2010), the Court banned LWOP for juveniles not convicted of homicide. In *Miller v. Alabama* (2012), the Court banned the mandatory imposition of LWOP for juveniles. In other words, states can still impose a LWOP sentence on a juvenile, but only after individualized consideration of the juvenile and the juvenile's offense. *Montgomery v. Louisiana* (2016) made *Miller* retroactive. As a result of these decisions, 28 states and the District of Columbia have revised their laws for juveniles convicted of homicide. For example, Nevada and West Virginia specify mandatory 15-year minimums, and Texas and Nebraska have 40-year mandatory minimum sentences. On the other hand, 25 states and the District of Columbia have now prohibited LWOP sentences for juveniles (Nellis, 2021; Rovner, 2021b).

In its most recent ruling on juvenile LWOP, *Jones v. Mississippi* (2021), the Supreme Court has ruled that a judge does not have to find a youth "permanently incorrigible" before it can sentence him to juvenile LWOP. The judge simply has to have the discretion to consider a defendant's youth in sentencing. The dissent has objected that the Court's prior rulings in *Miller* and *Montgomery* clearly indicate that "a lifetime in prison is a disproportionate sentence for all but the rarest children, those whose crime reflect 'irreparable corruption'" (Justice Sotomayor, joined by Justice Breyer and Justice Kagan). Liberals were disappointed by this Court decision, as they were hoping that the Court would have pushed further against LWOP sentences for juveniles.

The Supreme Court decisions on life without parole and state law changes concerning life without parole may be a pyrrhic victory; that is, critics of LWOP may have won a battle but lost the war. Since states may deny parole for various reasons and since many youths may die before their 50 years are up, both life with parole and virtual life sentences can easily translate to life without parole in fact. It appears that some states are sentencing youths who commit homicide or even other crimes to sentences that are the functional equivalent of life without parole.

The growth in the use of LWOP and related sentences for juveniles was expected, given the *Roper* decision banning the death penalty for juveniles. Absent the death penalty, LWOP is arguably the harshest sentence a state can impose, followed by virtual life and life with parole. If a juvenile is convicted of a heinous murder, it is logical that judges, responding to prosecutors, juries, the public, and the press, would impose the harshest alternative available: some version of a life sentence. With Supreme Court restrictions on LWOP, it is logical for state courts to impose the next harshest sentences: life with parole, virtual life, or simply a lengthy sentence.

Sentencing a juvenile to any type of life sentence, whether life without parole, life with the possibility of parole, or a virtual life sentence, raises serious questions. One problem is unfair implementation. For example, one report showed that in 11 states, black youths arrested for murder were more likely to be sentenced to a life without parole sentence than white youths arrested for murder (Human Rights Watch, 2008). That report also noted that in both California and Connecticut, the ratio of black youths arrested for murder

In this June 12, 2018 photo, Dana Barker, left, and Leigh Ann Zaepfel, right, both serving life sentences without parole for crimes they committed as juveniles, participate in an interview at the Mabel Bassett Correctional Center in McLoud, Oklahoma.

CREDIT: AP Photo/Sue Ogrocki

sentenced to LWOP was more than five times higher than that for white youths arrested for murder. Just as some criticized racial discrimination in the administration of the death penalty, critics see racial problems continuing in the use of LWOP sentences.

Critics also point to other problems in meting out LWOP sentences to juveniles. First, one report showed that the majority—59 percent—of juveniles with LWOP sentences were first-time offenders with no prior adult criminal record or juvenile adjudication record. Second, it is estimated that one-quarter (26 percent) of the juveniles with LWOP sentences were convicted of felony murder. That is, they were an accomplice; for example, their co-defendant actually committed the murder during another felony crime. Third, frequently the juvenile committed the crime with an adult, and in many cases the adult received a more lenient sentence.

A study of 1,579 juvenile lifers found that many had suffered from socioeconomic disadvantages, school failure, and abuse. Specifically, 79 percent had witnessed violence in their homes, almost half (47 percent) had been physically abused, and 77 percent of the girls had been sexually abused. About one-third were raised in public housing, and 18 percent were not living with a close relative just prior to their incarceration. Only 47 percent had been attending school at the time of their offense, and 84 percent had been either suspended or expelled from school at some point in their past (Nellis, 2012). The criminological term for this is ACE: Adverse Childhood Experiences. In general, ACEs are clearly related to both delinquency and criminal behavior (see, e.g., Baglivio et al., 2014). Another problem is that youths sentenced to LWOP are experiencing severe trauma in prison, including knifings, threats, and suicidal thoughts (Human Rights Watch, 2008).

Still another criticism is that while sentences usually serve multiple goals, including rehabilitation, LWOP, life with parole (if parole is rare), and virtual life sentences have little or no rehabilitative aspects. They simply give up on any hope of change for the offender. In fact, many prisons deny access to programs such as education to inmates serving life sentences. With juveniles, however, there is usually considerable chance for change. One might object that the possibility of parole does leave room open for rehabilitation. The recent pushback—if not abolition—on granting parole, however, is clear indication of scant concern for rehabilitation.

Perhaps the most serious criticism of any type of life sentence for juveniles is the question of responsibility. Barry Feld, for example, argues that the reasoning behind the *Roper* decision that made the death penalty unconstitutional for juveniles applies with equal vigor to LWOP sentences and "de facto life sentences"—life with parole (with little chance of parole) and virtual life sentences. If a juvenile is too immature and too susceptible to peer pressure to be executed, argues Feld, the same logic dictates that he or she is not mature enough for a sentence of LWOP or life. In Feld's words: "Adolescents' personalities are in transition and it is unjust and irrational to continue harshly to punish a fifty- or sixty-year-old person for the crime that an irresponsible child committed several decades earlier" (Feld, 2008:36; see also, Feld, 2018). Most recently, Feld (2013b; 2018) has argued that the reasoning in *Roper*, *Graham*, and *Miller* is sound rationale to have a youth discount for all juvenile sentences, and that the harshest sentence available should be no more than 20 or 25 years.

A number of authorities concur with Feld that LWOP is overly harsh for juveniles. Human Rights Watch, for example, notes that the United States is "an international anomaly" as the only country in the world that imposes LWOP sentences on juveniles (Human Rights Watch, 2008:8). Michael Tonry argues that LWOP is one of several American inhumane policies that is "unimaginable in most other Western countries" (Tonry, 2008:3).

On the other side, some argue that LWOP and related sentences are reasonable and should be available for those juveniles who commit extremely violent murders and are a danger to society. Heritage Foundation authors Stimson and Grossman (2009) describe 16 horrific murders committed by juveniles as evidence for this position. For example, one youth told his friend that he needed some money and was going to steal it. He proceeded to approach a woman and her daughter in their car as the mother was making an ATM withdrawal to buy ice cream for her daughter and herself on a summer evening. The youth shot the mother, and the same bullet also killed the daughter. The Heritage Foundation makes a straightforward claim: horrendous acts of violence and cruelty are the worst harms individuals can inflict. Even adolescents know or should know that such acts of violence are wrong and deserve punishment, either the death penalty or LWOP. Since the Supreme Court has ruled out the death penalty for juveniles (*Roper v. Simmons*, 2005), society has a deontological duty to impose LWOP on such despicable murderers, despite their youthfulness.

Besides ignoring the developmental evidence that adolescents do not fully mature until their twenties, the second major weakness in the argument by Stimson and Grossman is that they present no background information on the murderers they describe. No one is alleging that even a horribly abusive childhood exonerates a teen who commits a brutal murder. But many would agree that having a father who is abusive to his children and their mother, who regularly drinks to excess, and shows no pattern of concern for his children might well mitigate against the harshest sentences and instead call for a sentence that is punitive but also takes into consideration a horrible childhood.

If one objects that 15 or 20 years is much too short a punishment for a murderer, consider what a 15- to 20-year sentence actually means for a juvenile age 16 who commits a murder. If he had not committed the murder, in the next 15 to 20 years he could graduate from high school, go to college, begin a career, advance in that career, marry, and possibly have children who would be in junior high or high school in 15 or 20 years. So sentencing him to such a sentence would mean that he would have missed all of those milestones in life. In other words, 15 or 20 years is a very significant slice of life, a real punishment, and not just "a slap on the wrist."

WEB ACTIVITY

Human Rights Watch has criticized LWOP for juveniles, available at www.hrw.org.

The Heritage Foundation sponsored a major report in favor of LWOP for juveniles, available at www.heritage.org. (Search for "Adult Time for Adult Crimes.")

Trulson and Caudill (2017) caution that some sentences can be too short for juvenile homicide offenders. Their study of 247 juvenile homicide offenders in Texas showed that on average their sample served four years in prison and that half of the released juvenile murderers were rearrested within the three-year follow-up period. As length of incarceration was a significant negative predictor of recidivism, these authors note that keeping juvenile homicide offenders in prison for longer than four years could act as a protective factor against recidivism.

Still another problem is that mistakes can be made. This is due to "the inability of judges and juries to accurately render individualized assessments about whether a teenager's immaturity and developmental deficits attenuates his or her culpability" (Fagan, 2007:742). Part of the problem is that juries sometimes treat youthful age as a factor characterizing juveniles as more dangerous, rather than seeing incomplete development as making them less responsible.

LWOP in particular, and life sentences in general, for juveniles have not attracted the same outcry that capital punishment for juveniles did. The death penalty is dramatic because it is so extreme. A life sentence can be seen as a considerable improvement over the death penalty and can lull juvenile justice reform advocates into a sense of victory that they have stopped a horrible injustice. However, if Barry Feld is correct that the same reasoning that destroys the justification for a juvenile death penalty also destroys that for a juvenile life sentence, then juvenile justice advocates need to get ready for another fight—the fight to overturn any type of life sentence for juveniles.

The Sentencing Project has been speaking out against life sentences for years. Similar to Feld, it recommends a sentence maximum of 20 years. First, such a maximum should be plenty of time for society to address the problems of such offenders. Second, if society (e.g., a prosecutor) thinks that the prisoner still poses a risk to society, society (that prosecutor) could seek a civil commitment of the offender. The Sentencing Project even questions the necessity of 20 years of confinement and thus recommends "second look" provisions. This means that courts would review 20-year sentences at perhaps 10 years and/or again at 15 years to determine if the offender needs 10 or five more years of prison, or if it would be safe to release him at the time of review (Nellis, 2021).

JURISDICTION OVER STATUS OFFENSES

Also related to the fundamental issue of the philosophy and continued existence of juvenile court is the issue of divestiture, that is, eliminating juvenile court jurisdiction over status offenders. Assuming that a state chooses not to eliminate juvenile court completely, should it continue to exercise control over disobedient, runaway, and truant adolescents? As noted, the state of Washington has opted to continue juvenile court but to eliminate jurisdiction over status offenses. Maine has written full divestiture into law. Most states have retained jurisdiction but implemented policies of deinstitutionalization (stopped confining status offenders in state institutions). In many places, private drug treatment and mental health facilities have stepped in to fill the void that juvenile court previously occupied (Feld, 1999).

Despite such efforts, status offenses and status offenders continue to take up a considerable portion of juvenile court time and effort. In 2018, juvenile courts handled an estimated 97,800 petitioned status offense cases. More than half involved truancy petitions. Although this is a considerable decrease from the 137,000 cases handled in 2010, it still involves a sizable number of children. Despite more than a decade of discussion about ending juvenile court jurisdiction over status offenses, approximately 2,300 youths were adjudicated status offenders and placed in out-of-home placements in 2018. On the positive side, 65 percent of the status offense petitioned cases were not adjudicated (Hockenberry & Puzzanchera, 2020). The 2019 census of juveniles in custody showed over 1,400 youths in placement for a status offense (OJJDP, 2021). Another positive note is that racial disparity is less of a factor in status offense cases than delinquency cases (Rovner, 2021a).

Michel (2011) suggests that jurisdictions stop using probation officers in initial work with status offenders. Instead, states should set up a new program that hires recent college graduates and trains them to produce more favorable outcomes for youths and avoid all the negative labeling of juvenile court processing.

WEB ACTIVITY

The Coalition for Juvenile Justice advocates divestiture. See its website at www.juvjustice.org.

Arguments for Ending Jurisdiction

There are several arguments in favor of complete divestiture. First, it allows the juvenile court more time and resources to deal with juvenile delinquents—especially violent and chronic delinquents. Because the court does not have to process or supervise status offenders, probation officers, prosecutors, public defenders, judges, and correctional program employees are able to focus on more serious delinquents. Related to this, a study of first-time referral status offenders in Florida found that almost half later committed a delinquent act. The author concludes that formal court processing of status offenders "stigmatizes the youth and does not buffer the majority of them from entry into the juvenile justice system" (Jennings, 2011:184). Second, the elimination of status offense jurisdiction prevents any possible violations of the due process rights of status offenders, such as being prosecuted for very vague charges. For example, how disobedient does a child have to be before he or she is "incorrigible," or how truant before he or she is eligible for a truancy petition? Status offense statutes typically are unclear and vague. Third, elimination of this jurisdiction recognizes the reality that juvenile courts are not adequately staffed and equipped to deal with status offenders. Most probation officers often have only bachelor's degrees and are not qualified to do the social work and psychological counseling necessary to assist troubled teenagers and their families. Thus, status offenders should be diverted to private agencies with trained social workers and counselors who are better equipped to handle the complex problems of these youths and their families. Furthermore, eliminating juvenile court jurisdiction would force any intervention to be voluntary, which some argue is the proper way to deal with status offenders.

Meda Chesney-Lind (1987) believes that status offenses are intricately intertwined with the place of women in American society. She questions whether the concern over maintaining jurisdiction is one of concern or control:

> What is really at stake here is not "protection" of youth so much as it is the right of young women to defy patriarchy. Such defiance by male youth is winked at, both today and in the past, but from girls such behavior is totally unacceptable. (Chesney-Lind, 1987:21)

Much of the concern, therefore, about status offenders is not so much for the children as for maintaining a patriarchal society. Thus, like the critics of the child savers discussed in Chapter 2, Chesney-Lind questions the intentions of those concerned with the protection of status offenders.

Simmons (2006) argues that mandatory mediation for status offenses is superior to processing such children in juvenile court and can better address the root problems behind status offending. Simmons reports on three programs that had considerable success in dealing with status offenders (Simmons, 2006). On the other hand, recent experience in juvenile court shows that a number of courts charge status offenders with violations of court orders (VCOs) as a way to "bootstrap" them into delinquency charges and even to place them in secure confinement.

In fiscal year (FY) 2006–2007, Connecticut reformed how it handled status offenders in an attempt to reduce court handling, to eliminate detention for status offenders, and to direct status offenders to community services and the education system. A study of results in FY 2007–2008 and 2008–2009 showed that complaints declined over 40 percent, there were no Families with Service Needs youth confined in a secure detention facility in FY 2008–2009, and that juvenile courts only handled 4 percent of status offense complaints in 2009. Subsequent referrals and arrests also dropped (Ryon, Devers, Early, & Hand, 2012). This indicates that states can be successful in drastically reducing juvenile court involvement in status offense cases if they set up community services and educational interventions for such cases.

Several prominent organizations—the MacArthur Foundation, Models for Change, and the Vera Institute of Justice—support divestiture.

> In sum, regardless of the issues underlying a status offense, families require a faster response and a different kind of response than courts and the juvenile justice system can offer ... [The juvenile court should reserve] costly resources and disruptive proceedings for young people who pose a significant risk to others. (Salsich & Trone, 2013:4)

People take part in a June 2021 news conference to call on the Los Angeles United School District Board of Education to defund and eliminate the L.A. School Police Department.

CREDIT: Ringo Chiu via AP

In contrast to the call for divestiture, some see schools and courts as opening back doors to allow for continuing supervision over adolescent misbehavior. School experts claim that teachers, counselors, principals, and police in schools are criminalizing status offense behaviors, such as minor disciplinary infractions. Thus, student misbehavior results in arrest instead of the teacher or the principal handling the matter. Critics of SROs and harsh school responses, such as Zero Tolerance Policy, to what used to be considered simply school discipline matters contend that schools are overreacting when they turn to arrest as a quick response to adolescent misbehavior (Mallett, 2016). (See Chapter 7 for further discussion.) Similarly, some see judges as criminalizing status offense behavior by issuing Valid Court Orders (VCOs) for status offenders who violate probation. This allows those youth to be handled as delinquents, including possible detention (Blitzman, 2015).

Arguments for Continuing Jurisdiction

Some still think, however, that juvenile court jurisdiction over status offenses is both desirable and necessary. Proponents of continued jurisdiction contend that parents and schools need the court backing to impress adolescents with the need to obey their parents, attend school, and not run away from home. Concerning truancy, Rubin argues that repeal of status offense jurisdiction would "effectively eradicate compulsory education" and that "children will be free to roam the streets with impunity" (Rubin, 1985:65). Furthermore, such total freedom would "deny children the necessary preparation for achievement in a complex technological society" (Rubin, 1985:65). Second, proponents of court jurisdiction argue that private agencies in the community will not handle (or will not be able to handle) all of the status offense cases if the juvenile court cannot intervene. Private agencies intervene only with willing clients, and many status offenders taken to such agencies simply refuse assistance. Moreover, some agencies do not provide the services they claim to provide (Schneider, 1985).

Proponents also contend that status offenders often escalate into delinquent activity and note that truants are linked with daytime burglary and vandalism

(Baker et al., 2001). Therefore, they claim, early intervention can prevent current and future delinquency. However, the escalation hypothesis is controversial. Some proportion of status offenders do indeed escalate or progress, but most do not (Lab, 1984; Rojek & Erickson, 1982; Shannon, 1982). Hence, it is questionable whether all status offenders should be subject to juvenile court jurisdiction. A similar argument is that many status offenders become involved in very dangerous situations that can cause serious harm to the child. For example, one study of runaways found that more than 50 percent dealt drugs and about 20 percent (including 19 percent of the male runaways) engaged in acts of prostitution to support themselves (Miller, Miller, Hoffman, & Duggan, 1980). One study found little difference between status offenders and delinquents. Both groups had similar histories of abuse and placement, peer influences, and psychiatric diagnosis (Steinke & Martin, 2014). Research on street children has shown that many turn to theft, prostituting, rolling johns, and selling drugs to survive (Hagan & McCarthy, 1997). Proponents of court jurisdiction argue that courts might prevent some children from running away and becoming involved in associated dangerous behaviors. A related argument is that because states intervene "to protect adults from their own harmful conduct" (Ryan, 1987:64), they should protect juveniles from the harmful consequences of their actions.

Another argument in favor of continued jurisdiction is that it prevents status offenders from being processed as delinquents. That is, where divestiture has occurred, there is some evidence of treating status offenders as minor delinquents (Schneider, 1985). Finally, there is concern that total removal of status offense jurisdiction from juvenile court "changes the character of the court and may substantially weaken attempts to consider the child status of delinquent" (Mahoney, 1987:29). In other words, Mahoney fears that removal of status offense jurisdiction, with a concentration on delinquency only, may lead to a view of the juvenile court as concerned with crime only and, hence, a belief that adult criminal courts can exercise that function. Thus, removal of status offense jurisdiction may very well be the beginning of the end of the juvenile court. At present, the debate over divestiture has changed. In the Justice Department's research and writing on delinquency, there is little mention of status offenses as such. Instead of debate about divestiture, the Office of Juvenile Justice and Delinquency Prevention emphasizes prevention strategies that help youngsters at risk of becoming delinquent by building up protective factors. Such protective factors include caring parents who supervise their children, personal attributes such as conventional beliefs and conflict resolution skills, and schools that have caring teachers and help youths succeed in school (Coordinating Council on Juvenile Justice and Delinquency Prevention, 1996). The Coordinating Council is concerned with such programs as truancy reduction programs that have the police round up truants so that parents can be notified and come pick up their children (see also Chapter 8). Also mentioned are mentoring programs including Bigs in Blue, which matches high-risk youths with police officer mentors who try to help youths cope with peer pressure and also do well in school. Noted as well are conflict resolution programs in schools and community efforts such as community policing cooperative arrangements that attack community risk factors such as easy avail-ability of drugs and firearms (Coordinating Council on Juvenile Justice and Delinquency Prevention, 1996; see also Baker et al., 2001).

Unlike a decade ago, the emphasis is not so much on the status offender as a distinct problem, but on those risk factors that can lead to serious, violent, or chronic delinquency. Attention to reducing risk factors and enhancing protective factors is considered to be the way to prevent such problematic delinquency.

CONCLUSION

Most of the proposals for the future of the juvenile justice system have some merit. The authors of these proposals care about juveniles and about how the juvenile court system should attempt to prevent and control delinquency.

The suggestion to get the juvenile justice system to return to its *parens pat-riae* roots—to attempt to get juvenile court to truly implement rehabilitation efforts based on valid empirical research findings—is a positive one. The goal is noble: Genuine assistance for juveniles. Obstacles include funding problems, lack of societal commitment to the disadvantaged youths that are the clientele of juvenile court, vestiges of racism, and punitive strains in some politicians.

Bazemore's call to make a drastic change and pursue the path of restorative justice is also positive (Bazemore, 2012). Advantages of this proposal are that it can appeal to both liberals and conservatives. Both parties like the fact that restorative justice puts renewed emphasis on the victim. Restitution, for example, is desirable because it restores the victim to the condition he or she was in prior to the crime. Perhaps the major question about this proposal is whether citizens will commit to participate. Putnam's (2000) concerns about the decline of community in America raise the question that citizens are not as civically involved today as they were even 50 years ago. A number of communities, including the state of Vermont (Karp et al., 2004), have implemented restorative justice practices, though, so this does not appear to be a pipedream.

In the last 20 years, developmental psychology has examined the incomplete development of adolescent brain functioning and maturity, the Supreme Court has issued rulings on the death penalty and LWOP for juveniles based in part on those findings, and several states have reverted to age 18 for initial crim-inal court jurisdiction and/or limited transfer provisions and sentencing. As noted, Bishop and Feld (2012) first saw signs of rebalancing or a new balan-cing between traditional juvenile court *parens patriae* philosophy and the "get tough" movement of the 1990s and early 2000s. Since then, a number of states have revised their laws to moderate many of the "get tough" provisions of the 1990s and turn to evidence-based practices in what some call the "fourth wave" of juvenile justice reform (also called "smart on juvenile justice"). Thus, a number of states are following this recent trend to mitigate the harsh reforms enacted in response to what now appears to have been a baseless moral panic over an imagined juvenile crime spree by "superpredators" that never should have been predicted in the first place.

Feld (2018) calls for **harm reduction** via decriminalization, deinstitutionalization, and delinquency prevention. He also calls for limits on police interrogation, full access to defense attorneys, sentencing discounts, age 18 as the age of criminal court jurisdiction, and the elimination of life sentences for juveniles. In short, he suggests critical changes in how the police and juvenile court treat delinquent youths. (For similar suggestions, see Tonry, 2011, 2014.)

Character education or the reintroduction of the spiritual dimension into juvenile corrections also merits serious consideration. If Staples (2000) is correct that problems such as school violence stem, at least in part, from excessive emphasis on the consumer culture and inattention to the search for meaning, creativity, and engagement, then superficial changes in juvenile court are not critical. If such terms as "character education" or a "search for the spiritual" are simply ploys to avoid funding meaningful programs for youths in trouble, then they are hypocritical and dangerous. However, if calls for character education and the reintroduction of the spiritual dimension go along with education, job training, substance-abuse counseling, and other efforts to address all the needs of problem youths, both material and spiritual, then they hold promise. Critics of our consumer culture are accurate that there is more to life than purchasing increasingly more goods.

Perhaps the most dramatic and drastic reform proposal is that of Elliott Currie who calls for an attack on social and economic disadvantage and segregation (Currie, 2020). He argues that these factors are primarily responsible for violence by and against blacks. He calls for the government to address these issues by spending on jobs and measures to address disadvantaged neighborhoods. Unlike calls to implement evidence-based interventions, Currie's proposal sees social and economic conditions as largely responsible for crime and delinquency. As a result, simply addressing risk levels and individual needs will not solve the problem. Although his proposal would require significant government spending, he argues that the current situation also poses high economic costs: The costs of crime and prisons.

In light of highly publicized police shootings, the steps outlined to reform policing also stand out as essential. Policing in particular and justice in general demand that both citizen and police officer concerns be addressed and be addressed as soon as possible. It is not acceptable that too many blacks think that police treat black citizens unfairly. It is not acceptable that police either hesitate to act or fear that reasonable police actions will be condemned. Change is needed so that both citizens and police can feel assured of fair treatment by each other and by the media.

The founders of the juvenile court had it at least half right: kids do need help. That was true back in 1899 and is as true today in the twenty-first century. The problem is that in seeking solutions for youth problems and problem youths, we prefer to ignore this truth and seek refuge in simplistic slogans like "adult time" and "Scared Straight." As Currie has pointed out, violence, structural disadvantage, lack of jobs, and problematic policing confront all too many black youths on an everyday basis. We are a lot like dieters seeking to lose weight; we want the easy way out. Just as persons trying to lose weight have to face the hard facts of diet and exercise, American society has to face the facts of delinquency. There is no easy solution. Whatever proposal for the future of juvenile court wins out, it will not be an answer unless it addresses the problems of youths who break the law.

DISCUSSION QUESTIONS

1. Discuss the reform proposals for juvenile court. Which proposal(s) do you favor? Why? The current trend among the states appears to be trying to be "smart on crime" (or the fourth wave of reform), which translates into risk assessment, evidence-based practices, and diversion of less serious offenses. Discuss this trend compared to suggestions to re-emphasize the *parens patriae* philosophy and the balanced and restorative model.

2. Discuss Elliott Currie's argument that racial segregation and structural disadvantage are strong factors in the problem of crime and delinquency. Discuss his point that reform must involve social and economic reform, not simply efforts to help individual delinquents.

3. Police shootings, investigations of police officers, and citizen demonstrations against the police have dominated media coverage in the last few years. As noted, scholars say there is a crisis of legitimacy in policing. Any reform of juvenile justice must address changes in policing. What changes do you think are necessary in policing? What changes are called for in how citizens regard and treat the police? Do the police reform bills passed in states or at the federal level adequately address police reform?

4. Do you favor the death penalty for juveniles? Discuss this in light of the recent Supreme Court decision making the juvenile death penalty unconstitutional.

5. Discuss LWOP for juveniles. Although the Supreme Court did not completely abolish this sentence for juvenile murderers, it expressed the hope that such sentences would be very rare. Do you think states should abolish LWOP for juveniles altogether? In *Graham v. Florida*, dissenting Chief Justice Roberts raises the question of what an appropriate sentence would be for a juvenile who rapes an 8-year-old girl and leaves her to die, or juveniles who gang-rape a woman and force her to perform oral sex on her own 12-year-old son (real cases)? Justice Roberts thinks that an LWOP sentence might be the appropriate sentence in such cases. What do you think? Are virtual life sentences or life with the possibility of parole sentences any different from LWOP sentences or do they present the same problems?

6. What role, if any, should juvenile court have with status offenders? Do you agree with some experts that all status offenders should be handled in diversion programs or other community treatment programs, and that juvenile court should have no control over status offenses and status offenders?

Glossary

A

abandonment: the permanent desertion of a child; an acceptable practice from the fourth to the thirteenth centuries when a child was an economic burden to a household.

abuse: any nonaccidental infliction of injury that seriously impairs a child's physical or mental health.

adjudication: the process of determining whether there is enough evidence to find a youth to be a delinquent, a status offender, or a dependent.

affective interventions: an approach to drug use prevention that focuses attention on the individual in order to build self-esteem, self-awareness, and feelings of self-worth.

aftercare: (parole in the adult system) supervision of released offenders by probation or aftercare officers who seek to assist and monitor their charges.

anomie: Emil Durkheim's concept of the state of normlessness in society.

Antisocial Personality Disorder (APD): "a mental health condition in which a person has a long-term pattern of manipulating, exploiting, or violating the rights of others." (MedlinePlus, 2021)

apprenticeship: a situation in which one is bound by indenture to serve another for a prescribed period with a view to learning an art or trade.

atavistic: a term describing ape-like physical qualities of the head and body that were supposed by Cesare Lombroso to be indicative of the individual's developmental state.

Attention Deficit Hyperactivity Disorder (ADHD): disorder characterized by being persistently disruptive, acting impulsively, easily frustrated, experiencing wide mood swings, and acting inappropriately.

avoidance: a common reaction to actual or potential victimization in which an individual stays away from particular locations where or individuals by whom victimization is anticipated.

B

balanced approach: a recent approach in juvenile corrections that places emphasis on the offender, the victim, and community safety. One aim is to restore the victim and the community, as much as possible, to his or her pre-crime status.

behavior modification: a therapeutic approach based on the work of B.F. Skinner and Hans J. Eysenck that entails the use of reinforcements to increase the probability of desired behaviors and a lack of reinforcement, or punishment stimuli, to decrease the probability of undesirable behaviors.

Big Brothers/Big Sisters (BB/BS): a nonprofit organization, the goal of which is to help children reach their potential through professionally supported, one-to-one relationships with volunteer mentors.

biosociology: also known as sociobiology, the idea that the biological makeup of the organism and the surrounding environment are intimately related.

blended sentencing: a development in juvenile justice in which either the juvenile court or the adult court imposes a sentence that can involve either the juvenile or the adult correctional system or both.

bond to society (also called social bond): in Travis Hirschi's control theory, the connections an individual has to the social order; the four elements of the bond are attachment, commitment, involvement, and belief.

boot camp: a short-term program that resembles basic military training by emphasizing physical training and discipline; boot camps often include educational and rehabilitative components.

Boston Gun Project: a project that targeted firearms use by gangs by using a "pulling levers" (zero-tolerance) approach.

Breaking the Cycle (BTC) program: a program that seeks to identify offenders with substance-abuse problems early in their system processing, assess the appropriate treatment needs of the offender, and establish an integrated set of interventions (sanction, treatment, and rewards) for the individual.

Bridewell Institution: early English institution to handle youthful beggars.

"broken windows" policing: policing strategies based on the belief that signs of urban decay, such as broken windows, in a neighborhood serve to make the neighborhood more conducive to crime and more fear-inducing; police attend to both crime and disorder.

bullying: behavior including both physical and verbal aggression that is repeated over time and is meant to intentionally harm the victim.

C

capital punishment: the death penalty. The Supreme Court recently ruled that capital punishment is unconstitutional for juveniles.

Chancery Court: a body concerned with property matters in feudal England; responsible for overseeing the financial affairs of orphaned juveniles who were not yet capable of handling their own matters.

Chicago School: a perspective explaining deviance as the natural outgrowth of the location in which it occurs; named for the work performed by social scientists at the University of Chicago.

child maltreatment: a variety of actions in which children are harmed, either intentionally or unintentionally.

child protective services: a state's method of handling child abuse cases; usually responsible for accepting and investigating reports of abuse and neglect and for removing children from potential or actual abusive situations.

child saver: Anthony Platt's term for a person involved in the development of the juvenile court during the Progressive Era.

Children's Advocacy Center (CAC): an umbrella organization, independent of the criminal justice system, that brings together child protective services workers, law enforcement officers, the prosecutor's office, educators, mental health counselors, and medical personnel in an effort to provide a coordinated response and seamless service delivery to maltreated children.

civil abatement: procedures to control or eliminate locations that gang members frequent or own.

civil gang injunctions: court orders that prohibit certain behaviors linked to criminal activity.

Classicism: a school of thought that sees humankind as having free will, that is, humans calculate the pros and cons of an activity before choosing what to do (compare to **Positivism**).

collective efficacy: refers to the willingness and ability of the neighborhood to regulate or control behavior through both formal and informal means.

common-sense corrections: the use of various types of wilderness programs, ranging from relatively short stays in outdoor settings to long wagon train or ocean ship trips.

community/restorative justice: an approach to justice that focuses on helping community residents manage their own affairs, solve their own problems, and live together effectively and safely.

community policing: problem-oriented policing that relies on input from the public to define problems and establish police policy.

Community-Wide Approach to Gang Prevention, Intervention, and Suppression Program: a program aimed to initiate a comprehensive set of strategies: mobilizing communities, providing youths with opportunities, suppressing gang violence, providing social intervention (services) and street outreach, and facilitating organizational change and development in community agencies.

concerned adult role: a role assumed by some attorneys in juvenile cases in which the attorney acts as a "concerned adult" rather than a zealous advocate, sometimes encouraging youths to admit to petitions in cases in which an adversarial approach may have resulted in a dismissal of the petition.

concordance: similarity among groups in a study.

consent search: a search in which a defendant voluntarily allows the police to search person or effects without a search warrant.

containment theory: Walter Reckless's social control theory holding that behavior is controlled through outer containment (influences of family, peers, etc.) and inner containment (strengths within an individual), working in opposition to external pushes, external pressures, and external pulls.

corporal punishment: physical punishment.

cottage system: a training school design that attempts to simulate home life more closely than would a prison-like institution; it divides the larger prison into smaller "cottages" for living.

Court-Appointed Special Advocate (CASA): a voluntary advocate for children in child abuse and neglect cases.

criminalized juvenile court: a suggested reform of juvenile court that advocates providing juveniles with all the procedural protections of adult criminal court and offering reduced penalties for juvenile offenders.

culture conflict: the conflict resulting when one set of cultural or subcultural practices necessitates violating the norms of a coexisting culture.

Currie's reform proposal: argues that structural disadvantage and segregation are the principal causes of the disparity in violent victimization of blacks, including black youths, and calls for a guarantee of meaningful employment for all Americans with wages that allow for a decent standard of living.

cyberbullying: involves the use of the internet and other technologies to attack the victim.

cycle of violence: the idea that a child who is abused or who witnesses abuse will grow up to be an abuser.

D

dark figure of crime: crimes that are unreported to the police.

day–evening center: a detention alternative in which a center was formed to devote time to formal education and remedial and tutorial work in the day and recreational programs in the evening.

deadly force: police actions that have the potential to cause the death of the offender.

deinstitutionalization: the practice of avoiding any involuntary residential placements of status offenders; also, the general idea of removing any youths from institutional control.

delinquency: in general, conduct that subjects a juvenile individual to the jurisdiction of the juvenile court (for more on the various definitions that fall under this term, see Chapter 1).

detached worker program: a program designed to place system workers into the environment of the gang.

detention decision: the decision whether to keep a juvenile in custody or to allow the youth to go home while awaiting further court action.

determinism: a theory or doctrine holding that acts of the will, occurrences in nature, and social or psychological phenomena are causally determined by preceding events or natural laws.

detoxification: a treatment approach that attempts to remove an individual from an addiction by weaning him or her off drugs.

developmental theories: theories that explain the changes and stability that characterize the trajectory of an individual's behavior or time.

differential association: Edwin Sutherland's theory suggesting that criminal behavior is learned when an individual encounters an excess of definitions favoring deviant definitions over those that conform to the law.

differential identification: a concept proposing that personal association is not always necessary for the transmission of behavioral cues; fictional presentations provide information concerning acceptable behavior.

differential reinforcement: a theory that proposes that an individual can learn from a variety of sources, both social and nonsocial, and that the differing levels of reinforcement received will help shape future behavior.

disposition: the process of determining what intervention to give a juvenile offender upon his or her adjudication as a delinquent.

disproportionate minority contact (DMC): the fact that minority youths are more likely to be arrested or adjudicated delinquent compared to their proportion of the population.

dispute resolution: bringing together adversarial parties in an attempt to arrive at a mutually agreeable solution.

divestiture: elimination of juvenile court jurisdiction over status offenses.

domestic relations court: a civil court devoted to issues involved in divorce, child support, and related matters.

dopamine: hormone that acts in the opposite way from serotonin; higher dopamine levels result in greater action and pleasure-seeking behaviors; aggression is similarly enhanced from higher dopamine levels in the body.

dowry: the money, goods, or estate that a woman would bring to her husband in marriage.

drift: the concept that individuals are pushed and pulled toward different modes of activity at different times in their lives (that is, a person can "drift" in and out of crime).

Drug Abuse Resistance Education (D.A.R.E.) program: a school-based, police-taught program aimed at elementary students that attempts to reduce drug use by focusing on enhancing the social skills of the individual.

drug courts: specialized courts that attempt to help drug offenders stop using drugs by providing services and judicial supervision.

Due Process Period: period from 1967 to the early 1980s when due process was emphasized in juvenile proceedings.

E

Early Head Start (EHS): incorporates interventions with expectant parents, infants, and children prior to age 3.

ecological fallacy: the fallacy of attributing results based on grouped data to the individual level.

ecological perspective: an approach that seeks to explain deviance as a natural outgrowth of the location in which it occurs.

effectiveness: whether interventions have an impact on any measure of the crime problem.

ego: in Freudian theory, the social identity of an individual; actual behavior; conscious activity.

elaboration model: a perspective that takes components of various theories in order to construct a single explanation that incorporates the best parts of the individual theories.

Elmira Prenatal/Early Infancy Project: a program that targets the earliest stage of a child's development, specifically when the child is still in the womb, the centerpiece of which is home visitation by nurses beginning during pregnancy and lasting through the child's second birthday.

emphasis on status offenses: a focus on status offenses such as truancy; see status offense.

enhancement model: a model of the delinquency–gang relationship that strikes a middle ground in which gangs recruit delinquency-prone youths and enhance their deviance.

epigenetics: study of how DNA can be altered by the environment.

epinephrine: hormone that increases adrenaline; influences fight or flight reactions.

external pressures: poverty, unemployment, inequality.

external pulls: deviant peers, subcultures, media.

F

family court: a court designated to deal with family matters.

family group conferencing (FGC): a strategy involving the community of people most affected by the crime in deciding the resolution of a criminal or delinquent act.

focal concerns: the concerns designated by Walter Miller to represent the cultural values of the lower class; they include trouble, toughness, smartness, excitement, fate, and autonomy.

foray: an attack, usually by two or three youths, upon one or more rival gang members (e.g., a drive-by shooting).

fourth wave: see smart on juvenile justice/the fourth wave/new balance effort.

free will: the tenet that people choose to act the way that they do after calculating the pros and cons of an activity.

freedom of speech: the right to speak freely without censorship or limitation; for students, the Supreme Court has ruled that the right of free speech is to be balanced with the school's interest in education and discipline.

FRIENDS: a cognitive therapy intervention targeting anxiety and stress in youths; FRIENDS stands for: Feelings, Relax, I can try, Encourage, Nurture, Don't forget—be brave, Stay happy.

G

gang: in general, a group that exhibits characteristics that set them apart from other affiliations of juveniles, often involved in deviant activity (for more on the various definitions that fall under this term, see Chapter 5).

Gang Resistance Education and Training (G.R.E.A.T.) program: a program operated by the Bureau of Alcohol, Tobacco, Firearms, and Explosives in which local police officers present a curriculum to middle-school children designed to induce them to resist the pressure to join a gang.

ganging: the process of developing gangs.

gatekeeper role: means that police officers exercise considerable discretion with juveniles and are often the ones who decide whether a juvenile is processed in the juvenile justice system or not.

general strain theory: Robert Agnew's theory positing that the removal of valued stimuli or the presentation of negative stimuli can lead to strain and, perhaps, deviance.

goal confusion: the state of affairs in which judges, probation and aftercare officers, probation directors, state legislators, juvenile justice experts, and others in the system disagree about the objectives of juvenile court and community supervision.

graduated licensing: a strategy in which young drivers acquire on-the-road driving experience in lower-risk settings, then learning time is increased and drivers are gradually introduced to more difficult driving situations; they "graduate" to greater driving responsibility as they master the previous steps.

group hazard hypothesis: a contention that delinquency committed in groups has a greater chance of being detected and acted upon by the juvenile and criminal justice systems.

guardian ad litem: an individual appointed by the court to serve as an advocate for a child in a child abuse or neglect case (also see **Court-Appointed Special Advocate**).

H

harm reduction (Feld): focus on decriminalization, deinstitutionalization, and delinquency prevention, and critical changes in how the police and juvenile court treat delinquent youths.

Head Start: a federal-funded early childhood program designed to provide comprehensive services to young children, and which emphasizes parent engagement.

hedonistic calculus: the belief that individuals seek to maximize pleasure.

home detention: programs that supervise juveniles at home instead of in custody while they are awaiting further court action.

hormones: natural chemicals produced in the body that control many of the basic bodily functions, including growth, reproduction, and functioning of the central nervous system.

houses of refuge: early institutions for children that were designed to separate the youths from the detrimental environment of the city.

hybrid gangs: gangs that are mixed racially or ethnically or gangs whose members may belong to more than one gang.

hypoglycemia: a condition of low blood sugar, it manifests itself in a lack of energy, lethargy, nervousness, and, in the extreme, a coma.

I

id: in Freudian theory, unconscious desires, drives, instincts.

in camera testimony: testimony given outside the courtroom, often used for the testimony of children in abuse and neglect cases.

incidence: how many times something (e.g., a drug) was used.

Incredible Years program: a series of interlocking, evidence-based programs for parents, children, and teachers, the goal of which is to prevent and treat young children's behavior problems and promote their social, emotional, and academic competence.

Index crime: an offense included in Part I of the Uniform Crime Reports. The eight crimes included are murder, rape, robbery, aggravated assault, burglary, larceny, motor vehicle theft, and arson.

infanticide: the deliberate killing of young children, a common practice prior to the fourth century, when a child was an economic burden to a household.

informal adjustment: informal handling of an offense without the filing of a petition (e.g., a probation intake officer orders the payment of restitution).

inner containment: direct control over the individual from inside sources.

institutional life: refers to the demands of daily life in institutions such as detention centers and state training schools where all aspects of life are regulated. Inmates typically make adjustments to such institutions that often work against the objectives of staff.

intake decision: the decision whether to file a court petition of delinquent, status offense, abuse, or dependency.

intelligence quotient (IQ): a test, developed by Alfred Binet, that provides a numerical representation of the mental ability of an individual. The formula is IQ = (mental age/chronological age) × 100.

internal pushes: restlessness, discontent, anxiety.

internet banging: the use of violent threats and insults online.

Interpersonal Maturity Levels (I-levels): developed by Sullivan et al. (1957), the seven levels that reflect the progressive development of social and interpersonal skills.

interstitial areas: areas that are deteriorating and in a state of disorganization.

intraindividual theory: in explanations of child maltreatment, a theory that views child maltreatment as an internal defect of the abuser.

involuntary servitude: selling or trading a youth to another for service.

J

jurisdiction over status offenders: the juvenile court's prerogative to exercise control over juveniles who have committed status offenses (e.g., disobedient, runaway, and truant adolescents); see status offense.

"Just Say No": a school- and media-based program designed to encourage children to make a personal decision to refuse any offer to use illicit drugs in the face of peer influences.

justice by geography: juvenile courts vary from jurisdiction to jurisdiction in how they process cases. For example, rural courts may vary considerably from urban courts.

juvenile: a minor. (The precise definition of a juvenile varies from jurisdiction to jurisdiction, currently ranging from under age 16 to under age 18.)

juvenile curfew laws: laws that state that juveniles must stay inside their homes at specific times, enacted in an effort to reduce victimization of and by juveniles.

K

Keepin' It REAL: the new version of the D.A.R.E. program, in which police officers teach a 10-session curriculum to children and adolescents in schools; the focus of the program has shifted from drug prevention to teaching resistance skills; REAL stands for Refuse, Explain, Avoid, and Leave.

knowledge approach: an approach to drug use prevention that entails providing youths with information on different types of drugs and the possible legal consequences of using them.

L

labeling: the contention that the fact of being labeled deviant by society leads an individual to act in accordance with that label.

Lancaster State Industrial School for Girls: early industrial school for girls in Massachusetts.

legal drinking age: the age at which a person is allowed to legally purchase and consume alcohol.

legislative waiver: state laws that provide for automatic transfer of a juvenile to adult court, as opposed to judicial waiver or transfer (see waiver).

life-course theories: see developmental theories.

life skills training: educational programs that include basic personal and social skills development (which deal with general life situations and how to deal with them) as well as specific resistance skills aimed directly at substance-abuse issues.

lifestyle explanations: see routine activities theory.

looking-glass self: the idea that individuals view themselves in the way other people look at them.

Lyman School for Boys: opened in 1848 by the state of Massachusetts and eliminated the housing of adult and juvenile offenders.

M

maintenance program: a drug treatment program that seeks to establish a state in which the individual does not experience withdrawal symptoms.

medical model: a perspective that approaches the deviant act as a symptom of a larger problem (or "disease").

mentalistic construct: refers to something that relies on the mindset and attitude of the individual involved.

mentoring: pairing adult volunteers with youths in need of friendship, emotional support, guidance, and advice.

meta-analysis: a statistical technique that uses data from a number of studies to compute a common statistic in order to compare results across studies.

Minnesota Multiphasic Personality Inventory (MMPI): a 556-question inventory that serves as a standardized method for tapping personality traits in individuals.

mission distortion: in probation, the phenomenon describing what happens when probation officers no longer see themselves as service providers or social workers but instead over-identify with a law enforcement role.

modeling: a form of learning that entails copying the behavior of others.

modes of adaptation: according to Merton, the various ways of adapting to strain; the five modes of adaptation are conformity, innovation, ritualism, retreatism, and rebellion.

Monitoring the Future (MTF) Project: a self-report survey, administered annually to high school seniors, college students, and young adults, that includes both serious and less serious offenses, such as robbery, aggravated assault, hitting teachers, use of weapons, group fighting, and drug usage.

monoamine oxidase A (MAOA) gene: facilitates or inhibits the transfer of information from neuron to neuron, thus altering possible reactions to inputs.

moral development: Kohlberg's theory that individuals progress through six stages of "moral development," which are arranged into three levels: preconventional, conventional, and postconventional (principled).

motivational interviewing: a style of communication designed to make it more likely that offenders will listen, will be engaged in the process, and will be more ready to make changes.

Multi-Dimensional Family Therapy (MDFT): therapy centered on the family, peers, and community influences around youths.

N

National Child Abuse and Neglect Data System (NCANDS): a voluntary national data collection and analysis system created in response to the requirements of the Child Abuse Prevention and Treatment Act.

National Crime Victimization Survey (NCVS): a victim survey administered by the U.S. Census Bureau.

National Incident-Based Reporting System (NIBRS): replaces the traditional UCR Summary Reporting System; collects detailed information on 23 categories with 52 total offenses.

National Survey on Drug Use and Health: a survey of the prevalence, patterns, and consequences of alcohol, tobacco, and illegal drug use and abuse of the general U.S. civilian noninstitutionalized population, age 12 and older, conducted by the Substance Abuse and Mental Health Services Administration (SAMHSA).

National Youth Survey (NYS): a self-report survey administered to 11- to 17-year-old youths that taps information on Index offenses.

nature–nurture controversy: the debate as to whether intelligence is inherited (nature) or whether it is an outcome of growth in the environment (nurture).

near group: an assembly of individuals characterized by a relatively short lifetime, little formal organization, a lack of consensus between members, a small core of continuous participants, self-appointed leadership, and limited cohesion.

neglect: the failure to provide life's essentials (e.g., food, shelter, clothing, etc.) to a child.

neighborhood reparative boards (NRBs): boards made up of community members that seek to restore victims and community to pre-offense states, require the offender to make amends, and aid the offender in understanding the impact of his or her actions on the victim and community.

Neoclassicism: the middle ground between Classicism and Positivism, the contention that humankind exercises some degree of free will, but that choices are limited by a large number of factors both within and outside of the individual (also called soft determinism).

net-widening: the practice of handling youths (or other offenders) who normally would have been left alone.

neurotransmitters: chemicals involved in the transmission of electrical impulses through the nervous system.

new balance: see smart on juvenile justice/the fourth wave/new balance effort.

nonsecure detention: the placement of a delinquent youth in a small group home that is not as securely locked to await further court action (compare to secure detention).

norepinephrine: hormone that leads to increased heart rates and energy levels; influences fight or flight reactions.

nullification: a refusal to enforce the law or impose a punishment.

O

offense rate: the number of offenses per 100,000 persons.

Olweus Bullying Prevention Program (OBPP): a bullying prevention program that attempts to raise awareness about the problem of bullying, establish rules and regulations governing behavior and responses to offending, train school staff on how to integrate bullying discussions into curriculum, require meetings between parents and teachers, and hold meetings between bullies and their victims.

"once an adult, always an adult" provisions: state laws that mandate that certain juvenile offenders be processed in adult court after an initial processing in adult criminal court.

operant conditioning: the reinforcement of behavior through a complex system of rewards.

Operation Ceasefire: deterrence project which targeted firearms use by gangs; used an approach referred to as pulling levers (also known as the Boston Gun Project).

orthomolecular factors: chemicals that are introduced to the body or altered through diet or other influences.

outer containment: direct control over the individual from outside sources.

outpatient drug-free program: a nonresidential form of drug treatment that emphasizes the provision of a supportive, highly structured, family-like atmosphere within which a patient can be helped to alter his or her personality and develop social relationships conducive to conforming behavior.

P

panel design: a study design in which the same set of individuals are interviewed repeatedly over an extended number of years.

parens patriae: a legal doctrine under which the state is seen as a parent.

Part I offenses: murder, rape, robbery, aggravated assault, burglary, larceny, motor vehicle theft, and arson (also known as Index offenses).

Part II offenses: all other offenses that do not fall into the Part I offense category.

peacemaking: a perspective that supports efforts of corrections workers, whether prison counselors or probation officers, to help offenders find greater meaning in their lives.

peacemaking/sentencing circles: a community-directed process, conducted in partnership with the criminal justice system, to develop consensus on an appropriate sentencing plan that addresses the concerns of all interested parties; the process takes place post-conviction to determine a sentence.

peer mediation: a program in which disputants in a matter are brought together with a third-party peer (youth) mediator in an effort to resolve the dispute to the satisfaction of both parties.

Perry Preschool Project: a preschool program that seeks to provide students with a positive introduction to education by involving the children in the planning of activities, a low child–teacher ratio, enhanced reinforcement of student achievement, and frequent home visits with parents.

petition: the document filed in juvenile court alleging that a juvenile is a delinquent, status offender, or dependent.

phrenology: the study of the shape of a person's skull.

physiognomy: the study of facial features.

plea bargaining: negotiation between the prosecutor and the defense attorney concerning the petition (charge) and/or the disposition (sentence).

police effectiveness: whether police are accomplishing their objectives such as controlling crime, improving the quality of life, or solving problems.

police use of excessive force: intentional use of brutality by police.

Positivism: a school of thought based upon determinism, wherein what an individual does is determined by factors beyond the control of the individual (compare to Classicism).

predisposition report: see social history investigation.

prevalence: how many respondents report the use of something (e.g., a drug).

preventive detention: detention to prevent further delinquency while awaiting court action on an earlier charge.

primary deviance: those actions that are rationalized or otherwise dealt with as functions of a socially acceptable role (compare to secondary deviance).

probation: a type of community corrections in which an offender is under the supervision of a probation officer. The court orders the offender to follow certain rules and to report regularly to a probation officer.

problem-oriented policing: addressing the underlying causes of problems (such as delinquency) rather than simply addressing the symptoms.

professional policing: also known as the 911 model of policing, a model of policing that emphasizes rapid response to citizen calls for service. This model includes greater emphasis on police patrol in cruisers rather than foot patrol.

program effectiveness: the question of whether programs achieve their objectives.

Project HOPE: emphasizes swift and certain sanctions.

Project TOUGH: (Taking Out Urban Gang Headquarters–Los Angeles) this project entails the employment of civil abatement procedures to control or eliminate locations that gang members frequent or own.

Promoting Alternative Thinking Strategies (PATHS): a five-year curriculum offered in elementary schools that is intended to reduce both behavioral and emotional problems, while building self-control and problem-solving abilities.

prosecutorial waiver: a waiver or transfer by the prosecutor of a juvenile case to adult court.

psychoanalysis: pioneered by Freud, an approach to understanding human behavior, the major premise of which is that unconscious, and perhaps instinctual, factors account for much of the behavior displayed by individuals.

psychopharmacological perspective/explanations: the perspective that drugs have a direct causal impact on crime by inducing the user to act out in a certain way.

pulling levers: an approach wherein the police strictly enforce any and all codes and regulations (i.e., zero tolerance) in an attempt to change the behavior of a target group.

punitive direction in probation: placing emphasis on accountability.

Punitive Period: started in the 1980s when increased use of waiver, mandatory sentencing, and less emphasis on rehabilitation and treatment was evident.

R

racial tension: discord based on differences in racial background.

rational choice theory: the theory that potential offenders make choices based on various factors in the physical and social environments.

reactive hypoglycemia: changes in the blood sugar level, both higher and lower, as a result of dietary intake.

reasonable doubt standard: the standard of proof used in both adult criminal cases and juvenile delinquency cases: doubt based on reason that a reasonable man or woman might entertain.

reciprocal relationship: a relationship in which two behaviors being studied (e.g., drug use and delinquency) feed one another.

reduced use of probation (Mendel): limiting probation to serious or chronic offenders with most youths getting diversion.

reintegrative shaming: an idea postulated by Braithwaite that offers shaming as a key mechanism for showing societal disapproval. The shaming needs to be imposed in such a fashion as to draw the offending party into conforming society.

resistance skills training: training involving a set of ideas dealing with recognizing problematic situations and issues, dealing with peer pressure, recognizing pressure from media presentations, knowing proper responses to temptations, building self-esteem and assertiveness, and knowing how and when to take a stand.

Resolving Conflict Creatively Program (RCCP): a school-based intervention that focuses on character education and social and emotional learning, and aims to teach children self-management, cooperation, and problem-solving skills and promote interpersonal effectiveness and intercultural understanding.

restitution: the practice of offenders paying for all or part of the damage inflicted on persons or property damaged by the offense.

restorative justice: a model of justice that is concerned with repairing the damage or harm inflicted through processes of negotiation, mediation, empowerment, and reparation.

restorative justice conferences: meetings in which victims and offenders face one another in an attempt at restorative justice; for example, a burglary victim meets a juvenile burglar and explains precisely how the burglary impacted the victim. Supporters for both sides are present and, with the help of a leader, they work out an agreement on how the offender can make amends.

restorative justice juvenile court: a juvenile court focused on building community so that neighborhoods can better respond to and prevent delinquency. With such a court, communities would be more involved in sentencing through community panels or conferences or dispute resolution programs.

retributive justice: justice that focuses on the lawbreaker and the imposition of sanctions for the purposes of deterrence, vengeance, and/or punishment.

reverse waiver: the act of the adult criminal court returning certain cases received from juvenile court via waiver back to the juvenile court.

right to intervention: *Commonwealth v. Fisher* (1905) determined that a juvenile has a right to intervention rather than a right to freedom; the juvenile court was granted a free hand in dealing with youths.

risk factors: indicators of who may become deviant in the future.

role-taking: the process in which an individual (a child) assumes the role of a person or character whom they have observed (see modeling).

routine activities theory: a perspective that assumes that the normal, day-to-day behavior of individuals contributes to deviant events; that is, the convergence of motivated offenders, suitable targets, and an absence of guardians allows for the commission of crime.

rumble: a gang fight.

S

school prayer: prayer that takes place in the school setting; it is debated whether school prayer represents the promotion of religion by the school.

school resource officers (SROs): police officers in schools who provide traditional police activity as well as mentoring and referrals, training to teachers and parents, teaching programs such as Drug Abuse Resistance Education (D.A.R.E.), and chaperoning school events.

school-to-prison pipeline: refers to a combination of factors that appear to criminalize much youthful behavior and facilitate the eventual placement of youths in our nation's prisons.

search and seizure: can include searches of persons, places, and things, and actions such as taking into custody (arrest); the Fourth Amendment protects against unreasonable searches and seizures.

Seattle Social Development Project (SSDP): a long-term study that looks at the development of positive and problem behaviors among adolescents and young adults.

secondary deviance: deviance that occurs when deviant behavior is used as a means of adjusting to society's reactions (compare to primary deviance).

secure detention: the placement of a youth in a locked facility with other youths who are awaiting either further court action or transfer to a state correctional facility.

selection model: a model of the delinquency–gang relationship that maintains that gangs recruit or attract already delinquent youths.

self-control theory: Gottfredson and Hirschi's (1990) theory holding that self-control, internalized by individuals early in life, is what constrains a person from involvement in deviant behavior.

self-report measures: surveys that attempt to gauge the level of delinquency by asking individuals to tell of their own participation in deviant activity.

serotonin: hormone that is an inhibitor of behavior, particularly aggressive and impulsive behaviors.

sexting: the sending of sexually explicit texts or nude or partially nude images of minors by minors.

shock incarceration: alternatives to traditional incarceration in which participants are involved in an intensive curriculum of discipline, work, strenuous physical activities, education, and other programs; boot camps are a common form.

Short–Nye instrument: developed by James Short and Ivan Nye, this early self-report survey asked youths to note the frequency with which they committed each of 23 items, dominated by status and minor offenses.

smart on juvenile justice/the fourth wave/new balance effort: an approach to juvenile justice that softens the punitive strains of the "get tough" era to rebalance and focus on risk assessment, evidence-based practices, and diversion of less serious offenses.

social concern theory: rests on four elements that can impact on crime: a concern about the welfare of others; the desire to build ties to others; following moral intuitions about what is right and wrong; conforming to the views of others and social norms.

social control theories: theories that seek to find factors that keep an individual from becoming deviant.

social disorganization: the state of a community in which the people in that community are unable to exert control over those living there.

social facilitation model: a model of the delinquency–gang relationship that maintains that belonging to a gang is the cause of increased deviance.

social history investigation: an investigation performed by a probation officer into the legal and social history of a delinquent youth and his or her family, similar to a presentence investigation in adult court.

social learning approach: in explanations of child maltreatment, an approach that contends that an individual learns to be abusive or neglectful by observing past behavior of that type.

social support theory: the theory that social support reduces antisocial and criminal/delinquent behavior.

sociocultural explanation: in explanations of child maltreatment, an explanation that emphasizes the role of society and the environment in leading to deviant behavior.

soft determinism: see Neoclassicism.

somatotypes: physiques (e.g., ectomorph, endomorph, and mesomorph) supposedly corresponding to particular temperaments.

spiritual dimension in corrections: a suggestion that corrections should go beyond providing education and counseling to also focus on such issues as the meaning of life and the importance of personal values in one's life.

spiritualistic/demonological explanations: the belief that deviant acts are the result of the battle between good and evil, God and the devil.

spurious relationship: a relationship in which two occurrences have no causal connection yet it may be inferred that they do, due to a certain third factor that causes both behaviors being studied (e.g., drug use and delinquency).

state training schools: residential placement centers for juveniles who have been adjudicated delinquent. They are youth prisons that may have a cottage structure and educational programming.

status offense: an action illegal only for persons of a certain status (i.e., juveniles); an action for which only a juvenile can be held accountable (e.g., runaway behavior, truancy).

statutory exclusion: a state legislature's rule that certain offenses, such as murder, automatically go to adult court; see legislative waiver.

STEP Act: California's Street Terrorism Enforcement and Prevention Act of 1988, which effectively criminalizes membership in a street gang.

strain theory: Robert Merton's theory that deviance results from a disjuncture between the goals approved by a culture and the means approved for reaching those goals.

student search: search of a student's possessions or person in a school.

subculture: a smaller part of a larger culture that exists within and is part of the larger culture.

Summary Reporting System (SRS): name for the traditional UCR reporting system.

superego: in Freudian theory, learned values, behaviors; moral character of the individual; outlines the acceptable and unacceptable; may be conscious or unconscious.

symbolic interactionism: the process through which an individual creates his or her self-image through interaction with the outside world.

Syracuse Family Development Research Program (FDRP): a comprehensive early childhood program aimed to develop child and family functioning through home visitation, parent training, and individualized daycare.

systemic violence: violence due to factors related to the sale and marketing of drugs.

T

tautological: leading to circular reasoning.

techniques of neutralization: techniques outlined by Sykes and Matza that allow a juvenile to accommodate deviant behavior while maintaining a positive self-image.

teen courts: a diversion option in which youths act as judge, prosecutor, defense attorney, and jury in minor cases such as status offenses and misdemeanors. The most common penalty is community service.

theory: an attempt to answer the question "why?"

therapeutic community: a residential form of drug treatment that emphasizes the provision of a supportive, highly structured, family-like atmosphere within which a patient can be helped to alter their personality and develop social relationships conducive to conforming behavior.

token economy programs: a behavior modification strategy, often used in training schools and other residential facilities, in which point or dollar values are assigned to particular behaviors and are used as a way of rewarding appropriate behavior.

training school: an institution that houses delinquents considered to be unfit for probation or another lesser punishment.

transfer: see waiver.

transfer of evil: moving the attribution of evil from the act to the actor.

transporter genes: genes that influence the processing of information in the brain.

U

Uniform Crime Reports (UCR): data collected yearly by the Federal Bureau of Investigation, which provides information on 29 categories of offenses known to the police. It includes two offense subgroups: the first eight offenses are known as the Part I crimes or Index crimes; all remaining offenses fall within the Part II category.

use, abuse, and addiction: three common terms used in discussing the drug problem. *Use* means the utilization of a drug. *Abuse* refers to the use of any drug beyond that legally prescribed for a medical condition. *Addiction* refers to chronic use of a drug to the point at which the individual develops a need to continue use of the drug, increases the amount used over time, and develops a psychological or physical dependence on the drug.

V

vertical integration: stable neighborhoods with strong private and parochial networks may not be able to marshal the public support needed for effective delinquency control.

victim–offender mediation (VOM): a formal mediation program in which victim and offender are clearly identified and the participation of the offender is often a requirement of the court; also known as Victim–Offender Reconciliation Programs (VORPs).

victimization: in general, being victimized by a crime or delinquent act such as assault or theft. In reference to institutional life, victimization refers to an assault (physical or sexual) or theft experienced in a facility such as a state training school.

victimless crimes: behaviors in which the offender does not typically have a victim besides himself or herself.

W

waiver: the process by which an individual who is legally a juvenile is sent to the adult criminal system for disposition and handling (also called **legislative waiver** or **transfer**).

wet-nursing: the practice of employing a surrogate mother to care for and suckle a child.

wilderness program: a program in which youths undergo an outdoor experience that is designed to teach self-reliance, independence, and self-worth.

Z

zealous advocate role: defense attorney role that emphasizes strong tactics to prove the juvenile defendant innocent or get the least severe penalty (contrasted to the concerned adult model in which the attorney acts like a parent seeking the best treatment outcome for the youth).

References

Abadinsky, H. (1989). *Drug abuse: An introduction*. Chicago, IL: Nelson-Hall.

Aber, J.L., Pedersen, S., Brown, J.L., Jones, S.M., & Gershof, E.T. (2003). *Changing children's trajectories of development: Two-year evidence for the effectiveness of a school-based approach to violence prevention*. New York: National Center for Children in Poverty.

Abram, K.M., Paskar, L.D., Washburn, J.J., & Teplin, L.A. (2008). Perceived barriers to mental health services among youths in detention. *Journal of the American Academy of Child and Adolescent Psychiatry, 47*, 291–300.

Abram, K.M., Teplin, L.A., King, D.C., Longworth, S.L., Emanuel, K.M., Romero, E.G., … & Olson, N.D. (2013). *PTSD, trauma, and comorbid psychiatric disorders in detained youth*. Washington, DC: Office of Juvenile Justice and Delinquency Prevention.

Abt Associates. (1994). *Conditions of confinement: Juvenile detention and corrections facilities: Research report*. Washington, DC: U.S. Department of Justice.

Acoca, L. (1998). Outside/inside: The violation of American girls at home, on the streets, and in the juvenile justice system. *Crime & Delinquency, 44*, 561–589.

Adams, K. (2003). The effectiveness of juvenile curfews at crime prevention. *Annals of the American Academy of Political and Social Science, 587*, 136–159.

Adams, K. (2007). Abolish juvenile curfews. *Criminology & Public Policy, 6*, 663–670.

Adams, L.R. (1974). The adequacy of differential association theory. *Journal of Research in Crime and Delinquency, 11*, 1–8.

Adamson, C. (1998). Tribute, turf, honor and the American street gang: Patterns of continuity and change since 1820. *Theoretical Criminology, 2*, 57–84.

Administration on Children, Youth and Families. (2020). *Child Maltreatment 2018*. Retrieved from www.acf.hhs.gov/cb/research-data-technology/statistics-research/child-maltreatment.

Administration on Children, Youth and Families. (2021). *Child Maltreatment 2019*. Retrieved from www.acf.hhs.gov/cb/research-data-technology/statistics-research/child-maltreatment.

Agnew, R. (1992). Foundation for a general strain theory of crime and delinquency. *Criminology, 30*, 47–87.

Agnew, R. (1994). The techniques of neutralization and violence. *Criminology, 32*, 555–580.

Agnew, R. (2001). An overview of general strain theory. In R. Paternoster & R. Bachman (Eds.), *Explaining criminals and crime* (pp. 161–174). Los Angeles: Roxbury.

Agnew, R. (2006a). *Pressured into crime: An overview of general strain theory*. Los Angeles: Roxbury.

Agnew, R. (2006b). General strain theory: Current status and directions for future research. In F.T. Cullen, J.P. Wright, & K.R. Blevins (Eds.), *Taking stock: The status of criminological theory* (pp. 101–123). New Brunswick, NJ: Transaction.

Agnew, R. (2014). Social concern and crime: Moving beyond the assumption of simple self-interest—2013 presidential address to the American Society of Criminology. *Criminology, 52*, 1–32.

Agnew, R. (2016). Strain, economic status, and crime. In A.R. Piquero (Ed.), *The handbook of criminological theory.* (pp. 209–229). West Sussex: John Wiley and Sons.

Agnew, R., & Peters, A.A.R. (1986). The techniques of neutralization: An analysis of predisposing and situational factors. *Criminal Justice and Behavior, 13*, 81–97.

Ahlin, E.M., & Hummer, D. (2019). Sexual victimization of juveniles incarcerated in jails and prisons: An exploratory study of prevalence and risk factors. *Victims & Offenders, 14*, 793–810.

Aikens, N., Kopack Klein, A., Tarullo, L., & West, J. (2013). *Getting ready for kindergarten: Children's progress during Head Start.* FACES 2009 Report. OPRE Report 2013-21a. Washington, DC: Office of Planning, Research and Evaluation, Administration for Children and Families, U.S. Department of Health and Human Services. Retrieved from www.acf.hhs.gov/sites/default/files/opre/faces_2009_child_outcomes_brief_final.pdf

Akers, R.L. (1985). *Deviant behavior: A social learning approach.* Belmont, CA: Wadsworth.

Akers, R.L. (2001). Social learning theory. In R. Paternoster & R. Bachman (Eds.), *Explaining criminals and crime* (pp. 192–210). Los Angeles: Roxbury.

Akers, R.L., Krohn, M.K., Lonza-Kaduce, L., & Radosevich, M. (1979). Social learning and deviant behavior: A specific test of a general theory. *American Sociological Review, 44*, 636–655.

Alarid, L.F., Sims, B.A., & Ruiz, J. (2011). Juvenile probation and police partnerships as loosely coupled systems: A qualitative analysis. *Youth Violence and Juvenile Justice, 9*, 79–95.

Alexander, M. (2012). *The New Jim Crow: Mass incarceration in the age of colorblindness* (Revised ed.). New York: The New Press.

Alexander, M., & Vanbenschoten, S. (2008). The evolution of supervision within the federal probation and pretrial system. *Journal of Offender Rehabilitation, 47*, 319–337.

Allen, T.T. (2005). Taking a juvenile into custody: Situational factors that influence police officers' decisions. *Journal of Sociology and Social Welfare, 32*, 121–129.

Alm, S.S. (2016). HOPE probation: Fair sanctions, evidence-based principles, and therapeutic alliances. *Criminology & Public Policy, 15*, 1195–1214.

Altschuler, D.M. (1998). Intermediate sanctions and community treatment for serious and violent juvenile offenders. In R. Loeber & D.P. Farrington (Eds.), *Serious and violent juvenile offenders: Risk factors and successful interventions* (pp. 367–385). Thousand Oaks, CA: Sage.

American Civil Liberties Union (ACLU). (2013). *The war on marijuana in black and white.* New York: ACLU.

American Dietetics Association. (1984). Position paper of the American Dietetics Association on diet and criminal behavior. *Journal of the American Dietetics Association, 85*, 361–362.

Anderson, E. (1994). The code of the streets. *Atlantic Monthly, 273*(5), 81–94.

Anderson, G.S. (2007). *Biological influences on criminal behavior.* Boca Raton, FL: CRC Press.

Andrews, D.A. (2006). Enhancing adherence to risk-need-responsivity: Making quality a matter of policy. *Criminology & Public Policy, 5*, 595–602.

Anglin, M.D., & Hser, Y. (1987). Addicted women and crime. *Criminology, 25*, 359–397.

Anglin, M.D., & Hser, Y. (1990). Treatment of drug abuse. In M. Tonry & J.Q. Wilson (Eds.), *Drugs and crime* (pp. 393–460). Chicago, IL: University of Chicago Press.

Anglin, M.D., & Speckart, G.R. (1988). Narcotics use and crime: A multisample, multimethod analysis. *Criminology, 26*, 197–233.

Anglin, M.D., Speckart, G.R., Booth, M.W., & Ryan, T.M. (1989). Consequences and costs of shutting off methadone. *Addictive Behaviors, 14*, 307–326.

Annie E. Casey Foundation. (2017). *JDAI at 25*. Foundation Retrieved from www.aecf.org.

Aos, S., & Drake, E. (2013). *Prison, police, and programs: Evidence-based options that reduce crime and save money* (Doc. 13-11-1901). Olympia, WA: Washington State Institute for Public Policy.

Aos, S., Miller, M., & Drake, E. (2006). *Evidence-based public policy options to reduce future prison construction, criminal justice costs, and crime rates* (Washington State Institute of Public Policy Report 06-10-1201). Olympia, WA: Washington State Institute for Public Policy. Retrieved from www.wsipp.wa.gov

Applegate, B.K., Davis, R.K., & Cullen, F.T. (2009). Reconsidering child saving: The extent and correlates of public support for excluding youths from the juvenile court. *Crime & Delinquency, 55*, 51–77.

Araujo, W. (2012). Punishing cyberbullies: Using Supreme Court guidance beyond Tinker to protect students and school officials. *Thomas Jefferson Law Review, 34*, 325–372.

Aries, P. (1962). *Centuries of childhood*. New York: Knopf.

Ash Institute. (2008). *Division of youth services honored as innovations in American Government award winner*. Cambridge, MA: Harvard University Press.

Austin, J., Johnson, K.D., & Weitzer, R. (2005). *Alternatives to the secure detention and confinement of juvenile offenders*. Washington, DC: U.S. Department of Justice.

Ba, H., & Hawkins, J. (1996). *Resolving conflict creatively: Program evaluation project*. New York: Education Development Center.

Bachman, J.G., Johnson, L.D., & O'Malley, P.M. (2014). *Monitoring the future: Questionnaire responses from the nation's high school seniors, 2012*. Ann Arbor, MI: Institute for Social Research.

Baglivio, M.T., & Epps, N. (2016). The interrelatedness of adverse childhood experiences among high-risk juvenile offenders. *Youth Violence & Juvenile Justice, 14*, 179–198.

Baglivio, M.T., Epps, N., Swartz, K., Sayedul, M., Sheer, A., & Hardt, N.S. (2014). The prevalence of Adverse Childhood Experiences (ACE) in the lives of juvenile offenders. *Journal of Juvenile Justice, 3*(2), 1–23.

Baglivio, M., Wolff, K.T., Piquero, A.R., Greenwald, M.A., & Epps, N. (2017). Racial, ethnic disproportionality in psychiatric diagnoses and treatment in a sample of serious juvenile offenders. *Journal of Youth & Adolescence, 46*, 1424–1451.

Baker, M.L., Sigmon, J.N., & Nugent, M.E. (2001). *Truancy reduction: Keeping students in school*. Washington, DC: Office of Juvenile Justice and Delinquency Prevention.

Ball, J.C., Shaffer, J.W., & Nurco, D.N. (1983). The day-to-day criminality of heroin addicts in Baltimore: A study in the continuity of offense rates. *Drug and Alcohol Dependence, 12*, 119–142.

Bandura, A., & Walters, R.H. (1963). *Social learning and personality development*. New York: Holt, Rhinehart and Winston.

Bannister, A.J., Carter, D.L., & Schafer, J. (2001). A national police survey on juvenile curfews. *Journal of Criminal Justice, 29*, 233–240.

Barnert, E.S., Abrams, L.S., Maxson, C., Gase, L., Soung, P., Carroll, P., & Bath, E.C. (2017). Setting a minimum age for juvenile justice jurisdiction in California. *International Journal of Prisoner Health, 13*, 49–56.

Barnes, J.C., Boutwell, B.B., & Beaver, K.M. (2016). Contemporary biosocial criminology: A systematic review of the literature, 2000–2012. In A.R. Piquero (Ed.), *The handbook of criminological theory* (pp. 75–99). West Sussex: John Wiley and Sons.

Barnes, J.C., Wright, J.P., Boutwell, B.B., Schwartz, J.A., Connolly, E.J., Nedelec, J.L., & Beaver, K.M. (2014). Demonstrating the validity of twin research in criminology. *Criminology, 52*, 588–626.

Barnoski, R. (2009). *Providing evidence-based programs with fidelity in Washington state juvenile courts: Cost analysis.* Olympia, WA: Washington State Institute for Public Policy. Retrieved from www.wsipp.wa.gov.

Barnum, R. (1987). The development of responsibility: Implications for juvenile justice. In F.X. Hartman (Ed.), *From children to citizens: Volume II: The role of the juvenile court* (pp. 67–79). New York: Springer-Verlag.

Barr, A., & Gibbs, C.R. (2017). *Breaking the cycle? Intergenerational effects of an anti-poverty program in early childhood.* Retrieved from https://static1.squarespace.com/static/563b9 5a2e4b0c51a8b87767c/t/59b2e1d259cc681cdd587b22/1504895485410/Barr+%26+ Gibbs_Intergenerational_2017.pdf.

Barrett, P., Farrell, L., Ollendick, T., & Dadds, M. (2006). Long-term outcomes of an Australian universal prevention trial of anxiety and depression symptoms in children and youth: An evaluation of the Friends Program. *Journal of Clinical Child and Adolescent Psychology, 35,* 403–411. DOI: 10.1207/s15374424jccp3503_5.

Bartollas, C., & Sieverdes, C.M. (1981). The victimized white in a juvenile correctional system. *Crime & Delinquency, 27,* 534–543.

Barton, W.H. (2012). Detention. In B.C. Feld & D.M. Bishop (Eds.), *The Oxford handbook of juvenile crime and juvenile justice* (pp. 637–663). New York: Oxford University Press.

Batchelor, S. (2009). Girls, gangs, violence: Assessing the evidence. *Probation Journal, 56,* 399–414.

Bazemore, G. (1999). The fork in the road to juvenile court reform. *Annals of the American Academy of Political and Social Science, 564,* 81–108.

Bazemore, G. (2012). Restoration, shame, and the future of restorative practice. In B.C. Feld & D.M. Bishop (Eds.), *The Oxford handbook of juvenile crime and juvenile justice* (pp. 695– 722). New York: Oxford University Press.

Bazemore, G., & Maloney, D. (1994). Rehabilitating community service: Toward restorative service in a balanced justice system. *Federal Probation, 58,* 24–35.

Bazemore, G., & Schiff, M. (2005). *Juvenile justice reform and restorative justice: Building theory and policy from practice.* Portland, OR: Willan.

Bazemore, G., & Umbreit, M. (1994). *Balanced and restorative justice: Program models.* Washington, DC: Office of Juvenile Justice and Delinquency.

Bazemore, G., & Umbreit, M. (2001). *A comparison of four restorative conferencing models.* Washington, DC: U.S. Department of Justice, Office of Juvenile Justice and Delinquency Prevention.

Beaver, K.M., Rowland, M.W., Schwartz, J.A., & Nedelec, J.L. (2011). The genetic origins of psychopathic personality traits in adult males and females: Results from an adoption-based study. *Journal of Criminal Justice, 39,* 426–432.

Beck, A.J., & Rantala, R.R. (2016). *Sexual victimization reported by juvenile correctional authorities, 2007–12.* Washington, DC: Bureau of Justice Statistics.

Beck, A.J., Kline, S.A., & Greenfield, L.A. (1988). *Survey of youth in custody, 1987.* Bureau of Justice Statistics Special Report. Washington, DC: U.S. Department of Justice.

Behrman, M. (2015). When gangs go viral: Using social media and surveillance cameras to enhance gang databases. *Harvard Journal of Law and Technology, 29,* 315–338.

Beldon, E. (1920). *Courts in the U.S. hearing children's cases.* Washington, DC: U.S. Children's Bureau.

Belknap, J. (1984). The effect of local policy on the sentencing patterns of state wards. *Justice Quarterly, 1,* 549–561.

Belknap, J. (1987). Routine activity theory and the risk of rape: Analyzing ten years of national crime survey data. *Criminal Justice Policy Review, 2,* 337–356.

Bell, D., & Lang, K. (1985). The intake dispositions of juvenile offenders. *Journal of Research in Crime and Delinquency, 22*, 309–328.

Bellis, D.J. (1981). *Heroin and politicians: The failure of public policy to control addiction in America.* Westport, CT: Greenwood.

Belsky, J. (1978). Three theoretical models of child abuse: A critical review. *Child Abuse & Neglect, 2*, 37–49.

Benda, B.B. (2002). Religion and violent offenders in boot camp: A structural equation model. *Journal of Research in Crime and Delinquency, 39*, 91–121.

Benekos, P.J., & Merlo, A.V. (2008). Juvenile justice: The legacy of punitive policy. *Youth Violence and Juvenile Justice, 6*, 28–46.

Bennett, T., Holloway, K., & Farrington, D. (2008). The statistical association between drug misuse and crime: A meta-analysis. *Aggression and Violent Behavior, 13*, 107–118.

Bentham, J. (1948). *An introduction to the principles of morals and legislation.* New York: Hafner.

Bergseth, K.J., & Bouffard, J.A. (2012). Examining the effectiveness of a restorative justice program for various types of juvenile offenders. *International Journal of Offender Therapy and Comparative Criminology, 57*, 1054–1075.

Berrueta-Clement, J.R., Schweinhart, L.J., Barnett, W.S., Epstein, A.S., & Weikart, D.P. (1984). *Changed lives: The effects of the Perry Preschool Program on youths through age 19.* Ypsilanti, MI: High/Scope Press.

Bettman, J.E., Gillis, H.L., Speelman, E.A., Parry, K.J., & Case, J.M. (2016). A meta-analysis of wilderness therapy for private pay clients. *Journal of Child and Family Studies, 25*, 2659–2673.

Big Brothers/Big Sisters of America. (2021). Retrieved from www.bbbs.org/national-office/.

Bilchik, S. (1998). *A juvenile justice system for the 21st century.* Washington, DC: U.S. Department of Justice.

Bishop, D.M. (2000). Juvenile offenders in the adult criminal justice system. In M. Tonry (Ed.), *Crime and justice: A review of research* (Vol. 27, pp. 81–167). Chicago, IL: University of Chicago Press.

Bishop, D.M. (2005). The role of race and ethnicity in juvenile justice processing. In D.F. Hawkins & K. Kempf-Leonard (Eds.), *Our children, their children: Confronting racial and ethnic differences in American juvenile justice* (pp. 23–82). Chicago, IL: University of Chicago Press.

Bishop, D.M. (2006). Public opinion and juvenile policy: Myths and misconceptions—reaction essay. *Criminology & Public Policy, 5*, 653–664.

Bishop, D.M., & Feld, B.C. (2012). Trends in juvenile justice policy and practice. In B.C. Feld & D.M. Bishop (Eds.), *The Oxford handbook of juvenile crime and juvenile justice* (pp. 898–926). New York: Oxford University Press.

Bishop, D.M., & Leiber, M.J. (2012). Racial and ethnic differences in delinquency and justice system responses. In B.C. Feld & D.M. Bishop (Eds.), *The Oxford handbook of juvenile crime and juvenile justice* (pp. 445–484). New York: Oxford University Press.

Bjerregaard, B. (1989). Televised testimony as an alternative in child sexual abuse cases. *Criminal Law Bulletin, 25*, 164–175.

Bjerregaard, B. (2002). Operationalizing gang membership: The impact of measurement on gender differences in gang self-identification and delinquent involvement. *Women & Criminal Justice, 13*, 79–100. DOI: doi.org/10.1300/J012v13n02_05.

Bjerregaard, B. (2010). Gang membership and drug involvement: Untangling the complex relationships. *Crime & Delinquency, 56*, 3–34.

Bjerregaard, B., & Lizotte, A. (1995). Gun ownership and gang membership. *Journal of Criminal Law and Criminology, 86*, 37–58.

Bjerregaard, B., & Smith, C. (1993). Gender differences in gang participation, delinquency, and substance use. *Journal of Quantitative Criminology, 4*, 329–355.

Blackburn, S. (2019). Juvenile justice in Pennsylvania: Mission-driven, performance-based, outcome focused. *Juvenile and Family Court Journal, 70*, 73–87.

Blair, L., Sullivan, C., Latessa, E., & Sullivan, C.J. (2015). *Juvenile drug courts: A process, outcome, and impact evaluation.* Washington, DC: Office of Juvenile Justice and Delinquency Prevention.

Blitzman, J.D. (2015). Are we criminalizing adolescence? *Criminal Justice, 30*, 22–28.

Bloch, H.A., & Niederhoffer, A. (1958). *The gang: A study in adolescent behavior.* New York: Philosophical Library.

Bohman, M. (1996). Predisposition to criminality: Swedish adoption studies in retrospect. *Ciba Foundation Symposium, 194*, 99–109.

Bolin, R.M., & Applegate, B.K. (2016). Adultification in juvenile corrections: Examining the orientations of juvenile and adult probation and parole officers. *American Journal of Criminal Justice, 41*, 321–339.

Bolin, R.M., Applegate, B.K., & Ouelette, H.M. (2021). Americans' opinions of juvenile justice: Preferred aims, beliefs about juveniles, and blended sentencing. *Crime & Delinquency, 67*, 262–286.

Bonnett, P.L., & Pfeiffer, C.L. (1978). Biochemical diagnosis for delinquent behavior. In L.J. Hippchen (Ed.), *Ecologic-biochemical approaches to treatment of delinquents and criminals* (pp. 183–205). New York: Van Nostrand Reinhold.

Bonnies, R.J., Johnson, R.L., Chemers, B.M., & Schuck, J.A. (Eds.). (2013). *Reforming juvenile justice: A developmental approach.* Washington, DC: The National Academies Press.

Bonta, J., Wallace-Capretta, S., Rooney, J., & McAnoy, K. (2002). An outcome evaluation of a restorative justice alternative to incarceration. *Contemporary Justice Review, 5*, 319–338.

Bookin-Weiner, H., & Horowitz, R. (1983). The end of the youth gang: Fad or fact? *Criminology, 21*, 585–602.

Booth, A., & Osgood, D.W. (1993). The influence of testosterone on deviance in adulthood: Assessing and explaining the relationship. *Criminology, 31*, 93–118.

Booth, B., Van Hasselt, V.B., & Vecchi, G.M. (2011). Addressing school violence. *FBI Law Enforcement Bulletin, 80*(5), 1–9.

Borrero, M. (2001). The widening mistrust between youth and police. *Families in Society: The Journal of Contemporary Human Services, 82*, 399.

Bortner, M.A., & Williams, L.M. (1997). *Youth in prison: We the people of unit four.* New York: Routledge.

Botvin, G.J. (1990). Substance abuse prevention: Theory, practice and effectiveness. In M. Tonry & J.Q. Wilson (Eds.), *Drugs and crime* (pp. 461–520). Chicago, IL: University of Chicago Press.

Botvin, G.J., & Dusenbury, L. (1989). Substance abuse prevention and the promotion of competence. In L.A. Bond & B.E. Compas (Eds.), *Primary prevention and promotion in the schools* (pp. 146–178). Newbury Park, CA: Sage.

Botvin, G.J., Epstein, J.A., Baker, E., Diaz, T., & Ifill-Williams, M. (1997). School-based drug abuse prevention with inner-city minority youth. *Journal of Child and Adolescent Substance Abuse, 6*, 5–19.

Botvin, G.J., Griffin, K.W., Paul, E., & Macaulay, A.P. (2003). Preventing tobacco and alcohol use among elementary school students through life skills training. *Journal of Child and Adolescent Substance Abuse, 12*, 1–18.

Bouchard, J., & Wong, J.S. (2017). A jury of their peers: A meta-analysis of the effects of Teen Court on criminal recidivism. *Journal of Youth Adolescence, 46*, 1472–1487.

Bracey, J.R., Geib, C.F., Plant, R., O'Leary, J.R., Anderson, A., Herscovitch, L., ... & Vanderploeg, J.J. (2013). Connecticut's comprehensive approach to reducing in-school arrests: Changes in statewide policy, systems coordination and school practices. *Family Court Review, 51,* 427–434.

Brady, K.P., Balmer, S., & Phenix, D. (2007). School–police partnership effectiveness in urban schools: An analysis of New York City's Impact Schools Initiative. *Education and Urban Society, 39,* 455–478.

Braga, A.A. (2008). Pulling levers focused deterrence strategies and the prevention of gun homicide. *Journal of Criminal Justice, 36,* 332–343.

Braga, A.A. (2015). *New perspectives in policing: Crime and policing revisited.* Washington, DC: National Institute of Justice.

Braga, A.A., & Bond, B.J. (2008). Policing crime and disorder hot spots: A randomized controlled trial. *Criminology, 46,* 577–607.

Braga, A.A., Kennedy, D.M., Piehl, A.M., & Waring, E.J. (2001). *The Boston Gun Project: Impact evaluation findings.* Washington, DC: National Institute of Justice.

Braga, A.A., Papachristos, A.V., & Hureau, D.M. (2014). The effects of hot spots policing on crime: An updated systematic review and meta-analysis. *Justice Quarterly, 31,* 633–663.

Braga, A.A., Pierce, G.L., McDevitt, J., Bond, B.J., & Cronin, S. (2008). The strategic prevention of gun violence among gang-involved offenders. *Justice Quarterly, 25,* 132–162.

Braithwaite, J. (1989). *Crime, shame and reintegration.* Cambridge, England: Cambridge University Press.

Braithwaite, J. (1999). Restorative justice: Assessing optimistic and pessimistic accounts. In M. Tonry (Ed.), *Crime and justice: A review of research* (Vol. 25, pp. 1–127). Chicago, IL: University of Chicago Press.

Braswell, M., Fuller, J., & Lozoff, B. (2001). *Corrections, peacemaking, and restorative justice: Transforming individuals and institutions.* Cincinnati: Anderson.

Brennan, P.A., Mednick, S.A., & Jacobsen, B. (1996). Assessing the role of genetics in crime using adoption cohorts. *Ciba Foundation Symposium, 194,* 115–123.

Brennan, P.A., Mednick, B.R., & Mednick, S.A. (1993). Parental psychopathology, congenital factors, and violence. In S. Hodgins (Ed.), *Mental disorder and crime.* Newbury Park, CA: Sage.

Brennan, P.A., Mednick, S.A., & Volavka, J. (1995). Biomedical factors in crime. In J.Q. Wilson & J. Petersilia (Eds.), *Crime* (pp. 65–90). San Francisco: ICS Press.

Brenzel, B.M. (1983). *Daughters of the state: A social portrait of the first reform school for girls in North America, 1856–1903.* Cambridge, MA: MIT Press.

Brewer, D.D., Hawkins, J.D., Catalano, R.F., & Neckerman, H.J. (1995). Preventing serious, violent, and chronic offending: A review of evaluations of selected strategies in childhood, adolescence, and the community. In J.C. Howell, B. Krisberg, J.D. Hawkins, & J. Wilson (Eds.), *Sourcebook on serious, violent, and chronic juvenile offenders* (pp. 61–141).Thousand Oaks, CA: Sage.

Brewster, M.P. (2001). An evaluation of the Chester County (PA) drug court program. *Journal of Drug Issues, 31,* 171–206.

Brick, B.T., Taylor, T.J., & Esbensen, F. (2009). Juvenile attitudes towards the police: The importance of sub-cultural involvement and community ties. *Journal of Criminal Justice, 37,* 488–495.

Bridges, G.S., & Steen, S. (1998). Racial disparities in official assessments of juvenile offenders: Attributional stereotypes as mediating mechanisms. *American Sociological Review, 63,* 554–570.

Britt, C.L., & Rocque, M. (2016). Control as an explanation of crime and delinquency. In A.R. Piquero (Ed.), *The handbook of criminological theory* (pp. 182–208). West Sussex: Wiley Blackwell.

Britt, H., Toomey, T.L., Dunsmuir, W., & Wagenaar, A.C. (2006). Propensity for and correlates of alcohol sales to underage youth. *Journal of Alcohol and Drug Education, 50*(2), 25–42.

Brooks, K., & Kamine, D. (2003). *Justice cut short: An assessment of access to counsel and quality of representation in delinquency proceedings in Ohio.* Columbus: Ohio State Bar Association.

Brooks-Gunn, J., Love, J.M., Raikes, H.H., & Chazan-Cohen, R. (2013). Conclusions and implications. In J.M. Love, R. Chazan-Cohen, H. Raikes, & J. Brooks-Gunn (Eds.), What makes a difference: Early Head Start evaluation findings in a developmental context. *Monographs of the Society for Research in Child Development, 306*(1).

Brown, R.A., & Frank, J. (2006). Race and officer decision making: Examining differences in arrest outcomes between black and white officers. *Justice Quarterly, 23,* 96–126.

Brown, R.A., Novak, K.J., & Frank, J. (2009). Identifying variation in police officer behavior between juveniles and adults. *Journal of Criminal Justice, 37,* 200–208.

Brunson, R.K. (2007). "Police don't like black people": African-American young men's accumulated police experiences. *Criminology & Public Policy, 6,* 71–102.

Brunson, R.K., & Miller, J. (2006). Gender, race, and urban policing: The experience of African American youths. *Gender and Society, 20,* 531–552.

Brunson, R.K., & Wade, B.A. (2019). "Oh hell no, we don't talk to police:" Insights on the lack of cooperation in police investigations of urban gun violence. *Criminology & Public Policy, 18,* 623–648.

Bureau of Justice Assistance. (2003). *Juvenile drug courts: Strategies in practice.* Washington, DC: Bureau of Justice Assistance.

Bureau of Justice Statistics. (2021). *NCVS Victimization Analysis Tool (NVAT).* Retrieved from www.bjs.gov/index.cfm?ty=nvat.

Burgess, A.W., & Laszlo, A.T. (1976). When the prosecutrix is a child: The victim consultant in cases of sexual assault. In E.C. Viano (Ed.), *Victims & society.* Washington, DC: Visage Press.

Burgess, E.W. (1925). The growth of the city. In R.E. Park, E.W. Burgess, & R.D. McKenzie (Eds.), *The city.* Chicago, IL: University of Chicago Press.

Burke, J.D., Mulvey, E.P., & Schubert, C.A. (2015). Prevalence of mental health problems and service use among first time juvenile offenders. *Journal of Child & Family Studies, 24,* 3774–3781.

Burke, M.N. (2005). Juvenile justice supreme court provides uniformity in juvenile procedure rules. *Pennsylvania Law Weekly, 28*(17), 5.

Burruss, G.W., & Kempf-Leonard, K. (2002). The questionable advantage of defense counsel in juvenile court. *Justice Quarterly, 19,* 37–68.

Burruss, G.W., Peck, J.H., & Cameron, A.L.J. (2020). Fifty years post Gault: A meta-analysis of the impact of attorney representation on delinquency outcomes. *Journal of Criminal Justice, 66,* 1–13.

Bursik, R.J., & Grasmick, H.G. (1993). *Neighborhoods and crime: The dimensions of effective community control.* New York: Lexington.

Burt, C.H., & Simons, R.L. (2014). Pulling back the curtain on heritability studies: Biosocial criminology in the postgenomic era. *Criminology, 52,* 223–262.

Buss, E. (2000). The role of lawyers in promoting juveniles' competence as defendants. In T. Grisso & R.G. Schwartz (Eds.), *Youth on trial: A developmental perspective on juvenile justice* (pp. 243–265). Chicago, IL: University of Chicago Press.

Butts, J.A. (1994). *Offenders in juvenile court, 1992.* Juvenile Justice Bulletin. Washington, DC: U.S. Department of Justice.

Butts, J.A., & Pfaff, J. (2019). Private confinement facilities in juvenile justice. *Criminology & Public Policy, 18,* 361–378.

Butts, J.A., & Roman, J.K. (2014). *Line drawing: Raising the minimum age of criminal court jurisdiction in New York*. New York: Research & Evaluation Center, John Jay College of Criminal Justice, City University of New York.

Butts, J.A., Buck, J., & Coggeshall, M.B. (2002). *The impact of teen court on young offenders*. Washington, DC: Urban Institute Press.

Butts, J.A., Roman, J.K., & Lynn-Whaley, J. (2012). Varieties of juvenile court: Nonspecialized courts, teen courts, drug courts, and mental health courts. In B.C. Feld & D.M. Bishop (Eds.), *The Oxford handbook of juvenile crime and juvenile justice* (pp. 606–635). New York: Oxford University Press.

Butts, J.A., Zweig, J.M., & Mamalian, C. (2004). Defining the mission of juvenile drug courts. In J.A. Butts & J. Roman (Eds.), *Juvenile drug courts and teen substance abuse* (pp. 137–184). Washington, DC: Urban Institute Press.

Calleja, N.G. (2020). Assessing and treating trauma in detained adolescents: A pre-post within subjects evaluation. *Journal of Child and Family Studies, 29*, 934–941.

Camp, S.D., Klein-Saffran, J., Kwon, O., Daggett, D.M., & Joseph, V. (2006). An exploration into participation in a faith-based prison program. *Criminology & Public Policy, 5*, 529–550.

Campbell, A. (1984). Girls' talk: The social representation of aggression by female gang members. *Criminal Justice and Behavior, 11*, 139–156.

Campbell, A. (1990). Female participation in gangs. In C.R. Huff (Ed.), *Gangs in America* (pp. 163–182). Newbury Park, CA: Sage.

Canada, K.E., & Ray, B. (2016). Mental health courts participants' perspectives of success: What key outcomes are we missing? *International Journal of Forensic Mental Health, 15*, 352–361.

Capaldi, D.M., & Patterson, G.R. (1996). Can violent offenders be distinguished from frequent offenders? Prediction from childhood to adolescence. *Journal of Research in Crime and Delinquency, 33*, 206–231.

Carpenter, C., Glassner, B., Johnson, B.D., & Loughlin, J. (1988). *Kids, drugs, and crime*. Lexington, MA: Lexington Books.

Carson, E.A. (2020). *Prisoners in 2019 (NCJ 255115)*. Washington, DC: U.S. Department of Justice.

Carson, E.A., & Cowhig, M.P. (2020). *Mortality in state and federal prisons, 2001–2016—statistical tables* (NCJ 251920). Washington, DC: U.S. Department of Justice.

Cashel, M.L. (2003). Validity of self-reports of delinquency and socio-emotional functioning among youth on probation. *Journal of Offender Rehabilitation, 37*, 11–23.

Caspi, A., McClay, J., Moffitt, T.E., Mill, J., Martin, J., Craig, I.W., Taylor, A., & Poulton, R. (2002). Role of genotype in the cycle of violence in maltreated children. *Science, 297*(5582), 851–854. DOI: https://doi.org/10.1126/science.1072290.

Catalano, R.F., & Hawkins, J.D. (1996). The social development model: A theory of antisocial behavior. In J.D. Hawkins (Ed.), *Delinquency and crime: Current theories* (pp. 149–197). New York: Cambridge University Press.

Catalano, R.F., Park, J., Harachi, T.W., Haggerty, K.P., Abbott, R.D., & Hawkins, J.D. (2005). Mediating the effects of poverty, gender, individual characteristics, and external constraints on antisocial behavior: A test of the social development model and implications for developmental life-course theory. In D.P. Farrington (Ed.), *Integrated developmental and life-course theories of offending: Advances in criminological theory* (Vol. 14) (pp. 93–124). New Brunswick, NJ: Transaction.

Catalano, R.F., Hawkins, J.D., Kosterman, R., Bailey, J.A., Oesterle, S., Cambron, C., & Farrington, D.P. (2021). Applying the Social Development Model in middle childhood to promote healthy development: Effects from primary school through the 30s and across generations. *Journal of Developmental and Life Course Criminology, 7,* 66–86. DOI: https://doi.org/10.1007/s40865-020-00152-6.

Cate, S. (2016). Devolution, not decarceration: The limits of juvenile justice reform in Texas. *Punishment & Society, 18,* 578–609.

Cavan, R.S., & Ferdinand, T.N. (1981). *Juvenile delinquency* (4th ed.). New York: Harper and Row.

Cerda, M., Wall, M., & Feng, T. (2016). Association of state marijuana laws with adolescent marijuana use. *JAMA Pediatrics, 171*(2), 142–149.

Chaiken, J.M., & Chaiken, M.R. (1982). *Varieties of criminal behavior.* Santa Monica, CA: RAND.

Chaiken, M.R. (2004). *Community policing beyond the big cities.* Washington, DC: National Institute of Justice.

Chan, J.P.K., & Ireland, J.L. (2009). Fear of bullying among adult, young and juvenile prisoners: Its association with perpetration, victimization, and behavioural predictors. *International Journal of Prisoner Health, 5,* 223–232.

Chandler, N. (2000). *Best practices for establishing a children's advocacy center program* (3rd ed.). Washington, DC: National Children's Alliance. Retrieved on June 2, 2013, from www.fncac.org/file.php/2129/BEST+PRACTICES.pdf.

Chappell, A.T., Maggard, S.R., & Higgins, J.L. (2012). Exceptions to the rule? Exploring the use of overrides in detention risk assessment. *Youth Violence and Juvenile Justice, 11,* 332–348.

Charters, C.A. (1994). Volunteer work assumes a new role in public high school: *Steirer v. Bethlehem Area School District. Journal of Law and Education, 23,* 607–613.

Chavaria, F.P. (1997). Probation and cognitive skills. *Federal Probation, 61,* 57–60.

Chen, F.R., Gao, Y., Glenn, A.L., Niv, S., Portnoy, J., Schug, R., & Raine, A. (2016). Biosocial bases of antisocial and criminal behavior. In A.R. Piquero (Ed.), *The handbook of criminological theory* (pp. 355–379). West Sussex: John Wiley and Sons.

Chesney-Lind, M. (1977). Judicial paternalism and the female status offender: Training women to know their place. *Crime & Delinquency, 23,* 121–130.

Chesney-Lind, M. (1987). *Girls' crime and woman's place: Toward a feminist model of female delinquency.* Paper presented at the Annual Meeting of the American Society of Criminology, New Orleans, LA.

Chesney-Lind, M., & Shelden, R.G. (1992). *Girls, delinquency, and juvenile justice.* Pacific Grove, CA: Brooks/Cole.

Child Welfare Information Gateway. (2019). *What is child abuse and neglect? Recognizing the signs and symptoms.* Washington, DC: U.S. Department of Health and Human Services, Children's Bureau.

Chin, K., Fagan, J., & Kelly, R.J. (1992). Patterns of Chinese gang extortion. *Justice Quarterly, 9,* 625–646.

Christiansen, K.O. (1974). Seriousness of criminality and concordance among Danish twins. In R. Hood (Ed.), *Crime, criminology, and public policy.* New York: Free Press.

Clark, R.D., & Lab, S.P. (1995). *The relationship between victimization and offending among junior and senior high school students.* Paper presented at the Annual Meeting of the Academy of Criminal Justice Sciences, Boston, MA.

Clarke, J.P., & Tifft, L.L. (1966). Polygraph and interview validation of self-reported deviant behavior. *American Sociological Review, 31,* 516–523.

Clarke, R.V., & Felson, M. (1993). *Routine activities and rational choice.* New Brunswick, NJ: Transaction.

Clarke, S.H., & Koch, G.G. (1980). Juvenile court: Therapy or crime control, and do lawyers make a difference? *Law and Society Review, 14,* 263–308.

Clayton, R.R., Cattarello, A., & Walden, K.P. (1991). Sensation seeking as a potential mediating variable for school-based prevention interventions: A two-year follow-up of DARE. *Journal of Health Communications, 3*, 229–239.

Clear, T.R. (1994). *Harm in American penology: Offenders, victims, and their communities.* Albany, NY: SUNY Press.

Clear, T.R. (2011). A private-sector, incentives-based model for justice reinvestment. *Criminology & Public Policy, 10*, 585–608.

Clear, T.R. (2020). Reinventing punitive justice and the community justice system: Address to the Asian Criminological Society. *Asian Journal of Criminology, 15*, 185–193.

Clear, T.R., Clear, V.B., & Braga, A.A. (1997). Correctional alternatives for drug offenders in an era of overcrowding. In M. McShane & F.P. Williams (Eds.), *Criminal justice: Contemporary literature in theory and practice* (pp. 24–44). New York: Garland.

Cleary, H.M.D. (2013). Police interviewing and interrogation of juvenile suspects: A descriptive examination of actual cases. *Law and Human Behavior, 38*, 272–282.

Cloninger, C.R., Sigvardsson, S., Bohman, M., & von Knorring, A.I. (1982). Predisposition to petty criminality in Swedish adoptees: II. Cross-fostering analysis of gene–environment interaction. *Archives of General Psychiatry, 39*, 1242–1247.

Cloward, R., & Ohlin, L. (1960). *Delinquency and opportunity: A theory of delinquent gangs.* New York: Free Press.

Cobbina, J.E., Miller, J., & Brunson, R.K. (2008). Gender, neighborhood danger, and risk-avoidance strategies among urban African-American youths. *Criminology, 46*, 673–707.

Cohen, A.K. (1955). *Delinquent boys: The culture of the gang.* Glencoe, IL: Free Press.

Cohen, E., & Pfeifer, J. (2011). Mental health services for incarcerated youth: Report from a statewide survey. *Juvenile and Family Court Journal, 62*(2), 22–34.

Cohen, L.E., & Felson, M. (1979). Social changes and crime rate trends: A routine activities approach. *American Sociological Review, 44*, 588–608.

Cohen, L.E., & Kluegel, J.R. (1979). Selecting delinquents for adjudication: An analysis of intake screening decisions in two metropolitan juvenile courts. *Journal of Research in Crime and Delinquency, 16*, 143–163.

Colantonio, A., Kim, H., Allen, S., Asbridge, M., Petgrave, J., & Brochu, S. (2014). Traumatic brain injury and early life experiences among men and women in a prison population. *Journal of Correctional Health Care, 20*, 271–279.

Cole, D. (2003). The effect of a curfew law on juvenile crime in Washington, DC. *American Journal of Criminal Justice, 27*, 217–232.

Collaborative for Academic, Social and Emotional Learning. (2021). *Resolving Conflict Creatively Program (RCCP).* Retrieved from https://pg.casel.org/resolving-conflict-creatively-program-rccp/.

Collins, B.J., Cuddy, K., & Martin, A.P. (2017). Assessing the effectiveness and cost-effectiveness of drug intervention programs: UK case study. *Journal of Addictive Diseases, 36*, 5–13.

Collins, J.J., Hubbard, R.L., & Rachal, J.V. (1985). Expensive drug use and illegal income: A test of explanatory hypotheses. *Criminology, 23*, 743–764.

Colwell, B. (2002). Shocking the conscience: Excessive discipline of elementary and secondary students. *School Law Reporter, 44*, 1–3.

Colwell, B. (2003). Student speech at graduation: When does it violate the establishment clause? *School Law Reporter, 45*(5), 75–78.

Conger, R.D., & Simons, R.L. (1997). Life-course contingencies in the development of adolescent antisocial behavior: A matching law approach. In T.P. Thornberry (Ed.), *Advances in criminological theory* (pp. 55–99). New York: Aldine.

Connell, A., Farrington, D.P., & Ireland, J.L. (2016). Characteristics of bullies and victims among incarcerated male young offenders. *Journal of Aggression, Conflict, and Peace Research, 8*, 114–123.

Cook, A.C., Leung, G., & Smith, R.A. (2020). Marijuana decriminalization, medical marijuana laws, and fatal traffic crashes in U.S. cities 2010–2017. *American Journal of Public Health, 110*, 363–369.

Cook, P.J., Moore, M.H., & Braga, A.A. (2002). Gun control. In J.Q. Wilson & J. Petersilia (Eds.), *Crime: Public policies for crime control* (pp. 291–330). Oakland, CA: ICS Press.

Cooley, C.H. (1902). *Human nature and the social order.* New York: Scribner.

Cooper, C.N. (1967). The Chicago YMCA detached workers: Current status of an action program. In M.W. Klein (Ed.), *Juvenile gangs in context* (pp. 183–193). Englewood Cliffs, NJ: Prentice Hall.

Coordinating Council on Juvenile Justice and Delinquency Prevention. (1996). *Combating violence and delinquency: The national juvenile justice action plan.* Report. Washington, DC: U.S. Department of Justice.

Corbett, R.P. (2001). Juvenile probation on the eve of the next millennium. In J.L. Victor & J. Naughton (Eds.), *Annual edition: Criminal justice 01/02* (pp. 141–151). Guilford, CT: Dushkin.

Corbett, R.P. (2002). Reinventing probation and reducing youth violence. In G.S. Katzmann (Ed.), *Securing our children's future: New approaches to juvenile justice and youth violence* (pp. 175–199). Washington, DC: Brookings Institution Press.

Corbett, R.P. (2015). The burdens of leniency: The changing face of probation. *Minnesota Law Review, 99*, 1697–1733.

Cordner, G. (2020). *Evidence-based policy in 45 small bytes.* Washington, DC: National Institute of Justice.

Cornell, D.G. (2020). Threat assessment as a school violence prevention strategy. *Criminology & Public Policy, 19*, 235–252.

Cornish, D.B., & Clarke, R.V. (1986). *The reasoning criminal.* New York: Springer-Verlag.

Corsaro, N., Brunson, R.K., & McGarrell, E.F. (2009). Problem-oriented policing and open-air drug markets: Examining the Rockford pulling levers deterrence strategy. *Crime & Delinquency, 59*, 1085–1107.

Cortes, J.B. (1972). *Delinquency and crime.* New York: Seminar Press.

Costanzo, M. (1997). *Just revenge: Costs and consequences of the death penalty.* New York: St. Martin's Press.

Council of State Governments Justice Center. (2015). *Locked out: Improving educational and vocational outcomes for incarcerated youth.* New York: The Council of State Governments Justice Center.

Council of State Governments Justice Centre. (2016, May 31). *Risk and needs assessment and race in the criminal justice system.* Retrieved from www.csgjusticecenter.org.

Council of State Governments Justice Center. (2017). *Mental health courts.* Retrieved from https://csgjusticecenter.org.

Cox, S.M., Davidson, W.S., & Bynum, T.S. (1995). A meta-analytic assessment of delinquency-related outcomes of alternative education programs. *Crime & Delinquency, 41*, 219–234.

Crank, J.P., & Caldero, M. (1991). The production of occupational stress in medium-sized police agencies: A survey of line officers in eight municipal departments. *Journal of Criminal Justice, 19*, 339–349.

Crawford, A., & Newburn, T. (2003). *Youth offending and restorative justice: Implementing reform in youth justice.* Portland, OR: Willan.

Crean, H.F., & Johnson, D.B. (2013). Promoting Alternative Thinking Strategies (PATHS) and elementary school aged children's aggression: Results from a cluster randomized trial. *American Journal of Community Psychology, 52*, 56–72. DOI: https://doi.org/10.1007/s10 464-013-9576-4.

Crime and Justice Institute. (2017). *Improving outcomes for youth: A look at juvenile justice reform implementation in six states.* Retrieved from www.crgj.org.

Cristall, J., & Forman-Echols, L. (2009). *Property abatements: The other gang injunction— Project T.O.U.G.H.* National Gang Center Bulletin 2. Washington, DC: Bureau of Justice Assistance.

Cronin, R.C. (1994). *Boot camps for adult and juvenile offenders: Overview and update.* Washington, DC: National Institute of Justice.

Cullen, F.T. (1994). Social support as an organizing concept for criminology: Presidential address to the Academy of Criminal Justice Sciences. *Justice Quarterly, 11*, 527–59.

Cullen, F.T. (2007). Make rehabilitation corrections' guiding paradigm. *Criminology & Public Policy, 6*, 717–728.

Cullen, F.T., & Wright, J.P. (1995). The future of corrections. In B. Maguire & P. Radosh (Eds.), *The past, present, and future of American criminal justice* (pp. 198–219). New York: General Hall.

Cullen, F.T., Blevins, K.R., Trager, J.S., & Gendreau, P. (2005). The rise and fall of boot camps: A case study in common sense corrections. *Journal of Offender Rehabilitation, 40*, 53–70.

Cullen, F.T., Pratt, T., & Turanovic, J.J. (2016). It's hopeless: Beyond zero-tolerance supervision. *Criminology & Public Policy, 15*, 1215–1227.

Cullen, F.T., Pratt, T.C., Turanovic, J.J., & Butler, L. (2018). When bad news arrives: Project HOPE in a post-factual world. *Journal of Contemporary Criminal Justice, 34*, 13–34.

Cullen, F.T., Wright, J.P., & Chamlin, M.B. (1999). Social support and social reform: A progressive crime control agenda. *Crime & Delinquency, 45*, 188–207.

Cummings, S., & Monti, D.J. (1993). Public policy and gangs: Social science and the urban underclass. In S. Cummings & D.J. Monti (Eds.), *Gangs: The origins and impact of contemporary youth gangs in the United States* (pp. 305–320). Albany, NY: SUNY Press.

Currie, E. (2020). *A peculiar indifference: The neglected toll of violence on black America.* New York: Metropolitan Books; Henry Holt & Co.

Curry, G.D., & Decker, S.H. (1998). *Confronting gangs: Crime and community.* Los Angeles: Roxbury.

Curry, G.D., Ball, R.A., & Decker, S.H. (1996). *Estimating the national scope of gang crime from law enforcement data.* Research in Brief. Washington, DC: U.S. Department of Justice, Office of Justice Programs, National Institute of Justice.

Curry, G.D., Fox, R.J., Ball, R.A., & Stone, D. (1993). *National assessment of law enforcement anti-gang information resources: Final report.* Washington, DC: U.S. Department of Justice, Office of Justice Programs, National Institute of Justice.

Dabbs, J.M., Carr, T.S., Frady, R.L., & Riad, J.K. (1995). Testosterone, crime and misbehavior among 692 male prison inmates. *Personality and Individual Differences, 18*, 627–633.

Dadds, M.R., Spence, S.H., Holland, D.E., Barrett, P.M., & Laurens, K.R. (1997). Prevention and early intervention for anxiety disorders: A controlled trial. *Journal of Consulting and Clinical Psychology, 65*, 627–635.

Daly, K. (2002). Restorative justice: The real story. *Punishment and Society, 4*, 5–79.

Dannefer, D., & Schutt, R.K. (1982). Race and juvenile justice processing in court and police agencies. *American Journal of Sociology, 87*, 1113–1132.

Daugherty, C. (2013). *State trends: Legislative victories from 2011–2013 removing youth from the adult criminal justice system.* Washington, DC: Campaign for Youth Justice.

Davis, R., & O'Donnell, J. (2005). Some teenagers call tracking driving an invasion of privacy. *USA Today*, 1B.

Davis, S.M., & Schwartz, M.D. (1987). *Children's rights and the law*. Lexington, MA: D.C. Heath.

Davis, S.M., Scott, E.S., Wadlington, W., & Whitebread, C.H. (1997). *Children in the legal system: Cases and materials* (2nd ed.). Westbury, NY: Foundation Press.

deBeus, K., & Rodriguez, N. (2007). Restorative justice practice: An examination of program completion and recidivism. *Journal of Criminal Justice, 35*, 337–347.

Decker, S., & Van Winkle, B. (1994). Slinging dope: The role of gangs and gang members in drug sales. *Justice Quarterly, 11*, 583–604.

Decker, S., Pennel, S., & Caldwell, A. (1997). *Illegal firearms: Access and use by arrestees*. Washington, DC: National Institute of Justice.

Decker, S.H., Melde, C., & Pyrooz, D.C. (2013). What do we know about gangs and gang members and where do we go from here? *Justice Quarterly, 30*, 369–402.

DeFleur, M.L., & Quinney, R. (1966). A reformulation of Sutherland's differential association theory and a strategy for empirical verification. *Journal of Research in Crime and Delinquency, 3*, 1–22.

DeJong, W. (1993). *Building the peace: The Resolving Conflict Creatively Program (RCCP)*. NIJ Program Focus. Washington, DC: Department of Justice.

DeJong, W., & Blanchette, J. (2014). Case closed: Research evidence on the positive public health impact of the age 21 minimum legal drinking age in the United States. *Journal of Studies of Alcohol and Drugs Supplement, 17*, 108–114.

DeLeon, G., & Rosenthal, M.S. (1989). Treatment in residential therapeutic communities. In T.B. Karasu (Ed.), *Treatment of psychiatric disorders: A task force report of the American Psychiatric Association* (Vol. 2, pp. 1379–1396). Washington, DC: American Psychiatric Association.

DeLisi, M., Angton, A., Behnken, M.P., & Kusow, A.M. (2015). Do adolescent drug users fare the worst? Onset type, juvenile delinquency, and criminal careers. *International Journal of Offender Therapy and Comparative Criminology, 59*, 180–195.

DeMuro, P. (2008). Boot camps revisited. *Journal for Juvenile Justice Services, 22*, 49–60.

Denno, D.W. (1990). *Biology and violence: From birth to adulthood*. Cambridge, England: Cambridge University Press.

DeSilver, D., Lipka, M., & Fahmy, D. (2020). *10 things we know about race and policing in the US*. Washington, DC: Pew Research Center. Retrieved from www.pewresearch.org.

DeWit, D.J., DuBois, D., Erdem, G., Larose, S., & Lipman, E.L. (2016). The role of program-supported mentoring relationships in promoting youth mental health, behavioral and developmental outcomes. *Prevention Science: The Official Journal of the Society for Prevention Research, 17*(5), 646–657. DOI: https://doi.org/10.1007/s11121-016-0663-2.

Dijkstra, S., Creemers, H.E., Asscher, J.J., Deković, M., & Stams, G.J.J.M. (2016). The effectiveness of family group conferencing in youth care: A meta-analysis. *Child Abuse & Neglect, 62*, 100–110. DOI: https://doi.org/10.1016/j.chiabu.2016.10.017.

Dodson, K.D., Cabage, L.N., & Klenowski, P.M. (2011). An evidence-based assessment of faith-based programs: Do faith-based programs work to reduce recidivism? *Journal of Offender Rehabilitation, 50*, 367–383.

Doerner, W.G., & Lab, S.P. (2021). *Victimology* (9th ed.). New York: Routledge.

Donnelly, E.A. (2017). The politics of racial disparity reform: Racial inequality and criminal justice policymaking in the states. *American Journal of Criminal Justice, 42*, 1527.

Donnelly, E.A. (2019). Do disproportionate minority (DMC) mandate reforms change decision-making in the juvenile justice system? *Youth Violence and Juvenile Justice, 17*, 288–308.

Döring, N. (2014). Consensual sexting among adolescents: Risk prevention through abstinence education or safer sexting? *Cyber Psychology, 8.* DOI: https://doi.org/10.5817/CP2014-1-9.

Doumas, D.M., Esp, S., Turrisi, R., Bond, L., & Flay, B. (2020). Efficacy of the eCHECKUP TO GO for high school seniors: Differences in risk factors, protective behavioral strategies, and alcohol use. *Journal of Studies on Alcohol and Drugs, 81,* 135–143.

Drake, E. (2013). *The effectiveness of declining juvenile court jurisdiction of youthful offenders* (Doc. 13-12-1902). Olympia, WA: Washington State Institute for Public Policy.

Drug Courts Program Office. (2000). *About the Drug Courts Program Office.* Washington, DC: U.S. Department of Justice.

Drug Policy Alliance. (2021). *Good Samaritan fatal overdose prevention laws.* New York: Drug Policy Alliance. Retrieved from www.drugpolicy.org.

Drug Strategies. (2005). *Bridging the gap: A guide to drug treatment in the juvenile justice system.* Washington, DC: Drug Strategies.

DuBois, D.L., Holloway, B.E., Valentine, J.C., & Cooper, H. (2002). Effectiveness of mentoring programs for youth: A meta-analytic review. *American Journal of Community Psychology, 30,* 157–197.

DuBois, D.L., Portillo, N., Rhodes, J.E., Silverthorn, N., & Valentine, J.C. (2011). How effective are mentoring programs for youth? A systematic assessment of the evidence. *Psychological Science in the Public Interest, 12,* 57–91.

DuBois, D.L., Herrera, C., & Rivera, J. (2018). *Investigation of long-term effects of the Big Brothers Big Sisters community-based mentoring program: Final technical report for OJJDP.* Retrieved from https://ojjdp.ojp.gov/library/publications/investigation-long-term-effects-big-brothers-big-sisters-community-based.

Dum, C.P., & Fader, J.J. (2013). These are kids' lives! Dilemmas and adaptations of juvenile aftercare workers. *Justice Quarterly, 30,* 784–810.

Dunworth, T. (2000). *National evaluation of the youth firearms initiative.* Washington, DC: U.S. Department of Justice.

Durkheim, E. (1933). *The division of labor in society.* (Translated by G. Supson). New York: Free Press.

Dvorak, P. (2018, Dec. 27). Millions of kids fear being killed at school. It's time for adults to say: enough. *Washington Post.* Retrieved from www.washingtonpost.com/local/millions-of-kids-fear-being-killed-at-school-its-time-for-adults-to-say-enough/2018/12/27/faa0cf62-0a06-11e9-88e3-989a3e456820_story.html?utm_term=.67c6089fea24.

Eck, J., & Maguire, J. (2000). Have changes in policing reduced violent crime? An assessment of the evidence. In A. Blumstein & J. Wallman (Eds.), *The crime drop in America* (pp. 207–265). Cambridge, England: Cambridge University Press.

Education Week. (2019). *The school shootings of 2018: What's behind the numbers?* Retrieved from www.edweek.org/ew/section/multimedia/the-school-shootings-of-2018-whats-behind.html.

Egley, A., & Howell, J.C. (2011). *Highlights of the 2009 National Youth Gang Survey.* Washington, DC: Office of Juvenile Justice and Delinquency Prevention.

Egley, A., Howell, J.C., & Harris, M. (2014). *Highlights of the 2012 National Youth Gang Survey.* Washington, DC: Office of Juvenile Justice and Delinquency Prevention. Retrieved June 1, 2017, from www.ojjdp.gov/pubs/248025.pdf.

Egley, A., Howell, J.C., & Major, A.K. (2004). Recent patterns of gang problems in the United States: Results from the 1996–2002 National Youth Gang Survey. In F. Esbensen, S.G. Tibbetts, & L. Gaines (Eds.), *American youth gangs at the millennium* (pp. 90–108). Long Grove, IL: Waveland.

Ehrenkranz, J., Bliss, E., & Sheard, M.H. (1974). Plasma testosterone: Correlation with aggressive behavior and social dominance in man. *Psychosomatic Medicine, 36,* 469–475.

Eisen, M., Zellman, G.L., Massett, H.A., & Murray, D.L. (2002). Evaluating the lions-quest "skills for adolescence" drug education program: First year behavior outcomes. *Addictive Behaviors, 27,* 619–632.

Ekins, E. (2016). *Policing in America: Understanding public attitudes toward the police. Results from a national survey.* Washington, DC: Cato Institute. Retrieved from www.cato.org.

Elliott, D.S. (1994). Serious, violent offenders: Onset, developmental course, and termination. *Criminology, 32,* 1–21.

Elliott, D.S. (2000). Editor's introduction. In D. Olweus and S. Limber (Eds.), *Bullying prevention program: Blueprints for violence prevention.* Boulder, CO: Institute of Behavioral Science.

Elliott, D.S., & Menard, S. (1996). Delinquent friends and delinquent behavior: Temporal and developmental patterns. In J.D. Hawkins (Ed.), *Delinquency and crime: Current theories* (pp. 28–67). Cambridge: Cambridge University Press.

Elliott, D.S., Huizinga, D., & Ageton, S.S. (1985). *Explaining delinquency and drug use.* Beverly Hills: Sage.

Ellis, L., & Walsh, A. (2000). *Criminology: A global perspective.* Boston, MA: Allyn & Bacon.

Emmers, E., Bekkering, G.E., & Hannes, K. (2015). Prevention of alcohol and drug misuse in students: An overview of systematic reviews. *Nordic Studies on Alcohol and Drugs, 32,* 183–198.

Empey, L.T. (1982). *American delinquency: Its meaning and construction.* Homewood, IL: Dorsey Press.

Engel, R.S., McManus, H.D., & Isaza, G.T. (2020). Moving beyond "best practice," Experiences in police reform and a call for evidence to reduce officer-involved shootings. *Annals of the American Academy of Political and Social Sciences, 687,* 146–165.

Engel, R.S., Tillyer, M.S., & Corsaro, N. (2013). Reducing gang violence using focused deterrence: Evaluating the Cincinnati initiative to reduce violence (CIRV). *Justice Quarterly, 30,* 403–439.

Engle, B., & MacGowan, M.J. (2009). A critical review of adolescent substance abuse group treatments. *Journal of Evidence-Based Social Work, 6,* 217–243.

Erdem, G., & Kaufman, M.R. (2020). *Mentoring for preventing and reducing substance use and associated risks among youth.* Washington, DC: National Mentoring Center, Office of Juvenile Justice and Delinquency Prevention. Retrieved from www.nationalmentoringresourcecenter.org.

Erickson, M.L. (1971). The group context of delinquent behavior. *Social Problems, 19,* 114–129.

Erickson, M.L. (1973). Group violations and official delinquency: The group hazard hypothesis. *Criminology, 11,* 127–160.

Esbensen, F., & Carson, D.C. (2012). Who are the gangsters? An examination of the age, race/ethnicity, sex, and immigration status of self-reported gang members in a seven-city study of American youth. *Journal of Contemporary Criminal Justice, 28,* 465–481.

Esbensen, F., & Huizinga, D. (1991). Juvenile victimization and delinquency. *Youth and Society, 23,* 202–228.

Esbensen, F., & Huizinga, D. (1993). Gangs, drugs and delinquency in a survey of urban youth. *Criminology, 31,* 565–590.

Esbensen, F., & Osgood, D.W. (1997). *National evaluation of G.R.E.A.T.* NIJ Research in Brief. Washington, DC: National Institute of Justice.

Esbensen, F., Brick, B.T., & Melde, C. (2008). The role of race and ethnicity in gang membership. In F., van Gemert, D. Peterson, & L. Inger-Lise (Eds.), *Street gangs, migration and ethnicity* (pp. 117–139). New York: Routledge.

Esbensen, F., Osgood, D.W., Peterson, D., Taylor, T.T., & Carson, D.C. (2013). Short- and long-term outcome results from a multisite evaluation of the G.R.E.A.T. program. *Criminology and Public Policy, 12*, 375–412.

Esbensen, F., Peterson, D., Taylor, T.J., Freng, A., & Osgood, D.W. (2004). Gang prevention: A case study of a primary prevention program. In F. Esbensen, S.G. Tibbetts, & L. Gaines (Eds.), *American youth gangs at the millennium* (pp. 274–351). Long Grove, IL: Waveland.

Esbensen, F., Peterson, D., Taylor, T.J., Freng, A., Osgood, D.W., Carson, D.C., & Matsuda, K.N. (2011). Evaluation and evolution of the gang resistance education and training (G.R.E.A.T.) program. *Journal of School Violence, 10*, 53–70.

Esthappan, S., Lacoe, J., & Young, D. (2019). *Juvenile probation transformation: Applying the approach in Lucas, County (OH) and Pierce County (WA)*. Washington, DC: The Urban Institute.

Eysenck, H.J., & Gudjonsson, G.H. (1989). *The causes and cures of criminality*. New York: Plenum.

Fabricant, M. (1983). *Juveniles in the family courts*. Lexington, MA: Lexington Books.

Fagan, J. (1990). Social process of delinquency and drug use among urban gangs. In C.R. Huff (Ed.), *Gangs in America* (pp. 183–219). Newbury Park, CA: Sage.

Fagan, J. (2002). Policing guns and youth violence. *Children, Youth and Gun Violence, 12*, 133–151.

Fagan, J. (2007). End natural life sentences for juveniles. *Criminology & Public Policy, 6*, 735–746.

Fagan, J., & Weis, J.G. (1990). *Drug use and delinquency among inner city youth*. New York: Springer-Verlag.

Fagan, J., Weis, J.G., & Cheng, Y. (1990). Delinquency and substance use among inner city students. *Journal of Drug Issues, 20*, 351–402.

Faggiano, F., Vigna-Taglianti, F., Versino, E., Zambon, A., Barracino, A., & Lemon, A. (2005). *School-based prevention for illicit drug use. The Cochrane database of systematic reviews, 2*, CD003020. https://doi.org/10.1002/14651858.CD003020.pub2.

Fareed, A., Vayalapalli, S., Stout, S., Casarella, J., Drexler, K., & Bailey, S.P. (2011). Effect of methadone maintenance treatment on heroin craving: A literature review. *Journal of Addictive Diseases, 30*, 27–38.

Farrington, D.P. (1989). Early predictors of adolescent aggression and adult violence. *Violence and Victims, 4*, 79–100.

Farrington, D.P. (1996). The explanation and prevention of youthful offending. In J.D. Hawkins (Ed.), *Delinquency and crime: Current theories*. Cambridge: Cambridge University Press.

Farrington, D.P. (1997). The relationship between low resting heart rate and violence. In A. Raine, P.A. Brennan, D.P. Farrington, and S.A. Mednick (Eds.), *Biosocial bases of violence*. New York: Plenum.

Farrington, D.P., & Loeber, R. (1998). Transatlantic replicability of risk factors in the development of delinquency. In P. Cohen, C. Slomkowski, & L.N. Robbins (Eds.), *Where and when: Geographic and generational influences on psychopathology*. Mahwah, NJ: Erlbaum.

Faust, F.L., & Brantingham, P.J. (1979). *Juvenile justice philosophy: Readings, cases and comments*. St. Paul, MN: West Group.

Federal Bureau of Investigation. (2015). *National Incident-Based Reporting System*. Washington, DC: FBI. Retrieved from https://ucr.fbi.gov/about-us/cjis/ucr/nibrs/2014/resource-pages/incidents-and-offenses_f.pdf.

Federal Bureau of Investigation. (2019). *2018 National Incident-Based Reporting System*. Retrieved from https://ucr.fbi.gov/nibrs/2018/tables/data-tables.

Federal Bureau of Investigation. (2020a). *2019 National Incident-Based Reporting System*. Retrieved from https://ucr.fbi.gov/nibrs/2019/tables/data-tables.

Federal Bureau of Investigation. (2020b). *Crime in the United States, 2019*. Retrieved from www.fbi.gov .

Federal Forum on Child and Family Statistics. (2020). *America's children in brief: Key national indicators of well-being, 2020*. Washington, DC: U.S. Government Printing Office. Retrieved from www.childstats.gov.

Feld, B.C. (1981). A comparative analysis of organizational structure and inmate subcultures in institutions for juvenile offenders. *Crime & Delinquency, 27*, 336–363.

Feld, B.C. (1998). Juvenile and criminal justice systems' responses to youth violence. In M. Tonry & M.H. Moore (Eds.), *Youth violence* (pp. 189–261). Chicago, IL: University of Chicago Press.

Feld, B.C. (1999). *Bad kids: Race and the transformation of the juvenile court*. New York: Oxford University Press.

Feld, B.C. (2006). Juveniles' competence to exercise Miranda rights: An empirical study of policy and practice. *Minnesota Law Review, 91*, 26–100.

Feld, B.C. (2008). A slower form of death: Implications of Roper v. Simmons for juveniles sentenced to life without parole. *Notre Dame Journal of Law, Ethics & Public Policy, 22*(1), 9–65.

Feld, B.C. (2012). Procedural rights in juvenile courts: Competence and consequences. In B.C. Feld & D.M. Bishop (Eds.), *The Oxford handbook of juvenile crime and juvenile justice* (pp. 664–691). New York: Oxford University Press.

Feld, B.C. (2013a). Real interrogation: What actually happens when cops question kids. *Law & Society Review, 47*, 1–35.

Feld, B.C. (2013b). Adolescent criminal responsibility, proportionality, and sentencing policy: Roper, Graham, Miller/Jackson and the youth discount. *Law and Inequality, 31*, 263–330.

Feld, B.C. (2018). Punishing kids in juvenile and criminal court. *Crime & Justice, 47*, 417–474.

Feld, B.C., & Bishop, D.M. (2012). Transfer of juveniles to criminal court. In B.C. Feld & D.M. Bishop (Eds.), *The Oxford handbook of juvenile justice* (pp. 801–842). New York: Oxford University Press.

Feld, B.C., & Moriearty, P.L. (2020). Race, rights, and the representation of children. *American University Law Review, 69*, 743–803.

Feld, B.C., & Schaefer, S. (2010). The right to counsel in juvenile court: Law reform to deliver legal services and reduce justice by geography. *Criminology & Public Policy, 9*, 327–356.

Fenwick, C.R. (1982). Juvenile court intake decision making: The importance of family affiliation. *Journal of Criminal Justice, 10*, 443–453.

Ferrer-Wreder, L., Lorente, C.C., Briones, E., Bussell, J., Berman, S., & Arrufat, O. (2002). Promoting identity development in marginalized youth. *Journal of Adolescent Research, 17*, 168–187.

Feyerherm, W. (1980). The group hazard hypothesis: A reexamination. *Journal of Research in Crime and Delinquency, 17*, 58–68.

Filges, T., Rasmussen, P.S., Andersen, D., & Jorgensen, A.K. (2015). *Multidimensional family therapy (MDFT) for young people in treatment for non-opioid drug use: A systematic review*. Oslo: Campbell Systematic Reviews. Vol. 11, No. 8.

Finckenauer, J.O. (1982). *Scared Straight! and the panacea phenomenon*. Englewood Cliffs, NJ: Prentice-Hall.

Fisak, B.J., Jr, Richard, D., & Mann, A. (2011). The prevention of child and adolescent anxiety: A meta-analytic review. *Prevention Science: The Official Journal of the Society for Prevention Research, 12*(3), 255–268. DOI: https://doi.org/10.1007/s11121-011-0210-0.

Fishbein, D., Dariotis, J.K., Ferguson, P.L., & Pickelsimer, E. (2016a). Relationships between traumatic brain injury and illicit drug use and their association with aggression in inmates. *International Journal of Offender Therapy and Comparative Criminology, 60,* 575–597.

Fishbein, D.H., Domitrovich, C., Williams, J., Gitukui, S., Guthrie, C., Shapiro, D., & Greenberg, M. (2016b). Short-term intervention effects of the PATHS curriculum in young low-income children: Capitalizing on plasticity. *The Journal of Primary Prevention, 37*(6), 493–511. DOI: https://doi.org/10.1007/s10935-016-0452-5.

Fishbein, D., Miller, S., Winn, D.M., & Dakof, G. (2009). Biopsychological factors, gender, and delinquency. In M. Zahn (Ed.), *The delinquent girl.* Philadelphia: Temple University Press.

Fishman, L.T. (1988). *The vice queens: An ethnographic study of black female gang behavior.* Paper presented at the Annual Meeting of the American Society of Criminology, Chicago, IL.

Flexon, J.L., Lurigio, A.J., & Greenleaf, R.G. (2009). Exploring the dimensions of trust in the police among Chicago juveniles. *Journal of Criminal Justice, 37,* 180–189.

Forman, R. (2017). *Locking up our own: Crime and punishment in Black America.* New York: Farrar, Straus, and Giroux.

Fox, D. (2018). *Family Group Conferencing with children and young people: Advocacy approaches, variations and impacts.* London: Palgrave. DOI: 10.1007/978-3-319-71492-9.

Fox, J.R. (1985). Mission impossible? Social work practice with black urban youth gangs. *Social Work, 30,* 25–31.

Franzese, R.J., Covey, H.C., & Menard, S. (2016). *Youth gangs.* Springfield, IL: Charles C. Thomas.

Freisthler, B., Gaidus, A., Tam, C., Ponicki, W.R., & Gruenewald, P.J. (2017). From medical to recreational marijuana sales: Marijuana outlets and crime in an era of changing marijuana legislation. *Journal of Primary Prevention, 38,* 249–263.

FRIENDS. (2015). *The FRIENDS Program.* Retrieved from http://friendsprograms.com.

Gaarder, E., & Belknap, J. (2004). Little women: Girls in adult prison. *Women & Criminal Justice, 15*(2), 51–80.

Gal, T., & Moyal, S. (2011). Juvenile victims in restorative justice: Findings from the Reintegrative Shaming Experiments. *British Journal of Criminology, 51,* 1014–1034. DOI: doi:10.1093/bjc/azr052.

Gallup. (2014, July 24). *Americans still oppose lowering the drinking age.* Retrieved from www.gallup.com.

Gallup. (2017, July 10). *Confidence in police back at historical average.* Retrieved from www.gallup.com.

Gang Resistance Education and Training. (2021). *What is GREAT?* www.great-online.org/About/What-Is-GREAT.

Garbarino, J., & Gilliam, G. (1980). *Understanding abusive families.* Lexington, MA: Lexington Books.

Garces, E., Thomas, D., & Currie, J. (2002). Longer-term effects of Head Start. *American Economic Review, 92*(4): 999–1012.

Garland, D. (2001). *The culture of control: Crime and social order in contemporary society.* Chicago, IL: University of Chicago Press.

Gase, L.N., Kuo, T., Lai, E.S., Stoll, M.A., & Pone, N.A. (2016). The impact of two Los Angeles County teen courts on youth recidivism: Comparing two informal probation programs. *Journal of Experimental Criminology, 12,* 105–126.

Gase, L.N., Schooley, T., DeFosset, A., Stoll, M.A., & Kuo, T. (2015). The impact of Teen Courts on youth outcomes: A systematic review. *Adolescent Research Review, 1,* 51–67.

Gates, L.B., & Rohe, W.M. (1987). Fear and reactions to crime: A revised model. *Urban Affairs Quarterly, 22*, 425–453.

Geary, D.P. (1983). Nutrition, chemicals and criminal behavior: Some psychological aspects of anti-social conduct. *Juvenile and Family Court Journal, 34*, 9–13.

Geiselman, R.E., Bornstein, G., & Saywitz, K.J. (1992). *New approach to interviewing children: A test of its effectiveness*. Washington, DC: U.S. Department of Justice.

Geller, A., & Fagan, J. (2010). Pot as pretext: Marijuana, race, and the new disorder in New York City street policing. *Journal of Empirical Legal Studies, 7*, 591–633.

Gelles, R.J. (1980). Violence in the family: A review of research in the 70s. *Journal of Marriage and the Family, 42*, 873–885.

Gendreau, P. (1996). The principles of effective intervention with offenders. In A.T. Harland (Ed.), *Choosing correctional options that work: Defining the demand and evaluating the supply* (pp. 117–130). Thousand Oaks, CA: Sage.

Gendreau, P., Smith, P., & French, S.A. (2017). The theory of effective correctional interventions: Empirical status and future directions. In F.T. Cullen, J.P. Wright & K.R. Blevins (Eds.), *Taking stock: The status of criminological theory*. New York: Routledge.

Giallombardo, R. (1974). *The social world of imprisoned girls*. New York: John Wiley.

Gibson, J., Werner, S., & Sweeney, A. (2015). Evaluating an abbreviated version of the PATHS curriculum implemented by school mental health clinicians. *Psychology in the Schools, 52*, 549–561. DOI: 10.1002/pits.21844.

Gil, D. (1971). *Violence against children: Physical child abuse in the United States*. Cambridge, MA: Harvard University Press.

Gilberstadt, H. (2020). *A month before George Floyd's death, black and white Americans differed sharply in confidence in the police*. Washington, DC: Pew Research Center. Retrieved from www.pewresearch.org

Girshick, L.B. (1999). *No safe haven: Stories of women in prison*. Boston: Northeastern University Press.

Glaser, D. (1956). Criminality theories and behavioral images. *American Journal of Sociology, 61*, 434–444.

Glaser, D. (1964). *The effectiveness of a prison and parole system*. Indianapolis: Bobbs-Merrill.

Glueck, S., & Glueck, E. (1956). *Physique and delinquency*. New York: Harper.

Goddard, H.H. (1920). *Efficiency and levels of intelligence*. Princeton, NJ: Princeton University Press.

Goddard, T., & Myers, R.R. (2017). Against evidence-based oppression: Marginalized youth and the politics of risk. *Theoretical Criminology, 2*, 151–167.

Goddard, T., & Myers, R. (2018). *Youth, community, and the struggle for social justice*. New York: Routledge.

Goffman, E. (1961). *Asylums: Essays on the situation of mental patients and other inmates*. Garden City, NY: Anchor Books.

Gold, M. (1970). *Delinquent behavior in an American city*. Belmont, CA: Brooks/Cole.

Gold, M., & Mann, D. (1972). Delinquency as defense. *American Journal of Orthopsychiatry, 42*, 463–477.

Goldstein, A.P. (1993). Gang intervention: A historical review. In A.P. Goldstein & C.R. Huff (Eds.), *The gang intervention handbook* (pp. 21–51). Champaign, IL: Research Press.

Goldstein, H. (1990). *Problem-oriented policing*. New York: McGraw-Hill.

Goldstein, P.J. (1989). Drugs and violent crime. In N.A. Weiner & M.E. Wolfgang (Eds.), *Pathways to criminal violence* (pp. 16–48). Newbury Park, CA: Sage.

Gordon, J.A., Moriarty, L.J., & Grant, P.H. (2003). Juvenile correctional officers' perceived fear and risk of victimization: Examining individual and collective levels of victimization in two juvenile correctional centers in Virginia. *Criminal Justice and Behavior*, *30*, 62–84.

Gordon, R.A., Lahey, B.B., Kawai, E., Loeber, R., Stouthamer-Loeber, M., & Farrington, D.P. (2004). Antisocial behavior and youth gang membership: Selection and socialization. *Criminology*, *42*, 55–88.

Goring, C. (1913). *The English convict: A statistical study*. Montclair, NJ: Patterson Smith.

Gottfredson, D.C. (1987). Examining the potential of delinquency prevention through alternative education. *Today's Delinquent*, *6*, 87–100.

Gottfredson, D.C., & Barton, W.H. (1993). Deinstitutionalization of juvenile offenders. *Criminology*, *31*, 591–611.

Gottfredson, D.C., Crosse, S., Tang, Z., Bauer, E.L., Harmon, M.A., Hagen, C.A., & Greene, A.D. (2020). Effects of school resource officers on school crime and responses to school crime. *Criminology & Public Policy*, *19*, 905–940.

Gottfredson, G.D., & Gottfredson, D.C. (2001). *Gang problems and gang programs in a national sample of schools*. Ellicott City, MD: Gottfredson Associates.

Gottfredson, M.R., & Hirschi, T. (1990). *A general theory of crime*. Stanford, CA: Stanford University Press.

Gover, A.R., & MacKenzie, D.L. (2003). Child maltreatment and adjustment to juvenile correctional institutions. *Criminal Justice and Behavior*, *30*, 374–396.

Grasmick, H.G., Tittle, C.R., Bursik, R.J., & Arneklev, B.J. (1993). Testing the core empirical implications of Gottfredson and Hirschi's general theory of crime. *Journal of Research in Crime and Delinquency*, *30*, 5–29.

Gray, G.E., & Gray, L.K. (1983). Diet and juvenile delinquency. *Nutrition Today*, *18*, 14–21.

Greenberg, M.T., & Kusche, C. (1996). *The PATHS Project: Preventive intervention for children: Final report*. Washington, DC: National Institute of Mental Health.

Greenberg, M.T., & Kusche, C. (1997). *Improving children's emotion regulation and social competence: The effects of the PATHS curriculum*. Paper presented at the Society for Research in Child Development Meeting, Washington, DC.

Greenberg, M.T., & Kusche, C. (1998). *Promoting alternative thinking strategies (paths): Blueprints for violence prevention*. Boulder, CO: Institute of Behavioral Science.

Greenberg, M.T., Kusche, C., Cook, E.T., & Quamma, J.P. (1995). Promoting emotional competence in school-aged children: The effects of the PATHS curriculum. *Development and Psychopathology*, *7*, 117–136.

Greenwood, P. (2008). Prevention and intervention programs for juvenile offenders. *The Future of Children*, *18*, 185–210.

Greenwood, P.W., & Turner, S. (2012). Probation and other noninstitutional treatment: The evidence is in. In B.C. Feld & D.M. Bishop (Eds.), *The Oxford handbook of juvenile justice* (pp. 723–747). New York: Oxford University Press.

Griffin, P. (2005). *National overviews. State Juvenile Justice Profiles*. Pittsburgh: National Center for Juvenile Justice. Retrieved from www.ncjj.org/stateprofiles.

Griffin, P., & King, M. (2006). *National overviews. State juvenile justice profiles*. Pittsburgh: National Center for Juvenile Justice. Retrieved from www.ncjj.org/stateprofiles/.

Griffin, P., & Thomas, D. (2004). The good news: Measuring juvenile outcomes at case closing. *Pennsylvania Progress*, *10*(2), 1–6.

Griffin, P., & Torbet, P. (2002). *Desktop guide to good juvenile probation practice*. Pittsburgh: National Center for Juvenile Justice.

Grisso, T.P., & Schwartz, R.G. (2000). *Youth on trial: A developmental perspective on juvenile justice*. Chicago, IL: University of Chicago Press.

Grogger, J. (2002). The effects of civil gang injunctions on reported violent crime: Evidence from Los Angeles County. *Journal of Law and Economics, 4,* 69–90.

Grossman, E.R., & Miller, N.A. (2015). A systematic review of the impact of juvenile curfew laws on public health and justice outcomes. *American Journal of Preventive Medicine, 49*(6), 945–951.

Grossman, E.R., Jernigan, D.H., & Miller, N.A. (2016). Do juvenile curfew laws reduce underage drinking? *Journal of Studies on Alcohol and Drugs, 77,* 589–595.

Grossman, J.B., & Tierney, J.P. (1998). Does mentoring work? An impact study of the Big Brothers Big Sisters program. *Evaluation Review, 22,* 403–426.

Guevara, L., Spohn, C., & Herz, D. (2004). Race, legal representation, and juvenile justice: Issues and concerns. *Crime & Delinquency, 50,* 344–371.

Hagan, J., & McCarthy, B. (1997). *Mean streets: Youth crime and homelessness.* New York: Cambridge University Press. (In collaboration with P. Parker and J. Climenhage.)

Hagedorn, J.M. (1988). *People and folks: Gangs, crime and the underclass in a rustbelt city.* Chicago, IL: Lakeview Press.

Hagedorn, J.M. (1994). Homeboys, dope fiends, legits, and new jacks. *Criminology, 32,* 197–220.

Hardt, R.H., & Peterson-Hardt, S. (1977). On determining the quality of delinquency self-report method. *Journal of Research in Crime and Delinquency, 14,* 247–261.

Harrell, E., & Davis, E. (2020). *Contacts between police and the public, 2018: Statistical tables.* Washington, DC: Bureau of Justice Statistics.

Harris, J.A. (1999). Review and methodological considerations in research on testosterone and aggression. *Aggression and Violent Behavior, 4,* 273–291.

Harris, N. (2003). Evaluating the practice of restorative justice: The case of family group conferencing. In L. Walgrave (Ed.), *Repositioning restorative justice* (pp. 121–135). Portland, OR: Willan.

Hawkins, J.D., Arthur, M.W., & Catalano, R.F. (1995). Preventing substance abuse. In M. Tonry & D.P. Farrington (Eds.), *Building a safer society: Strategic approaches to crime prevention.* Chicago, IL: University of Chicago Press

Hawkins, J.D., Catalano, R.F., Kosterman, R., Abbott, R., & Hill, K.G. (1999). Preventing adolescent health-risk behaviors by strengthening protection during childhood. *Archives of Pediatric and Adolescent Medicine, 153,* 226–234.

Hawkins, J.D., Smith, B.H., Kosterman, K.G., & Catalano, R.F. (2007). Promoting social developments and preventing health and behavior problems during the elementary grades: Results from the Seattle Social Development Project. *Violence and Offenders, 2,* 161–181.

Hayes, H., & Daly, K. (2004). Conferencing and re-offending in Queensland. *Australian and New Zealand Journal of Criminology, 37,* 167–191.

Hayes, L.M. (2004). *Juvenile suicide in confinement: A national survey.* Baltimore, MD: National Center on Institutions and Alternatives.

Haynes, S.H., Cares, A.C., & Ruback, R.B. (2014). Juvenile economic sanctions: An analysis of their imposition, payment, and effect on recidivism. *Criminology & Public Policy, 13,* 31–60.

Hecht, M.L., Graham, J.W., & Elek, E. (2006). The Drug Resistance Strategies Intervention: Program effects on substance use. *Health Communication, 20,* 267–276.

Hecht, M.L., Marsiglia, F.F., Elek-Fisk, E., Wagstaff, D.A., Kulis, S., Dustman, P., & Miller-Day, M. (2003). Culturally-grounded substance use prevention: An evaluation of the keepin' it R.E.A.L. curriculum. *Prevention Science, 4,* 233–248.

Heckman, J.J., & Karapakula, G. (2019). *Intergenerational and intragenerational externalities of the Perry Preschool Project.* National Bureau of Economic Research. DOI: 10.3386/w25889. Retrieved from www.nber.org/papers/w25889.

Henderson, C.E., Young, D.W., Jainchill, N., Hawke, J., Farkas, S., & Davis, R.M. (2007). Program use of effective drug abuse treatment practices for juvenile offenders. *Journal of Substance Abuse Treatment, 32*, 279–290.

Hennigan, K.M., & Sloane, D. (2013). Improving civil gang injunctions: How implementation can affect gang dynamics, crime, and violence. *Criminology and Public Policy, 12*, 7–42.

Henning, K. (2010). Denial of the child's right to counsel, voice, and participation in juvenile delinquency proceedings. *Child Welfare, 89*, 121–138.

Henretta, J.C., Frazier, C.E., & Bishop, D.M. (1985). *Juvenile justice decision-making: An analysis of the effects of prior case outcomes.* Paper presented at the Annual Meeting of the American Society of Criminology, San Diego, CA.

Henretta, J.C., Frazier, C.E., & Bishop, D.M. (1986). The effect of prior case outcomes on juvenile justice decision-making. *Social Forces, 65*, 554–562.

Herrnstein, R.J., & Murray, C. (1994). *The bell curve: Intelligence and class structure in American life.* New York: Free Press.

Hill, P.L., Roberts, B.W., Grogger, J.T., Guryan, J., & Sixkiller, K. (2011). Decreasing delinquency, criminal behavior, and recidivism by intervening on psychological factors other than cognitive ability: A review of the intervention literature. In P.J. Cook, J. Ludwig, & J. McCrary (Eds.), *Controlling crime: Strategies and tradeoffs* (pp. 367–406). Chicago, IL: University of Chicago Press.

Hills, S.L. (1980). *Demystifying social deviance.* New York: McGraw-Hill.

Hindelang, M.J. (1971). The social versus solitary nature of delinquent involvement. *British Journal of Criminology, 11*, 167–175.

Hindelang, M.J. (1973). Causes of delinquency: A partial replication and extension. *Social Problems, 20*, 470–487.

Hindelang, M.J. (1975). *Public opinion regarding crime, criminal justice, and related topics.* Washington, DC: U.S. Department of Justice.

Hindelang, M.J., Gottfredson, M.R., & Garofalo, J. (1978). *Victims of personal crime: An empirical foundation for a theory of personal victimization.* Cambridge, MA: Ballinger.

Hindelang, M.J., Hirschi, T., & Weis, J.G. (1981). *Measuring delinquency.* Beverly Hills: Sage.

Hingson, R., & White, A. (2014). New research findings since the 2007 Surgeon General's Call to Action to Prevent and Reduce Underage Drinking: A review. *Journal of Studies on Alcohol and Drugs, 75*, 158–169.

Hinton, E. (2016). *From the war on poverty to the war on crime: The making of mass incarceration in America.* Cambridge, MA: Harvard University Press.

Hippchen, L.J. (1978). *Ecologic-biochemical approaches to treatment of delinquents and criminals.* New York: Van Nostrand Reinhold.

Hippchen, L.J. (1981). Some possible biochemical aspects of criminal behavior. *International Journal of Biosocial Research, 2*, 37–48.

Hipple, N.K., Gruenewald, J., & McGarrell, E.F. (2014). Restorativeness, procedural justice, and defiance as predictors of reoffending of participants in Family Group Conferences. *Crime & Delinquency, 60*(8), 1131–1157. DOI: https://doi.org/10.1177/0011128711428556.

Hipple, N.K., Gruenewald, J., & McGarrell, E.F. (2015). Restorativeness, procedural justice, and defiance as long-term predictors of reoffending of participants in Family Group Conferences. *Criminal Justice and Behavior, 42*(11), 1110–1127. DOI: https://doi.org/10.1177/0093854815601153.

Hirschel, J.D., Dean, C.W., & Dumond, D. (2001). Juvenile curfews and race: A cautionary note. *Criminal Justice Policy Review, 12*, 197–214.

Hirschfield, P.J., & Celinska, K. (2011). Beyond fear: Sociological perspectives on the criminalization of school discipline. *Sociology Compass, 5*, 1–12.

Hirschi, T. (1969). *Causes of delinquency.* Berkeley: University of California Press.

Hirschi, T., & Hindelang, M.J. (1977). Intelligence and delinquency: A revisionist review. *American Sociological Review, 42,* 572–587.

Hockenberry, S. (2020). *Juveniles in residential placement, 2017.* Washington, DC: Office of Juvenile Justice and Delinquency Prevention.

Hockenberry, S. (2021). *Delinquency cases waived to criminal court, 2018.* Washington, DC: Office of Juvenile Justice & Delinquency Prevention.

Hockenberry, S., & Puzzanchera, C. (2017). *Juvenile court statistics 2014.* Pittsburgh: National Center for Juvenile Justice.

Hockenberry, S., & Puzzanchera, C. (2020). *Juvenile court statistics 2018.* Pittsburgh, PA: National Center for Juvenile Justice.

Hockenberry, S., & Sladky, A. (2020). *Juvenile residential facility census, 2018.* Washington, DC: Office of Juvenile Justice and Delinquency Prevention.

Holtz, L.E. (1987). Miranda in a juvenile setting: A child's right to silence. *The Journal of Criminal Law and Criminology, 78,* 534–556.

Honig, A.S., Lally, J.R., & Mathieson, D.H. (1982). Personal and social adjustment of school children after five years in the family development research program. *Child Care Quarterly, 11,* 136–146.

Hope, T. (1997). Inequality and the future of community crime prevention. In S.P. Lab (Ed.), *Crime prevention at a crossroads* (pp. 143–158). Cincinnati: Anderson.

Horowitz, R. (1983). *Honor and the American dream: Culture and identity in a Chicano community.* New Brunswick, NJ: Rutgers University Press.

Howell, J.C. (1997). *Youth gangs.* OJJDP Fact Sheet #72. Washington, DC: Office of Juvenile Justice and Delinquency Prevention.

Howell, J.C. (2000). *Youth gang programs and strategies: Summary.* Washington, DC: Office of Juvenile Justice and Delinquency Prevention.

Howell, J.C. (2010). *Gang prevention: An overview of research and programs.* Juvenile Justice Bulletin. Washington, DC: Office of Juvenile Justice and Delinquency Prevention.

Howell, J.C., Egley, A., Tita, G.E., & Griffiths, E. (2011). *U.S. gang problem trends and seriousness, 1996–2009.* National Gang Center Bulletin No. 6. Washington, DC: National Gang Center.

Howell, J.C., & Griffiths, E. (2019). *Gangs in America's communities* (3rd ed.). Los Angeles: Sage.

Hser, Y., Anglin, M.D., & Chou, C. (1988). Evaluation of drug abuse treatment: A repeated measure design assessing methadone maintenance. *Evaluation Review, 12,* 547–570.

Hsia, H.M., Bridges, G.S., & McHale, R. (2004). *Disproportionate minority confinement 2002 update: Summary.* Washington, DC: U.S. Department of Justice.

Hsieh, M., Woo, Y., Hafoka, M., van Wormer, J., Stohr, M.K., & Hemmens, C. (2016). Assessing the current state of juvenile probation practice. *Journal of Offender Rehabilitation, 55,* 329–354.

Huang, D.T. (2001). Less unequal footing: State courts' per se rules for juvenile waivers during interrogation and the case for their implementation. *Cornell Law Review, 86,* 437.

Huba, G.J., & Bentler, P.M. (1983). Causal models of the development of law abidance and its relationship to psychosocial factors and drug use. In W.S. Laufer & J.M. Day (Eds.), *Personality theory, moral development and criminal behavior* (pp. 165–215). Lexington, MA: D.C. Heath.

Huebner, B.M., Schafer, J.A., & Bynum, T.S. (2004). African American and white perceptions of police service: Within- and between-group variation. *Journal of Criminal Justice, 32,* 123–135.

Huey, S.J., Lewine, G., & Rubenson, M. (2016). A brief review and meta-analysis of gang intervention trials in North America. In C.L. Maxson & F. Esbensen (Eds.), *Gang transitions and transformations in an international context*. New York: Springer.

Huff, C.R. (1990). Denial, overreaction, and misidentification: A postscript on public policy. In C.R. Huff (Ed.), *Gangs in America* (pp. 310–317). Newbury Park, CA: Sage.

Huff, C.R. (1993). Gangs in the United States. In A.P. Goldstein & C.R. Huff (Eds.), *The gang intervention handbook* (pp. 3–20). Champaign, IL: Research Press.

Huizinga, D., & Elliott, D.S. (1987). Juvenile offenders: Prevalence, offender incidence, and arrest rates by race. *Crime & Delinquency, 33*, 206–223.

Huizinga, D., Loeber, R., & Thornberry, T.P. (1995). *Urban delinquency and substance abuse: Research summary*. Washington, DC: Office of Juvenile Justice and Delinquency Prevention.

Huizinga, D., Menard, S., & Elliott, D. (1989). Delinquency and drug use: Temporal and developmental patterns. *Justice Quarterly, 6*, 419–456.

Huizinga, D., Thornberry, T.P., Knight, K.E., Lovegrove, P.J., Loeber, R., Hill, K., & Farrington, D.P. (2007). *Disproportionate minority contact in the juvenile justice system: A study of differential minority arrest/referral to court in three cities*. An unpublished report submitted to the Office of Juvenile Justice and Delinquency Prevention. Available from the National Criminal Justice Reference Service.

Human Rights Watch. (2001). No escape: Male rape in U.S. prisons. Retrieved from www. hrw.org.

Human Rights Watch. (2006). *Custody and control: Conditions of confinement in New York's juvenile prisons for girls*. New York: Human Rights Watch.

Human Rights Watch. (2008). *The rest of their lives: Life without parole for youth offenders in the United States in 2008*. New York: Human Rights Watch.

Human Rights Watch. (2014a). *Branded for life: Florida's prosecution of children as adults under its "direct file" law*. New York: Human Rights Watch.

Human Rights Watch. (2014b). *Profiting from probation: America's "offender funded" probation industry*. New York: Human Rights Watch.

Human Rights Watch. (2016). *Every 25 Seconds: The human toll of criminalizing drug use in the United States*. New York: Human Rights Watch. Retrieved from www.hrw.org.

Humes, E. (1996). *No matter how loud I shout: A year in the life of juvenile court*. New York: Simon & Schuster.

Hunter, A. (1985). Private, parochial and public school orders: The problem of crime and incivility in urban communities. In G.D. Suttles & M.N. Zald (Eds.), *The challenge of social control: Citizenship and institution building in modern society*. Norwood, NJ: Ablex.

Hunter, S.B., Ramchand, R., Griffin, B.A., Suttorp, M.J., McCaffrey, D., & Morral, A. (2012). The effectiveness of community-based delivery of an evidence-based treatment for adolescent substance abuse. *Journal of Substance Abuse & Treatment, 43*, 211–220.

Hurst, Y.G., Frank, J., & Browning, S.L. (2000). The attitudes of juveniles toward the police: A comparison of black and white youth. *Policing: An International Journal of Police Strategies & Management, 23*, 37–53.

Husak, D. (2003). Four points about drug decriminalization. *Criminal Justice Ethics, 30*, 21–29.

Hutchings, B., & Mednick, S.A. (1977). Criminality in adoptees and their adoptive and biological parents: A pilot study. In S.A. Mednick & K.O. Christiansen (Eds.), *Biosocial bases of criminal behavior* (pp. 127–141). New York: Gardner Press.

Hutchinson, R., & Kyle, C. (1993). Hispanic street gangs in Chicago's public schools. In S. Cummings & D.J. Monti (Eds.), *Gangs: The origins and impact of contemporary youth gangs in the United States* (pp. 113–136). Albany, NY: SUNY Press.

Inciardi, J.A., Horowitz, R., & Pottieger, A.E. (1993). *Street kids, street drugs, street crime: An examination of drug use and serious delinquency in Miami.* Belmont, CA: Wadsworth.

Incredible Years. (2012). *Incredible Years: Parents, teachers and children's training series.* Retrieved from www.incredibleyears.com/program/Incredible-Years_factsheet.pdf.

Inderbitzin, M. (2006a). A look from the inside: Balancing custody and treatment in a juvenile maximum-security facility. *International Journal of Offender Therapy and Comparative Criminology, 51,* 348–362.

Inderbitzin, M. (2006b). Lessons from a juvenile training school: Survival and growth. *Journal of Adolescent Research, 21,* 7–26.

Institute of Judicial Administration–American Bar Association (IJA–ABA). (1980). *Juvenile justice standards project: Standards relating to adjudication* (2nd ed.). Cambridge, MA: Ballinger. Retrieved from www.ojp.gov.

Institute of Judicial Administration–American Bar Association (IJA–ABA). (1982). *Juvenile justice standards project: Standards for juvenile justice: A summary and analysis* (2nd ed.). Cambridge, MA: Ballinger. Retrieved from www.ojp.gov.

Ishida, K., Clarke, E., & Reed, D. (2014). *Automatic adult prosecution of children in Cook County, Illinois.* Evanston, IL: Juvenile Justice Initiative.

Jablecki, L.T. (2005). A critique of faith-based prison programs. *The Humanist, 65,* 11–16.

Jamieson, K.M., & Flanagan, T. (1987). *Sourcebook of criminal justice statistics: 1986.* Washington, DC: U.S. Department of Justice.

Jang, S.J., & Johnson, B.R. (2001). Neighborhood disorder, individual religiosity, and adolescent use of illicit drugs: A test of multilevel hypotheses. *Criminology, 39,* 109–144.

Jennings, W.G. (2011). Sex disaggregated trajectories of status offenders: Does CINS/FINS status prevent male and female youth from becoming labeled delinquent? *American Journal of Criminal Justice, 36,* 177–187.

Jeong, S., McGarrell, E.F., Hipple, N.K. (2012). Long-term impact of family group conferences on re-offending: The Indianapolis restorative justice experiment. *Journal of Experimental Criminology, 8,* 369–385. DOI: 10.1007/s11292-012-9158-8.

Johnson, B.D., Goldstein, P.J., Prebel, E., Schmeidler, J., Lipton, D.S., Spunt, B., & Miller, T. (1985). *Taking care of business: The economics of crime by heroin abusers.* Lexington, MA: Lexington Books.

Johnston, L.D., Miech, R.A., O'Malley, P.M., Bachman, J.G., Schulenberg, J.E., & Patrick, M.E. (2021). *Monitoring the future: National survey results on drug use, 1975–2020: 2020 Overview: Key findings on adolescent drug use.* Ann Arbor, MI: Institute for Social Research: University of Michigan.

Johnston, L.D., O'Malley, P.M., & Bachman, J.G. (1987). *National trends in drug use and related factors among American high school students and young adults, 1975–1986.* Rockville, MD: National Institute on Drug Abuse.

Johnston, L.D., O'Malley, P.M., & Eveland, L.K. (1978). Drugs and delinquency: A search for causal connections. In D.B. Kandel (Ed.), *Longitudinal research on drug use: Empirical findings and methodological issues* (pp. 137–156). Washington, DC: Hemisphere.

Johnstone, J.W.C. (1981). Youth gangs and black suburbs. *Pacific Sociological Review, 58,* 355–375.

Jones, J.B. (2004). *Access to counsel.* Washington, DC: U.S. Department of Justice.

Jones, L.M., Cross, T.P., Walsh, W.A., & Simone, M. (2005). Criminal investigations of child abuse: The research behind "best practices." *Trauma, Violence, & Abuse, 6,* 254–268.

Jordan, K.L., & Myers, D. (2011). Juvenile transfer and deterrence: Re-examining the effectiveness of a "get tough" policy. *Crime & Delinquency, 57*(2), 247–270.

Justice Policy Institute. (2014). *$ticker $hock: Calculating the full price tag for youth incarceration.* Washington, DC: Justice Policy Institute.

Juvenile Justice Update. (1995). Juveniles subject to warrantless search as a probation condition have no expectation of privacy. *Juvenile Justice Update, 2*, 8.

Kandel, D.B., Simcha-Fagan, O., & Davies, M. (1986). Risk factors for delinquency and illicit drug use from adolescence to young adulthood. *Journal of Drug Issues, 16*, 67–90.

Kandel, E., & Mednick, S.A. (1991). Perinatal complications predict violent offending. *Criminology, 29*, 519–529.

Kanter, D., & Bennett, W. (1968). Orientation of street-corner workers and their effects on gangs. In S. Wheeler (Ed.), *Controlling delinquents*. New York: Wiley.

Karp, D.R. (2001). The offender/community encounter: Stakeholder involvement in the Vermont reparative boards. In D.R. Karp & T. Clear (Eds.), *What is community justice? Case studies of restorative justice and community supervision* (pp. 61–86). Thousand Oaks, CA: Sage.

Karp, D.R., Bazemore, G., & Chesire, J.D. (2004). The role and attitudes of restorative board members: A case study of volunteers in community justice. *Crime & Delinquency, 50*, 487–515.

Katz, C.M., & Maguire, E.R. (Eds.). (2020). *Transforming the police: Thirteen key reforms*. Long Grove, IL: Waveland Press.

Katz, C.M., & Webb, V.J. (2003). *Police response to gangs: A multi-site study—final report*. Washington, DC: National Institute of Justice.

Katz, J., & Chamblis, W.J. (1995). Biology and crime. In J.F. Sheley (Ed.), *Criminology: A contemporary handbook* (pp. 275–304). Belmont, CA: Wadsworth.

Kelley, T.M., Kennedy, D.B., & Homant, R.J. (2003). Evaluation of an individualized treatment program for adolescent shoplifters. *Adolescence, 38*, 725–733.

Kelling, G. (1975). Leadership in the gang. In D.S. Cartwright, B. Tomson, & H. Schwartz (Eds.), *Gang delinquency* (pp. 111–126). Monterey: Brooks/Cole.

Kelling, G.L., & Coles, C.M. (1996). *Fixing broken windows: Restoring order and reducing crime in our communities*. New York: Touchstone.

Kelly, R. (2013, July 22). The NYPD: Guilty of saving 7,383 lives. *Wall Street Journal*. Retrieved from http://online.wsj.com/news/articles/SB10001424127887324448104578616333588719320.

Kelly, W.R., Macy, T.S., & Mears, D.P. (2005). Juvenile referrals in Texas: An assessment of the criminogenic needs and the gap between needs and services. *Prison Journal, 85*, 467–489.

Kempf-Leonard, K. (2012). The conundrum of girls and juvenile justice processing. In B.C. Feld & D.M. Bishop (Eds.), *The Oxford handbook of juvenile crime and juvenile justice* (pp. 485–525). New York: Oxford University Press.

Kennedy, D. (1998). Pulling levers: Getting deterrence right. *National Institute of Justice Journal, 236*, 2–8.

Kennedy, L.W., & Forde, D.R. (1990). Routine activities and crime: An analysis of victimization data in Canada. *Criminology, 28*, 137–152.

Kennedy, R. (2021). *Corporal punishment is still legal in many states*. Retrieved from www.boardingschoolreview.com.

Kim, B., Matz, A.K., Gerber, J., Beto, D.R., & Lambert, E. (2013). Facilitating police–probation/parole partnerships: An examination of police chiefs' and sheriffs' perceptions. *Policing: An International Journal of Police Strategies & Management, 36*, 752–767.

Kim, C.Y., Losen, D.J., & Hewitt, D.T. (2010). *The school-to-prison pipeline: Structuring legal reform*. New York: NYU Press.

Kim, S. (1988). A short- and long-term evaluation of Here's Looking at You alcohol education program. *Journal of Drug Education, 18*, 235–242.

Kim, S., McLeod, J.H., & Shantzis, C. (1993). An outcome evaluation of here's looking at you 2000. *Journal of Drug Education, 23,* 67–81.

Kim-Cohen, J., Caspi, A., Taylor, A., Williams, B., Newcombe, R., Craig, I., & Moffitt, T.E. (2006). MAOA, maltreatment, and gene–environment interaction predicting children's mental health: New evidence and a meta-analysis. *Molecular Psychiatry, 11,* 903–913.

Kirk, D.S., & Sampson, R.J. (2013). Juvenile arrest and collateral educational damage in the transition to adulthood. *Sociology of Education, 86,* 36–62.

Kleiman, M.A.R. (2011). Justice reinvestment in community supervision. *Criminology & Public Policy, 10,* 651–659.

Klein, M.W. (1969). Gang cohesiveness, delinquency, and a street-work program. *Journal of Research in Crime and Delinquency, 6,* 135–166.

Klein, M.W. (1971). *Street gangs and street workers.* Englewood Cliffs, NJ: Prentice Hall.

Klein, M.W. (1995). *The American street gang: Its nature, prevalence and control.* New York: Oxford University Press.

Klein, M.W., & Maxson, C.L. (1989). Street gang violence. In N.A. Weiner & M.E. Wolfgang (Eds.), *Violent crime, violent criminals* (pp. 198–234). Newbury Park, CA: Sage.

Klein, M.W., & Maxson, C.L. (2006). *Street gang patterns and policies.* New York: Oxford University Press.

Klingele, C. (2013). Rethinking the use of community supervision. *Journal of Criminal Law and Criminology, 103,* 1015–1070.

Knox, G.W. (1991). *An introduction to gangs.* Berrien Springs, MI: Vande Vere.

Kochel, T.R., Wilson, D.B., & Mastrofski, S.D. (2011). Effect of suspect race on officers' arrest decisions. *Criminology, 49,* 473–512.

Kohlberg, L. (1981). *The philosophy of moral development.* San Francisco: Harper and Row.

Kolivoski, K.M., & Shook, J.J. (2016). Incarcerating juveniles in adult prisons: Examining the relationship between age and prison behavior in transferred juveniles. *Criminal Justice & Behavior, 43,* 1242–1259.

Kovach, G.C. (2008, May 12). To curb truancy, Dallas tries electronic monitoring. *New York Times.* Retrieved from www.nytimes.com/2008/05/12/education/12dallas.html?_r/1&partner/rssnyt&emc/rss&ore/slogin/&_r=0.

Kreuz, L.E., & Rose, R.M. (1972). Assessment of aggressive behavior and plasma testosterone in a young criminal population. *Psychosomatic Medicine, 34,* 321–332.

Krisberg, B. (2005). *Juvenile justice: Redeeming our children.* Thousand Oaks, CA: Sage.

Krisberg, B. (2012a). Juvenile corrections: An overview. In B.C. Feld & D.M. Bishop (Eds.), *The Oxford handbook of juvenile justice* (pp 748–770). New York: Oxford University Press.

Krisberg, B. (2012b). There is no juvenile crime wave: A call to end the war against children. In M. Mauer & K. Epstein (Eds.), *To build a better criminal justice system: 25 experts envision the next 25 years of reform* (pp. 32–33). Washington, DC: The Sentencing Project.

Krisberg, B., & Austin, J. (1978). *The children of Ishmael.* Palo Alto, CA: Mayfield.

Krisberg, B., & Austin, J. (1993). *Reinventing juvenile justice.* Newbury Park, CA: Sage.

Krisberg, B., & Howell, J.C. (1998). The impact of the juvenile justice system and prospects for graduated sanctions in a comprehensive strategy. In R. Loeber & D.P. Farrington (Eds.), *Serious and violent juvenile offenders: Risk factors and successful interventions* (pp. 313–345). Thousand Oaks, CA: Sage.

Krisberg, B., Austin, J., & Steele, P.A. (1989). *Unlocking juvenile corrections: Evaluating the Massachusetts Department of Youth Services.* San Francisco: National Council on Crime and Delinquency.

Krisberg, B., Currie, E., Onek, D., & Wiebush, R.G. (1995). Graduated sanctions for serious, violent, and chronic juvenile offenders. In J.C. Howell, B. Krisberg, J.D. Hawkins & J.J.

Wilson (Eds.), *Serious, violent, and chronic juvenile offenders: A sourcebook* (pp. 142–170). Thousand Oaks, CA: Sage.

Kroes, W.H., Margolis, B.L., & Hurrell, J.J. (1974). Job stress in policemen. *Journal of Police Science and Administration, 2,* 145–155.

Krohn, M.D., & Thornberry, T.P. (2008). Longitudinal perspectives on adolescent street gangs. In A. Lieberman (Ed.), *The long view of crime: A synthesis of longitudinal research.* New York: Springer.

Krohn, M., & Massey, J. (1980). Social control and delinquent behavior: An examination of the elements of the social bond. *Sociological Quarterly, 21,* 529–543.

Kuanliang, A., Sorensen, J.R., & Cunningham, M.D. (2008). Juvenile inmates in an adult prison system: Rates of disciplinary misconduct and violence. *Criminal Justice and Behavior, 35,* 1186–1201.

Kulis, S., Nieri, T., Yabiku, S., Stromwall, L.K., & Marsiglia, F.F. (2007). Promoting reduced and discontinued substance use among adolescent substance users: Effectiveness of a universal prevention program. *Prevention Science, 7,* 123–144.

Kupchik, A. (2014). The school-to-prison pipeline: Rhetoric and reality. In F.E. Zimring & D.S. Tanenhaus (Eds.), *Choosing the future for American juvenile justice* (pp. 94–119). New York: New York University Press.

Kurki, L. (2000). Restorative and community justice in the United States. In M. Tonry (Ed.), *Crime and justice: A review of research* (Vol. 27, pp. 235–303). Chicago, IL: University of Chicago Press.

Kurlychek, M., Torbet, P.M., & Bozynski, M. (1999). *Focus on accountability: Best practices for juvenile court and probation.* Washington, DC: U.S. Department of Justice and Delinquency Prevention.

Lab, S.P. (1984). Patterns in juvenile misbehavior. *Crime & Delinquency, 30,* 293–308.

Lab, S.P., & Allen, R.B. (1984). Self-report and official measures: A further examination of the validity issue. *Journal of Criminal Justice, 12,* 445–456.

Lab, S.P., & Clark, R.D. (1996). *Discipline, control and school crime: Identifying effective intervention strategies.* Final Report. Washington, DC: National Institute of Justice.

Lab, S.P., & Whitehead, J.T. (1994). Avoidance behavior as a response to in-school victimization. *Journal of Security Administration, 17*(2), 32–45.

Lacey, J.H., Kelly-Baker, T., Berning, A., Romano, E., Ramirez, A., Yao, J., … & Compton, R. (2016). *Drug and alcohol crash risk: A case-control study.* Washington, DC: National Highway Safety Administration.

Lally, J.R., Mangione, P.L., & Honig, A.S. (1987). *The Syracuse University Family Development Research Program: Long-range impact of an early intervention with low-income children and their families.* New York: W.T. Grant Foundation.

Lally, J.R., Mangione, P.L., & Honig, A.S. (1988). The Syracuse University Family Development Research Program: Long-range impact on an early intervention with low-income children and their families. In D.R. Powell & I.E. Sigel (Eds.), *Parent education as early childhood intervention: Emerging direction in theory, research, and practice* (pp. 79–104). Norwood, NJ: Ablex.

Lane, J., Turner, S., Fain, T., & Sehgal, A. (2005). Evaluating an experimental intensive probation program: Supervision and official outcomes. *Crime & Delinquency, 51,* 26–52.

Larson, J., Mattu, S., Kirchner, L., & Angwin, J. (2016, May 23). *How we analyzed the COMPAS recidivism algorithm.* ProPublica. Retrieved from www.ProPublica.org.

Latessa, E.J., Johnson, S.L., & Koetzle, D. (2020). *What Works (and Doesn't) in Reducing Recidivism* (2nd ed.). New York: Routledge.

Latimer, J., Dowden, C., & Muise, D. (2005). The effectiveness of restorative justice practices: A meta-analysis. Ottawa, Canada: Canada Department of Justice. (Cited in

Rodriguez, N. (2007). Restorative justice at work: Examining the impact of restorative justice resolutions on juvenile recidivism. *Crime & Delinquency, 53*, 355–379.)

Lattimore, P.K., Krebs, C.P., Graham, P., & Cowell, A.J. (2005). *Evaluation of the juvenile breaking the cycle program: Final report.* Washington, DC: National Institute of Justice.

Lauritsen, J.L., Sampson, R.J., & Laub, J.H. (1991). The link between offending and victimization among adolescents. *Criminology, 29*, 265–292.

Lederman, C.S., & Brown, E.N. (2000). Entangled in the shadows: Girls in the juvenile justice system. *Buffalo Law Review, 48*, 909–925.

Lee, J.M., Steinberg, L., & Piquero, A.R. (2010). Ethnic identity and attitudes toward the police among African American juvenile offenders. *Journal of Criminal Justice, 38*, 781–789.

Lehman, P.S., Chiricos, T., & Bales, W.D. (2017). Sentencing transferred juveniles in the adult criminal court: The direct and interactive effects of race and ethnicity. *Youth Violence and Juvenile Justice, 15*, 172–190.

Lehman, P.S., Chiricos, T., & Bales, W.D. (2018). Juveniles on trial: Mode of conviction and the adult court sentencing of transferred juveniles. *Crime and Delinquency, 64*, 563–586.

Leiber, M.J. (2013). Race, pre- and postdetention, and juvenile justice decision making. *Crime & Delinquency, 59*, 396–418.

Leiber, M.J., & Fix, R. (2019). Reflections on the impact of race and ethnicity on juvenile court outcomes and efforts to enact change. *American Journal of Criminal Justice, 44*(4), 581–608. DOI: https://doi.org/10.1007/s12103-019-09479-3.

Leiber, M.J., & Mack, K.Y. (2003). The individual and joint effects of race, gender, and family status on juvenile justice decision-making. *Journal of Research in Crime and Delinquency, 40*, 34–70.

Lemert, E.M. (1951). *Social pathology: A systematic approach to the theory of sociopathic behavior.* New York: McGraw-Hill.

Levine, M., & Battistoni, L. (1991). The corroboration requirement in child sex abuse cases. *Behavioral Sciences and the Law, 9*, 3–20.

Liebow, E. (2003). *Tally's corner: A study of Negro streetcorner men.* Lanham, MD: Rowman & Littlefield.

Liederbach, J. (2007). Controlling suburban and small-town hoods: An examination of police encounters with juveniles. *Youth Violence and Juvenile Justice, 5*, 107–124.

Lilly, J.R., Cullen, F.T., & Ball, R.A. (1995). *Criminological theory: Context and consequences* (2nd ed.). Thousand Oaks, CA: Sage.

Lilly, J.R., Cullen, F.T., & Ball, R.A. (2019). *Criminological theory: Context and consequences* (7th ed.). Los Angeles: Sage.

Lim, L., & Day, A. (2014). Mental health diversion courts: A two-year recidivism study of a South Australian mental health court program. *Behavioral Sciences and the Law, 32*, 539–551.

Limber, A.P., Olweus, D., Wang, W., Masiello, M., & Breivik, K. (2018). Evaluation of the Olweus Bullying Prevention Program: A large scale study of U.S. students in grades 3–11. *Journal of School Psychology, 69*, 56–72. DOI: https://doi.org/10.1016/j.jsp.2018.04.004.

Lindner, C. (1981). The utilization of day–evening centers as an alternative to secure detention of juveniles. *Journal of Probation and Parole, 13*, 12–18.

Lipsey, M.W. (1999). Can intervention rehabilitate serious delinquents? *Annals of the American Academy of Political and Social Science, 564*, 142–166.

Lipsey, M.W. (2009). The primary factors that characterize effective interventions with juvenile offenders: A meta-analytic overview. *Victims and Offenders, 4*, 124–147.

Lipsey, M.W., & Derzon, J.H. (1998). Predictors of violent or serious delinquency in adolescence and early adulthood: A synthesis of longitudinal research. In R. Loeber and

D.P. Farrington (Eds.), *Serious and violent juvenile offenders: Risk factors and successful interventions* (pp. 86–105). Thousand Oaks, CA: Sage.

Lipsey, M.W., & Wilson, D.B. (1998). Effective intervention for serious juvenile offenders: A synthesis of research. In R. Loeber & D.P. Farrington (Eds.), *Serious and violent juvenile offenders: Risk factors and successful intervention* (pp. 313–345). Thousand Oaks, CA: Sage.

Lipton, D.L. (1995). *The effectiveness of treatment for drug abusers under criminal justice supervision.* Washington, DC: U.S. Department of Justice.

Lizotte, A., & Sheppard, D. (2001). *Gun use by male juveniles: Research and prevention.* Juvenile Justice Bulletin. Washington, DC: U.S. Department of Justice.

Loeber, R., & Stouthamer-Loeber, M. (1986). Family factors as correlates and predictors of juvenile conduct problems and delinquency. In M. Tonry & N. Morris (Eds.), *Crime and justice: An annual review of research* (Vol. 7) (pp. 29–149). Chicago, IL: University of Chicago Press.

Loeber, R., Green, S.M., Keenan, K., & Lahey, B.B. (1995). Which boys will fare worse? Early predictors of the onset of conduct disorder in a six-year longitudinal study. *Journal of the American Academy of Child and Adolescent Psychiatry, 34,* 499–509.

Loeber, R., Wung, P., Keenan, K., Giroux, B., Stouthamer-Loeber, M., VanKammen, W.B., & Maughan, B. (1993). Developmental pathways in disruptive child behavior. *Development and Psychopathology, 5,* 103–133.

Lombroso, C. (1876). *On criminal man.* Milan, Italy: Hoepli.

Loney, J., Whaley-Klahn, M.A., Kosier, T., & Conboy, J. (1983). Hyperactive boys and their brothers at 21: Predictors of aggressive and antisocial outcomes. In K.T. Van Dusen & S.A. Mednick (Eds.), *Prospective studies of crime and delinquency.* Boston: Kluwer-Nijhof.

Los Angeles City Attorney's Office. (2009). *Gang injunctions: How they work* (The City Attorney's report). Retrieved from www.atty.lacity.org/stellent/groups/electedofficials/@atty_contributor/documents/contributor_web_content/lacityp_006877.pdf.

Love, J.M., Kisker, E.E., Ross, C.M., Schochet, P.Z., Brooks-Gunn, J., Paulsell, D., Boller, K., Constantine, J., Vogel, C., Sidle Fuligni, A., & Brady-Smith, C. (2002). *Making a difference in the lives of infants and toddlers and their families: The impacts of early Head Start. Volumes I-III: Final technical report and appendixes and local contributions to understanding the programs and their impacts.* Washington, DC: Administration for Children and Families. Retrieved from www.mathematica-mpr.com/~/media/publications/PDFs/ehsfinalsumm.pdf.

Lowery, P.G., & Smith, C.S. (2020). The impact of concentrated affluence and disadvantage on the pre-adjudication detention decision: A status characteristics approach. *Crime & Delinquency, 66,* 915–948.

Lowrey-Webster, H.M., Barrett, P.M., & Dadds, M.R. (2001). A universal prevention trial of anxiety and depressive symptomatology in childhood: Preliminary data from an Australian study. *Behavior Change, 18,* 36–50.

Lozoff, B., & Braswell, M. (1989). *Inner corrections: Finding peace and peace making.* Cincinnati: Anderson.

Lu, R., Willits, D., Markin, M.K., Snyder, J., Lovrich, N., Meize, M., ... & Hemmens, C. (2021). The cannabis effect on crime: Time-series analysis of crime in Colorado and Washington State. *Justice Quarterly, 38,* 565–595.

Lugo, K., & Przybylski, R. (2018). *Estimating the financial costs of crime: Final report.* Washington, DC: Justice Research and Statistics Association.

Lundman, R.J. (1994). Demeanor or crime? The Midwest City Police–Citizen Encounters Study. *Criminology, 32,* 631–656.

Lyons, M.J. (1996). A twin study of self-reported criminal behavior. In G.R. Bock & J.A. Goode (Eds.), *Genetics of criminal and antisocial behavior* (pp. 61–69). Chichester, England: John Wiley and Sons.

Mack, J.W. (1909). The juvenile court. *Harvard Law Review, 23*, 104–119.

MacKenzie, D.L. (2006). *What works in corrections: Reducing the criminal activities of offenders and delinquents.* New York: Cambridge University Press.

MacKenzie, D.L., & Farrington, D.P. (2015). Preventing future offending of delinquents and offenders: What have we learned from experiments and meta-analyses? *Journal of Experimental Criminology, 11*, 565–595.

MacKenzie, D.L., & Freeland, R. (2012). Examining the effectiveness of juvenile residential programs. In B.C. Feld & D.M. Bishop (Eds.), *The Oxford handbook of juvenile justice* (pp. 771–798). New York: Oxford University Press.

MacNeill, A. (2020, December 9). *Over 1,000 readers respond: Here's what they think about the legal drinking age.* Boston.com. Retrieved from www.boston.com.

Maggard, S.R., Higgins, J.L., & Chappell, A.T. (2013). Pre-dispositional juvenile detention: An analysis of race, gender, and intersectionality. *Journal of Crime and Justice, 36*, 67–86.

Maguin, E., & Loeber, R. (1996). Academic performance and delinquency. In M. Tonry & N. Morris (Eds.), *Crime and justice* (Vol. 20). Chicago, IL: University of Chicago Press.

Mahoney, A.R. (1985). Jury trial for juveniles: Right or ritual? *Justice Quarterly, 2*, 553–565.

Mahoney, A.R. (1987). *Juvenile justice in context.* Boston: Northeastern University Press.

Maier, S.L., Mannes, S., & Koppenhofer, E.L. (2017). The implications of marijuana decriminalization and legalization on crime in the United States. *Contemporary Drug Problems, 44*(2), 125–146.

Maitland, A.S., & Sluder, R.D. (1998). Victimization and youthful prison inmates: An empirical analysis. *Prison Journal, 78*, 55–73.

Males, M.A. (2000). Vernon, Connecticut's juvenile curfew: The circumstances of youths cited and effects on crime. *Criminal Justice Policy Review, 11*, 254–267.

Mallett, C.A. (2016). The school-to-prison pipeline: A critical review of the punitive paradigm. *Child and Adolescent Social Work Journal, 33*, 15–24.

Mallett, C.A. (2018). Disproportionate minority contact in juvenile justice: Today's and yesterday's, problems. *Criminal Justice Studies, 31*, 230–248.

Malloy, L.C., Shulman, E.P., & Cauffman, E. (2014). Interrogations, confessions, and guilty pleas among serious adolescent offenders. *Law and Human Behavior, 36*, 181–193.

Marier, C.J., & Fridell, L.A. (2020). Demonstrations, demoralization, and de-policing. *Criminology & Public Policy, 19*, 693–719.

Martinez, J.Y. (2008). Character education in juvenile detention. *Corrections Today, 70*, 150–154.

Marzell, M., Bavarian, N., Paschall, M.J., Mair, C., & Saltz, R.F. (2015). Party characteristics, drinking settings, and college students' risk of intoxication: A multi-campus study. *Journal of Primary Prevention, 36*, 247–258.

Maslach, C., & Jackson, S.E. (1979). Burned-out cops and their families. *Psychology Today, 12*(12), 59–62.

Mathis, K.J. (2007). American Bar Association: Adult justice system is the wrong answer for most juveniles. *American Journal of Preventive Medicine, 32*, S1–S2.

Matz, A. (2014). Do youth mentoring programs work? A review of the empirical literature. *Journal of Juvenile Justice, 3*, 83–101.

Mause, L. (1974). *The history of childhood.* New York: Psychohistory Press.

Maxson, C.L. (2011). Street gangs. In J.Q. Wilson & J. Petersilia (Eds.), *Crime and public policy* (pp. 158–182). New York: Oxford University Press.

Maxson, C.L., & Whitlock, M.L. (2002). Joining the gang: Gender differences in risk factors for gang membership. In C.R. Huff (Ed.), *Gangs in America* (3rd ed.) (pp. 19–36). Thousand Oaks, CA: Sage.

Maxson, C.L., Hennigan, K.M., Sloane, D.C., & Kolnick, K.A. (2004). *Can civil gang injunctions change communities? A community assessment of the impact of civil gang injunctions.* Washington, DC: National Institute of Justice.

Maxson, C.L., Woods, K., & Klein, M.W. (1996). Street gang migration: How big a threat? *NIJ Journal, 230,* 26–31.

Maxwell, J.C., & Mendelson, B. (2016). What do we know now about the impact of the laws related to marijuana? *Journal of Addictions Medicine, 10,* 3–12.

Mayo Clinic. (2010). *Antisocial personality disorder.* Retrieved from www.mayoclinic.com/health/antisocial-personality-disorder/DS00829.

Mays, G.L., Fuller, K., & Winfree, L.T. (1994). Gangs and gang activity in southern New Mexico: A descriptive look at a growing rural problem. *Journal of Crime and Justice, 17,* 25–44.

Mazerolle, L., & Terrill, W. (2018). Making every police-citizen interaction count: The challenges of building a better cop. *Criminology & Public Policy, 17,* 89–96.

Mazerolle, L.G., Roehl, J., & Kadleck, C. (1998). Controlling social disorder using civil remedies: Results from a randomized field experiment in Oakland, California. In L.G. Mazerolle & J. Roehl (Eds.), *Civil remedies and crime prevention* (pp. 141–159). Monsey, NY: Criminal Justice Press.

McCarthy, B.R. (1987). Preventive detention and pretrial custody in the juvenile court. *Journal of Criminal Justice, 15,* 185–200.

McCarthy, B.R., & Smith, B.L. (1986). The conceptualization of discrimination in the juvenile justice process: The impact of administrative factors and screening decisions on juvenile court dispositions. *Criminology, 24,* 41–64.

McClelland, G.M., Teplin, L.A., & Abram, K.M. (2004). Detection and prevalence of substance use among juvenile detainees. *Juvenile Justice Bulletin.* Washington, DC: U.S. Department of Justice, Office of Juvenile Justice and Delinquency Prevention.

McCold, P. (2003). A survey of assessment research on mediation and conferencing. In L. Walgrave (Ed.), *Repositioning restorative justice* (pp. 67–120). Portland, OR: Willan.

McCord, J. (1979). Some child-rearing antecedents of criminal behavior in adult men. *Journal of Personality and Social Psychology, 37,* 1477–1486.

McDowall, D., Loftin, C., & Wiersema, B. (2000). The impact of youth curfew laws on juvenile crime rates. *Crime & Delinquency, 46,* 76–91.

McElvain, J.P., & Kposowa, A.J. (2008). Police officer characteristics and the likelihood of using deadly force. *Criminal Justice and Behavior, 35,* 505–521.

McGarrell, E.F., & Hipple, N.K. (2007). Family group conferencing and re-offending among first-time juvenile offenders: The Indianapolis experiment. *Justice Quarterly, 24,* 221–246.

McGarrell, E.F., Chermak, S., Wilson, J.M., & Corsaro, N. (2006). Reducing homicide through a "lever-pulling" strategy. *Justice Quarterly, 23,* 214–231.

McGarrell, E.F., Olivares, K., Crawford, K., & Kroovand, N. (2000). *Returning justice to the community: The Indianapolis juvenile restorative justice experiment.* Indianapolis: Hudson Institute.

McGarvey, A. (2005, September). A culture of caring. The American Prospect, A12–A14.

McGee, T.R., & Farrington, D.P. (2016). *Developmental and life-course theories of crime.* In A.R. Piquero (Ed.), *The handbook of criminological theory.* West Sussex: John Wiley and Sons.

McKeehan, J. (2017, August 21). *What does the child curfew statute actually say?* The Knoxville Focus. Retrieved from www.knoxfocus.com.

McMahon, M. (1999). *Women on guard: Discrimination and harassment in corrections.* Toronto, Canada: University of Toronto Press.

Mead, G.H. (1934). *Mind, self and society.* Chicago, IL: University of Chicago Press.

Meade, B., & Steiner, B. (2010). The total effects of boot camps that house juveniles: A systematic review of the evidence. *Journal of Criminal Justice, 38,* 841–853.

Mears, D.P. (2000). Assessing the effectiveness of juvenile justice reforms: A closer look at the criteria and the impacts on diverse stakeholders. *Law and Policy, 22,* 175–202.

Mears, D.P., Hay, C., Gertz, M., & Mancini, C. (2007). Public opinion and the foundation of the juvenile court. *Criminology, 45,* 223–257.

MedlinePlus. (2021). *Antisocial personality disorder.* https://medlineplus.gov/ency/article/000 921.htm.

Mednick, S.A., & Christiansen, K.O. (1977). *Biosocial bases of criminal behavior.* New York: Gardner.

Megargee, E.I., & Bohn, M.J. (1979). *Classifying criminal offenders: A new system based on the MMPI.* Beverly Hills: Sage.

Melde, C. (2015). Gang membership in developmental perspective. In J. Morizot & L. Kazemian (Eds.), *The development of criminal and antisocial behavior.* New York: Springer.

Melde, C., & Esbensen, F. (2011). Gang membership as a turning point in the life course. *Criminology, 49,* 513–552.

Melde, C., & Esbensen, F. (2013). Gangs and violence: Disentangling the impact of gang membership on the level and nature of offending. *Journal of Quantitative Criminology, 29,* 143–166.

Melton, G.B. (1980). Psycholegal issues in child victims' interaction with the legal system. *Victimology, 5,* 274–284.

Melton, G.B., Limber, S.P., Cunningham, P., Osgood, D.W., Chambers, J., Flerx, V., … & Nation, M. (1998). *Violence among rural youth: Final report.* Washington, DC: Office of Juvenile Justice and Delinquency Prevention.

Mendel, R.A. (2001). *Guiding lights for reform in juvenile justice.* Washington, DC: American Youth Policy Forum.

Mendel, R.A. (2011). *No place for kids: The case for reducing juvenile incarceration.* Baltimore: MD: The Annie E. Casey Foundation.

Mendel, R.A. (2015). *Maltreatment of youth in U.S. juvenile correctional facilities: An update.* Baltimore, MD: The Annie E. Casey Foundation.

Mendel, R.A. (2018) *Transforming juvenile probation: A vision for getting it right.* Baltimore, MD: The Annie E. Casey Foundation.

Merton, R.K. (1938). Social structure and anomie. *American Sociological Review, 3,* 672–682.

Metropolitan Life. (1993). *Violence in America's public schools.* New York: Louis Harris and Associates.

Meyer, J.R., & Reppucci, N.D. (2007). Police practices and perceptions regarding juvenile interrogation and interrogative suggestibility. *Behavioral Sciences and the Law, 25,* 757–780.

Mezzacappa, E.S. (1999). Epinephrine, arousal and emotion: A new look at a two-factor theory. *Cognition and Emotion, 13,* 181–199.

Michel, D.A. (2011). The CHINS don't stand a chance: The dubious achievements of child in need of services ("CHINS") jurisdiction in Massachusetts & a new approach to juvenile status offenses. *Boston University Public Interest Law Journal, 20,* 321–352.

Midgette, G., & Reuter, P. (2020). Has cannabis use increased after changes in its legal status? A commentary on use of Monitoring the Future for analyses of changes in state cannabis laws. *Prevention Science, 21,* 137–145.

Miech, R.A., Johnston, L.D., O'Malley, P.M., Bachman, J.G., Schulenberg, J.E., & Patrick, M.E. (2020). *Monitoring the future: National survey results of drug use 1975–2019: Volume I: Secondary school students.* Ann Arbor, MI: University of Michigan: Institute for Social Research.

Miethe, T.D., Stafford, M.C., & Long, J.S. (1987). Social differentiation in criminal victimization: A test of routine activities lifestyle theory. *American Sociological Review, 52,* 184–194.

Miller, D., Miller, D., Hoffman, F., & Duggan, R. (1980). *Runaways: Illegal aliens in their own land—implications for service*. New York: Praeger.

Miller, J. (2001). *One of the guys? Girls, gangs and gender*. New York: Oxford University Press.

Miller, J., & Palmer, K. (2020). Juvenile probation officer decision making in a reforming state. *Criminal Justice & Behavior, 47*, 1136–1155.

Miller, J.Y. (2005, May 14). Six aides lose jobs after a boy dies. *Atlanta Journal-Constitution*, A9–A10.

Miller, W.B. (1958). Lower class culture as a generating milieu of gang delinquency. *Journal of Social Issues, 15*, 5–19.

Miller, W.B. (1975). *Violence by youth gangs and youth groups as a crime problem in major American cities*. Washington, DC: National Institute for Juvenile Justice and Delinquency Prevention.

Miller, W.B., Gertz, H., & Cutter, H.S.G. (1961). Aggression in a boys' street-corner group. *Psychiatry, 24*, 283–298.

Miller-Wilson, L.S., & Puritz, P. (2003). *Pennsylvania: An assessment of access to counsel and quality of representation in delinquency proceedings*. Washington, DC, and Philadelphia: American Bar Association Juvenile Justice Center and Juvenile Law Center in collaboration with the National Juvenile Defender Center and the Northeast Juvenile Defender Center. Retrieved from www.jlc.org/sites/default/files/publication_pdfs/PA%20Assesment%20of%20Access%20to%20Counsel.pdf.

Minor, K.I., Hartmann, D.J., & Terry, S. (1997). Predictors of juvenile court actions and recidivism. *Crime & Delinquency, 18*, 295–318.

Minor, W.W. (1981). Techniques of neutralization: A reconceptualization and empirical examination. *Journal of Research in Crime and Delinquency, 18*, 295–318.

Mitchell, O., Wilson, D.B., Eggers, A., & MacKenzie, D.L. (2012). Assessing the effectiveness of drug courts on recidivism: A meta-analytic review of traditional and non-traditional drug courts. *Journal of Criminal Justice, 40*, 60–71.

Moffitt, T.E., Brammer, G.L., Caspi, A., Fawcett, J.P., Raleigh, M., Yuwiler, A., & Silva, P. (1998). Whole blood serotonin relates to violence in an epidemiological study. *Biological Psychology, 43*, 446–457.

Moffitt, T.E., Caspi, A., Fawcett, P., Brammer, G.L., Raleigh, M., Yuwiler, A., & Silva, P.A. (1997). Whole blood serotonin and family background relate to male violence. In A. Raine, P.A. Brennan, D.P. Farrington, & S.A. Mednick (Eds.), *Biosocial bases of violence*. New York: Plenum.

Moffitt, T.E., Ross, S., & Raine, A. (2011). Crime and biology. In J.Q. Wilson & J. Petersilia (Eds.), *Crime and public policy*. New York: Oxford University Press.

Montgomery, J.M., Foley, K.L., & Wolfson, M. (2006). Enforcing the minimum drinking age: State, local and agency characteristics associated with compliance checks and Cops in Shops programs. *Addiction, 101*, 223–231.

Monti, D.J. (1993). Origins and problems of gang research in the United States. In S. Cummings & D.J. Monti (Eds.), *Gangs: The origins and impact of contemporary youth gangs in the United States* (pp. 3–26). Albany, NY: SUNY Press.

Moore, D., & O'Connell, T. (1994). Family conferencing in Wagga Wagga: A communitarian model of justice. In C. Adler & J. Wundersitz (Eds.), *Family conferencing and juvenile justice: The way forward or misplaced optimism?* (pp. 15–44). Canberra, Australia: Australian Institute of Criminology.

Moore, J. (1991). *Going down to the barrio: Homeboys and homegirls in change*. Philadelphia: Temple University Press.

Moore, J. (1993). Gangs, drugs, and violence. In S. Cummings & D.J. Monti (Eds.), *Gangs: The origins and impact of contemporary youth gangs in the United States* (pp. 27–46). Albany, NY: SUNY Press.

Morash, M. (1984). The establishment of a juvenile police record: The influence of individual and peer group characteristics. *Criminology, 22*, 97–112.

Morgan, E., Salomon, N., Plotkin, M., & Cohen, R. (2014). *The school discipline consensus report: Strategies from the field to keep students engaged in school and out of the juvenile justice system*. New York: The Council of State Governments Justice Center.

Morin, R., Parker, K., Stepler, R., & Mercer, A. (2017). *Behind the badge: What police think about their jobs*. Washington, DC: Pew Research Center. Retrieved from www.pewresearchcenter.org.

Morrow, W.J., Nuno, L.E., & Mulvey, P. (2018). Examining situational and suspect predictors of police use of force among a juvenile arrestee population. *Justice Policy Journal, 15*, 1–22.

Morse, S. (1999). Delinquency and desert. *Annals of the American Academy of Political and Social Science, 564*, 56–80.

Muhammad, D. (2019). *A positive youth justice system*. Oakland, CA: National Institute for Criminal Justice Reform. Retrieved from www.nicjr.org.

Muller, C., Sampson, R.J., & Winter, A.S. (2018). Environmental inequality: The social causes and consequences of lead exposure. *Annual Review of Sociology, 44*(1), 263–282. DOI: http://dx.doi.org/10.1146/annurev-soc-073117-041222.

Mulvey, E.P., & Schubert, C.A. (2012). *Transfer of juveniles to adult court: Effects of a broad policy change in one court*. Washington, DC: Office of Juvenile Justice and Delinquency Prevention.

Mulvey, E.P., Schubert, C.A., & Chassin, L. (2010). *Substance use and delinquent behavior among serious adolescent offenders*. Washington, DC: Office of Juvenile Justice and Delinquency Prevention.

Mumola, C.J. (2005). *Suicide and homicide in state prisons and local jails*. Bureau of Justice Statistics Special Report. Washington, DC: U.S. Department of Justice.

Murphy, D., & Lutze, F. (2009). Police–probation partnerships: Professional identity and the sharing of coercive power. *Journal of Criminal Justice, 37*, 65–76.

Nadelmann, E.A. (2004). Criminologists and punitive drug prohibition: To serve or to challenge? Reaction essay. *Criminology & Public Policy, 3*, 441–450.

Nagin, D.S., & Telep, C.W. (2020). Procedural justice and legal compliance: A revisionist perspective. *Criminology & Public Policy, 19*, 761–786.

Najdowski, C.J., & Weintraub, J.N. (2020). Juror gender and confession evidence: An exploratory study of effects on empathy and trial outcomes. *Journal of Experimental Criminology, 16*, 595–606.

Nassi, A., & Abramowitz, S.I. (1976). From phrenology to psychosurgery and back again: Biological studies of criminality. *American Journal of Orthopsychiatry, 46*, 591–607.

National Association of Youth Courts. (2020). *Youth courts*. Baltimore: National Association of Youth Courts. Retrieved from www.youthcourt.net.

National CASA. (2017). *Court appointed special advocates for children*. Retrieved from www.casaforchildren.org.

National CASA. (2021). *State and local programs*. Retrieved from https://nationalcasagal.org/our-work/programs/.

National Center for Biotechnology Information. (2010). *Antisocial personality disorder*. Retrieved from www.ncbi.nlm.nih.gov/pubmedhealth/PMH0001919.

National Center for Juvenile Justice. (2017). *Juvenile justice: Geography, policy, practice & statistics website*. Retrieved from www.jjgps.org/juvenile-court.

National Children's Alliance. (2019). *One voice, stronger: Annual report 2019*.Retrieved from www.nationalchildrensalliance.org/wp-content/uploads/2020/04/AR2019-web.pdf.

National Conference of State Legislatures. (1993). *1993 state legislature summary*. Washington, DC: National Conference of State Legislatures.

National Conference of State Legislatures. (2015). *Trends in juvenile justice state legislation 2011–2015*. Retrieved from www.ncsl.org.

National Conference of State Legislatures. (2021). *Juvenile justice 2020 year-end report*. Retrieved from www.ncsl.org.

National Council on Crime and Delinquency. (1987). *The impact of juvenile court sanctions: A court that works—Executive summary*. San Francisco: National Council on Crime and Delinquency.

National Drug Court Resource Center. (2017). Home page. Retrieved from www.ndcrc.org.

National Gang Center. (2017). *National Youth Gang Survey analysis*. Retrieved June 5, 2017 from www.nationalgangcenter.gov/Survey-Analysis.

National Gang Center. (2021). *Frequently asked questions*. Retrieved from https://nationalgan gcenter.ojp.gov/about/faq#faq-1-what-is-a-gang.

National Gang Intelligence Center. (2015). *National Gang Report, 2015*. Retrieved May 20, 2017 from www.fbi.gov/file-repository/national-gang-report-2015.pdf/view.

National Highway Traffic Safety Administration (NHTSA), Governors Highway Safety Association, & the Volpe National Transportation Systems Center. (2017, June). *Impact of the legalization and decriminalization of marijuana on the DWI system: Highlights from the expert panel meeting* (Report No. DOT HS 812 430). Washington, DC: NHTSA.

National Institute for Criminal Justice Reform. (2021). *A framework for transforming police*. Oakland, CA: National Institute for Criminal Justice Reform. Retrieved from www. nicjr.org.

National Institute on Drug Abuse (NIDA). (1999). *Principles of drug addiction treatment: A research-based guide*. Washington, DC: National Institute on Drug Abuse.

National Institute on Drug Abuse (NIDA). (2011). *Lessons from prevention research*. Washington, DC: National Institute on Drug Abuse.

National Institute on Drug Abuse (NIDA). (2014). *Lessons from prevention research*. Washington, DC: U.S. Department of Health and Human Services, National Institutes of Health.

National Institute on Drug Abuse (NIDA). (2018). *Treatment approaches for drug addiction drug facts*. Washington, DC: U.S. Department of Health and Human Services, National Institutes of Health. Retrieved from www.drugabuse.gov.

National Institute on Drug Abuse (NIDA). (2021). Retrieved from www.drugabuse.gov.

National Juvenile Defender Center. (2017). *Access denied: A national snapshot of states' failure to protect children's right to counsel*. Washington, DC: National Juvenile Defender Center.

National Juvenile Defender Center. (2020). *Broken contracts: Reimagining hi-quality representation of youth in contract and appointed counsel systems*. Washington, DC: National Juvenile Defender Center.

National School Boards Association. (2013, June 12). Advocacy groups file DOJ complaint claiming truancy enforcement at Dallas area districts violates civil rights of disabled and LEP students. *San Francisco Chronicle*. Retrieved from http://legalclips.nsba.org/ 2013/06/20/advocacy-groups-file-doj-complaint-claiming-truancy-enforcement-at-dal las-area-districts-violates-civil-rights-of-disabled-and-lep-students.

National Youth Gang Center. (2014). *National Youth Gang Survey analysis*. Washington, DC: Office of Juvenile Justice and Delinquency Prevention.

Nellis, A. (2009). *Back on track: Supporting youth reentry from out-of-home placement to the community*. Washington, DC: Juvenile Justice and Delinquency Prevention Coalition, The Sentencing Project.

Nellis, A. (2012). *The lives of juvenile lifers: Findings from a national survey*. Washington, DC: The Sentencing Project.

Nellis, A. (2016). *The color of justice: Racial and ethnic disparity in state prisons*. Washington, DC: The Sentencing Project.

Nellis, A. (2017). *Still life: America's increasing use of life and long-term sentences*. Washington, DC: The Sentencing Project.

Nellis, A. (2021). *No end in sight: America's enduring reliance on Life imprisonment*. Washington, DC: The Sentencing Project.

Nelson, E.J. (2011). Custodial strip searches of juveniles: How Safford informs a two-tiered standard of review. *Boston College Law Review, 52*, 339–374.

Newman, D.J. (1986). *Introduction to criminal justice* (3rd ed.). New York: Random House.

Newman, H.H., Freeman, F.H., & Holzinger, K.J. (1937). *Twins: A study of heredity and environment*. Chicago, IL: University of Chicago Press.

Nicholl, C.G. (1999). *Community policing, community justice, and restorative justice: Exploring the links for the delivery of a balanced approach to public safety*. Washington, DC: Office of Community Oriented Policing Services.

Niederhoffer, A. (1967). *Behind the shield: The police in urban society*. Garden City, NY: Anchor Books.

Nix, J., Campbell, B.A., Byers, E.H., & Alpert, G.P. (2017). A bird's eye view of civilians killed by police in 2015. *Criminology & Public Policy, 16*, 309–340.

Novak, K.J., Frank, J., Smith, B.W., & Engel, R.S. (2002). Revisiting the decision to arrest: Comparing beat and community officers. *Crime & Delinquency, 48*, 70–98.

Nugent, W.R., Umbreit, M.S., Wiinamaki, L., & Paddock, J. (1999). Participation in victim-offender mediation and severity of subsequent delinquent behavior: Successful replications? *Journal of Research in Social Work Practice, 11*, 5–23.

Nurco, D.N., Kinlock, T.W., Hanlon, T.E., & Ball, J.C. (1988). Nonnarcotic drug use over an addiction career: A study of heroin addicts in Baltimore and New York City. *Comprehensive Psychiatry, 29*, 450–459.

O'Brien, D.M. (1997). *Constitutional law and politics* (Vol. 2) (3rd ed.). New York: W.W. Norton.

O'Brien, R.M. (1985). *Crime and victimization data*. Beverly Hills: Sage.

Office of Justice Programs. (2000). *Promising strategies to reduce substance abuse*. Washington, DC: Office of Justice Programs.

Office of Juvenile Justice and Delinquency Prevention (OJJDP). (2011). *Statistical briefing book*. Retrieved from www.ojjdp.gov/ojstatbb.

Office of Juvenile Justice and Delinquency Prevention (OJJDP). (2017). *OJJDP statistical briefing book*. Retrieved from www.ojjdp.gov/ojstatbb.

Office of Juvenile Justice and Delinquency Prevention (OJJDP). (2018). *Statistical briefing book*. Retrieved from www.ojjdp.gov/ojstatbb/.

Office of Juvenile Justice and Delinquency Prevention (OJJDP). (2021). *Statistical briefing book* (SSB). Washington, DC: OJJDP. Retrieved from www.ojjdp.gov.

Ohio Revised Code. (2017). Retrieved from http://codes.ohio.gov/orc.

Olds, D., Eckenrode, J., Henderson, C.R., Kizman, H., Powers, J., Cole, R., Petitt, L., Sidora, K., Morris, P., & Luckey, D.W. (1997). Long-term effects of nurse home visitation on maternal life course and child abuse and neglect: 15-year follow-up of a randomized controlled trial. *JAMA, 278*, 637–643.

Olds, D., Henderson, C.R., Cole, R., Eckenrode, J., Kitzman, H., Luckey, D., Petitt, L., Sidora, K., Morris, P., & Powers, J. (1998). Long-term effects of nurse home visitation on children's criminal and antisocial behavior: 15-year follow-up of a randomized controlled trial. *JAMA, 280*, 1238–1244.

Olive, P., Keen, J., Rowse, G., Ewins, E., Griffiths, L., & Mathers, N. (2010). The effect of time spent in treatment and dropout status on rates of convictions, citations and imprisonment over 5 years in a primary care-led methadone maintenance service. *Addiction, 105,* 732–739.

Olweus, D. (1993). Victimization by peers: Antecedents and long-term outcomes. In K.H. Rubin & J.B. Asendorf (Eds.), *Social withdrawal, inhibition, and shyness* (pp. 315–341). Hillsdale, NJ: Erlbaum.

Olweus, D. (1994). Bullying at school: Basic facts and effects of a school-based intervention program. *Journal of Child Psychology and Psychiatry and Allied Disciplines, 35,* 1171–1190.

Olweus, D. (1995). Bullying or peer abuse at school: Facts and intervention. *Current Directions in Psychological Science, 4,* 196–200.

Olweus, D., & Limber, S. (2000). *Bullying Prevention Program: Blueprints for violence prevention.* Boulder, CO: Institute of Behavioral Science.

Ott, B. (2005, July 26). *School prayer: Teen support hinges on type.* Gallup Poll Tuesday briefing, 1–2. Retrieved from https://news.gallup.com/poll/17494/school-prayer-teen-support-hinges-type.aspx.

Owen, T. (2012). The biological and the social in criminological theory. In S. Hall & S. Winslow (Eds.), *New directions in criminological theory.* New York: Routledge.

Padilla, F. (1993). The working gang. In S. Cummings & D.J. Monti (Eds.), *Gangs: The origins and impact of contemporary youth gangs in the United States* (pp. 173–192). Albany, NY: SUNY Press.

Paige, K.J. & Colder, C.R. (2020). Long-term effects of early adolescent marijuana use on attentional and inhibitory control. *Journal of Studies on Alcohol and Drugs, 81,* 164–172.

Paoline, E.A., Myers, S.M., & Worden, R.E. (2000). Police culture, individualism, and community policing: Evidence from two departments. *Justice Quarterly, 17,* 575–605.

Parent, D.G. (2003). *Correctional boot camps: Lessons from a decade of research.* Washington, DC: National Institute of Justice.

Parsloe, P. (1978). *Juvenile justice in Britain and the U.S.: The balance of needs and rights.* London: Routledge and Kegan Paul.

Paschall, M.J., Grube, J.W., & Biglan, A. (2017). Medical marijuana legalization and marijuana use among youth in Oregon. *Journal of Primary Prevention, 38,* 329–341.

Passini, S. (2012). The delinquency–drug relationship: The influence of social reputation and moral disengagement. *Addictive Behaviors, 37,* 577–579.

Patton, D.U., Eschmann, R.D., Elsaesser, C., & Bocanegra, E. (2016). Sticks, stones and Facebook accounts: What violence outreach workers know about social media and urban-based gang violence in Chicago. *Computers in Human Behavior, 65,* 591–600.

Patton, D., Eschmann, R., & Butler, D. (2013). Internet banging: New trends in social media, gang violence, masculinity and hip hop. *Computers in Human Behavior, 29.* A54–A59. 10.1016/j.chb.2012.12.035.

Pealer, J.A. (2017). *Correctional rehabilitation and therapeutic communities: Reducing recidivism through behavior change.* New York: Routledge.

Pealer, J., Terry, A.N., & Adams, K.R. (2017). Voices from inside the walls: Views of the juvenile justice system from the youthful offenders. *Corrections: Policy, Practice, and Research, 2,* 130–147.

Pearson, D.A.S., McDougall, C., Kanaan, M., Bowles, A., & Torgerson, D.J. (2011). Reducing criminal recidivism: Evaluation of citizenship, an evidence-based probation supervision process. *Journal of Experimental Criminology, 7,* 73–102.

Petersilia, J. (1997). Probation in the United States. In M. Tonry (Ed.), *Crime and justice: A review of research* (Vol. 22, pp. 149–200). Chicago, IL: University of Chicago Press.

Phillips, M.D. (2012). Assessing the impact of drug use and drug selling on violent offending in a panel of delinquent. *Journal of Drug Issues, 42*, 298–316.

Phillips, M.D. (2017). A factor analytic model of drug-related behavior in adolescence and its impact on arrests at multiple states of the life course. *Journal of Quantitative Criminology, 33*, 131–155.

Piquero, A.R. (2008). Disproportionate minority contact. *The Future of Children, 18*, 59–79.

Piquero, A.R., & Jennings, W.G. (2017). Research note: Justice system-imposed financial penalties increase the likelihood of recidivism in a sample of adolescent offenders. *Youth Violence & Juvenile Justice, 15*, 325–340.

Piquero, A.R., Farrington, D.P., Welsh, B.C., Tremblay, R., & Jennings, W.G. (2009). Effect of early family/parent training programs on antisocial behavior and delinquency. *Journal of Experimental Criminology, 5*, 83–120.

Piquero, A.R., MacIntosh, R., & Hickman, M. (2000). Does self-control affect survey response? *Criminology, 38*, 897–930.

Piquero, N.L., Langton, L., & Schoepfer, A. (2008). *Completely out of control or the desire to be in complete control? An examination of low self-control and the desire-for-control.* Unpublished.

Pisciotta, A.W. (1979). *The theory and practice of the New York house of refuge, 1857–1935.* Unpublished PhD dissertation, Florida State University.

Pisciotta, A.W. (1982). Saving the children: The promise and practice of *parens patriae*, 1838–1898. *Crime & Delinquency, 28*, 410–425.

Pisciotta, A.W. (1983). Race, sex and rehabilitation: A study of differential treatment in the juvenile reformatory, 1825–1900. *Crime & Delinquency, 29*, 254–269.

Platt, A.M. (1977). *The child savers: The invention of delinquency.* Chicago, IL: University of Chicago Press.

Podolsky, E. (1964). The chemistry of murder. *Pakistan Medical Journal, 15*, 9–14.

Poole, E.D., & Regoli, R.M. (1979). Parental support, delinquent friends and delinquency. *Journal of Criminal Law and Criminology, 70*, 188–193.

Pope, C.E., & Snyder, H.N. (2003). *Race as a factor in juvenile arrests.* Washington, DC: U.S. Department of Justice.

Pratt, T., & Cullen, F.T. (2000). The empirical status of Gottfredson and Hirschi's general theory of crime: A meta-analysis. *Criminology, 38*, 931–964.

Prescott, P.S. (1981). *The child savers: Juvenile justice observed.* New York: Knopf.

President's Commission on Law Enforcement and the Administration of Justice. (1967). *The challenge of crime in a free society.* Washington, DC: United States Government Printing Office. Retrieved from www.ncjrs.gov/pdffiles1/nij/42.pdf.

President's Task Force on 21st Century Policing (2015). *Final report of the President's task force on 21st century policing.* Washington, DC: Office of Community Oriented Policing Services.

Propper, A.M. (1982). Make-believe families and homosexuality among imprisoned girls. *Criminology, 20*, 127–138.

Puritz, P., Burrell, S., Schwartz, R., Soler, M., & Warboys, L. (1995). *A call for justice: An assessment of access to counsel and quality of representation in delinquency proceedings.* Washington, DC: American Bar Association Juvenile Justice Center.

Putnam, R.D. (2000). *Bowling alone: The collapse and revival of American community.* New York: Simon & Schuster.

Puzzanchera, C. (2020). *Juvenile arrests, 2018.* Washington, DC: U.S. Department of Justice.

Puzzanchera, C. (2021). *Juvenile arrests, 2019.* Washington, DC: U.S. Department of Justice.

Pyrooz, D.C. (2013). Gangs, criminal offending, and an inconvenient truth: Considerations for gang prevention and intervention in the lives of youth. *Criminology & Public Policy, 12*, 427–436.

Pyrooz, D.C. (2014). From your first cigarette to your last dyin' day: The pattern of gang membership in the life course. *Journal of Quantitative Criminology, 30,* 349–372.

Pyrooz, D.C., Decker, S.H., & Moule, R.K. (2015). Criminal and routine activities in online settings: Gangs, offenders, and the internet. *Justice Quarterly, 32,* 471–499.

Pyrooz, D.C., Decker, S.H., Wolfe, S.E., & Shjarback, A. (2016). Was there a Ferguson Effect on crime rates in large U.S. cities? *Journal of Criminal Justice, 46,* 1–8.

Quaranta, K. (2021). California to phase out Division of Juvenile Justice, creating an opportunity for substantial reform. *KOLD News13.* Retrieved from www.KOLD.com.

Rada, R.T., Laws, D.R., & Kellner, R. (1976). Plasma testosterone levels in the rapist. *Psychosomatic Medicine, 38,* 257–268.

Raine, A. (1993). *The psychopathology of crime: Criminal behavior as a clinical disorder.* San Diego: Academic Press.

Raine, A. (2008). From genes to brain to antisocial behavior. *Current Directions in Psychological Science, 17,* 323–328.

Raine, A. (2013). *The anatomy of violence: The biological roots of crime.* New York: Pantheon.

Raine, A., Venables, P.H., & Williams, M. (1995). High autonomic arousal and electrodermal orienting at age 15 years as protective factors against criminal behavior at age 29 years. *American Journal of Psychiatry, 152,* 1595–1600.

Rasmussen, A. (2004). Teen court referral, sentencing, and subsequent recidivism: Two proportional hazards models and a little speculation. *Crime & Delinquency, 50,* 615–635.

Ray, B., & Richardson, N.J. (2017). Traumatic brain injury and recidivism among returning inmates. *Criminal Justice and Behavior, 44,* 472–486.

Reading Eagle (2008, January 26). *Berks County juveniles pay off fines by serving community.* Retrieved from www2.readingeagle.com/article.aspx?id=77795.

Reckless, W.C. (1962). A non-causal explanation: Containment theory. *Excerpta Criminologica, 1,* 131–134.

Reckless, W.C. (1967). *The crime problem.* New York: Appleton, Century, Crofts.

Redding, R.E. (2010). *Juvenile transfer laws: An effective deterrent to delinquency?* OJJDP Juvenile Justice Bulletin. Washington, DC: Office of Juvenile Justice and Delinquency Prevention.

Reidy, T.J., Sorensen, J.R., & Cihan, A. (2018). Institutional misconduct among juvenile offenders serving a blended sentence. *Journal of Criminal Justice, 57,* 99–105.

Reinart, R.J. (2020). *Nurses continue to rate highest in honesty, ethics.* Retrieved from www.news.gallup.com.

Reiss, A.J., Jr., & Rhodes, A.L. (1961). The distribution of juvenile delinquency in the social class structure. *American Sociological Review, 26,* 720–732.

Reiss, A.J., Jr., & Roth, J.A. (1993). *Understanding and preventing violence* (Vol. 1). Washington, DC: National Academy Press.

Reynolds, K.M., Seydlitz, R., & Jenkins, P. (2000). Do juvenile curfew laws work? A timeseries analysis of the New Orleans law. *Justice Quarterly, 17,* 205–230.

Rhee, S.H., & Waldman, I.D. (2012). Genetic and environmental influences on antisocial behavior: A meta-analysis of twin and adoption studies. *Psychological Bulletin, 128,* 490–529.

Rhodes, J.E. (2008). Improving youth mentoring interventions through research-based practice. *American Journal of Community Psychology, 41,* 35–42.

Riffkin, R. (2014, September 25). *In U.S., support for daily prayer dips slightly.* Retrieved from www.gallup.com.

Ringwalt, C.L., Ennett, S.T., & Holt, K.D. (1991). An outcome evaluation of project D.A.R.E. *Health Education Research: Theory and Practice, 6,* 327–337.

Ringwalt, C.L., Messerschmidt, P., Graham, L., & Collins, J. (1992). *Youth's victimization experiences, fear of attack or harm, and school avoidance behaviors: Final report.* Washington, DC: National Institute of Justice.

Robin, G.D. (1967). Gang member delinquency in Philadelphia. In M.W. LeKlein (Ed.), *Juvenile gangs in context* (pp. 15–24). Englewood Cliffs, NJ: Prentice Hall.

Robin, G.D. (1982). Juvenile interrogations and confessions. *Journal of Police Science and Administration, 10,* 224–228.

Rocca, G., Verde, A., & Gatti, U. (2019). Impact of alcohol and cannabis use on juvenile delinquency: Results from an international multi-city study. *European Journal on Criminal Policy and Research, 25,* 259–271.

Rodgers, A., & Dunsmuir, S. (2015). A controlled evaluation of the "FRIENDS for Life" emotional resiliency programme on overall anxiety levels, anxiety subtype levels and school adjustment. *Child and Adolescent Mental Health, 20,* 13–19.

Rodriguez, N. (2005). Restorative justice, communities, and delinquency: Whom do we reintegrate? *Criminology & Public Policy, 4,* 103–130.

Rodriguez, N. (2007). Restorative justice at work: Examining the impact of restorative justice resolutions on juvenile recidivism. *Crime & Delinquency, 53,* 355–379.

Rodriguez, N. (2010). The cumulative effect of race and ethnicity in juvenile court outcomes and why preadjudication detentions matters. *Journal of Research in Crime and Delinquency, 47,* 391–413.

Rojek, D.G., & Erickson, M.L. (1982). Juvenile diversion: A study of community cooptation. In D.G. Rojek & G.F. Jensen (Eds.), *Readings in juvenile delinquency* (pp. 316–321). Lexington, MA: D.C. Heath.

Roncek, D.W., & Maier, P.A. (1991). Bars, blocks, and crimes revisited: Linking the theory of routine activities to the empiricism of "hot spots." *Criminology, 29,* 725–753.

Roodbeen, R.T.J., Kruize, A., Bieleman, B., Friele, R., van de Mheen, D., & Schelleman-Offermans, K. (2020). The right time and place: A new approach for prioritizing alcohol enforcement and prevention efforts by combining the prevalence and the success rate for minors purchasing alcohol themselves. *Journal of Studies on Alcohol and Drugs, 81,* 719–724.

Rosenbaum, D.P. (2007). Just say no to D.A.R.E. *Criminology & Public Policy, 6,* 815–824.

Rosenbaum, D.P., & Hanson, G.S. (1998). Assessing the effects of school-based drug education: A six-year multilevel analysis of project D.A.R.E. *Journal of Research in Crime and Delinquency, 35,* 381–412.

Rosenbaum, D.P., Flewelling, R.L., Bailey, S.L., Ringwalt, C.L., & Wilkinson, D.L. (1994). Cops in the classroom: A longitudinal evaluation of Drug Abuse Resistance Education (DARE). *Journal of Research in Crime and Delinquency, 31,* 3–31.

Rosenberg, I.M. (2008). Gault turns 40: Reflections on ambiguity. *Criminal Law Bulletin, 44,* 330–354.

Rossman, S.B., Butts, J.A., Roman, J., DeStefano, C., & White, R. (2004). What juvenile drug courts do and how they do it. In J.A. Butts & J. Roman (Eds.), *Juvenile drug courts and teen substance abuse* (pp. 55–106). Washington, DC: Urban Institute Press.

Rossow, L.F., & Parkinson, J.R. (1994). Yet another student strip search: *Cornfield by Lewis v. Consolidated High School District No. 230. School Law Reporter, 36*(3), 1–2.

Rossum, R.A., Koller, B.J., & Manfredi, C.P. (1987). *Juvenile justice reform: A model for the states.* Clairmont, CA: Rose Institute of State and Local Government and the American Legislative Exchange.

Roth, J.J. (2013). Commentary: Place-based delinquency prevention—Issues and recommendations. *OJJDP Journal of Juvenile Justice, 3,* 110–119.

Rothman, D.J. (1971). *The discovery of the asylum: Social order and disorder in the new republic.* Boston: Little, Brown.

Rothman, D.J. (1980). *Conscience and convenience: The asylum and its alternatives in progressive America*. Boston: Little, Brown.

Roush, D.M., & McMillen, M. (2000). *Construction, operations, and staff training for juvenile confinement facilities*. Washington, DC: Office of Juvenile Justice and Delinquency Prevention.

Rovner, J. (2016a). *How tough on crime became tough on kids: Prosecuting teenage drug charges in adult court*. Washington, DC: The Sentencing Project.

Rovner, J. (2016b). *Racial disparities in youth commitments and arrests*. Washington, DC: The Sentencing Project.

Rovner, J. (2021a). *Racial disparities in youth incarceration persist*. Washington, DC: The Sentencing Project. Retrieved from www.sentencingproject.org.

Rovner, J. (2021b). *Juvenile life without parole: An overview*. Washington, DC: The Sentencing Project. Retrieved from www.sentencingproject.org.

Rowe, D.C. (2002). *Biology and crime*. Los Angeles: Roxbury.

Rubin, H.T. (1985). *Juvenile justice: Policy, practice, and law* (2nd ed.). New York: Random House.

Rubin, H.T. (2013). Juveniles in solitary confinement. *Juvenile Justice Update, 19*, 1–10.

Russell, S.F. (2015). Jury sentencing and juveniles: Eighth Amendment limits and Sixth Amendment rights. *Boston College Law Review, 56*, 553–616.

Ryan, C.M. (1987). Juvenile court jurisdiction: Intervention and intrusion. In F.X. Hartmann (Ed.), *From children to citizens: Volume II: The role of the juvenile court* (pp. 56–64). New York: Springer-Verlag.

Ryan, J.P., Abrams, L.S., & Huang, H. (2014). First-time violent juvenile offenders: Probation, placement, and recidivism. *Social Work Research, 38*, 7–18.

Ryerson, E. (1978). *The best-laid plans: America's juvenile court experiment*. New York: Hill and Wang.

Ryon, S.B., Devers, L., Early, K.W., & Hand, G.A. (2012). Changing how the system responds to status offenders: Connecticut's families with service needs initiative. *Juvenile and Family Court Journal, 63*, 37–46.

Ryon, S.B., Early, K.W., Hand, G., & Chapman, S. (2013). Juvenile justice interventions: System escalation and effective alternatives to residential placement. *Journal of Offender Rehabilitation, 52*, 358–375.

Sagatun, I.J., & Edwards, L.P. (1995). *Child abuse and the legal system*. Chicago, IL: Nelson-Hall.

Salsich, A., & Trone, J. (2013). *From courts to communities: The right response to truancy, running away, and other status offenses*. New York: Vera Institute of Justice.

SAMHSA. (2004). *Graduated driver licensing and drinking among young drivers*. Washington, DC: Substance Abuse and Mental Health Services Administration. Retrieved from www.drugabusestatistics.samhsa.gov.

SAMHSA. (2012). *Incredible years*. Retrieved from www.nrepp.samhsa.gov/ViewIntervention.aspx?id=93#std174.

SAMHSA. (2020). *Key substance use and mental health indicators in the United States: Results from the 2019 National Survey on Drug Use and Health*. Rockville, MD: SAMHSA. Retrieved from www.samhsa.gov/data.

Samples, F., & Aber, L. (1998). Evaluations of school-based violence prevention programs. In D.S. Elliott, D.P. Farrington, & K.R. Williams (Eds.), *Violence in American schools*. Cambridge, England: Cambridge University Press.

Sampson, R.J. (1986). Effects of socioeconomic context on official reaction to juvenile delinquency. *American Sociological Review, 51*, 876–885.

Sampson, R.J., & Laub, J. (2003). Life-course desisters? Trajectories of crime among delinquent boys followed to age 70. *Criminology, 41*, 555–592.

Sampson, R.J., & Laub, J.H. (1993). *Crime in the making: Pathways and turning points through life*. Cambridge, MA: Harvard University Press.

Sampson, R.J., & Lauritsen, J. (1994). Violent victimization and offending: Individual-, situational-, and community-level risk factors. In A.J. Reiss & J.A. Roth (Eds.), *Understanding and preventing violence: Vol. 3. Social influences*. Washington, DC: National Academy Press.

Sampson, R.J., Raudenbush, S.W., & Earls, F. (1997). Neighborhood and violent crime: A multilevel study of collective efficacy. *Science, 277*, 918–924.

Sanborn, J. (2001). A parens patriae figure or impartial fact finder: Policy questions and conflicts for the juvenile court judge. *Criminal Justice Policy Review, 12*, 311–332.

Sanders, W.B. (1994). *Gangbangs and drive-bys: Grounded culture and juvenile gang violence*. New York: Aldine de Gruyter.

Sante, L. (1991). *Low life: Lures and snares of old New York*. New York: Vintage Books.

Saunders, J., Midgette, G., Taylor, J., & Faraji, S. (2021). A hidden cost of convenience: Disparate impacts of a program to reduce burden on probation officers and participants. *Criminology & Public Policy, 20*, 71–122.

Schaffner, L. (2006). *Girls in trouble with the law*. New Brunswick, NJ: Rutgers University Press.

Schaps, E., Moskowitz, J.M., Malvin, J.H., & Schaeffer, G.A. (1986). Evaluation of seven school-based prevention programs: A final report of the Napa project. *International Journal of the Addictions, 21*, 1081–1112.

Schauss, A.G. (1980). *Diet, crime and delinquency*. Berkeley, CA: Parker House.

Schiff, A. (1999). The impact of restorative interventions on juvenile offenders. In G. Bazemore & L. Walgrave (Eds.), *Restorative juvenile justice: Repairing the harm of youth crime*. Monsey, NY: Criminal Justice Press.

Schlossman, S.L. (1977). *Love and the American delinquent: The theory and practice of "progressive" juvenile justice, 1825–1920*. Chicago, IL: University of Chicago Press.

Schnebly, S.M. (2008). The influence of community-oriented policing on crime-reporting behavior. *Justice Quarterly, 25*, 223–251.

Schneider, A.L. (1985). *The impact of deinstitutionalization on recidivism and secure confinement of status offenders*. Washington, DC: U.S. Department of Justice.

Schneider, A.L. (1988). A comparative analysis of juvenile court responses to drug and alcohol offenses. *Crime & Delinquency, 34*, 103–124.

Schneider, A.L., & Schram, D.D. (1986). The Washington State juvenile justice reform: A review of findings. *Criminal Justice Policy Review, 2*, 211–235.

Schneider, M.E. (2008). HIV rates are low in high-risk adolescent group studied. *Pediatric News, 42*, 10.

Schubert, C.A., & Mulvey, E.P. (2014). *Behavioral health problems, treatment, and outcomes in serious youthful offenders*. Washington, DC: Office of Juvenile Justice and Delinquency Prevention.

Schwadel, P. (2013). Changes in Americans' views of prayer and reading the Bible in public schools: Time periods, birth cohorts, and religious traditions. *Sociological Forum, 28*, 261–282.

Schwalbe, C.S. (2012). Toward an integrated theory of probation. *Criminal Justice and Behavior, 39*, 185–201.

Schwartz, R.G. (2018). A 21st century developmentally appropriate juvenile probation approach. *Juvenile and Family Court Journal, 69*, 41–54.

Schwartz, I.M., Fishman, G., Rawson Hatfield, R., Krisberg, B.A., & Eisikovits, Z. (1987). Juvenile detention: The hidden closets revisited. *Justice Quarterly, 4*, 219–235.

Schwartz, M.D. (1989). Family violence as a cause of crime: Rethinking our priorities. *Criminal Justice Policy Review, 3,* 115–132.

Schweinhart, L.J. (1987). Can preschool programs help prevent delinquency? In J.Q. Wilson & G.C. Lowrey (Eds.), *From children to citizens. Vol. 3. Families, schools and delinquency prevention* (pp. 135–153). New York: Springer-Verlag.

Schweinhart, L.J., Barnes, H.V., & Weikart, D.P. (1993). *Significant benefits.* Ypsilanti, MI: High/Scope Press.

Sealock, M.D., Gottfredson, D.C., & Gallagher, C.A. (1997). Delinquency and social reform: A radical perspective. In L. Empey (Ed.), *Juvenile justice* (pp. 245–290). Charlottesville: University of Virginia Press.

Sedlak, A.J. (2016). *Survey of youth in residential placement: Conditions of confinement. SYRP Report.* Rockville, MD: Westat.

Sedlak, A.J., & Bruce, C. (2010). *Youth's characteristics and backgrounds: Findings from the survey of youth in residential placement.* Washington, DC: U.S. Department of Justice.

Sedlak, A.J., & Bruce, C. (2016). *Survey of youth in residential placement: Youth characteristics and backgrounds. SYRP Report.* Rockville, MD: Westat.

Sedlak, A.J., & McPherson, K.S. (2010a). *Conditions of confinement: Findings from the survey of youth in residential placement.* Washington, DC: U.S. Department of Justice.

Sedlak, A.J., & McPherson, K.S. (2010b). *Youth's needs and services: Findings from the survey of youth in residential placement.* Washington, DC: U.S. Department of Justice.

Sedlak, A.J., McPherson, K.S., & Basena, M. (2013). *Nature and risk of victimization: Findings from the survey of youth in residential placement.* Washington, DC: Office of Juvenile Justice and Delinquency Prevention.

Seffrin, P.M., & Domahidi, B.I. (2014). The drugs–violence nexus: A systematic comparison of adolescent drug dealers and users. *Journal of Drug Issues, 44,* 394–413.

Sells, S.B., & Simpson, D.D. (1979). Evaluation of treatment outcomes for youths in the drug abuse reporting program (DARP): A follow-up study. In G.M. Beschner & A.S. Friedman (Eds.), *Youth drug abuse* (pp. 571–628). Lexington, MA: Lexington Books.

Sentencing Project. (2018). *Report to the United Nations on racial disparities in the U.S. criminal justice system.* Washington, DC: The Sentencing Project. Retrieved from www.sentencingproject.org.

Shah, S.A., & Roth, L.H. (1974). Biological and psychophysiological factors in criminality. In D. Glaser (Ed.), *Handbook of criminology* (pp. 101–173). New York: Rand McNally.

Shane, C. (2019, November 13). *Kids, the cops may not be setting your curfew for long.* Retrieved from www.ozy,com.

Shannon, L.W. (1982). *Assessing the relationship of adult criminal careers to juvenile careers.* Iowa City: Iowa Urban Community Research Center.

Shannon, L.W. (1991). *Changing patterns of delinquency and crime: A longitudinal study in Racine.* Boulder, CO: Westview.

Shannon, S., & Hauer, M. (2018). A life table approach to estimating disproportionate minority contact in the juvenile justice system. *Justice Quarterly, 35,* 330–355.

Shaw, C.R., & McKay, H.D. (1942). *Juvenile delinquency and urban areas.* Chicago, IL: University of Chicago Press.

Shaw, C.R., Zorbaugh, F.M., McKay, H.D., & Cottrell, L.S. (1929). *Delinquency areas.* Chicago, IL: University of Chicago Press.

Sheldon, W.H. (1949). *Varieties of delinquent youth: An introduction to correctional psychiatry.* New York: Harper and Brothers.

Sheley, J.F., McGee, Z.T., & Wright, J.D. (1995). *Weapon-related victimization in selected innercity high school samples.* Washington, DC: National Institute of Justice.

Sher, G. (2003). On the decriminalization of drugs. *Criminal Justice Ethics, 22*, 30–33.

Sherman, L.W. (2020). Evidence-based policing and fatal police shootings: Promise, problems, and prospects. *Annals of the American Academy of Political and Social Science, 687*, 8–26.

Sherman, L.W., Strang, H., Mayo-Wilson, E., Woods, D.J., & Ariel, B. (2015). Are restorative justice conferences effective in reducing repeat offending? Findings from a Campbell systematic review. *Journal of Quantitative Criminology, 31*, 1–24.

Shine, J., & Price, D. (1992). Prosecutors and juvenile justice: New roles and perspectives. In I.M. Schwartz (Ed.), *Juvenile justice and public policy: Toward a national agenda* (pp. 101–133). New York: Lexington Books.

Short, J.F. (1960). Differential association as a hypothesis: Problems of empirical testing. *Social Problems, 8*, 14–25.

Short, J.F., & Nye, I. (1958). Extent of unrecorded delinquency: Tentative conclusions. *Journal of Criminal Law, Criminology and Police Science, 49*, 296–302.

Short, J.F., & Strodbeck, F.L. (1965). *Group process and gang delinquency.* Chicago, IL: University of Chicago Press.

Shufelt, J.S., & Cocozza, J.C. (2006). *Youth with mental health disorders in the juvenile justice system: Results from a multi-state prevalence study.* Delmar, NY: National Center for Mental Health and Juvenile Justice.

Sickmund, M., & Puzzanchera, C. (2014). *Juvenile offenders and victims: 2014 national report.* Pittsburgh: National Center for Juvenile Justice. Retrieved May 21, 2017 from: www.ncjj.org/pdf/NR2014.pdf.

Sickmund, M., Sladky, A., & Kang, W. (2020). *Easy access to juvenile court statistics: 1985–2018.* Online. Retrieved from www.ojjdp.gov/ojstatbb/ezajcs/.

Sickmund, M., Sladky, T.J., Kang, W., & Puzzanchera, C. (2019). *Easy access to the census of juveniles in residential placement.* Retrieved from www.ojjdp.gov/ojstatbb/ezacjrp/.

Sickmund, M., Snyder, H.N., & Poe-Yamagata, E. (1997). *Juvenile offenders and victims: 1997 update on violence.* Washington, DC: Office of Juvenile Justice and Delinquency Prevention.

Siegel, M. (2020). Racial disparities in fatal police shootings: An empirical analysis informed by critical race theory. *Boston University Law Review, 100*, 1069–1092.

Sierra-Arevalo, M., & Nix, J. (2020). Gun victimization in the line of duty: Fatal and nonfatal assaults on police officers in the United States, 2014–2019. *Criminology & Public Policy, 19*, 1041–166.

Silver, J. (2020). Space between concern and crime: Two recommendations for promoting the adoption of threat assessment model and encouraging bystander reporting. *Criminology & Public Policy, 19*, 253–270.

Simmons, T.J. (2006). Mandatory mediation: A better way to address status offenses. *Ohio State Journal of Dispute Resolution, 21*, 1–31.

Simpson, D.D., & Sells, S.B. (1982). Effectiveness of treatment for drug abuse: An overview of the DARP research program. *Advances in Alcohol and Substance Abuse, 2*, 7–29.

Singer, S.I. (1996). *Recriminalizing delinquency: Violent juvenile crime and juvenile justice reform.* New York: Cambridge University Press.

Skinner, B.F. (1953). *Science and human behavior.* New York: Macmillan.

Skogan, W.G. (1981). On attitudes and behavior. In D.A. Lewis (Ed.), *Reactions to crime.* Beverly Hills: Sage.

Skogan, W.G. (1990). *Disorder and decline: Crime and the spiral of decay in American neighborhoods.* New York: Free Press.

Skogan, W.G., & Hartnett, S.M. (1997). *Community policing, Chicago style.* New York: Oxford University Press.

Skogan, W.G., & Maxfield, M.G. (1981). *Coping with crime: Individual and neighborhood reactions.* Beverly Hills: Sage.

Skolnick, J. (1966). *Justice without trial.* New York: John Wiley and Sons.

Skolnick, J., Bluthenthal, R., & Correl, T. (1993). Gang organization and migration. In S. Cummings & D.J. Monti (Eds.), *Gangs: The origins and impact of contemporary youth gangs in the United States* (pp. 193–218). Albany, NY: SUNY Press.

Skowyra, K., & Cocozza, J.J. (2006). *A blueprint for change: Improving the system response to youth with mental health needs involved with the juvenile justice system.* National Center for Mental Health and Juvenile Justice Research and Program Brief. Delmar, NY: National Center for Mental Health and Juvenile Justice.

Smith, E.L., & Stroop, J. (2019). *Sexual victimization reported by youth in juvenile facilities, 2018.* Washington, DC: Office of Juvenile Justice and Delinquency Prevention.

Snyder, H.N., & Sickmund, M. (2006). *Juvenile offenders and victims: 2006 national report.* Pittsburgh: National Center for Juvenile Justice.

Social Development Research Group. (2012). Home page. Retrieved from www.sdrg.org.

Soler, H., Vinayak, P., & Quadagno, D. (2000). Biosocial aspects of domestic violence. *Psychoneuroendocrinology, 25,* 721–739.

Sommers, C.H. (2000). *The war against boys: How misguided feminism is harming our young men.* New York: Touchstone.

Speckart, G.R., & Anglin, M.D. (1985). Narcotics and crime: A causal modeling approach. *Journal of Quantitative Criminology, 2,* 3–28.

Spergel, I.A. (1966). *Street gang work: Theory and practice.* Reading, MA: Addison-Wesley.

Spergel, I.A. (1984). Violent gangs in Chicago: In search of social policy. *Social Service Review, 58,* 199–226.

Spergel, I.A. (1986). The violent gang problem in Chicago: A local community approach. *Social Service Review, 60,* 94–131.

Spergel, I.A., & Curry, G.D. (1993). The national youth gang survey: A research and development process. In A.P. Goldstein & C.R. Huff (Eds.), *The gang intervention handbook* (pp. 359–400). Champaign, IL: Research Press.

Spergel, I.A., Curry, G.D., Chance, R., Kane, C., Ross, R., Alexander, A., Simmons, E., & Oh, S. (1990). *National youth gang suppression and intervention program: Executive summary, stage 1: Assessment.* Arlington, VA: National Youth Gang Information Center.

Spergel, I.A., Wa, K.M., & Sosa, R.V. (2001*). Evaluation of the Bloomington-Normal comprehensive gang program—Final report.* Washington, DC: Office of Juvenile Justice and Delinquency Prevention.

Spergel, I.A., Wa, K.M., & Sosa, R.V. (2002). *Evaluation of the Mesa gang intervention program (MGIP)—Final report.* Washington, DC: Office of Juvenile Justice and Delinquency Prevention.

Spergel, I.A., Wa, K.M., & Sosa, R.V. (2003). *Evaluation of the Riverside comprehensive community-wide approach to gang prevention, intervention and suppression—Final report.* Washington, DC: Office of Juvenile Justice and Delinquency Prevention.

Spergel, I.A., Wa, K.M., & Sosa, R.V. (2004a). *Evaluation of the Tucson comprehensive community-wide approach to gang prevention, intervention and suppression: Final report.* Washington, DC: Office of Juvenile Justice and Delinquency Prevention.

Spergel, I.A., Wa, K.M., & Sosa, R.V. (2004b). *Evaluation of the San Antonio comprehensive community-wide approach to gang prevention, intervention and suppression: Final report.* Washington, DC: Office of Juvenile Justice and Delinquency Prevention.

Spinney, E., Cohen, M., Feyerherm, W., Stephenson, R., Yeide, M., & Shreve, T. (2018). Disproportionate minority contact in the U.S. juvenile justice system: A review of the DMC literature, 2001–2014, Part I. *Journal of Crime and Justice, 41,* 573–595.

Spohn, C., Piper, R.K., Martin, T., & Frenzel, E.D. (2001). Drug courts and recidivism: The results of an evaluation using two comparison groups and multiple indicators of recidivism. *Journal of Drug Issues, 31*, 149–176.

Staff, J., Osgood, D.W., Schulenberg, J.E., Bachman, J.G., & Messersmith, E.E. (2010). Explaining the relationship between employment and juvenile delinquency. *Criminology, 48*, 1101–1131.

Stallard, P., Simpson, N., Anderson, S., Carter, T., Osborn, C., & Bush, S. (2005). An evaluation of the FRIENDS programme: A cognitive behaviour therapy intervention to promote emotional resilience. *Archives of Disease in Childhood, 90*, 1016–1019.

Staples, J.S. (2000). Violence in schools: Rage against a broken world. *Annals of the American Academy of Political and Social Science, 567*, 30–41.

Staples, W.G. (1987). Law and social control in juvenile justice dispositions. *Journal of Research in Crime and Delinquency, 24*, 7–22.

Starbuck, D., Howell, J.C., & Lindquist, D.J. (2001). *Hybrid and other modern gangs*. OJJDP Juvenile Justice Bulletin. Washington, DC: Office of Juvenile Justice and Delinquency Prevention.

Steele, B.F., & Pollock, C.B. (1974). A psychiatric study of parents who abuse infants and small children. In R.E. Helfer & C.H. Kempe (Eds.), *The battered child* (2nd ed.; pp. 80–133). Chicago, IL: University of Chicago Press.

Stein, D.M., Deberard, S., & Homan, K. (2013). Predicting success and failure in juvenile drug treatment court: A meta-analytic review. *Journal of Substance Abuse Treatment, 44*, 159–168.

Steiner, B., & Wright, E. (2006). Assessing the relative effects of state direct file waiver laws on violent juvenile crime: Deterrence or irrelevance? *Journal of Criminal Law and Criminology, 96*, 1451–1477.

Steinke, C.M., & Martin, E.M. (2014). Status offenders and delinquent youth: Actual or artificial taxonomy. *Child Welfare, 93*, 71–90.

Stephens, R.C. (1987). *Mind-altering drugs: Use, abuse, and treatment*. Newbury Park, CA: Sage.

Stephens, R.D., & Arnette, J.L. (2000). *From the courthouse to the schoolhouse: Making successful transitions*. Washington, DC: Office of Juvenile Justice and Delinquency Prevention.

Stevens, J., May, D., Rice, N., & Jarjoura, G.R. (2011). Nonsocial versus social reinforcers: Contrasting theoretical perspectives on repetitive serious delinquency and drug use. *Youth Violence and Juvenile Justice, 9*, 295–312.

Stimson, C.D., & Grossman, A.M. (2009). *Adult time for adult crimes: Life without parole for juvenile killers and violent teens*. Washington, DC: The Heritage Foundation.

Stoddard, C., Steiner, B., Rohrbach, J., Hemmens, C., & Bennett, K. (2015). All the way home: Assessing the constitutionality of juvenile curfew laws. *American Journal of Criminal Law, 42*, 177–211.

Straus, M.A. (1983). Ordinary violence, child abuse, and wife battering: What do they have in common? In D. Finkelhor, R.J. Gelles, G.T. Hotaling & M.A. Straus (Eds.), *The dark side of families: Current family violence research*. Beverly Hills: Sage.

Strickland, R.A. (2004). *Restorative justice*. New York: Peter Lang.

Stuart, B. (1996). Circle sentencing: Turning swords into ploughshares. In B. Galaway & J. Hudson (Eds.), *Restorative justice: International perspectives*. Monsey, NY: Criminal Justice Press.

Studt, E. (1973). *Surveillance and service in parole: A report of the parole action study*. Washington, DC: National Institute of Corrections.

Sullivan, C.J., Blair, L., Latessa, E., & Sullivan, C.C. (2016). Juvenile courts and recidivism: Results from a multisite outcome study. *Justice Quarterly, 33*, 291–318.

Sullivan, C.J., Dollard, N., Sellers, B., & Mayo, J. (2010). Rebalancing response to school-based offenses: A civil citation program. *Youth Violence and Juvenile Justice, 8*, 279–294.

Sullivan, C.J., Piquero, A.R., & Cullen, F.T. (2012). Like before, but better: The lessons of developmental, life-course criminology for contemporary juvenile justice. *Victims and Offenders, 7*, 450–471.

Sullivan, C., Grant, M.Q., & Grant, J.D. (1957). The development of interpersonal maturity: Applications to delinquency. *Psychiatry, 20*, 373–385.

Sutherland, E.H. (1939). *Principles of criminology* (3rd ed.). Philadelphia: Lippincott.

Sutherland, E.H., & Cressey, D.R. (1974). *Criminology* (9th ed.). Philadelphia: Lippincott.

Sutphen, R.D., & Ford, J. (2001). The effectiveness and enforcement of a teen curfew law. *Journal of Sociology and Social Welfare, 28*, 55–78.

Swank, J.M., & Gagnon, J.C. (2016). Mental health services in juvenile correctional facilities: A national survey of clinical staff. *Journal of Child and Family Studies, 25*, 2862–2872.

Sykes, G.M., & Matza, D. (1957). Techniques of neutralization: A theory of delinquency. *American Sociological Review, 22*, 664–670.

Szymanski, L.A. (2002, September). *Juvenile delinquents' right to a jury trial*. NCJJ Snapshot, 7(9).

Takagi, P., & Shank, G. (2004). Critique of restorative justice. *Social Justice, 31*, 147–163.

Tanehaus, D.S. (2004). *Juvenile justice in the making*. New York: Oxford University Press.

Tannenbaum, F. (1938). *Crime and the community*. New York: Columbia University Press.

Tanner-Smith, E.E., Lipsey, M.W., & Wilson, D.B. (2016). Juvenile drug court effects on recidivism and drug use: A systematic review and meta-analysis. *Journal of Experimental Criminology, 12*, 477–513.

Taxman, F.S. (2008). No illusions: Offender and organizational change in Maryland's pro-active community supervision efforts. *Criminology & Public Policy, 7*(2), 275–302.

Taylor, C.S. (1990). Gang imperialism. In C.R. Huff (Ed.), *Gangs in America* (pp. 103–115). Newbury Park, CA: Sage.

Taylor, T.J., Turner, K.B., Esbensen, F., & Winfree, T. (2001). Coppin' an attitude: Attitudinal differences among juveniles toward police. *Journal of Criminal Justice, 29*, 295–305.

Teigen, A. (2021). *Juvenile justice 2020 year-end report*. Washington, DC: National Conference of State Legislatures. Retrieved from www.ncsl.org.

Terrill, W. (2020). Reduce use of force. In C.M. Katz & E.R. Maguire (Eds.), *Transforming the police: Thirteen key reforms* (pp. 73–89). Long Grove, IL: Waveland Press.

Thomas, S.A., & Stich, C. (2019). Why (jury-less) juvenile courts are unconstitutional. *Emory Law Journal, 69*, 273–319.

Thornberry, T.P. (1998). Membership in youth gangs and involvement in serious and violent offending. In R. Loeber & D.P. Farrington (Eds.), *Serious and violent offenders*. Newbury Park, CA: Sage.

Thornberry, T.P., & Christenson, R.L. (1984). Unemployment and criminal involvement: An investigation of reciprocal causal structures. *American Sociological Review, 49*, 398–411.

Thornberry, T.P., & Krohn, M.D. (2005). Applying interactional theory to the explanation of continuity and change in antisocial behavior. In D.P. Farrington (Ed.), *Integrated developmental and life-course theories of offending: Advances in criminological theory* (Vol. 14). New Brunswick, NJ: Transaction.

Thornberry, T.P., Huizinga, D., & Loeber, R. (1995). The prevention of serious delinquency and violence: Implications from the program of research on the causes and correlates of delinquency. In J.C. Howell, B. Krisberg, J.D. Hawkins, & J.J. Wilson (Eds.), *Sourcebook on serious, violent, and chronic juvenile offenders*. Thousand Oaks, CA: Sage.

Thornberry, T.P., Krohn, M.D., Lizotte, A.J., & Chard-Wierschem, D. (1993). The role of juvenile gangs in facilitating delinquent behavior. *Journal of Research in Crime and Delinquency, 30*, 55–87.

Thornberry, T.P., Moore, M., & Christiansen, R.L. (1985). The effect of dropping out of high school on subsequent criminal behavior. *Criminology, 23*, 3–18.

Thrasher, F.M. (1936). *The gang.* Chicago, IL: University of Chicago Press.

Thurman, Q.C. (1984). Deviance and the neutralization of moral commitment: An empirical analysis. *Deviant Behavior, 5*, 291–304.

Tobey, A., Grisso, T., & Schwartz, R. (2000). Youths' trial participation as seen by youths and their attorneys: An exploration of competence-based issues. In T. Grisso & R.G. Schwartz (Eds.), *Youth on trial: A developmental perspective on juvenile justice* (pp. 225–242). Chicago, IL: University of Chicago Press.

Tobler, N.S. (1986). Meta-analysis of 143 adolescent drug prevention programs: Quantitative outcome results of program participants compared to a control or comparison group. *Journal of Drug Issues, 16*, 537–567.

Tobler, N.S. (1997). Meta-analysis of adolescent drug prevention programs: Results of the 1993 meta-analysis. In W.J. Bukoski (Ed.), *Meta-analysis of drug abuse prevention programs* (pp. 5–68). Rockville, MD: National Institute on Drug Abuse.

Tolan, P.H., Henry, D.B., Schoeny, M.S., Lovegrove, P., & Nichols, E. (2014). Mentoring programs to affect delinquency and associated outcomes of youth at risk: A comprehensive meta-analytic review. *Journal of Experimental Criminology, 10*, 179–206.

Tolan, P., Henry, D., Schoeny, M., & Bass, A. (2008). *Mentoring interventions to affect juvenile delinquency and associated problems.* Oslo: The Campbell Collaboration. Retrieved from www.campbellcollaboration.org.

Tonry, M. (2008). Crime and human rights: How political paranoia, protestant fundamentalism, and constitutional obsolescence combined to devastate black America—The American Society of Criminology 2007 presidential address. *Criminology, 46*, 1–33.

Tonry, M. (2011). Making peace, not a desert: Penal reform should be about values not justice reinvestment. *Criminology & Public Policy, 10*, 637–649.

Tonry, M. (2014). Remodeling American sentencing: A ten-step blueprint for moving past mass incarceration. *Criminology & Public Policy, 13*, 503–533.

Torbet, P.M. (1996). *Juvenile probation: The workhorse of the juvenile justice system.* Washington, DC: U.S. Department of Justice.

Toseland, R.W. (1982). Fear of crime: Who is most vulnerable? *Journal of Criminal Justice, 10*, 199–210.

Toy, C. (1992). A short history of Asian gangs in San Francisco. *Justice Quarterly, 9*, 647–666.

Travis, L.F., & Coon, J.K. (2005). *The role of law enforcement in public school safety: A national survey.* Washington, DC: National Institute of Justice.

Trebach, A.S. (1987). *The great drug war and radical proposals that could make America safe again.* New York: Macmillan.

Tremblay, R. (2007). Targeted and situational prevention of physical violence: In response to Eisner's and Homel's comments. *European Journal on Criminal Policy and Research, 13*, 179–181.

Trojanowicz, R., Kappeler, V.E., Gaines, L.K., & Bucqueroux, B. (1998). *Community policing: A contemporary perspective* (2nd ed.). Cincinnati: Anderson.

Trulson, C.R. (2007). Determinants of disruption: Institutional misconduct among state-committed delinquents. *Youth Violence and Juvenile Justice, 5*, 7–34.

Trulson, C.R. & Caudill, J. (2017). Juvenile homicide offenders recidivism. *Journal of Criminal Psychology, 7*, 93–104.

Trulson, C.R., DeLisi, M., Caudill, J.W., Belshaw, S., & Marquart, J.W. (2010). Delinquent careers behind bars. *Criminal Justice Review, 35*, 200–219.

Teigen, A. (2018). *Much needed guidance on how to close juvenile facilities.* Washington, DC: National Conference of State Legislatures. Retrieved from www.ncsl.org.

Trulson, C., DeLisi, M., & Marquart, J.W. (2011). Institutional misconduct, delinquent background, and rearrest frequency among serious and violent delinquent offenders. *Crime and Delinquency, 57*, 709–731.

Tyler, T.R. (2006). *Why people obey the law* (2nd ed.). Princeton, NJ: Princeton University Press.

Tyler, T.R. (2017). Procedural justice and policing: A rush to judgment? *Annual Review of Law and Social Science, 13*, 29–53.

Umbreit, M.S. (1999). Avoiding the marginalization and McDonaldization of victim-offender mediation: A case study in moving toward the mainstream. In G. Bazemore & L. Walgrave (Eds.), *Restorative juvenile justice: Repairing the harm of youth crime* (pp. 213–234). Monsey, NY: Criminal Justice Press.

Umbreit, M.S., & Coates, R.B. (1992). *Victim offender mediation: An analysis of programs in four states of the U.S.* St. Paul, MN: Center for Restorative Justice and Peacemaking.

Umbreit, M.S., Coates, R.B., & Vos, B. (2001). *Juvenile offender mediation in six Oregon counties.* Salem, OR: Oregon Dispute Resolution Commission.

Umbreit, M.S., Vos, B., Coates, R.B., & Brown, K.A. (2003). *Facing violence: The path of restorative justice and dialogue.* Monsey, NY: Criminal Justice Press.

Underwood, J. (1994). Prayer in the schools. *Schools and the Courts, 20*(May), 1039–1050.

Urban, L.S. (2008). Court-orders curfew: the application of graduated sanctions for juvenile offenders. *Justice Policy Journal, 5*, 1–35.

Urban, L.S., St. Cyr, J.L., & Decker, S.H. (2003). Goal conflict in the juvenile court: The evolution of sentencing practices in the United States. *Journal of Contemporary Criminal Justice, 19*, 454–479.

U.S. Bureau of the Census. (2011). *Annual population estimates 2002 to 2009.* Washington, DC: U.S. Bureau of the Census. Retrieved from www.census.gov/popest.

U.S. Department of Education. (2020, January 16). *Guidance on constitutionally protected prayer and religious expression in public elementary and secondary schools.* Washington, DC: U.S. Department of Education.

U.S. Department of Justice. (2006). *National CASA program: Audit report 07-04.* Washington, DC: U.S. Department of Justice, Office of the Inspector General.

U.S. Department of Justice. (2015). *Investigation of the Ferguson Police Department.* Washington, DC: U.S. Department of Justice Civil Rights Division.

U.S. Dept. of Justice Civil Rights Division & U.S. Attorney's Office, Northern District of Illinois. (2017). *Investigation of the Chicago Police Department.* Washington, DC: U.S. Department of Justice.

U.S. Government Accountability Office (GAO). (2021). *Drug misuse: Most states have Good Samaritan Laws and research indicates they may have positive effects.* Washington, DC: U.S. Government Accountability Office (GAO). Retrieved from www.gao.org.

Valdez, A. (2000). *Gangs: A guide to understanding street gangs* (3rd ed.). San Clemente, CA: Law Tech.

van den Haag, E., & Conrad, P. (1983). *The death penalty: A debate.* New York: Plenum.

Van Kammen, W.B., & Loeber, R. (1994). Are fluctuations in delinquent activities related to the onset and offset in juvenile illegal drug use and drug dealing? *The Journal of Drug Issues, 24*, 9–24.

Van Ness, D.W., & Strong, K.H. (2015). *Restoring justice: An introduction to restorative justice* (5th ed.). Boston: Elsevier (Anderson Publishing). Now published by Routledge.

Van Voorhis, P., & Salisbury, E.J. (2016). *Correctional counseling and rehabilitation* (9th ed.). New York: Routledge.

Van Voorhis, P., Braswell, M., & Lester, D. (2007). *Correctional counseling and rehabilitation* (6th ed.) (p. 44). Newark, NJ: LexisNexis Matthew Bender.

Vandervort, F.E., & Ladd, W.E. (2001). The worst of all possible worlds: Michigan's juvenile justice system and international standards for the treatment of children. *University of Detroit Mercy Law Review, 78*, 202–258.

Vigil, J.D. (1993). The established gang. In S. Cummings & D.J. Monti (Eds.), *Gangs: The origins and impact of contemporary youth gangs in the United States* (pp. 95–112). Albany, NY: SUNY Press.

Vigil, J.D. (1997). *Learning from gangs: The Mexican American experience.* ERIC Digest Document No. RC020943.

Vigil, J.D. (2010). *Gang redux: A balanced anti-gang strategy.* Long Grove, IL: Waveland.

Viglione, J., Rudes, D., Nightingale, V., Watson, C., & Taxman, F. (2018). The many hats of juvenile probation officers: A latent class analysis of work-related activities. *Criminal Justice Review, 43*, 252–269.

Viljoen, J.L., Klaver, J., & Roesch, R. (2005). Legal decisions of preadolescent and adolescent defendants: Predictors of confessions, pleas, communication with attorneys, and appeals. *Law and Human Behavior, 29*, 253–277.

Vingilis, E.R., & DeGenova, K. (1984). Youth and the forbidden fruit: Experiences with changes in legal drinking age in North America. *Journal of Criminal Justice, 12*, 161–172.

Virkkunen, M., Goldman, D., & Linnoila, M. (1996). Serotonin in alcoholic violent offenders. In G.R. Bock & J.A. Goode (Eds.), *Genetics of criminal and antisocial behavior* (pp. 168–176). Chichester, England: John Wiley and Sons.

Vogel, C.A., Xue, Y., Moiduddin, E.M., Kisker, E.E., & Carlson, B.L. (2010). *Early Head Start children in grade 5: Long-term follow-up of the Early Head Start Research and Evaluation Study sample.* OPRE Report # 2011–8, Washington, DC: Administration for Children and Families. Retrieved from www.acf.hhs.gov/sites/default/files/opre/grade5.pdf.

Vold, G.B., & Bernard, T.J. (1986). *Theoretical criminology* (3rd ed.). New York: Oxford University Press.

von Hentig, H. (1941). Remarks on the interaction of perpetrator and victim. *Journal of Criminal Law, Criminology and Police Science, 31*, 303–309.

W. Haywood Burns Institute. (2016). *Stemming the rising tide: Racial & ethnic disparities in youth incarceration & strategies for change.* Oakland, CA: author.

Wachtel, T. (1995). Family group conferencing: Restorative justice in practice. *Juvenile Justice Update, 1*(4), 1–2, 13–14.

Wadlington, W., Whitebread, C.H., & Davis, S.M. (1983). *Cases and materials on children in the legal system.* Mineola, NY: Foundation Press.

Walker, S. (1992). *The police in America: An introduction.* New York: McGraw-Hill.

Walker, S. (2011). *Sense and nonsense about crime, drugs, and communities* (7th ed.). Stamford, CT: Cengage Learning.

Walker, S. (2015). *Sense and nonsense about crime, drugs, and communities* (8th ed.). Stamford, CT: Cengage Learning.

Walker, S., Spohn, C., & Delone, M. (2018). *The color of justice: Race, ethnicity, and crime in America.* Boston, MA: Cengage Learning.

Walsh, A. (2009). *Biology and criminology: The biosocial synthesis.* New York: Routledge.

Walsh, B.A., & Mortenson, J.A. (2020). *Transforming Early Head Start home visiting: A family life education approach.* New York: Routledge.

Walsh, T. (2014). Juvenile economic sanctions: A logical alternative. *Criminology & Public Policy, 13*, 69–77.

Walters, G.D. (1992). A meta-analysis of the gene–crime relationship. *Criminology, 30*, 595–613.

Walters, G.D. (2014). Crime and substance misuse in adjudicated delinquent youth: The worst of both worlds. *Law and Human Behavior, 38*, 139–150.

Walters, G.D. (2017). The drug–crime connection in adolescent and adult respondents: Interaction versus addition. *Journal of Drug Issues, 47*(2), 205–216.

Walters, S.T., Clark, M.D., Gingerich, R., & Meltzer, M.L. (2007). *A guide for probation and parole: Motivating offenders to change.* Washington, DC: U.S. Department of Justice, National Institute of Corrections.

Walters, S.T., Vader, A.M., Nguyen, N., Harris, T.R., & Eells, J. (2010). Motivational interviewing as a supervision strategy in probation: A randomized effectiveness trial. *Journal of Offender Rehabilitation, 49*, 309–323.

Wang, K., Chen, Y., Zhang, J., and Oudekerk, B.A. (2020). *Indicators of school crime and safety: 2019* (NCES 2020-063/NCJ 254485). National Center for Education Statistics, U.S. Department of Education, and Bureau of Justice Statistics, Office of Justice Programs, U.S. Department of Justice. Washington, DC.

Ward, A.C. (2000). *Evidentiary use of biological disorder: Ethics and justice.* Thesis, Simon Fraser University.

Ward, G., & Kupchik, A. (2010). What drives juvenile probation officers? Relating organizational contexts, status characteristics, and personal convictions to treatment and punishment orientations. *Crime & Delinquency, 56*, 35–69.

Ward, K.C., Lucas, P.A., & Murphy, A. (2019). The impact of marijuana legalization on law enforcement in states surrounding Colorado. *Police Quarterly, 22*, 217–242.

Ward, T. (2010). The good lives model of offender rehabilitation: Basic assumptions, aetiological commitments, and practice implications. In F. McNeil, P. Raynor, & C. Trotter (Eds.), *Offender supervision: New directions in theory, research, and practice* (pp. 41–64). New York: Willan.

Washington Post (2021, June 10). *Fatal force.* Retrieved from www.washingtonpost.com.

Washington State Institute for Public Policy (WSIPP). (2016). *Benefit–cost results.* Olympia, WA: WSIPP. Retrieved from www.wsipp.wa.gov.

Washington State Institute for Public Policy (WSIPP). (2017). *Updated inventory of programs for the prevention and treatment of youth cannabis use.* Olympia, WA: WSIPP. Retrieved from www.wsipp.wa.gov.

Watkins, A.M., & Maume, M.O. (2012). Rethinking the study of juveniles' attitudes toward the police. *Criminal Justice Studies, 25*, 279–300.

Watts, S.J., & McNulty, T.L. (2015). Delinquency peers and offending: Integrating social learning and biosocial theory. *Youth Violence and Juvenile Justice, 13*, 190–206.

Watts, W.D., & Wright, L.S. (1990). The relationship of alcohol, tobacco, marijuana, and other illegal drug use to delinquency among Mexican-American, black, and white adolescent males. *Adolescence, 25*, 171–181.

Webster-Stratton, C. (2001). The Incredible Years: Parent, teacher and child training series. In *Blueprints for violence prevention.* Boulder: University of Colorado.

Webster-Stratton, C., & Hammond, M. (1997). Treating children with early-onset conduct problems: A comparison of child and parent training interventions. *Journal of Consulting and Clinical Psychology, 65*, 93–109.

Wechsler, H., & Nelson, T.F. (2010). Will increasing alcohol availability by lowering the minimum legal drinking age decrease drinking and related consequences among youths? *American Journal of Public Health, 100*, 986–992.

Weerman, F.M., Maxson, C.L., Esbensen, F., Aldridge, J., Medina, J., & van Gemert, F. (2009). *Eurogang program manual.* Retrieved from https://eurogangproject.files.wordpress.com/2018/06/eurogang-manual.pdf.

Weisel, D.L., & Shelley, T.O. (2004). *Specialized gang units: Form and function in community policing—Final report*. Washington, DC: National Institute of Justice.

Weiss, G. (2013). *The fourth wave: Juvenile justice reforms for the twenty-first century*. National Campaign to Reform State Juvenile Justice Systems.

Wells, L.E., & Rankin, J.H. (1988). Direct parental controls and delinquency. *Criminology, 26*, 263–285.

Welsh, B.C., & Farrington, D.P. (2007). Save children from a life of crime. *Criminology & Public Policy, 6*, 871–880.

Werb, D., Kamarulzaman, A., Meacham, M.C., Rafful, C., Fischer, B., Strathdee, S.A., & Wood, E. (2016). The effectiveness of compulsory drug treatment: A systematic review. *International Journal of Drug Policy, 28*, 1–9.

Werner, A. (2014, April 16). Don't TASE students at school, activists say. *CBS News*. Retrieved from www.cbsnews.com/news/tasers-plus-teenagers-equal-a-dangerous-mix-activists-say.

West, D.J., & Farrington, D.P. (1973). *The delinquent way of life*. New York: Crane Russack.

Whitaker, C., & Bastian, L. (1991). *Teenage victims: A national crime survey report*. Washington, DC: U.S. Department of Justice.

White, C. (2016). Incarcerating youth with mental health problems: A focus on the interaction of race, ethnicity, and mental illness. *Youth Violence and Juvenile Justice, 14*, 426–447.

White, G.F. (1990). The drug use–delinquency connection in adolescence. In R. Weisheit (Ed.), *Drugs, crime and the criminal justice system*. Cincinnati: Anderson.

White, H.R., Pandina, R.J., & LaGrange, R.L. (1987). Longitudinal predictors of serious substance use and delinquency. *Criminology, 25*, 715–740.

White, M.D., & Fradella, H.F. (2016). *Stop and frisk: The use and abuse of a controversial policing tactic*. New York: New York University Press.

White House. (2016). *National drug control strategy*. https://obamawhitehouse.archives.gov/ondcp/policy-and-research/ndcs.

Whitehead, J.T., & Braswell, M.C. (2000). The future of probation: Reintroducing the spiritual dimension into correctional practice. *Criminal Justice Review, 25*, 207–233.

Whitney, I., Rivers, I., Smith, P., & Sharp, S. (1994). The Sheffield project: Methodology and findings. In P. Smith & S. Sharp (Eds.), *School bullying: Insights and perspectives*. London: Routledge.

Wiatrowski, M., Griswold, D., & Roberts, M. (1981). Social control theory and delinquency. *American Sociological Review, 46*, 525–541.

Widom, C.S. (1989). Child abuse, neglect and violent criminal behavior. *Criminology, 27*, 251–271.

Widom, C.S. (1995). *Childhood victimization and violent behavior*. Paper presented at the Annual Conference on Criminal Justice Research and Evaluation, Washington, DC.

Wiebush, R.G., Wagner, D., McNulty, B., Wang, Y., & Le, T.N. (2005). *Implementation and outcome evaluation of the intensive aftercare program: Final report*. Washington, DC: Office of Juvenile Justice and Delinquency Prevention.

Wiehe, V.R. (1992). *Working with child abuse and neglect*. Itasca, IL: F.E. Peacock.

Wilson, D.B., Gill, C., Olaghere, A., & McClure, D. (2016). Juvenile curfew effects on criminal behavior and victimization: A systematic review. *Campbell Systematic Reviews, 3*. DOI: 10.4073/csr.2016.3.

Wilson, D.M., Jordan, S.P., Meyer, I.H., Flores, A.R., Stemple, L., & Herman, J.L. (2017). Disproportionality and disparities among sexual minority youth in custody. *Journal of Youth and Adolescence, 46*, 1547–1561.

Wilson, J.Q., & Herrnstein, R.J. (1985). *Crime and human nature*. New York: Simon & Schuster.

Wilson, S.J., & Lipsey, M.W. (2003). Wilderness challenge programs for delinquent youth: A meta-analysis of outcome evaluations. *Evaluation and Program Planning, 23*, 1–12.

Wish, E.D., Toborg, M.A., & Bellassai, J.P. (1988). *Identifying drug users and monitoring them during conditional release.* Washington, DC: U.S. Department of Justice.

Wolfgang, M.E. (1961). Pioneers in Criminology: Cesare Lombroso (1825–1909). *Journal of Criminal Law and Criminology, 52*, 361–91. Retrieved from https://scholarlycommons.law.northwestern.edu/jclc/vol52/iss4/1.

Womer, S., & Bunker, R.J. (2010). Surenos gangs and Mexican cartel use of social networking sites. *Small Wars and Insurgencies, 21*, 81–94.

Wong, J.S., Bouchard, J., Gravel, J., Bouchard, M., & Morselli, C. (2016). Can at-risk youth be diverted from crime? A meta-analysis of restorative diversion programs. *Criminal Justice and Behavior, 43*(10), 1310–1329. DOI: https://doi.org/10.1177/0093854816640835.

Wood, P.B., Pfefferbaum, B., & Arneklev, B.J. (1993). Risk-taking and self-control: Social psychological correlates of delinquency. *Journal of Crime and Justice, 16*, 111–130.

Wood, W.R. (2012). Correcting community service: From work crews to community work in a juvenile court. *Justice Quarterly, 29*, 684–711.

Wooden, K. (1976). *Weeping in the playtime of others: America's incarcerated children.* New York: McGraw-Hill.

Wooden, W.S., & Blazak, R. (2001). *Renegade kids, suburban outlaws: From youth culture to delinquency* (2nd ed.). Belmont, CA: Wadsworth.

Worden, R.E. (1996). The causes of police brutality: Theory and evidence on police use of force. In W.A. Geller & H. Toch (Eds.), *Police violence: Understanding and controlling police abuse of force* (pp. 23–51). New Haven, CT: Yale University Press.

World Health Organization. (1964). *WHO expert committee on addiction producing drugs: 13th Report.* Geneva: author.

World Health Organization. (2004). *Prevention of mental disorders: Effective interventions and policy options.* Geneva: author.

Worrall, J.L., & Gaines, L.K. (2006). The effect of police–probation partnerships on juvenile arrests. *Journal of Criminal Justice, 34*, 579–589.

Wright, J.P. (2011). Parental insults and the development of persistent criminal behavior. In M. DeLisi and K.M. Beaver (Eds.), *Criminological theory: A Life-course approach* (pp. 51–67) Burlington, MA: Jones and Bartlett.

Wright, J.P., & Beaver, K.M. (2005). Do parents matter in creating self-control in their children? A genetically informed test of Gottfredson and Hirschi's theory of low self-control. *Criminology, 43*, 1169–1202.

Wright, J.P., & Cullen, F.T. (2000). Juvenile involvement in occupational crime. *Criminology, 38*, 863–896.

Wright, J.P., Barnes, J.C., Boutwell, B.B., Schwartz, J.A., Connolly, E.J., Nedelec, J.L., & Beaver, K.M. (2015). Mathematical proof is not minutiae and irreducible complexity is not a theory: A final response to Burt and Simons and a call to criminologists. *Criminology, 53*, 113–120.

Wright, J.P., Cullen, F.T., & Williams, N. (1997). Working while in school and delinquent involvement: Implications for social policy. *Crime & Delinquency, 43*, 203–221.

Wu, G., Boateng, F.D., & Lang, A. (2020). The spillover effect of recreational marijuana legalization on crime: Evidence from neighboring states of Colorado and Washington State. *Journal of Drug Issues, 50*, 392–409.

Yablonsky, L. (1962). *The violent gang.* New York: Macmillan.

Young, D.W., Farrell, J.L., & Taxman, F.S. (2013). Impacts of juvenile probation training models on youth recidivism. *Justice Quarterly, 30*, 1068–1089.

Zane, N.Z., Welsh, B.C., & Mears, D.P. (2016). Juvenile transfer and the specific deterrence hypothesis: Systematic review and meta-analysis. *Crime and Public Policy*, *15*, 901–925.

Zane, S.N. (2016) Do criminal court outcomes vary by juvenile transfer mechanism? A multi-jurisdictional, multilevel analysis. *Justice Quarterly*, *34*, 542–569.

Zehr, H. (1990). *Changing lives: A new focus for crime and justice*. Scottdale, PA: Herald Press.

Zhai, F., Brooks-Gunn, J., & Waldfogel, J. (2011). Head Start and urban children's school readiness: A birth cohort study in 18 cities. *Developmental Psychology*, *47*, 134–152.

Ziemer, D. (2005, July 13). Juvenile interrogations must be recorded. *Wisconsin Law Journal*. Retrieved from http://wislawjournal.com/2005/07/13/juvenile-interrogations-must-be-recorded.

Zimring, F.E. (1982). *The changing legal world of adolescence*. New York: Free Press.

Zimring, F.E. (2007). *The great American crime decline*. New York: Oxford University Press.

Zimring, F.E. (2012). *The city that became safe: New York's lessons for urban crime and its control*. New York: Oxford University Press.

Zimring, F.E., & Tanenhaus, D.S. (Eds.). (2014). *Choosing the future for American juvenile justice*. New York: New York University Press.

Court Cases

Bethel School District No. 403 v. Fraser, 478 U.S. 675, 106 S. Ct. 3159, 92 L.Ed.2d 549 (1986).

Blakely v. Washington, 542 U.S. 296 (2004).

Board of Education of Independent School District No. 92 of Pottawatomie County et al. v. Lindsay Earls et al., 536 U.S. 822 (2002).

Breed v. Jones, 421 U.S. 519 (1975).

Brown v. Gwinnett County School District, 112 F.3d 1464 (11th Cir. 1997).

Chicago v. Morales, 527 U.S. 41 (1999).

Commonwealth v. Fisher, 213 Pa. 48 (1905).

Deborah Morse, et al. v. Joseph Frederick, 551 U.S. 393 (2007).

Doe v. Renfrow, 451 U.S. 1022 (1981).

Ex parte Crouse, 4 Whart. 9 (Pa. 1839).

Fare v. Michael C., 442 U.S. 707 (1979).

G.C. v. Owensboro Public Schools, 711 F.3d 623 (2013).

Gonzalez v. Mailliard, Civ. No. 50424, N.D. Cal. 2/9/71, Appeal U.S. No. 70-120 4/9/71 (1971).

Good News Club v. Milford Central School, 533 U.S. 98 (2001).

Graham v. Connor, 490 U.S. 386 (1989).

Graham v. Florida, 560 U.S. 48 (2010).

Hazelwood School District v. Kuhlmeier, 484 U.S. 260 (1988).

In re Gault, 387 U.S. 1 (1967).

In re Tyrell, 8 Cal.4th 68 (1994).

In re Winship, 397 U.S. 358, 90 S. Ct. 1068, 25 L.Ed.2d 368 (1970).

Ingraham v. Wright, 430 U.S. 651 (1977).

J.D.B. v. North Carolina, 564 U.S. 261 (2011).

Johnson v. City of Opelousas, 658 F.2d 1065 (5th Cir. 1981).

Jones v. Clear Creek Independent School District, 977 F.2d 963 (5th Cir. 1992).

Jones v. Mississippi, 593 U.S. ___ (2021).

Kent v. United States, 383 U.S. 541 (1966).

Lee v. Weisman, 505 U.S. 577 (1992).

Mahanoy Area School District v. B.L., A Minor, by and through her Father, Levy, et al.; 594 U.S. ___ (2021).

McKeiver v. Pennsylvania, 403 U.S. 528 (1971).

Miller v. Alabama, 567 U.S. 460 (2012).

Montgomery v. Louisiana, 577 U.S. 190 (2016).

New Jersey v. T.L.O., 469 U.S. 325 (1985).

P.B. v. Koch, 96 F.3d 1298 (9th Cir. 1996).

People v. Turner, 55 Ill. 280 (1870).

Qutb v. Strauss, 11 F.3d 488 (5th Cir. 1993).

R.L. v. Cent. York School, 183 F. Supp.3d 625 (2016).

Roper v. Simmons, 543 U.S. 551 (2005).

Safford Unified School District v. Redding, 557 U.S. 364 (2009).

Santa Fe Independent School District v. Doe, 530 U.S. 290 (2000).

Schall v. Martin, 467 U.S. 253 (1984).

Schneckloth v. Bustamonte, 412 U.S. 218 (1973).

Settle v. Dickson County School Board, 53 F.3d 152 (6th Cir. 1995).

Steirer v. Bethlehem Area School District, 987 F.2d 989 (3rd Cir. 1994).

Tennessee v. Garner et al., 83 U.S. 1035 (1985).

Thompson v. Carthage School District, 87 F.3d 979 (8th Cir. 1996).

Tinker v. Des Moines Independent Community Schools District, 393 U.S. 503 (1969).

Todd v. Rush County Schools, 133 F.3d 984 (7th Cir. 1998).

United States v. Mark James Knights, 278 F.3d 920 (9th Cir. 2002).

Vernonia School District v. Acton, 515 U.S. 646 (1995).

Yarborough, Warden v. Alvarado, 541 U.S. 652 (2004).

Index